Wissenschaftliche Untersuchungen zum Neuen Testament

430

James R. Harrison

Paul and the Ancient Celebrity Circuit

The Cross and Moral Transformation

Mohr Siebeck

James R. Harrison, born 1952; 1976 BADipEd; 1989 MA; 1997 PhD (Macquarie University); 2002–12 Head of the School of Theology, Wesley Institute, Sydney, Australia; currently Research Director, Sydney College of Divinity, Macquarie Park, Australia.

ISBN 978-3-16-154615-0 / eISBN 978-3-16-157019-3
DOI 10.1628/978-3-16-157019-3

ISSN 0512-1604 / eISSN 2568-7476
(Wissenschaftliche Untersuchungen zum Neuen Testament)

The Deutsche Nationalbibliothek lists this publication in the Deutsche Nationalbibliographie; detailed bibliographic data are available at *http://dnb.dnb.de*.

The book was typeset and printed on non-aging paper by Gulde Druck in Tübingen. It was bound by Buchbinderei Spinner in Ottersweier.

Printed in Germany.

Preface

My interest in the "celebrity circuit," ancient and modern, was first provoked as an undergraduate student at Macquarie University in 1973. In a striking lecture that formed part of an ancient history unit called *The Roman Nobility*, Edwin Judge, Professor of History, drew upon the documentary evidence to unveil the boasting culture of the republican *nobiles* ("nobles").[1] As I listened, I sensed that there was a collision of cultures occurring here between the humility espoused by the apostle Paul, who gloried in Christ and repudiated any self-elevation before God, and the self-advertisement of the Roman nobles, who sought not only to equal but also to surpass the glory of their famous consular ancestors. The more I thought about Judge's lecture in subsequent years, the more I realised that Paul's critique of the Roman boasting tradition had important implications for the relentless quest for fame pursued by late twentieth and early twenty-first century media luminaries.

I was also intrigued by the fact that some of the more reflective rock musicians of my generation aired ambivalence in their songs about the ephemeral nature of fame and the vacuousness of the Hollywood celebrity circuit. The Kinks' superb song, *Celluloid Heroes*, underscored the tension existing between the allurement of the Hollywood star system and the vulnerability of its casualties (Greta Garbo, Bette Davis, Marilyn Monroe), while nevertheless acknowledging that we all secretly desire to live in an insulated "fantasy world of celluloid villains and heroes."[2] The case is relentlessly pressed to breaking point by Bob Dylan in his 1965 song *Desolation Row.*[3] There Dylan, the 2016 winner of the Nobel Prize in Literature, reduces a cavalcade of celebrated figures from Western civilisation, fictional and historical, to absurdity in his desperate vision of a world gone awry. This "apocalyptic" song, ranking in quality and stature with T.S. Eliot's magnum opus *The Waste Land*, posed intriguing questions for me in relation to the gospel of the apostle Paul.

[1] For full details, see James R. Harrison, "Preface", in E.A. Judge, *The First Christians in the Roman World: Augustan and New Testament Essays*, ed. James R. Harrison, WUNT 229 (Tübingen: Mohr Siebeck, 2008), ix–x.

[2] For the lyrics of "Celluloid Heroes", accessed 27/08/2019, see https://www.lyrics.com › lyric › The+Kinks › Celluloid+Heroes.

[3] For the lyrics of "Desolation Row", accessed 27/08/2019, see https://bobdylan.com › songs › desolation-row. For the lyrics of Dylan's songs, see his official website above and Bob Dylan, *The Lyrics 1961–2012* (New York: Simon & Schuster, 2016).

Was the apostle Paul, in radically dismissing all human boasting, speaking directly to the spiritual heart of the Roman world in a manner similar to Dylan in the late twentieth century? And with what transformative purpose morally? How did the shame of the cross overturn the deeply entrenched Graeco-Roman culture of esteem and, in a surprising case of social levelling, establish humility as its crowning virtue for the great man and his dependents? Why did Paul's leadership paradigm of "power in weakness" ultimately trump the famous "reluctance" of Augustus, who had consistently refused further powers when pressed upon him by an adoring Roman public? Should we speak about the "failure" of Augustus, as E.A. Judge has provocatively argued,[4] and, by contrast, about the unexpected and unconventional triumph of the apostle Paul's gospel in the Western intellectual tradition? And how did this cultural collision, still reverberating today, affect the civic ethics of Paul's converts, their communal ethos and paradigms of group identity, their pedagogical curriculum, and their understanding of honour and dishonour? It became clear that these questions could only be resolved by a detailed investigation of the phenomenon of celebrity culture in its modern and ancient context. The ethos of the Roman culture of self-advertisement had to be investigated from the republican perspective of the orations of Cicero, as much as from the paradoxical paradigm of Augustan leadership, which, in the intention of the Princeps, was designed to raise up a new generation of Roman leaders in his age of overflowing grace.

In addition to the introduction and conclusion, three new studies (Chapters 2–3, 6) appear in this collection of essays. Five previous studies of mine (Chapters 4–5, 7–9) have also been updated for the contribution that they make to our understanding of how the cross effected moral transformation in the face of the self-assertive values espoused by the luminaries of the ancient celebrity circuit. Each study has been given copyright release by their publishers. I express my gratitude to each press, all noted below, in allowing the republication of these essays.[5]

I am also deeply grateful for the support of the Mohr Siebeck staff after I aired the possibility of a third monograph with the press. I am indebted to Pro-

[4] E.A. Judge, *The Failure of Augustus: Essays on the Interpretation of a Paradox* (Newcastle upon Tyne: Cambridge Scholars, 2019).

[5] James R. Harrison, "Paul and the Athletic Ideal in Antiquity: A Case Study in Wrestling with Word and Image," in *Paul's World. Pauline Studies: Volume IV*, ed. Stanley E. Porter (Leiden: Brill, 2007), 81–109; *idem*, "Paul and the Gymnasiarchs: Two Approaches to Pastoral Formation in Antiquity," in *Paul: Jew, Greek, and Roman. Pauline Studies: Volume V*, ed. Stanley E. Porter (Leiden: Brill, 2008), 141–78; *idem*, "The Imitation of the Great Man in Antiquity: Paul's Inversion of a Cultural Icon," in *Christian Origins and Classical Culture: Social and Literary Contexts for the New Testament*, ed. Stanley E. Porter and Andrew W. Pitts, TENTS 9 (Leiden: Brill, 2013), 213–54; *idem*, "Paul and Ancient Civic Ethics: Redefining the Canon of Honour in the Graeco-Roman World," in *Paul's Graeco-Roman Context*, ed. Cilliers Breytenbach, BETL 227 (Leuven: Peeters, 2015), 75–118; *idem*, "Paul and the Cultic Associations," *Reformed Theological Review* 58.1 (1999): 31–47.

fessor Jörg Frey, the managing editor of *Wissenschaftliche Untersuchungen zum Neuen Testament*, who has welcomed the book's inclusion in the series. The help of Elena Müller, Programme Director Theology and Jewish Studies, and Tobias Stäbler, Editorial Assistant Theology and Jewish Studies, has been invaluable in finalising the script. The encouragement of Dr. Henning Zietbritzki, the Managing Director of Mohr Siebeck, has also been a constant feature in my dealings with the press since my first 2003 publication. I have always appreciated Henning's warm interest in my scholarship. Many thanks to the Associate Editors who gave helpful feedback on the initial book proposal and especially to Professor J. Ross Wagner who encouraged me to consider submitting a third monograph to Mohr Siebeck.

The writing of the book has been enhanced by the many audiences that have heard elements of Chapters 2–9 delivered at various conferences around the world. By being asked penetrating questions after presentations and upon receiving helpful feedback in such contexts, I have experienced the truth of Proverbs 27:17: "As iron sharpens iron, so one person sharpens another" (NIV). I am especially thankful to a wide range of Pauline and ancient history scholars, far too many to be named, who, through their personal friendship and deep familiarity with the Graeco-Roman world, have contributed to my thinking in rich and diverse ways. Above all, without the support, love and encouragement of my wife, Elisabeth, this book would not have reached its completion.

This book is dedicated to Emeritus Professor Edwin Judge who, in his ninety-first year, has already published two books this year.[6] He awaits the appearance in print of the "Corpus of Christian Papyri" project, his great labour of love conducted in partnership with his Macquarie University colleagues since 1972 in its various evolutions, now submitted to a press for consideration for publication.[7]

---

[6] E.A. Judge, *Paul and the Conflict of Cultures: The Legacy of His Thought Today*, ed. James R. Harrison (Eugene: Cascade, 2019); *idem*, *The Failure of Augustus*.

[7] The "Corpus of Christian Papyri" project, formerly called the *Corpus Papyrorum Christianarum* (C.P.C.), was renamed "Papyri from the Rise of Christianity in Egypt" (P.C.E) from 1980 onwards. In private correspondence, Professor Judge summed up the results of the project thus: "'Papyri from the Rise of Christianity in Egypt', a long-term collective project of the Documentary Research Centre at Macquarie, reviewing 400 texts palaeographically, and re-editing 200 non-literary ones with extensive historical commentary and translation, is currently being considered by a press for publication."

Table of Contents

List of Abbreviations

ABR	*Australian Biblical Review*
AC	*L'antiquité classique*
AJA	*American Journal of Archaeology*
AJP	*American Journal of Philology*
Anc. Soc.	*Ancient Society*
AncW	*The Ancient World*
ANRW	*Aufstieg und Niedergang der römischen Welt*, ed. H. Temporini
ASSH Bulletin	*Australian Society for Sports History Bulletin*
Ath. Mitt.	*Mitteilungen des Deutschen Archäologischen Instituts, Athenische Abteilung*
BA	*The Biblical Archaeologist*
BBR	*Bulletin for Biblical Research*
BCH	*Bulletin de correspondance hellénique*
Bib	*Biblica*
BICS	*Bulletin of the Institute of Classical Studies*
BTB	*Biblical Theology Bulletin*
CA	*Classical Antiquity*
CB	*Classical Bulletin*
CBQ	*Catholic Biblical Quarterly*
CIG	*Corpus Inscriptionum Graecarum*, eds. A. Boekhio and I. Franzius
CIJ	*Corpus Inscriptionum Iudaicarum*, ed. J.B. Frey
CIL	*Corpus Inscriptionum Latinarum*, eds. T. Mommsen, W. Henzen, et al.
CJ	*Classical Journal*
CPh	*Classical Philology*
CPJ	*Corpus Papyrorum Judaicarum*, ed. V. Tcherikover
CQ	*Classical Quarterly*
CTM	*Concordia Theological Monthly*
CurTM	*Currents in Theology and Mission*
DHA	*Dialogues d'histoire ancienne*
DocsAug	*Documents Illustrating the Reigns of Augustus and Tiberius*, eds. V. Ehrenberg and A.H.M. Jones
DocsGaius	*Documents Illustrating the Principates of Gaius, Claudius and Nero*, ed. E.M. Smallwood
EvQ	*Evangelical Quarterly*
FD	*Fouilles de Delphes*, ed. E. Bourget et al.
G&R	*Greece & Rome*
GRBS	*Greek, Roman, and Byzantine Studies*
HSCPh	*Harvard Studies in Classical Philology*
HTR	*Harvard Theological Review*

IAssos	*Die Inschriften von Assos*, ed. R. Merkelbach
ICreticae	*Inscriptiones Creticae*, ed. M. Guarducci
IDelos	*Inscriptions de Délos*, ed. A. Plassart et al.
IEph	*Die Inschriften von Ephesos*, ed. H. Wankel et al.
IG	*Inscriptiones Graecae*, ed. F.H. von Gaertringen et al.
IGLSyr	*Inscriptions grecques et latines de la Syrie*, eds. L. Jalabert and R. Mouterde
IGRR	*Inscriptiones Graecae ad res Romanas pertinentes*, R. Cagnat et al.
IIasos	*Die Inschriften von Iasos*, ed. W. Blümel
IKyzikos	*Die Inschriften von Kyzikos und Umgebung*, ed. E. Schwertheim
ILaodikeia am Lykos	*Die Inschriften von Laodikeia am Lykos*, ed. T. Corsten
ILS	*Inscriptiones Latinae Selectae*, ed. H. Dessau
IMagnesia	*Die Inschriften von Magnesia am Maeander*, ed. O. Kern
IMilet	*Milet. I.1–9*, ed. A. Rehm
IMylasa	*Die Inschriften von Mylasa. I. Inschriften der Stadt*, ed. W. Blümel
IPriene	*Die Inschriften von Priene*, ed. F. Hiller von Gaertringen
ISestos	*Die Inschriften von Sestos und des thrakischen Chersones*, ed. J. Krauss
IvO	Olympia: die Ergebnisse der *von dem Deutschen Reich veranstalteten Ausgrabung. V. Die Inschriften*, eds. W. Dittenberger and K. Purgold
JAC	*Jahrbuch für Antike und Christentum*
JBL	*Journal of Biblical Literature*
JETS	*Journal of the Evangelical Theological Society*
JGRChJ	*Journal of Greco-Roman Christianity and Judaism*
Jh. Österr	*Jahreshefte des Österreichischen Archäologischen Institutes in Wien*
JHS	*Journal of Hellenic Studies*
JJMJS	*Journal of the Jesus Movement in Its Jewish Setting*
JRA	*Journal of Roman Archaeology*
JRS	*Journal of Roman Studies*
JSJ	*Journal for the Study of Judaism*
JSNT	*Journal for the Study of the New Testament*
JSNTPHRP	*Journal for the Study of Judaism in the Persian, Hellenistic and Roman Period*
JSNTSup	*Journal for the Study of the New Testament Supplement Series*
JTS	*Journal of Theological Studies*
MAAR	*Memoirs of the American Academy in Rome*
MAMA	*Monumenta Asiae Minoris Antiqua*, ed. W.M. Calder et al.
MH	*Museum Helveticum*
Michel	*Recueil d'inscriptions grecques*, ed. C. Michel
Neot	*Neotestamentica*
New Docs	*New Documents Illustrating Early Christianity*, eds. G.H.R. Horsley (vols. 1–5); S.R. Llewelyn (vols. 6–9), and S.R. Llewelyn and J.R. Harrison (vol. 10)
NovT	*Novum Testamentum*
NTS	*New Testament Studies*
OGIS	*Orientis Graeci Inscriptiones Selectae*, ed. W. Dittenberger

P. Univ. Athen. inv. 2782	A.N. Oikonomides, "*The Lost Delphic Inscription with the Commandments of the Seven and P. Univ. Athen. 2782,*" *Zeitschrift für Papyrologie und Epigraphik 37 (1980): 179–83*
P. Brem.	*Die Bremer Papyri*, ed. U. Wilcken
PBSR	*Papers of the British School at Rome*
PCPS	*Proceedings of the Cambridge Philological Society*
PGM	*The Greek Magical Papyri in Translation*, ed. H.D. Betz
P. Kramer	"*... vor dem Papyrus sind alle gleich!*" *Papyrologische Beiträge zu Ehren von Bärbel Kramer*, ed. R. Eberhard et al.
P. Lond.	*Greek Papyri in the British Museum*, ed. F.G. Kenyon et al.
P. Mich.	*Michigan Papyri. I. Zenon Papyri*, ed. C.C. Edgar
PMLA	*Publications of the Modern Language Association of America*
P. Oxy.	*Oxyrhynchus Papyri*, eds. B.P. Grenfell and A.S. Hunt et al.
RAC	*Reallexikon für Antike und Christentum*
RE	Realencyclopädie der classischen Altertumswissenschaft
REG	*Revue des études grecques*
REL	*Revue des études latines*
ResQ	*Restoration Quarterly*
RIC[2]	*Royal Imperial Coinage*
RIDA	*Revue internationale des droits de l'antiquité*
RTR	*Reformed Theological Review*
SEG	*Supplementum Epigraphicum Graecum*
SIG[3]	*Sylloge Inscriptionum Graecarum*, ed. W. Dittenberger
SJT	*Scottish Journal of Theology*
SR	*Studies in Religion/Sciences Religieuses*
TAM	*Tituli Asiae Minoris*, ed. E. Kalinka et al.
TAPA	*Transactions of the American Philological Association*
TDNT	*Theological Dictionary of the New Testament*
TrGF	*The Context of Ancient Drama*, eds. E. Csapo and W.J. Slater
TynBul	*Tyndale Bulletin*
USQR	*Union Seminary Quarterly Review*
VC	*Vigiliae Christianae*
VEv	*Vox Evangelica*
VSpir	*La vie spirituelle*
WUNT	*Wissenschaftliche Untersuchungen zum Neuen Testament*
YCS	*Yale Classical Studies*
ZPE	*Zeitschrift für Papyrologie und Epigraphik*
ZWT	*Zeitschrift für wissenschaftliche Theologie*

Chapter 1

"The Bold and the Beautiful": Fame and Celebrity in Antiquity and the Modern World

The idea that history may be explained by the study of the "great man" began in the modern era with a pioneering publication of Thomas Carlyle (1795–1881) in 1840.[1] Although Jean-Jacques Rousseau had been Carlyle's immediate predecessor in reviving the long-lost interest in the classical ideal of heroic virtue,[2] Carlyle seized the popular imagination by producing not only a moral-philosophical assessment of the heroic past but also by proposing an ethical interpretation of the role that political leaders, the modern inheritors of the heroic mantle, should now play in the world.[3] Carlyle depicted the great man as a divinity, prophet, poet, priest, man of letters and king. For Carlyle, the "Man of Letters" was the ultimate hero.[4] He endorsed Fichte's estimate that the literary elites were a "perpetual priesthood" unfolding "the Godlike to men."[5] In so doing, Carlyle bypassed Napoleon, the kingly paradigm of heroic virtue,[6] preferring instead to make his own quiet gambit for deflected glory as a Scottish "man of letters." Carlyle also sought to endorse the divine right of the aristocratic elites to rule by promoting a society governed by the excellent, or, as he pompously

---

[1] The phrase employed in the chapter's title, "The Bold and the Beautiful", alludes to the most-watched television soap opera in the world. The show premiered on CBS on March 23, 1987, and it depicts the celebrity family members connected with the fictional fashion house, Forrester Creations, based in Los Angeles. Regarding the "great man" in history, see T. Carlyle, *On Heroes, Hero-Worship, and the Heroic in History: Six Lectures* (New York: Longmans, Green, and Co., 1906; orig. London: Chapman and Hall, 1841). Carlyle (*ibid.*, 28) sums up his thesis with these words: "No great man lives in vain. The History of the world is but the Biography of great men." For discussion of Carlyle's views, see E. Bentley, *The Cult of the Superman: A Study of the Idea of Heroism in Carlyle and Nietzsche with Notes on Other Hero-Worshippers of Modern Times* (London: R. Hale, 1947); D. Garofalo, "Communities in Mourning: Making Capital Out of Loss in Carlyle's Past and Present and Heroes," *Texas Studies in Literature and Language* 45.3 (2003): 293–314.

[2] See J.-J. Rousseau, "Discourse on the Virtue a Hero Most Needs or On Heroic Virtue," in *idem*, *The "Discourses" and Other Early Political Writings*, ed. V. Gourevitch, Cambridge Texts in the History of Political Thought (Cambridge: Cambridge University Press, 1997).

[3] L. Eriksonas, *National Heroes and National Identities: Scotland, Norway and Lithuania*, "Multiple Europes" 26 (Brussels: Peter Lang, 2005), 32.

[4] Carlyle, *On Heroes*, 149–88

[5] Carlyle, *On Heroes*, 189–235

[6] Carlyle, *On Heroes*, 151.

categorised this spiritual elite, the "Able-man".[7] However, the "great man" model for understanding the evolution of history came under serious attack at the hands of Herbert Spencer, dislodging the approach from mainstream historical investigation of the past.[8] In the view of Spencer, "great" men were simply the products of their social environment. While some monographs still attribute historical agency primarily to the actions of great men,[9] researchers now situate historical figures within the complex and variegated currents of society at large, though there has been a recent explosion in "heroic" studies across many disciplines.[10] Thus it should not surprise us that no satisfying history of celebrity has yet been written. The deep interconnectedness of celebrities with their social and historical context makes analysis difficult. Moreover, the fan base of celebrities must also be factored in as an actor on the historical stage of celebrity if the phenomenon is to be properly evaluated.

However, writers in antiquity celebrate the rise, achievements, and virtues of the "great man". Plutarch not only wrote contrasting biographies of Greek and Roman leaders, but also prefaced his parallel lives with a comparison (συγκρίσις) of the figures whom he was discussing. The anonymous *De Viris Illustribus* ("Deeds of Famous Men") provides seventy-seven biographical sketches of republican luminaries for its audience to consider as *exempla*. Last, Valerius Maximus' *Facta et Dicta Memorabilia* ("Memorable Doings and Sayings") also

[7] Carlyle, *On Heroes*, 206–08. Note, *ibid.*, 166: "Find in any country the Ablest Man that exists there; raise him to the supreme place, and loyally reverence him: you have a perfect government for that country; no ballot-box, parliamentary eloquence, voting, constitution-building, or other machinery whatsoever can improve it a whit. It is in the perfect state; an ideal country."

[8] H. Spencer (*The Study of Sociology* [New York: D. Appleton and Co., 1896], 31) writes: "If it may be a fact that the great man may modify his nation in its structure and actions, it is also a fact that there must have been those antecedent modifications constituting national progress before he could be evolved. Before he can re-make his society, his society must make him. So that all those changes of which he is the proximate initiator have their chief causes in the generations he descended from. If there is to be anything like a real explanation of these changes, it must be sought in that aggregate of conditions out of which he and they have arisen."

[9] For example, S.B. Ferrario (*Historical Agency and the "Great Man" in Classical Greece* [Cambridge and New York: Cambridge University Press, 2014]) argues that a development occurs from the agency of the polis displayed at the time of early Athenian democracy to the emergence of individual agency under the unprecedented conquests of Alexander the Great. In Ferrario's view (*ibid.*, 354), Alexander represents the "culmination" of the individualism that led to the emergence of the "great man" theory. On the great man in antiquity, see E.A. Judge, "The Changing Idea of the Great Man," in *Paul and the Conflict of Cultures: The Legacy of His Thought Today*, ed. J.R. Harrison (Eugene: Cascade Books, 2019), 122–137.

[10] See M. Jones, "What Should Historians Do with Heroes? Reflections on Nineteenth- and Twentieth-Century Britain," *History Compass* 5.2 (2007): 493–54; J. Price, *Everyday Heroism: Victorian Constructions of the Heroic Civilian* (London and New York: Bloomsbury Academic, 2014). For bibliographic references to "heroism" across the disciplines, see "Heroism Science: Promoting the Transdisciplinary Study of Heroism in the 21st Century," at https:// www.heroismscience.wordpress.com/, accessed 11.05.2017.

recounts *exempla*, Roman and foreign, for the consideration of posterity.[11] Whereas modern scholars are reticent about speaking of the influence that individuals can *singehandedly* impose upon history, there was no such reticence in antiquity. These virtuous figures, precisely because of their fame and accomplishments, were worthy of imitation. This book, collecting together previously published essays and new contributions on the topic of celebrity, is interested in the moral transformation that the ancients thought such figures offered to their contemporaries and posterity. The collision of this venerable moral tradition, indissoluably linked to the accomplishments of ancient luminaries, with the gospel of the apostle Paul represents a significant flashpoint in the western intellectual tradition and in the development of social relations in antiquity, the reverberations of which continue to be felt in our culture today. What, then, is the nature of celebrity in its modern and ancient context?

1.1. Research on Celebrity in Its Modern and Ancient Context

1.1.1. Scholarship on the Modern Phenomenon of Celebrity

Precisely when the phenomenon of "celebrity" began in the modern era remains a moot point in scholarship.[12] No authoritative history of celebrity has been written, though, as we will see, R. Garland, not unreasonably, traces the beginnings of the celebrity cult back to ancient times.[13] But, in many respects, the

[11] For full details, see Chapter 7.

[12] For books from 2000 onwards discussing celebrity, see R. Shickel, *Intimate Strangers: The Culture of Celebrity in America*, 2nd ed. (Chicago: Ivan R. Dee, 2000; orig. 1985); G. Turner et al., *Fame Games: The Production of Celebrity in Australia* (Cambridge and New York: Cambridge University Press, 2000); C. Rojek, *Celebrity* (London: Reaktion, 2001); M. Orth, *The Importance of Being Famous: Behind the Scenes of the Celebrity-Industrial Complex* (New York: H. Holt, 2004); P.D. Marshall, *The Celebrity Culture Reader* (New York: Routledge, 2006); J. Gaffney and D. Holmes, *Stardom in Postwar France* (New York: Berghahn Books, 2007); D.A. Herwitz, *The Star as Icon: Celebrity in the Age of Mass Consumption* (New York: Columbia University Press, 2008); K.O. Ferris and S.R. Harris, *Stargazing: Celebrity, Fame, and Social Interaction* (New York and London: Routledge, 2011); R. van Krieken, *Celebrity Society* (New York and London: Routledge, 2012); K. Sternheimer, *Celebrity Culture and the American Dream: Stardom and Mobility*, 2nd ed. (New York: Routledge, 2015). See also D. Beer and R. Penfold-Mounce, "Researching Glossy Topics: The Case of the Academic Study of Celebrity," *Celebrity Studies* 1.3 (2010): 360–65. For a Marxist approach to celebrity, see P.D. Marshall, *Celebrity and Power: Fame in Contemporary Culture* (Minneapolis: University of Minnesota Press, 1997).

[13] See R. Garland, *Celebrity in Antiquity: From Media Tarts to Tabloid Queens* (London: Duckworth, 2006). Note also L. Braudy (*The Frenzy of Renown: Fame and Its History* [New York: Vintage Books, 1997], 3–113), who traces the origins of celebrity back to Alexander the Great, followed hard on the heels by Cicero and Augustus. In sharp contrast, contrast F. Inglis (*A Short History of Celebrity* [Princeton: Princeton University Press, 2010]) who argues that the history of celebrity was set in motion by the Romantics during the eighteenth century. Because of the Romantic emphasis upon living for the passions, new ideologies about self-

answer to the question about the origins of modern celebrity is predetermined by the perspective (entertainment, politics, literature, philosophy, military?) with which the scholar, consciously unconsciously, approaches the question.[14] Furthermore, consideration must also be given to the countries and continents (Europe? England? America?) from which the choice of the majority of celebrities has been made, including the urban sophistication and media penetration of the regions in which each celebrity operated.[15] Once again, each of these factors will largely predetermine one's answers regarding the origins and development of celebrity, either at a national or trans-national level. What follows, therefore, is in no way meant to be a history of the rise of the modern celebrity. Rather the selection, spanning the eighteenth to the early twenty-first century, is illustrative of the phenomenon of fame and is provided as a useful counterpoint to our ensuing discussion of ancient celebrity. Needless to say, the selection below is determined, to some extent, by my personal interests.

1.1.1.1. The So-Called "Origins" of Modern Celebrity from the Eighteenth to the Twentieth Century: A Survey of Representative Figures

What candidates might be mooted as possibilities for being the originator of the modern celebrity cult? If one considers celebrity from a political perspective, then Giuseppe Garibaldi (1807–1882) looms large as a potential candidate for being the first modern celebrity. His numerous scandals, exotic war stories, adventuring spirit, and lofty idealism in spearheading the unification of Italy

hood and individuality emerged. Outlining a complex interaction of diverse forces, Inglis (*ibid.*, 5) posits the following pathway of development from the individualisation of the emotions towards the ultimate emergence of celebrity: "The rise of urban democracy, the two-hundred-year expansion of its media of communication, together with the radical individualisation of the modern sensibility made fame a much more transitory reward and changed public acclaim from an expression of devotion into one of celebrity."

[14] S.J. Morgan, in his review of Inglis, *A Short History of Celebrity*, correctly observes: "… the problem facing any student of celebrity is the sheer volume and bewildering variety of available subjects. Any choice of case studies will therefore be highly personal." See http://www.history.ac.uk/reviews/review/994, accessed 19.04.2017.

[15] S.J. Morgan (review of Inglis, *A Short History of Celebrity*) makes a telling point about the importance of locale in the development of celebrity: "… the eastern United States played a vibrant role in international fame culture after the opening up of the literary lecture circuit in the 1830s, not to mention the intercontinental promotional activities of Phineas Barnum, who among other triumphs introduced the 'Swedish Nightingale' Jenny Lind to enraptured audiences across America in the 1850s. However, it does draw out very neatly the importance of major urban centres in providing the *necessary conditions* for the first celebrity cultures to thrive, including places to see and be seen, proximity to the centres of political and/or financial power, a thriving press and a large, literate audience. These are factors often ignored by contemporary theorists, who hold that the mass audiences and means of communication which enable the culture of celebrity to survive did not exist before the 20th century" (my emphasis). See http://www.history.ac.uk/reviews/review/994, accessed 19.04.2017.

meant that he dominated the attention of the international printing presses.[16] "Garibaldimania" even spread to Britain, but whether it permeated all the English provinces, or was merely a locally contested event fought out between the radicals and conservatives, as a recent study of 1854–1861 Newcastle-upon-Tyne has argued,[17] is beyond the scope of this work to determine.

By contrast, if the origins of modern celebrity are explored from the perspective of literature, then "Byromania" is another equally viable option.[18] The widespread international celebrity of Lord Byron (1788–1824), it has recently been argued,[19] was less generated by the publication of his poetry volumes than by his widespread fame in periodicals, newspapers and magazines of the time. However, there are other candidates who emerge as genuine possibilities for being among the first celebrities in the modern era, at least in an American context. The American poet Walt Whitman (1819–1892), for example, was famous for his volume of poems, the *Leaves of Grass*, rewritten and expanded over his career until the original 12 poems numbered over 400. But equally important for the promotion of Whitman's fame was a photograph taken of the poet by a Philadelphian firm, operated by Samuel Broadbent and W. Curtis Taylor. The much celebrated "Butterfly" portrait of Walt Whitman was taken by Taylor in the spring of 1877. It shows Whitman, in smoking jacket and large felt hat, looking intently at his extended right index finger, upon which had alighted a delicate butterfly with expanded wings.[20] As has been well observed of the photograph,[21] Whitman was a poseur of epic proportions who understood well "that photography was one of several cultural developments that would change the way in which literature was promoted and produced." Each of these potential candidates for first modern celebrity understood the centrality of the print media and photography for a much wider dissemination of their fame than they could achieve political and literary careers alone.

Irrespective of who might be thought to be the "first" celebrity from our three examples above, by the early twentieth century, famous literary elites (Ezra Pound, T.S. Eliot, James Joyce, Wyndham Lewis) continued to create

[16] L. Riall, *Garibaldi: Invention of a Hero* (New Haven and London: Yale University Press, 2007); *idem*, "Garibaldi: The First Celebrity," *History Today* 57.8 (2007): 41–47.

[17] M.P. Sutcliffe, "Negotiating the 'Garibaldi Moment' in Newcastle-upon-Tyne (1854–1861)," *Modern Italy*, 15.2 (2010): 129–44.

[18] On Byromania, see F. Wilson, ed., *Byromania: Portraits of the Artist in Nineteenth and Twentieth Century Culture* (Basingstoke: Palgrave Macmillan, 1999); T. Mole, *Byron's Romantic Celebrity: Industrial Culture and the Hermeneutic of Intimacy* (Houndmills and New York: Palgrave MacMillan, 2007); G. McDayter, *Byromania and the Birth of Celebrity Culture*, Studies in the Long Nineteenth Century Literature (Albany: State University of New York Press, 2009).

[19] See McDayter, *Byromania and the Birth of Celebrity Culture*.

[20] For the picture, see D.H. Blake, *Walt Whitman and the Culture of American Celebrity* (New Haven and London: Yale University Press, 2006), 2.

[21] Blake, *Walt Whitman*, 4.

markets for their works and the establishment of their fame by networking, reviewing and editing their literary productions, even though they rejected the baseness of popular culture in preference for their own elite cultural products.[22] Similar networks operated between the American novelists Jack Kerouac and William S. Burroughs, the Beat Poets (Allen Ginsburg, Lawrence Ferlinghetti, Gregory Corso, among others), and Bob Dylan in the late 1950's and the early 1960's. Media influences were again prominent in these interconnections of fame. Ginsburg's photograph appeared on the album cover of *Bringing It All Back Home*, whereas in D.A. Pennebaker's documentary film, *Don't Look Back*, covering Dylan's 1965 UK tour, Ginsberg made a cameo appearance in the clip for Dylan's song *Subterranean Homesick Blues*.[23] Thus, by the time of the early twentieth century, media and literary networking was clearly a crucial step for the famous to acquire the exalted status of celebrity.

Also interesting for our purposes is how the mythology of celebrity was constructed and deconstructed in the twentieth century. Two examples from the American literary world will suffice. The American novelist Ernest Hemingway was often captured in iconic outdoor photographs, either fishing, hunting or attending bull fights. During the 1950's he was involved in two plane crashes, won the Nobel Prize, and five films were made from his fiction. Consequently, the "Hemingway myth" became inextricably entwined with his masculinity and the perception that he was a literary genius. Hemingway's quasi-mythological status as a male was reinforced at a popular cultural level by a host of articles titled "Hemingway, Rogue Male," "Hemingway: America's No 1 He-Man," "Hemingway: War, Women, Wine, and Words," and "Hemingway: King of the Vulgar Words and Seduction." Surprisingly, these were published in the trashy men's pulp magazines of the 1950's as opposed to the more elite male publications of Esquire and Playboy. This lurid and misogynistic genre of popular publishing enhanced Hemingways' status as a literary giant with a new audience, while also establishing him as an American mid-century icon of machismo.[24]

By contrast, the famous American novelist Philip Roth – winner of the 1960 National Book Award in Fiction with his first novella *Goodbye, Columbus* (1959) and author of the controversial *Portnoy's Complaint* (1969) – went on to win the Pulitzer Prize with his novel *American Pastoral* (1997). But, after this

---

[22] See A. Jaffe, *Modernism and the Culture of Celebrity* (Cambridge and New York: Cambridge University Press, 2004).

[23] See M. Jacobi, "Bob Dylan and Collaboration" and D.R. Schumway, "Dylan as Cultural Icon," in *The Cambridge Companion to Bob Dylan*, ed. K.J.H. Dettmar (Cambridge and New York: Cambridge University Press, 2009), respectively, 69–79 and 110–21.

[24] See D.M. Earle, *All Man!: Hemingway, 1950s Men's Magazines, and the Masculine Persona* (Kent: Kent State University Press, 2009); T. Strychacz, "Masculinity," in *Ernest Hemingway in Context*, ed. D.A. Moddelmog and S. Del Gizzo (Cambridge: Cambridge University Press, 2013), 277–86. More generally, see J. Smith, *The Thrill Makers: Celebrity, Masculinity, and Stunt Performance* (Berkeley: University of California Press, 2012).

high-point of fame, Roth re-evaluated the celebrity he had acquired, while, ironically, his subsequent novels went on to win further plaudits. The paradox is potent. A late surge of creativity in his mid-sixties after the Pulitzer Prize resulted in a series of novels whose quality was hailed by literary critics across the world.[25] However, as Roth explains in his valedictory interview with Alan Yentob for the BBC in 2014, summarised in *The Guardian* (May 17, 2004), he withdrew from the "celebrity game" while writing these new works:

> (Roth) reports that, in old age, "the last thing I wanted to do was to make myself more visible then I already was. The visibility unnerved me. And so I moved to the country." Roth retreated to an isolated farmhouse in Connecticut. He describes, almost for the first time, the conditions under which he wrote the sequence of novels that followed *American Pastoral*. "I find it very congenial to live in the natural beauty of the place I have in Connecticut. I work during the day, do some exercise late in the day" – he swims regularly – "and so I haven't lost contact with what I've been doing all day."[26]

Roth's abdication from the celebrity circuit finds its counterparts in other modern writers and entertainers who, while remaining in the public eye of their profession, nevertheless critiqued the shallowness of the celebrity industry.[27]

---

[25] See *I Married a Communist* (1998), *The Human Stain* (2000), *The Dying Animal* (2001) and *The Plot Against America* (2004). For discussion, see M. Shipe, "The Twilight of the Superheroes: Philip Roth, Celebrity, and the End of Print Culture," in *Roth and Celebrity*, ed. A. Pozorski (Lanham, MD: Lexington Books, 2013), 101–18.

[26] See "Bye-bye ... Philip Roth talks of fame, sex and growing old in last interview," at https://www.theguardian.com › Arts › Books › Philip Roth, accessed 16.04.2017. For further discussion of Philip Roth and the phenomenon of celebrity, Pozorski, *Roth and Celebrity*, *passim*.

[27] For example, Mark Twain, the American novelist, writes regarding the universal seduction of fame: "Celebrity is what a boy or a youth longs for more than for any other thing. He would be a clown in a circus; he would be a pirate, he would sell himself to Satan, in order to attract attention and be talked about and envied. True, it is the same with every grown-up person; I am not meaning to confine this trait to the boys." Mark Twain, *Autobiography of Mark Twain, Vol. 2*, ed. H.E. Smith et al. (Berkeley: University of California Press, 2013), 232. Numerous pop and rock stars show strong ambivalence about fame in their songs: e.g. David Bowie ("Fame;" "The Stars [Are Out Tonight]"); Harry Chapin ("W.O.L.D."); Counting Crows ("Have You Seen Me Lately"); Eagles ("After the Thrill is Gone"); Lady Gaga ("Paparazzi"); Billy Joel ("The Entertainer"); Josh Joplin ("Camera One"); Alanis Morissette ("Celebrity"); The Kinks ("Celluloid Heroes"); The Smashing Pumpkins ("Bullet with Butterfly Wings"); Peter Sarstedt ("Where Do You Go To My Lovely?"); Chris Rea ("Tennis"); Warren Zevon ("Splendid Isolation"). Supremely, Bob Dylan's song, "Desolation Row" – an apocalyptic depiction of the demise of modernity ranking in quality with T.S. Eliot's "The Waste Land" – invokes famous figures from the Bible (Noah, Cain, Abel, Good Samaritan), history (Einstein, Nero), fiction (Ophelia, Romeo, Cinderella), and literature (Ezra Pound, T.S. Eliot) as characters or allusions in the song. Dylan reduces these celebrated symbols of Western civilisation to absurdity in his desolate vision of the modern world. For an insightful discussion of the song, see C.H. Jones, *Bob Dylan and the End of the (Modern) World* (PhD diss., University of Texas, Dallas, 2013), 112–20. There is little doubt that the lyrical quality of songs like "Desolation Row" earned Dylan, controversially in the perspective of some, the Nobel Prize for Literature in October 2016.

The withdrawal of Roth from celebrity and his continuing literary success in self-imposed exile is diametrically opposed to how the American novelist Scott Fitzgerald, along with his manic depressive wife Zelda, were eventually undone by their celebrity. With the success of Scott's novel *This Side of Paradise* (1920), the Fizgeralds skilfully courted public fame by exploiting the (up till then) little ventured avenues of the popular press, magazines, theatre and cinema through the twenties and early thirties.[28] Scott dubbed Zelda as "the first American Flapper" of the Jazz Age[29] and portrayed himself as hedonistic and intellectual. But by 1935 their ascendant star had waned, plunging Scott into drunken degradation and a declining literary output until his eventual death in 1940,[30] while Zelda was confined to specialist clinics until her death by an outbreak of fire in her hospital in 1948.

The powerful role of the photojournalism in promoting celebrity in the first half of the twentieth century must not be underestimated.[31] R. Linkof, in an excellent thesis, explores the democratising effect of tabloid celebrity. He argues that between 1890 and 1940 there was a dissolution of the Victorian aristocratic social system, resulting in the emergence of the "photojournalistic culture of celebrity."[32] The traditional social hierarchies were overcome by bridging the distance between the privileged elites and mass audiences through the photos taken of the elites, which were published for all to see in the popular tabloids (e.g. *Picture Post*, *Tatler*, *Illustrated News*, *Daily Mirror*).[33] A radical change in conceptions of class and social difference occurred with the emergence of the press photographer as a social actor.[34] The glamourous "debutante" balls of the aristocracy were widely photographed,[35] and, with the gradual decline of the aristocracy, all their social events became an excuse for a torrent of self-advertisement in the tabloids.[36] This was not by any means the preserve of the aristocracy: the "lighter side of the war" in 1916 was captured with pictures of smiling

---

[28] See T.W. Galow, *Writing Celebrity: Stein, Fitzgerald, and the Modern(ist) Art of Self-Fashioning* (New York: Palgrave Macmillan, 2011); R. Prigozy, "Introduction: Scott, Zelda, and the Culture of Celebrity," in *The Cambridge Companion to Scott Fitzgerald*, ed. R. Prigozy (Cambridge: Cambridge University Press 2002), 1–27.

[29] The Jazz Age is brilliantly depicted in Fitzgerald's *The Great Gatsby* (1925) and in Baz Luhrmann's 2013 film of the novel. See the interesting comparison between the book and the film provided by D.R. Shumway "Gatsby, the Jazz Age, and Luhrmann Land," *The Journal of the Gilded Age and Progressive Era* 14 (2015): 132–37. On the Jazz Age, see F. Scott Fitzgerald's essay, "Echoes of the Jazz Age," *Scribner's Magazine* 90.5 (1931): 459–65.

[30] *The Last Tycoon* remained unfinished at Fitzgerald's death and was published in 1941.

[31] See R. Linkof, *The Public Eye: Celebrity and Photojournalism in the Making of the British Tabloids, 1904–1938* (PhD thesis, University of Southern California, 2011).

[32] Linkof, *The Public Eye*, 33.

[33] Linkof, *The Public Eye*, 41–47, 55–59.

[34] Linkof, *The Public Eye*, 31–32, 53.

[35] Linkof, *The Public Eye*, 301–22.

[36] Linkof, *The Public Eye*, 320.

nurses and soldiers on the Western Front.[37] Thus the consolidation of Fleet Street in the first half of the twentieth century as the mainstay of the newspaper industry led inexorably to the rise of the paparazzi and the stalking of celebrities which are so much part of modern culture.

Last, the famous book of D.J. Boorstin revealed with great clarity for his American readers the image-dominated celebrity culture that had begun to emerge in the USA by the early 1960's.[38] Boorstin argued that American culture was being increasingly infiltrated by "the menace of unreality"[39] in the form of a media-constructed reality, which was orchestrated by "pseudo-events" (e.g. the ubiquitous television debate). These pseudo-events, Boorstin opined, tended "to be more interesting and more attractive than spontaneous events," because they were controlled and calculated, but, consequently, less "real."[40] In particular, the *human* pseudo-event increasingly dominated twentieth century society. Here untalented celebrities become media fabrications "known for (their) well-knownness" (e.g. Zsa Zsa Gabor) as opposed to any accomplishment of lasting social or cultural value.[41] Boorstin's analysis was prophetic. The rampantly narcissistic worlds of Paris Hilton, the Kardashians, and Donald Trump would inevitably appear at the beginning of the new century.[42]

But even before the self-absorption of banal celebrities, along with their adoring cohorts, had gripped popular culture, an increasing preoccupation with public fame is reflected in the shift in value priorities espoused in the top "tween" TV shows from 1967 to 2007.[43] This change in value priorities is particularly telling. "Fame" was rated as the top value in 2007, followed hard on the heels by "Achievement" and "Popularity" in second and third place, whereas "Fame" had only been rated fifteenth (out of sixteen) in previous decades. By contrast, "Community Feeling" dropped to eleventh in 2007, whereas it had been first in 1967, 1977, and 1997, and second in 1987.[44] But, by 2007, self-assertion and individualism had eclipsed the moral tradition of social consciousness in "tween"

---

[37] Linkof, *The Public Eye*, 97–101.

[38] D.J. Boorstin, *The Image: A Guide to Pseudo-events in America* (New York: Atheneum, 1961). For a helpful discussion of the significance of Boorstin's book, see N. Gabler, "Toward a New Definition of Celebrity – the Norman Lear Center," at https://learcenter.org/pdf/Gabler.pdf, accessed 07.09.2017.

[39] Boorstin, *The Image*, 57.

[40] Boorstin, *The Image*, 37.

[41] Boorstin, *The Image*, 57; cf. "A sign of a celebrity is often that his name is worth more than his services" (*ibid.*, 220).

[42] On celebrity and Donald Trump, see P. Dreier, "Zsa Zsa, Donald, and America's Celebrity Culture," at http://www.huffingtonpost.com/peter-dreier/zsa-zsa-and-donald_b_13716396.html, accessed 07.09.2017.

[43] See Y.T. Uhls and P.M. Greenfield, "The Rise of Fame: An Historical Content Analysis," Cyberpsychology 5.1. (2011) at https://cyberpsychology.eu/article/view/4243/3289, accessed 08.09.2017.

[44] See Uhls and Greenfield, "The Rise of Fame," Table 4.

TV culture. Y.T. Uhls and P.M. Greenfield conclude regarding TV shows like *Hannah Montana*, which depict highly successful teenagers living out their "career dream" amidst their drab and dull peers: "it is likely that tweens observing teenage characters with high status jobs that emphasize public recognition and material success will aspire to be like these social models."[45] This slavish imitation of vacuous "show biz" icons will inevitably breed a superficial and self-obsessed set of "disciples" who will not sacrificially invest themselves for others beyond either their immediate circle or their own self-interest. Nor will they experience the radical moral transformation that occurs from the early Christian understanding of our indebtedness to God and, consequently, our obligation to meet the needs of others (Rom 13:8–10), no matter who that might be (12:9–21; cf. Luke 6:27–36).

What features of celebrity are prominent in the early years of the first quarter of the twenty-first century?

1.1.1.2. Celebrity in the Early Twenty-First Century

In this section, the new trends in the international celebrity cult are briefly flagged and analysed. At the outset, perhaps the most important trend among the recent developments of international celebrity, departing from its largely elite focus, is the "decisive turn towards the ordinary."[46] First, the advent of reality TV (e.g. *Big Brother*, *Survivor*, *The Apprentice*, *The Bachelor*, *The X Factor*, *The Voice*) and the Internet has spawned a "celebrity culture ... increasingly populated by unexceptional people who have become famous and by stars who have been made ordinary."[47] There is a distinct cycle of fame (or "six stages of celebrity") for participants in these programmes.[48] Even elite versions of these shows have been devised (*Dancing with the Stars*, *Celebrity Survivor*).[49]

[45] Uhls and Greenfield, "The Rise of Fame."

[46] J. Gamson, "The Unwatched Life Is Not Worth Living: The Elevation of the Ordinary in Celebrity Culture," *PMLA* 126.4 (2011): 1061–69, at 1061–62. See also P.D. Marshall, "The Promotion and Presentation of the Self: Celebrity as a Marker of Presentational Media," *Celebrity Studies* 1.1 (2010): 35–48.

[47] Gamson, "The Unwatched Life," 1062. Whereas in the old Hollywood studio system before the late 1940's "celebrity was tightly controlled," now "one often encounters photos that demonstrate simultaneously celebrities' extraordinary glamour and awesome beauty on the red carpet and their just-like-us, unglamorous trips to the grocery store or a restaurant." Further, from the 1970's onwards the gossip columns and tabloids "puncture the public image of celebrities with the often sordid or ugly 'truths' of their private lives, their ordinary human foibles, their feet of clay" (*ibid.*, 1063).

[48] See R.A. Deller, "Star Image, Celebrity Reality Television and the Fame Cycle," *Celebrity Studies* 7.3 (2016): 373–89. See also L.C. Hellmueller and N. Aeschbacher, "Media and Celebrity: Production and Consumption of 'Well-Knownness'," *Communication and Research Trends* 29.4 (2010): 3–35.

[49] Gamson, "The Unwatched Life," 1065, 1066. As Gamson explains (*ibid.*, 1065), "The Internet drastically widens the pool of potential celebrities by lowering the entry barriers – a

The Web 2.0 phenomena (*YouTube*, *Myspace*, *Facebook*) have resulted in a "bottom-up ... self-made, do-it-yourself celebrity." The Internet phenomenon and its consequences are nicely encapsulated in these words:

> Internet celebrity culture has, then, made it easy for ordinary people to build an audience, bypassing the traditional celebrity industry; elevated the role of fans or audiences, turning them into powerful producers of celebrities, hyperaware of their star-making capacity; and moved to the forefront new celebrity characters and narratives that seem to defy the traditional celebrity system.[50]

Second, the celebrity funeral, along with the mourning rituals attached to it, official and general public, has become increasingly a part of modern culture. These rituals, of course, were played out with great solemnity in the case of the funerals of the ruler Augustus (Dio Cassius 56.34–47) and his relative Germanicus (*infra*, § 1.2.3) in the early imperial age, among many others in previous civilisations. But while these rituals were largely confined to royalty and the political elites in antiquity, the mourning now attached to deaths of media figures and entertainers has reached vast proportions. What was essentially a private sphere of celebrity death has moved into the public domain of the popular media, consuming the attention of the fan networks of the deceased, as well as interested onlookers.[51] The death of the Australian Steve Irwin on 4 September 2006, the "crocodile hunter" and "wildlife warrior," produced "communities of mourning" across the world, continuing a trend already in place with the deaths of Princess Diana (1997),[52] Mother Teresa (1997), the terrorist attack of Septem-

---

computer and a bit of moxie, and you've got a shot – and bypassing the tightly controlled publicity system and the tightly controlling middle people of Hollywood."

[50] Gamson, "The Unwatched Life," 1067.

[51] J. Garde-Hansen, "Measuring Mourning with Online Media: Michael Jackson and Real-time Memories," *Celebrity Studies* 1.2. (2010): 233–35. On the "fame monster" associated with Michael Jackson's career, see K. Grennel, *The Making of the "Fame Monster": Disability, Aesthetics, Bodily Deviance, and Celebrity Culture* (PhD thesis, New York: State University of New York, 2016), 34–67.

[52] On the twentieth anniversary of the death of Princess Diana (August 31, 2017), Hilary Mantel, the *Wolf Hall* novelist, wrote an incisive article in *The Guardian* (August 26, 2017) on the discrepancy between the celebrity icon and the young woman born Diana Spencer. He argues that Diana "arrived on the scene in an era of gross self-interest, to distract the nation from the hardness of its own character." The general public was complicit in the myth-building of Diana's public persona: "The princess we invented to fill a vacancy had little to do with an actual person." Consequently, her death unleashed dismay and "a salt ocean" of tears. As Mantel sums up, "As Diana was a collective creation, she was also a collective possession. The mass-mourning offended the taste police. It was gaudy, it was kitsch – the rotting flowers in their shrouds, the padded hearts of crimson plastic, the teddy bears and dolls and broken-backed verses. But all these testified to the struggle for self-expression of individuals who were spiritually and imaginatively deprived, who released their own suppressed sorrow in grieving for a woman they did not know." See "The Princess Myth: Hilary Mantel on Diana" at https://www.theguardian.com › Arts › Books › Hilary Mantel, accessed 07.09.2017.

ber 11 (2001), and Pope John Paul II (2005).[53] The death of Michael Jackson on 25 June 2009 led to such a global internet surge that Google had to disseminate its 403 Forbidden error message, thereby denying any service access, and forcing Google to crash because it could no longer distinguish between legitimate human internet activity and illegitimate internet activity (i. e. spying, viruses).[54] Last, the unprecedented pace of celebrity deaths in 2016 shook the world as familiar faces from the arenas of sport,[55] literature,[56] music,[57] TV and film,[58] as well as non-elite photo icons[59] – many of whom the Baby Boomer generation had grown up with as "family" friends over TV dinners – were wrenched from the personal possession of their fans and consigned to the oblivion of the past. Barely had this long roll call of celebrity deaths passed, but another icon of American TV sitcoms and film, Mary Tyler Moore, died on January 25, 2017. In 2018 deaths of celebrities in academia and in the medium of radio/televange-

[53] M. Gibson, "Guest Editorial: Some Thoughts on Celebrity Deaths: Steve Irwin and the Issue of Public Mourning," *Mortality* 12.1 (2007): 1–3. Gibson also observes that "Steve Irwin embodied a mythology of Australian working-class masculinity; the image of the true blue (patriotic) Australian who presents himself honestly, without deception or dissimulation."

[54] Garde-Hansen, "Measuring Mourning." See also P. McCurdy, "The King Is Dead, Long Live the King: Meditations on Media Events and Michael Jackson," *Celebrity Studies* 1.2 (2010): 236–38.

[55] Richard Adams (*Watership Down*), Edward Albee (*Who's Afraid of Virginia Woolf?*), E.R. Braithwaite (*To Sir, With Love*), Jim Harrison (poet and novelist, *Legends of the Fall*), Harper Lee (*To Kill a Mockingbird*), Umberto Eco (*The Name of the Rose*), Alvin Toffler (*Future Shock*). 2017: John Ashbery (American poet); Michael Bond (creator of Paddington Bear). 2018: Peter Mayle (*A Year on Provence*), Philip Roth (see our discussion *supra*), Neil Simon (*The Odd Couple*), Tom Wolfe (*Bonfire of the Vanities*).

[56] Muhammad Ali, Arnold Palmer.

[57] 2016: David Bowie, Leonard Cohen, Keith Emerson (Emerson, Lake and Palmer), Glen Frey (Eagles), Merle Haggard, Greg Lake (Emerson, Lake and Palmer), Paul Kanter (Jefferson Airplane), George Martin (producer of The Beatles), George Michael, Prince, Leon Russell, Maurice White (Earth, Wind and Fire). The deaths of other music icons continue to impact upon the public consciousness. 2017: Chuck Berry, Glen Campbell, Fats Domino, Tom Petty, Malcolm Young (AC/DC). 2018: Aretha Franklin. On the American rapper, Kanye West, and the quest for celebrity, see M.B. Stephens and G. Deal, "The God Who Gives Generously: Honour, Praise, and Celebrity Culture," *SJT* 71.1 (2018): 52–66.

[58] 2016: Joe Alaskey (the voice of Bugs Bunny and Daffy Duck in the Looney Tunes cartoons), Kenny Baker (R2-D2 in *Star Wars*), William Christopher (M*A*S*H), Michael Cimino (director of *The Deer Hunter*), Patty Duke, Carrie Fisher, Zsa Zsa Gabor, Florence Henderson (*The Brady Bunch*), George Kennedy, Joseph Macolo (*Days of Our Lives*), Alan Rickman, Debbie Reynolds, Doris Roberts (*Everyone Loves Raymond*), Gary Shandling (*The Larry Sanders Show*), Alan Young (*Mr Ed*), Robert Vaughn (*The Man from U.N.C.L.E.*), Gene Wilder. The widespread reporting of the deaths of entertainment celebrities continues unabated in the media. 2017: David Cassidy (*The Partridge Family*), John Hurt, Martin Landau, Jerry Lewis, Roger Moore, Jim Nabors (*Gomer Pyle, U.S.M.C*), Erin Moran (*Happy Days*), Don Rickles, Adam West (*Batman*), David Cassidy (*The Partridge Family*). 2018: John Mahoney (*Frazier*), Burt Reynolds.

[59] Greta Zimmer Friedman (photographed kissing a sailor celebrating the end of World War II in Times Square). For the photo, see http//www.nbcnews.com/.../greta-zimmer-fried man-nurse-iconic-wwii-kissing-photo-dies-9..., accessed 17.04.2017.

lism have also been deeply felt and widely reported (Stephen Hawking, Billy Graham).

Third, the ephemeral nature of athletic fame was underscored by the intense media attention given to the trial of the convicted murderer Oscar ("The Blade-runner") Pistorius, the famous Paralympian, over the shooting and killing of his partner Reeva Steenkamp.[60] In an Australian context, the sexual orientation of two Olympic champions, the diver Matthew Mitcham and the swimmer Ian Thorpe, has almost absorbed as much attention as their victories.[61] The intrusiveness of the celebrity cult draws no boundaries.

Fourth, the issue of celebrity and its relation to people with physical disabilities has become an important issue in academic discussion. The female British Paralympic champion, Tanni Grey-Thompson, has been hailed as an iconic celebrity in the modern Paralympic movement. Speaking of such athletes, J. Hargreaves says:

> Elite performers transform the stereotypes of disabled women as weak, inactive victims into incredible, dynamic sports performers, blurring the able-bodied/disabled body divide. The female stars of disabled sport signal an identity which is resistant to being reduced to "the Other". They also symbolize a challenge to ableist ideology, a reinvention of the (dis)abled body and a redefinition of the possible. [...] [I]t is important to have heroic images of disabled sportswomen for popular consumption in order to change public consciousness and overturn ableism. Disabled sports heroines are active agents in the conversion from exclusion and invisibility to inclusion and visibility.[62]

Yet this estimation over-simplifies the complex politics of "celebrity" in Paralympic competition. In Olympic and Paralympic contexts, select athletes move from being a successful competitor alone to acquiring celebrity status before an adoring public, with the fame acquired being either relatively brief or long-lived. However, in the Paralympic selection process, there is a hierarchy of "acceptable" physical impairment, in which "the majority of representations of athletes with a disability are from the less impaired classes of any given sport so as to not 'offend' the public." Celebrities in a Paralympic context, therefore, will necessarily be the "less impaired": an unannounced selection process is being

[60] Notably, the arrest of O.J. Simpson – NFL running back, broadcaster, and movie star – for the alleged murders of Nicole Browne Simpson and Ron Goldman in 1994 led to the most famous celebrity trail of the late twentieth century. The trial (and acquittal) of the silent film star, Roscoe Conkling "Fatty" Arbuckle, for the rape and manslaughter of actress Virginia Rappe is another example in the early twentieth century (1921–1922).

[61] B. McDonald and D. Eagles, "Matthew Mitcham: The Narrative of a Gay Sporting Icon," *Celebrity Studies* 3.3 (2012): 297–318. Note the media presentation of Ian Thorpe as a "metrosexual" in 2008 before he outed himself as gay in 2014. See D. Coad, *The Metrosexual: Gender, Sexuality, and Sport* (Albany: State University of New York Press, 2008), 173–81. On the reasons for his outing, see https://www.theguardian.com › Sports › Ian Thorpe, accessed 17.04.2017.

[62] J. Hargreaves, *Heroines of Sport: The Politics of Difference and Identity* (London: Routledge, 2000), 199.

carried out. Furthermore, in the era of Late Capitalism, Tanni Grey-Thompson's commodified persona has diverse elements. Not only does her hard physical work gain her fame because of her athletic prowess, but also continued public consumption maintains her celebrity status, touching on how the complex issues of gender, disability and personal identity are publicly worked out in her case.[63]

In the case of the modern American pop diva, Lady Gaga, her brand has been described as "overarching deviance." Gaga aims "to provide non-normative representations of bodily difference, deviancy, sexuality, and gender as an artist."[64] It is beyond the scope of our discussion to analyse in depth Lady Gaga's depiction of people with disabilities and to assess her artistic vision for the acceptance of deviance more generally.[65] Suffice it to say, Lady Gaga

(a) glamorises disability as "chic" when she sits in a bedazzled wheelchair, walks down a stairway in a silver body suit on crutches and in high heels, with images of dead bodies interspersed between her singing and dancing scenes (*Paparazzi* video clip);
(b) devised a catalogue of three photos, titled the *Lady Gaga Disability Project*, drawing upon her *Paparazzi* video for inspiration;[66]
(c) released her song "Born in This Way," which "solidified Gaga as the defender of the Other, misfits and deviant bodies everywhere;"[67]
(d) appeared in a 2011 French concert and at the Sydney Town Hall in Australia, dressed as her alter-ego Yüyi the Mermaid while sitting in a wheel-chair, with the result that critics and disability groups were divided around the world.

The more inclusive approach of Lady Gaga towards deviance, whatever its social and ideological limitations might be,[68] finds no real counterpart in the world of antiquity, except for the Kingdom community of Jesus that included people with disabilities (Luke 14:7–14). In the early imperial era, the Graeco-Roman elites ceased to view the dwarf, giant, hunchback and living skeleton as prodigies, but rather introduced them into their families as household "pets,"

---

[63] See P.D. Howe and A. Parker, "Celebrating Imperfection: Sport, Disability, and Celebrity Culture," *Celebrity Studies* 3.3 (2012): 270–82.

[64] Grennel, *The Making of the "Fame Monster,"* 116, citing K.J. Lieb, *Gender, Branding, and the Modern Music Industry: The Social Construction of Female Popular Music Stars* (New York: Routledge, 2013), 15.

[65] For full details, see Grennel, *The Making of the "Fame Monster,"* 110–48.

[66] See https://www.thesocietypages.org/socimages/2010/01/22/lady-gagas-disability-project/, accessed 25.04.2017.

[67] See Grennel, *The Making of the "Fame Monster,"* 138.

[68] See the insightful and nuanced comments of Grennel, *The Making of the "Fame Monster,"* 146–47, on the deficits and strengths of Lady Gaga's representations of bodily deviance, including disability.

who, when used as entertainers at public banquets,[69] acquired an inverted type of celebrity as "freaks", or who became objects of humour among the guests (e.g. Cicero, *De Or.* 2.58.238–239; Plutarch, *Mor.* 621e). Indeed, there was a "monster market" in Rome where slaves with physical disabilities were sold and sought out by the elites for precisely for such entertainment purposes (Plutarch, *Mor.* 520c). Intriguingly, Lady Gaga also depicts herself as Mama Monster to her "little monsters" both in her concerts and songs (*You're All My Little Monsters*). Significantly in terms of her celebrity, the same song became part of a Simpsons episode, with Lady Gaga singing it to the citizens of Springfield, while she hovers over the crowd in a flaming bra. Celebrity entertainment, therefore, does periodically involve people with disabilities, whether actual or artistically conceived, in both its modern and ancient contexts. Whereas in the ancient world this type of entertainment was confined to the banquets of the slave-owning elites, in the case of Lady Gaga the audience ranges across the social divide as she constructs an inclusive version of bodily deviance for her adoring fans.

Two final observations. The expansion of celebrities into charitable and humanitarian causes shows interesting connections with the Victorian philanthropists of the past.[70] In the ancient world, too, benefaction was an important way of enhancing ancestral prestige of Roman nobles questing for glory, as well as ensuring the ascendancy of the provincial elites throughout the Mediterranean basin. Again, in a study based upon the Getty Museum dataset of celebrity photos, G. Ravid and E. Currid-Halkett have found that the individuals depicted formed a "small-world network," exhibiting "cumulative advantage and rich-get-richer attributes." Seemingly, although celebrities were often disconnected, the fact that they *were* celebrities nevertheless brought connection.[71] The status of "celebrity" *itself* created networks of wealth and interconnection that enabled the elites to remain visible to the public, both as benefactors and socialites.

[69] For discussion, see C.A. Barton, *The Sorrows of Ancient Romans: The Gladiator and the Monster* (Princeton: Princeton University Press, 1993), 85–87; V. Dasen, "*Infirmitas* or Not? Short-statured Persons in Ancient Greece," in *Infirmity in Antiquity and the Middle Ages: Social and Cultural Approaches*, ed. A. Krötzl et al. (London and New York: Routledge, 2015), 29–50; L.A. Gosbell, *"The Poor, the Crippled, the Blind, and the Lame": Physical and Sensory Disability in the Gospels of the New Testament*, WUNT II 469 (Tübingen: Mohr Siebeck, 2018).

[70] See J. Littler, "The New Victorians? Celebrity Charity and the Demise of the Welfare State," *Celebrity Studies* 6.4 (2015): 471–85. Many modern celebrities have also set up their own charitable foundations. See the acerbic assessment of George Packer, "Celebrating Inequality," *The New York Times*, May 10, 2013, Opinion Pages, Page A21, accessed 13.05.2017 at http://www.nytimes.com/2013/05/20/.../inequality-and-the-modern-culture-of-celebrity.htm.

[71] See G. Ravid and E. Currid-Halkett, "The Social Structure of Celebrity: An Empirical Network Analysis of an Elite Population," *Celebrity Studies* 4.2 (2013): 182–201.

Having covered the general terrain of the celebrity circuit from the eighteenth to the twenty-first century, the question now to be addressed is how celebrity was understood in antiquity. What differences and similarities were there between the ancient and modern celebrities in their quest for fame before posterity, their elite contemporaries, and the ever watchful public?

1.1.2. Scholarship on the Ancient Phenomenon of Celebrity: Robert Garland on "Media Tarts and Tabloid Queens"

Prior to discussing modern scholarship on celebrity in the ancient world, several preliminary comments about the Roman terminology of "celebrity" are apposite. In terms of the Roman *nobilis*, there was a conglomeration of terms denoting the various aspects of the public renown that an aristocrat acquired in the estimation of his elite competitors and social superiors, as well as in the popular estimation: namely, *fama* ("reputation," "rumour"), *dignitas* ("status," "authority"), *existimatio* ("reputation," "civil honour," "standing in society"), *amplitudo* ("greatness," "importance"), *decus* ("glory," "splendour," "honour," "distinction") and *gloria* ("renown," "glory").[72] Whereas *fama* attached itself to a man in a negative or a positive way,[73] the best men (*boni*) from the political aristocracy appraised the reputation of those individuals who were deemed to possess the requisite glory (*gloria*, *decus*) to be called *nobilis* ("noble").[74] In the case of *existimatio*, the term referred to the public perception or image of a Roman politician from the perspective of the people, based on birth, official position, and wealth.[75] Last, *dignitas*, as defined by the literature of the late republic,

[72] Garland (*Celebrity in Antiquity*, 5) argues that "neither Greek nor Latin possesses a word that exactly conforms to the abstract English noun celebrity." For Greek approximations, Garland proposes *axiôma*, *charisma*, *doxa*, *epiphaneia*, *kleos*, *lamprotês*, *philotimia*, *time*, *epiphanês*, and *lampros*. As an important aside, note the absence of *charisma* as a Greek term denoting celebrity. For its modern use in historical studies, see E. Berenson and E. Giloi, eds., *Constructing Charisma: Celebrity, Fame, and Power in Nineteenth-Century Europe* (New York: Berghahn Books, 2010); E. Berenson, *Heroes of Empire: Five Charismatic Men and the Conquest of Africa* (Berkeley: University of California Press, 2011). For the Latin approximations, see *claritas*, *gloria*, *laus*, *popularitas*, *auctoritas*, *ambitio*, *honos*, *illustris*, *clarus*, *famosis*, and *gloriosus*. Only a brief range of terminology confined to the notability of the Roman *nobiles* and the public esteem in which they were held will be discussed below, given our focus on republican and early imperial Rome in Chapters 2 and 3.

[73] On *fama*, see J.-P. Neraudau, "La Fama dans la Rome antique," *Médiévales* 12.24 (1993): 27–34; P. Hardie, *Rumour and Renown: Representations of* Fama *in Western Literature* (Cambridge: Cambridge University Press, 2012); T. J. Chiusi Tiziana, "'Fama' and 'Infamia' in the Roman Legal System: The Cases of Afrania and Lucretia," in *Judge and Jurist: Essays in Memory of Lord Rodger of Earlsferry*, ed. A. Burrows et al. (Oxford: Oxford University Press, 2013), 143–65.

[74] See J. R. Harrison, *Paul and the Imperial Authorities at Thessalonica and Rome: A Study in the Conflict of Ideology*, WUNT I 273 (Tübingen: Mohr Siebeck, 2011), 205–32.

[75] Z. Yavetz, "*Existimatio*, *Fama*, and the Ides of March," *HSCP* 78 (1974): 35–65, at 56.

denoted the political prestige acquired though holding significant offices in the cursus *honorum*, distinguishing itself from *gloria* by virtue of the fact that it "attaches to a man permanently and is inheritable by his descendants."[76] There is little doubt that the celebrity that accrued to the great man of Rome, whether a republican noble of the past or their representatives of the Julio-Claudian house, would have been pinpricked by Paul's rejection of all human boasting in the face of the unconditioned and unmerited grace of the crucified Christ.

What has modern scholarship said about the celebrity circuit in Graeco-Roman antiquity? The Roman and eastern Mediterranean elites have been extensively covered in recent French scholarship and in several older classic works of Roman historians.[77] But when one turns to an investigation of celebrity as a phenomenon in antiquity, surprisingly only one monograph on the issue has been written: R. Garland's well-researched and engagingly written book.[78] Employing a variety of ancient media in his discussion of ancient self-promotion (literary texts, coins, portraits, building programmes), Garland proceeds by looking at the success of famous historical personages and a host of other celebrities (entertainers, athletes, loose women, philosophers etc.), differentiating the ancient phenomenon of fame from the rise of the 1960's British "celebrity class." Furthermore, Garland posits that the ancient celebrities did not pose the threat to the political and social "establishment" that their modern counterparts do.[79]

However, Garland's analysis of the celebrities in a predominantly narrative genre disconnects the individuals discussed from the social values, ideologies,

---

[76] D.C. Earl, *The Political Thought of Sallust* (Cambridge: Cambridge University Press, 1961), 53. Additionally, see Rolf Rilinger, *Ordo und dignitas: Beiträge zur römischen Verfassungs- und Sozialgeschichte* (Stuttgart: Franz Steiner Verlag, 2007).

[77] M. Cébeillac-Gervasoni and L. Lamoine, eds., *Les élites et leurs facettes: les élites locales dans le monde hellénistique et romain* (Rome: École française de Rome; Clermont-Ferrand: Presses universitaires Blaise-Pascal, 2003); M. Cébeillac-Gervasoni et al., eds., *Autocélébration des élites locales dans le monde romain: contextes, images, textes, IIe s. av. J.C.- IIIe s. ap. J.-C.* (Clermont-Ferrand: Centre de recherche sur les civilisations antiques, 2004); H. Fernoux, *Notables et élites des cités de Bithynie aux époques hellénistique et romaine (IIIe siècle av. J.-C. –IIIe siècle ap. J.-C.), Essai d'histoire sociale*, Collection de la Maison de l'Orient et de la Méditerranée 31, Série Épigraphique et Historique 5 (Paris: Collection de la Maison de l'Orient et de la Méditerranée, 2004); L. Capdetrey and Y. Lafond, eds., *La cité et ses élites: pratiques et représentation des formes de domination et de contrôle social dans les cités grecques. Actes du colloque de Poitiers, 19–20 octobre 2006* (Pessac: Ausonius, 2010). On the Roman nobility, see M. Gelzer, *The Roman Nobility*, tr. Robin Seager, 2nd ed. (Oxford: Basil Blackwell, 1975; Gmn. orig. 1912); T.D. Barnes, "Who Were the Nobility of the Roman Empire?" *Phoenix* 28.4 (1974): 444–49. On elite self-identity at Rome and in the Empire, see E.S. Gruen, "The Roman Oligarchy: Image and Perception," in *Imperium Sine Fine: T.S. Roberts and the Roman Republic*, ed. J. Linderski (Stuttgart: Franz Steiner Verlag, 1966), 215–34; H.I. Flower, "Elite Self-Representation in Rome," in *The Oxford Handbook of Social Relations in the Roman World*, ed. M. Peachin (Oxford and New York: Oxford University Press, 2011), 271–85.

[78] Garland, *Celebrity in Antiquity.*

[79] Garland, *Celebrity in Antiquity*, 145–46.

political and cultural developments of the wider Graeco-Roman world. The following comments on the limitations of Garland's book are made with full awareness of the strictures placed on the author by the series in which he is writing ("necessarily brief").[80] Notwithstanding, we gain no real sense of the contribution of fame as a phenomenon in shaping communal morality and identity, nor of the legacy of famous individuals themselves to their societies other than the continually changing and ephemeral curiosity of fame. How did ancient celebrities provoke the widespread phenomenon of exemplarity among each upcoming generation of the aristocrats and the upwardly mobile? Surprising too is the lack of attention paid to the public inscriptions, the visual repositories of elite fame in each city of the Mediterranean basin, accompanied by the public proclamations of the contents of eulogistic decrees themselves. By contrast, methodologically, the epigraphic evidence will be the springboard for much of our investigation below and the book generally.

Last, the collision of early Christianity with the self-promoting values of the Graeco-Roman elites – seen in its emphasis on humility as opposed to celebrity and in its cruciform service of the weak over against the adulation of the elites – is also bypassed. Surely the dissonance of voices that speak out against fame must be engaged as much as the endless chatter about the famous? What is it about celebrity as a phenomenon that provokes (culturally speaking) these surprisingly dissonant responses?[81] In his discussion of Christ,[82] Garland rightly recognises that "Christ wanted to delimit the terms of his own celebrity."[83] Yet he overlooks the teaching of Christ on personal and corporate humility among his disciples (Matt 18:1–4; 19:30; 20:16; Luke 14:7–11), his establishment of an alternative "servant" community of the marginalised (Mark 10:44–45; Luke 14:7–23), and his rejection of the self-advertisement and self-serving power of the imperial and Herodian elites (Luke 22:25).[84] Furthermore, Paul's deconstruction of the Graeco-Roman *cursus honorum* with a *cursus pudorum* (Phil 2:5–11) finds its rationale in the historic teaching of Christ as much as in the shame of the cross.[85] Why does Paul pivot God's choice of the weak and foolish community of believers over against the cardinal values of the ancient celebrity cult (viz. wisdom, power, and noble birth: 1 Cor 1:26–29)? Why is the early Christian community, which recognises the importance of honour rituals

[80] Garland, *Celebrity in Antiquity*, 10.

[81] This dissonance was not confined to the early Christians. Note, too, the criticism of honorific crowning rituals in antiquity: J. R. Harrison, "'The Fading Crown': Divine Honour and the Early Christians," *JTS* 54.2 (2003): 493–529.

[82] Garland, *Celebrity in Antiquity*, 96–98.

[83] Garland, *Celebrity in Antiquity*, 97.

[84] Garland (*Celebrity in Antiquity*, 54) correctly notes this disposition in Augustus too, notwithstanding the enormity of the self-advertisement of the Julian house.

[85] J. Hellerman, *Reconstructing Honor in Roman Philippi: Carmen Christi as* Cursus Pudorum, SNTSMS 132 (Cambridge: Cambridge University Press, 2005).

(Rom 13:7; 1 Peter 3:13–14, 17a), so opposed to (what the rest of antiquity considers to be) the legitimate boasting and the rightful celebrity of the powerful and beautiful? These, of course, are not the concerns of Garland's book, but clearly they deserve attention from a new generation of Pauline scholars interested in the celebrity context of his thought.

However, before exploring these issues in the rest of book, a crucial preliminary question must be answered. How did the ancient elites commend themselves?

1.2. The Commendation of the Ancient Elites and Their Families

1.2.1. Eulogies of the Graeco-Roman Elites from the Republic to the Imperial Period

The self-advertisement of the aristocratic elites in Rome and the provincial elites in the cities of the eastern Mediterranean basin, recorded in inscriptions on monuments erected in prominent civic places or placed in hallowed sanctuaries in family tombs, was a foundational aspect of Graeco-Roman boasting culture from the republican to the imperial period. The apostle Paul pinpricked the culture of boasting at Rome (Rom 2:17, 23; 3:27; 4:2; 15:17; 5:2, 3, 11),[86] reducing the importance of the great man to a cipher in God's vast re-ordering of the hierarchical first-century society in the Body of Christ (1 Cor 1:26–29).[87] In this section, select documentary evidence from Rome, the Italian peninsula, Corinth, Philippi, and Ephesus will be explored in order to establish the nature of the "celebrity culture" that contributed substantially to the endless "chatter" of the public inscriptions in the ancient cities.

The Roman conception of "nobility" (*nobilitas*) was an aristocracy of esteem, based upon the "notability" of the famous Roman houses in the capital from early republican times. Many of their family members had achieved the consulship,[88] the highest magistracy in the *cursus honorum* ("course of offices"), had secured military victories resulting in triumphal processions and, correspondingly, the addition of eulogistic nomenclature ("Africanus," Numidicus," "Macedonicus," "Asiaticus," "Creticus"), established far-flung *clientelae* in foreign lands,[89] and funded civic projects in the city. Not only were these elite achievements celebrated on stone monuments, but they were also recorded in diverse literary memorials and vaunted in the literary compositions of various writers. The elogia inscribed on the sarcophagi of the Roman noble family of the

[86] See Harrison, *Paul and the Imperial Authorities*, 201–69.
[87] See Harrison, "The Erasure of Honour."
[88] See Harrison, *Paul and the Imperial Authorities*, 205–06.
[89] E. Badian, *Foreign Clientelae (264–70 BC)* (Oxford: Clarendon Press 1958).

Scipios are particularly revealing in this regard and readers are referred to their discussion in Chapter 7.

Elsewhere I have examined the important honorific inscription and monument of Gaius Duilius,[90] consul of 260 BC and the naval victor over the Carthaginian fleet at Mylae, a member of the powerful Roman noble family of the Duilii. Situated in the Roman forum, the inscription was inscribed on the base of a large column. It was probably topped with a statue of Duilius and bronze ramming "beaks" (*rostra*) of the captured Carthaginian ships (Pliny, *NH* 34.20; Silius Italicus *Pun.* 6.663–669; Quintilian 1.7.12; Servius, *ad Georg.* 3.29) adorned the length of the entire column. The inscription's catalogues of Duilius' victories over the town of Macella and the Carthaginian navy, its rhetorical use of numbers as a mnemonic, and the fourfold repetition of "first" (*primos*) for Duilius' unprecedented accomplishments establishes the glory and primacy of Duilius over every rival at Rome. This inscription helps us to see, if only by contrast, the breathtaking depths of Paul's self-humiliation and the "foolishness" of his self-mockery in 2 Corinthians 11:16–12:10, as he boasts in his weaknesses in order to shame and lampoon the self-commendation of the apostolic interlopers and their supporters at Corinth.[91]

But other inscriptions are equally instructive for our purposes. Lucius Mummius, the Roman general and consul of 146 BC, razed Corinth to the ground and received his triumph in 145 BC, recorded on a tablet of stone found at Rome on the Mons Caelius:

> Lucius Mummius, consul of Lucius. Under his leadership his auspices and his command was taken, and Corinth laid waste. He then returned to Rome in a triumph. In recompense for these exploits prosperously achieved, he the commander is the dedicator of this temple of Hercules the Conqueror, which he had vowed in the war.[92]

Here Mummius is not only lauded for his military victory, but also for his public piety towards the gods, not forgetting from whom his victory had ultimately come (Hercules the Conqueror), and also reciprocating the prosperity divinely allocated to him in battle by building the temple for the god in fulfilment of a vow.

By contrast, the military tribune G. Publicius Bibulus (209 BC?) is honoured, the inscription having been found at Rome on a tomb, "because of his worthi-

---

[90] For a translation, see E.H. Warmington, *Remains of Old Latin: Archaic Inscriptions* (Cambridge, MA: Harvard University, 1953), § 1. For discussion, see Harrison, *Paul and the Imperial Authorities*, 223–24; E. Kondratieff, "Column and Coinage of C. Duilius," *Scripta classica Israelica* 23 (2004): 1–39.

[91] See J.R. Harrison, "In Quest of the Third Heaven: Paul and His Apocalyptic Imitators," *VC* 58.1 (2004): 24–55, at 46–55.

[92] CIL I.2.626. Similarly, in CIL I.2.652, Gaius Sempronius Tuditanus (cos. 129 BC) gave a temple to the river-god Timavus, "restored to him his pristine worship, and entrusted it to overseers," because of his victory and triumph over the Iapydes of Istria.

ness (*honoris virtutisque*)."[93] There is no hint here of any reciprocation on the honorand's part to the gods for their prior beneficence. Rather the honorand's *own* virtue has to be acknowledged by the State and the People as a matter of legitimate recompense in the operations of the reciprocity system. To ignore the claims of his worthiness would risk the cardinal sin of antiquity: namely, ingratitude towards one's benefactors.[94]

Public gifts to communities throughout the Italian peninsula are also *de rigeur* if one is to enhance one's notability as a member of the Roman elites. On the front of a temple at Aletrium (c. 135–90 BC), 6 miles due north of Frusino in Italy, Lucius Betilienes Varus is eulogised for all the public works that he had built:

> Lucius Betilienes Varus, son of Lucius, by a vote of the Senate superintended the construction of the works which are recorded below: all the street-paths in the town; the colonnade along which the people walk to the stronghold; a playing-field; a sun-dial; a meat-market; the liming of the town-hall; seats; a bathing pool; he constructed a reservoir by the gate; an aqueduct about 340 feet long leading into the city and to the height; also the arches and good sound water-pipes. In reward for these works the Senate made him censor twice and ordered that his son be exempt from military service; and the people bestowed the gift of a statue on him over the title of Censorinus.[95]

Other gifts to towns the Italian peninsula are recorded in the Latin inscriptions. Lucius Papius Pollio provides public services in 60 BC, including a feast of mead and pastry at Sinuessa and Caedex, as well as a show of gladiators and a dinner to the colonists at Sinuessa.[96] Gaius Quinctius and Marcus Porcius (100–80 BC) also provide shows at their own expense for the colonists at Pompeii.[97] Publius Popillius Laenas (cos. 132 BC) built bridges, milestones, and sign-posts from Regia to Capua: further, as praetor in Sicily, he caught the runaway slaves of Italians, constructed a Market and public buildings, and looked after the interests of the plowmen over against the cattle-breeders as far as land usage.[98] The well-known motif of the "endangered" benefactor, in which the benefactor expends himself to rescue his dependents from a perilous plight, is employed in an inscription from Interamna (82 BC):[99] "the whole borough was, through his services, released and preserved from the greatest dangers and difficulties (*ex summis pereiculeis et difficultatibus*)." Last, E. Forbis has studied the civic

[93] CIL I.2.834.

[94] J.R. Harrison, *Paul's Language of Grace in Its Graeco-Roman Context*, WUNT II 172 (Tübingen: Mohr Siebeck, 2003), *s.v.* Index of Subjects: "Ingratitude".

[95] CIL I.2.1529.

[96] CIL I.2.1578.

[97] CIL I.2.1632.

[98] CIL I.2.638. Also note CIL I.2.1903 which refers to the "permanent bathing-room" built by Quintus Poppaeus and Gauis Poppaeus at Interamna for "their townsmen, settlers, other residents, strangers, and visitors."

[99] CIL I.2.2510. On the inscriptional "endangered benefactor" motif, see F.W. Danker, *Benefactor: Epigraphic Study of a Graeco-Roman and New Testament Semantic Field* (St. Louis: Clayton Publishing Inc., 1982), 417–35.

virtues recorded on honorific inscriptions from municipal Italy in the imperial period.[100] The summons to exceptional virtues (e.g. *rarissimus, singularis, incomparabilis*) in many of these inscriptions, Forbis argues, rather than deterring people by their exceptionally high standards, actually encouraged the more competitive onlookers to emulate the honorands in their civic-mindedness.[101] The important motif of the emulation of the "great man" in antiquity will be further engaged in Chapter 7.

Turning now from Rome and the Italian peninsula to the Roman colonies of Corinth and Philippi, the same pattern of self-advertisement emerges among the elites, replicating the heavy Roman emphasis upon the *cursus honorum* in the capital. We see this in the carefully calculated presentation of magistracies at Corinth in the honorific inscriptions of the *agōnothetai,* which, I have argued elsewhere,[102] either ascend or descend in their order of progression of magistracies, as the rhetoric of the situation warranted. An intriguing inscription found on a stone at Corinth details the exploits of Hirrus in 10 BC:

> Learn you of an exploit such as no man has attempted and no man will hazard hereafter, so that we may make renown of a hero's achievements. Under the command of Marcus Antonius, proconsul, a fleet was carried over the Isthmus and sent across the sea. Marcus himself set out upon his voyage to Sida. Hirrus, as proprietor, stationed his fleet at Athens because of the season of the year. All this was accomplished in a few days with little turmoil; sound strategy and safe deliverance attended it. He who is upright (*probus*) has praise for him, and he who is otherwise, looks askance at him (*quei contra est in[videt illum]*). Let men envy (*invid[ea]nt*) so long as they have reverence for what is seemly.[103]

The strategic and expedited docking of the fleet by Hirrus at Athens, at a time when unseasonable weather imperiled the very safety of the fleet, is spotlighted. A measure of hyperbole exists in the first line of the inscription regarding the unparalleled significance of the feat, immediately grabbing the attention of the reader for what is to come. Much to the reader's surprise the sensitive issue of *invidia* is delicately aired at the end of the inscription. Such a feat like that of Hirrus, the inscription states, will provoke *invidia* ("envy", "jealousy"), a result characteristic of the heated competitions between the ancient elites. Our inscription underscores the fact that the "upright" person praises the elites for what they have accomplished: *invidia*, however, is inevitably aroused by the fame and celebrity accrued to the honorand from such an act. But, on this occasion, the jealousy is quite legitimate, our inscription concludes, as long as those

---

[100] E. Forbis, *Municipal Virtues in the Roman Empire: The Evidence of Italian Honorary Inscriptions* (Stuttgart and Leipzig: B.G. Teubner, 1996).

[101] Forbis, *Municipal Virtues*, 90.

[102] J.R. Harrison, "Paul and the *agōnothetai* at Corinth: Engaging the Civic Values of Antiquity," in *The First Urban Churches. Volume 2: Roman Corinth*, ed. J.R. Harrison and L.L. Welborn (Atlanta: SBL Press, 2016), 271–326, at 286–91.

[103] CIL I.2.2662.

consumed with *invidia* reverence what actually has been achieved by Hirrus, irrespective of the wider tensions existing between the elites at Corinth because of their intense civic competition.

In the case of the Roman colony of Philippi, an inscription honoring a senator, found in the city's forum, eulogises its honorand thus:

For Gaius Julius Maximus Mucianus, the son of Gaius, of the tribe Voltinia, a *vir clarissimus*, honoured with the *latus clavus* by the divine (Antoninus) Pius, quaestor, pro praetor of Pontus and Bithynia, aedile of the grain supply, designated praetor, also decurion of Philippi and in the province of Thracia, for his brother Gaius Iulius Teres, the Thracharch, father of senators, (has set up this inscription) in the place determined by a decree of the decurions.[104]

J. Hellerman notes that the term *vir clarissimus* ("highly regarded man") immediately identifies Mucianus as belonging to the senatorial class. Furthermore, the reference to *latus clavus* is striking. Hellerman explains its full significance: "An aristocrat like Gaius, appearing in the forum attired in his citizen toga, decorated with the broad purple senatorial stripe (*latus clavus*) would have impressed observers as a rare and notable sight in Roman Philippi."[105] The fact that members of the decurion council makes the decree also demonstrates "their desire to recognize two of their own" in the case of the brothers.[106] Even the seemingly incidental mention of the tribe "Voltinia" links the family of Mucianus to the traditional citizen groupings of Rome, demonstrating how the ethos of the elites in the colony of Philippi mimicked the ancient tribal structures in the capital as much as its pursuit of civic offices in the *cursus honorum*.

Last, an Ephesian inscription eulogising the elite family of the Vedii is worth close attention. In a tombstone in honour of Vedia, a priestess of Artemis, an extraordinary roll call of civic merit is recounted:

[To Vedia ... priestess of] most pure Artemis, daughter of Vedius Servilius Gaius *philosebastos*, *eques*, granddaughter of Vedius Gaius Sabinianus *philosebastos*, high priest of the god Lucius and high priest of Asia, grandson of Dionysios who sat in judgement over law suits instead of the proconsul Vibius Bassus and of Ulpia Sev(ilia) Bassilla *matrona stolata*, daughter of the priestess (Servilia) Bassilla, called Andronike and granddaughter of the *prytanis* Servilius Menander and of Antonius Salvius *philosebastos*, secretary of the people and agonothete of the Great world-wide Ephesia, great-granddaughter of Vedia Iusta priestess and *kosmetira* and *prytanis* and of Antonia Frugilla *prytanis*; descendant of Vedius Gaius *philosebastos*, sole secretary of the people who whilst in the office of

[104] Tr., with discussion, Hellerman, *Reconstructing Honor*, 93–94.

[105] Hellerman, *Reconstructing Honor*, 94. For inscriptions reserving seats for *viri clarissimi* ("most honourable men"), *clarissimi iuvenes* ("most honourable young men"), and *clarissimi pueri* ("most honourable boys") – designations pointing to high status individuals from senatorial families – in the amphitheatre of Carthage, see T. Jones, *Seating and Spectacle in the Graeco-Roman World* (PhD diss., McMaster University, 2008), 305–06 (§ 58), 308 (§ 59), 308 (§ 60), 309 (§ 61).

[106] Hellerman, *Reconstructing Honor*, 94.

secretary received the lord Lucius the god Augustus, (descendant) of the great-uncles Claudius Zeno asiarch of the temples here and Claudius Salvius asiarch of the temples in Smyrna; being of a family (supplying) to all levels (of government) many *prytaneis*, sole secretaries, a former high-priest in the five *metropoleis*, a queen of the Ionians and senators and men of consular rank. (Vedia) furnished the customary distributions to all the guilds and completed the mysteries on account of her father Gaius and of her family worthily. Her father (erected this in honour of) his most longed-for daughter.[107]

There are several things worthy of note about this inscription, stratospheric as it is in its boastfulness. First, the support of the Vedii family for the imperial house at Rome is relentlessly driven home by the fourfold repetition of *philosebastos* (literally, "lover of Augustus"). Connections with the imperial house are further highlighted by the appointment of Vedius Gaius Sabinianus to the prestigious high-priesthood of the imperial cult in the province of Asia. Second, the family members of the Vedii, by birth and by marriage, are depicted in all their glory. Some

- had received the emperor Lucius Verus himself, presumably during his visit to Asia Minor in 162 AD;
- had acted as judges of law suits in the place of the pro-consul of Asia;
- were secretaries of the people and, in one case, the "sole secretary";
- were appointed as high-priests of the five *metropoleis* (Ephesus, Pergamum, Smyrna, Sardis, Cyzicus);
- were *prytaneis* ("presidents", i.e. civic magistrates) in Ephesus;
- were asiarchs (cf. Acts 19:31) of the temples in *both* Ephesus and Sardis, each city being, significantly, a *neokoros* (temple-warden) of the imperial cult and rivals for the ruler's patronage;[108]
- were priestesses of the mystery cult of Artemis;
- were royal descendants of an Ionian queen;
- were benefactors of the local associations (guilds);
- had acted as organisers and financial underwriters (*agonothetes*) of the local Ephesian games;[109]
- were Roman women of important rank, indicated by the designation *matrona stolata* ("women wearing a stole").

Third, what is really surprising is that this extensive roll call of merit is unfolded for a young Vedian priestess of the Artemis mysteries and benefactor of the guilds.[110] What has precipitated this extraordinary paean of praise to a virtually

[107] IEph VII 1.3072. For the family stem, see R. Merkelbach, et al., ed., *Die Inschriften von Ephesos Teil VII, I* (Bonn: Rudolf Habelt Verlag, 1981), 76.

[108] R.S. Ascough, ed., *Religious Rivalries and the Struggle for Success in Sardis and Smyrna*, SCJ 14 (Waterloo: Wilfrid Laurier University Press, 2005).

[109] See Harrison, "Paul and the *agōnothetai*," 286–91.

[110] J.R. Harrison, "Family Honour of a Priestess of Artemis," *New Docs* 10 (2012): 30–36, §7.

unknown member of the Vedian family so unexpectedly here? The answer is provided by other inscriptions. It was the habit of elites to bolster the epigraphic commemoration of dead relatives who had been cut off in their prime before they had any chance to advance their career. We see this type of career "apologetic" in the 160 BC (?) inscription of Lucius Cornelis Scipio, son of Gnaeus, grandson of Gnaeus. The elogium boasts in the "non-achievements" of this prematurely dead member of the famous Scipio family of Rome thus:

Great virtues and great wisdom holds this stone with tender age. Whose life but not his honour fell short of honours, he that lies here was never outdone in virtue; twenty years of age to burial-places he was entrusted. Seek not honour; which unto this man was not entrusted.[111]

Similarly, Publius Cornelius Scipio, probably a son of Scipio Africanus, died in c. 170 BC and was honoured with the elogium below, even though he had only ever held an inconsequential and honorific priesthood. It is readily admitted that Publius did not have the time in his brief life to surpass the glory of his Scipionic ancestors through the conventional acquisition of civic offices, military victories, and deeds of beneficence. Nevertheless, his personal and public virtues, conspicuous to all, would have allowed him to excel not only his contemporaries from the other rival noble houses but also, in a striking hyperbole, all the amassed honours of his Scipionic forebears:

You who have worn the honoured cap of Jupiter's holy priest: Death caused all your virtues, your honour, good report, and valiance, your glory and your talents to be short-lived. If you had but been allowed long life in which to enjoy them, an easy thing it would have been for you to surpass by great deeds the glory of your ancestors. Wherefore, O Publius Cornelius Scipio, begotten son of Publius, joyfully does Earth take you to her bosom.[112]

Both of these Scipionic inscriptions mount a defense of character as a bulwark against criticism. By the time of the early Roman Empire onwards, however, a subtle shift in emphasis occurred. The focus is more on military victories, civic magistracies held, ancestral dignitaries, benefactions dispensed, clientage and diplomatic embassies undertaken, and so on. Intrinsic character traits recede into the background, as the relentless lists of achievement (office, campaigns, gifts) in the *Res Gestae* shows,[113] though Augustus ends his boasting with a

---

[111] CIL I.2.11.

[112] CIL I.2.10. For another example, see the epitaph (c. AD 210–250: Prusias ad Hypium, Bithynia) of Ulpius Titius Calpurnianus Fado, who died prematurely young before he could fulfil his projected equestrian career. In the epitaph his prestigious family lineage is outlined and, significantly, he is spoken of as "a hero ... honoured of the public horse *ex quisitione*, first among the people of his age by his education and his virtues." See Fernoux, *Notables et élites des cités de Bithynie*, 438–39, no. 18.

[113] E. A. Judge noted in a 1973 undergraduate unit study guide for the Macquarie Univer-

variation on the four cardinal virtues (*RG* 34.2), voted to him by the Roman Senate.

In sum, the unmarried virgin priestess at Ephesus had probably died during or after completing her year-long service of Artemis, but before she had the opportunity to marry a male of high social status after her priesthood, enhancing thereby the fame of the Vedius family by another dynastic marriage of the type articulated several times in the inscription. The Vedian roll call of fame, therefore, compensates for the loss of future honour because of Vedia's tragic death in her prime. Any hint of virtuous character in the case of the young priestess, other than the scant reference to her performing the cult "worthily", is expunged in the Vedian epitaph. This stands in sharp contrast to the fore-fronting of virtue in the two Scipionic epitaphs above. The extraordinary pedigree of the Vedian family, it seems, could stand on its own without any reference to the moral bearing of Vedia as an individual.

1.2.2. The Heroic Virtue of the Well-Born: The Evidence of a Laodikeian Tombstone

Another intriguing feature of the phenomenon of fame and celebrity that emerges from the first century AD onwards is the link sometimes made in some epitaphs of the deceased with Homeric and royal heroes. In an epigram from a tomb at Laodikeia (ILaodikeia am Lykos § 81 [I cent. CE]) praises the σωφροσύνη and appearance of its honorand, Epigonos, claiming that he is superior in virtue and descent to the mythological heroes of the Trojan War: namely, the Greek Achilleus and the Trojan Hector. The inflated claim is extraordinarily bold when one remembers that Rome derived her mythological origins solely from the Trojan heroes, Aeneas and his family, who had fled the war upon the sack of the city by the Greeks:

> Tomb none other you see, passers by, than that of Epigonos, whose virtue (τὰν ἀρετάν) Time will not quench, leaving behind first place in the presence of the living on account of his prudence (σωφροσύνας) and his most godlike shape (θειοτάτος μορφᾶς); even Achilleus, Hector, son of Priam, and Hippolytus, who fled his father's marriage bed, were not as Epigonos, the son of Andreas, the well-born (εὐγενετα), a king of same father. But Epigonos remains with the survivors on a monument; also Achilleus the son of Thetis, did not escape Fate (μοιρ[ᾶ]ν) ...[114]

sity Ancient History Department ("The Roman Nobility: Study Guide No. 2," 3) that "The strictly personal element has been reduced to a stereotype in the Augustan publicity."

[114] For another Homeric epigraphic example, see *IG* II 3² 10051 in S. Mitchell, "The Ionians of Paphlagonia," in Whitmarsh, *Local Knowledge and Microidentities*, 95. Additionally, see SEG XXXV 1233, tr. A. Rostad, *Human Transgression – Divine Retribution: A Study of Religious Transgressions and Punishments in Greek Cultic Regulations and Lydian-Phrygian Reconciliation Inscriptions* (PhD thesis, University of Bergen, 2006), 167–68.

Whereas Fate had triumphed over the Greek hero Achilleus, the virtue of Epigonos not only trumps Time itself but also outshines the illustrious reputation of all Homeric heroes, Greek and Trojan. But that is not the end of the mythological allusions in the epigram. Hippolytus, the illegitimate son of the Athenian king Theseus, was killed after rejecting the sexual advances of his stepmother Phaedra ("who fled his father's marriage bed"). Once again, Epigonos is not only vastly superior in virtue to the adulterous royal house of Athens but also, in contrast to its tragic illegitimate prince Hippolytus, is "well-born." The latter, of course, jars with Paul's point to the Corinthians that not many of them were "well born" (1 Cor 1:26b: οὐ πολλοὶ εὐγενεῖς): being well-born ensured celebrity status in the eyes of others.

In reality, this pretentious funerary epigram was a curious expression of a wider phenomenon of the Second Sophistic, best exemplified by Philostratus' *On Heroes*. In that literary work, readers were exposed to what was claimed to be a truer and more accurate version of the Trojan War than Homer's version, reflecting through the epic tradition the continuing historical importance of hero cults in the third century AD.[115] Readers of this Laodikeian tombstone would have been impressed by the deflected glory that accrued to the honorand by means of its astute appeal to the heroic and royal past. Alternatively, others may have been quietly amused by its pomposity and sense of burlesque in claiming inappropriately heroic honours. Either way, the extraordinary status being asserted by this well-born member of Laodikeia could not be ignored.

1.2.3. The Funeral of Germanicus: The Ticklish Question of Honouring or Dishonouring the Deceased and His Family Line

On October 10th AD 19, the charismatic Roman general Germanicus – grandson of Augustus, heir-designate of the Roman Empire under Tiberius, and father of Caligula – died at Antioch. In the years prior to his death, Germanicus had put down a mutiny of the Rhine regions (AD 14), conquered the German tribe of the Chatti, recovered the lost standards of Varus' legions (AD 15), and, after quelling further disturbances in the East (AD 16), returned to Rome triumphant in AD 17. After acquiring the consulship in the following year, Germanicus embarked in AD 19 on grand tour of the eastern Mediterranean with his wife Agrippina the Elder, exhibiting personal éclat and reaping rapturous responses from local populations, stopping at various cities in Greece (Actium, Athens), Asia Minor (ancient Troy), and Egypt (Alexandria), before finally ar-

115 E.B. Aitken and J.K. Berenson McLean, tr., Flavius Philostratus, *On Heroes* (Atlanta: Society of Biblical Literature, 2001). See also the excellent discussion of A.J. Armstrong (*Roman Phrygia: Cities and Their Coinage* [PhD thesis, University College London, 1998], 157–64, esp. at 163–64) on the social pretentiousness of Laodikeia in placing Homer on the reverse of a Neronian coin.

riving at Syrian Antioch. The circumstances of Germanicus' death in the city are well-known and need not detain us.[116] More important for our purposes is what our ancient literary sources say about the issues of honour and dishonour attached to his funeral.

Tacitus tells us that Germanicus' body was cremated at Antioch. It had been exposed in the forum beforehand before the funeral, the occasion of which was "devoid of ancestral images or procession" and "distinguished by eulogies and recollections of his virtues (*Ann.* 2.73)." Popular comparisons of Germanicus with Alexander the Great were made at Antioch, emphasising his personal moral probity and military skills as a general,[117] and suggesting that, had Germanicus lived longer, he would have exceeded the Macedonian king "in clemency, moderation, and all other good qualities" (Tacitus, *Ann.* 2.73). Upon Agrippina's arrival in Rome with the ashes of Germanicus in an urn at Rome (AD 20), the remains were consigned to the mausoleum of Augustus. However, an absence of the pageantry normally associated with the state funerals of the Roman nobility was noted in the case of Germanicus' internment. Tacitus develops most effectively the sharp contrast between the earlier funeral of Augustus and that of Germanicus:

> In the bitterest of the winter, the sovereign had gone in person as far as Ticumum, and, never stirring from the corpse, had entered the capital along with it. The bier had been surrounded with the family effigies of the Claudian and Livian houses; the dead had been mourned in the Forum, eulogised upon the Rostra; every distinction which our ancestors had discovered, or their posterity invented, was showered upon him. But to Germanicus had fallen not even the honours due to every and any noble! ... His brother had gone no more than one day's journey to meet him; his uncle not even to the gate. Where were those usages of the ancients – the images placed at the head of the couch, the set poems to the memory of departed virtue, the panegyrics, the tears, the imitations (if no more) of sorrow?[118]

We see here the results of the *invidia* ("jealousy") that had been provoked in the Roman ruler Tiberius by the ever-increasing rise in popularity of the charismatic Germanicus, greatly enhanced by his military victories over the German tribes and his pacification of the East.[119] It is beyond our purpose here to discuss the rhetorical aims of Tacitus in his presentation Germanicus' burial rites.[120] Moreo-

[116] See B. Levick, *Tiberius the Politician* (London: Croom Helm, 1976), 124; R. Seager, *Tiberius*, 2nd ed. (Oxford: Blackwell, 2005), 88–94.

[117] D.R. Dudley (*The World of Tacitus* [London: Secker and Warburg, 1968], 100) writes: "Germanicus is indeed the one truly virtuous figure in the pages of Tacitus – the only one, that is to say, who is both good and great. Nor is Tacitus alone in this. A very similar picture is to be found in Suetonius, and it is echoed in Dio." See Suetonius, *Cal.* 3; Dio Cassius 57.18.7–8.

[118] Tacitus, *Ann.* 3.5.

[119] For discussion, see T. Strunk, *History after Liberty: Tacitus on Tyrants, Sycophants, and Republicans* (Ann Arbor: University of Michigan Press, 2017), 54–62.

[120] For discussion, see R. Syme, "Obituaries in Tacitus," *AJP* 79 (1958): 18–31; M.T. Gin-

ver, O'Gorman correctly notes that some of the absences in ritual at Germanicus' funeral in Rome spotted by contemporary observers *were* actually present in the celebrations at Antioch previously, with the main omission at Rome being only that of the *imagines* ("images").[121] Suffice it to say for our purposes, the episode alerts us to the alertness of the Roman public to the rituals associated with the funerals of the aristocratic elites in the capital from the republic through to imperial times. Funerals were a crucial means of maintaining the celebrity of the family of the deceased before a watching and easily excitable public.

Notwithstanding the intense contemporary debate on what were the elements of dishonour in the funeral of Germanicus at Rome by way of its omissions, the provinces of the Roman Empire and the Italian peninsula experienced their own opportunity to participate in the memorialisation of the dead Germanicus. We see this in the extensive Tabula Siarensis, fragments of which have been found at Siarum in Baetica (modern Seville in Spain) and in Heba in Etruria (Italy).[122] There the honours to be offered for the dead Germanicus are extensively detailed, which are also subsequently recounted in the narrative of Tacitus (*Ann.* 2.83). There is mention of

- the erection of marble archways at the Circus Flaminius in Rome (with the wording of its dedicatory inscription fulsomely recounted), at Amanis in Syria (with an accompanying statue of Germanicus), and on the banks of the Rhine (with a tomb of Germanicus showing the supplication of the Germans and Gauls);
- the building of a sepulchre to Germanicus at Antioch;
- the performance of ceremonies to the spirit of Germanicus;
- the erection of a statue of Germanicus in a triumphal cloak alongside the statues of Gaius and Lucius Caesar;
- the erection of statues of Germanicus and his family at the Palatine in the portico of the temple of Apollo (i.e. the tutelary god of Augustus);
- the establishment of a honorary curule chair for Germanicus;
- sacrifices to the dead Germanicus before his tomb and the closure of temples on the anniversary of his death each year.

In conclusion, the dissemination of honour for the dead Germanicus across the Empire, as well as the performance of sacrificial rituals in memory of him, not

gras, "Annalistic Format, Tacitean Themes and the Obituaries of 'Annals' 3," *CJ* 87.3 (1992): 241–56; E. O'Gorman, *Irony and Misreading in the Annals of Tacitus* (Cambridge: Cambridge University Press, 2004), 65–69.

[121] O'Gorman, *Irony and Misreading*, 67.

[122] R.K. Sherk, ed. and tr., *The Roman Empire: Augustus to Hadrian*, Translated Documents of Greece and Rome 6 (Cambridge: Cambridge University Press, 1988), §36. For discussion, see A.C. Spencer, *The Value of Imperial Virtues in the* Tabula Siarensis *and the Senatus Consultum de Cn. Pisone Patre* (MA thesis, University of North Carolina, Chapel Hill, 2009), 40–69.

only underscore the centrality of the imperial cult for the Julian house but also its determination that the fame of its ancestors was continually brought before the Roman public and its provincial clients. The politics of honour and funereal dishonour, hotly debated at Rome, were quickly swept aside as the Julian family continued its dominance in the capital.

1.3. The Ancient Celebrity Circuit and Processional Culture

1.3.1. Athletic Competitions: The Periodos and Circuits of Victory

One of the groups in antiquity that achieved international glory were the athletes who travelled from competition to competition in a well-established circuit of games. Not only were their victories recorded in personal inscriptions throughout the eastern Mediterranean basin, but also the victors of the games themselves were recorded in inscriptions at the local sites of the games (e.g. Olympia, Athens, Corinth).[123] Two inscriptions will suffice to establish the celebrity which attended ancient athletes.[124] First, the victory inscription of the boxer Photion, whose home city was Laodikeia ad Lycum, recounts with precision his victories by age division, region, and order of occurrence (IEph V 1605 [after AD 174). The victories of Photium in the age division of "young men" in Asia Minor are detailed in this manner: (a) two victories in Ephesus (Koina of Asia in Ephesos; Epinikia in Ephesos); (b) two in his home town (Koina of Asia in Laodikea; Ecumenical Deia Sebasta in Laodikea); (c) one in Miletos (Didymeia in Miletos). These provincial fights are followed by his fights in the age division of "men". Photion expands internationally his range of competitions by moving from further victories in Asia Minor (Traianeia Deiphileia in Pergamon; Ecumenical Deia Sebasta in Laodikea; Ephesea) to fights in Italy and the Peloponessus (Eusebeia in Puteoli, Sebasta in Naples; Aspis in Argos), and then, as an internationally famous boxer, returning again to further bouts in Asia Minor (Artemeisia in Ephesos).[125]

We know the result of Photion's boxing career after the sequence of fights outlined above. He went on to win at Olympia, as a papyrus (Pap. Lon. 3.1178.84

[123] For the list of names of victors in the various competitions of the Olympic games, see POxy II.222 (S.G. Miller, *Arete; Greek Sports from Ancient* Sources, 2nd ed. [Berkeley and Los Angeles: University of California Press, 1991], § 86). For the Panathenaic games (Athens), see IG II² 2311 (*ibid.*, § 84). For the Isthmian games (Corinth), see B.D. Meritt, ed., *Corinth Vol VIII. Part I: Greek Inscriptions 1896–1927* (Cambridge, Mass.: Harvard University Press, 1931), §§ 14–19.

[124] For further examples of athletic inscriptions illustrating the celebrity of the athlete, see Miller, *Arete*, §§ 15, 71, 106, 109b, 150, 153.

[125] For commentary on this inscription, see S.A. Brunet, *Greek Athletes in the Roman World: The Evidence from Ephesus* (PhD diss., University of Texas, 1998), 343–45, § 28.

[AD 194]) indicates by according the boxer the honorific "Olympionikes" (Φωτίων Καρπίνος Λαδίκευς καὶ Ἐφέσιος. πύκτης. Ὀλυμπιονείκης). Photion organised his boxing career strategically, gaining experience in the lower age division by competing in familiar local and regional bouts, before, upon moving to the higher age competition, testing himself on the international stage and gaining the ultimate prize at Olympia. This inscription gives us keen insight into the peripatetic world of the ancient athlete, who sought personal glory contest-by-contest, region-by-region, and continent-by-continent, with a view to enhancing the honour of his family and his city. The athletic elites, like their modern counterparts, were always travelling to the next contest. Ephesus, like other ancient cities, deeply imbibed this culture of the beautiful, strong, and victorious.[126]

Second, another important Ephesian inscription (IEph V 1613 [post AD 132]; cf. IEph IV 1133) honours a runner who has won the original athletic *periodos* ("circuit") of ancient Greece (i.e. Olympia in Prusa, Pythia in Delphi, Nemeia and Isthmia).[127] Several other important claims are made about this athlete. He was "unbeaten" ([ἄλ]ειπτος) and, very unusually, he had won victories in the *stadion* (180 m.) and *diaulos* (c. 400 m.) races, as well as in the pentathlon,[128] in the same session at Isthmia "once for all" (ἅπαξ). Most striking of all, in an unnamed race, he had arrived "alone and first (μό[νο]ς καὶ πρπῶτ[ος]) coming into the registration (of competitors) having stopped all (his) rivals" well before the race had begun. His towering reputation had scared all the other competitors away! Other victories occurred at the Panathenaia in Athens, the Panhellenic games, and the Hadrianeia. What we are witnessing here is not only the inflated boasting of ancient athletes and their cities, but also how increasingly difficult it was becoming by the second century AD to establish new claims of athletic primacy that had not already been accomplished before.[129] Ancient cities were assiduous record keepers of their various athletic competition results, as were the athletes themselves.[130] Remarkably, our Ephesian competitor had established new grounds for boasting in an already jam-packed arena of fame.

---

[126] On male beauty contests in antiquity, see N.B. Crowther, "Male Beauty Contests in Greece: The *Euandria* and *Euexia*," *AC* (1985): 285–91; J.R. Harrison, "Paul and the Ancient Athletic Ideal," in *Paul's World*, PAST 4, ed. S.E. Porter (Leiden and Boston: Brill, 2008), 81–110, at 102–03.

[127] For discussion, with a differently restored text to IEph at various junctures, see Brunet, *Greek Athletes in the Roman World*, 332–34 § 28. The IEph editor's claim that the athlete is possibly Demaratos is to be rejected since he was active in the Augustan age whereas our athlete competed in the reign of Hadrian (*ibid.*, 334).

[128] Brunet (*Greek Athletes in the Roman World*, 332 § 28) restores [ὁπλίταν] (a footrace in hoplite armour) instead of [πένταθλον] in the IEph edition.

[129] For discussion, see Brunet, *Greek Athletes in the Roman World*, 21–41, 82–84.

[130] The *agōnothetēs* determined the wording of the inscription, in conjunction with the athletes (Brunet, *Greek Athletes in the Roman World*, 93–94), with cities and synods being assiduous record keepers (*ibid.*, 41–58).

1.3.2. The International Fame of the Ecumenical Synod of Dionysiac Artists

"Synods" or guilds of artists (i.e. professional performers in the theatre) developed in the third century BC at Athens under the patronage of the god Dionysios. However, by the late republic, there had developed a "world-wide" (*oikoumenikos* or ecumenical) synod of Dionysiac artists, the privileges of which were reaffirmed by the Roman ruler Hadrian,[131] with the Diocletian later tightening the rules of admission into the synod's contests.[132] Under imperial patronage this synod became "an empire-wide association of victors in the major international music contests."[133] Not only were the artists in the synod celebrated internationally by winning the contests, but their benefactors were honoured locally. This is evident in the decree of the Dionysiac Artists for T. Aelius Alkibiades, who was from the city of Nysa but in this case is honoured by the city of Ephesus. The decree sets out the reasons for his public honours:

> Since Aelius Alkibiades, a man excelling in learning and magnanimity as well as adorned with other fine (qualities) of virtue, continues for a long and for twelve years even to benefact greatly all the musicals, and for honour and magnificence to assist the synod also with many self-benefactions to us and the confederation, yet also he has adorned with wonderful books the holy shrine in Rome of the world's artists, and provides magnificent gifts of the land by having assigned a stable, from which we will reap eternal and continuous income, distributing the incomes yearly on the birthday of the divine Hadrian, on account of which repaying his kindness the artist in Rome have voted also other appropriate honours to him, have designated him high priest for all time, and have deemed him worthy to be in the order of the other high priests by being listed first on the diptychs for which he adorned the immortal memory of Hadrian and displayed the synod more glorious by his gifts when it sent embassies and performed costly festivals ...[134]

Here we see how local benefactors from cities in Asia Minor can become "celebrity players" on the international stage of beneficence by benefitting the synod of the Dionysiac Artists, acquiring not only reciprocation of honour from the synod for himself and his home town but also an eternal high priesthood and the informal recognition of Hadrian himself (IEph 1a 22 *ll.*68–70). Strategic beneficence, astutely placed, brings international recognition.[135]

---

[131] For the letters of Hadrian dealing with the issue, see J.H. Oliver, *Greek Constitutions of Early Roman Emperors from Inscriptions and Papyri* (Philadelphia: American Philosophical Society, 1989), §96A-C. He especially encouraged the Athenian Synod of musical arts (*ibid.*, §97), devoting quite a few epistles to the group (§§98–104). Since Oliver's collection, three new letters have been published: G. Petzl and E. Schwertheim, *Hadrian und die dionysischen Künstler: drei in Alexandria Troas neugefundene Briefe des Kaisers an die Künstler-Vereinigung* (Bonn: Habelt, 2006).

[132] See E.A. Judge, "The Ecumenical Synod of Dionysiac Artists," in *Jerusalem and Athens: Cultural Transformation in Late Antiquity*, WUNT I 265, ed. A. Nobbs (Tübingen: Mohr Siebeck, 2010), 137–39.

[133] Judge, "The Ecumenical Synod of Dionysiac Artists," 138.

[134] IEph 1a.22 *ll.* 8–34.

[135] See in this regard the remarkable eulogistic inscription honouring the Lycian benefac-

1.3.3. *The Endowment of Vibius Salutaris at Ephesus*

A singular example of processional culture and the celebrity that it spawned is the procession of the statues through the city of Ephesus, established by an exceptionally wealthy Ephesian benefactor at the beginning of the second century AD. The foundation of Caius Vibius Salutaris (AD 104: IEph 1a 27), spanning 568 lines in the inscription, outlines in minute detail how the money was to be used by the boule and demos of Ephesus. A procession took place through the streets of Ephesus for important festivals and occasions, probably as regularly as, if G.M. Rogers is correct, every two weeks, occurring on the days that the assembly met.[136] The procession left the temple of Artemis, proceeded through the city in a roughly circular route, and returned to the temple again, passing three important sites honouring the founder of Ephesus, Androklos, in the process.[137]

In terms of Salutaris' bequest, the inscription mentions a yearly scheme of lotteries and distributions, from which were given

- monetary donations to the crowds in the temple of Artemis on the re-enactment of her birthday and to the provincial officials of the imperial cult for the sacrifices during the celebration of the mysteries;[138]
- the donation of 31 gold and silver type-statues for the "procession of the statues," which moved in a circular route throughout the city, beginning and ending at the temple of Artemis, as well as money for the care of the statuary;[139]
- donations for unspecified tasks, in strict hierarchical order, to the citizens of the tribes, members of the boule, members of the gerousia, and the ephebes.[140]

The birth of Artemis, an Olympian deity, legitimised the social hierarchy of Ephesus,[141] pointed to her existence before the Greek city,[142] affirmed the Roman contribution to the city through the processional map,[143] and gave the city its sacred identity and civic unity.[144]

---

tor Opramoas, containing a sequence of decrees and official correspondence (including rescripts from the Roman ruler Antoninus Pius), in Danker, *Benefactor*, § 19.

136 G.M. Rogers, *The Sacred Identity of Ephesos: Foundation Myths of a Roman City* (London and New York: Routledge, 1991), 83.

137 For a map showing the route of the procession, see Rogers, *The Sacred Identity*, 145–46 Figs. 1, 2. On the honorific sites of Androklos that the procession passed, see D.Y. Ng, *Manipulation of Memory: Public Buildings and Decorative Programs in Roman Cities of Asia Minor* (PhD diss., University of Michigan, 2007), 183–233.

138 Rogers, *Sacred Identity*, 1, 48–50.

139 Rogers, *Sacred Identity*, 45–48, 83–86. Nine of the statues depicted Artemis, with dedications from different groups within the city (see the table, *ibid.*, 84–85).

140 Rogers, *Sacred Identity*, 50–65.

141 Rogers, *Sacred Identity*, 69.

142 Rogers, *Sacred Identity*, 112–13.

143 Rogers, *Sacred Identity*, 113–15.

144 Rogers, *Sacred Identity*, 145–47.

Our interest, however, is more focused on how Salutaris is honoured in highly adulatory moral terms that define what true civic virtue was for elite Ephesians (IEph 1a 27 *ll.* 14–24; cf. *ll.* D. 370–389):

> ... [Gaius] Vibius Salutaris, a man
> 15 of the equestrian order, conspicuous by birth and personal worth, and with military commands
> and procuratorships by our lord *imperator* adorned,
> our citizen and (a member) of the bouleutic council, and in the sight of (his) father
> managing (his life) with a good disposition, since, from fortune to the better
> (intending) to crown (his) prosperity by the gravity of (his) morals, piously making
> 20 donations he has been zealous regarding the foundress with diverse plans concerning
> the cult, and with generous donations he has honoured the city in every way,
> and further now coming forward in the assembly in the assembly he has promised
> to dedicate nine type-statues, one of gold, on which is
> gold-gilded silver, and eight other type statues, and twenty silver images ...

This densely worded accolade resonates with the high morality expected of Ephesian benefactors. Salutaris' life is lived out before the watchful eyes of his father, causing Salutaris to demonstrate the type of internal disposition that invariably leads to a controlled lifestyle. The gravity (σεμνότητι ["dignity"]) of his morals (ἠθῶν ["character") is the secret of his success, with the result that he shows *eusebeia* ("piety") towards Artemis, the foundress of the city, generously (φιλοοτεί[μως]) carrying out his promises about honouring her cult. As the preamble of the inscription has already articulated (IEph 1a 27 *ll.* 8–14), precisely because of the qualities of benefactors like Salutaris, the honours of the present had to be commensurate with those accorded to benefactors of the past, so that it would act as an incentive to a new generation of benefactors seeking the same honours in the future. Consequently, Afrianus Flavianus, the *legatus pro praetore*, emphasises the importance for the Ephesians to reciprocate Salutaris commensurately by a fitting acknowledgement of his favours and personal merit (IEph 1a 27 *ll.* 389–395): "Wherefore I think it is owed to him by you, with a view toward being more equally enthusiastic, if this man should appear to be worthy of recompense according to merit. And it would be especially gratifying and the sweetest of things to me, if, the man whom especially of friends I honour and love, among you should be seen as worthy of recognition and honour."[145]

[145] Note D. Knibbe's assessment ("*Via Sacra Ephesiaca*: New Aspects of the Cult of Artemis," in *Ephesos: Metropolis of Asia. An Interdisciplinary Approach to Its Archaeology, Religion, and Culture*, ed. H. Koester [Valley Forge: Trinity International Press, 1995], 141–155, at 154) of C. Vibius Salutaris. He argues that the processions had "no relationship to the cult of Artemis," but were honouring instead Salutaris, who had become very rich in serving tax-collectors in Sicily and in his equestrian career. As Knibbe concludes (*ibid.*, 154), "Returning to Ephesos as a private citizen, he did something that would make him immortal." In my view, two motives drove Salutaris: honour of Artemis and, equally, honour of himself. The more that Salutaris honoured Artemis, the more Salutaris, as the benefactor of the goddess, was honoured by Ephesus and immortalised in the city's memory.

In sum, the officials of the Roman ruler in provincial Asia, aware that cities like Ephesus and Sardis were *neokoroi* of the imperial cult, were keen to see that powerful local benefactors were publicly honoured for their social contribution to the religious status quo in their cities. Furthermore, as G.M. Rogers rightly comments,[146] the increased devotion to Artemis not only honours the goddess abroad but also enhances the financial well-being of Ephesus through the increased goods and services required for all the new extra holy days and festival celebrations. Ephesus, through the endowment of Salutaris, nurtures her own goddess and profits financially in so doing. The recognition of the inherent virtue of Salutaris because of his benefactions to Artemis, therefore, not only increases his personal glory as a civic celebrity but also enhances the glory of Artemis and the welfare of her city.

1.3.4. The Circuit of Charioteers and the Arena of Gladiators

Another "circuit" of celebrity in antiquity was the chariot races.[147] Three examples will suffice. The famous inscription of Gaius Appuleius Diocles, charioteer of the Red Faction and from the Spanish Lusitanian people,[148] reveals that he won more than 35 million sesterces in prizes over a career of 4,257 races in which he had 1,462 victories.[149] Although rare, female charioteers also gained fame throughout the Greek world:

> Kings of Sparta were my fathers and brothers. Kyniska, victorious at the chariot race with her swift-footed horses, erected this statue. I assert that I am the only woman in all Greece who won this crown.[150]

---

[146] G.M. Rogers, *The Mysteries of Artemis of Ephesos: Cult, Polis, and Change in the Graeco-Roman World*, Synkrisis (New Haven and London: Yale University Press, 2012), 224.

[147] See J.H. Humphrey, *Roman Circuses: Arenas for Chariot Racing* (Berkeley: University of California Press, 1986); F. Meijer, *Chariot Racing in the Roman Empire: Spectacles in Rome and Constantinople*, tr. L. Waters (Baltimore: The Johns Hopkins University Press, 2010); S. Bell, "Roman Chariot Racing Charioteers, Factions, Spectators," in *A Companion to Sport and Spectacle in Greek and Roman Antiquity*, ed. P. Christesen and D.G. Kyle (Malden: Wiley-Blackwell, 2014), 492–504.

[148] For curse tablets summoning the underground gods to impede drivers from the Blue and Red factions, see A. Futrell, *The Roman Games: A Sourcebook* (Malden and Oxford: Blackwell, 2006), 203–04. See also A. Cameron, *Circus Factions: Blues and Greens at Rome and Byzantium* (Oxford: Clarendon Press, 1976); P. Lee-Stectum, "Dangerous Reputations: Charioteers and Magic in Fourth-Century Rome," *G&R* 53.2 (2006): 224–34.

[149] *CIL* 14.2884, tr. Futrell, *The Roman Games*, 200. For discussion, see D.S. Potter, "Entertainers in the Roman Empire," in *Life, Death, and Entertainment in the Roman Empire*, ed. D.S. Potter and D.J. Mattingly (Ann Arbor: The University of Michigan Press, 1999), 256–325, at 296–99. See also the famous charioteer Porphyrius (b. AD 480), discussed by A. Cameron, *Porphyrius the Charioteer* (London: Oxford University Press, 1973). On entertainment generally, see H. Leppin, "Between Marginality and Celebrity: Entertainers and Entertainments in Roman Society," in *The Oxford Handbook of Social Relations in the Roman World*, ed. M. Peachin (Oxford and New York: Oxford University Press, 2011), 660–78.

[150] IvO 160 (369 BC: Miller, *Arete*, § 98b).

The popularity of the individual gladiators among spectators across the Roman Empire is reinforced by a first-century AD glass beaker from Cholchester. It depicts a race between four chariot teams, with the acclamations of the spectators for their favourites written in the top register of the beaker: "Go Hierax! Go Olympus! Go Antilochus! Hail Cresces!"[151] In the Magical Papyri, we find a victory charm for the races, the following inscription was to be incised on the hoofs of the racing horse: "Give me success, charm, reputation, glory in the stadium."[152]

In terms of gladiators, D. S. Potter has drawn attention to the ambiguity of the Roman amphitheater.[153] Its high-status gladiators represented the quintessential virtues of the Roman aristocracy, but, nonetheless, "aristocratic society seems to have closed ranks against public combatants more forcefully than against any other type of entertainer."[154] Notwithstanding this ambiguity, C. A. Barton has highlighted the interplay that occurred between the love of glory and death animating the gladiator and the character traits similarly animating late republican and early imperial society. Faced with the horror of the civil wars and the "feeling of humiliation and insecurity" under the early imperial period, the aristocratic literary elites (e.g. Lucan, Seneca, Petronius, Martial, Juvenal) looked elsewhere for compensation and found it in the arena. The gladiator became more than just another Roman entertainer, but, simultaneously, at a quasi-mythological level, "a victim under direct compulsion" and "a redeemer, both of himself and his audience."[155] The glory and degradation of

---

[151] For a picture of the beaker, see Futrell, *The Roman Games*, 75 Figure 2.10. For the inscription (RIB 2419), see *ibid*, 76.

[152] PGM VII. 390–93.

[153] Potter, "Entertainers in the Roman Empire," 323–24.

[154] Potter, "Entertainers in the Roman Empire," 323. On gladiators, see L. Robert, *Les gladiateurs dans l'orient grec* (Amsterdam: Adolf M. Hakkert, 1971); T. Wiedemann, *The Emperors and Gladiators* (London and New York: Routledge, 1992); Barton, *The Sorrows of Ancient Romans*; T. Ritti and S. Yilmaz, *Gladiatori e venationes a Hierapolis di Frigia* (Rome: Accademia Naz. dei Lincei, 1998); M. Carter, *The Presentation of Gladiatorial Spectacles in the Greek East: Roman Culture and Greek Identity* (PhD diss., McMaster University, 1999); W. Pietsch et al., *Gladiatoren in Ephesos: Tod am Nachmittag. Eine Ausstellung im Ephesos Museum Seluk Seit 20. April 2002* (Wein: ÖAI, 2002); C. Mann, *'Um keinen Kranz, um das Leben kämpfen wir!': Gladiatoren im Osten des Römischen Reiches und die Frage der Romanisierung*, Studien zur Alten Geschichte, 14 (Berlin: Antike, 2011); C. W. Concannon, "'Not for an Olive Wreath, but Our Lives': Gladiators, Athletes, and Early Christian Bodies," *JBL* 133.1 (2014): 193–214; H. Dodge, "Amphitheaters in the Roman World," in *A Companion to Sport and Spectacle*, 543–60; A. Cadwallader, "Assessing the Potential of Archaeological Discoveries for the Interpretation of New Testament Texts: The Case of a Gladiator Fragment from Colossae and the Letter to the Colossians," in *The First Urban Churches I: Methodological Foundations* (Atlanta: SBL Press, 2015), 41–66. On the culture of death and the arena, see P. Plass, *The Game of Death in Ancient Rome: Arena Sport and Political Suicide* (London: The University of Wisconsin Press, 1995); D. G. Kyle, *Spectacles of Death in Ancient Rome* (London and New York: Routledge, 1998).

[155] Barton, *The Sorrows of Ancient Romans*, 46.

the gladiator spoke deeply to a culture immersed in its own hopelessness.[156] Having set out some of the wider ideological terrain regarding the role Roman gladiators in elite culture, what follows concentrates on how their fame was rendered in the honorific inscriptions and graffiti.

Long periods of successful fights by veteran gladiators ultimately ensured their survival, because their ardent fans, who wished to see them fight again, intervened by calling for their reprieve (*missio*),[157] thereby rewarding their skill or courage in fights where they had been disarmed or defeated:[158]

> To the ... spirits. Asiaticus, first fighter, released after 53 combats, his wife had this made.[159]

In other cases, a singular achievement is emphasised, such as the dismissal of a gladiator from the arena with its highest accolade (*summa rudis*):

> To the departed spirits of Cornelius Eugenianus, awarded the *summa rudis*, and of Cornelia Rufina. Their daughter has made this for her well-deserving and sweetest parents.[160]

However, the boasting and public rivalry between gladiators is very well illustrated in an inscription of the Thessalonian gladiator, Victor. In his epitaph Victor rejects outright (what he considers to be) the deceitful lies of Pinnas, his boastful conqueror and killer in the arena, attributing instead his loss to the machinations of "Doom".[161] Victor then claims post-mortem vindication over Pinnas, his now-dead opponent, who had been subsequently killed by Victor's "fellow-gladiator," Polyneikes. Reputation was a fragile commodity in antiquity and it had to be strongly defended before the critical eyes of posterity, in this case by a clever conflation of rhetorical rebuttal with a calculated boast in one's vicarious victory over one's opponent, even if the victory is retrospectively claimed. Significantly, all this is achieved by one who is "left handed." Why is this feature highlighted? Although left-handers comprise only 10 % of the population, physical competition favours the unusual and thus the left-handedness of a combatant gives an advantage in a fight, a feature worth boasting in:[162]

---

156 Barton, *The Sorrows of Ancient Romans*, 46.

157 See the graffito of the Pompeian gladiator Attilius granting *missio* to the disarmed and unhelmeted Felix (Futrell, *The Roman Games*, 100 Figure 3.8).

158 A. Futrell, *The Roman Games: A Sourcebook* (Malden and Oxford: Blackwell, 2006), 144.

159 CIL XII 5837 (Futrell, *The Roman Games*, 144). For other examples, *ibid.*, 144–45.

160 CIL VI 10201 (Futrell, *The Roman Games*, 151).

161 A twenty-three year old gladiator, Glauco, winner of seven contests until his death on the eighth (CIL 5.3466 [Futrell, *The Roman Games*, 153]), warns regarding the deceitfulness of the god of retribution on his epitaph: "I advise you to find your own star: do not trust Nemesis: That's how I was deceived."

162 D. M. Abrams and M. J. Panaggio, "A Model Balancing Cooperation and Competition? Can Explain Our Right-Handed World and the Dominance of Left-Handed Athletes?" *Journal of the Royal Society Interface* 9.75 (2012): 2718–22.

Victor, left-handed, lies here, but my homeland was Thessalonica. Doom killed me, not the liar Pinnas. No longer let him boast. I had a fellow gladiator, Polyneikes, who killed Pinnas and avenged me. Claudius Thallus set up this memorial from what I left behind as a legacy.[163]

As a final example of celebrity among Roman entertainers, we touch on an important part of gladiator (and, more widely, athletic and military) culture found in the graffiti of Pompeii: the physical beauty of the strong and their sexual allure.[164] In the cases of the Pompeian graffiti, it is uncertain whether this adulation represents the boasting of the gladiators themselves or, indeed, the sexual tributes of their female fans:[165]

Celadus the *Thraex*, the sigh of the girls, three combats, three victories.[166]
Celadus the *Thraex*, the glory of the girls.[167]
Crescens the *retarius*, doctor ... of nighttime dollies.[168]

In conclusion, although an ambiguous and low status figure among the Roman elites, the gladiator captured the popular imagination in ways that many powerful elite figures in the provinces did not.

1.3.5. Celebrity Entertainers in Antiquity

In addition to the athletic *periodos* in the Greek world, discussed above, there were also competitions in artistic performance at the games and festivals of the ancient cities, including drama, music, mime, poetry, and comedy. Some of these performers, like their modern counterparts, became international celebrities in their own right, commemorated with honorific inscriptions outlining their victories or eulogised for their art on their tombstones. Our focus will be primarily on the inscriptional evidence relating to ancient mime artists.[169] This

163 Robert, *Les gladiateurs*, § 34 (Futrell, *The Roman Games*, 149).

164 Plautus emphasises the sexual allure of the comic Roman general Pyrgopolynices in Plautus, *Mil. Glor.* 41–47, 52–58. For discussion, see Harrison, *Paul and the Imperial Authorities*, 223–25. Note, too, the emphasis on the beauty of Lucius Cornelius Scipio Long-beard "whose fine form matched his bravery surpassing well" (CIL I.2.7), as well as the reference to the "most godlike shape (θειοτάτος μορφᾶς)" of Epigonos (ILaodikeia am Lykos § 81), noted above. See also the reference to the beauty of Melancomas, the boxer (Dio Chrysostom, *Or.* 28.5–6), discussed in Chapter 4. On male beauty, see Crowther, "Male Beauty Contests in Greece."

165 Futrell, *The Roman Games*, 146.

166 CIL IV 4342 (Futrell, *The Roman Games*, 146).

167 CIL IV 4345 (Futrell, *The Roman Games*, 146).

168 CIL IV 4353 (Futrell, *The Roman Games*, 146).

169 On ancient mime and pantomime, see G. M. A. Richter, "Grotesques and the Mime," *AJA* 17.2 (1913): 149–56; A. Fountoulakis, "The Artists of Aphrodite," *L'antiquité classique* 69.1 (2000): 133–47; L. L. Welborn, *Paul, the Fool for Christ: A Study of 1 Corinthians 1–4 in the Comic-Philosophic Tradition* (London and New York: T&T Clark, 2005); I. Lada-Richards, *Silent Eloquence: Lucian and Pantomime Dancing* (London and New York: Blooms-

is an interesting group of performers to investigate because the association of the Dionysiac artists considered the mime "as a sub-dramatic form of artistic expression,"[170] especially because of the low social status of many of its performers and the dubious morality of the erotic content associated with much mime performance.[171] As a result, the Dionysiac artists excluded the mime performers from their association, with the result that the mimes were not allowed to participate in the sacred dramatic contests. Consequently, the mime artists belonged to associations called in the Latin inscriptions *Parisiti Apollinis*, *Mimarii*, and *Commune Mimorum*, being regarded as inferior to the prestigious Dionysiac artists, who considered themselves as "ministers of religion" because of their performances in religious festivals.[172] It was only towards the end of the second century AD that the mime artists were re-admitted to the Dionysiac artists, probably as full members, enabling them once again to enter fully the normal circuit of competitions.[173]

Many inscriptions recount the victories of mime/pantomime artists in competitions: three will suffice. First, in an inscription from Tivoli (AD 199), the performer and freedman, Memphius, lists all the pantomime roles "in the general contest" that he performed in and emerged as victor, nearly all of which were adapted from the tragedian Euripides, with the sole exception of a play from Sophocles (*Tympanistae*). E. Csapo and W.J. Slater observe that the reference to the "general context" shows that Memphius, presumably the victor in the "choral background adapted from these plays," was "the overall victor in the festival as well."[174] The vignette of Memphius being a threefold "sacred victor" is also milked for its unprecedented novelty, although the phrase establishing this is a cliché in the mime inscriptions ("first of his time"):

Heracles, *Orestes*, *Tympanistae*, in the general contest, *Trojan Women*, *Bacchae*, *Hippolytus*, in the general contest: for L. Aurelius Apolaustus Memphius, freedman of Augusti, pantomime, three times sacred victor, first of his time, ...[175]

Second, an epitaph in the theatre of Aquileia (AD 220) demonstrates the widespread impact of a female mime artist on the stage and in musical contests throughout the Greek cities:

bury Academic, 2007); E. Hall and R. Wyles, eds., *New Directions in Ancient Pantomime* (New York: Oxford University Press, 2008); R. Webb, "The Nature and Representation of Competition in Pantomime and Mime," in *L'Organisation des spectacles dans le monde Romain*, Entretiens sur l'Antiquité classique 58, ed. K. Coleman and J. Nelis-Clément (Vandoeuvres and Genève: Fondation Hardt, 2011), 221–56, 364–65.

[170] Fountoulakis, "The Artists of Aphrodite," 137.

[171] Fountoulakis, "The Artists of Aphrodite," 136–37.

[172] Fountoulakis, "The Artists of Aphrodite," 136.

[173] Fountoulakis, "The Artists of Aphrodite," 137.

[174] E. Csapo and W.J. Slater, *The Context of Ancient Drama* (Ann Arbor: University of Michigan Press, 1994), 382.

[175] *TrGF* 1, p. 344 *ad* 14a (Csapo and Slater, *The Context of Ancient Drama*, § 34).

She won resounding fame on the stage earlier among many people and many cities for manifold excellence among mimes, often in musical contests. Herakleides, a good speaker and character mime, set up <this> memorial to the mime actress Basilla, the tenth Muse, thus not dead; though she is a corpse, she has won life as her fair reward, having found a resting place for her body, in the soil of the Muses. That's life. Your fellow performers say to you: "Take heart Basilla: nobody is immortal."[176]

An especially striking honorific marks this inscription over and above its arresting cameo at the outset about Basilla's international career in the Greek world of mime and music. She has become the "tenth Muse", "thus not dead," joining the other nine Muses, the Greek goddesses who presided over the arts and the sciences, and thus continues to provide inspiration for participants in the artistic pursuits. But it is Basilla's reputation and celebrity as a performer that has acquired her immortal life with the Muses "as her fair reward" for her "manifold excellence" and which now motivates all future generations to perform in the discipline: there is no sense of apotheosis being claimed here for Basilla. This point is pressed home by her fellow performers reminding her of the ubiquitous formula found in the Greek epitaphs about making one's heart glad before the sadness and tragedy of inevitable death.

Third, the international career and victories of the pantomime Tiberius Iulius Apolaustus, a megastar in his particular discipline of the performing arts, is recounted in several fragmentary inscriptions from Delphi (FdD III 1.551), Magnesia (IMagnesia 192 fr. A, B), Ephesus (IEph VI.2070+1071) and Corinth (*Corinth* VIII. 3 fr. 693, 370).[177] During the final years of the second century AD, Apolaustus won many competition prizes in the prestigious games of the imperial period (e.g. Epheseia, Isthmia, Koina Asias, Leukophryneia, Olympeia Asklepieia, Pythia, among others), being showered with special honours, imperial favours, statues, the crown of the Actian games,[178] and civic accolades (e.g. councillorships, citizenships) from the cities of Asia Minor and Greece.[179] The reason for this plethora of awards is briefly summed up in FdD III 1 551 *ll.* 29–30 thus: "... because of the precision of (his) art and the well-ordered place of (his) life." As an aside at this juncture, the civic awards allocated to Apolaustus also illustrate another feature of the careers of mimes in antiquity: namely,

[176] IG XIV 2342 (Csapo and Slater, *The Context of Ancient Drama*, § 18).

[177] See W. J. Slater, "The Pantomime Tiberius Iulius Apolaustus," *GRBS* 36 (1995): 263–92 for all the inscriptions and commentary.

[178] Note the coronal award in ICreticae IV 222A (Csapo and Slater, *The Context of Ancient Drama*, § 26): "Lucius Furius Celsus, son of Lucius of the Falerian tribe, dancer of myths. Crowned in the theatre with a golden crown, the greatest according to law, *proxenos* of the [Gortynians], a citizen himself and his descendants."

[179] See Slater, "The Pantomime Tiberius Iulius Apolaustus," 286–88, for a useful summary of Apolautus' honours, comparing each inscription city by city.

the upward mobility of some mimes due to imperial patronage and their own benefactions to local associations.[180]

Last, an inscription in a performing arts field other than pantomime is worth noting. An Ephesian inscription honouring a boy comedian victor in the games speaks in conventional terms about reasons for his victory:

"The council and people of the first and greatest metropolis of Asia, twice Temple warden of the Augusti, the city of the Ephesians, honour T. Flavius Sarpedon, the Acmonean and Ephesian, a boy comedian, as a reward for his excellence and his studious training, and his care bestowed on his acting, after winning the contest at the great festival of the Artemesia; the president of the games being Lucius A[ureliu]s Philo."[181]

From what has been established above, there was a celebrity circuit attending victors in the performing arts in the ancient games of the Mediterranean basin, which was no different in this respect to the notoriety associated with the gladiators or to the ubiquitous athletic ideal that the apostle Paul engaged in his epistles (1 Cor 9:24–27).

1.3.6. The Eastern Mediterranean Tours of the Roman Rulers and Their Family Members

Finally, we touch briefly on the excitement that the tours of the Roman ruler and his relatives generated among his clients in the provinces of the Greek East. Two examples will suffice. First, an unidentified individual in a papyrus (*P. Oxy.* 2435) – undoubtedly the charismatic Roman general Germanicus – visits Alexandria in Egypt in AD 19 and creates a sensation by delivering an informal speech upon his arrival in the city. His reception by the crowd of ordinary citizens and the Greek civic officials is nothing but rapturous, with his impromptu speech being punctuated by excited cries of "Good luck!", "You will gain blessings!", and "Well done! May you live the longer!".[182] Succinctly put, we are witnessing here the entirely understandable reaction to the visit of any celebrity to a major city in antiquity.

[180] For an imperially sponsored career of a mime that acquires substantial social prestige as a result, see ILS 5193 (Csapo and Slater, *The Context of Ancient Drama*, § 33B [AD 181]): "For the freedman of M. Aurelius Augustus, Agilius Septenptrio, pantomime, first of his time, priest of the *synodus*, Parasite of Apollo, alumnus of Faustina, launched by M. Aurelius Commodus Antonius Pius Felix Augustus, decorated with the *ornamenta* of a Decurion by decree of the order, and adopted into the *iuvenes*." For the benefactions of a wealthy mime to the theatrical guild at Bovillae in Italy, see CIL XIV 2408 (Csapo and Slater, *The Context of Ancient Drama*, § 7). Additionally, see ILS 5186 (Csapo and Slater, *The Context of Ancient Drama*, § 33A [AD 191]): "For Lucius Aurelius Plyades, freeman of Augustus, first pantomime of his time, crowned four times in the sacred games, patron of the *Parasiti* of Apollo, priest of the association, honoured at Puteoli with the grant of decurion and duumviral honours ..."

[181] IEph V 1606.

[182] For a translation, see B. W. Jones and R. D. Milns, *The Use of Documentary Evidence in the Study of Roman Imperial History* (Netley: Sydney University Press, 1984), § 91.

Second, in AD 67 Nero visited Greece as a dedicated participant in the major festivals, including the chariot race and acting competitions, winning some 1,808 prizes. In November of the same year, he delivered a rhetorically effusive speech, recorded for us in an inscription from the small town of Akraiphia in Boeotia, in which he promised the freedom of Hellas from Roman taxation and jurisdiction. While his speech has intrinsic interest because of its self-perception and its understanding of grace and mercy, equally revealing is the response of the high priest Epameinondas to Nero's "unexpected" gift and "unhoped-for" generosity. Undoubtedly, excessive flattery is *de rigeur* on such on occasion, but one does sense the intense excitement generated by such "celebrity beneficence."

Epameinondas' accolades for Nero fall hard and fast upon the ears of his audience. The Roman beneficent ruler and his wife are said to be the "New Sun shining upon the Greeks," "Greece-loving [[Nero]] Zeus the Deliverer," "Zeus the Deliverer, Nero forever", and "the goddess Augusta [[Messalina]]."[183] The motion made in response to Nero's declaration of freedom exudes a tone of exultation because the benefactor of the world had come to Greece, had participated in the games, and had delivered something akin to the generosity of Zeus through his spectacular gift to Greece. Both of these visits to Egypt and Greece by Germanicus and Nero respectively afford us insight into rapturous response aroused when the Roman ruler and his family members actually left the boundaries of Rome and entered the territory of their provincial subjects.

In light of our discussion of the modern and ancient celebrity circuits, what questions emerge for our interpretation of Paul's gospel in its first-century "celebrity" context?

1.3.7. What Differentiates Ancient and Modern Celebrity?

The similarities between the elite-sponsored popular entertainment for the masses in antiquity, with its high profile celebrities, finds its counterpart in the modern entertainment and sports industries, with its respective "star" systems. Even the more disquieting interest of the ancients in people with disabilities as "entertainers" at feasts has its counterparts the modern world, though much more humanely focussed, in the Paralympic movement and in the construction of a "deviant" community by Lady Gaga. The communities of mourning, illustrated in the death of Steve Irwin and Princess Diana, finds "parallels" with the popular grief over the death of the charismatic figure of Germanicus. More similarities could be adduced, but the familiar contours of celebrity are found equally in the ancient and modern world.

Much could be said about the differences, but two key issues are worth airing. First, it might be mistakenly thought that the crucial role of the media was the

[183] DocsGauis 64. Tr. Sherk, *The Roman Empire*, §71.

key differentiator between celebrity in the ancient world and our modern era. The ancient world, it could be proposed, lacked the ability to mount the phenomenon of fame as widely on media platforms in the same way as modern society. But such a conclusion represents a naive inference from the explosion in the variety of media from the early twentieth century onwards. The Augustan age, for example, showed immense sophistication in its varied use of media in celebrating the triumph of the Julian house, whether that is by means of sculpture, iconography, numismatics, public ceremony and ritual, the architectural interrelation of buildings in Augustan Rome, and so on.[184] Moreover, the presence of the public inscriptions throughout the cities of the Mediterranean basin ensured the wide dissemination of the fame of the great man. The media are vastly different, but the imperial media penetration of the far-flung Roman Empire was highly effective and sophisticated.

Second, celebrity in the ancient world was inextricably bound to the ancient elites and their sponsorship of entertainment for the masses throughout the *poleis* in the Mediterranean basin. In other words, ancient society was hierarchical in a way that modern societies largely are not. We have seen, however, with the advent of print culture and the arrival of the Web 2.0 phenomena, that a self-made, do-it-yourself celebrity has now become viable for the everyday person in the modern era. Whether it is the viral video on YouTube, or an avalanche of website hits on a newly launched site, celebrity can be established overnight. To be sure, its longevity in the popular consciousness may last no longer than Andy Warhol's proverbial 15 minutes of fame, but the ability for the every-day person to establish immediate celebrity without any connection to the "elites" is now a possibility in modern society that was not open to the lower classes in antiquity. To be sure, part of attraction of the local associations antiquity was that their mixed social constituency could mimic the practices of the elites: but, notwithstanding, they still sought out elite benefactors to sponsor their activities.

1.4. The Cross, Celebrity and Moral Transformation: The Aim and Structure of the Book

The absence of any definitive historical study on the origins of celebrity has been noted above. The fact that Robert Garland's book is the only coverage of the phenomenon in antiquity underlines the lack of attention given to the issue

[184] See P. Zanker, *The Power of Images in the Age of Augustus*, tr. A. Shapiro (Ann Arbor: The University of Michigan Press, 1990); K. Galinsky, *Augustan Culture: An Interpretative Introduction* (Princeton: Princeton University Press, 1996); P. Rehak, *Imperium and Cosmos: Augustus and the Northern Campius Martius*, ed. J.G. Younger (Wisconsin: University of Wisconsin Press, 2006); J.R. Harrison, "Paul among the Romans," in *All Things to All Cultures: Paul Among Jews, Greeks, and Romans*, ed. M. Harding and A. Nobbs (Grand Rapids: Eerdmans, 2013), 143–76, at 144–46.

by ancient historians. To be sure, many monographs deal with the fame of individuals from particular civilisations in the ancient world. However, the approach taken is either too atomistic or generalist to be helpful for a proper analysis of celebrity and its origins as a phenomenon. The situation in modern historical studies of celebrity is not much better. As far as modern historical analyses of the issue, S. Morgan makes the following assessment of the state of the debate:

> While some of these give relatively little sense of the wider culture in which their subjects existed, a few of the more scholarly have made a genuine contribution to our understanding of that culture: particularly the extent to which their subject's celebrity status was the result of a deliberate process of self-promotion and media manipulation, and how far they were simply objectified by an emerging mass culture based on print and mass-produced commodities.[185]

Furthermore, in the case of celebrity in antiquity, little attention has been paid to the early Christians as critics of the "great man". Thus the collision in value systems between early Christianity and the Graeco-Roman world that gradually emerged in the western intellectual tradition over the seduction of fame has been overlooked in studies of celebrity, ancient and modern. The demonstration of humility came to be viewed as more important than the Graeco-Roman tradition of boasting in the "great man". The giftedness of all stood opposed to the privilege of the elite few. Obligation to others replaced the Stoic cultivation of a state of self-sufficiency or indifference. Consideration of the needs of the weak and disabled came to have priority over deference to the rights of the strong and abled. The moral and social transformation of communities in the crucified Christ through the Spirit undermined the static construct of the ancient virtues, which, it was believed, had been assigned to the social elites from birth, with the result that the status quo was entrenched and any significant social change was therefore profoundly feared. What brought about this dramatic shift in social attitudes towards celebrity and the urban elites?

This book will argue that Paul's apocalyptic and eschatological gospel challenged the ancient celebrity circuit by establishing a new understanding of where human achievement, virtue, and identity before God and others actually resided: that is, in the atoning work of the crucified, risen, and reigning Christ. Paul argues that the Spirit of Christ indwells and empowers his charismatic communities of mercy and beneficence, reconciling Jews and Gentiles to God and to each other, with the result that the attitudes of ethnic and cultural superiority of the powerful elites living in the capital and in the provinces towards their social inferiors were now anathema in the Body of Christ. Consequently, a new set of social relations and moral values have been established in the communal life of believers, so that they might continue to seek the welfare of the

[185] See http://www.history.ac.uk/reviews/review/994, accessed 19.04.2017.

city in a manner radically different to the self-interested monopolies of the elites, as believers waited for Christ's return from the heavenly city of Jerusalem and God's establishment of the new creation.

Our study focuses, therefore, on an important aspect of the outworking of the soteriology of the cross in the first-century Graeco-Roman world that has been little explored by New Testament scholars: the moral transformation of the early believers in a world dominated by the civic ethics of the ancient elites.[186] Thus this study not only contributes to an understanding of the collision of the early Christian communities with the civic ethics and celebrity culture of the provincial and imperial elites, including the games, entertainment and spectacles that they sponsored, but also it provides another aperture through which we can better appreciate the gradual impact of Paul's theology of the cross in Graeco-Roman society, that led, ultimately, to the ideological transformation of important aspects of the western intellectual tradition.[187] As such, it is hoped that the book will contribute to the growing literature on the social significance of the death of Jesus in New Testament scholarship.[188]

In concentrating upon the social emphasis of the cross in this book, we are in no way denying or playing down the traditional soteriological emphases of Christ's work associated with Pauline theology:[189] namely, salvation, the fulfil-

---

[186] For literature, see Chapter 8.

[187] See Judge, *Paul and the Conflict of Cultures.*

[188] See H.-R. Weber, *The Cross: Tradition and Interpretation*, tr. E. Jessett (London: SPCK, 1979: Gmn. orig. 1975), 64–82; S. Barton, "Paul and the Cross: A Sociological Approach," *Theology* 85 (1982): 13–19; C.B. Cousar, *A Theology of the Cross: The Death of Jesus in the Pauline Epistles* (Minneapolis: Fortress, 1990), 135–48; R. Pickett, "The Death of Christ as Divine Patronage in Romans 5:1–11," *SBL Seminar Papers* 1993, 726–39; *idem*, *The Cross in Corinth: The Social Significance of the Death of Jesus*, JSNTSup 143 (Sheffield: Sheffield Academic Press, 1997); A.R. Brown, *The Cross and Human Transformation: Paul's Apocalyptic Word in 1 Corinthians* (Minneapolis: Fortress, 1995); T.B. Savage, *Power Through Weakness: A Historical and Exegetical Examination of Paul's Understanding of the Christian Ministry in 2 Corinthians*, SNTSMS 86 (Cambridge: Cambridge University Press, 1996); M.J. Gorman, *Cruciformity: Paul's Narrative Spirituality of the Cross* (Grand Rapids: Eerdmans, 2001), 214–303; *idem*, *Inhabiting the Cruciform God: Kenosis, Justification, and Theosis in Paul's Narrative Theology* (Grand Rapids: Eerdmans, 2009), 137–60; D.L. Balch, "Paul's Portrait of Christ Crucified (Gal 3:1) in Light of Paintings and Sculptures of Suffering and Death in Pompeiian and Roman Houses," in *Early Christian Families in Context: An Interdisciplinary Dialogue*, ed. D.L. Balch and C.A. Oseik (Grand Rapids: Eerdmans, 2003), 84–108; Welborn, *Paul, the Fool of Christ*; *idem*, "'Extraction from the Mortal Site": Badiou on the Resurrection in Paul," *NTS* 55.3 (2009): 295–314; J.R. Harrison, "Paul and the Social Relations of Death at Rome (Rom 5:14, 17, 21)," in *Paul and His Social Relations. Pauline Studies: Volume VII*, PAST 7, ed. S.E. Porter (Leiden: Brill, 2012), 85–123; *idem*, "The Erasure of Honour: Paul and the Politics of Dishonour," *Tyn Bul* 66.2 (2016): 161–84.

[189] See D.J. Dupont, ΣΥΝ ΧΡΙΣΤΩΙ: *L'Union avec le Christ suivant Saint Paul* (Paris: Desclée de Brouwer, 1952); B. Caird, *Principalities and Powers: A Study in Pauline Theology* (Oxford: Clarendon Press, 1956); L. Morris, *The Apostolic Preaching of the Cross*, 3rd ed. (London: Tyndale Press, 1965); *idem*, *The Cross in the New Testament* (Exeter: Paternoster Press, 1967); R.C. Tannehill, *Dying and Rising with Christ* (Berlin: Alfred Töpelmann, 1967);

ment of Old Testament sacrificial types, vicarious atonement, propitiation, redemption, ransom, justification, reconciliation, imputed righteousness, baptism in and union with Christ, and the apocalyptic triumph over evil powers. We are simply saying that there is also an outworking of the work of the cross that inverts social relations in unexpected ways, unleashing a moral transformation that challenges the hierarchical, celebrity-and-status-driven mores of the ancient and modern worlds.

The gallows humour attached to crucifixion by the ancients is highly revealing in this regard.[190] A witty epigram of Lucillius, an unknown writer from the reign of Nero, lampoons the crucified by attributing to them exactly the same invidious drive for celebrity and social ascendancy at the moment of their death as the elites of antiquity.[191] The epigram, which acerbically highlights implication the social envy characteristic of the elites, states that

> Envious Diophon, seeing another man near him crucified on a higher cross than himself, fell into a decline.[192]

While the envy of the crucified man may just be limited to his rival's "more impressive cross", as J.G. Cook has argued,[193] it is more likely that the *higher position* of the cross, symbolic of social superiority in a world of grandiose elite monuments, also consumes the victim.

A joke from the *Philogelos* ("The Laughter-Lover"), an ancient joke book dateable to after 391 AD, presents the continued competition of an athlete on the cross with this wry observation about his superior "athletic" status:

> On seeing a runner who had been crucified, an Abderite remarked, "By the Gods, now he does fly – literally!" [194]

H. Ridderbos, *Paul: An Outline of His Theology* (Grand Rapids: Eerdmans, 1975), 159–204; J.C. Beker, *Paul the Apostle: The Triumph of God in Life and Thought* (Edinburgh: T&T Clark, 1980), 182–212; R.P. Martin, *Reconciliation: A Study of Paul's Theology* (London: Marshall, Morgan and Scott, 1981); Cousar, *A Theology of the Cross*; M.A. Seifrid, *Justification by Faith: The Origin and Development of a Central Pauline Theme* (Leiden: Brill, 1992); C.-S. Han, *Raised for Our Justification: An Investigation on the Significance of the Resurrection of Christ within the Theological Structure of Paul's Message* (Kampen: Uitgeverij Kok, 1995), 33–68, 159–301; T.R. Schreiner, *Paul, Apostle of God's Glory in Christ: A Pauline Theology* (Downers Gove: IVP, 2002), 219–49; U. Schnelle, *Apostle Paul: His Life and Theology* (Grand Rapids: Baker Academic, 2005), 443–71; M. Wolter, *Paul: An Outline of His Theology*, tr. R.L. Brawley (Waco: Baylor University Press, 2015), 951–24.

[190] On the gallows-humour attached to crucifixion in antiquity, see Welborn, *Paul, the Fool of Christ*, 124–47.

[191] On the grandiose funeral monuments of the Roman elites and imperial rulers from the republic to the late Empire, see P.J.E. Davies, *Death and the Emperor: Roman Imperial Funerary Monuments from Augustus to Marcus Aurelius* (Austin: University of Texas Press, 2004), 1–48.

[192] Lucillius, *Anthologia Graeca* 11.192.

[193] J.G. Cook, *Crucifixion in the Mediterranean World*, WUNT I 327 (Tübingen: Mohr Siebeck, 2014), 10.

[194] B. Baldwin, *The Philogelos or Laughter-Lover* (Amsterdam: J.C. Gieben, 1982), § 121.

Further, Gaius Maecenas – the famous Roman literary patron, writer and friend of Augustus – prays to live longer no matter what suffering still remained ahead of him. Given the depiction of people with disabilities in ancient and modern entertainment contexts, noted above, it is worth observing that the ancients did not baulk at linking the experience of the crucified on the cross to people suffering with physical disabilities. Both groups belonged, in the view of the ancient elites, to the contemptible "no accounts" of society:

Fashion me with a palsied hand,
Weak of foot, and a cripple;
Build upon me a crook-backed hump;
Shake my teeth till they rattle;
All is well, if my life remains.
Save, oh, save it, I pray you,
Though I sit on the piercing cross.[195]

In other words, the cross was seen by Paul's contemporaries as so antithetical to the ancient celebrity circuit that they could devise jokes about the crucified competing for social status and ascendancy while pinioned to the cross and still get a humorous rise of recognition from their audience. The gospels, too, reveal variations on this grim cruciform humour when the two crucified rebels alongside Christ derisively heap insults upon him (Mark 15:27–32), rejecting this failed would-be Messiah and Prophet who could not save himself or fulfil any of his prophecies. Furthermore, the scene of the cross is prefaced by the mock-homage paid by the Roman soldiers to Christ as King of the Jews, spoofing a royal coronal investiture by offering him the purple robe and crown of thorns (Mark 15:16–19). The cross of Jesus, therefore, is inherently social in its ideological outworking, precisely because it was inextricably enmeshed with the power of the elites over the condemned in a first-century context, as much as it belonged to soteriological categories in the eternal plan of God. Paul spoke adeptly into *both* contexts, social and theological, displaying the paradoxical triumph of Christ in abject weakness and foolishness for all to see (1 Cor 1:18–31; 2:8).[196]

The argument of the book is structured around a series of case studies that touch on the ethos and values of the elites from the late republic to the early imperial period, generally focusing on what might be labelled "civic ethics" in a variety of contexts. In Chapter 2 the ethos and social values of late republican society at Rome, as articulated by Cicero, are set out. Paul's radical reconfiguration of the social relations and morality of Roman society is then explored,

[195] Seneca, *Ep.* 101.11. For full discussion, see Harrison, "Paul and the Social Relations of Death at Rome," 122–23.

[196] Wolter (*Paul*, 124) writes: "Therefore the theology of the cross – especially that of Paul – has in fact primarily a 'polemical' and 'critical' function. In this respect, it is anything but a coincidence that for Paul ... the theology of the cross comes up for discussion as theological *Sachkritik*. It asserts that God's action always goes hand in glove with a transvaluation of those values and norms that hold validity in the symbolic universes constructed by humans."

employing Romans 12–16 as the basis for discussion. In Chapter 3 the paradoxical leadership styles of Augustus and the apostle Paul are compared and contrasted, with a view to understanding why Paul's legacy of "leadership" triumphed over that of Augustus in the western intellectual tradition. In Chapter 4 the ancient athletic ideal is analysed from the visual evidence and brought into dialogue with Paul's athletic metaphors in his epistles. How was Paul's appropriation of the athletic ideal for the believer different to its sponsorship by the elites and the popular exaltation of the athletes by an enthusiastic public? In Chapter 5 the elite values and curriculum of the ancient gymnasium, along with the pastoral role of its main official, the gymnasiarch, are discussed in their civic context and compared to the teaching and example of Paul. Subsequently, in Chapter 6, the curriculum of the ancient gymnasium, the Dephic canon, is investigated for its ethical framework and is examined against the backdrop of the cruciform and pneumatic paradigms of moral transformation promoted by the apostle in his alternative communities of grace. With this background in place, we are then well placed to examine the exemplary and honorific culture of the eastern and western Mediterranean elites and the local associations in Chapters 7 and 8, with a view to appreciating how the Paul handled the formative pedagogy for civic life and social conventions of antiquity. Last, in Chapter 9 the charismatic community of the Body of Christ is compared to the local associations, which mimicked the values and institutional conventions of the urban elites. What similarities and differences emerge? A conclusion will draw out the implications of our argument for understanding the Pauline theology of the cross, especially in regard to its transformative role in subverting or reconfiguring the civic ethics of the Mediterranean elites in surprising ways. What difference did Paul's teaching ultimately make to the western intellectual tradition over against the traditions of the classical world?

The standard conventions of abbreviation are used throughout. Abbreviations for the inscriptions follow the epigraphic checklist of G. H. R. Horsley and J. A. L. Lee,[197] whereas abbreviations for the papyri are to be found in the web edition of the "Checklist of Editions of Greek, Latin, Demotic and Coptic Papyri, Ostraca and Tablets."[198] In the case of the classical, biblical, and Jewish authors, abbreviations conform to SBL conventions and *The Oxford Classical Dictionary*,[199] whereas abbreviations for periodicals, reference works, and serials follow SBL conventions and *L'Année Philologique*.

---

[197] G. H. R. Horsley and J. A. L. Lee, "A Preliminary Checklist of Abbreviations of Greek Epigraphic Volumes," *Epigraphica* 66 (1994): 129–70.

[198] J. F. Oates et al., eds., *Checklist of Editions of Greek, Latin, Demotic and Coptic Papyri, Ostraca and Tablets Web Edition* http://scriptorium.lib.duke.edu/papyrus/texts/clist.html.

[199] P. H. Alexander, et al., ed., *The SBL Handbook of Style for Ancient Near Eastern, Biblical, and Early Christian Studies*, 2nd ed. (Atlanta: SBL Press, 2014); S. Hornblower and A. Spawforth *The Oxford Classical Dictionary*, 3rd ed. (Oxford: Oxford University Press, 1996).

Chapter 2

Romans and the Reconfiguration of Roman Society: Paul and Cicero Compared

2.1. Cicero as Evidence for Roman Social Attitudes in the Imperial Age

A comparison of the social thought of Cicero (106–43 BC) with the apostle Paul has not as yet provoked the interest of New Testament scholars. Only recently has an article appeared devoted *exclusively* to a comparison of an aspect of Cicero's social thought (Roman civil litigation) with a pericope from 1 Corinthians (1 Cor 6:1–8).[1] Interest in Cicero's contribution to our understanding of Paul's epistles has concentrated on either his rhetorical technique or philosophy.[2] In terms of social ideology, I have touched on Cicero's understanding of the reciprocity *(gratia)* in relation to Paul's teaching about divine and human grace, as well as Cicero's commitment to and re-definition of the Roman quest for glory in relation to Romans.[3] Generally, however, Cicero's writings are subsumed under the evidence of the other philosophers or rhetoricians, with little attention given to historical context, and are not studied in their own right for the riches they might reveal. While many studies have been written comparing Paul to the writings of specific philosophers, Greek and Roman,[4] no one has considered the

---

[1] R. Edsall, "When Cicero and St Paul Agree: Intra-Group among Luperci and the Corinthian Believers," *JTS* 64.1 (2013): 25–36.

[2] On rhetoric, see A.D. Litfin, *St. Paul's Theology of Proclamation: 1 Corinthians 1–4 and Greco-Roman Rhetoric*, SNTSMS 79 (Cambridge and New York: Cambridge University, 1993), 91–100; J. Patrick, "Insights from Cicero on Paul's Reasoning in 1 Corinthians 12–14: Love Sandwich or Five Course Meal," *TynBul* 55.1 (2004): 43–64; R.N. Gaines, "Cicero, Philodemus, and the Development of Late Hellenistic Rhetorical Theory," in *Philodemus and the New Testament*, NovTSup 111, ed. J.T. Fitzgerald et al. (Leiden: Brill, 2004), 91–100. On philosophy, see M.V. Lee, *Paul, the Stoics, and the Body of Christ*, SNTSMS 137 (Cambridge: Cambridge University Press, 2006).

[3] J.R. Harrison, *Paul's Language of Grace in Its Graeco-Roman Context*, WUNT II 172 (Tübingen: Mohr Siebeck, 2003), 199–209; *idem*, *Paul and the Imperial Authorities at Thessalonica and Rome: A Study in the Conflict of Ideology*, WUNT I 273 (Tübingen: Mohr Siebeck, 2011), 212–19.

[4] Several prominent examples may be cited: N.W. De Witt, *St. Paul and Epicurus* (Minneapolis: University of Minnesota Press, 1954); J.N. Sevenster, *Paul and Seneca*, NovTSup 4 (Leiden: Brill, 1961); P.E. Oakes, "Epictetus (and the New Testament)," *VEv* 23 (1993): 39–56; C.E. Glad, *Paul and Philodemus: Adaptability in Epicurean and Early Christian Psychagogy*, NovTSup 81 (Leiden: Brill, 1995); J.R. Dodson and D.E. Briones, eds., *Paul and Seneca in Dialogue* (Leiden: Brill, 2017).

most important Roman republican orator and philosopher, Cicero, worthy of extended comparison with Paul. How do we explain this scholarly tunnel vision? The issue is complex, reflecting the fluctuating popularity of Cicero in classical and New Testament scholarship. Two brief observations will suffice.

First, the historically artificial division of Roman history into "Republic" and "Empire", with the Augustan principate eclipsing what went before, has relegated Cicero's writings to irrelevance. New Testament scholars have ransacked the Roman historians and biographers, poets and satirists, inscriptions, iconography and numismatics to uncover the imperial world in which Paul lived. Faced with this wealth of evidence, Cicero is regarded an anachronism or consigned to the arcane interest of antiquarian researchers.

But we never pause to ask whether there is greater continuity in Roman social attitudes from the time of Cicero to the early imperial period than is initially imagined. Do we observe in Cicero's orations social developments that would flower after his death, some of which he would have disapproved? Does Cicero represent the conservative voice of the republic that gradually declined as the Julian house outcompeted its noble rivals? Does Cicero provide us valuable insight into the later opposition to Julio-Claudian rule, only available to us now in a few snippets of anti-imperial propaganda?[5] Why did Romans continue to read the orations of Cicero in the imperial age, apart from the desire to improve their rhetoric?[6]

Second, classical scholarship dismissed for a long time the intellectual worth of Cicero's orations. Theodore Mommsen delivered the death knell for Cicero in this regard with one damning sentence: "The dreadful barrenness of thought in the Ciceronian orations must revolt every reader of feeling and judgment."[7] This scholarly disinterest in Cicero emerged in the eighteenth century after the heady days of his popularity in the Renaissance and Enlightenment. It coincided with wider criticism of Cicero as a Roman philosopher that has persisted until recently.[8]

[5] Harrison, *Paul and the Imperial Authorities*, 177–85.

[6] See T.J. Keeline, *A Rhetorical Figure: Cicero in the Early Empire* (PhD diss., Harvard University, 2014).

[7] T. Mommsen, *History of Rome* Vol. 5 (London: J.M. Dent, 1911), 506. The unfairness of Mommsen's judgement is compounded by the fact that we only have fragments of earlier Roman oratory: how can we make such a sweeping denunciation of Cicero when we cannot judge him against his predecessors? In an online review of I. Gildenhard's *Creative Eloquence* [n. 11 *infra*]: *Bryn Mawr Classical Review* 2011.08.07), J. Zetzel observes: "we are often simply not in a position to know just when Cicero is being 'original'." S.E. Smethurst ("Politics and Morality in Cicero," *Phoenix* 9.3 [1955]: 111–21, at 111) argues that the divided opinion over Cicero's reputation is attributable to the "complex personality of the man himself" and the difficulty that Cicero had in reconciling his idealism with party politics. More fully, see W.J. Nicorgski, "Cicero and the Rebirth of Political Philosophy," *The Political Science Reviewer* 8 (1978): 63–101.

[8] Note, however, the discussion of Cicero's *On Duties* and modern business ethics in G. Bragues, "Profiting with Honour: Cicero's Vision of Leadership," *Journal of Business Ethics* 97 (2010): 21–33. For an excellent coverage of the "rise" and "fall" of Cicero in scholarly

The substance of the critique is that Cicero was no more than an unoriginal epitomiser of Plato, Aristotle, Epicurus and the Stoics.[9]

However, there has been a strong resurgence of scholarship on Cicero, not only in terms of his intrinsic interest for the troubled history of his times, but also in terms of the philosophical worth of his orations and the importance of his social thought more generally. But, so far, the 1988 work of N. Wood still remains the only major English discussion of the social and political contours of Cicero's thought across his diverse works.[10] However, I. Gildenhard, in his 2011 book on the orations of Cicero, argues that the orator creatively and conceptually infuses his orations with his philosophy:

> (Cicero's) speeches document enact discursive constructions of realities at the level of the human being and the human condition, politics, society, and culture, and the sphere of the supernatural, which presuppose a significant degree of theoretical reflection.[11]

In other words, Cicero's orations function at an anthropological, sociological and theological level.[12] These categories are worth pursuing in our own investigation. However, apart from two examples (§§2.2.3, 2.2.5 *infra*), we will not pursue the impact of Stoic thought upon Cicero and its relation to Romans because of the extensive debate on the issue generated by the monograph of T. Engberg-Pederson.[13]

There remains another dimension to the orations of Cicero that makes them worth investigating, though with caution, for their social realities. Gildenhard has drawn attention to the idiosyncratic and polemical nature of Cicero's evaluation of Roman culture in the orations:

> Cicero's manner of appraising and defining Rome's human resources, his commentary on legal and political matters, and his premises about how the world works (or ought to work) are, in various ways, highly idiosyncratic and frequently at variance with routine views, approaches, and convictions in Roman public discourse.[14]

---

estimation over the centuries, see N. Wood, *Cicero's Social and Political Thought* (Berkeley and Los Angeles: University of California Press, 1988), 1–11.

[9] J.W. Mohr, "Cicero: Persons and Positions," in *Sociological Insights of Great Thinkers*, ed. C. Edling and J. Rydgren (Santa Barbara: Praeger, 2011), 123–32, at 123. For a strong defense of the substantial contribution that Cicero made philosophically in comparison to other social philosophers, see Wood, *Cicero's Social and Political Thought*, 11–12.

[10] Wood, *Cicero's Social and Political Thought*. See also G. Remer, "Political Oratory and Conversation: Cicero versus Deliberative Democracy," *Political Theory* (1999): 39–44. On Cicero as a philosopher, see J. G. F. Powell, ed. *Cicero the Philosopher* (Oxford: Clarendon Press, 1995); R. Stem, "Cicero as Orator and Philosopher: The Value of the *Pro Murena* for Ciceronian Political Thought," *The Review of Politics* 68 (2006): 206–31.

[11] I. Gildenhard, *Creative Eloquence: The Construction of Reality in Cicero's Speeches* (Oxford and New York: Oxford University Press, 2011), 2–3.

[12] Gildenhard, *Creative Eloquence*, 3.

[13] T. Engberg-Pedersen, *Paul and the Stoics* (Edinburgh: T&T Clark, 2000).

[14] Gildenhard, *Creative Eloquence*, 7.

Because of Cicero's rhetorical intent and his personal convictions, the orations highlight, if only by way of contrast on occasion, what was really important ideologically and socially for the Romans. Cicero speaks as a *novus homo*, the first of his family to achieve consular status, with everything to lose socially and politically if he, along with the *nobiles*, did not maintain the *mos mairoum* ("ancestral custom") of republican society.[15] In other words, the very same convictions of Roman public discourse, from which Cicero occasionally diverged, also exercised an invisible restraint upon his worldview.

Therefore, the 29 orations of Cicero, polished for publication after their delivery and spanning the period of his public life (89–44 BC), represent a rich repository of Roman values, expressed in the rhetoric of the law courts. The social values of Cicero's orations provide us sympathetic insight into how the original auditors of Paul's epistle to the Romans might have responded to aspects of the social implications of his gospel. While we have to be careful regarding the ideological continuity and discontinuity of Cicero's orations in an imperial context, the comparison may also help us to appreciate the extent to which the apostle challenged the impact of Roman values, traditional and emergent, in the lives of believers living in the capital of the empire. We will isolate several motifs that recur throughout the orations (§§2.2.1–2.2.7) and include another motif that, although incidental to the orations (§2.2.8), is the kerygmatic basis of the apostle's gospel (1 Cor 1:23). From there we will compare the motifs with the evidence of Romans, but will focus especially on Roman 12:1–16:25. It is perhaps in those final chapters of the epistle that we see most clearly Paul's reconfiguration of Roman society.

2.2. *The Social Ideology of Cicero*

2.2.1. *The gods and Roman Rule*

It is a curiosity for modern readers the scrupulous attention that Cicero devotes to the gods in his speeches, but it spotlights the intimate connection between the prosperity of the Roman Empire and divine blessing.[16] Jupiter was the "most ancient custodian" of Rome (*Cat.* 1.5.11), having established the city under his auspices, and continuously protecting both its inhabitants and empire (1.13.33; 2.13.29). The blessings of the gods upon Rome are routinely mentioned through-

[15] Gildenhard, *Creative Eloquence*, 51–54.

[16] For a proper study of Cicero and the gods, the following Ciceronian works should be consulted: *De divinatione*, *De haruspicum responso*, *De natura deorum*. As far as secondary literature, see J. O. Leneghan, *A Commentary on Cicero's Oration* De haruspicum responso (The Hague and Paris: Mouton, 1969); R. G. Short, *Religion in Cicero* (PhD diss., Harvard University, 2012); R. Woolf, *Cicero: The Philosophy of a Roman Sceptic* (London and New York: Routledge, 2015), 34–92.

out his oration against Cataline. In the past, the famous Cornelian family was promised, through the Sibylline books and soothsayers, "the rule and sway of this city" (2.4.9). In the present era, Cicero credits the enlarging of the statue of Jupiter, looking out upon the forum and senate-house, with the uncovering of Cataline's conspiracy against the State in 65 BC (3.8.18–3.9.22). Cicero, consequently, encourages the Roman citizens to show appropriate piety (2.13.29):

You ought, citizens, to pray to them, to beseech them and implore them since they have ordained this city to be most beautiful, most flourishing, most powerful, and since they have overwhelmed the hosts of all foreign foes by land and sea, to defend this city from the outrageous plot of nefarious traitors.

The dishonouring of the immortal gods, whether it is through ingratitude (*Leg.* 16.47) or the impiety of a Verres (*Verr.* 2.1.4 § 9), requires the restitution of divine honour at the highest level. Thus Cicero ends his oration against Verres, the corrupt governor of Sicily, with a remarkable prayer. Its address to the deities invokes fifteen Roman deities, as well as other non-identified gods, listing in each case the despoliation and plundering of their sanctuaries perpetrated by Verres (*Verr.* 2.5.72 §§ 184–188), before calling for his conviction by the court (2.5.72 §§ 188–189). Augustus would later show the same commitment to the honour of the Roman gods and the priestly colleges in the *Res Gestae* (7.3; 8.1; 1.1–2; 20.1, 3–4; 24.1–2).

2.2.2. *The Roman World of Honour and the Obligation of Gratitude*

The Romans, like the rest of the ancient world, believed in a hierarchical world of honour in which the reciprocation of gratitude was *de rigeur.*[17] Cicero spells out clearly the hierarchy of honour, with its graduation of indebtedness, in his oration delivered after his return from exile (*Post. red.* 1.2). Addressing the Conscript Fathers, he says:

So it comes about that, while our debt to you is considerable, to the Roman people great, and to our parents infinite, while to the immortal gods we owe everything, whereas hitherto we have been debtors to each of you in regard to what each has given us, to you it is that we owe it today that we find ourselves once more in possession of the whole.[18]

---

[17] On honour in the Roman world, see J.E. Lendon, *Empire of Honour: The Art of Government in the Roman World* (Oxford: Oxford University Press, 2002, rpt.); M.T. Finney, *Honour and Conflict in the Ancient World: I Corinthians in Its Greco-Roman Social Setting* (London and New York: Bloomsbury/T&T Clark, 2012), 34–46. In terms of Cicero, see Bragues, "Profiting with Honour."

[18] Cicero highlights the debt of gratitude (*Balb.* 1.1; 26.59; *Agr.* 2.36.100; *Planc.* 30.74: "fetters of obligation"; 33.81) and the difficulty of adequate requital of honour (*Post. red.* 9.24). Note, too, the inflated honorific language used of Caius Caesar (i.e. C. Octavianus, the future Augustus: *Phil.* 5.8.23: "by the favour of the Immortal gods, with a heaven-given greatness of spirit"; 14:9.25: "begotten by the favour of the Gods for the benefit of the State"). Of Gauis Marius, Cicero says: "whose divine and outstanding bravery was our stay after grievous dis-

Indeed, as was the case with Cicero, the demands of reciprocation to many benefactors could create uncertainty about the hierarchy of honour (*Planc.* 32.78). He admits being

perplexed, not because I have many creditors, for the obligation which a kindness imposes is but a light burden, but because the several claims upon me of my various benefactors are often mutually conflicting, and the result, I fear, is that it is impossible for me to seem grateful, at one and the same time, to all.

Cicero observes that whereas he could discharge the pecuniary obligations to his benefactors and settle all debts once and for all, a moral obligation is an entirely different affair. Cicero elaborates: "in a moral debt, when I pay I keep, and when I keep, I pay by the very act of keeping" (*Planc.* 28.68). The cryptic nature of what Cicero is saying is subsequently clarified. Even if Cicero discharged his debt to Plancius – the accused whom Cicero was defending (56 BC) – by winning the case for him, Cicero would "not thereby cease to be his debtor." Rather he would continue repaying his debt to Plancius by "his good wishes" (*Planc.* 28.68). The reason for this is clear. Because Plancius had looked after Cicero, as well as his brother and children, during the humiliation of Cicero's exile in 58 BC, Cicero could never look upon them, to borrow his words, "without recalling the obligation I am under to him" (*Planc.* 28.69). In sum, Cicero's idea of a lasting moral obligation arising out of favours experienced and which cannot ever be adequately reciprocated has interesting intersections with Paul's thought worth exploring.

2.2.3. Ancestral Virtue and Cicero's Redefinition of Glory

As a *novus homo*, Cicero was well aware that republican noble houses, which had achieved the curule offices, had the "right to have images in their family" (*Agr.* 2.1.1: 63 BC), either in the atrium of their house or in funeral processions. Cicero draws upon these ancestral traditions when he challenges Clodia – who had previously seduced Cicero's defendant, Caelius, and subsequently accused him of attempting to poison her in 63 BC – regarding her family honour. In a clever rhetorical tactic, Cicero pictures the famous deceased relative of Clodia, Appius Claudius the Blind, summoned up from the dead, accusing her, the manipulative seductress, in this manner:

When you had passed, by marriage, from a family of high nobility into a most illustrious house, why was Caelius so closely connected with you? Kinsman/Relative by marriage? Friend of your husband? None of these. What then was your reason, if it was not some reckless passion? If the images of the men of our family did not touch your heart, did not

---

asters and losses suffered by the Roman people" (*Prov. cons.* 13.32). Of Pompey, see *Leg. man.* 16.48.

even the famous Quinta Claudia, a daughter of my own race, rouse you to show yourself a rival of those virtuous women who have brought glory (*gloria*) upon our house?[19]

In a different tactic, Cicero, prosecuting Verres for his corrupt governorship of Sicily (70 BC), reminds the praetor hearing the case, Manilius Acilius Glabrio, of his prestigious family reputation so that he would judge justly. Thus Cicero charges Glabrio that he should show the "keen vigour" of his father, the "foresight" of his grandfather, the "steadfastness" of his father-in-law, not allowing the praetor "to forget the high honour (his) family has won" (*Verr.* 1.17.52).

As far as the military achievement of ancestral glory (*Mur.* 14.31–32), Cicero underwent a shift in perspective regarding its acquisition. The great man, Cicero admits, may have had "a heaven-born light within their souls," leading them on to attain glory and virtue without the aid of education (*Arch.* 7.15). However, as a man of letters, Cicero suggests education as an alternate pathway for the great man seeking glory, citing weighty ancestral precedent in support (*Arch.* 7.15–16):

Yet I do at the same time assert that when a lofty and brilliant character is applied the moulding influence of abstract studies, the result is often inscrutably and unapproachably noble. Such a character her forefathers were privileged to behold in the divine figure of Scipio Africanus; such were those patterns of continence and self-control, Gauis Laelius and Gaius Furius; such was the brave and venerable Marcus Cato, the most accomplished man of his day.

Consequently, there is a cultural imperialism in Roman ancestral virtue and glory. Cicero encapsulates the attitude succinctly with these words: "our ancestors have surpassed other nations, not only in arms, but also in wisdom and prudence" (*Rosc. Amer.* 25.69).[20]

As the republic lurched towards civil war, another shift occurred in Cicero's thought about ancestral glory. Cicero distinguished between "false glory" and "true glory." Self-serving careerists such as Caesar, Cicero claims, had violated the *mos maorum* in their ruthless pursuit for "false glory" by pandering to "popular humours" (*Phil.* 5.49), whereas others – Cicero, his senatorial supporters, and the young Octavian – sought "true glory" by deeds performed in service of the *res publica* (5.49–50).[21]

---

[19] Cicero, *Cael.* 14.34; cf. 17:39: "... nothing in life was worth striving for unless it was united with glory and honour ... Such I think were those famous Camilli, Fabricii, Curii, and all those who made Rome so great that was once so small." For another cavalcade of ancestral luminaries (including, Cicero's contemporary, Pompey), see *Balb.* 17.40 (56 BC). On Cicero on glory, see the Dutch work of A.D. Leeman, *Gloria: Cicero's waardering van de roem en haar achtergrond in de Hellenistische wijsbe geerte en de Romeinse samenleving* (with an extensive summary in English) (Diss. Leiden; Rotterdam: N.V. Drukkerij M. Wijt & Zonen, 1949).

[20] On the competitive nature of generals for military victories and senatorial jurists for office and honours in the late republic, see J. Harries, *Cicero and the Jurists: From Citizen's Law to Lawful State* (London: Duckworth, 2006).

[21] See Harrison, *Paul and the Imperial Authorities*, 217–19; Gildenhard, *Creative Elo-*

What elements of discontinuity and continuity exist in this case between Cicero's thought and the Julio-Claudian rulers? Although Augustus presented himself in the *Res Gestae* as scrupulously maintaining ancestral tradition at Rome during his principate, Cicero's fears for the survival of the traditional mores belonging to aristocratic Roman society were justified. Two examples from Neronian Rome will suffice. By that time the nobility was such a spent force that the descendants of the old noble families demeaned themselves by performing in Nero's games (Juvenal, *Sat.* 8). Second, Seneca, Nero's tutor, committed himself unflinchingly to Stoic ethics in an alternate quest for glory over against the autocracy of the Roman ruler and his sycophantic clients, a decision that cost Seneca his life. The richness of republican ancestral tradition, therefore, had inevitably declined in the face of the unparalleled triumph of the Julian house from 31 BC onwards. Ultimately, the opportunities that the Augustan principate spawned for the acquisition of glory, achieved by the upwardly mobile securing posts in the imperial *cursus honorum*, supplanted the old noble pathways of honour.

2.2.4. Imitatio

We will limit our investigation of the *imitatio* motif to Cicero's *Philippics*, a series of pungent attacks on Mark Antony delivered in 44–43 BC, and the oration on behalf of Rabirius (54 BC).[22] Cicero praises Decimus Brutus for promising to keep the province of Gaul in the jurisdiction of the Senate and Roman people. This desire to maintain liberty marked Brutus as "an imitator of his ancestors (*imitatoremque maiorum*)," referring to the famous consul who expelled the Roman tyrant Tarquin in 510 BC (*Phil.* 3.4.8).[23] Elsewhere Cicero heightens the moral force of the exemplum of Brutus with grandiloquent language: "That

quence, 159–67. In other works such as the *De Officiis*, Cicero emphasises that commitment to moral duties, summed up in "true glory" elsewhere, is established in youth, maintaining that in life ethical character is the only thing worth striving for. See T.J. Husband, *Cicero and the Moral Education of Youth* (PhD thesis, Georgetown University, 2013). The pursuit of "honour" and "glory" was also related conceptually to "greatness of soul" (*magnitudo animi*; μεγαλοψυχία), a subject of discussion of both Aristotle and Cicero. See H. Cullyer, *Greatness of Soul from Aristotle to Cicero: The Genealogy of a Virtue* (PhD thesis, Yale University, 1999).

[22] On *imitatio*, see W.P. de Boer, *The Imitation of Paul: An Exegetical Study* (Kampen: J.H. Kok, 1962) and Chapter 6 in this volume. On Ciceronian imitation, see D.P. Hanchey, *Cicero the Dialogician: The Construction of Community at the End of the Republic* (PhD diss., University of Texas, 2009), 18–68.

[23] Cicero, *Phil* 1.14.35: "look back on your ancestor, and so direct the State that your fellow-citizens may rejoice that you were born"; 13.14.29: "Publius Scipio, a man of great distinction and most resembling (*simillimum*) his ancestors." Note also Cicero, *Mur.* 31.66: "But still you who are descended from him can more easily imitate his character than any one of us, yet he is set up as an example for my imitation (*ad imitandum exemplar*) quite as much as for yours."

deed in itself is not only illustrious and godlike (*divinum*), but also set before us for our imitation (*ad imitandum*), all the more because they achieved such a glory (*gloriam*) as seems scarce to be bounded by heaven itself" (*Phil.* 2.44.114).

In his *apologia* against Antony, Cicero is not reluctant to set his own civic virtue forward as an exemplum (*Phil.* 14.6.17), though he is well aware that such public prominence may well elicit the envy of his enemies, having just recently exposed himself to potential massacre (14.6.15) and, ultimately, to assassination subsequently on December 7, 43 BC:

I have interpreted these remarks, Conscript fathers, not so much as an apology for myself ... as that I might advise, as I have always done, certain persons of too puny and narrow a spirit to regard the virtue of excellent citizens as worthy of imitation (*imitatione*), not of envy (*invidia*). Great is the field open in the State, as Crassus wisely used to say; many are they for whom the path to fame is open.

Cicero expects, as the Scipionic funeral *elogia* enunciate,[24] that each Scipionic descendent would uphold and surpass his ancestral fame on the battlefield and in magistracies. Equally, the descendants of the Decii would emulate the exemplary self-sacrifice of their noble forebears (*Rab. Post.* 1.2):

... the virtues of their fathers are perpetuated by the speech and recollection of the world; so did Scipio emulate the military renown (*in gloria rei militaris*) of Paulus; so also did his son emulate Maximus; so also Publius Decius was imitated (*imitatus est*) by his son in the sacrificing of his life and in the very manner of his death.[25]

There remains a strong commitment to *imitatio* similar to Cicero in the exemplary practice of the Julio-Claudian period. This is illustrated by (a) Augustus' adherence to ancestral practice, as well as his statue program in the *forum Augustum* (*RG* 8.5; 27.1; 31.5);[26] (b) the exhortation to the imitation of Augustus and Tiberius in a senatorial decree;[27] (c) the suggestion of Claudius as the supreme *exemplum* by the proconsul of Asia to his fellow governors in an inscription (*I. Eph.* Ia. 18a *ll.* 11–17); and, last, the appeal to Augustan precedent by the Julio-Claudian heirs.[28] What

24 For discussion, see Harrison, *Paul and the Imperial Authorities*, 219–25.

25 Cicero, *Rab. Post.* 1.2. Additionally, see *Scaur.* 3.2–3; *Mur.* 66.

26 See M. Spannagel, EXEMPLARIA PRINCIPIS: *Untersuchungen zu Entstehung und Ausstattung des Augustusforums* (Heidelberg: Verlag Archäologie und Geschichte, 1999); E.A. Judge, "The Eulogistic Inscriptions of the Augustan Forum: Augustus on Roman History," in *idem*, *The First Christians in the Roman World: Augustan and New Testament Essays*, WUNT I 229, ed. J.R. Harrison (Tübingen: Mohr Siebeck, 2008), 52–58; Harrison, *Paul and the Imperial Authorities*, 170–77.

27 See A.E. Cooley (*Res Gestae Divi Augusti: Text, Translation, and Commentary* [Cambridge: Cambridge University Press, 2009], 40), who cites a senatorial decree that exhorts the senate to model its behaviour on Augustus and Tiberius (W. Eck [et al., eds.], *Da Senatus Consultum de. Cn. Pisone Patre* [Munich: Beck, 1996], 44).

28 This is especially evident in the coinage of the Augustan successors. Coins of Tiberius: *RIC* 1^2 Tiberius §49 (reverse seated radiate Augustus, feet on a stool, holding laurel branch, before an altar, with the obverse legend DIVO AVGVSTO S P Q R ["For divine Augustus. The Senate and People of Rome"]); *RIC* 1^2 Tiberius §§70–83 (obverse radiate head of Augus-

changed over the course of time, however, was the concentration of exemplary virtue in the Roman ruler and his house.[29]

2.2.5. Misericordia, Clementia, *and* Humanitas

In considering the extension of forgiveness and its relationship to pity (*misericordia*) and kindness (*humanitas*), Cicero is well aware of the dictums of the Stoic Zeno about the ethics of the wise man in his social relations (*Mur.* 29.61–31.66). According to Zeno, the sage should be never swayed by generosity or favour, does not pardon human error, and is not moved by the unstable emotion of pity.[30] However, Cicero adjusts the boundaries of Stoic ethics in encouraging the prosecutor Cato the Younger, the great-grandson of the revered Stoic Cato the Elder, to mollify the punishment being proposed for Cicero's defendant, Lucius Murena. Cicero reminds Cato the Younger of his great-grandfather, whose reputation for kindness (*humanitas*) he must imitate (*Mur.* 31.66). Thus Cicero asks Cato the Younger to act more moderately, but strictly within the limits of *humanitas* as opposed to the excesses of *misericordia* (31.65):

> "You will forgive (*ignoveris*) nothing." Rather something – not all. "You will do nothing because of influence (*gratiae*)." Rather resist influence when duty and honour shall demand. Be not moved by pity (*misericordia*)". Yes, in tempering cruelty, but still kindness (*humanitatis*) deserves some praise (*laus*). "Abide by your opinion". Yet, unless some better opinion shall prevail over your opinion.

Conversely, while Cicero praises the *clementia* of Caesar in his orations,[31] Cicero is well aware of what is (in his view) the dark underside of its social operation. In his attack upon Mark Antony in the *Philippics*, Cicero sums up the deleterious impact that the *clementia* of the wealthy military leader can have upon the social psychology of a community (*Phil.* 2.45.116):

---

tus, with the obverse legend DIVVS AVGVSTVS PATER ["divine Augustus Father"]). Obverse issues: radiate Augustus before altar (*RIC* 1² Tiberius § 49); radiate Augustus in quadriga of elephants (*RIC* 1² Tiberius § 47). Coins of Gaius: *RIC* 1² Gaius §§ 15, 23 31 (reverse radiate head of Augustus, with legend DIVVS AVG PATER PATRIAE ["divine Augustus Father of the Fatherland"]). Coins of Claudius: *RIC* 1² Claudius § 101 (obverse head of Augustus between S – C; reverse of seated Livia, holding coin ears and torch, with legend DIVA AVGVSTA). Coins of Nero: *RIC* 1² Nero §§ 6–7 (reverse quadriga of elelphants, bearing two chairs, seated with Divus Claudius and Divus Augustus); *RIC* 1² Nero §§ 8–43 (obverse laureate head of Claudius).

[29] See Harrison, *Paul and the Imperial Authorities*, 138–41.

[30] See D. Konstan, *Before Forgiveness: The Origins of a Moral Idea* (Cambridge: Cambridge University Press, 2010).

[31] Cicero, *Deiot.* 8, 33, 37; *Lig.* 5, 10, 13, 14, 16; *Marc.* 9, 12; *Phil.* 116; *Vat.*, 21. On Cicero's attitude to Caesar in the orations, see Gildenhard, *Creative Eloquence*, 224–43. On *clementia*, see M.B. Dowling, *Clemency and Cruelty in the Roman World* (Ann Arbor: University of Michigan, 2006).

… by shows, buildings, largesses, banquets he had conciliated the ignorant crowd; his own followers he had bound to him by rewards, his adversaries by a show of clemency (*clementiae*): in brief, he had already brought to a free community – partly by fear, partly by endurance – a habit of servitude (*serviendi*).

Finally, since Cicero's view of *humanitas* in social relations is complex and wide-ranging and demands coverage beyond the scope of this chapter,[32] we will concentrate on its operation in the area of ethnic relations. Cicero's oration in defence of Lucius Flaccus (*Flac.* 11.24: 59 BC) is fascinating for the way that the orator contrasts the humanity of the Roman citizenry with the fickle savagery of the Greek witnesses for the prosecution at the trial:

If I were defending a man of low birth, of no personal distinction, with no reputation to commend him, but still a citizen, I would entreat of you as citizens, according to the law of common humanity and pity (*communis humanitatis iure et misericordia*), not to surrender your fellow citizen and suppliant to unknown and frenzied witnesses, the companions, guests, and intimate friends of the prosecutor, to men Greek in their fickleness and savages in their cruelty, lest you set up a dangerous precedent for others to imitate in the future.

In writings other than the orations of Cicero, the same picture emerges. In terms of the oversight of provincial governor over the nations (*Quinct.* 1[I.1]27–28), Cicero says that there is strong line of demarcation to be maintained between the civilised (the Greeks) and the uncivilized (the barbarians). In this regard, Cicero believed that contemporary Greeks were vastly inferior to their illustrious ancestors (1[I.1]16).[33] But, significantly, Romulus and Romans were destined to bring the universal process of *humanitas* to its glorious culmination by ruling over the barbarians through their customs (*Res.* 1.58). Here Cicero's attitude of Roman ethnic superiority, arising from *humanitas*, is consistent with the later Julio-Claudian triumphalism over the conquered and humiliated barbarian peoples, illustrated graphically by the iconography of many Augustan triumphal arches and the Sebasteion of Aphrodisias.[34]

2.2.6. *Ethnicity*

We have already noted Cicero's attitude to the barbarians above (cf. *Prov. cons.* 13:33; *pace*, *Planc.* 29.71), so we will not revisit familiar terrain. In regards to the Jews and Syrians, Cicero dismisses them as "peoples born to be slaves" (*Prov.*

[32] On *humanitas* in Cicero, see R. Bauman, *Human Rights in Ancient Rome* (London: Routledge, 2000), 36–50; Gildenhard, *Creative Eloquence*, 201–16.

[33] Cicero has a strong "barbarian" stereotype: "men unknown to us or known only as wild, savage and warlike – tribes which no one who ever lived would not wish to see crushed and subdued" (*Prov. cons.* 13.33).

[34] See D.C. Lopez, *Apostle to the Conquered: Reimagining Paul's Mission* (Minneapolis: Fortress Press, 2008), 26–55.

cons. 5.10). The practice of Diaspora Jews sending money to Jerusalem for maintenance of the Temple is also dismissed as a "barbaric superstition" (*Flac.* 28.67: cf. "a state ... given to superstition and calumny" [*ibid.*, 68]). As far as the Greeks, Cicero is more equivocal in his judgement. He lauds the civilized Greeks of classical times, but is highly critical of the current generation. In the 62 BC trial in defence of Lucius Valerius Flaccus, the governor of Asia, Cicero appropriates popular ethnic stereotypes to blacken the Greek witnesses against his client. Cicero asserts that the witnesses for the prosecution were "Greeks in their fickleness and savages in their cruelty" (*Flac.* 11.24; cf. 7.17; 8.19; 24.57, 71; *Red. Sen.* 5.14: "miserable Greeks"). Moreover, Cicero cites a series of demeaning ethnic "put-downs" that were abroad in popular culture (e.g. "A Phrygian is usually improved by whipping") to humiliate further the Asian Greek witnesses present at the trial for Flaccus (*Flac.* 27.64–66).[35] Cicero's distaste for contemporary Greeks over against the Greek worthies of old is seen in his other writings, where, for example, he derogatively dismisses Paconius as "not even a Greek, but a Mysian, or rather a Phrygian" (*Quint.* 1 [I.1]19).

In his speech delivered before the Senate after his return from exile (57 BC), Cicero attacked Lucius Calpurnius Piso Caesoninus, the consul of 58 BC who had been involved with Clodius in exiling Cicero. Cicero mockingly discredits him by calling him by the Gallic name of his maternal grandfather ("Caesoninus Calventius": *Red. sen.* 6.13; cf. *Prov. Cons.* 13; *Pis.* 14) and then, in a comic vignette, stigmatises him by using Cappodocian ethnic stereotypes (*Red. sen.* 6.13–14):

Had you chanced to see in passing that unkempt, boorish, sullen figure, you might have judged him to be uncouth and churlish, but scarcely a libertine or a renegade. To hold converse with such a man as this, or with a post in the forum, would be all one in your eyes; you would call him stockish, insipid, tongue-tied, a dull and brutish clod, a Cappadocian plucked from some slave-dealer's stock in trade.

Looking ahead to Julio-Claudian times, the same Roman ethnic superiority, which Paul struggled against in writing Romans, was deeply rooted in the antisemitism of the Roman mid-50's intelligentsia, the cultural elitism of the Romans over Greek and barbarian, and the iconographic humiliation of barbarian captives.[36]

---

[35] Somewhat inconsistently, Cicero airs annoyance when similar put-downs are wielded by Antony against his personal friends. Caius Caesar, whose mother was from the borough of Aricia in central Italy, is dismissed as a mere "provincial": "'His mother was from Aricia' – you might think that he was speaking of a woman from Tralles or Ephesus!" (*Phil.* 3.6.15). Here Cicero, in response to the slur against Caius, vaunts the *ethnic* superiority of Italy over the Greek Asian cities.

[36] On the anti-Semitism of the Roman intelligentsia, see J. G. Gager, *The Origins of Anti-Semitism: Attitudes Toward Judaism in Pagan and Christian Antiquity* (New York and Oxford: Oxford University Press, 1985); W. Wiefel, "The Jewish Community in Ancient Rome and the Origins of Roman Christianity," in *The Romans Debate: Revised and Expanded Edi-*

2.2.7. Enmity

The lifetime of Cicero spanned a period of protracted internal division and personal acrimony at Rome. Political alliances were made and unmade as political careerists sought unprecedented powers, magistracies and glory at the expense of the senatorial elites and the *mos mairorum*. Consequently, the outbreak of enmity and the loss of honour produced a volatile and fractious society that was unwilling to reconcile or to be reconciled, insisting upon its own rights and civic esteem, while cultivating the favour of powerful and ignoring the socially marginalized and dishonoured.[37] Cicero's comments on the outbreak of personal enmity provide us an insider's view of this process. Although the advent of the Augustan principate brought its much-heralded peace to Rome, its inauguration had come through the bloodbath of the civil war, and the highly competitive and status-conscious society that emerged meant that personal affronts were much feared and contested. One example of Cicero' venomous hatred from the orations will be cited, although others could be appealed to.[38]

In his oration cross-examining Publius Vatinius during the trail of P. Sestius in 57 BC – published independently of his proceedings in defence of Sestius – Cicero attacks a despised enemy who had been complicit in exiling Cicero in 58 BC. Indeed, the entire speech, apart from *Vat.* 1–3 and 40–41, impugns the character of Vatinius. But even at the outset, Cicero sets on public record the difficulty he has in setting aside his hatred of his political enemy:

> For because of my hatred for you – which ought to have been greater than that of all the others, owing to your crime against me, but almost seems to be less – I was so carried away that, although I despised you no less than I hated you, yet I preferred to let you go in confusion rather than in contempt. Accordingly, in case you should perhaps be surprised that I do you the honour in questioning you, when no one deems you worthy of his converse or his acquaintance, no one deems you worthy of a vote, of citizenship, or even of the light of day, I declare that nothing would have induced me to do so, except my desire to curb your violence, to crush your effrontery, and to put a check on your loquacity, by embarrassing you with a few questions.

The intensity of the invective arising from the personal hatred that Cicero bears towards Vatinus is seen in *Vat.* 3.8–9. There he pompously contrasts the honour

---

tion, ed. K.P. Donfried, 2nd ed. (Peabody: Hendrickson, 1991), 85–101; J.C. Walters. *Ethnic Issues in Paul's Letter to the Romans: Changing Self-Definitions in Earliest Roman Christianity* (Valley Forge: Trinity Press International, 1993), 19–68; D. Schäfer, *Judeophobia: Attitudes towards the Jews in the Ancient World* (London and Cambridge, Mass.: Harvard University Press, 1997). On Roman attitudes to barbarians in the monumental iconography, documentary and numismatic evidence and the ancient literature, see J.R. Harrison, "'More Than Conquerors' (Rom 8:37): Paul's Gospel and the Augustan Triumphal Arches of the Greek East and Latin West," *Buried History* 47 (2011): 3–21; *idem*, "Paul's 'Indebtedness' to the Barbarian (Rom 1:14) in Latin West Perspective," *NovT* 55.4 (2013): 311–48.

[37] On dishonour, see Cicero, *Planc.* 31.88; *Sull.* 31.88–89.

[38] Cicero, *Prov. Cons.* 10.24; 18.43; *Phil.* 12.8.19; 12.12.30; *Cat.* 1.9.23; *Mil.* 13.33.

of his return from exile with the shame of Vatinus, the universally loathed and hated pariah:

... what more honourable could have happened to me, what more desirable for an immortality of glory and everlasting perpetuation of my name, than all my fellow-citizens should think that the welfare of the State was bound up with the welfare of my single self? I give you tit for tat. For as you said that I was dear to the Senate and the Roman People, not so much for my own sake as for the sake of the State, so in return I say that you, foulest of men though you are, in all your horror and monstrosity, are yet an object of hatred to the State, not so much on your own account as on that of the State.

Finally, the serious implications of political enmity were graphically spotlighted in the circumstances of Cicero's death and the subsequent dishonouring of his body. Cicero's end came with reprehensible savagery when he was caught fleeing from his house in Naples for the East in 43 BC. His severed hands were publicly displayed in vengeance for his bitter denunciations of Antony in the *Philippics,* and, after decapitation, his head was derisively nailed to the Speakers' Rostrum in the Roman Forum. But the latter did not occur until Antony's wife, Fulvia, had first taken Cicero's head on her knees, cursed and spat on it, opened the mouth and pulled out the tongue, piecing it with her hair pin and making brutal jests about the orator (Dio Cassius 47.8.4). Cicero's most potent weapon – the oratory emanating from his tongue – had been finally pinioned by a woman in post-mortem revenge.[39]

2.2.8. Cicero and the Cross

In a brief but significant aside, Cicero makes several revealing comments regarding the punishment of crucifixion.[40] In the Verrine orations (*Verr.* 2. 65. 169: 70 BC) Cicero sets out the depths of the public humiliation of a Messanian victim, possibly a Roman citizen, who was crucified by the order of Verres, the corrupt Roman governor of Sicily (74–70 BC). The ironic interplay of the language of "slavery" and "freedom" is instructive for Paul's language of crucifixion in Romans:

You were the enemy, I say again, not of that individual man, but of the common liberties of us all. What else was the meaning of your order to the Messanians, who had followed their regular custom by setting up the cross on the Pompeian Road behind the town, to set it up in the part of the town that looks over the Straits? And why did you add words ... that you purposely chose this spot to give this man, since he claimed to be a Roman citizen, a view of Italy and a prospect of his home country as he hung on the cross? This place with its view of Italy was deliberately picked out by Verres, that his victim, as he

[39] For the Roman criteria for deciding who is an "enemy," see Dionysius of Harlicarnassus, *Roman Antiquities* 13.1–2.

[40] For full discussion of crucifixion in the Ciceronian corpus, see J. G. Cook, *Crucifixion in the Mediterranean World*, WUNT I 327 (Tübingen: Mohr Siebeck, 2014), 62–78.

died in pain and agony, might feel how yonder narrow channel marked the frontier between slavery and the land of freedom, and that Italy might see her son, as he hung there, suffer the worst extreme of the tortures inflicted upon slaves.

In similar manner, at the trial of Rabirius for the murder of a tribune (63 BC), Cicero had to head off the prosecutor's proposed punishment of the defendant by crucifixion through the revival of the ancient charge of *perduellio*. Cicero reminds the court that this punishment violated Roman liberty and clemency, belonging, as it did, to the reign of Roman tyrant Tarquin, whose infamous motto was: "'Veil his head, hang him to the tree of shame (*arbori infelici*)'" (*Rab. Post.* 4.13; *id.*, 5.16: "the dread of the cross").[41]

2.2.9. Summing Up

Although the intersection of Julio-Claudian values with the epistle to the Romans has been studied,[42] the continuing contribution of the iconic Cicero to Roman social conservatism and tradition in the imperial period has been underestimated. We have seen in our study of several important Ciceronian motifs in the orations that, while there are areas of ideological discontinuity between Cicero and the early imperial age, nevertheless substantial continuities of social practice remain. Furthermore, many of the discontinuities represent more the concentration of social practice and values in the Julio-Claudian house rather than their eclipse as values, though Cicero would have seen in the Julio-Claudian principate the fatal outcome of the self-serving quest for "false" glory in the late republic. It is intriguing, therefore, that Paul, in unfolding the ethical and social consequences of transformation in Christ (Rom 12:1–2), prefaces his exposition with his alternate to the republican and imperial political "bodies politic" in the "body of Christ" metaphor (12:3–7). Paul concludes his epistle with a rich portrait of the social cohesion of the house churches at Rome, Corinth, and Cenchrea, spanning geographically the Greek East and Latin West with the projected mission to Spain in view (16:1–16, 21–23; cf. 15:19, 24–28). In his contemporary Roman context, Paul presents the "body of Christ" not only as an

[41] M. Hengel, *Crucifixion in the Ancient World and the Folly of the Message of the Cross* (Philadelphia: Fortess, 1977); H.-R. Weber, *The Cross: Tradition and Interpretation* (London: SPCK, 1979; Gmn. orig. 1975); L. L. Welborn, *Paul, the Fool of Christ: A Study of 1 Corinthians 1–4 in the Comic-Philosophic Tradition* (2005: T&T Clark, 2005), 131–47; W. Shi, *Paul's Message of the Cross as Body Language*, WUNT II 254 (Tübingen: Mohr Siebeck, 2008), 20–52; W. G. Samuelson, *Crucifixion in Antiquity: An Enquiry into the Background and Significance of the New Testament* Terminology, WUNT II 310, 2nd ed. (Tübingen: Mohr Siebeck, 2013), 37–208; L. W. Hurtado, "The Staurogram: Earliest Depiction of Jesus' Crucifixion," *BAR* 39.2 (2013): 49–52, 63; B. Witherington III, "Images of Crucifixion: Fresh Evidence," *BAR* 39.2 (2013): 28, 66; Cook, *Crucifixion in the Mediterranean World.*

[42] R. Jewett, *Romans: A Commentary*, Hermeneia (Minneapolis: Fortress, 2007); N. Elliott, *The Arrogance of Nations: Reading Romans in the Shadow of Empire* (Minneapolis: Fortress, 2008); Harrison, *Paul and the Imperial Authorities.*

alternative to Cicero's selfless service of the "body of the republic" (*Off.* 1.25.85; cf. 3.5.22), but also to Seneca's version of the "body of state" being Nero himself (*Clem.* 1.4.1–1.5.2).[43] How, then, would Paul's reconfiguration of Roman values have interacted with Cicero and his ideological legacy?

2.3. Paul and the Reconfiguration of Roman Society in Romans 12–16

In coming to grips with the spectrum of motifs common to Cicero and Paul, we will concentrate on their appearance in Romans 12:1–16:1 where possible. In those chapters Paul explains how the new identity in Christ unites the Roman believers as they minister to people, influential and non-influential, inside and outside of the house churches and tenement churches.[44] But, in a remarkable rhetorical strategy, Paul reconfigures social relationships within the Body of Christ in such an unexpected and transformative way that the old Roman assumptions about ethnic, ancestral and cultural superiority, providentially ordered by the gods, start to fall apart at the centre. Moreover, he addresses the social legacy of the competition for personal glory among the leading men from the late republic to the early imperial age: namely, issues of personal enmity, triumphal attitudes towards social inferiors, and outbreaks of factionalism.

---

[43] On the latter, see Harrison, *Paul and the Imperial Authorities*, 294–97. More generally, E.A. Judge, "Demythologising the Church: What is the Meaning of the 'Body of Christ'?" in *idem*, The *First Christians in the Roman World: Augustan and New Testament Essays*, WUNT I 229, ed. J.R. Harrison (Tübingen: Mohr Siebeck, 2008), 586–96; T.P. Wiseman, "Cicero and the Body Politic," *Politica Antica* 1 (2012): 133–40. J. Connolly (*The State of Speech: Rhetorical and Political Thought in Ancient Rome* [Princeton: Princeton: Princeton University Press, 2007], 118) interprets the Ciceronian "body" metaphor as "the embodied proof of republican virtue", whereas Judge (*The First Christians*, 589) sees it as referring to the "collective leadership by the great men of the state."

[44] For the existence of tenement churches at Rome, see the arguments of R. Jewett, *Romans*, 53–55, 64–70; D.L. Balch, "Rich Pompeiian Houses, Shops for Rent, and the Huge Apartment Building in Herculaneum as Typical Spaces for Pauline House Churches," *JSNT* 27.1 (2004): 27–46; J.R. Harrison, "The First Urban Churches: Introduction," in *The First Urban Churches. Volume 1: Methodological Foundations*, ed. J.R. Harrison and L.L. Welborn (Atlanta: SBL Press, 2015), 1–40, at 33–35. On the tenement churches at Thessalonica, see R. Jewett, "Tenement Churches and Communal Meals in the Early Church: The Implications Form-Critical Analysis of 2 Thessalonians 3:10," *Biblical Research* 38 (1993): 23–43. Contra, R.S. Ascough, "Of Memories and Meals: Greco-Roman Associations and the Early Jesus-Group at Thessalonikê," in *From Roman to Early Christian Thessalonikê: Studies in Religion and Archaeology*, Harvard Theological Studies 64, ed. L. Nasrallah, C. Bakirtzis, and S.J. Friesen (Cambridge, MA: Harvard University Press, 2010), 49–72, at 63–67. On the variety of places where the early Christians met and worshipped, see E. Adams, *The Earliest Christian Meeting Places: Almost Exclusively Houses?* LNTS 450 (London and New York: Bloomsbury T&T Clark, 2013). See also R.W. Gehring, *House Church and Mission: The Importance of Household Structures in Early Christianity* (Peabody: Hendrickson, 2004).

Irrespective of one's place in the social order, Romans simply assumed that this was how life was conducted at Rome. Roman Gentile converts in the capital had lived and breathed this culture, without ever considering the possibility of an alternative lifestyle, other than perhaps a Stoic retreat into imperturbability.[45] Paul hoped that the Body of Christ (Rom 12:3–8) would provide a powerful counterpoint to the republican "body politic" and the Senecan "body of state" incarnated in Nero. Therefore, throughout Romans 13:1–16:27, Paul appeals to the example and teaching of the historical Jesus,[46] the apocalyptic hope (Rom 13:11–14; 14:10–12),[47] and his theology of obligation (1:14a; 4:4; 13:8; 15:1, 27).[48] As a result, believers are encouraged to live out "the obedience of faith" (Rom 1:5; 10:16; 15:18; 16:19), exhibited in love without pretence (Rom 12:9–21),[49] and in service of the brethren "in Christ" (16:3, 7, 9, 10)/"in the Lord" (16:2, 8, 11, 12 [2x], 13, 22).[50] Moreover, in learning to overcome their internal divisions (Rom 15:7–13) through the example of Christ (15:1–6), the Roman believers would ensure that they would be financial partners with Paul in mission to Spain and the Latin West (Rom 15:24).[51] In so doing, Roman believers would conform to Paul's apostolic understanding of the identity of the new covenantal missionary community.

First, in terms of the nexus between the piety towards the traditional gods and the blessing of the Roman empire, Paul responds with a traditional Jewish denunciation of Roman *religio* as idolatrous, though with a clever inversion culled from benefaction rhetoric In seeking "honour" and "favour" for the Roman nation by means of a scrupulous cultic *pietas*, one was in reality dishonoring the Creator by worshipping his creation and therefore demonstrating rank ingratitude towards God (Rom 1:19–23). Rather than divine blessing, the empire was presently experiencing divine wrath, evidenced in the moral and social

---

[45] See the G. Reydams-Schils, *Roman Stoics: Self, Responsibility and Affection* (Chicago and London: University of Chicago Press, 2005); R.M. Thorsteinsson, *Roman Christianity and Roman Stoicism: A Comparative Study of Ancient Morality* (Oxford: Oxford University Press, 2010).

[46] M. Thompson, *Clothed with Christ: The Example and Teaching of Jesus in Romans 12:1–15:13*, JSNTSup 59 (Sheffield: Sheffield Academic, 1991).

[47] M. Reasoner, "The Theology of Romans 12:1–15:13," in *Pauline Theology Volume III: Romans*, ed. D.M. Hay and R.E. Johnson (Minneapolis, 1995), 287–99. On Jewish apocalyptic in Romans, see L.E. Keck, *Romans* (Nashville: Abingdon, 2005), *passim*.

[48] On Paul's theology of obligation in Romans, see Harrison, "Paul's 'Indebtedness' to the Barbarian."

[49] W.T. Wilson, *Love Without Pretense: Romans 12:9–21 and Hellenistic-Jewish Wisdom Literature*, WUNT II 46 (Tübingen: Mohr Siebeck, 1991).

[50] A.B. Du Toit, "Shaping a Christian Lifestyle in the Roman Capital," in *idem*, *Focusing on Paul: Persuasion and Theological Design in Romans and Galatians*, BZNW 151, ed. C. Breytenbach and D.S. Du Toit (Berlin and New York: De Gruyter, 2007), 371–403.

[51] C.N. Toney, *Paul's Inclusive Ethic: Resolving Community Conflicts and Promoting Mission in Romans 14–15*, WUNT II 252 (Tübingen: Mohr Siebeck, 2008), 91–125. On Paul's mission to Spain and its relation to the occasion of Romans, see Jewett, *Romans*, 74–91.

turpitude of its inhabitants (1:18–31). Rather than trusting in the antiquity of the sacred Sybilline oracles, the Romans should consult the unveiling of the mystery in the Jewish prophetic writings, hidden for long ages past, but now made known by the eternal God in Christ (1:1–5; 16:25–27; cf. 4:1–25; 5:12–21; 9:1–11:36).

Second, the apostle endorses the Roman quest for honour (Rom 2:7) and, concomitantly, the obligation of gratitude, but it is radically reconfigured in the process within the Body of Christ, and subjected to eschatological judgement (2:9–11).[52] In terms of society at large, the imperial authorities are appointed by God and are to be obeyed (Rom 13:1b–2a, 5). They should be rendered full compliance (Rom 13:6–7), with the wealthy believer,[53] as occasion arose and, if financially able, to make some type of civic contribution to the life of the capital, thereby winning the ruler's praise through civic beneficence (13:3–4). However, the likelihood that early Christians, given their low socio-economic status, could compete with elite Roman benefactors in the city would be highly doubtful. Paul, of course, could just be speaking hypothetically with the future in mind, should God bring such a financially well-placed benefactor-believer into their midst later on. More likely, Paul is reconfiguring benefaction culture among the Roman churches in the capital, given their limited resources, so that those who are more moderately well off among believers (e.g. Aquila and Priscilla) would look after (as they were able) those facing privation within the Body of Christ, while taking opportunities to minister to needy outsiders on the fringes of their communities (e,g. Acts 9:39b; Rom 12:13). In this way the early Christians would win the praise of the Roman ruler by breaking down the prominent stereotype of the Christian movement as "haters of mankind", acquired by virtue of the perceived social isolationism of the early believers (Tacitus, *Ann.* 14.44; *Hist.* 5.5; Minucius Felix, *Octavius* 9.5–6). Last, we would do well to remember the modest contributions made by some members of local associations to various civic projects in their cities.[54] With the boons made to

[52] On Paul and the Roman ruler at Rome, see Harrison, *Paul and the Imperial Authorities*, 271–323. On honour in the Roman Empire, see J.E. Lendon, *Empire of Honour: The Art of Government in the Roman World* (Oxford: Clarendon Press, 1997). On Paul and honour in 1 Corinthians, see M.T. Finney, *Honour and Conflict in the Ancient World: 1 Corinthians in Its Greco-Roman Social Setting* (London and New York: Bloomsbury T&T Clark, 2112). On honour in Graeco-Roman culture more generally, see Chapter 8, *infra*.

[53] The Greek singular ("do what is good": τὸ ἀγαθὸν ποίει) indicates that the ministry of a wealthy believing benefactor is envisaged in Romans 13:4. See B.W. Winter, *Seek the Welfare of the City: Christians as Benefactors and Citizens* (Carlisle/Grand Rapids: Paternoster/Eerdmans, 1994), 25–40. However, see J.R. Harrison ("Sponsors of *Paideia*: Ephesian Benefactors, Civic Virtue and the New Testament," *Early Christianity* 7 [2016]: 346–67, at 362–64) for caveats to Winter's arguments.

[54] For a potent example of the range of monetary contributions (as well as building materials), ranging from the modest (5 denarii) to the more substantial (50 denarii), that was offered for the construction of the toll office in Ephesus by the association of fishermen and fish

the coffers of the church through occasional donations, acquired by "one off" sales of personal possessions at Rome (e.g. elsewhere: Acts 2:45; 4:37; 5:1–2), one could conceive how Roman believers, adding to this base of capital the very modest contributions from the more economically challenged believers, might fund specific projects with a more "civic ministry" focus in the same way as the local associations financed their own special projects in some cities.

Further, the ruler is to be accorded honour, along with others deserving honour (Rom 13:7b). However, in line with the LXX, the ruler is demoted to "servant" status (13:4, 6), stripping him of the honorific plaudits of the imperial propaganda and the stratospheric praise of Jewish clients like Philo (*Legat.* 8, 143–158).[55] Moreover, the apostle reconfigures the operation of the reciprocity system, upon which the return of honour and gratitude depends, with its consequent obligation. Once the return of honour has been made and the obligation of gratitude evinced (13:8a), believers still owe everyone the debt of love (13:8b–10), understood in light of the social obligation to the marginalised enunciated in Leviticus 19:18, 34 (cf. vv. 9–18, 32–36), and summed up in the teaching and example of Christ (Matt 22:36–40). Last, in terms of honorific rituals within the Body of Christ, the priority is the honoring of others ahead of oneself (12:9b), soberly evaluating rather than over-estimating one's gifts (12:3), and associating with the lowly rather than the powerful elites (12:16).

Third, in terms of the glory emanating from Roman ancestral virtue, Paul's understanding of the quest for glory is entirely God-centered (Rom 2:7, 9–11; 9:4, 23), focused in and mediated through the soteriological work of Christ (6:4; 16:27), and fully revealed by God at the eschaton (8:18, 21, 30; 9:23). Consequently, Paul glories in his service in Christ (Rom 15:17), while the Gentiles, in response, glory in the Father (15:6, 9). In other words, the apostle has pinpricked the anthropocentric nature of Roman glory (3:23) and its performance-based boasting in ancestral culture (Rom 3:27; 4:1–5). Critically, in this regard, it is because Christ has confirmed the patriarchal promises by becoming a servant of the Jews (Rom 15:8),[56] that the Roman gentiles, in company with the other nations (15:9b–12), are able to glory God for his mercy (15:9a). Thus Roman ethnocentrism has also been overturned in this dismantling of Roman ancestral glory.

---

dealers, see R.S. Ascough, ed. et al., *Associations in the Greco-Roman World: A Sourcebook* (Waco: Baylor Press/De Gruyter, 2012), § 162.

[55] Regarding Philo's exaltation of Augustus as a virtuous benefactor, M. Hadas-Lebel (*Jerusalem against Rome* [Leuven/Dudley: Peeters, 2006], 57) writes: "Philo's praise of Augustus, benefactor of humanity, was only equaled in the *Carmen Saeculare* or the *Odes* of Horace. Philo credits him with superhuman virtues (*Legatio* 143), short of refusing to consider the Emperor divine, there was little to distinguish his admiration from that of any Roman."

[56] N.T. Wright ("Romans," in *New Interpreters Bible Volume X*, ed. L.E. Keck [Nashville: Abingdon, 2002], 747) sums up the ethical implication of Romans 15:7 thus: "The Messiah became a servant of the circumcision – so you Gentile Christians should love and serve your Jewish brothers and sisters in the Messiah."

Fourth, as far as the Roman ethos of *imitatio*, Paul does not employ the language of "imitation" in Romans, as he does elsewhere in his other epistles.[57] This, however, does not mean that the concept is absent from Romans. We are conformed to the image of Christ (Rom 8:28) and we are able to accept the "other" because of the *exemplum* of Christ accepting us as the "other" (15:7). But, in the departing greetings to the Roman believers in 16:3–16, we see how Paul's alternative to Roman boasting culture – namely, the corporate culture of greeting and honoring Roman brothers and sisters in Christ (16:16) – enables the apostle to establish exempla for people to ponder and imitate. The roll call of Christian "virtue" at Rome is impressive. Prisca and Aquila had acted as endangered benefactors upon Paul's behalf (Rom 16:4a), engendering the gratitude of all the Gentile churches (16:4b); Epenetus, Paul's first Asian convert, continued to be a loyal friend to the apostle (16:5b); Mary, Tryphena, Tryphosa, and Persis had all worked hard in the Lord for the Roman house churches (16:6, 12, 12b); Andronicus and Junias had counted the cost of Christian discipleship by being imprisoned with Paul (16:7); Apelles was tested and approved in Christ (16:10); the mother of Rufus had been a "mother" to Paul as well (16:13). Here we see how, in being conformed to the image of Christ, the Roman believers become not only exempla to themselves but also to other believers more widely.

Fifth, Paul engages the key Roman concepts – *humanitas* ("nature", "civilization", "kindness"), *clementia* ("mercy"), and *misericordia* ("pity") – in ways that Romans would have found challenging.[58] Fist, Paul would have had little sympathy for the Ciceronian superiority of Roman civilization, given his searing portrayal of the fallenness of mankind (Rom 1:18–32; 3:10–18; 5:12–21). Second, Paul avoids totally the Greek equivalent (ἐπιείκεια: "fairness", "clemency") for the Roman Latin word *clementia*, preferring instead the LXX ἔλεος ("mercy", "pity"). The latter word, of course, would have opened up for Romans the Stoic concern about the instability of "pity" as an emotion (*misercordia*; ἔλεος). But Paul is adamant about the issue. God does not deal with us on the basis of "fairness" (ἐπιείκεια; *clementia*), but chooses instead, as LXX Exodus 33:19b (Rom 9:14; cf. vv. 16, 18, 23–24) states, to act on the basis of his sovereign and electing right to choose those whom he blesses: "I will have mercy (Ἐλεήσω) upon whom I have mercy (ἐλεῶ)."

The Stoic issue of the (so-called) instability of "pity" as an emotion, which in Seneca's view jeopardised one's ability to act justly (*Clem.* 2.7.1–3), does not enter the Jewish world-view of the apostle. God acts justly (3:5–6; 9:14), *not* compromising his justice by ignoring the sins of the past (3:25b–26a), but rather justifying those in Christ through faith (3:26b) because of God's provision of

[57] On imitation in Paul, see Chapter 7, *infra*.

[58] For discussion, see Harrison, *Paul and the Imperial Authorities*, 292–299; *idem*, "Who is the 'Lord of Grace'? Jesus' Parables in Imperial Context," in *Border: Terms, Ideologies and Performances*, WUNT I 336, ed. A. Weissenrieder (Tübingen: Mohr Siebeck, 2016), 383–417.

his *hilasterion* (3:25a: ἱλαστήριον). In this process, Paul continuously reminds the Romans of the compassion (Rom 9:14b: οἰκτιρήσω, οἰκτίρω) and the kindness of God (2:4a: χρηστότητος), without obviating the necessity of God as judge of all to act justly. Precisely because of the Roman believers' experience of covenantal mercy (11:30–33; 12:1),[59] some are to exercise the ministry of mercy – and others generally by contributing to the needs of believers and by being hospitable to strangers (12:13) – in cheerfulness (12:8b: ὁ ἐλεῶν ἐν ἱλαρότητι).[60]

Sixth, in terms of ethnicity, while Paul recognizes elements of ethnic difference (Jew and Gentile: 1:16), covenantal privilege (3:1–2; 9:1–5; 11:1–2a), and cultural diversity (Greek, barbarian, Roman: 1:14–15), they are not considered impediments to approaching God in Christ (3:9, 29; 4:11–12; 10:12) or acceptance within the body of Christ (Rom 14:1–15:11). Rather Paul reverses cultural expectation by stating that he is equally obligated to barbarian and Greek (Rom 1:14), while the servanthood of Christ towards the Jews and the patriarchal promises (15:8–9; cf. 11:16, 29–29a) ensures the mutual acceptance of Jew and Gentile in the Body of Christ (15:7). Similarly, the Jerusalem collection does not represent a gift, which, in the understanding of ancient benefaction ideology, the Jewish believers had to reciprocate to their Gentile patrons sometime in the future, or for which they had to express continual gratitude. Rather the truth was the reverse: the Gentile believers are reciprocating the Jewish believers for their prior spiritual blessing through the gospel (15:27) and are acknowledging, thereby, the covenantal priority of the Jews (1:16b; 2:9b, 10b; 3:1–2), as well as evincing gratitude to them.[61] Furthermore, Roman attitudes attitude of military and ethnic superiority to the conquered Jews are undermined by God's continuing love and soteriological plans for Israel. Consequently, the Roman triumphalism and arrogance towards other ethnic groups was entirely misplaced (11:18–21) because they, like all the other Gentile nations, were merely the "wild olive" grafted into the vine of Israel (11:17). This stands in marked contrast to Cicero who dismisses the Jews because the *religio* and *mos maiorum* (traditions of the ancestors) of Rome are incompatible with

---

[59] On covenantal mercy in Romans, see S. Whittle, *Covenant Renewal and the Consecration of the Gentiles in Romans*, SNTSMS 161 (Cambridge: Cambridge University Press, 2015), *s.v.* Index of Subjects, "divine mercy".

[60] On whether ὁ ἐλεῶν ἐν ἱλαρότητι (Rom 12:8b) is limited to the restricted sense of Jewish almsgiving or embraces any act of mercy to others, see D. Moo, *The Epistle to the Romans* (Grand Rapids: Eerdmans, 1996), 769.

[61] For discussion of the Jerusalem collection in Romans 15:14–32, see D.J. Downs, *The Offering of the Gentiles: Paul's Collection for Jerusalem in Its Chronological, Cultural, and Cultic Contexts*, WUNT II 248 (Tübingen: Mohr Siebeck, 2008), 146–56. Regarding 2 Corinthians 8–9, see Harrison, *Paul's Language of Grace*, 294–321; S.J. Friesen, "Paul and Economics: The Jerusalem Collection as an Alternative to Patronage," in *Paul Unbound: Other Perspectives on the Apostle*, ed. M.D. Given (Peabody: Hendrickson, 2010), 27–54; R. Last, *The Pauline Church and the Corinthian Ekklêsia: Greco-Roman Associations in Comparative Context*, SNTSMS 164 (Cambridge: Cambridge University Press, 2016), 137–48, 166–76.

and superior to the sacred practices of the conquered and enslaved Jewish state (*Pro Flacco* 28:69; cf. Apion, cited in Josephus, *C. Ap.* 2.125):[62]

Each state, Laelius, has its own religious canon (*religio*) and we have ours. Even when Jerusalem was still standing and the Jews at peace with us, the practice of their sacred rites (*istorum religio sacrorum*) was incompatible with the glory of our empire, the dignity of our name, and the institutions of our ancestors (*maiorum institutis*); and now that the Jewish nation has shown by armed rebellion what are its feeling about our rule, it is even more so; how dear it was to the immortal gods has been shown by the fact that it has been conquered, farmed out to the tax collector and enslaved.[63]

Seventh, Paul addresses the issue of enmity between believers and outsiders (12:14, 17–21) and factionalism between believers themselves (12:16a; 14:1–15:11; 16:17) from a theological viewpoint. God has extinguished the enmity between humanity and himself (5:10) through the execution of his dishonoured benefactor on the cross (5:6–8).[64] The love prompting this act (5:8) explains the motif of love (12:9; 13:8–10) that frames Paul's discussion of believers' relations with insiders and outsiders in Romans 12:8–13:10.

Furthermore, Paul's teaching draws upon both dominical teaching (12:14, 21; cf. Matt 4:43–48; Luke 6:27–31) and LXX texts (12:19 [Deut 32:35]; 12:20 [Prov 25: 21, 22]). Significantly, in its original context, the Deuteronomic threat of divine vengeance is directed against the faithless and idolatrous Israelites, and not against their enemies.[65] Once again, the presumption on the part of some Roman believers that they would be somehow exempt from judgement in comparison to the other inferior enemy nations, routinely barbarian (cf. Rom 1:14), is challenged by the reference to the story of Israel as a hortatory paradigm (Rom 11:18–22). Rather Romans believers are to leave judgement in God's hands, whether it be God's eschatological judgement or his own judgement of other believers in the present (Rom 14:7–14). Moreover, readers familiar with the

[62] Josephus (*C. Ap.* 2.125) reports Apion as saying: "A clear proof, according to him (i.e. Apion), that our laws are unjust and our religious ceremonies erroneous is that we are not masters of an empire, but rather the slaves, first of one nation, then of another, and that calamity has more than once befallen our city."

[63] See Schäfer, *Judeophobia*, 182, for discussion. I have borrowed Schäfer's translation. The military and ethnic superiority of the Romans toward the Jews is also reinforced by the iconography of the Roman Empire where the Jews, with an inscribed base (*ETHNOUS IOUDAIŌN*) and a male Jewish face in the relief below on the panel, are displayed among the many other conquered races in the Sebasteion at Aphrodisias from the Claudian and Neronian period. See D.C. Lopez, *Apostle to the Conquered: Reimagining Paul's Mission* (Minneapolis: Fortress, 2008), 47 Fig. 12.

[64] For discussion, see Harrison, *Paul and the Imperial Authorities*, 185–97. On Republican enmity, see D.F. Epstein, *Personal Enmity in Roman Politics, 218–43 BC* (London: Croom Helm, 1987). There is a lacuna in studies on enmity in the early imperial period that needs to be addressed by ancient historians.

[65] For a different interpretative nuance regarding Romans 12:19 (Deut 32:35), see M.A. Seifrid, "Romans," in *Commentary on the New Testament Use of the Old Testament*, ed. G.K. Beale and D.A. Carson (Grand Rapids: Baker/Apollos, 2007), 680–81.

LXX text of Proverbs 25:21–22 would be aware that Paul, for his own reasons, has abridged the text, omitting Proverbs 25:22b. In the original LXX context, the fundamental motivation for feeding the hungry enemy and giving water to the thirsty enemy is the eschatological reward of God (Prov 25:22b).[66]

So why has Paul omitted this perfectly acceptable motivation? Perhaps a focus on eschatological reward, Paul feared, would distract from the real motivation for godly behaviour on the part of believers towards insiders and outsiders throughout this entire section (12:8–13:10): namely, love without pretense (12:9), summed up in the teaching of Christ (13:8–19), and supremely demonstrated in the cross towards the enemy (5:6–8, 10). In particular, Christ's cruciform love for his enemies (cf. Luke 6:27–36; 23:34; 1 Cor 4:9–13) moves the believer away from the worldly desire for retaliation against the offender towards the proper and godly response of non-retaliatory peace (12:18), empowered by Christ's indwelling love through the indwelling Spirit (Rom 5:5; 12:9; 13:8–10). This is demonstrated specifically by the believer's reaction of non-retaliation towards persecutors (12:17a, 19a), an attitude of blessing and beneficence towards them (12:14, 21), and patience under affliction throughout the entire process (12:12a). Additionally, just as Christ welcomed Jew and Gentile, vegetarian and non-vegetarian (Rom 14:1–15:11), into his messianic banquet through the shame of the cross (15:8–9), so believers were to welcome their enemies and outsiders to their own earthly "love feasts" through the exercise of hospitality (12:13b; 12:20a).[67]

Another possibility for Paul's exclusion of Proverbs 25:22b is that, at the level of biblical intertextual echo, Paul was well aware that just the brief LXX allusion to personal vengeance (Prov 25:21–22a [Rom 12:20]), as well as the vengeance of the Lord (Deut 32:35 [Rom 12:19]), and the priority of love towards the vengeful (12:9a; 13:8–10), would evoke other texts in the corpus of Proverbs that touched on exactly the same motifs (i.e. Prov 10:12; 20:22; 24:29; cf. 25:21–22a), over and above the omitted section of Proverbs 25:22b itself. The impact of the Old Testament wisdom literature upon Paul's ethical exhortation, therefore, should not be underestimated here in his decisions to abbreviate LXX texts and to write allusively instead.[68]

Eighth, we have noted Cicero's telling story about the public humiliation of a Messanian victim who was publicly crucified with the view of the freedom of Italy across the Straits, held perpetually before him until he died, thereby humiliating the victim through the knowledge that that he would never regain that freedom. Thus the gospel of Christ crucified, for Roman auditors with views similar to Cicero, must have been incomprehensible. Believers were baptised

[66] See the discussion of Jewett, *Romans*, 778.

[67] See M.J. Gorman, *Cruciformity: Paul's Narrative Spirituality of the Cross* (Grand Rapids: Eerdmans, 2001), 246–52.

[68] See I. Tadashi, *Paul's Use of Canonical and Non-canonical Wisdom Literature in Romans and the Corinthian Letters* (PhD thesis, Andrews University, 2003).

into the crucifixion of Christ and united with him in his resurrection (Rom 6:1–6; v.6: συνεσταυρώθη; cf. Gal 2:19–20).[69] Paradoxically, believers are freed from sin and death (Rom 6:7–11), only to experience servitude again – understood metaphorically as slavery to righteousness (6:15–23) or as marriage to a new messianic husband (7:1–6). One word, as Paul knew very well, summed up the content of this message for Roman Gentiles: "foolishness" (1 Cor 1:23).[70] However, Cicero's terminology of shame ("tree of shame") coheres with Paul's dishonour of the cross (cf. 1 Cor 1:18–31; Phil 2:8b) and, in Roman minds, the shame of the gospel preached by Paul (Rom 1:16a).

2.4. From Cicero's Republic to Augustus' Emergence as Pater Patriae: *Evaluating the Social Challenge Posed by Paul's Gospel*

In the nineteenth century Theodore Mommsen, in a memorable but damning phrase, lambasted Cicero for his "dreadful barrenness of thought". Cicero's reputation as a philosopher plummeted in modern scholarship from that time onwards, notwithstanding the philosopher's immense popularity in previous centuries. We are witnessing currently a resurgence of scholarly interest in Cicero as a thinker and rhetorician. It is surprising that Pauline scholars have, so far, little engaged this Ciceronian revival. The assumption is, as we have proposed, that Cicero is not relevant to New Testament studies because of the so-called transition from "Republic" to "Empire" that occurred with the establishment of Augustus' principate and the rule of the Julio-Claudians.

However, such a transition reflects the settled judgements of hindsight rather than the perspective of Cicero's contemporaries. Augustus legitimately spoke of a new age having begun for Rome with his victory over Antony and Cleopatra at Actium (31 BC),[71] because he was in total control, by universal consent, from

[69] Moo (*The Epistle to the Romans*, 376) highlights the significance of the believer's co-crucifixion effectively: "Paul's point, then, is that the real, though forensic, inclusion of the believer with Christ in his crucifixion means that our solidarity with, and dominance by, Adam, though whom we are bound to the nexus of sin and death, has ended." On the role of the cross in Paul's thought more widely, see R.C. Tannehill, *Dying and Rising with Christ: A Study in Pauline Theology* (Berlin: Alfred Töpelmann, 1966); C.B. Cousar, *A Theology of the Cross: The Death of Jesus in the Pauline Letters* (Minneapolis: Fortress, 1990); Gorman, *Cruciformity*.

[70] R. Penna, "The Wisdom of the Cross and Its Foolishness as Foundation of the Church," in *idem*, *Paul the Apostle: Wisdom and Folly of the Cross. Volume 2*, tr. T.P. Wahl (Collegeville: Michael Glazier, 1996), 45–60; L.L. Welborn, *Paul, the Fool of Christ: A Study of 1 Corinthians 1–4 in the Comic-Philosophic Tradition* (London and New York: T&T Clark, 2005), esp. 117–60.

[71] A.E. Cooley (*Res Gestae Divi Augusti: Text, Translation, and Commentary* [Cambridge: Cambridge University Press, 2009], 34, 158) points to the revealing phrases "before I was born" (13) and "my era" (16.1: ἀών in the Greek version of the *Res Gestae*).

the end of the civil wars onwards.[72] But when faced with relentless public pressure to accept even more extraordinary and unconstitutional powers in 27 BC (and again in 23), Augustus states in *Res Gestae* 34.1b that he "transferred the state (*res publicam*) from my power into the control of the Roman Senate and People," strongly resisting any imposition of exceptional honours contrary to republican tradition.

Ronald Syme has famously dismissed Augustus' tactic here as a calculated façade by which the *princeps*, cleverly strategising on many fronts, established an unassailable power base for the future.[73] Succinctly put, Augustus acquired unprecedented powers by his public charade of disavowing further powers.[74] Syme, however, was writing his portrait of the "Augustan revolution" against the backdrop of the rise of tyranny in pre-war Europe and found in Tacitus's venomous portrait of Augustus a congenial dialogue partner.[75] Indeed, Tacitus himself had composed his *Annals* under the shadow of the tyrannous reign of Domitian. Historians are often impacted by their own age in assessing the past and Tacitus and Syme were no exceptions to this tendency. But, as noted, the total dominance of Augustus by universal consent preceded the handing back of his powers to the Senate and the People by four years: the "façade" theory has no basis in reality. We can only conclude that Augustus was sincere in wanting to return powers that he considered incompatible with republican convention.

But because of the legacy of the "façade" theory,[76] many scholars have considered Augustus' self-presentation in the *Res Gestae* to be riddled with untruths, though like any historical document, it is selective in its presentation and we must not unfairly exaggerate its tendentiousness.[77] Consequently, any investiga-

[72] For the significance of the revised translation of *Res Gesate* 34.1a ("In my sixth and seventh consulships, after I had put an end to civil wars, although by everyone's agreement I had power over everything"), arising from the recent discovery of a new fragment of the text, see Cooley, *Res Gestae*, 257–58; E. A. Judge, "The Crux of RG 34.1 Resolved? Augustus on 28 BC," *New Docs* 10 (2012): 55–58, § 10; J. R. Harrison, "Augustan Rome and the Body of Christ: A Comparison of the Social Vision of the Res Gestae and Paul's Letter to the Romans," *HTR* 106.1 (2013): 1–36, at 27–28.

[73] This interpretation of Augustus' regime will be pursued and found wanting in Chapter 3, though, in what follows, its deficiencies are also exposed.

[74] R. Syme, *The Roman Revolution* (Oxford: Oxford University Press, 1939), 312–30, esp. 323–30. For an evaluation of Syme's contribution, see E. A. Judge, "The Second Thoughts of Syme on Augustus," in *idem*, *The First Christians in the Roman World: Augustan and New Testament Essays*, WUNT I 229, ed. J. R. Harrison (Tübingen: Mohr Siebeck, 2008), 314–45.

[75] Note the comment of R. Syme (*Tacitus Volume 1* [Oxford: Oxford University Press, 1958], 408) regarding the façade underlying the rule of Augustus: "Between the formula and the realities a wide gap yawned. The main elements in the supremacy of Augustus derive from sources outside the Roman constitution. Tacitus insists ever and again upon the contrast between words and substance."

[76] For E. A. Judge's critique of the façade theory, see *idem*, "The Second Thoughts of Syme," 316–28.

[77] On the untruthfulness of the *Res Gestae*, see especially R. Ridley, *The Emperor's Retrospect: Augustus' Res Gestae in Epigraphy, Historiography and Commentary* (Leuven and

tion of the leadership ideals of the apostle Paul with those of Augustus in the *Res Gestae* would be rendered suspect, it could be argued, because of the perceived slipperiness of Augustus' self-portrait.[78] Moreover, to compare the social vision of Paul's letters and Cicero's speeches, as we have done in this chapter, could also be considered a lost cause or, at the very least, a futile exercise in antiquarianism.

But, in actuality, there remained strong republican continuities under the Augustan principate because of the ruler's strong personal commitment to the *mos maiorum* ("ancestral custom"). Moreover, the quest for ancestral glory on the part of the surviving members of the Roman noble houses, along with the new men (*novi homines*), would only remain viable provided that the *cursus honorum* ("course of offices") and its completion for magistracies operated conventionally.[79] Therefore, Augustus only assumed normal offices wherever possible, not only to avoid the fatal mistakes that his adoptive father, Julius Caesar, had made in acting unconstitutionally at various junctures, but also in order to maintain in his principate what were the defining mores and practices of the Roman republic. The plurality of leadership of the Roman state, spoken of in a contemporary inscription just after the death of Augustus, underscores the continuance of republican conventions in leadership, standing in contrast to the so-called Augustan "tyranny" of Tacitus and Syme.[80]

To be sure, discontinuities with the republican past existed because of (a) the enormity of the military and civic triumph of the Julian house over the remaining old noble houses, (b) Augustus' unchallenged position as world benefactor, (c) his client-patron relationship with his personal armies in the imperial provinces, and (d) the loyalty of the provincial cities and their elites forged through

Dudley: Peeters, 2003), *passim*. It should be noted, however, that the genre of eulogistic literature, to which the *Res Gestae* belongs, is political and triumphal. Objectivity cannot be expected (A.E. Cooley, *Res Gestae Divi Augusti: Text, Translation, and Commentary* [Cambridge: Cambridge University Press, 2009], 35; cf. A.H.M. Jones, *Augustus* [New York: Norton, 1970], 168–69).

[78] See, however, Harrison, "Augustan Rome and the Body of Christ."

[79] Note, however, the "paralysis of competition" that nevertheless occurred despite Augustus' best intentions: E.A. Judge, "The Real Basis of Augustan Power," in *idem*, *The First Christians in the Roman World*, 116–20, at 120.

[80] Note the calendar of Amiternum, 13 September, AD 16, which states: "Holiday by resolution of the senate because on this day the evil plot against the life of T. Caesar and his children and other leaders (*principes*) of the state, and against the *res publica*, formed by M. Libo was condemned in the senate." *Docs Aug*, p. 52. The plurality of leadership ("other leaders": *principes*) spotlights how Augustus and Tiberius understood history in the tradition of the republic where nobles from the famous Roman houses competed against each other for honour in service of the state, reflecting exactly how the word *principes* "was used in the Ciceronian age two generations before" (E.A. Judge, "The Augustan Republic: Tiberius and Claudius on Roman History," in *idem*, *The First Christians in the Roman World*, at 127–39, at 135). For discussion of additional evidence, see J.R. Harrison, "Diplomacy over Tiberius Succession," *New Docs* 10 (2012): 64–75, at 70–71, § 12.

imperial beneficence and diplomacy on an unprecedented scale in comparison to republican times. But all of this "novelty" was subsumed under the entirely conventional paradigm of Roman patronage, summed up in the honorific accolade given to Augustus by the Senate: *Pater Patriae* (*Res Gestae* 35:1: "Father of the fatherland").[81] In sum, what we now call "Empire", with all the clarity of hindsight, only gradually emerged over time. This estimate is reflected in the hardened historical assessments of Augustus as "tyrant" (Tacitus, *Ann.* 1.1–5 [AD 58–117]), founder of "empire" (Suetonius, *Aug.* 28.1 [AD 69–post 122]), or constitutional "monarch", Dio Cassius, 52.1.1; 53.11.4 [AD 150–235]), each aired in literary sources post-dating the first century. But, significantly, the assessment of the Augustan principate by our contemporary source, Velleius Paterculus (2.89.3–4 [19 BC–AD 31]), is vastly different, reflecting the profound gratitude of Romans of the time for Augustus' preservation of the *mos maiorum* and the return of the operations of the *res publica* to normality and peace after the protracted civil war:

> The civil wars were ended after twenty years, foreign wars suppressed, peace restored, the frenzy of arms everywhere lulled to rest; validity was restored to the laws, authority to the courts, and dignity to the senate; the power of the magistrates was reduced to its former limits, with the sole exception that two were added to the eight existing praetors. The traditional form of the republic was restored (*rei publicae forma revocata*). Agriculture returned to the fields, respect to religion, to mankind freedom from anxiety, and to each citizen his property rights were now assured; old laws were usefully emended, and new laws passed for the general good; the revision of the senate, while not too drastic, was not lacking in severity. The chief mem of the state who had won triumphs and had held high office were at the invitation of Augustus induced to adorn the city. In the case of the consulship only, Caesar was not able to have his own way, but was obliged to hold that office consecutively until the eleventh time in spite of his frequent efforts to prevent it; but the dictatorship which the people persistently offered him, he as stubbornly refused.

Now that we understand slightly better Rome's political and social development from Cicero's republic to Augustan Rome, including the continuities and discontinuities between each period of rule, where does this leave us in assessing

[81] Augustus emerges as a type of "super-patron". As E. A. Judge ("*Contemptu famae contemni* virtutes: On the Morality of Self-advertisement among the Romans," in *idem*, The *First Christians in the Roman World*, 59–65, at 65) observes regarding the crucial placement of the honorific *pater patriae* in the *Res Gestae:* "The nature of this ascendancy is revealed in the concluding honour, the unanimous recognition of him as *Pater Patriae.* In other words, the personal moral superiority, exemplified in the lengthy catalogue of achievements and benefactions that goes before, has placed him a class apart from the rival patrons with their competitions in honour and massed client support. He has acquired a universal patronage over the republic." On *Pater Patriae*, see Cooley, *Res Gestae Divi Augusti*, 273–75, who concludes (*ibid.*, 275): the title "had multiple legal and religious resonances and evoked ideas of someone acting as a saviour, patron and god." The three roles, historically, are summed up under the rubric of benefactor in the ruler-cult.

the contribution of Cicero and Paul to civic and personal morality, each of whom aired their social vision for the inhabitants of Rome in rapidly changing epochs?

We have seen from our discussion of important motifs in Cicero's speeches that many of the traditional Roman values espoused by Cicero continued to play an important role in Roman society well into the imperial period. This remains an accurate appraisal even if K. Galinsky is correct in saying that Augustus' commitment to exemplary Roman traditions produced something socially akin to a "somnolent antiquarianism."[82] Furthermore, the continued popularity of Cicero's works in the imperial age, considered to be a high water mark in Roman rhetoric, meant that his social agenda remained well known, read and appreciated, and enthusiastically evaluated and debated. As such, Cicero remains an important source for understanding the political, social and religious ethos of Rome, including perceptions of how the elites should participate in civil life and replenish their ranks, without thereby imperilling the future of the state.

What would have been confronting was the challenge that Paul's gospel posed to traditional Roman values as the imperial authorities gradually became aware of the early Christian communities at Rome.[83] What are the ideological contours of this challenge? Paul's searing denunciation of Roman *religio* (Rom 1:18–31) put the safety of the capital at risk, secured as it was by Augustus' meticulous attention to traditional Roman morality and religious practices (*Res Gestae* 6.2, 13; 19.1, 2; 20.4). The Roman quest for honour and glory did not find its culmination in the Julian house, as the Augustan propaganda claimed, but rather in the risen Christ, the *telos* of the Law and the prophetic hope (Rom 1:2–6; 10:4; 16:25–27), the One in whom the Gentiles gloried (Rom 15:9–12). The Roman ethos of *imitatio*, focused on the famous ancestors of the noble houses during the republic and refocused in the person of Augustus during the principate, was undermined by God's predestinating plan to conform believers to the image of his crucified and risen Son (Rom 8:29). Clemency in the Roman world was only extended to the worthy, that is, to those who possessed the ability to change morally, for otherwise the demands of Roman justice would be diluted. For Paul, however, God had exercised his mercy towards his enemies (Rom 5:6–8), the morally dissolute and unrepentant who were unable and unwilling to change (Rom 3:9–18, 23; 5:12a, 13a, 14a, 15a, 16a, 17a, 18a, 19a, 20a, 21a), and, in this process of reconciliation, God upheld the strictest demands of his justice at the

---

[82] K. Galinsky, *Augustan Culture: An Interpretative Introduction* (Princeton: Princeton University Press, 1996), 139.

[83] I argue in a recent publication that the Roman authorities in the capital noticed the emergence of the early Christians in the capital much earlier than is normally posited by scholars. See J.R. Harrison, "The Persecution of Christians from Nero to Hadrian," in *Into All the World: Emergent Christianity in its Jewish and Greco-Roman Context*, ed. M. Harding and A. Nobbs (Grand Rapids: Eerdmans, 2017), 266–300.

cross of Christ (Rom 3:24–26). The superiority of Rome ethically, socially, culturally to the rest of the world was bypassed by Paul in the vast re-ordering of social relations occurring in the Body of Christ (Rom 1:14, 16; 10:12; 15:7–9). The indelible line between Rome and her enemies was totally compromised by Paul's counter-cultural teaching on revenge (Rom 12:4–21; 13:8–10). The crucifixion of the 6,000 survivors of Sparticus' slave revolt along the Appian Way in 71 BC from Capua to Rome underscored Roman disdain for the "non-entities" and "disposables" at the base of the social pyramid. Undoubtedly early believers who claimed that they were slaves of righteousness to a "Lord" recently crucified in Palestine (Rom 6:15–19) would have met with similar contempt. In sum, Cicero was an astute judge of what was central and valuable for Romans and he would have despised the early Christians, had he lived in the mid 50's of the imperial age.

But a fundamental question still remains unanswered, given the unlikelihood of traditional Romans responding favourably to this novel and dangerous cult. How did the paradoxical understanding of leadership enunciated by the apostle Paul gradually come to dislodge the equally paradoxical understanding of leadership on the part of Augustus in the Roman Empire? We turn to that intriguing issue in our next chapter.

Chapter 3

The Paradox of Paul's Apostolic Ministry (2 Cor 4:7–18) in Its Augustan and Apocalyptic Context

Throughout the Julio-Claudian period Augustus remained the iconic paradigm of civic virtue for each new generation. The rhetoric of the honorific inscriptions, erected by grateful clients of the Roman ruler in the Greek East, provided providential and prophetic perceptions of Augustus' beneficence.[1] In the Latin West, the *forum Augustum* presented Augustus as the culmination of republican history, holding him up as the exemplum for future Roman rulers. This was because Augustus had stepped decisively into the breach at the battle of Actium (31 BC) to end the protracted struggle for power among Rome's leading men which was ripping apart the state, in the same way that the famous republican *principes* ("leaders"), celebrated in the *forum Augustum* at Rome, had managed the crises of the past.[2] The heated quest among the Roman nobles for ancestral glory, which had plunged Rome into a century of bloody civil war, found its resolution in Augustus who brought peace and security to the state.[3] Consequently, Augustus and the Julian family became the repository of civic virtue and military glory.[4]

---

[1] J.R. Harrison, "Paul, Eschatology and the Augustan Age of Grace," *TynBul* 50.1 (1999): 79–91; *idem*, *Paul's Language of Grace in Its Graeco-Roman Context*, WUNT II 172 (Tübingen: Mohr Siebeck, 2003), *passim*.

[2] On the Augustan forum, see J. Luce, "Livy, Augustus and the Forum Augustum," in *Between Republic and Empire: Interpretations of Augustus and His Principate*, ed. K.A. Raaflaub and M. Toher (Oxford/Berkeley: University of California Press, 1990), 123–38; M. Spannagel, *Exemplaria Principis. Untersuchungen zu Entstehung und Ausstattung des Augustusforums* (Heidelberg: Verlag Archäologie und Geschichte, 1999); K. Galinsky, *Augustan Culture: An Interpretive Introduction* (Princeton: Princeton University Press, 1996), 197–213; P. Zanker, *The Power of Images in the Age of Augustus* (Ann Arbor: The University of Michigan, 1999), 210–15; E.A. Judge, "The Eulogistic Inscriptions of the Augustan Forum: Augustus on Roman History," in *idem*, *The First Christians in the Roman World: Augustan and New Testament Essays*, WUNT I 229, ed. J.R. Harrison (Tübingen: Mohr Siebeck, 2008), 165–81; J.R. Harrison, *Paul and the Imperial Authorities at Thessalonica and Rome: A Study in the Conflict of Ideology*, WUNT I 273 (Tübingen: Mohr Siebeck, 2011), 170–77.

[3] On 1 Thess 5:3 (ὅταν λέγουσιν, Εἰρήσιν καὶ ἀσφάλεια ["whenever they say, 'Peace and security'"]) and its significance in regards to the imperial propaganda, see Harrison, *Paul and the Imperial Authorities*, 61–62. Contra, see J.R. White, "'Peace and Security' (1 Thessalonians 5:3): Is It Really a Roman Slogan?" *NTS* 59.3 (2013): 382–95.

[4] On the culmination of virtue and glory in Augustus, see Harrison, *Paul and the Imperial Authorities*, 138–41, 225–32; *idem*, "The Brothers as the 'Glory of Christ' (2 Cor 8:23): Paul's *Doxa* Terminology in Its Ancient Benefaction Context," *NovT* 52.2 (2010): 156–88.

As the "super" patron of Rome and its provinces,[5] Augustus provided the opportunity of social advancement for his clients through the adaptations he made to the traditional *cursus honorum* ("course of honours"), fostering thereby the careers of senators and equestrian military personnel.[6] Further, as the "benefactor of the world,"[7] Augustus became the source of overflowing grace to a wide variety of groups: his army veterans, the urban plebs and cults of Rome, the leading figures of the literary world, and, last, the cities of the Mediterranean basin,[8] as well as their local elites who competed for priesthoods in the imperial cult.[9] The social, cultural, and moral program, founded upon Augustus' *auctoritas* ("influence"), revitalised the traditional *mores maiorum*

---

[5] Vitruvius (*On Architecture* 1.1–3; cf. Suetonius, *Aug.*, 28.3) speaks of Augustus' transformation of the city of Rome – in conjunction with his organisation of and beneficence to the provinces – through his building programs: "I saw that you were concerned not just for the welfare of the whole community and the establishment of the *res publica*, but also to provide [the *res publica*] with public buildings. Thus through your initiative the state was enriched with provinces, and at the same time its majestic imperial power was reflected in the pre-eminent authority of its civic constructions ... I began to write this for you because I observed that you have built extensively, that you continue to do so, and that in the future you will ensure that posterity will remember your public and private works alongside your other distinguished achievements."

[6] For discussion, see A.H.M. Jones, *Augustus* (New York: Norton, 1970), 136–39; P.A. Brunt, "Princeps and Equites," *JRS* 73 (1983): 42–75; *idem*, "The Role of the Senate in the Augustan Regime," *CQ* (1984): 434–44; D. Shotter, *Augustus*, 2nd ed. (London and New York: Routledge, 2005), 46–47.

[7] Note the inscriptions honouing Augustus, Tiberius, and Claudius respectively: "Divine *Augustus* Caesar, son of god, imperator of land and sea, the benefactor and saviour of the whole world, the people of the Myrians" (*DocsAug* § 72); "Tiberius Caesar, divine Augustus, the son of the divine Augusti, imperator of land and sea, the benefactor and saviour of the whole world, the people of the Myrians" (*DocsAug* § 88); "Euphanes, son of Charinus, a Rhodian, the present *stephanephorus* and priest of divine Augustus ... has dedicated from his own resources this statue of the saviour and benefactor of all mankind" (*DocsGaius* § 135). See also Velleius Paterculus 2.89.2. Note D.C. Earl's comment regarding Augustus as benefactor (*The Age of Augustus* [New York: Crown, 1968], 71): "All the inhabitants of the Roman world were his clients. The army and the Roman People were the twin pillars of his power and his hold over them was personal and beyond the constitution."

[8] On Augustus as a patron, see R.P. Saller, "Promotion and Patronage in Equestrian Careers," *JRS* 60 (1980): 38–49; A.K. Bowman, ed., et al., *The Cambridge Ancient History X: The Augustan Empire 43 BC–AD 69* (Cambridge: Cambridge University Press, 1996), *s.v.* Index: "Patronage: ('Augustus')"; Shotter, *Augustus*, 39–59; W. Eck, *The Age of* Augustus, 2nd ed. (Oxford: Blackwell, 2007), *s.v.* Index: "Clients", "Patronage." On Julio-Claudian patronage more generally, see R.P. Saller, *Personal Patronage Under the Early Empire* (Cambridge: Cambridge: Cambridge University Press, 1982), 41–78.

[9] On the social position of the municipal priests of Roma, see R. Mellor, "The Goddess Roma," *ANRW* 2.17.2 (1981): 998–99. More generally, J. Scheid, "Les prêtres officials sous les empereurs Julio-Claudiens," *ANRW* 2.16.1 (1979): 610–54. On the competition among cities and local elites in the Greek East and Latin West, see S.R.F. Price, *Rituals and Power: The Roman Imperial Cult in Asia Minor* (Cambridge: Cambridge University Press, 1984), 62–64, 89–91, 100, 122–23; Zanker, *The Power of Images*, 302–07, 316–23.

("customs of the ancestors") that had been so severely compromised during the civil war.[10]

This exalted status of Augustus caused his contemporaries to speak of the arrival of the "Golden Age" of Saturn during his principate.[11] Indeed, the extraordinary accumulation of honorific accolades culminates in his patronage being designated as "god-like".[12] This was encapsulated in the honorific titles of "Augustus" and "Pater Patriae" ("Father of the Country").[13] The moral ascendancy of Augustus would enable his Julio-Claudian successors to establish the legitimacy of their rule by appeal to Augustan precedent,[14] and, in Claudius' and Nero's case respectively, assert that either the new *saeculum* had occurred under their rule,[15] or that a new Golden Age had dawned upon their accession to power.[16] Seemingly the *auctoritas* of Augustus remained as potent after his death as it was during his life.

By contrast, Augustus' *Res Gestae* provides a more ambiguous and paradoxical construction of the power and influence than what is found in the court poets, the statue and *elogia* program of the *forum Augustum*, and the honorific

---

[10] On the literature, art and architecture of the Augustan age, see Galinsky, *Augustan Culture*, 141–287; T. Habinek and A. Schiesaro, eds., *The Roman Cultural Revolution* (Cambridge: Cambridge University Press, 1997), *passim*; Zanker, *The Power of Images*, 101–66.

[11] On the Golden Age of Saturn from Augustus to Nero, see Harrison, *Paul and the Imperial Authorities*, 101–04, 121–23; cf. A. Wallace-Hadrill, "The Golden Age and Sin in Augustan Ideology," *Past and Present* 95 (1982): 19–36.

[12] See S.R.F. Price, "Gods and Emperors: The Greek Language of the Roman Imperial Cult," *JHS* 104 (1984): 79–95. C. Damon (*Res Gestae Divi Augusti* [Bryn Mawr: Bryn Mawr College, 1995], 45) observes of the name "Augustus": "'Augustus' set him at the apex of mankind, but not quite in the realm of the immortals" (Suetonius, *Life of Augustus* 7.2). Of the incorporation of Augustus' name in the hymn of the Salii (*Res Gestae* 10.1), Damon (*Res Gestae*, 23) writes: "Augustus was not deified at Rome until after his death, but this honour puts him on a par with the ancestral gods on at least this respect."

[13] On the title "Augustus" (*Res Gestae* 34.2; Suetonius, *Aug.* 7.2; 21.8; Ovid, *Fast.* 1.589–590, 560–562, 608–616; *Tr.* 3.1.39–46; Dio Cassius 53.16.6–8; Velleius Paterculus 2.91.1; Florus 2.34.66), see J. Scheid, *Res Gestae Divi Augusti: hauts faits du divin Auguste* (Paris: Les Belles Lettres, 2007), 88–89; A.E. Cooley, *Res Gestae Divi Augusti: Text, Translation, and Commentary* (Cambridge: Cambridge University Press, 2009), 261–62. On the title "Pater Patriae" (*Res Gestae* 35.1; Suetonius, *Aug.* 58.1–2; Horace, *Carm.* 3.24.25–32; Ovid, *Fast.* 2 127–128; *Tr.* 2.574; Dio Cassius 55.10.10), see Scheid, *Res Gestae*, 92–93; Cooley, *Res Gestae*, 273–75.

[14] The Julio-Claudian successors to Augustus' principate appealed to Augustan precedent during their rule. See B. Levick, *Tiberius the Politician* (London: Routledge, 1999), 82; A.A. Barrett, *Caligula: The Corruption of Power* (London: B.T. Batsford, 1989), 250; T.E.J. Wiedemann, "Tiberius to Nero," in *The Cambridge Ancient History. Second Edition. X: The Augustan Empire 43 BC–AD 69*, ed. A.K. Bowman et al. (Cambridge: Cambridge University Press, 1996), 198–255, at 232; M.T. Griffin, *Nero: The End of a Dynasty* (New Haven/London: Yale University Press, 1984), *s.v.* Index of Persons, Human & Divine, "Augustus the Emperor"; E. Champlin, *Nero* (Cambridge, MA and London: Harvard University Press, 2003), 139–44.

[15] Harrison, *Paul and the Imperial Authorities*, 100.

[16] Harrison, *Paul and the Imperial Authorities*, 103; cf. Galinsky, *Augustan Culture*, 106–21.

inscriptions of the Greek East. Engraved on two pillars of bronze erected at the entrance to his Mausoleum in the Campus Martius, the *Res Gestae* recorded Augustus' achievements for posterity, ranging from his triumviral years to just prior to his death as the ruler of Rome. The inscription was composed in the final year of Augustus' life when he was seventy-six years old and in the thirty-seventh year of his tribunician power (*Res Gestae* 4.4; 35.2).

Because classical scholars have sometimes been too preoccupied with what Augustus has omitted to say in the *Res Gestae* regarding his Principate at the expense of what he actually said, a fundamental paradox in Augustus' self-presentation in the text has, to some extent, been overlooked. Undercutting the relentless emphasis on boasting and achievement throughout the *Res Gestae* is an unease that causes the princeps to draw back from overshadowing his contemporaries with his honours and powers and to place the good of the *res publica* ("the public property") at the centre of his concern. The contrasts in tone are intriguing. Augustus surpasses all previous competitors, while acting within the restraints of republican convention and precedent, excelling his contemporaries in influence (*auctoritas*), while possessing no more power (*potestas*) than his fellow magistrates, ruthlessly subduing the nations militarily, while attracting their diplomatic embassies from afar because of his reputation for justice and clemency. Furthermore, the text presents Augustus as strangely reluctant to seize honours, while readily shouldering the burdens of state.[17] This stands in sharp contrast to Tacitus' portrait of Augustus' duplicitous concealment of his powers in the *Annals*.[18] There is little doubt that these shifts in tone

---

[17] Horace, addressing the princeps (*Ep.* 2.1.1–3), sums up Augustus' shouldering of the burden of state thus: "Seeing that you alone carry the weight of so many great charges, guarding our Italian state with arms, gracing her with morals, and reforming her with laws." See especially T. Hillard, "Augustus and the Evolution of Roman Concepts of Leadership," *Ancient History: Resources for Teachers* 38.2 (2011): 107–52.

[18] For the argument that Augustus' "restoration of the republic" was a hypocritical façade and that Tacitus' dark version of the Augustan principate is to be preferred to the omissions, half-truths and lies of the *Res Gestae*, see R. Syme, *The Roman Revolution* (Oxford: Oxford University Press, 1939), 2–9, 322–30, 404–05. For Tacitus' evaluation of Augustus, see *idem*, *Tacitus, Volumes I & II* (Oxford: Oxford University Press, 1958), esp. Vol. I, 431–32; cf. D.R. Dudley, *The World of Tacitus* (London: Secker & Warburg, 1968), 76–78; K. Galinsky, *Augustan Culture: An Interpretative Introduction* (Princeton: Princeton University Press, 1996), 77–79. On the untruthfulness of the *Res Gestae*, see Jones, *Augustus*, 168–69; R. Ridley, *The Emperor's Retrospect: Augustus' Res Gestae in Epigraphy, Historiography and Commentary* (Leuven and Dudley: Peeters, 2003). However, for more balanced approaches to Augustus' *Res Gestae* – each incorporating the new restoration of *Res Gestae* 34.1 and canvassing the interpretative challenge that it issues to Augustus' (alleged) hypocritical "restoration of the republic" – see Scheid, *Res Gestae*; E.A. Judge, "Augustus in the *Res Gestae*," in *idem*, *The First Christians in the Roman World*, 182–223; E.A. Judge, "The Crux of RG 34.1 Resolved?' Augustus on 28 BC," in *New Documents Illustrating Early Christianity*, Vol. 10, ed. S.R. Llewelyn and J.R. Harrison (Grand Rapids: Eerdmans, 2012), 55–58, § 10; Cooley, *Res Gestae*. For an incisive critique of Syme and his interpretative legacy to Augustan studies, see E.A. Judge, "The Second Thoughts of Syme on Augustus," in *idem*, *The First Christians*,

are rhetorically crafted with great care, drawing upon well-known models in antiquity,[19] but it would be churlish to rule out the possibility of Augustus' sincerity at the outset.[20]

A series of important questions emerge at this point. How do we explain this oscillation in the *Res Gestae* between Augustus excelling others in influence (*auctoritas*) and his professing reluctance to accept honours? Would this unconventional *exemplum* raise up a new generation of leaders for Rome? How does Augustus' portrait of his principate intersect with Paul's apocalyptic gospel and its equally paradoxical understanding of apostolic ministry in 2 Corinthians 4:7–18? Why did Paul's "cruciform" and "apocalyptic" paradigm of ministry ultimately triumph in the West at the expense of the legacy of Augustus?

This chapter will argue that both the Roman ruler Augustus and the apostle Paul had a paradoxical understanding of their respective leadership roles. However, each figure overcomes the obstacles he faces by shouldering his responsibilities in vastly different but in equally effective ways. Both men also exhibited substantial differences in the ideological understanding of their leadership, reflecting in miniature the collision that would eventually emerge between the Classical and Christian tradition in western civilisation.

314–45; cf. F. Millar, ed., *La révolution romaine après Ronald Syme: bilans et perspectives* (Genève: Fondation Hardt, 2000), *passim*. For a nuanced exploration of what Augustus meant in returning "the *res publica* to the Senate and the people" (*Res Gestae* 34.1), see E. A. Judge, "*Res Publica Restituta*: A Modern Illusion?" in *idem*, *The First Christians*, 140–64; cf. J. Rich and J. H. C Williams, "Leges et iura P. R. restituit: A New Aureus of Octavian and the Settlement of 28–27 BC," *Numismatic Chronicle* 159 (1999): 169–213. A related shibboleth of Augustan studies is the purported monarchic pretensions of Augustus, particularly prevalent in German scholarship. For example, see A. Alföldi, *Die monarchische Repräsentation im römischen Kaiserreiche* (Darmstadt: Wissenschaftliche Buchgesellschaft, 1970), *passim*; Eck, *The Age of Augustus*, 3–5, 146–47; J. Bleicken, *Augustus: Eine Biographie* (Hamburg: Rowohlt Taschenbuch Verlag, 2010), 297–369, 509–40. Not only do these proposals overlook the historic Roman rejection of monarchy (510–509 BC) and Augustus' personal avoidance of monarchic perceptions (Cooley, *Res Gestae*, 34), but also they anachronistically impose upon Augustus' principate the monarchic assumptions of the late source, Dio Cassius (AD 150–235: cf. Dio Cassius 52.1.1; 53.11.4). See especially J. A. Crook, "Political History, 30 BC to AD 14," in *The Cambridge Ancient History. Second Edition. X: The Augustan Empire 43 BC–AD 69*, ed. A. K. Bowman et al. (Cambridge: Cambridge University Press, 1996), 70–112, at 71. Cf. A. Wallace-Hadrill, "Civilis Princeps: Between Citizen and King," *JRS* 72 (1982): 32–48. Last, the evaluation of Augustan power and authority in the new edition of the Cambridge Ancient History abandons Syme's portrait of Augustan rule as "a 'hoax', a 'cloak', or a 'veneer', masking 'brute power'." See J. A. Crook, "Augustus: Power, Authority, Achievement," in *The Cambridge Ancient History. Second Edition. X: The Augustan Empire 43 BC–AD 69*, ed. A. K. Bowman et al. (Cambridge: Cambridge University Press, 1996), 113–46, at 117, and especially 117–23 for a nuanced discussion of the entire issue.

[19] See Hillard, "Roman Concepts of Leadership," 131–43.

[20] See the neglected article of M. Hammond, "The Sincerity of Augustus," *HSCP* 69 (1965): 139–52.

3.1. *The Paradoxical Augustus: The Interplay Between "Reluctance" and "Influence" in Shaping the Princeps*

The *Res Gestae* sets out the achievements and accolades of Augustus' career in a dazzling panoply that attests to his personal pre-eminence after 31 BC: the honours (1–7) and special tributes achieved during his principate (9–13); the honours for his sons (14); his *impensae* ("expenses") incurred on behalf of the state and people of Rome (15–24); the *res gestae* (military "achievements") by which he subdued the world to the power of Rome (25–33; cf. "Heading", 1); and, last, his supreme position as an example of virtue (34–35). Most notably, a new fragment of *Res Gestae* 34.1 from Antioch has revealed that the words originally restored by T. Mommsen as *[potitus rerum omn]ium* ("after receiving the absolute control of affairs") are in reality *[po]tens re[r]um om[n]ium* ("although I had power over everything").[21] Thus the text should be translated:

> In my sixth and seventh consulships, after I had put an end to civil wars, although by everyone's agreement I had power over everything (*per consensum univorum [po]tens re[r]um om[n]ium*), I transferred the state (*rem publicam*) from my power (*ex mea potesate*) into the control of the Roman senate and people.[22]

The old scholarly consensus concerning Augustus' control of affairs was that total control was achieved by Augustus sometime after the second triumvirate in 32 BC, but before the time when Augustus handed back the *res publica* in his sixth and seventh consulships (28–27 BC).[23] However, the implication of the new fragment is that Augustus was already in total control, by universal consent, from the end of the civil wars in 31 BC.[24] This was because of his spectacular victory over Antony and Cleopatra at the battle of Actium in that year. The

---

[21] T. Mommsen, *Res Gestae Divi Augusti: Ex Monumentis Acyrano et Apolloniensi* (Berlin: Weidmann, 1883), lxxxxiv.

[22] The translation is Cooley, *Res Gestae*, 98. The aorist form (γενόμενος) of the Greek text of the *Res Gestae* (34.1: ἐνκρατὴς γενόμενος πάντων τῶν πραγμάτων ["although I was in control of all affairs"]) correctly translates the intention of the newly discovered fragment of the Latin text (34.1: *[po]tens re[r]um*). For discussion, see Judge, "The Crux of RG 34.1 Resolved?"; J.R. Harrison, "Augustan Rome and the Body of Christ: A Comparison of the Social Vision of the *Res Gestae* and Paul's Letter to the Romans," *HTR* 106.1 (2013): 1–36.

[23] J. Gagé, *Res Gestae Divi Augustae ex Monumentis Ancyrano et Antiocheno Latinis Ancyrano et Apolloniensi Graecis* (Paris: Les Belles Lettres, 1935), 144–45. H. Volkmann (*Res Gestae Divi AVGVSTI: Das Monumentum Ancyranum* [Berlin: Walter de Gruyter, 1969], 56) suggests this happened from 30 BC, whereas F.E. Adcock ("The Interpretation of *Res Gestae Divi Augusti*, 34.1," *CQ* 1 [1951]: 130–35) posits the date of 28 BC because of the renewed threat of civil war posed by Marcus Crassus' attainment of the *spolia opima* (Judge, "Augustus in the *Res Gestae*," 221).

[24] Note the comment of Scheid (*Res Gestae*, 86) regarding the significance of the new fragment of *Res Gestae* 34.1 from Antioch: "… un nouveau fragment de l'inscription d'Antioche … élimine définitivement *potitus* au profit de *potens*. Le *consensus universorum* constituera l'un des fondements du pouvoir impérial, et pour ainsi dire sa seule *légitimité* …".

imperial poets who singled out Actium as the providentially defining event in Augustus' rise to power, inaugurating thereby a "new age" of blessing for Rome, were correct in their propaganda.[25] Thus Augustus' return of the *res publica* – properly translated as "the public property" rather than "the state" or "the republic"[26] – to the senate and the Roman people in 27 BC acquires greater significance for our understanding of his honours and the overall nature of his rule. Augustus' divestment of his powers should be seen a sincere gesture on the part of the princeps as opposed to a cleverly staged and duplicitous concealment of his real powers, as Tacitus insinuates (*Ann.* 1.2). Furthermore, the honours given to Augustus in *Res Gestae* 34.2–35 not only celebrate the end of the civil war but also the re-establishment of constitutional propriety inaugurated by his divestment of his powers.[27] In Augustus' estimation (*Res Gestae* 34.2), therefore, the honours represent Rome's recognition of his pre-eminent merit (*quo pro merito*: "in return for this desert of mine" [tr. E.A. Judge]).[28] The most singular honour for Augustus is his acclamation as *pater patriae* (*Res Gestae* 35: "father of the fatherland"). As E.A. Judge observes, the new title "subjects everyone to a form of dependence, and elevates Augustus to a form of control ... founded upon personal and community relations rather than legal ones."[29]

Precisely because of his pre-eminent position, based on the universal consent of a war-weary public, Augustus could with legitimacy and without subterfuge claim about his rule: "After this time I excelled everyone in influence ([*a*]*uctoritate*), but I had no more power ([*potest*]*atis*) than the others who were my colleagues in each magistracy" (*Res Gestae* 34.3). Consequently, the *Res Gestae* is heavily weighted with the language of pre-eminence in ways that display continuity with the republican eulogistic tradition but which, because of the lavish excess of Augustus' achievements and honours, totally outstrip it.

A variety of techniques are employed in the inscription to highlight Augustus' personal supremacy. First, Augustus' relentless stress on primacy ("the first and only": *Res Gestae* 16.1; 'the first': 22.2; cf. 10.2; 12.1; 13; 26.4; 30.1; 31.1; 32.3; 34.3) underscores his superiority to his competitors, past and present. Second, Augustus' frequent use of superlatives and hyperbole in the *Res Gestae* points to how he excelled his contemporaries and created new precedents for posterity.[30] Third,

---

[25] For the evidence, see Harrison, *Paul and the Imperial Authorities*, 118–21.

[26] See Judge, "*Res Publica Restituta*"; Cooley, *Res Gestae*, 258.

[27] On *virtus*, *clementia*, *iustitia* and *pietas*, mentioned in *Res Gestae* 34.2, see E.S. Ramage, *The Nature and Purpose of Augustus' "Res Gestae"* (Stuttgart: Franz Steiner Verlag, 1987), 73–99.

[28] Cooley, *Res Gestae*, 260–61. F.W. Danker (*Benefactor: Epigraphic Study of a Graeco-Roman and New Testament Semantic Field* [St. Louis: Clayton Publishing House, 1982], 279) observes that there was no need to say anything extra regarding Augustus' merit other than the simple phrase "*pro merito meo*" because "his performance was the measure of his merit."

[29] Judge, "Augustus in the *Res Gestae*," 223.

[30] Examples from the *Res Gestae* are: "I have been the highest ranking member of the sen-

this is reinforced by phrases such as "under my authority" (28.2), "in my own name" (15.1; 22.1 [2x], 2, 3; 24.2), "under my auspices" (4.2; 26.5 ["under my command and auspices"]; 30.2), "as a private individual" (15.1), "with my own money" (17.1), "out of my personal assets" (17.2), "from my own granary and assets" (18), or "on my advice" (17.2). The accumulation of these expressions emphasises how Augustus considered his personal *auctoritas* ("influence") to be the real focus and impetus of his rule. Fourth, the frequent numerical catalogues detailing military victories (*Res Gestae* 3, 25), triumphs and thanksgivings (4), restoration of the Roman citizen body (8), donations to the plebs and veterans (15, 17), and games and spectacles (22) spotlight the unprecedented scope of Augustus' rule and beneficence.[31]

However, not only does Augustus surpass republican precedents in the *Res Gestae* – a focus, too, of the ideology of the *forum Augustum*[32] – but also he surpasses the luminaries of world history, with the expectation that he too, like his adoptive father Caesar, would be apotheosised. Augustus displays a clear consciousness in the *Res Gestae* that a "new age" for Rome had begun with his accession to rule, as the revealing phrases "before I was born" (13: *pr[iusquam] nascerer*) and "my era" (16.1: *aetatis meae*) demonstrate.[33] Another technique that Augustus employs is to emphasise implicitly how his achievements superseded the luminaries of the past: Romulus, Hercules, Alexander, Scipio Africanus, Pompey, Caesar, Antony and Cleopatra.[34] Augustus also engaged in (what might be called) "typology" by presenting the battle of Salamis in a public spectacle for the Roman people (*Res Gestae* 23) as a forerunner of his more glorious battle of Actium.[35] Moreover, the mausoleum of Augustus, with its Latin

ate until the very day on which I wrote this" (7.2); "from the whole of Italy a crowd, such as it is said had never before this time been at Rome, flooded together for my election" (10.1); "this honour has been decreed for no one except me up to this time" (12.1); "these handouts of mine never reached fewer than 250,000 men" (15.1); "I gave out distributions ... sometimes to 100,00 men, sometimes to many more" (18); "I neglected none which needed repair at this time" (20.4); "there were more than 700 senators ... among whom there were 83 who either before or afterwards up until the day on which these words were written were made consuls" (25.3); "the Pannonian peoples had never had an army of the Roman people come near them before I became leader" (30.1); "such as have not ever been seen before this time in the presence of any Roman general" (31.1); "while I have been leader very many other peoples have experienced the good faith of the Roman people ... previously no embassies or exchange of friendship had existed" (32.3).

[31] Ridley (*The Emperor's Retrospect*, 58–59) speaks of the "cataloguing quality" and "accounting vein" of the *Res Gestae*, as well as "Augustus' obsession with statistics and *aemulatio*" (*ibid.*, 116).

[32] See Harrison, *Paul and the Imperial Authorities*, 173–77.

[33] See Cooley, *Res Gestae*, 34, 158.

[34] Romulus: *Res Gestae* 4.1. Hercules: 10.1. Alexander: 21.1; 24.1; 26–33 (esp. 26.2; 31.1). Scipio Africanus: 1.1. Pompey: 1.1; 5.2; 20.1; 25.1; 26–33 (esp. 27.2; 31.2). Caesar: 4.1. Antony and Cleopatra 4.2; 27.2; 28.1–2. For the specific comparisons with Augustus, see Cooley, *Res Gestae, passim*.

[35] See Cooley, *Res Gestae*, 209–10.

original of the *Res Gestae*, might be seen as rivalling and surpassing the mausoleum of King Mausolos of Caria at Halicarnassos.[36] Last, as Bosworth argues, there are intimations of the hope of apotheosis in the inscription, even though Augustus is not claiming divine status while he was alive, given that the post-mortem deification of the ruler was the senate's prerogative.[37] In the Campus Martius, the spatial relationship between Augustus' mausoleum and the Agrippan Pantheon – with its statues of deities facing the mausoleum – also pointed symbolically to the possibility of future apotheosis.[38]

In spite of the exalted status of Augustus in the *Res Gestae* and the dynamism of his restoration of traditional values and practices, there remains in Augustus a reluctance to accept extraordinary honours and to act inconsistently with ancestral custom, despite considerable popular pressure to accept them. There is a paradox here, given that his adoptive father, Julius Caesar flouted republican convention in his rise to and maintenance of power. Moreover, there was a continuous demand on Augustus throughout his principate to conform to the expectations of a grateful and adulatory public. Why would Augustus make this "reluctance" such a feature of the *Res Gestae* when there was universal consensus from 31 BC that he "had power over everything" (*Res Gestae* 34.1)? What does it reveal about his understanding of his principate?

On two occasions in the *Res Gestae*, Augustus states that he declined the extraordinary powers offered to him ("I did not accept it": 5.1 [Velleius Paterculus 2.89.5; Suetonius *Aug.* 52]; 5.3 [Dio Cassius 54.6.1–3]). The first occasion was when he was offered the dictatorship, in absentia and then in person, by the senate and people in the consulship of Marcus Marcellus and Lucius Arruntius (*Res Gestae* 5.1: 22 BC). The second occasion was "when the consulship ... was conferred upon me at that time for a year and in perpetuity" (*Res Gestae* 5.3). Why would Augustus shrink back from these powers? In each case, Augustus

---

[36] Cooley, *Res Gestae*, 4.

[37] B. Bosworth, "Augustus, the *Res Gestae* and Hellenistic Theories of Apotheosis," *JRS* 89 (1999): 1–18. Although apotheosis of the ruler was the official prerogative of the Roman senate, there is iconographic evidence for apotheosis being attributed unofficially to members of the Julio-Claudian house (e.g. Caesar, Augustus, Germanicus). This type of material is clearly designed for the private consumption of the Julio-Claudian family members and their trusted *amici* ("friends"). On the gem and relief evidence for Julio-Claudian apotheosis, see L.J. Kreitzer, *Striking New Images: Roman Imperial Coinage and the New Testament World*, JSNTSup 134 (Sheffield: Sheffield Academic Press, 1996), 77 fig. 4, 79 fig. 5, 80 fig. 6; M. Beard, ed., et al., *Religions of Rome. Volume 1: A History* (Cambridge: Cambridge University Press, 1998), 187 fig. 4.3d.

[38] On the symbolic connection between the two circular buildings in the Campus Martius, Augustus' mausoleum and the Agrippan Pantheon, see Harrison, *Paul and the Imperial Authorities*, 115 n. 69. Augustus' modest house on the Palatine was also strategically placed adjacent to the temple of Apollo, Augustus' patron deity, and near to the hut of Romulus on the same hill, aligning the princeps with the gods and the birth of the city. See C. Edwards, *The Politics of Immorality in Rome* (Cambridge: Cambridge University Press, 1993), 167–68; A. Everitt, *Augustus: The Life of Rome's First Emperor* (New York: Augustus, 2006), 200–01.

resists public and senatorial expectations because, as he later explains (*Res Gestae* 6.1), he would accept no magistracy "that contravened ancestral custom." Augustus' acceptance of the dictatorship, given Julius Caesar's assassination as *dictator perpetuo* on the Ides of March (44 BC), would have invited a similar fate, whereas the perpetual consulship violated both the collegiality of the office and its annual tenure.[39]

But there are deeper reasons for Augustus' reluctance than the conventions associated with the *cursus honorum* in this instance. In a groundbreaking article, T. Hillard has argued that Augustus' reluctance finds its *exemplum* in the reluctance of Aeneas, as Virgil depicts him, in the *Aeneid*.[40] There the disconsolate and complaining Aeneas has to be cajoled and prodded to fulfil his divinely ordained destiny throughout his journey to Italy. Hillard's suggestion has merit, given that the Julian line of leaders in the statue program of the *forum Augustum* commences with the founder-figure of Aeneas (Ovid, *Fast.* 5.563–566).[41] The *exemplum* of personal reluctance, therefore, had, in terms of the Julian propaganda, ancestral precedent for Augustus.

But how did Augustus learn to overcome his reluctance? Hillard proposes an ideological solution to this problem. The *exemplum* of the "good king" in Hellenistic kingship theory,[42] with its emphasis on the ruler as a "caring" shepherd,[43] motivated Augustus to assume responsibility for the state. The Roman elite and their thinkers had long since been receptive to Greek culture and philosophy.[44] So, Augustus, overcoming his reluctance, dispelled the war-weariness of his generation by returning stability to Rome (cf. Ovid, *Carm.* 1.2).[45] I would add that Augustus' refusal to accept extraordinary honours also explains why he did not diminish the honours of other Romans by modifying their honorific monuments for his own self-promotion (*Res Gestae* 19.1; 20.1; cf. 24.2). As Hillard concludes, "The new mood required of Roman leadership moderation, even hesitancy, and something more than the quest of glory."[46] Thus the quest for ancestral glory, over which the republican luminaries had ripped apart the state, found its culmination in Augustus as the embodiment of

[39] Judge, "Augustus in the *Res Gestae*," 191.

[40] For discussion with references to Virgil's *Aeneid*, see Hillard, "Roman Concepts of Leadership," 114–20.

[41] See Harrison, *Paul and the Imperial Authorities*, 170–77.

[42] Hillard, "Roman Concepts of Leadership," 136–42. See also Harrison, *Paul and the Imperial Authorities*, 277–99.

[43] Hillard, "Roman Concepts of Leadership," 140. On the "shepherd" image, see Dio Chrysostom, *Or.* 1.12–13; 2.6; cf. 3.40–41; Ps-Ecphantus (Stob. 4.7.64 p. 276 He. *ll.* 1–5).

[44] Hillard, "Roman Concepts of Leadership," 137–40.

[45] Hillard, "Roman Concepts of Leadership," 142–43. Hillard (*ibid.*, 131–34, 135–36) also discusses republican examples of "reluctance" and suggests that the "new men" of late republican politics – the first of their family to attain the consulship – demonstrated an ethic of obligation to the state similar to that of Augustus.

[46] Hillard, "Roman Concepts of Leadership," 143.

a new type of glory:[47] that is, the paradox of the reluctant leader who assumed responsibility for the state in the time of crisis.

However, wedged between these two vignettes of "reluctance" (*Res Gestae* 5.1, 3) is another paradoxical vignette. In this case, Augustus "did *not* decline to manage the corn supply during a very severe grain shortage" (*Res Gestae* 5.2). The reason given for Augustus assuming the burden of state in this case is intriguing: "I administered it in such a way that within a few days I freed the entire community from pressing fear and danger (Latin: *metu et periclo praesenti*; Greek: [το]ῦ παρόντος φόβου καὶ κι[νδ]ύνου) through my expenditure and supervision." The terminology and ideology employed here resonates with motifs culled from traditional benefaction ideology: the "endangered" saviour-benefactor who delivers his dependents from "danger",[48] and the saviour-benefactor who steps into the breach in the "times of necessity".[49] It is worth remembering that Augustus devotes substantial space to his benefactions in *Res Gestae* 15–24. Thus, when *Res Gestae* 5.2 is considered within the context of 5.1 and 5.3, it is clear that Augustus' *auctoritas* ("influence") finds expression within his networks of patronage where the patron cares for his dependents,[50] notwithstanding the dangers and fears experienced by his clients, or his own reluctance to help initially.

In sum, what was innovative in this traditional construct was that Augustus, the benefactor of the world, had out-competed all his rivals, subjecting them to positions of dependence with its attendant rituals of reciprocity, for the benefit of the *res publica*. But, significantly, this was carried out overall within the framework of reluctance, where Augustus resisted popular demands to accept inappropriate honours, until he was eventually forced to act for the benefit of others by the pressing needs of the times. Augustus' resistance to acting as a *princeps*, preferring instead to be a "citizen on parity with the rest" (Velleius Paterculus 2.124.2), provided an unconventional and occasionally disconcerting portrait of the Roman ruler's conduct. The masses reacted against this perceived avoidance of leadership on Augustus' part by pressing ever greater honours

---

[47] See n. 4 *supra*.

[48] On the "endangered" benefactor, see Danker, *Benefactor*, 417–35.

[49] See J. R. Harrison, "Times of Necessity," *New Docs* 9 (2002): 7–8, §4. See also J. Reynolds, *Aphrodisias and Rome* (London: Society for the Promotion of Roman Studies, 1982), §§28, 30, 31.

[50] See Hillard, "Roman Concepts of Leadership," 141–42. Note, however, the comment of Judge ("Augustus in the *Res Gestae*", 191) on *Res Gestae* 5.2: "The stress upon the speed and personal cost of his solution may cover the fact that this post was also in effect a dictatorship under a less provocative title." Of Augustus' solution, P. A. Brunt and J. M. Moore (*Res Gestae Divi Augusti: The Achievements of the Divine Augustus* [Oxford and New York: Oxford University Press, 1967], 45) observe: "It is typical of Augustus' approach to running the state that he tried to solve a difficult problem by employing a remedy for which a Republican precedent existed, and only set up a novel organization after a long lapse of time, when it was shown that the earlier solution was not satisfactory."

upon him in 27 BC and 23 BC. However, the application of the positive models of the "endangered saviour-benefactor" and the Hellenistic caring "ruler-shepherd" to Augustan rule countered the implications of any long-term disinterest on the part of the Roman ruler.

Moreover, Augustus, in reproducing the reluctance of the fabled Aeneas and also the reluctance of two republican luminaries (Marius, Pompey),[51] gave the strategy a certain legitimation. It also explains why Augustus adopted such a tactical persona. It allowed the *princeps* to avoid making the fatal mistake of his adopted father, Julius Caesar, who ignored the boundaries of republican precedent and thereby provoked his own assassination. Alternatively, by adopting reluctance as a political strategy, Augustus avoided plunging the Roman state again into a new civil war again by precipitous and hubristic decisions. This was not a hypocritical ruse to gain even greater powers or to disguise the enormity of his current powers. Rather the life and continued rule of Augustus depended on his ability to walk the tightrope of being a merely a citizen among other citizens, while simultaneously outcompeting all rivals to the Julian house, and ensuring, as a cosmic benefactor, the continued welfare and preservation of the traditions of the Roman state and its people.

We turn now to the apocalyptic context (2 Cor 3:7–4:6) prefacing Paul's understanding of ministry in 2 Corinthians 4:7–18: what does it reveal about the apostle's strategies in building new communities of divine glory and grace across the Mediterranean basin?

3.2. The "Paradoxical" Paul: The Apocalyptic Interplay of Death, Life, and Glory in 2 Corinthians 4:7–18

3.2.1. The Polemical Context of the Pericope

In 2 Corinthians 4:7–18, which belongs to the larger literary unit of 2:13–7:4, Paul continues his response to the crisis in his relations with the Corinthians (1:15–2:12; 7:5–16). The pastoral crisis was precipitated by Paul's perceived inconsistency in visitation of his converts at Corinth (2 Cor 1:15–23; cf. 1 Cor 16:5–7) and by the local "wrongdoer" of 2 Cor 2:5–11 and 7:12 (ἕνεκεν τοῦ ἀδικήσαντος) who had publicly opposed Paul on his visit to Corinth on the way to Macedonia (1:16, 23).[52] The apostle penned the much-debated "letter of tears" in response (2 Cor 2:3–4, 9–11) and despatched Titus with the letter to intervene on his behalf at Corinth (2:12–13; 7:6–17). The crisis was also compounded by the ap-

[51] On the republican models of reluctance, see Hillard, "Roman Concepts of Leadership," 131–34.

[52] On the "wrongdoer", see the breakthrough work of L.L. Welborn, *An End to Enmity: Paul and the "Wrongdoer" of Second Corinthians* (Berlin and Boston: Walter de Gruyter, 2011).

pearance of the interloping opponents of 2 Cor 3:1b at the city. They had brought letters of recommendation from unidentified churches (3:1b; cf. 10:12a),[53] expecting similar commendation from the Corinthians (3:1b), with a view to establishing a counter-mission to Paul and his gospel (11:12b), violating thereby not only his apostolic jurisdiction (10:12–18) but also challenging his apostolic authority (10:7–11).[54] Arguably, the intruders exhibited "judaising" tendencies in their ministry (3:6b–7, 9a, 10a, 11a; cf. 11:22),[55] though without any stated

---

[53] P. Barnett (*The Second Epistle to the Corinthians* [Grand Rapids: Eerdmans, 1997], 163) postulates a Palestinian provenance for the intruders: "Possibly the source of recommendation lay with Greek-speaking members of the Pharisaic brotherhoods who were within the orbits of the churches of Judaea and who were profoundly disturbed by what appeared to be antinominian emphases in Paul's Gentile mission." Contra, B. Witherington III (*Conflict and Community in Corinth: A Socio-Rhetorical commentary on 1 and 2 Corinthians* [Grand Rapids: Eerdmans, 1995], 383), who argues for a Hellenistic provenance: "... they were Jewish, perhaps Jewish Christian, itinerant preachers who arrived in Corinth ... and ... drew on their Jewish heritage and on Hellenistic Jewish apologetics to win over the Corinthians." Similarly, V.P. Furnish, *II Corinthians* (New York: Doubleday, 1984), 53–54.

[54] Barnett, *Corinthians*, 163.

[55] On the "judaising" tendencies of the interlopers (2 Cor 3:1b), see D.W. Oostendorp, *Another Jesus: A Gospel of Jewish-Christian Superiority in II Corinthians* (Kampen: J.H. Kok, 1967), 80; C.C. Newman, *Paul's Glory-Christology: Tradition and Rhetoric*, NovTSup 69 (Leiden: E.J. Brill, 1992), 23; Barnett, *Corinthians*, 160–61; M.J. Harris, *The Second Epistle to the Corinthians* (Grand Rapids: Eerdmans, 2005), 85–87. Contra, D. Georgi, *The Opponents of Paul in Second Corinthians* (Edinburgh: T&T Clark, 1987), *passim*; M.E. Thrall, *The Second Epistle to the Corinthians. Volume I: I–VII* (Edinburgh: T&T Clark, 1994), 238–39, 241–42. Whether the interlopers are to be identified with the "super-apostles" of 2 Corinthian 10–13 (10:10–12; 11:3–5, 12–15, 18–22; 12:11) depends, among many issues, on whether (a) one views 2 Corinthians as a unity or not (for varying positions, see F. Young and D.F. Ford, *Meaning and Truth in 2 Corinthians* [Grand Rapids: Eerdmans, 1987], 27–59; Thrall, *II Corinthians*, 3–49; D.E. Garland, *2 Corinthians* [Nashville: Broadman & Holman, 1999], 33–44; Harris, *Corinthians*, 8–51; Welborn, *An End to Enmity*, xxix–xxviii); (b) whether the "letter of tears" (2 Cor 2:3–4, 9–11) is to be identified with 2 Corinthians 10–13, (c) whether 2:14–7:4 precedes or comes after 10–13, and, last, (d) the force of the aorist verbs in 12:18 in relation to the earlier references to Titus' visits to Corinth (2 Cor 8:17–18, 22; cf. 2:13; 7:6–7, 14–15: Harris, *Corinthians*, 39–40). The position taken in this chapter is that 2 Cor 1–9 precedes 10–13, with 10–13 having been written after the apostle received news of a renewed deterioration of affairs at Corinth after the reconciliation effected in 7:4–16. Thus 2 Cor 10--13 is either (a) second letter of Paul written in response to the news and subsequently attached to 1–9 by a later editor (Thrall, *II Corinthians*, 45–47), or (b) a rhetorical tour-de-force added by the apostle when he, having just finished writing his letter of reconciliation (2 Cor 1–9), received the news of renewed conflict at Corinth (F.F. Bruce, *1 and 2 Corinthians* [London: Oliphants, 1971], 169; Witherington, *Corinthians*, 336–39; Garland, *Corinthians*, 41–42). In a presentation at Macquarie University Ancient History Department in 2016 ("Papyrus Letters and Paul of Tarsus as Authentic Letter Writer"), Professor Peter Arzt-Grabner, from the Paris Lodron Universität, Salzburg (Austria), argued that the dramatic shifts in emotional tone seen in a single III AD cent. private letter from Alexandria (?) (P. Oxy. VII 1070) throw comparative rhetorical light on what might be happening in the transition from 2 Corinthians 1–9 to 10–13, assuming that the letter is a unity. In my opinion, the interlopers of 2 Corinthians 3:1b are probably to be identified with the super-apostles of 10–13, though the depth of the threat posed by them only became apparent when Titus had left Corinth, having effected what he

emphasis on circumcision, food laws, or the Sabbath.[56] However, they also embraced prominent Graeco-Roman values in their emphasis on *synkrisis* ("comparison": 10:12; 11:12b ["those who want an opportunity to be considered equal with us"]), boasting (10:12 ["some who commend themselves"]; 11:12b, 18, 21b), their commitment to rhetorical accomplishment (10:10b; 11:6a), and, finally, their sophistic practice of accepting monetary support (2:17; cf. 1 Cor 4:12a; 9:3–19; 2 Cor 12:14–16a). While caution has to be exercised in terms of "mirror-reading" the rhetoric of 2 Corinthians,[57] it is nevertheless likely that Paul's Corinthian detractors and the interlopers denigrated the apostle's character. He was probably depicted as an inconsistent and incompetent apostle (1:17; 3:5–6), lacking heart (4:1, 16), boldness (3:12; 7:4), and confidence (5:6; 5:8),[58] displaying insincerity (1:12; 2:17),[59] going about with cunning (4:2),[60] and adulterating the word of God (2:17; 4:2).[61]

How, then, does Paul rebut this ferocious attack in 2 Corinthians 3:1–4:6?

3.2.2. Paul's Use of "Glory" and "Creation" Motifs as Theological Descriptors of Apostolic Ministry in 2 Corinthians 3:1–4:6

In response to the Corinthian interlopers, Paul highlights the ever-increasing glory of the ministry of the new covenant of the Spirit and the concentration of glory in the risen Christ and Lord of all. The apostle contrasts the corporate transformation effected by the Spirit "from one degree of glory to another" with the "fading" (or "inoperative") glory of the intruders' ministry of death under the old covenant (2 Cor 3:4–18).[62] Confronting apocalyptic and targum-

---

had optimistically hoped would be a lasting reconciliation between the apostle and his converts (C. K. Barrett, *The Second Epistle to the Corinthians* [London: A & C Black, 1973], 107). However, the problem was more serious than Titus recognised.

[56] J. Lambrecht, *Second Corinthians* (Collegeville: Michael Glazier, 1999), 7; Witherington, *Corinthians*, 346.

[57] Furnish (*II Corinthians*, 50) writes: "One must not presume that every point made by Paul is designed to counter a point made by his rivals."

[58] 2 Cor 4:1: οὐκ ἐγκακοῦμεν; 4:16: οὐκ ἐγκακοῦμεν. 2 Cor 3:12: πολλῇ μοι παρρησίᾳ; 7:4: πολλῇ παρρησία. 2 Cor 5:6: θαρροῦντες; 5:8: θαρροῦμεν. This use of repetition throughout 2 Cor 1–7, while rhetorical, may also reflect repeated charges made against Paul.

[59] 2 Cor 1:12: ἐν ἁπλότητι καὶ εἰλικρινείας. 2 Cor 2:17: ἐξ εἰλικρινείας.

[60] 2 Cor 4:2: ἐν πανουργίᾳ

[61] 2 Cor 2:17: καπηλεύοντες τὸν λόγον τοῦ θεοῦ; 4:2: μηδὲ δολοῦντες τὸν λόγον τοῦ θεοῦ. S. Kim (*The Origin of Paul's Gospel* [Grand Rapids: Eerdmans, 1982], 233) argues regarding 2 Cor 4:2–3: "They also accused Paul of distorting the gospel by not requiring the Gentile converts to observe the law of Moses (4:2). They said that such a gospel was 'veiled' (4:3), meaning that it was unintelligible because it cut itself loose from God's revelation given to Moses on Sinai."

[62] For general discussion, see C. K. Stockhausen, *Moses' Veil and the Glory of the New Covenant* (Rome: Pontificio Istituto Biblico, 1989); S. J. Hafemann, *Paul, Moses, and the History of Israel: The Letter/Spirit Contrast and the Argument from Scripture in 2 Corinthians 3* (Peabody: Hendrickson, 1996).

like traditions about the unceasing and ever-increasing glory of the Mosaic law at Sinai,[63] Paul employs two christological arguments about the glory of Christ in 2 Corinthians 3:17–4:6: one brings new interpretative dimensions to his exegesis of LXX Exodus 34 (2 Cor 3:7–16), whereas the other pertains to the ongoing outcome of his Damascus road conversion experience in relation to his ministry (4:4, 6). In each case, Paul's comments regarding the glory of Christ outstripped traditional apocalyptic expectations.[64]

First, in 2 Corinthians 3:17a, Paul depicts the risen and ascended Christ, who is the "Lord" of the new covenant of the "Spirit" (3:3, 6, 8, 17a, 18b; 4:5; cf. Ezek 36:27; Jer 31:33), as "both the revelation and the revealer of God."[65] Paul explains this paradox more fully in 2 Corinthians 3:18. There the glory of the Lord (2 Cor 3:18a: τὴν δόξαν κυρίου) is set within the apocalyptic context of the ultimate revelation of the glory of Christ at the eschaton (3:18c: ἀπὸ δόξης εἰς δόξαν; 4:17–18).[66] The phrase εἰς δόξαν ("to glory": 2 Cor 3:18b), however, heralds the

[63] Note 4 *Ezra* 9.37: "… the Law, however, does not perish but remains in its glory." Cf. 2 Esd 3.19; 1 *En.* 99:2 (cf. 5:4; 99:14). See L.L. Belleville, *Reflections of Glory: Paul's Polemical Use of the Moses-Doxa Tradition in 2 Corinthians 3:1–18*, JSNTSup 52 (Sheffield: Sheffield Academic, 1991), 24–79, esp. 26–30. Hafemann (*Paul*, 287–313) argues that Belleville is incorrect in asserting that some traditions in Second Temple Judaism (Philo, Pseudo-Philo, etc.) espoused a "fading" glory on Moses' face (Belleville, *Reflections of Glory*, 31–35, 40–43, 63–72). Consequently, Hafemann proposes that Paul's use of τὴν καταργουμένην in 2 Cor 3:7 should be translated "which was being rendered inoperative" (alternatively, "which was being abolished": thus Barnett, *Corinthians*, 183 n. 23; Garland, *2 Corinthians*, 173–76), as opposed to "the [glory] [which] is fading" (Harris, *Corinthians*, 284–85; P.E. Hughes, *The Second Epistle to the Corinthians* [Grand Rapids: Eerdmans, 1962], 103–04).

[64] On the complex question of the definition of "apocalyptic," the reader is referred to J.J. Collins, "What is Apocalyptic Literature?" in *The Oxford Book of Apocalyptic Literature*, ed. J.J. Collins (Oxford: Oxford University Press, 2014), 1–16, and the literature cited in pp. 14–16. In saying that Paul has "apocalyptic" dimensions to his exegesis, I am not denying Paul's sharp exegetical focus on the LXX text of Exodus 34. See W.J. Dumbrell, "Paul's Use of Exodus 34 in 2 Corinthians 34," in *God Who is Rich in Mercy*, ed. P.T. O'Brien and D.G. Peterson (Homebush West: Lancer, 1986), 179–94.

[65] C.H. Giblin, *In Hope of God's Glory* (New York: Herder and Herder, 1970), 214–15. 2 Corinthians 3:16–17a remains one of the most hotly debated Pauline texts of the New Testament. The κύριος in vv. 16 and 17a has been viewed as referring either to God or Christ. For extensive discussion, see Thrall, *II Corinthians*, 278–82 and Harris, *Corinthians*, 309–12. The position taken in this chapter is that κύριος refers to Christ, following G. Theissen (*Psychological Aspects of Pauline Theology* [Edinburgh: T&T Clark, 1987], 129–30, esp. 130 n. 5), D.B. Capes (*Old Testament Yahweh Texts in Paul's Christology*, WUNT II 47 [Tübingen: Mohr Siebeck, 1992], 155–57), G.D. Fee (*Pauline Christology: An Exegetical-Theological Study* [Peabody: Hendrickson, 2007], 177–80) and L.W. Hurtado (*God in New Testament Theology* [Nashville: Abingdon, 2010], 91–93).

[66] Giblin (*In Hope of God's Glory*, 215; cf. Harris, *Corinthians*, 317) writes: "The change from "glory to glory" (v. 18) we may best construe in the over-all eschatological context of Paul's thought as a reference to the ultimate manifestation of Christ at the parousia, the realization of the new creation." Barnett (*Corinthians*, 208) also notes: "Unlike the glory of Moses, which was veiled because it was eschatologically circumscribed ('abolished'), the glory from the Lord is endless and ultimately infinite, as glorious as God himself." In regards to "higher"

final metamorphosis of believers to Christ's body of glory at the eschaton, a perspective found elsewhere in Paul (1 Cor 15:49; Phil 3:21; Col 3:4).[67] The eschatological shift that had occurred in terms of salvation history (2 Cor 6:2: ἰδοὺ νῦν … ἰδοὺ νῦν; cf. 3:14b) meant that the Sinaitic glory (Exod 34; cf. 2 Cor 3:7–16) had been abolished by the superior revelation of the risen and ascended Lord of glory.[68] Paul's christological reinterpretation of LXX Exodus 34 and the pseudepigraphic "glory" traditions not only reconfigured their eschatological focus from the future to the present,[69] but also located the source and culmination of divine glory in Christ as the risen and returning Lord.

Second, Paul's Christophany experience is further illustrated by "creation" motifs from Genesis – 2 Cor 4:4b ("Christ, who is the image of God": Gen 1:28) and 4:6a ("God who said 'Let light shine out of darkness'": Gen 1:3; cf. Isa 9:2) – which point to the inauguration of the new creation in Christ (2 Cor 5:17; cf. Gal 6:15).[70] For Paul, the intruders' ministry of death had been eclipsed by the new creation established by the ἀποκαλύψις of the all-glorious Father in the Lord of glory (cf. 1 Cor 2:8: τὸν κύριον τῆς δόξης). Christ, as the "image of God" (2 Cor 4:4b: εἰκὼν τοῦ θεοῦ), revealed the pristine glory of the pre-fall Adam, a "creation" motif discussed in the apocalyptic literature.[71] Furthermore, the passage points forward to how Christ, as the last Adam, would become a life-giving Spirit (1 Cor 15:45; 2 Cor 3:17–18).

In sum, the revelation of the eschatological glory of Christ, currently beheld reflected in a mirror (2 Cor 3:18b), but anticipating the immeasurable weight of eternal glory (4:17b), expresses the Lordship of Christ, the content of the apos-

stages of glory (2 Cor 3:18b: εἰς δόξαν), R.P. Martin (*2 Corinthians* [Waco: Word, 1986], 72) cites 2 Bar 51.3, 7, 10.

[67] Barnett, *Corinthians*, 320.

[68] J.-F. Collange, *Enigmes de la deuxième épître de Paul aux Corinthiens*, SNTSMS 18 (Cambridge: Cambridge University Press, 1972), 76.

[69] The apocalyptic and pseudepigraphic texts refer to "glory" in these contexts: Glory of God: 2 Esd 3.19; 1 *En.* 27.5; 36.4; 50.4; 55.4; 75.3; 81.3; *Sib. Or.* 4.30; *Gk. Apoc. Ezra* 6.9–10; *Apoc. El. (H)* 1.3, 5; 3 *Bar.* 16.4; *T. Levi* 18.6. Angels of glory: *T. Levi* 18.5; *Apoc. Ab.* 19.4. Throne of glory: 2 Esd 8.21; 1 *En.* 45.3; 47.3; *Apoc. Ab.* 19.4. Garments of glory: 1. *En.* 62.16; 63.6; 4 *Ezra* 2.40; *T. Jac.* 7.25. Glory of the Temple: *T. Levi* 18.6. Glory of the priesthood: *Apoc. Ab.* 25.4. Glory of the Mosaic law: 4 *Ezra* 9.37. Eschatological glory: 2 Esd 8.49; 4 *Ezra* 2.37; 8.49; 2 *Bar.* 51.16; 54.16; 3 *Bar.* 16.4.

[70] See the profusion of apocalyptic texts cited by D.S. Russell (*The Method and Message of Jewish Apocalyptic 200 BC–AD 100* [London: SCM, 1964], 282, 293) relating to the original creation predating Adam's fall and the new eschatological creation. For discussion and texts, see Rowland, *The Open Heaven*, *s.v.* Index of Subjects, "Creation"; Hafemann, "Paul's Argument", 300 n. 44.

[71] For the Jewish texts, see R. Scroggs, *The Last Adam: A Study in Pauline Anthropology* (Philadelphia: Fortress, 1966), 23–29; Harrison, *Paul and the Imperial Authorities*, 239. See also the exhaustive coverage of Adam traditions in C.M. Pate (*Adam Christology as the Exegetical and Theological Substructure of 2 Corinthians 4:7–5:21* [Lanham: University Press of America, 1991]), though Pate's argument for a full-scale Adam-Christology undergirding 2 Corinthians 4:7–5:10, in my opinion, over-interprets this Pauline pericope.

tolic proclamation (4:5b). This spectacular revelation of the reigning Lord of the new covenant and of the new creation (2 Cor 3:17–18; 4:6a) reduces all believers, including the apostles themselves, to the status of "slaves", who are summoned to serve their fellow-believers for the sake of Christ (4:5). The self-commending intruders (2 Cor 3:1–3; cf. 10:12–17), who appeal to an obsolete revelation, are in reality a spent force.

How, then, did Paul's apocalyptic eschatology inform his understanding of apostolic ministry? We turn to a discussion of 2 Corinthians 4:7–18 in its Jewish apocalyptic context.

3.2.3. Redefining the Apocalyptic Contours of Ministry in Light of the Death and Resurrection of Christ

It is worth remembering that Jewish apocalyptic "thrives on the paradoxical assurance that divine deliverance is guaranteed to take place in defiance of the present historical phenomena."[72] There is a polemical and rhetorical intent on Paul's part in playing up the paradoxical dimension of his apostolic ministry in 2 Corinthians 4:7–18. Paul's opponents probably depicted the apostle as "an inglorious suffering figure, a living denial of the fulfilment eschatology he had preached in Corinth."[73] How does apocalyptic literature view the ministry and ethics of the righteous who are undergoing suffering and experiencing opposition from their opponents? In what ways does Paul's perspective differ? The "ministry" perspective of apocalyptic literature is little discussed by scholars, with the focus of scholarship being on ethics,[74] but there is enough background evidence to situate Paul's attitude to the paradox of suffering in ministry within an apocalyptic context.

At the outset, there is a strong link between ethics and the final judgement in apocalyptic literature (cf. 2 Cor 5:9–10). This is understood in terms of God reciprocating the piety of his saints in the eschatological kingdom (e.g. *T. Jac.* 7.10–28), or his saints being exhorted to do good works with the promise of present and future reward (e.g. 4 *Ezra* 2.15–32; 2 *En.* 63.1 [J]). Given the pessimistic evaluation of the present evil age in apocalyptic thought (e.g. 4 *Ezra* 4.26–32; 2 *Bar.* 21.19–25 etc.),[75] what indications are there of practical pastoral concern for the suffering righteous remnant in apocalyptic literature?

---

[72] M. Bockmuehl, *Revelation and Mystery in Ancient Judaism and Pauline Christianity* (Grand Rapids: Eerdmans, 1990), 27. On the eschatology of our text, see J. Lambrecht, "The Eschatological Outlook in 2 Corinthians 4:7–15," in *To Tell the Mystery: Essays on New Testament Eschatology in Honor of Robert H. Gundry*, JSNTSup 100, ed. T.E. Schmidt and M. Silva (Sheffield: JSOT, 1994), 122–39.

[73] Barnett, *Corinthians*, 160 n.2. Paul, however, commends his suffering: 2 Cor 1:3–11; 2:14–17; 4:7–12; 6:3–10; 11:16–12:21; 13:4, 9.

[74] Russel, *Jewish Apocalyptic*, 100–03; Rowland, *The Open Heaven*, 133–35.

[75] Russel (*Jewish Apocalyptic*, 101), while acknowledging the emphasis on social and di-

Two examples will suffice. First, amidst the afflictions of the present age, Ezra is instructed to rebuke, comfort, and instruct his people, while continuing to renounce the corruption and the burdens of a world held captive by sin (4 *Ezra* 14.13–16). Second, a more paradoxical construction, approaching the tenor of 2 Corinthians 4:7–18, is found in 2 *En.* 66.6–8 [J]:

Walk, my children,
in long-suffering,
in meekness | honesty |,
in affliction,
in distress,
in faithfulness,
in truth,
in hope,
in weakness,
in derision,
in assaults,
in temptation,
in deprivation,
in nakedness,
having love for one another, until you go out from this age of suffering, so that you may become inheritors of the never-ending age. How happy are the righteous who shall escape the Lord's great judgement; for they shall be made to shine seven times brighter than the sun. For in that age everything is estimated sevenfold – light and darkness, and food and enjoyment and paradise and tortures | fire, frost, et cetera |.

Here we see a series of (what might be loosely called) "apocalyptic antinomies" that illustrate both the difficulty of and the paradigm for God's people walking in godliness in the present age.[76] The experience of the saints in this "age of suffering" (long-suffering, affliction, distress, weakness, derision, assaults, temptation, deprivation, nakedness) finds its counterpoint in the godly lifestyle (meekness, faithfulness, truth, hope) that emanates from the proper worship of God (cf. 2 *En.* 66.1–2). The surety of the saints inheriting the "never-ending age" and escaping God's "great judgement" is reinforced for the readers by the subsequent narrative of Enoch's ascension to heaven (2 *En.* 67.1–68.4).[77] What is intriguing about our text is its pastoral perspective, inculcating the ethos of communal love, but framed within the Jewish apocalyptic worldview of the "two ages."[78] Last,

vine righteousness in apocalyptic literature, nonetheless states: "So concerned were they, however, with the fast-approaching End that eschatology, not ethics, was their consuming interest."

[76] On "apocalyptic antinomies" in Paul, see J.L. Martyn, *Theological Issues in the Letters of Paul* (Edinburgh: T&T Clark, 1997), 111–23. Note the link of the "walking" motif in 2 *En.* 66.5 (cf. 67–68) with MT Gen 5:24a (*pace*, LXX Gen 5:24a: "Enoch was well-pleasing [εὐηρέστησεν] to God").

[77] On the transcendence of death in apocalyptic eschatology, see J.J. Collins, *Seers, Sibyls, and Sages in Hellenistic-Roman Judaism* (Leiden: Brill, 1997), 75–97.

[78] Garland (*Corinthians*, 227 n. 572) cites *T. Jos.* 1.3b–7 as background to 2 Cor 4:10–12, but

the stark apocalyptic antinomy between "light"/"darkness" and "paradise"/"torture" highlights the necessity of walking rightly with God, as Enoch did (Gen 5:24a), in order to be vindicated at the "Lord's great judgement". How, then, is Paul's understanding of ministry in 2 Corinthians 4:7–18 different to and consonant with the apocalyptic hope of Second Temple Judaism?

G. Theissen has argued that Paul speaks about his apostolic office in two ways in 2 Corinthians 2:14–6:10. Initially, Paul presents a "theology of glory" throughout 3:1–4:6 and, subsequently, a "theology of the cross" in 4:7–6:10. This is illustrated by the paradoxes punctuating 2:14–4:6 and 4:7–6:10 (2:14–16a; 4:7–12; 6:3–10) and by the "reconciliation" motif of 5:14–21.[79] In commencing 2 Corinthians 4:7–12, Paul speaks of his apostolic weakness in 2 Corinthians 4:7a (cf. 11:16–12:10; 13:4). The glorious treasure of the knowledge of God in the gospel of Christ (2 Cor 4:4, 6) was placed in "earthen vessels" (4:7a: ἐν ὀστρακίνοις σκεύεσιν), which, because of their fragility and cheapness, were expendable, though their contents were of incalculable value to God.[80] Nonetheless, it was always God's intention (2 Cor 4:7b: ἵνα) to show that the excess of divine power (4:7b: ἡ ὑπερβολὴ τῆς δυνάμεως), revealed in the sufferings of the apostles, originated with God alone (4:7b: μὴ ἐξ ἡμῶν).

Strikingly, Paul connects the paradox of apostolic ministry in 2 Corinthians 4:8–12 with the soteriological career of Christ in the present age. The "dying and rising with Christ" motif gives the passage its pastoral and theological coherence, uniting the "theology of the cross" with the "theology of glory" in complementary antitheses.[81] The antithetical structure of the "dying and rising" motif in vv. 8–12 is set out below:

"Dying with Christ"			"Rising with Christ"	
v. 8	in every [way] [we are]			
		hard-pressed	but not	crushed,
		at a loss	but not	at wit's end,
v. 9		persecuted	but not	forsaken,
		struck down	but not	destroyed,
v. 10	always			
		carrying about the dying of Jesus in the body,	so that also	the life of Jesus may be manifested in our body.

it lacks the apocalyptic perspective of the "two ages" found in 2 *En.* 66.6–8 [J]. Similarly, *T. Jos.* 1.1–7: see Russel, *Apocalyptic*, 101.

[79] I have slightly adapted Theissen's suggestion (*ibid.*). Notwithstanding the dominant "theology of the cross" found throughout 2 Corinthians 4:7–6:10, the "glory" motif still continues to appear in 4:7–18 (vv. 15b, 17b).

[80] For discussion, see Barnett, *Corinthians*, 230 n. 12; Thrall, *Corinthians*, 322–25.

[81] S.J. Hafemann, *2 Corinthians* (Grand Rapids: Zondervan, 2000), 186. On the "dying and rising" motif in 2 Corinthians 4:7–12, see R.C. Tannehill, *Dying and Rising with Christ: A Study in Pauline Theology* (Berlin: Alfred Töpelmann, 1966), 84–90.

v. 11	For always		
	we, who are alive,		
	are being handed over to death		
	because of Jesus,	so that also	the life of Jesus may be manifested in our mortal flesh.
v. 12	death is at work in us,	but	life in you.

Scholars have discussed in depth the meaning of the participles in vv. 8–9, along with the provenance of the "peristasis" catalogue itself, so further comment is not necessary.[82] But Barnett and Savage are correct in highlighting that there is probably a cumulative weight or progression in intensity of the physical and spiritual afflictions listed in the two verses.[83] However, in contrast to the apocalyptic worldview of 2 Enoch, the sufferings of the apostles are understood not in light of the career of Enoch who walked with God, but rather in light of the career of the crucified and risen Christ. Christ's "dying" (2 Cor 4:10a: τὴν νέκρωσιν τοῦ Ἰησοῦ) is experienced in the sufferings of his apostles (4:8–9: "hard-pressed", "at a loss", "persecuted", "struck down").[84] As with their Lord on the cross, the apostles are handed over by God in the present age to death (2 Cor 4:11a: παραδιδόμεθα),[85] precisely because of their costly commitment to the crucified Christ and his dependents (4:11a: διὰ Ἰησοῦν; cf. Mk 8:34 *et par.*; Rom 8:36; 1 Cor 15: 30–31; 2 Cor 1:8–9; 4:15a: τὰ γὰρ πάντα δι᾽ ὑμᾶς; 11:28–29; 12:19b: ὑπὲρ τῆς ὑμῶν οἰκοδομῆς; Gal 6:14; Col 1:24).[86] However, the dying of Christ has become for Paul an "apocalyptic" power "at work" in the lives of the apostles (2 Cor 4:12a: ὁ θάνατος ἐν ἡμιν ἐνεργεῖται; cf. 4:10a: τὴν νέκρωσιν τοῦ

---

[82] On the Cynic-Stoic diatribe, see R. Bultmann, *The Second Letter to the Corinthians* (Minneapolis: Augsburg, 1976), 113; J. T. Fitzgerald, *Cracks in an Earthen Vessel: An Examination of the Catalogue of Hardships in the Corinthian Correspondence*, SBLSS 99 (Atlanta: Scholars Press, 1988), 166–80; Witherington, *Corinthians*, 388–89; F. W. Danker (*II Corinthians* (Minneapolis: Augsburg, 1989), 67; Thrall, *Corinthians*, 329–31. In terms of *apocalyptic* Judaism, T. B. Savage (*Power Through Weakness: Paul's Understanding of the Christian Ministry in 2 Corinthians*, SNTSMS 86 [Cambridge: Cambridge University Press, 1996], 170) cites 1 *En.* 103.9–15 and 2 *En.* 66.6.

[83] Barnett, *Corinthians*, 233; Savage, *Power Through Weakness*, 171.

[84] For speculation regarding the context of Paul's afflictions mentioned in 2 Corinthians 4:7–12, see A. E. Harvey, *Renewal Through Suffering: A Study of 2 Corinthians* (Edinburgh: T&T Clark, 1996), 57. More generally, see J. Lambrecht, "The *nekrōsis* of Jesus: Ministry and Suffering in 2 Cor 4:7–15," in *L'Apôtre Paul*, ed. A. Vanhoye et al. (Leuven: Uitgeverij Peeters, 1986), 120–43.

[85] Garland, *Corinthians*, 232. Thrall (*Corinthians*, 336) argues that παραδιδόμεθα (2 Cor 4:11) is a divine passive that relates the apostle's sufferings to those of Jesus (παραδίδωμι: Mark 9:31; 10:33; 14:18, 21; Rom 4:25; 8:32; 1 Cor 11:23; Gal 2:20).

[86] On the force of διὰ Ἰησοῦν (2 Cor 4:11a), see Furnish, *Corinthians*, 257. See also P. E. Hughes, *The Second Epistle to the Corinthians* (Grand Rapids: Eerdmans, 162), 141–42. Regarding τὰ γὰρ πάντα δι᾽ ὑμᾶς (2 Cor 4:15a), Plummer (*Corinthians*, 134) observes: "All things that the Apostles and others do and suffer, as recounted in vv. 7–13, are done and suffered, not for their own benefit, but for that of their converts, and through their converts, not to their own glory, but to the glory of God."

Ἰησοῦ ἐν τῷ σώματι ἡμῶν περιφέροντες). God's extraordinary power is revealed in the weakness of the apostles, not only supporting them in the midst of their own affliction (2 Cor 1:10–11; 13:4b; cf. 1 Cor 1:25b; Gal 1:4), but also transforming others though the ministry that emanates from their affliction (4:12b: cf. 2 Cor 13:3, 4b, 9).

Thus "this age of suffering", to borrow the language of 2 Enoch 66.7, has been invaded by the superior power of the weak and crucified Christ, changing radically how suffering is to be understood in the present age by believers (2 Cor 1:3–7; 13:4). This novel element of early Christian belief has little precedent in apocalyptic Judaism, though Paul does appeal the example of the righteous sufferer of the Psalms as a pointer to how God would vindicate in Christ his suffering apostles (2 Cor 4:13–14: Ps 116:10 [LXX 115:10]).[87] He also possibly alludes to the suffering servant of Isaiah in 2 Corinthians 4:5 (4:5b: ἑαυτοὺς δὲ δούλους ὑμῶν διὰ Ἰησοῦν) and, more certainly, in 6:2 (LXX Isa 49:8).[88]

However, concomitant with the soteriological power of the cross in the present is the resurrection power of Jesus exhibited in the present and future age. Here we are witnessing the creative tension between the "already" of realised eschatology in Christ and the "not yet" of his glorious arrival at the eschaton. The former motif is another distinctive element of early Christian belief, marking off Paul's gospel from the apocalyptic tradition of the ascension of Enoch who, without dying, went to be with God (Gen 5:24; 2 *En*. 67.1–68.4). But it is precisely because Christ has poured out his life in death on behalf of others that God intervened in advance of the eschaton to vindicate his Son and his dependents. Indeed, the reality of death preceding the inauguration of resurrection age is strongly emphasised with Paul's phrase "our mortal flesh" (2 Cor 4: 11b; cf. 4:16b: "even though our outer nature is wasting away").[89] But Paul emphasises that the eschatological power of Jesus' resurrection is "at work" in the present age through God's physical and spiritual deliverance of his apostles from afflic-

[87] See Young and Ford, *Meaning and Truth*, 64–67; G.K. Beale, *A New Testament Biblical Theology: The Understanding of the Old Testament in the New* (Grand Rapids: Baker, 2011), 268–69.

[88] See Martin, *Corinthians*, 79–80; Pate, *Adam Christology*, 90–96; Garland, *Corinthians*, 304–05. P. Balla ("2 Corinthians," in *Commentary on the New Testament Use of the Old Testament*, ed. G.K. Beale and D.A. Carson [Grand Rapids: Baker, 2007], 768) writes regarding 2 Corinthians 6:2: "We cannot know whether the Corinthians could recall the context of the verse quoted from Isa. 49, but for Paul it may be a pointer to how he saw his ministry: he probably regarded Jesus as the "Servant" and saw himself called into the ministry of this Servant." See also L.J. Windsor, *Paul and the Vocation of Israel: How Paul's Jewish Identity Informs His Apostolic Ministry, With Special Reference to Romans*, BZNW 205 (Berlin and Boston: De Gruyter, 2014), 102, 104. Pace, on 2 Corinthians 6:2, see the more reserved position of M. Gignilliat, *Paul and Isaiah's Servants: Paul's Theological Reading of Isaiah 40–66 in 2 Corinthians 5:14–6:10*, LNTS 330 (London and New York: T&T Clark, 2007), regarding Paul's identification with the Isaianic servant.

[89] Thrall (*Corinthians*, 336) writes: "The replacement of ἐν τῷ σώματι by ἐν τῇ θνητῇ σαρκὶ ἡμῶν emphasises the weakness and mortality of earthly life."

tion (2 Cor 4:8–9: the fourfold ἀλλ' οὐκ ["but not"]; 4:11b; cf. 4:1, 16a: "we do not lose heart"; 4:16c: "our inner nature is being renewed day by day"; 6:9b: "as dying and behold we live").

Furthermore, the continuous experience of Christ's death in the sufferings of the apostles ("always": 2 Cor 4:10a [πάντοτε], 11a [ἀεί]) results in the extension of Jesus' resurrection "life" to the Corinthian converts (4:12b: ἡ δὲ ζωὴ ἐν ὑμῖν). Contextually, the new "life" that the Corinthian believers experience is the ever-increasing grace of God (2 Cor 4:15b: ἡ χάρις πλεονάσασα; cf. 2:16: ἐκ ζωῆς ἐις ζωήν), which causes an overflow of thanksgiving, to the glory of God (4:15c: τὴν εὐχαριστίαν περισσεύσῃ εἰς τὴν δόξαν τοῦ θεοῦ).[90] Indeed, Paul's reference to the inward renewal of believers (2 Cor 4:16; cf. 3:18; 5:5) captures the apocalyptic motif of the "new creation" through his use of the language of "newness" (4:16c: ἀνακαινοῦται ["is being renewed"]; cf. Col 3:10: τόν ἀνακαινούμενον ["the new self which is being renewed"]).[91] This continuous renewal explains Paul's ongoing capacity to minister in spite of his opponents' dismissal of him,[92] However, if one considers the immediate context of our passage (2 Cor 3:7–4:6), the new resurrection "life" (4:12b) also incorporates the idea of the transformation into the image of God in Christ from glory to glory through the Spirit of Jesus (3:17–18; 4:4, 6).[93] This represents another allusion, as we have argued above, to the "new creation" motif.

The resurrection hope, too, with its impress of the eternal weight of glory "from excess to excess" (2 Cor 4:17: καθ' ὑπερβολὴν αἰώνιον βάρος δόξης), belongs to traditional apocalyptic expectation.[94] Conventional, too, is Paul's emphasis on the "heaviness" of glory, implicit in the derivation of the Hebrew word for "glory" (*kābôd*).[95] However, the indissoluble link of glory to the life-giving power of the resurrected and ascended Jesus (4:10b, 11b) is a novelty in Second Temple Judaism. As noted, it stood in contrast to the Enochic tradition of ascension to heaven without prior death. But, just as the dying of Christ is viewed as an "apocalyptic" power at work in the apostles' weakness (2 Cor 4:10a [τήν νέκρωσιν τοῦ Ἰησοῦ ἐν τῷ σώματι περιφέροντες], 12a [ὁ θάνατος ἐν ἡμῖν ἐνεργεῖται]), so the glorious arrival of the resurrection age in Christ, vindicating

---

[90] Barnett, *Corinthians*, 238.

[91] Beale, *A New Testament Biblical Theology*, 269.

[92] Paul's opponents would later dismiss his outward appearance in his rhetorical performance at Corinth as of no account (2 Cor 10:10): "his bodily presence is weak (ἀσθενής), and his speech contemptible (ἐξουθενημένος)." While Paul concedes that the "outward man" is "wasting away" (2 Cor 4:16: διαφθείρεται), the reality for believers is that the "inner man" is being daily renewed in preparation for "an eternal weight of glory beyond all measure" (4:17).

[93] Savage, *Power Through Weakness*, 177–78.

[94] On the resurrection hope in apocalyptic, see Russel, *Jewish Apocalyptic*, 366–79.

[95] On glory in apocalyptic, see n. 69 *supra*. The Hebrew word *kābôd* ("glory") derived from *kābed* ("to be heavy") and came to be associated with the idea that those possessing glory were laden with riches (Gen 31:1), power (Isa 8:7) and position (Gen 45:13).

his suffering apostles (4:7–8, 17a), is also considered to be the outworking of "apocalyptic" power (4:17b: κατεργάζεται). It is this distinctive that marks off Paul's understanding of ministry from the eschatology and ethics of Jewish apocalyptic.

Having established the apocalyptic context of Paul's understanding of his apostolic ministry, we turn to our final enquiry. How does Augustus' unconventional portrait of his reluctance and shouldering of the burden of state intersect with Paul's eschatological gospel and its paradoxical understanding of ministry in 2 Corinthians 4:7–18? Why did Paul's "apocalyptic" paradigm of ministry ultimately triumph in the West?

3.3. The "Inadequate" Paul and the "Reluctant" Augustus: Comparing and Contrasting the Legacy of Two First-Century Leaders

We have argued that the realised eschatology of Paul's gospel may have sounded strangely familiar to auditors acquainted with the Julian propaganda. The imperial ideology of the inscriptions in the Greek East depicted Augustus as the unrivalled benefactor of the world, whose inexhaustible grace was truly "godlike". This was articulated in the imperial cult by means of its public rituals, media, and theatre, and reinforced through the diplomatic contact of the eastern city-states with the Roman ruler and his representatives. The same protocols existed in the Latin West, though, in the case of the *forum Augustum* and *Res Gestae* at Rome, Augustus' exalted status was more expressed in terms of his moral, religious, patronal and military superiority to the great men of the republican past. New Testament scholars have studied this phenomenon in recent years,[96] but what has been overlooked is how the puzzling paradigm of Augustan leadership in the *Res Gestae* interacted with the apocalyptic antinomies of Paul's understanding of ministry. In light of our discussion of *Res Gestae* 5.1–3 and 2 Corinthians 4:7–18, what conclusions might be drawn about the way that Augustus and Paul – each of whom announced vastly different reigns of grace (*Res Gestae* 15–24; Rom 5:12–21) – approached the needs of their respective communities? Two fundamental observations should be made.

First, there is a distinction to be made between Augustus' reluctance (*Res Gestae* 5.1, 3) – which is cleverly rhetorically balanced by his shouldering of responsibility (5:2) – and the subtlety of Paul's self-understanding as an apostle in 2 Corinthians 1–4. Not only does the intensity of Paul's self-revelation in 2 Corinthians stand at odds with (generally) the mundane and superficial content of the papyrus letters of antiquity, but also it presents a sharp contrast to the stylised and relentless boasting of the *Res Gestae*. In fact, Paul's honesty about

[96] Harrison, *Paul and the Imperial Authorities*, *passim*.

his ministry reversals and his catalogues of humiliations in service of Christ would have played into the hands of his detractors who despised his weakness.

How is Paul's weakness underscored in 2 Corinthians 1–4? The apostle despairs for his life in confronting deadly peril (2 Cor 1:8–10), avoids another painful visit to the Corinthians (2:1), is distressed and anguished (2:4), feels his incompetence and ordinariness (ἱκανός: 2:16; 3:5; "earthen vessels": 4:7), and fears losing heart (4:1, 16) in the face of constant suffering (1:3–9a; 2:14; 4:8–10a).

Notwithstanding his internal fears, Paul shoulders the burden of ministry with all its exhausting demands. The apostle boasts of his clear conscience concerning his conduct (1:12a, 15b), calls on God as his witness (1:23), tests the Corinthians regarding their obedience (2:9), speaks sincerely in Christ before God (2:17), is competent as the minister of the new covenant and its risen Lord (3:5b–6a; 4:5)[97], acts with boldness because of the hope of glory (3:12), commends himself to the conscience of everyone (4:12), does not lose heart because of God's mercy and strength (4:1, 16), displays God's treasure in earthen vessels (4:7), speaks with the same faith as the righteous sufferer of the Psalms and the Messiah himself (4:13 [MT Ps 116:10 = LXX Ps 115:1]),[98] and, although experiencing "momentary affliction", looks forward to what is unseen and eternal (4:17–18).[99]

For Paul, then, the paradigm of apostolic ministry is the paradox of divine strength experienced concurrently with human weakness (2 Cor 12:9–10; cf. 1 Cor 1:25b, 27b; 4:10b; 2 Cor 11:21, 30; 12:5; 13:4). In this regard, Paul heavily emphasises the total dependence of the apostles on God in 2 Corinthians 1–4. God consoles the afflicted apostles so that they can console others (1:4–7); their sufferings are the sufferings of Christ (1:5); the apostles experience death in the present so that they can rely on the God who raises from the dead (1:9–10); they are dependent on the Corinthian prayers to God for their deliverance (1:11); their conduct towards others is conditioned by the grace of God (1:12b); God establishes and anoints his apostles with his Spirit (1:21–22); the Lord opens evangelistic doors for Paul (2:12b); the apostles are the aroma of Christ in God's triumphal procession (2:14–15); the Corinthians are the Spirit-written letter of

[97] For discussion, see T.E. Provence, "'Who Is Sufficient for These Things?': An Exegesis of 2 Corinthians 2:15–3:18," *NovT* 24.1 (1982): 54–81.

[98] Thrall (*II Corinthians*, 340; similarly, Hafemann, *2 Corinthians*, 187) writes: Paul "... could see the speaker as representative of the righteous sufferer, as portrayed in the Psalms and elsewhere in the OT. In this case the psalmist would prefigure, as well as predict, the sufferings of Christ." Hafemann (*2 Corinthians*, 187) also observes that Paul is not citing proof-texts but is rather providing expository "footnotes" to the original Old Testament context: "For like the psalmist, Paul's preaching not only takes place in the midst of adversity, but also leads to even more adversity itself (Ps 116:10b)."

[99] For a brief exposition of 2 Corinthians 5:1–10 in apocalyptic context, see J.R. Harrison, "In Quest of the Third Heaven: Paul and His Apocalyptic Imitators," *VC* 58.1 (2004): 24–55, esp. 36–42.

the apostles (3:3); the competence and power of the apostles as ministers of the new covenant originates in God alone (3:5b–6a; 4:1a, 7b, 16b); their delivery over to will bring the apostles and the Corinthians into his presence (4:14). Moreover, Paul's theocentric emphasis in 2 Corinthians 1–4 is reinforced by his innovative use of Christophany – focused on LXX Exodus 34 – and his Damascus road experience, and is further enhanced by the extensive use of the "dying and rising" and "new creation" motifs.

By contrast, Augustus' emphasis is on the Roman gods in the *Res Gestae* points to his divine legitimation as the ruler of the state, his generosity as a benefactor of the cults, and his piety towards ancestral tradition. Moreover, the *Res Gestae* intended, among other aims, to underscore Augustus' claim to apotheosis after his death. But there is little sense that Augustus was ever in any doubt on the issue. The positioning of Augustus' mausoleum, which afforded a clear line of sight to Agrippa's Pantheon with its statues of the Roman gods (Dio Cassius 53.27.2–4), points to his expectation that the senate would apotheosise him upon his death, as had been the case with his adoptive father, Julius Caesar.[100] Paul, however, preaches himself as the δοῦλος of the risen and all-glorious Lord (2 Cor 4:5; cf. 6:2) and of the carping Corinthians. The reason for this abandonment of status on the apostle's part on the apostle's part is obvious enough. For Paul, the immeasurable weight of the eternal glory, to be fully revealed at the eschaton (2 Cor 4:17) and in the crucified and risen Lord of glory in the present (1 Cor 2:8), pinpricked the Roman boasting in the glory of Augustus and his house.[101]

Second, there is a similarity between Paul and Augustus in that each man, in spite of, respectively, his inadequacy and (humanly speaking) reluctance, assumes the burden of leadership by acting as a benefactor for his community in the time of crisis. Augustus explains his ability to overcome his reluctance, as I have proposed, by virtue of the paradigm of the "endangered" benefactor and, as Hillard has argued, by the Pythagorean ideal of the "shepherd-king". Furthermore, the paradigm of reluctance drew upon the Virgilian precedent of Rome's founder figure, Aeneas, and from the exemplum of republican worthies such as Marius and Pompey. By contrast, Paul is able to overcome his inadequacy and the discouragement of his sufferings (2 Cor 4:8a, 8c, 9a, 9c) through the "apocalyp-

[100] The 27 BC inscription on the Pantheon is M·AGRIPPA·L·F·COS·TERTIVM·FECIT ("Marcus Agrippa, son of Lucius, made [this building] when consul for the third time"). Dio Cassius (53.27.3), dating the erection of the building to 25 BC, states: "Agrippa, for his part, wished to place a statue of Augustus there also and to bestow on him the honour of having the structure named after him; but when the emperor would not accept either honour, he placed in the temple itself a statue of the former Caesar and in the ante-room statues of Augustus and himself." This is consistent with Augustus' refusal of divine honours when he was alive (*Res Gestae* 4.1; 5.1, 3; 10.2; 24.2; Suetonius, *Aug.* 52; Dio Cassius, 51.20.6–7). See M.P. Charlesworth, "The Refusal of Divine Honours: An Augustan Formula," *PBSR* 15 (1939): 1–10.

[101] See Harrison, *Paul and the Imperial Authorities*, 225–32.

tic" power of Jesus' soteriological death. This power is continuously at work in the apostle's life, conforming him to a cruciform understanding of existence, and delivering him either from self-absorption and self-pity (2 Cor 11:28–29), or from a personal retreat from the cost of the cross (2 Cor 5:15) and its social humiliation (1 Cor 1:18–31; 2 Cor 8:9; 13:4a; cf. 4:9–13; 2 Cor 6:8–10).

At the same time, the apocalyptic power of Christ's resurrection delivers Paul from potential destruction (2 Cor 4:8b, 8d, 9b, 9d, 10b, 11b), creating new spiritual life out of spiritual death in his converts (4:12b) because of his ministry to the Corinthians. Paul had become, by God's grace and empowering, a vessel of blessing to others in a vocation seemingly beyond his capacities and strength, at least in terms of his human ability to persevere in the discipleship demanded by the cross. Like other benefactors in antiquity, including the iconic Augustus (*Res Gestae* 5:2), Paul assumed the role of the endangered benefactor for his dependents (1 Cor 15:30: ἡμεῖς κινδυνεύομεν πᾶσαν ὥραν; 2 Cor 11:26: κινδύνοις), expending himself for his converts (2 Cor 12:15a). However, Paul's rationale for such a lifestyle is the paradigm of the self-impoverishment of Christ (2 Cor 8:9; cf. 1 Cor 4:11; 2 Cor 6:10; 11:27b) and his costly self-abandonment on the cross for others (1 Cor 1:18, 23; 2 Cor 13:4; Phil 2:5–8; cf. 1 Cor 4:9; 15:31; 2 Cor 1:8–9; 4:10a, 11a ["for Jesus' sake"], 12a, 15a ["everything is for your sake"]; 6:9b; 11:23b).[102] Indeed, in 2 Corinthians 4:7–18, Paul's emphasis is upon the dying of the apostles on behalf of others rather than their endangerment as apostolic benefactors, though, as we have seen, that emphasis is present elsewhere in his writings. Consequently, the apostle to the Gentiles returns all glory to the true Benefactor of the world (2 Cor 4:15b: εἰς τὴν δόξαν τοῦ θεοῦ), whose infinite grace extends far beyond the subjugated nations listed in the *Res Gestae* (4:15a: ἡ χάρις πλεονάσασα διὰ τῶν πλειόνων; cf. *Res Gestae* 25–33). This created an overflow of thanksgiving to God (2 Cor 4:15b: τὴν εὐχαριστίαν περισσεύσῃ) that made the Augustan "age of grace" pale into insignificance by comparison (cf. 1 Cor 7:31b).

Why did Paul's paradoxical understanding of ministry and leadership ultimately triumph in the West? This raises the vexed issue about the difference that Christianity made to the Roman Empire, as R. MacMullen famously formulated the question.[103] Furthermore, to come to grips properly with this question would necessitate coverage of the philosophical, political and social currents operating in Paul's world and their impact upon his original audiences, as well as the reception of his message, including its distinctive elements, by his contemporaries and subsequent generations, sympathetic and unsympathetic. Consequently, the four suggestions below are offered as a very tentative explanation

---

[102] On Christ as the "impoverished" benefactor, see Harrison, *Paul's Language of Grace*, 250–56.

[103] R. MacMullan, "What Difference Did Christianity Make?" *Historia* 35 (1986): 322–43.

of why Paul's gospel still remains at the centre of philosophical and social debate today,[104] as opposed to the once all-dominant Augustan paradigm of the "reluctant" leader.

First, the republican quest for ancestral glory culminated in the glory of Augustus and the Julian house, with the result that, from 19 BC onwards, Roman generals were not allowed to receive their own triumphal honours.[105] Paul, however, located all glory in the crucified and risen Christ (1 Cor 2:8), exalting him with the divine title of κύριος ("Lord": Phil 2:11a: cf. LXX Isa 45:23) in a coronation ceremony that reverberated entirely to God's glory (2:11b: εἰς δόξαν θεοῦ πατρός).[106] However, God's glory was extended to Christ's dependents in a spectacular transformation of ever-increasing glory (2 Cor 3:17–18), operative in the present until its culmination at the eschaton. By contrast, the static construct of Julian glory robbed the clients of Augustus of any hope other than just basking in the fame of their patron. Moreover, the hope of apotheosis was only formally extended to select individuals of the Julio-Claudian family (Caesar, Augustus, Livia, Claudius), whereas all believers were caught up in the eschatological glory of the resurrection age. The hierarchical nature of Augustan society was also pinpricked by the social levelling brought about by divine grace,[107] tearing down all human boasting (1 Cor 4:7; 2 Cor 10:17; 11:16–12:10; cf. Rom 3: 27–4:6; 10:18), while elevating believers to the same honour and status: valued servants of the Lord of glory who entrusted his treasure to earthen vessels (2 Cor 4:5, 7).

Second, precisely because Augustus was the iconic benefactor of the world, the old noble houses could no longer compete against the princeps in recruiting and retaining their traditional client-base. Their descendents would eventually become a cipher of their former greatness, demeaning themselves on the stage on behalf of the self-obsessed Nero (Juvenal, *Sat.* 8). Alternatively, some senators were disgruntled with the loss of their traditional pathways of honour under Augustus and baulked at their replacement by less prestigious pathways.[108] Everything, now, was dependent on the patronage of Augustus. However, Paul's understanding of the new covenant of the Spirit (2 Cor 3:7–18) and the arrival of the new creation in Christ (4:4b, 16b; 5:17) led believers into an empowering freedom (3:17) that would overflow in thankfulness to God as a mer-

---

[104] See A. Badiou, *Saint Paul: The Foundation of Universalism* (Stanford: Stanford University Press, 2003); G. Agamben, *The Time that Remains: A Commentary on the Letter to the Romans*, tr. P. Dailey (Stanford: Stanford University Press 2005); J.D. Caputo and L.M. Alcoff, eds., *St Paul among the Philosophers* (Bloomington: Indiana University Press, 2009); L.L. Welborn, *Paul's Summons to Messianic Life: Political Theology and the Coming Awakening* (New York: Columbia University Press, 2015).

[105] See Eck, *The Age of Augustus*, 69–70.

[106] Capes, *Old Testament Texts*, 157–60.

[107] On the hierarchical nature of Augustan society, see Jones, *Augustus*, 136–39.

[108] Galinsky, *Augustan Culture*, 72

ciful Benefactor (4:1, 15). In this regard, Paul's collection for the Jerusalem poor (1 Cor 16:1–4; 2 Cor 8:1–9:15) is announced with an explosion of the language of grace (χάρις and cognates) unparalleled in any contemporary inscription.[109] Paul's creation of small house churches, of mixed ethnicity and culture, which extended beneficence not only to their own communities but also to their enemies (Romans 12:14–21), creating thereby a network of mercy (12:8b) that criss-crossed the provinces of Roman empire, was an ethical and social novelty in the first century.

Third, the ethical change promoted by Augustus concentrated on the idealised republican past for social transformation, summed up in his commitment to and embodiment of its exemplary traditions for posterity.[110] However, what transpired could easily become, to borrow Galinsky's phrase, a "sort of somnolent antiquarianism."[111] By contrast, Paul's emphasis on the resurrection power operative in the lives of his converts – paradoxically unleashed by the dying of Christ in the apostles – looks forward to the transformation of all creation in Christ (2 Cor 4:16–5:17), experienced in advance through the down-payment of the Spirit who conforms believers to the image of Christ (1:22; 3:17–18; 4:4, 6; 5:5b). The forward-looking dynamism of Paul's apocalyptic understanding of ministry promoted lasting and continuing change within the communities of believers.

Fourth, the "inadequacy" of Paul, experienced daily in God's providential ordering of his ministry, provided a more realistic appraisal of human nature than the "reluctance" of Augustus. The reluctance of Augustus, pursued to its logical culmination, resulted in the withdrawal of Tiberius, Augustus' successor, from the rule of Rome to the isolation of Capri from 26 AD onwards, with the consequent unravelling of Roman government under his treacherous praetorian prefect, Sejanus. Thus Tiberius' absence from Rome and his inactivity in the daily affairs of government until his death in AD 37 pushed the example of the reluctant Aeneas to its breaking point.[112] Nor did the paradigm of reluctance necessarily generate selfless rulers who would shoulder the burden of state in the time of crisis as Augustus had hoped: the frenetic and self-absorbed reigns of Caligula and Nero point in a different direction.[113]

By contrast, the experience of resurrection power in the weakness of the cross overrode Paul's inadequacy and made his suffering ministry a blessing to the

---

[109] The closest inscription that I have found in terms of an explosion of grace language similar to Paul's is SEG XII 348. See Harrison, *Paul's Language of Grace*, 51.

[110] Galinsky, *Augustan Culture*, 73–77.

[111] Galinsky, *Augustan Culture*, 139. Galinsky (*ibid.*) cites Horace's complaints in his *Letter to Augustus* as indicative of the stultified atmosphere that an over-emphasis on the past engendered.

[112] See Hillard ("Roman Concepts of Leadership," 143–44) on Tiberius' avoidance of leadership.

[113] See Earl, *The Age of Augustus*, 190.

nations that Augustus had ruthlessly subdued (2 Cor 4:15b). Here, invisible to the rulers of the world (1 Cor 2:8a), was the beginning of a movement that would soon sweep across the Mediterranean basin and beyond. To this day it presents Western culture with a model of cruciform leadership that challenges its myopic predilection to idealise the past or to pursue self, enabling believers to embody in "servant" communities the in-breaking of God's new creation, and to persevere in that vocation until the eschatological renewal of all things in Christ.

3.4. Conclusion

The issue of "legacy" in any culture is a difficult issue to determine. Such an assessment runs the risk of simplifying highly complex historical, social, economic and ideological movements at the expense of their distinctive particularities by the broad brush strokes of generalisation. It was with considerable caution, therefore, that this chapter made some tentative suggestions as to why the "leadership" ideals of Augustus, modelled upon the paradigms of reluctance and the endangered shepherd-ruler, declined, whereas those of the apostle Paul, drawing upon Jewish apocalyptic and the risen power of the crucified Christ, gradually took hold in western civilisation, even though at a political level nothing would change for a long time in terms of family dynasties and their elite clients ruling the Roman Empire. Nevertheless, whereas the impact of Augustus and his adoptive father is indelibly marked in memoriam in the calendrical system of the West, Paul's communities of cruciform grace continue to challenge the self-serving and self-promoting paradigms of contemporary leadership by their paradoxical understanding of power in weakness in 2 Corinthians 4:7–18 and, consequently, have the capacity to bring new life where a "somnolent antiquarianism" resists the imperatives of change. In conclusion, the ambiguous leadership-styles of Augustus and Paul launched a series of unexpected and paradoxical consequences for first-century imperial society, the social tensions of which still reverberate down into our century.[114]

[114] On the ambiguous nature of Paul's leadership, see K. Ehrensperger, *Paul and the Dynamics of Power: Communication and Interaction in the Early Christ-Movement* (London and New York: T&T Clark, 2009), 98–116, 179–200, at 111–114 and 187–91.

Chapter 4

Paul and the Athletic Ideal in Antiquity: A Case Study in Wrestling with Word and Image

4.1. The Interplay of Word and Image: Paul and the "Beat" Poets

The older generation of American post-war poets and the new generation of "Beat" poets turned to the paintings of famous European masters for their inspiration. William Carlos Williams, Lawrence Ferlinghetti, and Gregory Corso, used the paintings of Brueghel, Goya, and Uccello for their reflections on the disparity between the rich and the poor, the absurdity of our technological society, and the inevitability of death. This interplay between word and image allowed these poets to draw their readers into the visually familiar and then to reorientate its imagery in a new construction of social reality.

We see this interplay in William Carlos Williams' magisterial poem *Paterson*. This five-volumed work, written during 1946–1958, investigates the resemblances between the life-thoughts of a man and the regional history of an American city. Both the man and the location are symbolised by the figure of Paterson, named after the New Jersey city near which Williams lived. At the beginning of Book V Section III, Williams describes the characters painted in Peter Brueghel's famous picture *The Adoration of the Kings* (AD 1564).[1] The poet's tone is discomforting, alternating between cynicism and pity for each group of figures. The contrast in Brueghel's picture between the wealth of the crowned and mitred Magi and the poverty of the soldiers in their ragged clothes underlines the social inequities of life. In a homily that concludes the poem, Paterson reflects on the poverty of the atomic age driven by corporate greed and technology:

It is no mortal sin to be poor – anything but this featureless tribe that has the money now – staring into the atom, completely blind – without grace or pity, as if they were so

[1] For a poem on the crucifixion based on the painting of an unknown Rhenish Master, see Zbigniew Herbert's *The Passion of our Lord painted by an anonymous hand from the circle of Rhenish Masters* (D. Curzon, *The Gospels in Our Image: An Anthology of Twentieth-Century Poetry Based on Biblical Texts* [New York et al.: Harcourt Brace and Co., 1995], 209). The Rhenish artist depicts the scene of the soldiers nailing Christ to the cross who carry out their grim task with disinterested efficiency. The detachment evinced by the artist in his painting comments ironically, in Herbert's view, on the deeper faith significance underlying the event itself ("As we said, the fine craftsmen are nailing our Lord to the cross").

many shellfish. The artist, Brueghel, saw them: the suits of his peasants were of better stuff, hand woven, than we can boast.[2]

Another example of the interplay between word and image is found in Lawrence Ferlinghetti's 1958 collection *A Coney Island of the Mind*. In the untitled poem introducing the collection, Ferlinghetti describes scenes of suffering, inhumanity, and insanity from Francisco de Goya's paintings as a prelude to his onslaught on contemporary American culture. The horror of Goya's universe finds its counterpart in the technology, consumerism, and existential angst tearing apart America. Americans, Ferlinghetti asserts, are part of Goya's "suffering humanity", albeit in a landscape of freeways, intersected with innocuous billboards advertising "imbecile illusions of happiness." Ferlinghetti concludes his comparison of mid twentieth-century America with Goya's surreal vision of the world's inhumanity towards the weak in this manner:

The scene shows fewer tumbrills
but more strung-out citizens
in painted cars
and they have strange license plates
and engines
that devour America.[3]

Finally, in the poem entitled *Uccello*, Gregory Corso turns to the battle scenes of the Early Renaissance painter Paolo Uccello for inspiration. Uccello's glorification of war, devoid of reference to death, stirs in Corso the illusory hope that life end might not end at the grave:

how I dream to join such a battle!
a silver man on a black horse with a red standard and striped
lance never to die but to be endless
a golden prince of pictorial war.[4]

As powerful as the preceding examples are, another way that modern poets explore the interplay of word and image is to focus on the life of a famous painter. Two examples will suffice. First, the poem of the Australian poet Gwen Harwood, entitled "Death of a Painter", was written in response to Van Gogh's

[2] William Carlos Williams, *Paterson*, rev. ed. (New York: New Directions, 1992), 225. For further examples of poems based on pictures, see William Carlos Williams, *Pictures from Brueghel and Other Poems: Collected Poems 1950–1962* (New York: New Directions Books, 1962): namely, *Pictures from Brueghel I–X*, *The Title* (based on Gauguin's *The Loss of Virginity*), and *Tribute to the Painters* (based on several Masters).

[3] See Lawrence Ferlinghetti, *These Are My Rivers: New and Selected Poems 1955–1993* (New York: New Directions, 1993), 79. For other examples of Ferlinghetti using famous painters and sculptors, see *ibid.*, 9–14, 18–19, 62, 65, 194. Ferlinghetti renders in haunting manner the iconic TV images of President Kennedy's funeral procession from Dallas to Washington: "we tune to a raga on the stereo and turn on Death TV without its sound." *Idem*, *Americus I* (New York: New Directions, 2003), 79–80.

[4] Ferlinghetti, *These Are My Rivers*, 204.

famous self-portrait of 1888.[5] The poem, exploring the reaction of Theo Van Gogh to his famous brother's death, explodes in imagery drawn from the frenzied canvasses of Arles. The brother sums up his ambiguous reaction to Vincent's death thus:

Flowers explode in torment,
the cypress whirls its crest
in frenzy, to encompass
the God who once possessed
this hand –
this hand assigns me
inviolable rest.[6]

Second, the French Surrealist post-war poet, Jacques Prévert, turns for inspiration to Vincent's tortured life in his poem *Vincent's Lament*. There the grisly episode of the crazed Vincent presenting his severed hear to a prostitute at Arles is recounted sympathetically with sparse imagery that evokes several of his paintings.[7] In both of these poems, we are witnessing how the poet invests an iconic figure of the art world with symbolic significance, though in a way that considers the artist's contribution to an understanding of our own humanity.

In sum, modern poets – not to mention Keats' *Ode to a Grecian Urn* before our era – have turned to the iconic images and figures of the art world, with a view to appropriating the impact of their visual imagery in a new verbal context.[8] The

[5] Note the comment of Gwen Harwood (*Collected Poems 1943–1995*, ed. A. Hoddinott and G. Kratzmann [St Lucia: University of Queensland Press, 2003], 575) regarding the poem in a letter to her life-long friend Thomas Riddel (02.11.1956): "the poem was directly inspired by the terrible self-portrait of 1888, where the face seems to be full of daemonic power, and by the painter's own words, 'The cypress is always occupying my thoughts ... I should like to make something of the cypresses like the canvass of the sunflowers; it astonishes me that they never have been done as I see them.'"

[6] Harwood, *Collected Poems 1943–1995*, 19. At the level of popular entertainment, the American song-writer, Don MacLean, achieved something similar with his song *Vincent*.

[7] Jacques Prévert, *Paroles: Selected Poems*, tr. Lawrence Ferlinghetti (San Francisco: City Lights Books, 1958), 105–07.

[8] For examples of French poets using the works of artists as the source of their inspiration, see Arthur Rimbaud's, *The Brilliant Victory of Saarebruck* (based on a full-colour Belgian print on sale in Charleroi for 35 centimes); Charles Baudelaire's, *Guiding Lights* (based on the corpus of eight Masters), *A Fantastic Engraving*, *A Martyr* (based on the drawing of an unknown Master). The ancients, too, were not averse to drawing inspiration from the visual arts, although primarily as a literary fiction. The *Tabula of Cebes* purports to be moralising exposition of curious votive tablet bearing a picture (*C.T.* 1.1–2.12; 4.2; 30.3). For discussion on whether a genuine tablet lay behind the Tabula's dialogue, see J.T. Fitzgerald and L.M. White, *The Tabula of Cebes* (Chico: Scholars Press, 1983), 35 n.49. The Greek rhetorician Philostratos (*Imagines* 2.6) claims to describe a painting of the pankratiast, Arrichion, who died victorious in the final round of the pankration (a form of all-in wrestling) at Olympia in 564 BC. However, the highly rhetorical nature of Philostratos' account casts doubt on the authenticity of its purported provenance. However, much more pointedly, wall paintings were used to satirise the official propaganda of Augustus as the "new Aeneas". Augustan propaganda had

imagery is then wielded with startling power in poems that critique the impoverishment of modern urban culture (Williams, Ferlinghetti), or reflect on the absurdity and pain of life (Corso, Harwood, Prévert).

This chapter – a case study in the responsible use of the visual arts as background to exegesis – proposes that the apostle Paul operates similarly in his interaction with the Greek athletic ideal as expressed in the ceramics, statuary, reliefs, mosaics, coins, seal stones and incised honorific decrees of the eastern Mediterranean basin. To be sure, Pindar and Bacchylides had elevated the athletic ideal to an art form through their odes to victors in the Greek games, and the philosophical tradition had transferred the true contest (ἀγῶν) to the arena of moral endeavour.[9] But, in 1 Corinthians 9:24–27, Paul interacts with the visual images that were part of the Greek "circuit" games (*periodos*),[10] as much as the verbal images that belonged to the moral discourse of the popular philosophers, reapplying them to the corporate relations of the divided Corinthian house churches.

Our methodology concentrates on the evidence of the visual arts as opposed to the written evidence of the poets and popular philosophers, though the evidence of the poets and philosophers will be referred to.[11] Commentators have

been quick to exploit the "Aeneas" literary tradition in its iconography by presenting Augustus as the second founder of Rome. In the statue program of the forum of Augustus, as Ovid informs us (*Fasti* 5.563–566), "(one) sees Aeneas laden with his precious burden, and so many members of Julian nobility." Also the *Ara Pacis* in the Campas Martias includes a representation of Aeneas arriving in Italy. Drawing upon the Virgilian portrait of Aeneas' flight from Troy (*Aen.* 2.680ff), wall paintings from the façade of a house at Pompeii operate within conventional artistic boundaries in depicting Aeneas with his father Anchises on his shoulders and his little son Ascanius by his side. But the critics of Augustus used the same motifs to lampoon the Aeneas group in the Forum of Augustus. A wall painting from a villa close to Stabiae, modelled on the Pompeian stereotype, caricatures the Aeneas group as dog-headed apes. See P. Zanker, *The Power of Images in the Age of Augustus* (Anne Arbor 1990), figs. 156a and 162.

[9] See S. Freyne, "Early Christianity and the Greek Athletic Ideal," in *Sport*, ed. G. Baum (Edinburgh: T&T Clark, 1989), 93–100.

[10] The locations of the four major athletic festivals in Greece, known as the "circuit" (*periodos*) games, included Corinth (Acts 18:1, 18), Delphi, Nemeia and Olympia. It is quite possible that Paul visited the Isthmian games in AD 51 (J. Murphy-O'Connor, "Corinth," in *The Anchor Bible Dictionary Volume I A–C*, ed. D. N. Freedman et al. [New York: Doubleday, 1992], 1138). On their location, see n. 25 *infra*. In the case of Athens (Acts 17:16–31), although the city did not feature in the Greek *periodos*, it nonetheless held local games as part of the Panathenaic festival. If Paul had journeyed south-east as far as the city wall, he would have seen the stadium on the far bank of the Ilissus, built in ca. 330 BC expressly for the Panathenaic games. See n. 25 *infra* on the principal games of the early Roman period.

[11] A proper discussion of the responsible use of visual evidence in interpreting literary texts cannot be provided in this chapter. The methodological problems are considerable. Unlike the literary evidence, artefacts may not have a clear context. To be sure, an inscription on an artefact may provide a significant clue regarding its context and interpretation (e.g. nn. 40, 42, 56, 76–77 *infra*). But a stone displaying the relief of an athlete may have been recycled from its original site to a new one (e.g. n. 33 *infra*). Further, an artefact may have gone through

conspicuously overlooked the visual arts in their exegesis of 1 Corinthians 9:24–27. The same neglect characterises wider scholarly discussions of early Christianity and the athletic ideal (though *pace*, P. F. Esler below).[12]

This is not the case, however, in other areas of biblical studies. Three examples will suffice. First, Othmar Keel's study of the impact of ancient near eastern iconography upon the Old Testament Psalms has been ground breaking for

different hands, contexts, and uses. Also, the precise site of an artefact may not have been recorded at its discovery. Other questions arise. How widely were such artefacts distributed and at what level of the social pyramid? Would Paul, for example, have seen the large amphorae bearing athletic motifs, which were given to athletes as prizes (e. g. n. 56) and buried with the victor upon his death? How widely were the smaller copies of these large amphorae disseminated (e. g. n. 34)? How do we know that we are correctly interpreting the athletic iconography of artefacts (e. g. n. 33)? Do the images represent the idealised views of the makers and consumers, with little correspondence to the real world they were living in? How do we relate the multiple images on the various surfaces of an artefact to each other? Are we being responsible in discussing artefacts that span several centuries, with little attempt at differentiation, and ignoring their local contexts and variations? For sophisticated discussion of the issues, see J. P. Crielard, et al., ed., *The Complex Past of Pottery: Production, Circulation and Consumption of Mycenaean and Greek Pottery* (Amsterdam: J.B. Gieben, 1999). I am indebted to Dr Rosalinde Kearsley, Department of Ancient History, Macquarie University, for this reference. In the view of E. Krentz ("Paul, Games, and the Military," in *Paul in the Greco-Roman World: A Handbook*, ed. J. P. Sampley [Harrisburg: Trinity Press, 2003] 352), Paul's description of athletics in 1 Cor 9:24–27 "is accurate for contemporary practice." See now the updated and new essay of A. H. Cadwallader, "Paul and the Games," in *Paul in the Greco-Roman World: A Handbook Volume 1*, ed. J. P. Sampley, 2nd ed. (London and New York: T&T Clark, 2016), 363–90.

[12] For discussions of the athletic ideal in early Christianity, see V. C. Pfitzner, *Paul and the Agon Motif: Traditional Athletic Imagery in the Pauline Literature* (Leiden: Brill, 1967); M. Poliakov, "Jacob, Jove, and Other Wrestlers: Reception of Greek Athletics by Jews and Christians in Antiquity," *Journal of Sport History* 11 (1984): 48–65; S. Freyne, "Early Christianity and the Greek Athletic Ideal," in Baum, *Sport*; R. Garrison, "Paul's Use of the Athlete Metaphor in 1 Corinthians 9," in *The Graeco-Roman Context of Early Christian Literature*, ed. R. Garrison (Sheffield: Sheffield University Press, 1997), 95–104; W. E. Henderson, "The Athletic Imagery of Paul," *Theological Educator* 56 (1997): 30–37; A. Papathomas, "Das agonistische Motiv 1 Kor 9.24ff. im Spiegel zeitgenössischer dokumentarischer Quellen," *NTS* 43.2 (1997): 223–41; N. Clayton Croy, *Endurance in Suffering: Hebrews 12:1–13 in Its Rhetorical, Religious and Philosophical Context* (Cambridge: Cambridge University Press, 1998), 40–76; R. F. Collins, *First Corinthians* (Collegeville: Michael Glazier/Liturgical Press, 1999), 357–63; D. J. Williams, *Paul's Metaphors: Their Context and Character* (Peabody: Hendrickson, 1999); J. R. C. Couslan, "Athletics," in *Dictionary of New Testament Background*, ed. C. A. Evans and S. E. Porter (Downers Grove-Leicester: IVP, 2000), 140–42; R. Metzner, "Paulus und der Wettkampf: Die Rolle des Sports in Leben und Verkündigung des Apostels (1 Kor 9.24–29; Phil 3.12–16)," *NTS* 46.4 (2000): 565–83; A. C. Thiselton, *The First Epistle to the Corinthians* (Carlisle: Eerdmans/Paternoster, 2000), 707–17; P. Fredricksen, "Paul at the Races. Some Sports Fans Consider Athletics a Religion: It Used to Be," *Bible Review* 18.3 (2002): 12, 42; D. E. Garland, *1 Corinthians* (Grand Rapids: Baker Academic, 2003), 438–45; Krentz, "Paul, Games and the Military," 344–83; M. Brändl (*Der Agon bei Paulus: Herkunft und Profil paulinischer Agonmetaphorik*, WUNT II 222 (Tübingen: Mohr Siebeck, 2006); Cadwallader, "Paul and the Games."

scholars who want to bring the visual arts into dialogue with the biblical text.[13] Until recently, Keel's innovative methodology has not sufficiently fired the interest of most Pauline scholars.[14]

But, second and most gratifyingly, this past negelect of the visual evidence by New Testament scholars has been recently overcome by the development of the "cutting edge" methodology of "visual exegesis". This has flourished in imperial studies of the New Testament for several years now, as the recent publications of D. Lopez, B. Kahl, R. Canavan, J.R. Harrison, and H.O. Meier show.[15] Also the methodology of using numismatic evidence in New Testament studies is still in its infancy, but the publications of M. Grant, R. Oster, L. Kreitzer, M.E. Hoskins Walbank, M. Amandry, B.J. Bitner and M. Theophilos need to be absorbed by New Testament scholars and the lessons learned there applied appropriated to the exegetical study of social and political realia in Paul's letters and to the New Testament more generally.[16]

---

[13] O. Keel, *The Symbolism of the Biblical World: Near Eastern Iconography and the Book of Psalms* (London: SPCK, 1978: Gmn. orig. 1972).

[14] Note, however, the following exceptions. J.L. White (*The Apostle of God: Paul and the Promise of Abraham* [Peabody: Hendrickson, 1999]) makes extensive use of the imperial iconography and statuary, drawing on the widely acclaimed study of P. Zanker, *The Power of Images in the Age of Augustus*, tr. A. Shapiro (Ann Arbor: The University of Michigan Press, 1990). L.L. Welborn (*Paul, the Fool of Christ: A Study of 1 Corinthians 1–4 in the Comic-Philosophic Tradition* [London and New York 2005]) employs visual arts materials in discussing the impact of the comic traditions of the *mimoi* upon Paul's presentation of the cruciform gospel as "foolishness" and himself as its "foolish" herald. For further examples, C.L. Thompson, "Hairstyles, Head-coverings, and St. Paul: Portraits from Roman Corinth," *BA* 51 (1988): 99–115; D.W.J. Gill, "The Importance of Roman Portraiture for Head-coverings in 1 Cor 11:2–16," *TynBul* 41 (1990): 245–60. For the new "visual exgesis" methodology now informing New Testament studies, see below.

[15] D.C. Lopez, *Apostle to the Conquered: Reimagining Paul's Mission* (Minneapolis: Fortress, 2008); B. Kahl, *Galatians Re-Imagined: Reading with the Eyes of the Vanquished* (Minneapolis: Fortress, 2010); J.R. Harrison, 'More Than Conquerors' (Rom 8:37): Paul's Gospel and the Augustan Triumphal Arches of the Greek East and Latin West," *Buried History* 47 (2011): 3–21; R. Canavan, *Clothing the Body of Christ at Colossae: A Visual Construction of Identity*, WUNT II 334 (Tübingen: Mohr Siebeck, 2012); H.O. Maier, *Picturing Paul in Empire: Imperial Image, Text and Persuasion in Colossians, Ephesians and the Pastoral Epistles* (London and New York: Bloomsbury, T&T Clark, 2013). See too the three articles on *Colloquium* on visual exegesis: R. Canavan, "Visual Exegesis: Interpreting Text in Dialogue with Its Visual Context," *Colloquium* 47.1 (2015): 141–51; H.O. Maier, "Come and See: The Promise of Visual Exegesis," *Colloquium* 47.1 (2015): 152–57; C. Renkin, "An Art Historian Reflects on Modes of Visual Exegesis," *Colloquium* 47.1 (2015): 158–61. See now the important collection of essays representing the new discipline in biblical studies, edited by V.K. Robbins et al., *The Art of Visual Exegesis: Rhetoric, Texts, Images*, Emory Studies in Early Christianity 19 (Atlanta: SBL Press, 2017).

[16] M. Grant, *Roman History from Coins: Some Uses of the Imperial Coinage to the Historian* (Cambridge: Cambridge University Press, 1968); R. Oster, "Numismatic Windows into the Social World of Early Christianity: A Methodological Enquiry," *JBL* 101 (1982): 195–223; *idem*, "'Show me a denarius': Symbolism of Roman Coinage and Christian Beliefs," *ResQ* 28.2 (1985–1986): 107–15; M. Amandry, *Le Monnayage des Duovirs Corinthiens* BCH Suppl. XV (Athens and Paris: École française d'Athènes, 1988); *idem*, "Le monnayage de la *Res*

Third, in a seminal collection essays, several scholars apply the iconographic method to the New Testament literature. As noted, P.F. Esler's study of Paul's agon motif against its ancient visual context is an innovative contribution to the study of the athletic ideal in Pauline studies.[17] In a review of modern scholarship on sporting-competition imagery, Esler notes the methodological flaw of interpreting historical data solely in terms of ideas and thereby disconnecting the data from its continuous dialogue with social structures. Even where visual arts evidence is acknowledged, the failure to use social-scientific methodology as part of one's analysis has a largely similar result. This has meant has meant that biblical scholars have either overlooked the visual arts evidence or have not interpreted the evidence properly.[18] Esler locates Paul's imagery within the grid of the Mediterranean anthropological models of "challenge-and-response" and "honour and shame".[19] He then discusses the events of the men's footrace, long-jump and combat sports, as well as the women's games.

Disappointingly, Esler discusses only five pieces of visual evidence, supplemented with one inscription and several references to ancient authors.[20] The visual evidence, with the exception of a head of a victorious athlete from the Isthmian games (II–I cent. BC), dates from the sixth to the fifth century BC and does not reflect in its provenance the athletic culture of the cities from which and to which Paul wrote his letters. As noted, the methodological problems in using this evidence are considerable. Finally, after a fine discussion of 1 Corinthians 9:24–27, Esler concludes:

> The overall impression that one obtains from 1 Cor. 9:24–27 is that Paul has adopted the language of sporting contests from the social world in which he lived and in a very positive manner. The way he has done so is redolent of Mediterranean culture, with its prioritising of honour as the primary good.[21]

Publica Coloniae Philippensium," in *Sonderdruck aus Edith Schönert-Geiss zum 65. Geburtstag*, Hrsg. S. Nomismatikos (Berlin: Akademie Verlag, 1998), 23–30; L.J. Kreitzer, *Striking New Images: Roman Imperial Coinage and the New Testament World* (Sheffield: Sheffield Academic Press, 1996); M.E. Walbank, "Image and Cult: The Coinage of Roman Corinth," in *Corinth in Context: Comparative Studies on Religion and Society*, ed. S.J. Friesen et al. (Leiden: Brill, 2011), 151–98; B.J. Bitner, "Coinage and Colonial Identity: Corinthian Numismatics and the Corinthian Correspondence" in *The First Urban Churches 1: Methodological Foundations*, ed. J.R. Harrison and L.L. Welborn (Atlanta: SBL Press, 2015), 151–87; M.P. Theophilos, "Ephesus and the Numismatic Background to 'νεωκόρος'," in *The First Urban Churches 3: Ephesus*, ed. J.R. Harrison and L.L. Welborn (Atlanta: SBL Press, 2018), 299–331.

[17] P.F. Esler, "Paul and the Agon: Understanding a Pauline Motif in Its Cultural and Visual Context," in *Picturing the New Testament: Studies in Ancient Visual Images*, WUNT II 193, ed. A. Weissenrieder et al. (Tübingen: Mohr Siebeck, 2005), 356–84. The massive new work of Brändl (*Der Agon bei Paulus*) does not discuss the visual evidence, confining himslef to the philosophers.

[18] Esler, "Paul and the Agon," 359–63.

[19] Esler, "Paul and the Agon," 363–70.

[20] Esler, "Paul and the Agon," 370–75.

[21] Esler, "Paul and the Agon," 397.

This is a very conservative social conclusion on Esler's part, given the radical contrast Paul draws between the φθαρτός and ἀφθαρτός coronal awards (1 Cor 9:25). Surely Paul was saying something more significant about the fate of athletic ideal other than endorsing the sporting status quo of his culture? Have Esler's anthropological models led him to see only what is only congruent with Graeco-Roman athletic culture and miss what is socially distinctive in Paul's approach?

Finally, R.S. Dutch has investigated in great depth the imagery of 1 Corinthians 9:24–27 from the perspective of a limited selection of the ancient visual evidence, with commendable attention to the Corinthian context and the wider ideology of the games. But, disappointingly, Dutch does not touch on Paul's figure of the κῆρυξ (1 Cor 9:27b: ἄλλοις κηρύξας), or upon the social significance of Paul's contrast between the φθαρτός and ἀφθαρτός coronal awards. Dutch's evaluation of the ideology of the athletic ideal concentrates more on the contributions of modern scholars than on the evidence of Paul at times, concluding that the apostle rejects the reward culture of ancient athletics and that he tailors his imagery to the educated Corinthian elite.[22] The perspective of Dutch is more polemically slanted at Paul's Corinthian opponents than at the social and theological challenge that Paul's thought presented to the Graeco-Roman athletic ideal.

Why, then, have New Testament exegetes largely overlooked the evidence of the visual arts in discussing the impact of the Greek athletic ideal upon early Christianity? In addition to Esler's suggestions above, probably exegetes are still held captive by the theological conflict between the *word-based* hermeneutic of northern European Protestantism and the *image-based* hermeneutic of the counter-Reformation in southern Europe.[23] Because this legacy still affects Pauline scholarship to a considerable extent, the use of visual materials as a methodology for the interpretation of Paul is only in its infancy. Therefore, an examination of the athletic imagery of 1 Corinthians 9:24–27 against the backdrop of the visual evidence celebrating the athletic ideal is long overdue.[24] This

---

[22] R.S. Dutch, *The Educated Elite in 1 Corinthians: Education and Community Conflict in Graeco-Roman Context*, JSNTS 271 (London and New York: T&T Clark International, 2005), 219–48.

[23] See the stimulating conversation between Neil Postman and Camille Paglia, "Dinner Conversation: She Wants Her TV! He Wants His Book!," *Harpers Magazine* (March 1991): 44–55. I am indebted to Dr Grenville Kent for this reference.

[24] For the visual evidence, see C. Alexander, *Greek Athletics* (New York: Metropolitan Museum of Art, 1925); E.N. Gardiner, *Athletics of the Ancient World* (Chicago: *Ares Publishers Inc.*, 1930); M.B. Poliakoff, *Combat Sports in the Ancient World: Competition, Violence, and Culture* (New Haven and London: Yale University Press, 1987); D. Sansone, *Greek Athletics and the Genesis of Sport* (Berkeley and Los Angeles: University of California Press, 1988); O. Tzachou-Alexandri, ed., *Mind and Body: Athletic Contests in Ancient Greece* (Athens: Catalogue of the Exhibition, Ministry of Culture and the National Hellenic Committee [ICOM], 1989); D. Vanhove, ed., *Le sport dans la Grèce antique: Du jeu à la compétition* (Bruxelles:

is not to deny that Paul may have visited the Isthmian games while he was at Corinth,[25] or one of many other local games scattered throughout the eastern Mediterranean.[26] Moreover, Paul would have been familiar with the athletic ideal from the time of his youth in Tarsus.[27] Nor am I excluding the possibility that

---

Palais des Beaux-Arts, 1992); J. Swaddling, *The Ancient Olympic Games*, 2nd ed. (London: British Museum Press, 1999); T. Measham et al., ed., *1000 Years of the Olympic Games: Treasures of Ancient Greece* (Sydney: Powerhouse Publishing, 2000); P. Valavanis, *Games and Sanctuaries in Ancient Greece: Olympia, Delphi, Isthmia, Nemea, Athens* (Los Angeles: J. Paul Getty Museum, 2004); Robert Weir, "Commemorative Cash: the Coins of the Ancient and Modern Olympics," in *Onward to the Olympics: Historical Perspectives on the Olympic Games*, ed. G.P. Schaus and S.R. Wenn (Waterloo: Wilfrid Laurier Press, 2007), 179–92.

[25] See n. 10 *supra*. As background to the Corinthian "runner" image (1 Cor 9:24, 26a; cf. Phil 3:12–14), for example, Paul may well have seen the starting-point and finishing-point of the racetrack (181.15 metres long) at the *later* stadium at Isthmia. This stadium – situated in a natural hollow at a small distance southeast of the sanctuary of Poseidon (ca. 250 m.) – was used during hellenistic and Roman times. Caution must be exercised here. The sanctuary was abandoned in the late hellenistic period, some time after the Roman destruction of 146 BC. The Isthmian games, however, continued under the supervision of Sicyon as long as Corinth lay deserted (Pausanias, 2.11.2). E.R. Gebhard ("The Isthmian Games and the Sanctuary of Poseidon in the Early Empire," in *The Corinthia in the Roman Period*, ed. T.E. Gregory [Ann Arbor: Journal of Roman Archaeology, 1993], 78–94) argues on the basis of the archaeological, inscriptional, and numismatic evidence that control of the Isthmian games returned to Corinth in 40 BC. But they did not return permanently to the sanctuary of Poseidon until AD 50–60 and they flourished once again when Nero enrolled as a competitor in the games in AD 67. However, M. Kajava ("When Did the Isthmian Games Return to the Isthmus? Rereading Corinth 8.3.153," *CPhil* 97 [2002]: 168–78) asserts that the games recommenced at the Isthmus in AD 43. Therefore, the location at which Paul may have seen the Isthmian and Caesarean games in AD 51 cannot be definitively determined. It was possibly still at Corinth or, more likely, at the Isthmian sanctuary itself. On the *later* stadium, see N. Papahatzis, *Ancient Corinth: The Museums of Corinth, Isthmia and Sicyon* (Athens: Ekdotike Helados S.A., 1994), 36–37; Valavanis, *Games and Sanctuaries*, 292–301. On the *earlier* Classical stadium (close to the temple of Poseidon) and its sophisticated starting arrangements, see O. Broneer, *Isthmia II: Topography and Architecture* (Princeton: American School of Classical Studies at Athens, 1973), 46–66, 137–42; Valavanis, *Games and Sanctuaries*, 286–91.

[26] The principal games in the early Roman period are set out in an inscription detailing the career of the athlete Titus Flavius Archibius of Alexandria (AD 107: IG XIV 747 [Provenance: Naples]; tr. S.G. Miller, *Arete: Greek Sports from Ancient Sources* [Berkeley et al.: University of California Press, 1991] § 150). Archibius competed at Olympia (220th/221st Olympiads), Rome (Great Capitoline Games; Heraklean Games); Delphi (Pythian Games); Nemea (Nemean Games); Corinth (Isthmian Games); Aktia (Aktian Games); Naples (festival games); Ephesos (Balbilleia Games); Antioch (sacred four-year games); Smyrna (League of Asia Games); Alexandria (sacred four-year games); Argos (Shield of Argos Games). The inscription highlights the likelihood that Paul either saw local games himself (1 Cor 9:21a: τοῖς ἀνόμοις ὡς ἄνομος) or encountered athletes on their way to and from games during his missionary travels. See also the wide-ranging victories of Marcus Aurelius Asclepiades (IG XIX 1102: tr. W.E. Sweet, *Sport and Recreation in Ancient Greece: A Sourcebook with Translations* [New York and Oxford: Oxford University Press, 1987], 146–47). Note, too, the victories of the Corinthian boy singer (J.H. Kent, *Corinth Vol. III/Pt. III The Inscriptions1926–1950* [Princeton; American School of Classical Studies at Athens, 1966], § 272 [=IKentKorinth § 272]) in the thymelic contests at Argos, Corinth, Sikyon, and Epidauros.

[27] Note the perceptive comment of C. Toussaint regarding Paul's use of athletic imagery,

Paul may have sourced his athletic imagery from the sermons of the popular philosophers delivered in the agora of Corinth or at the Isthmian games themselves.[28] Rather this chapter is intended to remind New Testament scholars that imagery is as much *visual* as it is literary in its origin and that Paul's sophisticated response to the Greek athletic ideal would have critiqued the visual icons of excellence as much its literary representations.

In the next section we will look at how Paul interacts with the athletic images of the runner and boxer in addressing the divisions in the Corinthian house churches. Finally, Paul's critique of crowning is explored in its epigraphic and visual arts context. Our choice of visual artefacts relating to the athletic ideal

---

arguing that it has its origins at Tarsus (*L'Hellénisme et l'apôtre Paul* [Paris: Émille Nourry, 1921], 202): "Paul n'a pas eu besoin d'aller aux jeux olympiques, lors de son séjour à Corinthe, pour prendre ses comparisons: il avait eudepuis longtemps, à Tarse, de pareils spectacles." Indeed, many diaspora Jews were frequenters of the games (e.g. Philo, *Omn. Prob. Lib.* 26). See H.A. Harris, *Greek Athletics and the Jews* (Cardiff: University of Wales Press, 1976), 51–95. On whether the nakedness of Greek athletes would prevent Jews from attending the games, see P.F. Esler, "Paul and the Agon," 375–76. It is even possible that Paul encountered diaspora Jews who had an ephebic education, with its emphasis on athletics for the body and philosophy for the mind, at the gymnasium of Tarsus (Dio Chrysostom, *Oration* 33.36: ἐν τῷ γυμνασίῳ) – though the remains of first-century Tarsus remain inaccessible, lying beneath the modern city – or at other eastern Mediterranean gymnasia. Philo, for instance, assumes a gymnasium education for upper class Alexandrian Jews and praises its educational outcomes (cf. L.H. Feldman (*Jew and Gentile in the Ancient World* [Princeton: Princeton University Press, 1993], 57–59). Moreover, it is likely that Jewish parents enrolled their sons in an ephebic education in order to gain Alexandrian citizenship (CPJ 153 Col III. *ll.* 53–59). Also, P. Borgen ("'Yes', 'No', 'How Far?': The Participation of Jews and Christians in Pagan Cults," in *Paul in His Hellenistic Context*, ed. T. Engberg-Pedersen [Edinburgh: T&T Clark, 1994], 30–59, at 41) observes that "Philo's writings even betray such an expert knowledge of Greek sports that he himself was active in athletics during his youth." For Jewish ephebic names and/or patronymics among the lists of gymnasium graduates at Cyrene, Iasos and Coronea, see M.H. Williams, *The Jews among the Greeks and Romans: A Sourcebook* (London: Duckworth, 1998), V.1, 2, 21–23. For an inscription, used as a seat marker in the *palaestra* at Hypaepa, mentioning an association of Jewish young men (νεώτεροι), see *ibid.*, V.24. In a papyrus (7–4 BC: Williams, *The Jews among the Greeks and Romans*, V.3), the Alexandrian Jew Helenos speaks of his having received, "as far as my father's means allowed, the appropriate education (*paideia*)," presumably at his father's "ancestral gymnasium." Finally, given that Paul characterises his childhood upbringing as being "a Hebrew of Hebrews" (Phil 3:5; 2 Cor 11:22; Acts 21:40; 22:2; 26:14), it is clear that Paul's parents never envisaged an ephebic education for their son (cf. Acts 22:3; 26:4; Gal 1:14). If Acts 22:3 (cf. 23:16) is historically correct, Paul was brought as a child in the city of Jerusalem (ἀνατεθραμμένος δὲ ἐν τῇ πόλει ταύτῃ) at the feet of Gamaliel. See the extensive discussion of C.S. Keener, *Acts: An Exegetical Commentary. Volume 3: 15:1–23:35* (Grand Rapids: Baker Academic, 2014), 3205–22.

[28] Dio Chrysostom (*Or.* 8.9–12) imagines Diogenes, the Cynic philosopher, presenting a moral diatribe replete with athletic imagery at the Isthmian Games (ca. 359 BC): "The man who is noble is the one who considers hardship as his greatest competitor and struggles with it day and night, and not, like some goat, for a bit of celery, olive, or pine, but for the sake of happiness and *arete* throughout his whole life." For discussion of the philosophers' appropriation of the athletic ideal, see Pfitzner, *Agon Motif*; Croy, *Endurance in Suffering*; R.F. Collins, *First Corinthians*; Brändl, *Der Agon bei Paulus.*

ranges from Classical times to the Roman period and spans the entire Mediterranean basin, though evidence from Corinth is highlighted where relevant visual images exist (nn. 36, 40, 43, 60, 90, 91, 96). Therefore, the bulk of the material cited is representative of the *types* of visual artefacts that Paul *may* have seen, dangers of anachronism notwithstanding.

What is required in terms of rigorous historical methodology is a *city-by-city* list of first-century visual artefacts found in the *poleis* visited by Paul, with a view to discussing imagery he uses. The foundation for such an approach is available to New Testament scholars through the *Harvard New Testament Archaeology Project* and the *Perseus Project* at Tufts University, though Pauline scholars have been until recently reticent to plumb the visual riches now available. It is, however, beyond the bounds of this chapter to mount such an ambitious exercise. Nonetheless, at the end of the article, we will ask what might be legitimately said about Paul's exposure to the visual imagery of the athletic ideal on the basis of the *local* Corinthian evidence, given our methodological caveats above.

4.2. Paul's Running and Boxing Images: A "Visual Arts" Approach

4.2.1. Paul's Image of the Runner (1 Corinthians 9:24–26a)

At the outset, we need to place Paul's games imagery in its immediate context.[29] Paul is writing to Corinthian house churches divided by internal leadership squabbles (1 Cor 1:12; 3:2–5, 21–23; 4:6, 14–15), sexual immorality (5:1–13; 6:9, 12–20), lawsuits (6:1–11), and asceticism (1 Cor 7:1–40). In particular, there were strong differences of opinion among believers regarding meat offered to idols and the associated cultural activities that occurred in the pagan temples, local associations, or private homes (8:1–11:1). The "strong" in the house churches despised the "weak" regarding their caution and timidity on these cultural and theological issues. Paul insists that the strong should demonstrate self-denial and not be a stumbling block to the weak by their culturally insensitive behaviour (1 Cor 8:9–13). The paradigm for this determination is the selfless death of Christ on behalf of the weak (1 Cor 8:11a) and the other-centered ministry of Paul as an apostle (9:1–23). Paul insists that he has demonstrated the radical self-sacrifice he demands of others, instancing his refusal of payment as an apostle (1 Cor 9:1–8) and his selfless identification with the needs and disposition of others as cases in point (9:19–23).[30]

[29] For discussion, see J.L. Sumney, "The Place of 1 Corinthians 9:24–27 in Paul's Argument," *JBL* 119.2 (2000): 24–27.

[30] On the Pythagorean understanding of the "weak" and "strong" as referring to the different temperaments of students, see C.E. Glad, *Paul and Philodemus: Adaptability in Epicurean and Early Christian Psychagogy*, NovTSup 81 (Leiden et al.: Brill, 1995), 236–332.

Therefore Paul appeals to the dedication and self-imposed abstinence of athletes (1 Cor 9:24a; 25a) as a further paradigm for Corinthian self-denial (9:24b, 25b). Self-control was necessary for the adaptable lifestyle of identification with others that Paul was advocating (1 Cor 9:19–22; 9:25; 10:33–11:1). The denial of personal rights was essential if one was to care for the weak and not be a stumbling block over the issue of food offered to idols (1 Cor 8:9–13; 10:28–29a, 31–32; cf. 9:4–15; 2 Cor 13:4).[31] Personal discipline was a prerequisite for those wanting to avoid the personal pitfalls of idolatry and its debilitating effects on the spiritual growth of the weak (1 Cor 5:9; 8:10; 10:1–22).[32] Thus Paul extends the scope of the Greek agonistic ideal to corporate relations in his house churches and deepens its force by reminding the Corinthians that the personal discipline of the spiritual athlete must have an other-centered focus, if the body of Christ was to function as a harmonious unit. In all of this, the "unfading crown" (1 Cor 9:25b) provides the eschatological incentive for the selfless lifestyle

[31] For discussion, see G.D. Fee, "Εἰδωλόθυτα Once Again: An Interpretation of 1 Corinthians 8–10," *Bib* 61 (1980): 172–97; W.L. Willis, *Idol Meat in Corinth: The Pauline Argument in 1 Corinthians 8 and 10*, SBL Dissertation Series 68 (Chico: Scholars Press, 1985); P.J. Tomson, *Paul and the Jewish Law: Halakha in the Letters of the Apostle to the Gentiles* (Minneapolis: Fortress, 1990), 187–220 P.D. Gooch, *Dangerous Food: 1 Corinthians 8–10 in Its Context*, Studies in Christianity and Judaism 5 (Ontario: Wilfrid Laurier University Press, 1993); B. Witherington III, "Not So Idle Thoughts about *Eidolothuton*," *TynBul* 44 (1993): 237–54; A.T. Cheung, *Idol Food in Corinth: Jewish background and Pauline Legacy* JSNTSup 176 (Sheffield: Sheffield Academic Press, 1999); J. Fotopoulos, *Food Offered to Idols in Roman Corinth: A Socio-Rhetorical Reconstruction of 1 Corinthians 8:1–11:1*, WUNT II 151 (Tübingen: Mohr Siebeck, 2003); D.G. Horrell, "Idol-Food, Idolatry and Ethics in Paul," in *Idolatry: False Worship in the Bible, Early Judaism and Christianity*, ed. S.C. Barton (London and New York: T&T Clark, 2007), 120–40; S.C. Barton, "Food Rules, Sex Rules and the Prohibition of Idolatry. What's the Connection?" in *idem*, *Idolatry*, 141–62; G.K. Beale, *We Become What We Worship: A Biblical Theology of Idolatry* (Downers Grove: IVP, 2008), 202–40; T.A. Rogers, *God and the Idols: Representations of God in 1 Corinthians 8–10*, WUNT II 427 (Tübingen: Mohr Siebeck, 2016).

[32] Garland (*1 Corinthians*, 438 n. 1) correctly notes that 1 Cor 9:24–27 "serves as an introductory transition to 10:1–13)." I am now less convinced than I was (cf. J.R. Harrison, 'The Fading Crown: Divine Honour and the Early Christians," *JTS* 54.2 [2003], 493–529, at 525) by B.W. Winter's suggestion (*Philo and Paul among the Sophists*, SNTSMS 96 [Cambridge: Cambridge University Press, 1997], 166–68) that 9:24–27 has an anti-sophistic thrust in Paul's portrayal of his conduct, building on his apologia in 1 Cor 9:1–18. Winter transposes the anti-sophistic concerns of 1 Corinthians 1–4 into a new context that deals with Corinthian concerns (1 Cor 8:1; cf. 7:1) over food offered to idols (8:1, 7; 10:25) and cultic feasts in pagan temples and private homes (8:10; 10:7, 14–22, 27). The athletic imagery of vv.24–27 is clearly part of Paul's rhetorical strategy addressing these cultic concerns and the communal divisions that had ensued (1 Cor 8:7, 9–13; 10:14, 21–22, 24). Moreover, Paul's apologia in 1 Cor 9:1–18 more provides an exemplum of self-sacrificial behaviour to be imitated by the "strong" (esp. vv. 15–18; cf. 11:1), who had run rough-shod over the sensibilities of the "weak" (8:1–3, 7, 9, 11–13; 10:27–29). There *may* be an implied contrast in 1 Cor 9:24–27 between the apostle and the self-indulgent sophists of 1 Cor 4:8, but it is somewhat muted on Paul's part. Contra, see Dutch, *The Educated Elite*, 247–48.

required of the Corinthians. But what of Paul's image of the "runner" in this regard? How does it function in its visual arts context?

In 1 Corinthians 9:24 Paul challenges the undisciplined Corinthians with a penetrating question and exhortation: "Do you not know that in a race all the runners run (οἱ ἐν σταδίῳ τρέχοντες πάντες μὲν τρέχουσιν), but only one gets the prize (τὸ βραβεῖον)? Run (τρέχετε) in such a way to get the prize." The runner's mind has to be entirely focused on winning, if he is to receive the crown of victory over against the rest of the pack relentlessly pursuing him (1 Cor 9:24). Therefore the determination of each believer must be to expend maximum effort in pursuit of the one goal: the acquisition of the victor's prize. The apostle follows up this admonition with the statement of his personal intention as a "runner" himself (1 Cor 9:26a; cf. Phil 2:16; 3:13–14; 2 Tim 4:7): "Therefore I do not run like a man running aimlessly (τρέχω ὡς οὐκ ἀδήλως)." No trace of hesitation should vitiate the believer's determination to win or distract him from the goal.

The visual arts evidence of athletes running in antiquity aligns with Paul's major emphases in vv. 24, 26a, outlined above. Several examples will suffice. First, the left side of a relief base of the funerary statue of a kouros depicts six athletes in different events and exercises.[33] In the centre are two runners, one with palms open contesting the sprint race (*stadion*), the other with clenched fists contesting the distance race (*dolichos*). Significantly, the two gesticulating athletes, to the right, who are watching the contest, distract neither runner.

Second, an Attic black-figure Panathenaic amphora – a smaller copy of the larger amphorae given to the victors in the Panathenaic games – depicts three

[33] Provenance Athens: 510 BC: Measham, *1000 Years*, 74 (found built into the Themistoclean Walls in 1922). M. Andronicos (et al., ed., *The Greek Museums* [London: Barrie & Jenkins, 1975], 68 plate 64; also, Alexander, *Greek Athletics* 30; Gardiner, *Athletics*, fig. 212; S. G. Miller, *Ancient Greek Athletics* [New Haven and London: Yale University Press, 2004], 173 fig. 255) interprets the scene differently. He argues that the six athletes are playing a ball game in two teams of three. If Andronichos is correct, the two figures to the extreme left and the two figures to the extreme right – ignoring for the moment the two central figures facing each other – are neither (respectively) exercising nor gesticulating, as Meascham (*1000 Years*, 74) suggests. Rather they are participating in the ball game. Which view, then, is correct? The relief is difficult to interpret definitively. A ball is visible in the right hand of the youth on the extreme left. The fact that the two sets of three figures are aligned to face each other does suggest a competitive ball game. The argument of Andronicos, therefore, has force. But, in favour of Meacham (*ibid.*) the hand positions of the two central figures facing each other on the left (open-palmed) and on the right (clench-fisted) are respectively the positions adopted by runners in the *stadion* (sprint) and the *dolichos* (long-distance) races. For the clench-fisted pose of the *diolos*, see Gardiner, *Athletics* figs. 92 and 93; for the open-palmed pose of the *stadion* race, see Gardiner, *Athletics*, fig. 89; Alexander, *Greek Athletics*, 8. That each set of three figures faces each other is simply intended for aesthetic effect. The youth on the extreme left, therefore, is preparing to throw the ball or is exercising with the ball, while his companion looks on. For an Attic grave relief (first half of IV cent. BC) showing an athlete exercising with a ball, see Valavanis, *Games and Sanctuaries*, 381 §550.

runners toiling towards the finish, with their fists clenched and arms held low.[34] The intent gaze of the three long-distance runners,[35] along with their vigorous wide stride and tautly muscled legs, underscores each man's determination to finish the *dolichos* as the victor.

Third, an Attic black-figure Kylix depicts a young athlete running to the right with his head turned back.[36] Clearly he is at the leader of the race and, determined to stay there, is checking how far his rivals are behind him.

Fourth, an Athenian drinking cup depicts the winner of the race-in-armour (*hoplitodromia*) taking off his helmet and looking at the runner-up who has abjectly thrown down his shield.[37]

Fifth, a bronze statuette of a runner leans forward in the starting position.[38] What is impressive about the statue is the steady gaze of the athlete ahead, given directional focus by the outstretched arms and the slightly raised left foot. Above all, the face sums up the athlete's attitude. As X. Arapoyianni notes, "The youthful face is framed by short hair and the large eyes gaze steadily ahead, giving the athlete an expression of decisiveness and inner concentration."[39] Significantly, the presence of the presiding deity at Olympia is emphasised by the votif inscription on the outside of the runner's right thigh (TO ΔΙΟΣ IMI: "I belong to Zeus").[40]

---

[34] Provenance: Kamiros on Rhodes; 500 BC: Measham, *1000 Years*, 84. See, too, the Panathenaic amphora (Provenance: Bologna: 440 BC: Gardiner, *Athletics*, fig. 91) that shows two boy runners vigorously striding, one running in self-contained manner, the other summoning all his strength and determination to spurt past his rival.

[35] Note the comment of Lucian (ca. 170 AD: *On Slander* 12): "Immediately the *hysplex* has fallen the good runner thinks only of what is in front of him, and stretching his mind towards the *terma* and putting his hope of victory in his feet, does not plot against the fellow next to him nor even consider his competitors." The tightly compressed lips and wide-eyed stare of a runner on a Panathenaic amphora (Provenance: Attica, 550 BC: Tzachou-Alexandri, *Mind and Body*, § 139) underscores the strain of the race.

[36] Provenance: Corinth; 570–560 BC: Measham, *1000 Years*, 80. See the Attic red-figure kylix (Gardiner, *Athletics*, fig. 96) that shows a race in armour: "Below we see three runners in full career, one of whom is committing an unpardonable offence, he is looking around" (*ibid.*, 142).

[37] Provenance: Athens; 500–475: J. Swaddling, *The Ancient Olympic Games*, 59. See also the unusual stele, forming part of a funeral monument, showing a nude running hoplite (Andronicos, *The Greek Museums*, 76 plate 63).

[38] Provenance: Olympia; 480–470: Measham, *1000 Years*, 76

[39] X. Arapoyianni, "Statuette of a Runner," in Measham, *1000 Years*, 76 picture 77. See the similar pose at the start of the race in armour on an Attic red-figure amphora (470 BC: Gardiner, *Athletics*, fig. 87). Additionally, note the runner poised at the start on a kylix, as well as the bronze statuette of an armed runner (*hoplitodromos*) practising starts (Alexander, *Greek Athletics*, 8–9). For an additional example, see Miller, "The Organization and Functioning of the Olympic Games," in *Sport and Festival in the Ancient Greek World*, ed. D.J. Philips and D. Pritchard (Swansea: The Classical Press of Wales, 2003), 28 fig. 26.

[40] Arapoyianni, "Statuette of a Runner", 76. See Measham, *1000 Years* 50, 78 for (respectively) a discus dedicated to Zeus ("In thanks to Olympian Zeus from Publius Asklepiades of

Sixth, the bronze statuette of a female runner also emphasises a total concentration of effort: not only is the young woman's musculature pronounced, but she also slightly raises the hem of her short chiton in order to make it easier to run.[41]

Seventh, and importantly for our context, at the Archaeological Museum of Isthmia a Panathenaic amphora, dedicated in the sanctuary by the Corinthian victor (DAMHΩN: "Damon") of the *dolichos* race, shows four runners intently competing in the event.[42] Corinthian bronze coins, stemming from the reign of Augustus, also show naked runners, one crouched ready to start, the other in full flight.[43]

Eighth, in 1 Corinthians 9:25a Paul generalises regarding the rigorous training regime of athletes, asserting that self-control' (ἐγκρατεύεται) was determinative for their success. As an illustration of their discipline, D.E. Garland points to Pausanias' statement that both athletes and trainers swore an oath on boar's flesh that they would sin against the Olympic games in nothing and then committed themselves to ten months of strict training.[44] The visual evidence corroborates this ceremony. The bezel of a cast gold ring shows a statue of Zeus Horkios ("Zeus of the Oaths") erected for this precise ritual.[45] The deity holds a thunderbolt in each hand and stands before the sacrificial boar and a flaming altar, the very place where the Olympic oath would be sworn.

Finally, in regards to the coronal image of 1 Corinthians 9:25b, Pindar devotes one of his Olympian odes to Xenephon of Corinth, a victor in the short foot race (464 BC). Pindar (*Olympian Odes* 13.23–40) speaks of Xenephon's victories thus:

Lord supreme of Olympia! That reigns and wide, O Father Zeus! ... grant a straight course to the fair breeze of Xenephon's good fortune, and accept from him the duly ordered triumph-band in honour of his crowns, being victor in the five events, as well as in the footrace. He has thus attained what no mortal man has ever attained before. And two wreaths of wild celery crowned him, when he appeared at the Isthmian festival; and

Corinth, Pentathlete") and the votive inscription to Athena on a statue of a long jumper ("Sacred to Athena: Philaios [dedicated me as] a tithe").

[41] Provenance: sanctuary of Zeus at Dodone; mid VI cent. BC: Measham, *1000 Years*, 82. See also the bronze statuette of a female runner in the same pose (Provenance: Sparta: 500 BC): Swaddling, *The Ancient Olympic Games*, 42. See also Vanhove, *Le sport dans la Grèce antique*, § 114 (Provenance: Palermo: 550–525 BC). An inscription from Corinth (IKent-Korinth § 155) speaks of Lucius Castricius Regulus establishing "[a contest for] girls." For additional ceramics of runners, see Vanhove, *Le sport dans la Grèce antique*, §§ 171–173, 175–177, 179; Tzachou-Alexandri, *Mind and Body*, §§ 137–138, 140; Valavanis, *Games and Sanctuaries*, 410–13 §§ 589–597.

[42] Valavanis, *Games and Sanctuaries*, 286 §§ 405–406.

[43] K.M. Edwards, *Corinth: Coins, 1896–1927* (Cambridge, MA: Harvard University Press, 1933), §§ 85, 87. See also Dutch, *Educated Elite*, 229.

[44] Garland, *1 Corinthians*, 441, citing Pausanias, *Descr.* 9.24.9–10.

[45] Swaddling, *The Ancient Olympic Games*, 39.

Nemea has shown no unkindly mood; and, at the steam of Alpheus, is stored up the glory won by the swift feet of his father, Thesalus. At Pytho, he has the fame of the single and the double foot-race, won within the circuit of the self-same sun; and, in the same month, at rocky Athens did one swift day fling over his hair three fairest crowns of victory, and seven times was victorious at the festival of Athenea Hellotis.[46]

We gain from Pindar a rich appreciation of the momentous achievements of the multiple crowned Xenephon. But while such runners were considered icons of virtue throughout the city states of the eastern Mediterranean, Paul democratises the victory of the Christian's race and postpones the allocation of its awards until the eschaton.[47] Moreover, he dismisses the coronal honours of athletes such as Xenephon as "fading" (φθαρτὸν στέφανον) in comparison to the "unfading" crown (ἄφθαρτον) of the believers (1 Cor 9:25). What we are witnessing in Paul's approach is a radical redefinition of the canons of honour in antiquity that would ultimately overturn its hierarchy of merit.

Having established the visual arts background of Paul's runner image, we turn now to the visual representation of the boxer in antiquity and its relevance for Paul's use of pugilistic imagery.

4.2.2. Paul's Image of the Boxer (1 Corinthians 9:26b–27)

In 1 Corinthians 9:26b–27 Paul issues a second challenge to the undisciplined Corinthians by means of the image of the boxer. Paul says,

> I do not fight like a man beating the air (πυκτεύω ὡς οὐκ ἀέρα δέρων). No, I beat my body (ὑπωπιάζω μου τὸ σῶμα) and make it my slave (δουλαγωγῶ) so that after I have preached to others (ἄλλοις κηρύξας), I myself will not be disqualified for the prize (μή πως αὐτὸς ἀδόκιμος γένωμαι).

The unusual jargon[48] – πυκτεύω ("I box"), δέρω ἀέρα ("I flail at the air"), ὑπωπιάζω ("I bruise": literally, "I give a black eye", "I strike under the eye"), and δουλαγωγῶ ("I subjugate") – underscores the savagery of boxing in the ancient games. Paul emphasises that he is now a battered and blooded competitor with

[46] Note too Bacchylides' *Isthmian Ode for Aglus of Athens* 10. Aglus won the foot race at the Corinthian isthmus and at other smaller games (Thebes, Argos, Sicyon, and Pellene): "In games of Poseidon, fine on the fields of praise you amazed the Greeks with a rushing sprint; no break and back to the ring's first mark – breath hot and short – you tensed, sprang, sprayed admirer's robes with oil, carved the roaring crowd on rounding the track's fourth lap. Isthmian victor twice proclaimed by infallible judges, twice near Nemea's altar holy to Cronian Zeus: famous Thebes, Argos starred with rings, and Sicyon received you grandly – joined by men of Pellene, Euboea thick with corn, and the hallowed isle of Aegina."

[47] Esler ("Paul and the Agon," 364–65) correctly emphasises that there was only one winner and one prize given in ancient races.

[48] Collins, *First Corinthians*, 362. Collins notes that these are the only occurrences of πυκτεύω, δέρω ἀέρα, and ὑπωπιάζω in the New Testament. E.-B. Allo (*Saint Paul: Première Épitre aux Corinthiens* [Paris: J. Gabalda, 1934], 228) says that ὑπωπιάζω is a "terme technique de boxe."

his chief opponent, the body, which remains the seat of his selfish desires and continuously demands self-gratification. Such a deceitful opponent must be dealt with ruthlessly if Paul is to receive his eschatological prize and if the self-seeking behaviour of the Corinthians towards their weaker brethren is to cease. How, then, does Paul's image of the boxer function in its ancient visual arts context?

Several examples from the Greek world confirm Paul's emphases. First, the bronze statuette of a boxer depicts the weariness of a boxer who, having probably lost his fight, raises his hand and squints through puffy eyes.[49] His knuckles are reinforced with rings of tougher leather and provide corroborating evidence for the bruising inflicted on opponents.[50] Second, another bronze statue shows a seasoned Greek boxer with a cauliflower ear and broken nose, seated in an exhausted pose.[51] Third, an Attic red-figure amphoriskos shows a boxer being spread-eagled by the well-timed punch of his opponent's left hand. The loser signals defeat by raising the index finger of his right hand.[52] Fourth, a Greek drinking cup shows two boxers on the left trying to deflect or land telling blows.[53] Fifth, two ceramic African boxers shows the loser reeling from a savage upper cut.[54] Sixth, an Athenian amphora depicts two boxers engaged in heated combat, one bleeding profusely from the nose.[55] Seventh, the boxer who was gaining the advantage in a fight is sometimes indicated by the figure of Nike standing nearby the fighter with a palm branch, as seen on side B of an Attic black-figure vase. This boxer has gained advantage in the contest by blocking his opponent's punch with his right arm and by throwing out his left arm while leaning back slightly, thereby not being hit in the face.[56] Eighth, on a krater two

---

[49] Provenance: unknown; I cent. BC; Measham, *1000 Years*, 105–06.

[50] Note the use of the *caestus* (a plate of ridged material, such as metal) covering the boxer's knuckles. For examples, see the bronze figurines and mosaics in Poliakoff, *Combat Sports*, 77–78 figs.78–80. On ancient boxing equipment, see Philostratos, *On Gymnastics* 34 (tr. Miller, *Arete*, 31 § 24).

[51] Provenance: unknown: I cent. BC: Poliakoff, *Combat Sports*, 74; cf. *ibid*., 78.

[52] Provenance: Aegina; V cent. BC; Measham, *1000 Years*, 110–11. See also Poliakoff, *Combat Sports*, 71 fig. 71; Alexander, *Greek Athletics*, 23; Gardiner, *Athletics*, 181 fig. 180, 199 fig. 173.

[53] 500–475 BC: Swaddling, *The Ancient Olympic Games*, 75. Gardiner, *Athletics*, 185 fig. 183, 207 fig. 186, 209 fig. 187.

[54] II or I cent. BC: Swaddling, *The Ancient Olympic Games*, 79. Note, too, the sixth century Greek vase showing a boxer striking his opponent's genitals (Poliakoff, *Combat Sports*, 86). For the physical damage done to boxers, see the epigram of Lucillius regarding the boxer Apollophanes cited in *ibid*., 87.

[55] 550–540 BC: Swaddling, *The Ancient Olympic Games*, 44. A black-figure amphora shows blood streaming from the faces of both boxers (Miller, "The Organization and Functioning of the Olympic Games," 26 fig. 23). See also Gardiner, *Athletics*, 215 fig. 190. For the bloody handprints on two competitors in the pankration (fragment of a red-figure kylix), see Miller, *Ancient Greek Athletics*, 58 fig. 96.

[56] Provenance: Cervetri: 336 BC. J.D. Beazley, *Attic Red-Figure Vase*-Painters, 2nd ed. (Oxford: Clarendon, 1963), 415, fig. 4. Note the inscription running down the shaft of the

boxers are depicted sparring with open hands,[57] learning to punch and counter-punch, and on other occasions – as Plato informs us[58] – practising on a lifeless effigy or shadowboxing.[59] Ninth, and once again significantly for the Corinthian context, Corinthian bronze coins show naked boxers facing each other, either landing blows while standing upright, or in one case, falling over backwards.[60]

The ancient visual representation of boxing, therefore, is consonant with the harsh treatment Paul metes out as a boxer and underlines his ruthlessness in ensuring that he wins his fight at all costs. Punches had to count: to have them blocked by one's opponent was a waste of vital energy; to flail at the air, appropriate for training, was a recipe for disaster in a real fight. The surprising thing is that Paul's real enemy is his own body and he calls the Corinthians, along with himself, to fight to the death the self-centeredness that vitiates corporate relationships in the house churches.

Once again, this differs manifestly from the quest for crowns – with its focus on personal fame and glory for one's city and family – that characterised the ancient athletes.[61] Pindar's Olympian Ode VII *ll.* 81–93 sums up memorably the quest of Diagoras of Rhodes, the most famous of Greek boxers (Pausanias, *Descr.* 6.7.1), for honour through boxing. Listing his four victories at the Isthmian games, among others, Pindar writes:

With flowers from that contest, twice has Diagoras crowned himself, and at the famous Isthmus four times, in his good fortune; and again and again, at Nemea and rocky Athens; while he is not unknown to the shield of bronze in Argos, and the works of art given as prizes in Arcadia and at Thebes, and to the duly ordered contests amid the Boetians, and to Pellana, and to Aegina, where he was six times victor, while in Megara the reckoning on the tablet of stone tells no other tale. But do you, O father Zeus, that rules over the height of Atabyrium, grant honour to the hymn ordained in praise of an Olympian victor, and to the hero who has found fame for his prowess as a boxer; and give him grace

right column on side A ("One of the prizes from Athens"). This provides the original context for the use of the vase and its intended distribution.

[57] Alexander, *Greek Athletics*, 23; see also Gardiner, *Athletics*, fig. 185. For additional ceramics and statues of boxers, see Vanhove, *Le sport dans la Grèce antique*, §§ 220, 231–233; Tzachou-Alexandri, *Mind and Body* §§ 169–172, 174; Valavanis, *Games and Sanctuaries*, 428–31 §§ 617–623.

[58] Plato, *Laws* 830a–c.

[59] On the uncertainty of the meaning of ἀέρα δέρων (shadowboxing? punches that miss the mark?), see Thiselton, *First Epistle*, 715. Esler ("Paul and the Agon," 377) argues that ἀέρα δέρων is an example of litoses current among boxers meaning "give a hiding to." While this is a possibility, we have also noted above visual evidence of boxers sparring open-handed and not landing full-fledged punches. This makes the interpretation of shadow-boxing more likely.

[60] Edwards, *Corinth: Coins*, §§ 83–84. Dutch, *Educated Elite*, 228–29 (citing O. Broneer, *Corinth: Terracotta Lamps* [Cambridge, MA: Harvard University Press, 1930], § 423, fig. 97, 172) also points to Corinthian terracotta lamps depicting boxers.

[61] On the motivations of athletes, see Esler, "Paul and the Agon," 363–65.

and reverence in the eyes of citizens and of strangers too. For he goes in a straight course along a path that hates insolence; he has learnt full well all the lessons prompted by the prudence which he inherits from goodly ancestors.[62]

There are other visual emphases in 1 Corinthians 9:27 that would have registered with an audience familiar with the athletic ideal. In verse 27b Paul fears that, notwithstanding his faithful heralding to others (ἄλλοις κηρύξας), he still might be disqualified and miss out on the eschatological prize (μὴ ατὸς ἀδόκιμος γένωμαι; cf. v.24b: τὸ βραβεῖον). Each feature of Paul's imagery here finds a visual arts counterpart in antiquity.

First, the prizes are regularly depicted on artefacts.[63] A fragment of a black-figure *dinos* (mid VI cent. BC) depicts two boxers sparring in front of a prize tripod.[64] An imperial bronze coin from Delphi shows a prize table bearing crowns, five apples, a vase and a crow.[65] A bronze coin of Elis shows the awards table with prizes on it, while on an Attic black-figure amphora a seated official crowns the victor, behind whom is born the heavy tripod prize.[66] It was for precisely such ephemeral prizes that runners and boxers devoted their ten months of training,[67] being subject to the threat that they would be disqualified if they did not do so.[68]

Second, the visual arts attest to the ever-present risk of disqualification, mentioned in verse 27b, that athletes faced as they participated in the games. On a vase (340/339 BC) we see the referee instructing two boxers before the fight.[69] On vases officials are shown striking boxers for clinching their opponent (510 BC) or grasping their opponent's arm (425 BC).[70] A seated official, probably a judge, is authoritatively placed before the finishing post on a Greek amphora

[62] In Bacchylides' *Isthmian Odes for Argeius of Ceos* I (cf. *ibid.*, II), the writer speaks of Argeius' boxing feats thus: "And now, one among all on his father's strength receives from Zeus of the rising throne an Isthmian win and fates of vital wreaths."

[63] For an inscription listing the prizes awarded at the Panathenaic games (IG II^2 2311: 400–350 BC), see Miller, *Arete*, § 84. On heralding at the Isthmian games, see Polybius, *Histories* 18.46.

[64] Gardiner, *Athletics*, fig. 184.

[65] Gardiner, *Athletics*, 35 fig. b.

[66] For the coin, see Miller, "The Organization and Functioning of the Olympic Games," 30 fig. 29. For the amphora, see Valavanis, *Games and Sanctuaries*, 114 § 144. For images of the prizes of an Athenian athlete, see Miller, *Ancient Greek Athletics*, 130 fig. 212.

[67] For the prizes for the chariot race, see Measham, *1000 Years*, 44, 114.

[68] Plato, *Laws* 840a, cited in G.D. Fee, *The First Epistle to the Corinthians* (Grand Rapids: Eerdmans, 1987), 436 n. 19. For additional prizes, see Valavanis, *Games and Sanctuaries*, 22 § 19, 370 §§ 531–533. See also the prizes mentioned in the papyrus of the athlete Dios in the National Museum at Berlin (number 6222), tr. Sweet, *Sport and Recreation*, 151 no. 8.

[69] Poliakoff, *Combat Sports*, 116 fig. 93; cf. *ibid.*, 79 fig. 81.

[70] Poliakoff, *Combat Sports*, 81 figs. 83 and 84 respectively. Note the amphora in Miller ("The Organization and Functioning of the Olympic Games," 26 fig. 22) where a judge prepares to flog a boxer who continues to hit his down-and-out opponent. On a black figure amphora showing two athletes in the pankration, the official signals a foul with his rod (Sweet, *Sport and Recreation*, 83 plate 29). Similarly, Miller, *Ancient Greek Athletics*, 59 fig. 102. For

(475–450 BC).[71] Finally, on a black figure amphora four runners are about to head around the *kampter* (turning post), while a seated official watches nearby for a foul with his right arm outstretched.[72]

Third, the heralding and trumpeting competitions, which prefaced all the athletic competitions in the games at Olympia,[73] are also seen on a Panathenaic amphora. The victor (a runner?) stands on the centre holding a palm branch. To the right the herald (κῆρυξ) proclaims in a loud voice the news of the victory, while a trumpeter stands watching nearby with a trumpet in his right hand.[74] Again, Paul's auditors would have been as familiar with the visual representations of the κήρυξ as the official himself at the games.

In the case of the believer, however, Paul holds out the prospect of the imperishable wreath (1 Cor 9:25) and a share in the blessings of the gospel (1 Cor 9:23b). Paul is merely the herald of the good news, commencing the competition for others (1 Cor 9:27b: ἄλλοις κηρύξας), but neither he nor his converts are yet victors in the contest (1 Cor 9:27b; Phil 3:14; 4:1; cf. 2 Tim 4:8). God alone allocates prizes to the successful spiritual athletes at the eschaton. Paul's warnings about apostasy and not entering the eschatological rest are disturbingly real in the context (1 Cor 10:1–14; cf. 4:4–5):[75] but the apostle mollifies the threat somewhat by reminding believers that God is faithful in times of trial (10:13) and that he will sustain them to the Judgement Day (1:8–9).

Finally, another piece of visual evidence throws light on a central aspect of the ancient athletic ideal. On side B of a red-figure kylix are depicted three nude athletes (two boxers and a javelin thrower) with their equipment (leather thongs, a looped boxing cord, a javelin). Significantly for our purposes, on sides A and B is written ΚΑΛΟΣ ("beautiful"), and on the interior, depicting a nude discus

judges in wrestling matches, running races, and boxing matches, see Miller, *Ancient Greek Athletics*, 15 fig. 10; 14 fig. 9; 36 fig. 43; 52 figs. 81, 83; 54 figs. 88–89; 55 fig. 92.

[71] Swaddling, *The Ancient Olympic Games*, 40.

[72] Sweet, *Sport and Recreation*, 28 plate 4. For additional examples of judges watching athletes (respectively, a discus thrower, two wresters) for disqualification, see Valavanis, *Games and Sanctuaries*, 149 §201, 331 §481. For judges watching discus throwers, singers and kithara and aulos players, and competitors in the *euandria*, see Miller, *Ancient Greek Athletics*, 62–63 figs. 108, 109, 112; 82–83 figs. 159–161; 140 fig. 224.

[73] Miller, "The Organization and Functioning of the Olympic Games," 10–11.

[74] Miller, "The Organization and Functioning of the Olympic Games," 11 fig. 6. See *ibid.*, n. 82, for a relief of a herald and trumpeter on the rostra (*bema*) of the thymelic games at Pamphylia. See Tzachou-Alexandri, *Mind and Body*, §200 for a similar scene on a Panathenaic amphora. On the left it shows a trumpeter puffing out his cheeks for the trumpet fanfare before the proclamation of the name of the winner, seen standing solemnly in the centre next to the referee. A red-figure amphora (500 BC) shows a discus thrower and a runner approaching the herald, who is about to announce the victor: see Miller, *Ancient Greek Athletics*, 123 fig. 208. On heralding generally, see P. Valavanis, "La proclamation des vainqueurs aux Panathénées," *BCH* 114 (1990): 325–59.

[75] Fee, *First Epistle*, 440.

thrower, is found ΚΑ[ΛΟΣ] and LUKΟΣ ("Lykos is beautiful").[76] Here we see how the cult of beauty dominated male athletics in antiquity.[77] Dio Chrysostom, speaking of the many-crowned boxer Melancomas, a competitor in the Carian and Olympic games, describes his beauty thus:

> Melancomas of Caria was the most courageous and the biggest of all mankind and the most beautiful. Had he remained a private citizen and not practised boxing at all, I believe that he would still have become widely known simply for his beauty. Even so all heads, even those who did not know who he was, turned wherever he went. And yet he dressed in such a way as to escape rather than to attract attention. No matter the number of boys, no matter the number of men who were exercising, when he stripped no one looked at anyone else. And although beauty customarily leads to softness, even for one who is only moderately beautiful, Melancomas was the most moderate of men despite his beauty. And though he despised his beauty, he preserved it none the less and despite his rough sport.[78]

In 1 Corinthians 9:24–27, however, Paul evinces no interest in the beauty of athletes. But when Paul later speaks of the body of Christ, he articulates social perspectives that would have stood opposed to the ideal of beauty in the mind of contemporary auditors. Paul says that the weaker members of Christ's body are indispensable, the less honourable are the most honourable, and the unpresentable members are treated with greater modesty at the expense of the more presentable parts (1 Cor 12:22–24a). Indeed, God has intervened to ensure that the inferior parts receive the most honour (1 Cor 12:24b; cf. 1 Cor 1:27–28). In other words, Paul undermines the aesthetic and social canons of athleticism in antiquity: the strong, the beautiful, and the honourable. The cruciform weak-

[76] Beazley, *Attic Red-Figure Vase-Painters*, 344, 64. For ΚΑΛΟΣ describing Athenodotos (ΑΘΕΝΟΔΟΤΟΣ ΚΑΛΟΣ) and the boy Laches (ΟΙ ΠΙΑΣ ΚΑΛΟΣ), see Measham, *1000 Years*, 52, 100. Note, too, the epigram (Valavanis, *Games and Sanctuaries*, 426) on the base of the statue of Milon of Kroton, one of the greatest wrestlers in the ancient world: "This beautiful statue is of beautiful Milon (Μίλωνος καλοῦ), who won six times without being thrown." For other examples of ΚΑΛΟΣ terminology, see Miller, *Ancient Greek Athletics*, 63 fig. 113, 86 fig. 185, 187 fig. 272, 189 fig. 273.

[77] P. Donnelly ("Red-Figure Kylix," in Measham, *1000 Years*, 100, pictures 100–01) comments that "In ancient Greece, athletes were *considered* the ultimate objects of beauty and desire, and Laches is the most popular *kalos* name used on the 100 or so cups attributed to the Antiphon painter." The inscription on an Attic red-figured kylix, ΑΘΕΝΟΔΟΤΟΣ ΚΑΛΟΣ ("Athenodotos the beautiful"), noted above, draws the comment from R. Proskynitopoulou (Tzachou-Alexandri, *Mind and Body*, § 29): "The handsome young man with the perfect profile and large, expressive eye, a figure epitomising the virtues of *gravitas* and modesty, represents the ideal of the Athenian ephebe. Every young man in Athens exercised his body and cultivated his mind as part of a daily routine designed to make him into a clean-limbed, virtuous citizen and a credit to his city."

[78] Dio Chrysostom, *Or.* 28.5–6. On the androcentric culture of ancient athletics, see the inscription of Drymos, son of Theodoros, a runner in the *dolichos*, recorded on the statue base (IG IV^2 1.618. Provenance: Epidauros; Miller, *Arete*, 23 § 15): "running to the glorious grove of the god, an example of manliness." On male beauty, see N.B. Crowther, "Male Beauty Contests in Greece: The *Euandria* and *Euexia*," *AC* 54 (1985): 285–91.

ness of God had triumphed over the strength of human beings (1 Cor 1:25b). God's intention, instead, was to destroy the Graeco-Roman agonistic spirit that led to discord in the body of Christ (1 Cor 12:18, 25a) and to replace the Stoic ethos of self-sufficiency (1 Cor 12:15–16, 26) with mutual care (1 Cor 12:25b).[79]

We turn now to an examination of the athletic awards against the backdrop of visual representations of the crowns awarded to victorious athletes.

4.3. Coronal awards and Paul's redefinition of athletic honours

4.3.1. 1 Corinthians 9:25 and the Visual Representations of Crowns

Crown portraits were often incised in the inscriptions or painted on various monuments.[80] This widespread epigraphic practice of the ancients is easily illustrated in the case of ancient athletics. Decrees in honour of athletes were ubiquitous and Paul would have seen them in his travels.[81] At Olympia a bronze plaque bears the names of the victors from Asia Minor and the Greek mainland from the first century BC to AD 385. Incised crowns sometimes accompany the entries, with the name of the victor repeated in the genitive.[82] A relief decoration has been found on the rostra (*bema*) where artists delivered their performance at the thymelic games of Pamphylia. It shows two games officials – the herald and trumpeter – standing either side of a large inscribed crown prize.[83] Finally, on an Athenian monument celebrating the athletic victories of Marcus Tullius [- - -] are several crowns inscribed inside with the names of the festivals he competed in.[84]

Thus the incised or painted representation of a crown visually reinforced the civic honour accorded the recipient after the proclamation of the crown(s) at the Theatre (or games) and the erection of the monument in a prominent place. Also it is noteworthy that multiple crowns often signalled multiple honours.

Moreover, there existed a wide range of artefacts, ubiquitous in the Greek poleis, and representative of the range of visual materials from which Paul could have sourced his coronal imagery. A late Roman mosaic found at Tusculum,

---

[79] For discussion, see J. R. Harrison, *Paul's Language of Grace in Its Graeco-Roman Context*, WUNT II 172 (Tübingen: Mohr Siebeck, 2003), 281–82.

[80] The inscriptions cited in § 3.1 and § 3.2 below draw on my article, Harrison, "The Fading Crown."

[81] For fragmentary victor lists at the Isthmian games, see IKentKorinth § 223 (footraces, pentathlon, pankration, wrestling, boxing), § 228 (pankration).

[82] SEG XLIV 412. Note that the cost of the victors' crowns at the games of the Sarapieia is listed at Tanagara (SEG XLI 481; cf. SEG XL 83).

[83] SEG XXXI 1288: (Ιερά Πύθια (AD 249–252).

[84] SEG XXXII 177: AD 114–116: Νέμ|εια, Παναθη|ναια, δὶς|Σεβαστά, ΕΦΕ||ΣΟΝ| Περγα|,|μύνων. ---.

replete with scenes from a gymnasium, shows an official crowning the palm-holding victor, while the nearby slave boy acclaims his master.[85] Coronal awards, such as the bay leaf wreath of the Pythian games, are found on imperial bronze coins from Delphi.[86] The winged figure of Agon holds two crowns on a coin of Peparethus,[87] while a coin of Syracuse displays Nike ("Victory") crowning a charioteer.[88] An Attic votif relief (c. 460 BC) of a naked victorious athlete, head shown in profile and body turned three quarters, shows him placing a wreath on his head with his right hand.[89] Finally, and significantly for the Isthmian and Corinthian context of Paul's imagery, there is the impressive marble victory stele at Isthmia (II cent. AD) which shows eight wreaths of various plants, inside of which are inscribed the names of the games (e.g. Olympia, Capitolia, Actia etc.) for which they were awarded.[90] Also, the South Stoa of Corinth, a mosaic portrays a nude male athlete after his triumph, rendered by the symbols of the wreath and palm, standing before the goddess of "Good Luck" (εὐτυχία).[91]

Given that coronal images from the games were spread across the visual media in the eastern Mediterranean basin, what is Paul attempting in distinguishing between the φθαρτός στέφανος ("fading") and ἀφθαρτός ("unfading") crown? How would such a distinction been heard by auditors immersed in the Greek athletic ideal?

---

85 Gardiner, *Athletics*, fig. 70.

86 Gardiner, *Athletics*, 35 fig. e. Athletes wear crowns of vegetation in a detail of a V cent. BC red-figure drinking cup (Sansone, *Greek Athletics* fig. 8). See too the picture (Alexander, *Greek Athletics*, 31) from a psykter showing a victorious athlete receiving a crown of wild olive. The athlete holds in his hand some of the branches showered on the victor by the spectators.

87 Gardiner, *Athletics*, 35 fig. a (tetradrachm: early V cent. BC).

88 Gardiner, *Athletics*, 35 fig. n (decadrachm: c. 412 BC). For a similar scene on an Attic Alabastron (480 BC), see Valavanis, *Games and Sanctuaries*, 284 § 402. On a seal stone, Nike crowns an athlete with an olive wreath (Swaddling, *The Ancient Olympic Games*, 91). Similarly, Miller, *Ancient Greek Athletics*, 128 fig. 211.

89 Measham, *1000 Years*, 132–33. Similarly, Tzachou-Alexandri, *Mind and Body*, § 206.

90 For the victory stele, see Valavanis, *Games and Sanctuaries*, 285 § 404. For additional coronal images, see Vanhove, *Le sport dans la Grèce antique*, §§ 280, 282.

91 H. Koester, ed., *Cities of Paul: Images and Interpretations from the Harvard New Testament Archaeology Project* (Minneapolis: Fortress, 2005) *s.v.* Corinth (Forum: go to 'South Stoa: Wreath Monument'). In the area encompassed by the South Stoa, the mosaic is found in room C, the *agononotheteion* (the presumed Corinthian office of the *agonothetes* for the Isthmian games). For a map of the site, see J. Murphy-OConnor, "Corinth", 1137. I am grateful to Professor Edgar Krentz for drawing my attention to this evidence at the *SBL 2004 Annual Meeting*, San Antonio, Texas, USA (Nov 20–23). For full discussion, see now B. A. Robinson, "'Good Luck' from Corinth: A Mosaic of Allegory, Athletics, and Civic Identity," *AJA* 116 (2012): 105–32; J. R. Harrison, "Paul and the *agōnothetai* at Corinth: Engaging the Civic Values of Antiquity," in *The First Urban Churches. Volume 2: Roman Corinth*, ed. J. R. Harrison and L. L. Welborn (Atlanta: SBL Press, 2016), 271–326, at 285–86.

4.3.2. Imperishable and Perishable Crowns (1 Cor 9:25): Paul's Dialogue with Honorific Culture

The language of "immortality" sometimes appeared in the honorific inscriptions celebrating the achievements of athletes and their benefactors. For example, P. Cornelius Ariston, Olympic victor in the pancratium (AD 49), sums up the never-fading glory of his career in this way: "Thus do I glorify my father Eirenaios and my fatherland Ephesos with immortal crowns (στέμμασιν ἀθανάτοις)".[92] Likewise, the synod of the world's Dionysiac artists – as well as the crowned victors and contestants of the quinquennial sacred games at Ephesos (c. AD 137–161) – decree that their benefactor Alkibiades should be perpetually honoured in every city with this proclamation: "that he has been honoured with a golden crown in the religious rites of the eternal contest (τοῦ διὰ πάντων ἀγώ[νος]])."[93]

Even where the language of immorality does not appear, the coronal honour is given precedence even over death. The epitaph of Agathos Daimon, found near Olympia, views his motivation to win as an expression of piety towards the deity:

> Agathos Daimon, nicknamed "the Camel" from Alexandria, a victor at Nemeia. Here [in Olympia] he died, boxing in the stadium, having prayed to Zeus for either wreath or death. Age 35. Farewell.[94]

Another inscription details the courage of the pankratiast named Tiberius Claudius Rufus. With great perseverance he fought his opponent until nightfall, securing a tied match in the end, but winning the accolade that he "considered it better to scorn life (τῆς ψυχῆς ὑπεριδεῖν) than the hope of the crown (τῆς περὶ τόν στέφανον ἐλπίδος)."[95]

However, in the agonistic context of 1 Corinthians 9:24–27, the "fading" coronal honours of the Greek athletic ideal belong to the passing age (1 Cor 7:31b). In the present age, there is for Paul no "eternal contest" on earth that warrants the award of the "immortal crown," as the agonistic inscriptions sometimes asserted. Even believers, upon whom the end of the ages had come (1 Cor 10:11b), wait for their imperishable crown (9:25). At a more mundane level, we must not forget the perishability of the withered celery crown awarded to the victorious athletes at the Isthmian games of Corinth.[96] If Paul is alluding to the local

[92] L. Moretti, *Inscrizioni agonistiche greche* (Roma: A. Signorelli, 1953), § 64. See also Dionysius of Halicarnassus, *Ant. Rom.* 14.9.6.

[93] IEph 1a 22 *ll.* 54–56.

[94] Cited in Poliakoff, *Combat Sports*, 90. Poliakoff (*ibid.*, 90–91) discusses a range of literary and inscriptional sources in which the athletes are said to prefer death to life in the struggle for victory.

[95] SIG³ 1073. Cited in Poliakoff, *Combat Sports*, 90–91.

[96] O. Broneer, "The Isthmian Victory Crown," *AJA* 66.3 (1962): 259–63. At the Archaeological Museum of Isthmia there is a fine Roman marble head of a young athlete wearing a

wreath – and he may have visited the Isthmian games in AD 51[97] – the apostle thereby underscores the fleeting nature of the Corinthian agonistic honours. Undoubtedly, those imbued with the athletic ideal would have found such a dismissive attitude to coronal honours confronting: but, conversely, those marginalised by the honour system may well have found the eschatological democritisation of coronal honours liberating.

4.4. Conclusion

This chapter has argued that Paul interacted with the rendering of the athletic ideal in the visual arts as much as with its moral appropriation by the popular philosophers or its expression in the games themselves. At the outset, we aired the methodological difficulties posed for the historical interpreter in using visual evidence responsibly as social background for Paul's letters (n. 11 *supra*). While the complex methodological issues have not been resolved here, the likelihood is that Paul would have been familiar with visual evidence pertinent to the athletic ideal while he was at Corinth and the Isthmus, or elsewhere in the eastern Mediterranean basin. We have seen that a wide variety of artefacts from Corinth and the Isthmus depict athletes running (a black-figure Kylix, an amphora, bronze coins), boxers fighting (bronze coins, terracotta lamps), and various victory wreaths (a marble stele, a marble head, bronze coins, and a mosaic). If we concede that the spread and volume of materials available for Paul to view in the first century AD would have been more extensive than the limited selection available to modern scholars because of the vagaries of archaeological survival, then it is probable that Paul was engaging in some type of critique of the athletic ideal in its visual expression in 1 Corinthians 9:24–27, notwithstanding the anachronism of using visual evidence far pre-dating the time of Paul.

What was radical about Paul's approach to the athletic ideal in antiquity? In emptying the athletic ideal of its elitism and myopic individualism, Paul democratised its discipline and postponed the allocation of its awards. No longer were its honours the preserve of the city-state and family of the winning athlete. Paul demythologised the deities presiding over the games (1 Cor 8:5–6 [cf. Gal 4:8]; 12:2),[98] demoting them to the demonic realm (10:14–22) or consigning them to non-existence (8:4a). Instead Paul located the divine presence in the assembled

pine (celery?) crown (Papahatzis, *Ancient Corinth*, 104). For coins of the Corinthian colony showing pine and *selinon* wreaths, see M. Amandry, *Le monnayage des duovirs corinthiens* (Paris: BCHsuppl.XV, 1988), type IV, pl. V, R1–5 (40 BC); type V, pl.VI, R1–8 (39–36 BC); type XXI, pl. XXXVII, RIIa1–RIIb11 (57/58 or 58/59 AD). For the literary evidence (ca. AD 100), see Plutarch, *Mor.* 675D-676F.

[97] See nn. 10, 25 *supra*.

[98] On the religious dimension of the games, see Fredricksen, "Paul at the Races"; Valavanis, *Games and Sanctuaries*.

body of Christ (1 Cor 14:24), as believers embraced its Lord's self-sacrifice in their social relations (1:18–29; 8:11b; 11:1b, 17–32), edified each other (1 Cor 14:3, 4, 5, 26), and maintained the unity established by the indwelling Spirit (3:16–17; 12:4, 13). In bringing the visual images of the athletic ideal into dialogue with the cruciform word of his gospel, Paul stripped the ancient city-state of its veneration of the "Great Man", whether in civic life or in the stadium. Instead, he elevated his house-churches as the arena in which the "weak" and "strong" were now mutually accepted (1 Cor 10:24, 31–33), as they sought to outdo each other in honour (12:24b, 26b) and beneficence (16:1–4; cf. 12:31; 13:3). In so doing, Paul had already begun the construction of a new social order that would ultimately transform antiquity.

Chapter 5

Paul and the Gymnasiarchs: Two Approaches to Pastoral Formation in Antiquity

During the last two decades the study of leadership in Paul's house churches has emerged as a growth industry. At the outset of these studies the approach of New Testament scholars was primarily theological,[1] sociological,[2] opponents-based,[3] or church-centered.[4] More recently, however, the examination of Paul's understanding of leadership in its eastern Mediterranean context has become widespread.[5] The organisation of the polis, household, synagogue and

[1] E.g. H. Doohan, *Leadership in Paul* (Wilmington: Michael Glazier, 1984); cf. A.T. Hanson, *The Pioneer Ministry*, rev. ed. (London: SPCK, 1975). This chapter has profited from the responses of scholars at the *SBL 2005 Annual Meeting*, Philadelphia, USA (Nov 19–22 2005) and at the *Twin Cities NT Trial Balloon Society*, Minnesota, USA (April 4 2006).

[2] E.g. J.H. Schutz, *Paul and the Anatomy of Apostolic Authority* (Cambridge: Cambridge University Press, 1975); B. Holmberg, *Paul and Power: The Structure of Authority in the Primitive Churches as Reflected in the Pauline Epistles* (Philadelphia: Fortress, 1980); G. Theissen, *The Social Setting of Pauline Christianity: Essays on Corinth* (Philadelphia: Fortress, 1982); E.A. Castelli, *Imitating Paul: A Discourse of Power* (Louisville: Westminster John Knox, 1991). For more recent sociological and political approaches, see P.F. Esler, *Conflict and Identity in Romans: The Social Setting of Paul's Letter* (Minneapolis: Fortress, 2003), 33–39; K. Ehrensperger, *Paul and the Dynamics of Power: Communication and Interaction in the Early Christ-Movement*, LNTS 325 (London and New York: T&T Clark, 2007); J. Barentson, "Stephanas as Model Leader: A Social Identity Perspective on Community and Leadership (Mis)Formation in Corinth," *Journal of Biblical Perspectives in Leadership* 3.2 (2011): 3–13; *idem*, *Emerging Leadership in the Pauline Mission: A Social Identity Perspective on Local Leadership Development in Corinth and Ephesus*, Princeton Theological Monograph Series 168 (Eugene: Pickwick, 2011).

[3] E.g. D. Georgi, *The Opponents of Paul in Second Corinthians* (Edinburgh: T&T Clark, 1987 [Gmn. orig. 1964]).

[4] E.g. A.L. Chapple, *Local Leadership in the Pauline Churches: Theological and Social Factors in Its Development. A Study Based on 1 Thessalonians, 1 Corinthians and Philippians* (PhD diss., Durham University, 1984).

[5] See the heavily epigraphic approach to honorific paradigms of civic leadership at Philippi in J.H. Hellerman, *Reconstructing Honor in Roman Philippi: Carmen Christi as* Cursus Pudorum, SNTSMS 132 (Cambridge: Cambridge University Press, 2005); cf. *idem*, *Embracing Shared Ministry: Power and Status in the Early Church and Why It Matters Today* (Grand Rapids: Kregel, 2013). Similarly, for Corinth, see L.L. Welborn, *An End to Enmity: Paul and the "Wrongdoer" of Second Corinthians* (Berlin and Boston: De Gruyter, 2011); J.K. Goodrich, *Paul as Administrator of God in 1 Corinthian*, SNTSMS 152 (Cambridge: Cambridge University Press, 2012); A.G. White, "Servants, Not Intellectual Clients: The Significance of Paul's Role as an *Oikonomos* in 1 Cor 4:1 and 9:17," *ABR* 62 (2014): 44–57. Additionally, see M.T. Finney, *Honour and Conflict in the Ancient World: 1 Corinthians in Its*

association has been analysed for similarities to early Christian leadership structures,[6] as has the Graeco-Roman reciprocity system for its impact upon patron-client relations in Paul's house-churches.[7] Epicurean psychagogy has also been profitably investigated for the light it throws on Paul's adaptability in ministering to the factionalised Corinthian house churches.[8] Consequently, we are better placed to appreciate the competing styles of leadership and group behaviour that Paul was forced to confront at Corinth. Whereas scholarship previously concentrated on the literary evidence, the recent focus on the docu-

---

Greco-Roman Social Setting, LNTS 460 (London and New York: Bloomsbury T&T Clark, 2012).

[6] J.N. Collins, *Diakonia: Re-interpreting the Ancient Sources* (Oxford: Oxford University Press, 1990); J.T. Burtchaell, *From Synagogue to Church: Public Services and Offices in the Earliest Christian Communities* (Cambridge: Cambridge University Press, 1992); A.D. Clarke, *Secular and Christian Leadership in Corinth: A Socio-Historical and Exegetical Study of 1 Corinthians 1–6* (Leiden: Brill, 1993); *idem*, *Serve the Community of the Church: Christians as Leaders and Ministers* (Grand Rapids: Eerdmans, 2000); R.A. Campbell, *The Elders: Seniority within Earliest Christianity* (Edinburgh: T&T Clark, 1994); S.J. Joubert, "Managing the Household: Paul as *Paterfamilias* of the Christian Household Group in Corinth," in *Modelling Early Christianity: Social-Scientific Studies of the New Testament in Its Context*, ed. P.F. Esler (London: Routledge, 1995), 213–23; R.A. Ascough, *Paul's Thessalonian Associations: The Social Context of Philippians and 1 Thessalonians*, WUNT II 161 (Tübingen: Mohr Siebeck, 2003); P.A. Harland, *Associations, Synagogues and Congregations: Claiming a Place in Ancient Mediterranean Society* (Minneapolis: Fortress, 2003); R.W. Gehring, *House Church and Mission: The Importance of Household Structures in Early Christianity* (Peabody: Hendrickson, 2004); E.D. MaGillivray, "Re-evaluating Patronage and Reciprocity in Antiquity and New Testament Studies," *JGRChJ* 6 (2009): 37–81; J.M. Ogereau, *Paul's* Koinonia *with the Philippians: A Socio-Historical Investigation of a Pauline Economic Partnership*, WUNT II 377 (Tübingen: Mohr Siebeck, 2014); R. Last, *The Pauline Church and the Corinthian Ekklêsia: Greco-Roman Associations in Comparative Context*, SNTSMS 164 (Cambridge: Cambridge University Press, 2016).

[7] J.K. Chow, *Patronage and Power: A Study of Social Networks in Corinth* (Sheffield: Sheffield Academic, 1992); B.W. Winter, *Seek the Welfare of the City* (Grand Rapids: Eerdmans, 1994); S. Joubert, *Paul as Benefactor: Reciprocity, Strategy and Theological Reflection in Paul's Collection* (Tübingen: Mohr Siebeck, 2000): D.W. Pao, *Thanksgiving: An Investigation of a Pauline Theme* (Downers Grove: IVP, 2002); J.R. Harrison, *Paul's Language of Grace in Its Graeco-Roman Context*, WUNT II 172 (Tübingen: Mohr Siebeck, 2003); Z.A. Crook, *Reconceptualising Conversion: Patronage, Loyalty, and Conversion in the Religions of the Ancient Mediterranean* (Berlin and New York: Walter de Gruyter, 2004); J. Rice, *Paul and Patronage: The Dynamics of Power in 1 Corinthians* (Eugene: Pickwick, 2013); P.J. Leithart, *Gratitude: An Intellectual History* (Waco: Baylor University Press, 2014); T. Morgan, *Roman Faith and Christian Faith:* Pistis *and* Fides *in the Early Roman Empire and Early Churches* (Oxford: Oxford Univeristy Press, 2015); T.R. Blanton, *A Spiritual Economy: Gift Exchange in the Letters of Paul* (London and New Haven: Yale University Press, 2017). For studies of χάρις in its Jewish context, see D. Zeller, *Charis bei Philon und Paulus* (Stuttgart: Verlag Katholisches Bibelwerk GmbH, 1990); J.M.G. Barclay, *Paul and the Gift* (Grand Rapids: Eerdmans, 2015); O. McFarland, *God and Grace in Philo and Paul*, NovTSup 164 (Leiden and Boston: Brill, 2015); K.B. Wells, *Grace and Agency in Paul and Second Temple Judaism: Interpreting the Transformation of the Heart*, NovTSup 157 (Leiden and Boston: Brill, 2015).

[8] C.E. Glad, *Paul and Philodemus: Adaptability in Epicurean and Early Christian Psychagogy* (Leiden: Brill, 1995).

mentary, numismatic and archaeological evidence has ensured a more balanced approach to ancient leadership ideals and structures than previously.

Insufficient attention has been paid to the educational context of ancient leadership theory and practice.[9] The main interest of scholars in this regard has been the disagreement between Paul and the Corinthians as to whether rhetorical eloquence – the chief educational instrument of antiquity – was an indicator of apostolic status, power and wisdom.[10] But New Testament scholars have overlooked the important role of the ancient gymnasium in shaping young men as civic leaders. This oversight is perhaps explained by the negative attitude of 1 and 2 Maccabees towards the Jerusalem gymnasium and by the scarcity of "gymnasium" terminology in the New Testament (γυμνάζω: 1 Tim 4:7; γυμνασία: 1 Tim 4:8).

More than a decade ago R.S. Dutch has argued that the Greek gymnasium was the primary venue for the education of elite Christians in Corinth. Dutch helpfully analyses the role of the gymnasium personnel (i.e. the *gymnasiarchos*) and its students (the *neoi* and *epheboi*) but, disappointingly, does not bring Paul's pastoral theology into dialogue with the ethical ideals of the gymnasium.[11] Instead, like many Corinthian interpreters before him, Dutch travels over well-worn exegetical ground in describing how Paul's self-presentation (e.g. 1 Cor 1:20; 3:1–4; 3:5–9; 4:6; 4:21; 7:17–24; 9:24–27) was polemically slanted at the educated elite opposing his ministry. The equally important task of cultural *synkrisis* ("comparison") is thereby bypassed.[12] Consequently, we fail to appreciate that the differences between Paul's gospel and the surrounding

[9] Note, however, the two articles cited in n. 20 *infra*. Additionally, see J.R. Harrison, "Sponsors of *Paideia*: Ephesian Benefactors, Civic Virtue and the New Testament," *Early Christianity* 7.3 (2016): 346–67.

[10] S.M. Pogoloff, *Logos and Sophia: The Rhetorical Situation of 1 Corinthians*, SBLDS 134 (Atlanta: Scholars, 1992); D. Litfin, *St Paul's Theology of Proclamation: 1 Corinthians 1–4 and Greco-Roman Rhetoric*, SNTSMS 79 (Cambridge: Cambridge University Press, 1994); B.W. Winter, *Philo and Paul among the Sophists*, SNTSMS 96 (Cambridge: Cambridge University Press, 1997); B.K. Peterson, *Eloquence and the Proclamation of the Gospel in Corinth*, SBLDS 163 (Atlanta: Scholars, 1998); C. Mihaila, *The Paul-Apollos Relationship and Paul's Stance toward Graeco-Roman Rhetoric*, LNTS 402 (London: T&T Clark, 2009). Not must we forget the impact of popular wisdom in the forms of proverbs, fables, exemplary stories and gnomic sayings. See T. Morgan, *Popular Morality in the Early Roman Empire* (Cambridge: Cambridge University Press, 2007).

[11] R.S. Dutch, *The Educated Elite in 1 Corinthians: Education and Community Conflict in Graeco-Roman Context*, JSNTS 271 (London and New York: T& T Clark, 2005), 95–167. See also the recent works of C.S. Smith, *Pauline Communities as "Scholastic Communities": A Study in the Vocabulary of "Teaching" in 1 Corinthians, 1 and 2 Timothy, and Titus*, WUNT II 335 (Tübingen: Mohr Siebeck, 2012); A.G. White, *Where is the Wise Man? Graeco-Roman Education as a Background to the Divisions in 1 Corinthians 1–4*, LNTS 536 (Harrisburg: T&T Clark, 2015).

[12] The Walter de Gruyter series, edited by D.B. Martin and L.L. Welborn, *Synkrisis: Invitations to Early Christianity in Greco-Roman Culture*, addresses this deficit in New Testament scholarship.

Graeco-Roman culture are just as revealing as the "parallels" posited by the *Relionsgeschichte Schule*.

Last, in a new monograph building upon Dutch's research, T.A. Brookins examines gymnasium education at Corinth,[13] arguing that, like Athens, 7–10 % of the urban population at Corinth may have received education through the gymnasium.[14] The "wise" at Corinth, therefore, would have received the level of philosophical intstuction commensurate with the ephebic curriculum of the gymnasium.[15] Brookins identifies the philosophy being purveyed by the "wise" and their teachers at Corinth as Stoic, given the Stoic philosophical undercurrents animating many of the topics in 1 Corinthians.[16] While this is a possibility, given the exposure of the elite Corinthians to a gymnasium education, Brookins is too sweeping in his conclusion that a "philosophical school" of Stoic persuasion was present in the Corinthian church. Many of the motifs of 1 Corinthians were also reflected in the moral philosophy the "seven sages" purveyed in the Dephic Canon, for example, taught to children throughout the Greek East well before the future civic elites entered the gymnasium as *epheboi*. In other words, attributing a *totally* gymnasium-based origin for the Corinthian attachment to wisdom, while having a certain validity in the case of the elites, underestimates the extent of more popular forms of wisdom that were abroad in Greek society and were not confined to elite audiences.[17] The ethical curriculum of the Dephic canon was taught in the preparatory schools prior to the gymnasium. This is demonstrated by the find of two second/third-century AD ostraka, each of which have Delphic maxims inscribed on them, and are probably exercises in student alphabet training.[18] Notwithstanding the quality of Brookins' work, the task of *synkrisis* is again bypassed, other than a comparison with (what he perceives to be) the Stoic dimension of the gymnasiun curriculum, a focus that I have suggested is too truncated in understanding the Corinthian context.

In sum, New Testament scholars have not realized that the pastoral role attributed to the gymnasiarchs in the honorific inscriptions constitutes important background for studies of pastoral leadership in Paul. The gymnasiarchal inscriptions highlight the commitment of the gymnasiarchs to ancestral honour

---

[13] T.A. Brookins, *Corinthian Wisdom, Stoic Philosophy, and the Ancient Economy*, SNTSMS 159 (Cambridge: Cambridge University Press, 2014), 132–41.

[14] Brookins (*Corinthian Wisdom*, 148–51) posits that for at church comprising fifty-plus members, five or six possessed moderate wealth and thus, possibly, access to gymnasium educational training.

[15] Brookins (*Corinthian Wisdom*, 151) speculates regarding the "wise" in the Corinthian church: "... some within their midst may indeed, against Paul's better wishes, have viewed their group as a kind of philosophical school, the gospel as a sort of philosophy, and their teachers as purveyors of its wisdom."

[16] Brookins, *Corinthian Wisdom*, 228.

[17] Morgan, *Popular Morality*.

[18] R. Pintaudi and Pieter J. Sijpesteijn, "Ostraka di contenuto scolastico provenienti da Narmuthis," *ZPE* 76 (1989): 85–92, Nos. 5, 6.

and high ethical standards, as well as the obligations of the reciprocity system. There are important echoes of Pauline concerns here that warrant investigation.

Additionally, several fragmentary inscriptions preserve ethical maxims, belonging to the Delphic Canon, which were taught to students in the eastern Mediterranean gymnasia.[19] What would have been Paul's attitude to these lofty ethical ideals? To what extent might Paul have endorsed or critiqued this theology of civic virtue? What do his disagreements with the gymnasium curriculum reveal about the personal and social dynamics of his gospel? We are presented with the opportunity to break out of the institutional approach to leadership studies characterising New Testament scholarship over recent decades. What is required by way of supplement to the fine work accomplished so far is a study of *leaders* from the documentary and literary evidence.[20] Only then will we avoid the danger of talking about ancient leadership ideals in abstraction.[21]

This chapter explores how the educational ideals of eastern Mediterranean gymnasia, as articulated in the honorific inscriptions, were expressed in the civic leadership and ethical behaviour of the *gymnasiarchoi*. The chapter demonstrates that Paul's cruciform gospel sought to transform the leaders of his house

[19] For the inscriptions and papyrus, with translation and commentary, see E.A. Judge, "Ancient Beginnings of the Ancient World," in *idem*, Jerusalem *and Athens: Cultural Transformation in Late* Antiquity, WUNT I 265, ed. A. Nobbs (Tübingen: Mohr Siebeck), 282–314, at 288–96, 305–09. In addition to the documents collected by Judge, see also these extra documents containing citations from the Delphic Canon: M. Huys, "P. Oxy. 61.4099: A Combination of Mythographic Lists with Sentences of the Seven Wise Men," *ZPE* 113 (1996): 205–12; Pintaudi and Sijpesteijn, "Ostraka di contenuto scolastico provenienti da Narmuthis," Nos. 5, 6; A. Papathomas, "14. Ein literarisches Fragment mit Sprüchen der Sieben Weisem," in "'... *vor dem Papyrus sind alle Gleich!': Papyrologische Beiträge zu Ehren von Bärbel Kramer (P. Kramer)*," ed. R. Eberhard et al. (Berlin and New York: Walter de Gruyter, 2009), 163–69.

[20] For two examples of the approach I am advocating, see E.A. Judge, "The Teacher as Moral Exemplar in Paul and in the Inscriptions of Ephesus," in *Social Distinctives of the Christians in the First Century: Pivotal Essays by E.A. Judge*, ed. D.M. Scholer (Peabody: Hendrickson, 2008), 175–88; R. Saunders, "Attalus, Paul and PAIDEIA: The Contribution of *I. Eph. 202* to Pauline Studies," in *Ancient History in a Modern University. Volume II: Early Christianity, Late Antiquity, and Beyond*, ed. T.W. Hillard et al. (Grand Rapids: Eerdmans, 1998), 175–83.

[21] Graeco-Roman writers speak of leadership idealistically and concretely. Examples of idealistic presentations are found in the kingship treatises of Dio Chrysostom (*Orations* 1–4, 56, 62) and the Pythagorean Περὶ βασιλείας literature (Diotogenes, Ps.-Ecphantus, Sthenidas). For discussion, see E.R. Goodenough, "The Political Philosophy of Hellenistic Kingship," *Yale Classical Studies* 1 (1928): 55–102; L. Delatte, *Les traités de la royauté d'Ecphante, Diotogène et Sthénidas* (Liége: Bibliothèque de la Faculté de Philosophie et Lettres de l'Université de Liége, 1942); B. Blumenfeld, *The Political Paul: Justice, Democracy and Kingship in a Hellenistic Framework* (Sheffield: Sheffield Academic, 2001), 189–274; J.R. Harrison, *Paul and the Imperial Authorities at Thessalonica and Rome: A Study in the Conflict of Ideology*, WUNT I 273 (Tübingen: Mohr Siebeck, 2011), 279–99. For concrete presentations in the *exempla*, see Augustus' *Res Gestae*, Valerius Maximus' *Memorable Doings and Sayings*, the anonymous *Deeds of Famous Men*, and the comparisons of Greek and Roman leaders in the introductions to Plutarch's *Lives*.

churches in order that they might act as ambassadors of divine reconciliation within the body of Christ and also within the network of client-patron relationships constituting Graeco-Roman society. Paul's gospel relativised hierarchies of merit and gender; it pinpricked a culture of self-sufficiency and fatalism; it redefined the operation of reciprocity – the lubricant of social relations in antiquity – in light of the divine love revealed in the cross. In this process of redefinition, wherever possible, Paul endorsed what was compatible with the gospel of grace, but deepened its application and redirected its rationale.

We turn to an overview of education in antiquity, with special emphasis on the gymnasium and the access that Paul would have had to its *paideia*.

5.1. What Contact Would Paul Have Had With the Gymnasium?

In the classical age the education of youth was the preserve of the land-owning elite.[22] The class bias of early Greek education had been reinforced by the aristocratic world-view of Homer. Although Homer venerated the battle-hardened noble in his poetry, he softened his portrait of the military hero by depicting his warriors as skilled musicians. This Homeric blend of aesthetic grace and military prowess characterised the aristocratic educational systems of the classical city-states. Even militaristic Sparta trained boys in music, reading, and writing, as much as in athletics and in the maneuvers of the hoplite phalanx.

But it was the Athenian system of education that provided the blueprint for the Hellenistic age. In classical Athens, education was private, fee-paying, and non-compulsory. The head teacher was a freeman, helped by assistant masters who were freemen or slaves. As regards curricula, there were three branches of elementary education: letters (reading, writing, arithmetic), athletics (gymnastics, games, deportment) and music (lyre-playing, lyric poetry). Beyond this lay

---

[22] On Graeco-Roman and Jewish education, see W. Jaeger, *Paideia: The Ideals of Greek* Culture, 3 vols. (Oxford: Blackwell, 1946); H.-I. Marrou, *A History of Education in Antiquity* (London and New York: Sheed and Ward, 1956); W. Barclay, *Educational Ideals in the Ancient World* (Grand Rapids: Eerdmans, 1974 repr. [orig. 1959]); J.T. Townsend, "Ancient Education in the Time of the Early Roman Empire," in *The Catacombs and the Colosseum: The Roman Empire as the Setting of Early Christianity*, ed. S. Benko and J.J. O'Rourke (London: Oliphants, 1972), 139–63; M.L. Clarke, *Higher Education in the Ancient World* (Albuquerque: University of New Mexico Press, 1971); S.F. Bonner, *Education in Ancient Rome: From the Elder Cato to the Younger Pliny* (London: Methuen, 1977); J.L. Crenshaw, *Education in Ancient Israel: Across the Deadening Silence* (New York: Doubleday, 1998); W.M. Bloomer, ed., *A Companion to Ancient Education* (Chichester: Wiley Blackwell, 2015); E.A. Judge, "Higher Education in the Pauline Churches," in *Learning and Teaching Theology: Some Ways Ahead*, ed. L. Ball and J.R. Harrison (Eugene: Wipf and Stock, 2015), 21–31; M.R. Hauge and A.W. Pitts, eds., *Ancient Education and Early Christianity* (London and New York: Bloomsbury T&T Clark, 2016); J.R. Harrison, "Sponsors of *Paideia*: Ephesian Benefactors, Civic Virtue and the New Testament," *Early Christianity* 7.3 (2016): 346–67.

the professional schools of law and medicine, rhetoric and philosophy, as well as the courses offered by itinerant sophists. During the fourth century BC Athens saw the establishment of Isocrates' school of rhetoric, Plato's Academy, Aristotle's Lyceum, and the Stoic and Epicurean schools of Zeno and Epicurus.

However, the Hellenistic education system progressively lost the aristocratic bias of the classical period as it focused on the needs of the common person. Public schools were established at Miletus, Teos, Rhodes and Delphi through the endowments of benefactors.[23] Although the trend towards free public education continued into the Roman empire, the creation of new elementary schools mostly lay in the hands of city councils, local benefactors, and parents with the means to pay. In regard to higher education, Athens continued to be the provider *par* excellence, but the beneficence of the emperors increasingly eclipsed competitors. Vespasian, for example, endowed a chair of literature and rhetoric at Rome, to which was appointed the incomparable Roman rhetorician Quintilian.[24]

Throughout the eastern Mediterranean, Greek public education was conducted in the gymnasia, the *palaestrae* (the wrestling schools) and temples devoted to the Muses (the Museum). Visiting teachers also rented private quarters, as Paul did at Rome (Acts 28:16, 30), or hired a guild hall like that of Tyrannus in first-century Ephesus (Acts 19:9).[25] In the case of the Jewish world, itinerant teachers such as Paul would have used the local synagogue (Acts 13:14–51; 14:1–6; 17:1–9, 10–15, 17; 18:1–12, 19; cf. Luke 4:16–28). But some Jews, including the Therapeutae of Egypt and the Covenanters of Qumran, lived with their teacher(s) in exclusivist communities of faith in remote locations. Others joined

[23] For decrees founding schools at Miletus (SIG[3] 577: 200/199 BC) and Teos (SIG[3] 578: II cent BC), see M.M. Austin, *The Hellenistic World from Alexander to the Roman Conquest: A Selection of Ancient Sources in Translation*, 2nd ed. (Cambridge: Cambridge University Press, 1981), §§ 138–139. For a Delphic decree honoring Attalos III for establishing an educational endowment (SIG[3] 672: 160/159 BC), see Austin, *The Hellenistic World*, § 242. A fragmentary Ephesian decree (IEph V 1618) honours a benefactor for "having given the prizes to the musicians and to the athletes at his own expense," as well as "having given the columns to the city for the old gymnasium." Theophrastus' will provided his garden, covered walk and buildings for the study of philosophy (Diogenes Laertius 5.52.3). The will of Epicurus (Diogenes Laertius 10.16–18) specified regarding the Epicurean school: "I entrust the school in the garden in perpetuity to those who are its members' so that the 'successors in philosophy ... [might] live and pursue philosophy therein."

[24] For Vespasian's edict (AD 74) on physicians' and teachers' privileges, see A.C. Johnson et al., eds., *Ancient Roman Statutes* (Austin: University of Texas Press, 1961), § 185. In AD 93/94 Domitian intervened to prevent the abuse of the provisions of Vespasian's patronage by unscrupulous entrepreneurs (Johnson, *Ancient Roman Statutes*, § 199). For Domitian's patronage of the philosopher Terentius Maximus, see Pliny, *Letters* 10.58.5. See also the letter of Plotina (Johnson, *Ancient Roman Statutes*, § 238: AD 121), widow of Trajan, to Hadrian regarding a successor to the presidency of the Epicurean school.

[25] On the nature of Tyrannus' hall in Acts 19:9, see A.J. Malherbe, *Social Aspects of Early Christianity* (Philadelphia: Fortress, 1983), 89–91.

the local Pharisaic table fellowships or attached themselves to wilderness figures such as John the Baptist or Bannus, the mentor of Josephus.

Because most cities had built at least one gymnasium, the gymnasium remained the most famous and popular educational institution in antiquity.[26] Hellenistic gymnasia not only offered physical education but also literature, philosophy and music. There were clear-cut educational age groups. The first seven years of a Greek boy's life was spent under the tutelage of his mother. Young boys, known as *paides* ("boys"), learned the rudiments at elementary school under the care of male teachers up to fourteen. The sons of well-off families, called *epheboi* ("adolescents"), were sent to the gymnasia from fifteen to seventeen. This included two years of compulsory military service called the *ephebeia* ("manhood").[27] Its aim was to usher the *ephebos* into the citizenship and to ensure a military reserve for the state. Notwithstanding, the gymnasium's military purpose virtually disappeared over time,[28] and the length of ephebic training was reduced from two years to one, resulting in "a reduction in the seriousness of the institution's intellectual component."[29] Last, students

---

[26] In the entire Hellenic area, we know of gymnasia existing in approximately 140 localities (J. Oehler, "Gymnasiarch," *RE* 7 [1912]: 2005–08). For evidence regarding the subjects taught, see the Teos decree (n. 23 *supra*). For the workings of a gymnasium, see S. G. Miller, *Arete: Greek Sports from Ancient Sources* (Berkeley and Los Angeles: University of California Press, 1991), § 126 (SEG XXVII 261). On the gymnasium, see J. Delorme, *Le Gymnase: Étude sur les monuments consacrés à l'éducation en Grèce* (Paris: Éditions E. de Boccard, 1960); O. Tzachou-Alexandri, "The Gymnasium: An Institution for Athletic and Education," in *Mind and Body: Athletic Contests in Antiquity*, ed. O. Tzachou-Alexandri (Athens: Ministry of Culture, The National Hellenic Committee I.C.O.M., 1989); D. Vanhove "Le gymnase," in *idem*, *Le sport dans le Grèce antique: Du jeu à la compétition* (Bruxelles: Universiteit Gent, 1992), 57–75; P. Gauthier, "Bienfaiteurs du gymnase au Létôon de Xanthos," *REG* 109.1 (1996): 1–34; D. Hawhee, *Bodily Arts: Athletic and Rhetorical Training in Antiquity* (PhD diss., The Pennsylvania State University, 2000), 139–208; B. Legras, "Violence ou douceur: Les normes éducatives dans les sociétés grecque et romaine," *Histoire de l'éducation* 118 (2008): 11–34; O. Curty and M. Piérart, *L'huile et l'argent, gymnasiarchie et évergétisme dans la Grèce hellénistique–Actes du colloque tenu à Fribourg, du 13 au 15 octobre 2005, publiés en l'honneur du Professeur Marcel Piérart à l'occasion de son 60e anniversaire* (Fribourg: Séminaire d'histoire ancienne, 2009); V. A. Troncoso, "The Hellenistic Gymnasium and the Pleasures of *Paideia*," *Symbolae Philologorum Posnaniensium Graecae et Latinae* 19 (2009): 71–84 (with further bibliography); P. Gauthier, "Notes sur le rôle du gymnase dans les cités hellénistiques," in *idem*, *Études d'histoire et d'institutions grecques: choix d'écrits (édité et indexé par Denis Rousset). École pratique des hautes études, sciences historiques et philologiques – III.* Hautes études du monde gréco-romain 47 (Genève: Librairie Droz, 2011), 531–50.

[27] See N. M. Kennell, "The Greek Ephebate in the Roman Period," in *Sport in the Cultures of the Ancient World: New Perspectives*, ed. Z. Papakonstantinou (Milton Park: Routledge, 2010), 175–94; A. S. Chankowski, *L'Éphébie hellénistique: Étude d'une institution civique dans les cités grecques des îles de la Mer Égée et de l'Asie Mineure*, Culture et cité 4 (Paris: De Boccard, 2010).

[28] Brookins, *Corinthian Wisdom*, 137.

[29] Brookins, *Corinthian Wisdom*, 138.

over eighteen were called *neoi* ("youths").[30] But by the end of the second century BC, it also included study of the humanities.

The pastoral and administrative role of the chief official at the gymnasium is worth highlighting. The *gymnasiarchos* ("leader of the gymnasium") supervised the training of gymnasium members, directed the operations of its teaching staff, and acted as a benefactor for the gymnasium (e.g. by supplying olive oil, providing prizes, paying teachers, and providing heating fuel for the hot baths).[31] The *gymnasiarchos* was regularly honoured in public inscriptions and embodied the Graeco-Roman ideal of civic leadership. Paul may have seen many such inscriptions erected in honour of gymnasium officials during his missionary travels throughout the eastern Mediterranean, or heard the same honours being proclaimed by a herald at a nearby prominent site.[32] In addition to the gymnasiarchal inscriptions, Paul may have noticed the ethical maxims of the seven sages – the Delphic canon being an important part of ephebic curriculum – inscribed on a *stele* at the local gymnasium or *palaestra*. He may have even listened to similar maxims expounded in the sermons of the popular philosophers at the market place, or heard them in conversations with interested inquirers or in interactions with his converts.

It is not inconceivable that Paul encountered *gymnasiarchoi* or visited a gymnasium, even though there were strict regulations as to who might enter a gymnasium.[33] Although some Jews had scruples about Hellenism and the idolatry of

[30] See C.A. Forbes, *NEOI: A Contribution to the Study of Greek Associations* (Middletown: American Philological Association, 1933). For the membership of women in gymnasia, see G. Tsouvala, "Women Members of a Gymnasium in the Roman East (ig iv 732)," in *Ancient Documents and Their Contexts: First North American Congress of Greek and Latin Epigraphy (2011)*, Brill Studies in Greek and Roman Epigraphy 5, ed. J. Bodel and N. Dimitrova (Leiden: Brill, 2014), 111–23.

[31] For gymnasiarchal benefactions, see IEph V 1618 (n. 23 *supra*); F.W. Danker, *Benefactor: Epigraphic Study of a Graeco-Roman and New Testament Semantic Field* (St. Louis: Clayton Publishing House, 1982), § 17 (Michel 327: 133/120 BC); A.R. Hands, *Charities and Social Aid in Greece and Rome* (London and Southampton: Thames and Hudson, 1968), §D54 (MDAI [A] 1907, 278), §D55 (OGIS 339), §D56 (SIG³ 714: 100 BC), §D57 (IG XII. 9[235]), §D58 (IG XII. 9[916]). On gymnasiarchal responsibilities, see the Teos decree (n. 23 *supra*).

[32] Menas (Danker, *Benefactor*, § 17) not only had his honorific decree inscribed and erected in the gymnasium, but his honours were to be proclaimed upon his annual crowning at the games. The gymnasiarch Boulagoras (J. Pouilloux, *Choix d'inscriptions Grecques: textes, traductions et notes* [Paris: Société d'édition Les Belles Lettres, 1960], § 3 [SEG I 366 [243/242 BC]) had his honours proclaimed during the tragedies of the Dionysia, in addition to the decree being inscribed on a stele and erected in the sanctuary of Hera. For the proclamation of the crowns awarded ephebes at multiple sites, see Miller, *Arete*, § 126 (SEG XXVII. 261: before 167 BC).

[33] Aeschines (*In Tim.* 12) cites a law setting out the strict regulations of entry into the gymnasium. On the exclusivist ethos of ancient gymnasia, see § 5.2.5 below; cf. S.G. Miller *Ancient Greek Athletics* (New Haven and London: Yale University Press, 2004), 189. The Greek *palaestrae* may have been easier for "outsiders" to enter without prohibition if Socrates' experience is representative (Plato, *Lysias* 203a–211a). Aristophanes (*Peace* 762–64) notes a character "hanging around *palaestrae* trying to seduce boys."

the gymnasium,[34] Philo assumes a gymnasium education for upper class Alexandrian Jews and praises its educational outcomes.[35] Inscriptional and papyrus evidence reveals that Jewish young men of the Diaspora received ephebic training at the gymnasium[36] Not surprisingly Herod the Great, the Hellenist and

---

[34] L.H. Feldman (*Jew and Gentile in the Ancient World* [Princeton: Princeton University Press, 1993], 480 n.69) cites *'Avodah Zarah* 18b, which lambasts Jews for visiting the stadia where naked athletic contests took place. Such attitudes would have been transported to the training institution responsible for the athletes. The authors of 1 and 2 Maccabees (1 Macc. 1:11–15; 2 Macc. 4.7–14) inveigh against the Hellenism of the high-priest Jason and his supporters who had set up a gymnasium at the foot of the citadel in Jerusalem (175 BC). Significantly, we do not hear of any popular revolt against Jason's reform. Either the majority supported Jason's Hellenistic reform at Jerusalem or in the view of many Jews the presence of the gymnasium in the holy city did not compromise Jewish covenantal identity. On the Maccabean sources, see L.L. Grabbe, *Judaism from Cyrus to Hadrian* (London: SCM, 1992), 277–84, esp. 280–81. However, the fact that the gymnasia were dedicated to various pagan deities, such as Hermes and Heracles, probably caused more rigorous Jews to view any Diaspora Jew undertaking an ephebic education as violators of the first and second commandments (Exod 20:3–6). The Miletus decree (SIG³ 577 [200/199 BC]: n.23 *supra*) stipulates that frankincense be burned to Hermes, the Muses, and Apollo, along with the presentation of prayers for the election of worthy officials. On fines being consecrated to Hermes, Heracles and the Muses, see SIG³ 578 (200/199 BC: n.16 above). On sacrifices being offered to Hermes and/or Heracles, see Hands, *Charities*, §§D55–D57. For the cult of the goddess Roma and the athletic games at Miletus, see R.K. Sherk, *Rome and the Geek East to The Death of Augustus* (Cambridge: Cambridge University Press, 1984), § 41 (IMilet I. 7: 130 BC). In the case of the gymnasium in Jerusalem, there is no evidence that the institution was ever dedicated to Hermes or any other pagan deity (Grabbe, *Judaism from Cyrus to Hadrian*, 278–79). As Grabbe states (*ibid.*, 279), the silence of the author of 2 Maccabees indicates that "neither nude exercise nor any pagan ceremonies were connected with Jason's gymnasium." Finally, the *palaestrae* (wrestling schools) were also dedicated to pagan divinities. A terracotta panel in the British museum (Brownley Collection GR 1805.7–3.390 BM Cat. *Terracottas* D632: Roman provenance, made in Italy, I cent. AD) is instructive in this regard. On the right side of the panel, a victorious boxer – whose left fist and forearm is bound with a boxing thong – holds a palm branch and a winner's ribbon. To the right of the panel, a bust of Hermes, patron god of the wrestlers, stands prominently on a pillar. For Cicero's comments on the figures of Hermes in the *palaestrae* and gymnasia, see *Att.* 1.8–1.10.

[35] See Feldman's discussion of Philo's evidence (*Jew and Gentile in the Ancient World*, 57–59). Also, A. Mendelson, *Secular Education in Philo of Alexandria* (Cincinnati: Hebrew Union College, 1982). Note P. Borgen's comment ("'Yes', 'No', 'How Far?': The Participation of Jews and Christians in Pagan Cults," in *Paul in His Hellenistic Context*, ed. T. Engberg-Pedersen [Edinburgh: T&T Clark, 1994], 15–43, at 41): "Philo's writings even betray such an expert knowledge of Greek sports that he himself was active in athletics during his youth."

[36] For Jewish ephebic names and/or patronymics among the lists of gymnasium graduates at Cyrene, Iasos and Coronea, see M.H. Williams, *The Jews among the Greeks and Romans: A Sourcebook* (London: Duckworth, 1998), V.1, 2, 21–23. For an inscription, used as a seat marker in the *palaestra* at Hypaepa, mentioning an association of Jewish young men (νεώτεροι), see Williams, *ibid.*, V.24. In a papyrus (7–4 BC: Williams, *ibid.*, V.3), the Alexandrian Jew Helenos speaks of his having received, "as far as my father's means allowed, the appropriate education," presumably at his father's "ancestral gymnasium." But, given that Paul characterises his childhood upbringing as being "a Hebrew of Hebrews" (Phil 3:5; 2 Cor 11:22; Acts 21:40; 22:2; 26:14), Paul's parents did not envisage an ephebic education for their son (cf. Acts 22:3; 26:4; Gal 1:14). If Acts 22:3 (cf. 23:16) is historically correct, Paul was brought up as a

benefactor, built gymnasia in Ptolemais, Tripolis, and Damascus. Paul as a Jew could not have not have escaped the pervasive influence of the gymnasium. Moreover, the apostle displays familiarity with the athletic ideal of the Greeks (1 Cor 9:24–27; cf. 1 Tim 4:7–8) and the honours it bestowed (9:25b; cf. 2 Tim 2:5), as was the case with many other first-century Jews.[37]

The honorific inscriptions of the gymnasium confronted Paul with leadership models of the highest civic merit. But while the ethical ideals of the athletic associations sometimes coincided with those of the apostle, more often than not they radically diverged. What were the consequences of this for Paul as a master builder of communities of faith (1 Cor 3:10)? Surely Paul would have considered how the personal and social transformation effected by the gospel of Christ differed from the transformation effected by the *paideia* ("education") of the gymnasium – or, for that matter, from the practices of the first-century associations more generally.[38]

In the next section, we discuss the inscriptional portrait of the *gymnasiarchos*. How does Paul respond to the aristocracy of civic merit promoted by the local gymnasia, in so far as his letters touch on areas of common concern? Our aim is gauge to what degree and in what manner Paul differentiated the transformation of his house church leaders from the character formation offered to the young men of the Hellenistic gymnasia.[39] Such a comparison provides in-

child in Jerusalem (ἀνατεθραμμένος δὲ ἐν τῇ πόλει ταύτῃ) at the feet of Gamaliel. For further discussion of Diaspora Jews' gymnasium education, see Dutch, *The Educated Elite*, 95–167. Additionally, see A. Kerkeslager, "Maintaining Jewish Identity in the Greek Gymnasium: A Jewish 'Load' in CPJ 3.519," *JSJ* 28 (1997): 12–33.

[37] See V. Pfitzner, *Paul and the Agon Motif* (Leiden: Brill, 1967); H. A. Harris, *Greek Athletics and the Jews* (Cardiff: University of Wales Press, 1967); R. Garrison, "Paul's Use of the Athlete Metaphor in 1 Corinthians 9," in *idem*, *The Graeco-Roman Context of Early Christian Literature* (Sheffield: Sheffield Academic 1997), 95–104; N. C. Croy, *Endurance in Suffering: Hebrews 12:1–13 in Its Rhetorical, Religious, and Philosophical Context*, SNTSMS 98 (Cambridge: Cambridge University Press, 1998), 40–58; M. Brändle, *Der Agon bein Paulus: Herkunft und Profil paulinischer Agonmetaphorik*, WUNT II 222 (Tübingen: Mohr Siebeck, 2006). On Jewish athletic ideals in 4 Maccabees, see D. A. deSilva, "The Noble Contest: Honor, Shame, and the Rhetorical Strategy of 4 Maccabees," *JSNT* 13 (1995): 31–57. C. Toussaint comments regarding Paul's use of athletic imagery (*L'Hellénisme et l'apôtre Paul* [Paris: Émile Nourry, 1921], 202): "Paul n'a pas eu besoin d'aller aux jeux olympiques, lors de son séjour à Corinthe, pour prendre ses comparisons: il avait eudepuis longtemps, à Tarse, de pareils spectacles." Presumably, Paul would have seen gymnsiarchal inscriptions – which embraced a range of leadership ideals, ethics and honours – at Tarsus as well.

[38] See Chapter 9. On teaching in the Pauline communities, based on a comprehensivive examination of its terminology, see now Smith, *Pauline Communities as "Scholastic Communities."*

[39] Whereas the *gymnasiarchos* oversaw the transition of the adolescent male body from immaturity to maturity in the civic life of the polis, Paul oversaw the transition of the local "body" of believers, transformed from glory to glory, towards their eschatological maturity in Christ (Rom 12:4–5; 1 Cor 12:12–13; 2 Cor 3:18; Eph 4:11–16; Phil 3:20–4:1). On the "body" in Paul in first-century context, see W. A. Meeks, *The Origins of Christian Morality: The First Two Centuries* (New Haven and London: Yale University Press, 1993), 130–35. The excellent

sight into the collisions and convergences between early Christian ideals of leadership and those of the late Hellenistic and early imperial city-states.

Admittedly, there remains a gulf between the civic context of the honorific inscriptions and the household context of Paul's letters, not to mention the different rhetorical function of each corpus.[40] The polis ensured that the higher moral training for boys of citizen class culminated in the education offered at the gymnasium and *palaestra*. But the rituals of patronage and friendship characterizing the urban elite – with which the gymnasiarch was familiar – trickled down to the local associations and immigrant cults through local benefactors. Paul's house churches, dependent on the generosity of patron-householders, linked themselves into the similar bonds of reciprocity and moral discourse animating the civic leadership of the polis. This line of social continuity (patronage, friendship, affiliation) makes comparison of the two different sets of documentary traditions profitable, especially where the same vocabulary appears in similar contexts.

5.2. *Paul and the Ancient Ideals of Civic Leadership*

The role of the ancient gymnasiarch has been little studied by classical scholars.[41] Unfortunately, O. Curty's recent collection of forty gymnasiarchal inscriptions has been poorly reviewed,[42] being criticised for concentrating too

---

discussion of D.B. Martin (*The Corinthian Body* [New Haven and London: Yale University Press, 1995], 25–28) on the upper-class ideology of the male "body" concentrates on Galen's evidence. Martin's discussion could be profitably expanded by a study of the gymnasiarchal inscriptions (§ 5.2.2 below) on the formation of the bodies of the *epheboi* and *neoi*.

[40] I am indebted to the excellent exposition of Meeks, *The Origins of Christian Morality*, 37–51.

[41] See Oehler, "Gymnasiarch," 1969–2004; B.A. van Groningen, *Les gymnasiarques des métropoles de l'Égypte Romaine* (Groningue: Noordhoff, 1924); Forbes, *NEOI*, 21–33; Delorme, *Le Gymnase*, Index *s.v.* "Gymnasiarque"; P.J. Sijpesteijn, *Liste de gymnasiarques des métropoles de l'Égypte romaine* (Amsterdam: Adolf M. Hakkert, 1967); P. Gauthier and M.B. Hatzopoulos, *La loi gymnasiarchique de Beroia* (Athens: Centre de recherches de l'antiquité grecque et romaine, 1993); A.J.S. Spawforth, "Gymnasiarch," in *The Oxford Classical Dictionary*, ed. S. Hornblower and A.J.S. Spawforth, 3rd ed. (Oxford: Oxford University Press, 1996), 659; G. Cordiano, *La Ginnasiarchia Nelle «Poleis» Dell'Occidente Mediterraneo Antico*, Studi e testi di storia antica diretti da Mauro Moggi 7 (1997: Ediozi ETS, 1997); A. Evangelos, "Educational Athletic Institutions in Thrace during the Hellenistic and Roman Periods," *ASSH Bulletin* 27 (1997): 15–20; Dutch, *The Educated Elite*, 111–17; P. Gauthier, "Un gymnasiarche honoré à Colophon," in *idem*, *Études d'histoire et d'institutions grecques: choix d'écrits (édité et indexé par Denis Rousset). École pratique des hautes études, sciences historiques et philologiques – III.* Hautes études du monde gréco-romain, 47 (Genève: Librairie Droz, 2011), 661–73.

[42] O. Curty, *Gymnasiarchika: recueil et analyse des inscriptions de l'époque hellénistique en l'honneur des gymnasiarques*, De l'archéologie à l'histoire, 64 (Paris: Éditions de Boccard, 2015).

much on the legislative role of the gymnasium and the administrative role of the gymnasiarch, as opposed to the crucial issue of the wider ideology of the gymnasium.[43] In particular, N.M. Kennell mentions that Curty fails to address the "qualities and virtues expected of gymnasiarchs and their charges through terms such as εὐκοσμία, εὐταξία, εὐανδρία, σωφροσύνη, and φιλαγαθία."[44] The omission, in my view, is telling for our project. In similar vein, the pastoral role of the gymnasiarch, with the exception of A.G. White,[45] has not fired the interest of New Testament scholars for the light it might throw on Paul as pastor and mentor. The philosophical traditions of pastoral care have been extensively studied in this regard, but not the gymnasiarchal epigraphic evidence.[46] What portrait of the gymnasiarch emerges from the honorific inscriptions?[47] What ideals, ethics and honours form the basis of his pastoral role? What type of community did he seek to build?[48] And how do the communities of the gymnasia compare with the communities of faith that Paul established across the eastern Mediterranean basin? A series of themes emerging from the inscriptions structures our discussion.

---

[43] See the review of N.N. Kennell (University of British Columbia) at *Bryn Mawr Classical Review* 2015.07.04: http//wwwbmcr.brynmawr.edu/2015/2015-07-04.html, accessed 05.04. 2017.

[44] See Kennell, *Bryn Mawr Classical Review*.

[45] See the 2013 Macquarie University PhD thesis of A.G. White, *Where is the Wise Man? Graeco-Roman Education as a Background to the Divisions in 1 Corinthians 1–4*, 47–49, for a coverage of the inscriptional portrait of the gymnasiarch as an exemplum of virtue. This section of the thesis is omitted from White's subsequent 2015 T&T Clark publication (*supra* n. 11).

[46] For discussion, see A.J. Malherbe, *Paul and the Thessalonians: The Philosophic Tradition of Pastoral Care* (Philadelphia: Fortress, 1987); *idem*, *Paul and the Popular Philosophers* (Minneapolis: Fortress, 1989), *idem*, *Light from the Gentiles: Hellenistic Philosophy and Early Christianity. Collected Essays, 1959–2012, by Abraham J. Malherbe*, ed. C.R. Halladay et al. (Leiden and Boston: Brill, 2013); Glad, *Paul and Philodemus*. See the introduction and translation of *Philodemus, On Frank Criticism: Introduction, Translation, and Notes*, Texts and Translations 43 Graeco-Roman 13, tr. D. Konstan et al. (Atlanta: Scholars Press, 1998).

[47] Limited visual evidence exists relating to the *gymnasiarchoi*. A red-figure kylix (Miller, *Ancient Greek Athletics*, 187 fig. 272: 480 BC) shows a *gymnasiarchos* supervising an aulos player and aulos singer, and a student performing recitation or spelling. See also the marble statue of a gymnasiarch (Musei Capitoloni, Rome, inv. no. 196), wrapped in his cloak and staring at the (imaginary) ephebes before him with fixed eyes and a severe expression (Vanhove, *Le sport dans la Grèce antique*, 213 § 72). For a useful list of gymnasiarchs (313 in total) in the inscriptions and papyri, see van Groningen, *Les gymnasiarques*, 12–27. This list needs to be supplemented with new gymnasiarchal inscriptions published in *SEG* and elsewhere since Groningen's work.

[48] The magisterial work of van Groningen on the gymnasiarchs adopts a "functional" approach in describing the role of the gymnasiarchs within the gymnasium (van Groningen, *Les gymnasiarques*, 46–116) and in relation to other municipal bodies and subordinate officials (*ibid.*, 116–30). However, due to the task-focused nature of Groningen's discussion, we do not gauge the *ethos* underlying the educational and pastoral formation of the *paides* implemented by the gymnasiarchs. My discussion below, focusing on the ethos of gymnasiarchal inscriptions and the curriculum of the Delphic canon, is intended to amplify Groningen's discussion at this juncture.

5.2.1. Motivations of the Gymnasiarch

The honorific inscriptions praise the motivation of the gymnasiarchs in upholding and surpassing ancestral honour, as well as bringing glory to the fatherland. Mantidoros of Eretria was said to have conducted his magistracy "worthily both of himself and of his forefathers," whereas Q. Flavius Lapianus shows "unparalleled generosity and munificence ... going beyond the generous gifts of his forefathers."[49] Menas encouraged the continuance of the cultural contributions of the Sestos gymnasium in order to "bring renown to his home city."[50] The inscription also states that he "aims to acquire for himself and his family imperishable glory."[51]

Clearly, ancestral honour was a dominant concern for those who aspired to excel in civic leadership in the first century. What role did ancestral honour play in the apostle Paul's thought? Did it motivate the early believers in the same way as it did the eulogistic culture around them?

Paul's attitude to Jewish ancestral honour is different to the civic eulogies of the gymnasiarchal inscriptions.[52] Paul does not reject the substantial privileges resulting from his Jewish ancestry (Rom 9:4–5 [cf. 3:1–2]; 11:1, 28b; Phil 3:4b–6). But, in contrast to his Jewish contemporaries, Paul claims that his former pursuit of Jewish ancestral tradition – in which he sought to outstrip his competitors in a way reminiscent of the honorific inscriptions (Gal 1:14) – was based on misguided zeal rather than on true knowledge of God (Rom 10:2). In Paul's "post-Damascus" perspective,[53] such a quest supplanted Christ's honour as soteriological Benefactor (Phil 2:9–11), misguidedly replacing it with law-keeping and boundary maintenance (Rom 10:3–4; 2 Cor 11:21b–23a; Phil 3:7–11). Indeed, to focus on ancestral privilege at the expense of the divine promise was to misconstrue the nature of covenantal grace: it was originally displayed to Abraham and his ancestors and had now found its fulfillment in Christ (Rom 9:6b–

---

[49] Hands, *Charities*, §D46 (AD 250).

[50] Danker, *Benefactor*, § 17 (Michel 327: 133/120 BC).

[51] The results of the beneficence of Straton of Pergamum (Hands, *Charities*, §D46) is "everlasting praise from those he has benefited, and for them ... the most valuable renewal of those things which are advantageous to life."

[52] See J. R. Harrison, "Excels Ancestral Honours," *New Docs* 9 (2002): 20–21, § 9.

[53] In using the term "post-Damascus perspective", I disagree with scholars who, in a polarised way, speak of Paul as being either prophetically "called" or undergoing the equivalent of a modern "psychological" conversion. In the first-century context, the evidence more points to Paul experiencing a Jewish prophetic call (Gal 1:15a: cf. Jer 1:5; Isa 49:1, 6), while also being the undeserving recipient of an extraordinary act of divine patronage that ensued in his commitment to a cruciform Benefactor (Gal 1:15b; cf. 2:20b). See Harrison, *Paul's Language of Grace*, 277–78. For an excellent critique of modern "psychological" approaches to Paul's conversion, see Crook, *Reconceptualising Conversion*, 13–52. Crook argues soundly that anachronistic psychological approaches should be abandoned in favour of the patronal and benefaction paradigms of the first-century if we are to understand properly Paul's change in loyalty commitment.

18; 10:4; cf. 4:1–5, 13–14; 9:10). Hence Paul parodies the Graeco-Roman and Jewish boasting conventions of his day – including its preoccupation with ancestral merit – in order to destroy the claims of the intruding apostles at Corinth who had boasted of their Abrahamic descent, among other qualifications (2 Cor 11:22–12:10).[54]

In sum, Jewish ancestry was advantageous and an occasion of praise to God, but only in so far that it directed its possessor through faith to the seed of Abraham, Jesus Christ (Rom 9:5; Gal 3:15–18). In contrast to his culture, there remains in Paul a reserve towards ancestral merit that was absent from the gymnasiarchal inscriptions. Unlike Menas of Sestos, Paul reserves "imperishable glory" for Christ and for those who labour in his service (1 Cor 2:7–8; 2 Cor 3:18; 4:4, 6; 8:23; Phil 3:20–21; 1 Thess 2:20).

5.2.2. The Pastoral Attitude of the Gymnasiarch and His Role as Benefactor

Another important feature of the inscriptional portrait of the gynmasiarch is the way that he cares for and develops the *epheboi* and *neoi*. Perhaps one of the most moving tributes paid to a gymnasiarch is the Ephesian inscription of the gymnasiarch Mithres:

> [...] he was not neglectful, not in the case of the y[oung men] [of their ...] and good bearing, treating them with respect, [and ...] with understatement and moderation, in all respects arranging his life-style in this place, and he gave attention also to the quality of the young men, both guiding them in training and, as for love of effort both in body and soul, making much of it for the sake of the reputation of the young men being fostered both in word and deed as befitted both the place's existing inherited dignity and fame.[55]

Another example is Straton of Pergamum. Upon entering his office as gymnasiarch, he "sacrificed a steer given by himself, praying to all the gods for the safety of the people and for their unity of heart."[56] Again, the educational and pastoral impact of Menas of Sestos upon young men is summed up in this manner:

> he not only shared his sacrificial offerings with the young men but through his personal dedication he impressed upon the young men the importance of cultivating discipline and tolerance of hardship, with the result that, being thus engaged in a competition for manliness, the personalities of the younger men are directed in the development of their character towards the goal of merit.[57]

[54] For discussion, see J. R. Harrison, "In Quest of the Third Heaven: Paul and His Apocalyptic Imitators," *VC* 58.1 (2004): 24–55, at 46–55.

[55] IEph Ia 6 (II cent. BC).

[56] Hands, *Charities*, §D54. The gymnasiarch Zosimos of Priene (IPriene 112) "has not displayed the fruitless return of honour" characteristic of the benefactor who maintains beneficence to the fatherland only while there are people still in need. Rather "(his) beneficence was bestowed towards the people for eternal fame."

[57] Danker, *Benefactor*, § 17.

From these examples one gains a keen sense of the comprehensive pastoral care that the young boys experienced under the gymnasiarchs. There are motifs here with which Paul would have surely agreed – the convergence of word and deed in personal transformation being a conspicuous example, as well as the centrality of unity.[58] But there are significant differences as well.

First, Paul's prayers for his converts express both the pastoral outworking of the gospel and his personal knowledge of the situation that his converts are facing.[59] They do not involve cultic approaches to the deity for favour and security, as is the case with the inscription of Straton of Pergamum, cited above, but are dynamic expressions of the Spirit at work in the body of Christ (Rom 8:15, 23, 26–28; Eph 6:18–19). Second, whereas there is a strong masculine tone to the gymnasiarchal pastoral role, Paul employs maternal and paternal images in depicting his pastoral concern for his converts (Gal 4:19; 1 Thess 2:7, 11). Third, over against gymnasiarchal culture, a competition for "manliness" is not the aim for Paul: rather it is the formation of the crucified and risen Christ in the church.[60]

Informative, too, are the descriptions of the role of gymnasiarchs as benefactors.[61] A Pergameme inscription unites the ethical merit of the gymnasiarch with his generosity towards the gymnasium: "not only was he exceedingly thoughtful in supplying many things for the upkeep of the gymnasium, he was also a man of surprising tact and sagacity."[62] In the world-view of the inscriptions, the gymnasiarch's beneficence expresses his conspicuous virtue as a citizen. Whereas civic virtue in the inscriptions is usually static, the fragmentary decree of Amphipolis portrays the justice of the gymnasiarch Philippus as exceeding conventional expectations:

Since Philippus, son of ..., on being elected gymnasiarch, tried to make the magistracy more conspicuous by his integrity and zeal, ... And in general he acted justly beyond our expectations, holding the leadership of the *neoi* and the charge of the gymnasium. For the first three months he supplied the oil at his own expense and furthermore, in a noble and magnificent spirit, he gave to the *neoi*, for oil all the money which was apportioned him from the public treasury.[63]

---

[58] Rom 13:11–14; Gal 2:14; Eph 2:8–10; 4:15–16; 4:22–24; Phil 1:9–11; 4:8–9; Col 1:9–12; 2:6–8; 3:9–10, 16–17; 1 Thess 1:3–7; 2:8; 2 Thess 2:16–17; 3:6–7, 9–10. On unity, see P.J. Achtemeier, *The Quest for Unity in the New Testament Church* (Philadelphia: Fortress, 1987); D.L. Peterlin, *Paul's Letter to the Philippians in the Light of Disunity in the Church*, NovTSupp 79 (Leiden et al.: Brill, 1995).

[59] See G.P. Wiles, *Paul's Intercessory Prayers: The Significance of the Intercessory Prayer Passages in the Letters of Paul*, SNTSMS 24 (Cambridge: Cambridge University Press, 1974); O. Cullmann, *Prayer in the New Testament, with Answer from the New Testament for Today's Questions*, tr. J. Bowden (London: SCM. 1995), 69–88.

[60] Rom 8:29; 2 Cor 3:18; Gal 4:19; Eph 1:11–12; 2:6; 20–21; 4:15–16; Phil 3:8–10, 20–21; Col 1:27–28; 2:19; 3:1–2, 11.

[61] See the discussion of Forbes, *NEOI*, 26–27.

[62] *Ath. Mitt.* xxxiii (1908): 376ff., No. 1. Cited by Forbes, *NEOI*, 24.

[63] *Jh. Österr.* I (1898): 180ff. Cited by Forbes, *NEOI*, 23.

Paradoxically, in contrast to the illustrious Philippus, Paul holds up a dishonoured and impoverished benefactor as the model for apostolic ministry (2 Cor 8:9; cf. 6:16b) and for those who, like the Macedonian churches, had stretched well beyond their ability as benefactors (2 Cor 8:9; cf. 8:1–3 [cf. Mark 12:41–44]).[64] We are witnessing here a dismantling of the inscriptional icons of civic virtue and their replacement by a cruciform Servant-Benefactor (2 Cor 13:4; Phil 2:5–8), notwithstanding the fact that Paul's portrait of Christ in 2 Corinthians 8:9 rhetorically functions as a paradoxical counterpart to the inscriptional vignettes of beneficence.[65]

Furthermore, a series of geographically, racially and socially diverse communities of faith are being encouraged to assume corporately the mantle of the Servant-Benefactor and thereby increase the thanksgiving given to God (2 Cor 9:10–11, 15; cf. 4:15). In the new communities of faith, believers are no longer reduced to a suppliant position before powerful civic benefactors, as in the world of the honorific inscriptions. Rather the return of gratitude is now redirected towards God. Prayer for one's benefactors, therefore, as well as longing in Christian love for them, are the appropriate responses of the grateful recipient (2 Cor 9:14).

5.2.3. The Ethics of the Gymnasiarch

Much could be said regarding the range of virtues (e.g. "love of fame and righteousness" [IEph 1.6]; "merit and goodwill" [Danker, *Benefactor*, § 17]; etc.) attributed to the gymnasiarchs in the honorific inscriptions. Such eulogies are consonant with the inscriptions erected to civic benefactors throughout the eastern Mediterranean basin. The virtues mentioned are little more than stereotyped circumlocutions for the benefactor's donations.[66] What we are looking for is the atypical description that says something striking about the ethical stance of the gymnasiarch. Consider, for instance, the comments of IEph 1.6 regarding Mithres:

> and for the remaining gymnasium affairs he took care, hating the bad and loving the good, in nothing neglectful of what relates to honour and fame for the sake of establishing as worth of memory and praise the preference he shows for the best.[67]

---

[64] For discussion, see Harrison, *Paul's Language of Grace*, 250–56.

[65] The inscriptions sometimes provide miniature portraits of beneficence, including the sketch of Epigone's generosity (cf. Hands, *Charities*, §D13) which is framed by the larger inscription in honour of her husband-benefactor, Euphrosynus.

[66] Note the pithy comment of Judge ("The Teacher as Moral Exemplar," 177): "money has purchased merit."

[67] A Pergameme inscription (*Ath. Mit.* xxxiii [1908]: 380, No. 2) speaks of the gymnasiarch Agias: "and thinking his watchful presence in the gymnasium most desirable, he never neglected anything in his oversight of the discipline of the *epheboi* and *neoi*; with an austere

Another captivating vignette is found in the decree honouring Zosimos of Priene. He is described as one who strives for "eternal fame,"

> rashly seeking after his own pleasure in nothing, and understanding that merit alone returns the greatest fruits and favours to those who treasure virtue in honour before foreigners and citizens.[68]

Finally, an insight into the corporate ethics of the gymnasiarchs can be gleaned from their oath of office, preserved for us on a large marble stele in Verroia in Macedonia. The words of the oath are as follows:

> I swear by [...] and by Heracles and by Hermes that I will be a *gymnasiarchos* in accordance with the gymnasiarchal law; and that I will do anything and everything not covered by the law in the most just manner I can; and I will not do special favours for my friends nor unjust injuries to my enemies; and from existing revenues for the young neither will I myself steal, nor will I allow anyone else to steal in any way that I might know or discover. I am true to my oath, may all be well with me; if not, may the opposite be my fate.[69]

There are echoes of Pauline sentiments in the ethics of the gymnasiarchal inscriptions. For example, Paul counsels believers to "hate what is evil, hold fast to what is good" (Rom 12:9; cf. 12:21; cf. 1 Thess 5:21). Believers should not please themselves or look only to their own interests (Rom 15:1b; 1 Cor 10:24, 33; Phil 2:4). Indeed, to show favoritism overlooks the impartiality of God (Rom 2:11). Retaliation and revenge are excluded (Rom 12:17–21; 1 Thess 5:15; Col 3:35). Paul takes seriously the truthfulness of his oaths in front of God (2 Cor 1:17–20, 23; 11:30–33). Finally, the thief should no longer steal, but work and use his spare money for the benefaction of the poor (Eph 4:28).

In all of this, Paul endorses commonplaces of Graeco-Roman and Jewish ethics without comment (Rom 12:17b; Phil 4:8). But there is a different dynamic behind Paul's exhortations. Paul's commonplaces are expressions of the new way of the Spirit who conforms believers to Christ in a way surpassing the righteous demands of the law (Rom 7:6; 8:4–5, 28–28). This transformed ethical life is tangible proof that believers are living under the reign of grace and are participating in the new creation.

---

loathing for evil, he made provision for the observance of good behaviour around the gymnasium."

[68] IPriene 112 (84 BC).

[69] Miller, *Arete*, § 126. As regards ethics, note the fines regarding the wrong use of money in the gymnasium (Austin, *The Hellenistic World*, § 139). The inscriptions sometimes contrast the integrity and competence of gymnasium officials (Pouilloux, *Choix d'inscriptions Grecques*, § 3): "and, elected director of the gymnasium by the people according to the law, on account of the deficiency of the gymnasiarch, (Boulagoras) supervised the good-conduct of the ephebes and the youths fairly and nobly."

5.2.4. The Honours Accorded to the Gymnasiarch

The return of honour to benefactors such as the gymnasiarchs ensured the operation of the Graeco-Roman reciprocity system.[70] It maintained the aristocracy of civic merit that was the preserve of benefactors and the worthy. It provided the motivation for benefactors to continue their beneficence towards the gymnasium and for new benefactors to compete for the same civic honours with gifts to the city.[71] Two brief examples will suffice.[72] For his generosity to the gymnasium of Sestos, the gymnasiarch Menas was to receive annually at the games a gold crown from the *epheboi* and *neoi*, front seating at the games for himself and his descendants, and the erection of a bronze statue of himself.[73] In the case of the Ephesian gymnasiarch Mithres, a statue was set up in his honour in the gymnasium so that it would encourage everyone "to become emulators of good deeds."[74]

---

[70] One of the reasons for the city Sestos honoring the benefactor Menas (Danker, *Benefactor*, § 17) is "in order that all might know that Sestos is hospitable to men of exceptional character and ability, especially those who from their earliest youth have shown themselves devoted to the common good and have given priority to the winning of a glorious reputation."

[71] The benefactor Menas (Danker, *Benefactor*, § 17) is honoured "(so) that also all others, as they see the People bestowing honours on exceptional men, might emulate the noblest qualities and be moved to virtue, to the end that the common good might be advanced as all aim ever to win a reputation for doing something beneficial for our home city."

[72] This chapter does not explore in depth the honours rendered to the imperial rulers by gymnasiarchs in local gymnasia. Adrustus, the gymnasiarch of Lapethus in Cyprus, set up in his gymnasium a cult statue of Tiberius 'from his own monies for his own god (i. e. Tiberius)' (OGIS 583 [I cent. AD], tr. B.W. Jones and R.D. Milns, *The Use of Documentary Evidence in the Study of Roman Imperial History* [Sydney: Sydney University Press, 1984] § 74). A first-century AD inscription from Arnaea honors Lallia as "priestess of the Emperor's cult and gymnasiarch" (see *infra* § 5.3.5 n. 110: M.R. Lefkowitz and M.B. Fant, *Women's Life in Greece and Rome: A Source Book in Translation* [Baltimore: John Hopkins University Press, 1982], 157 § 159). The original Hellenistic maxims of the Delphic canon, discussed in §§ 5.3.1–3.5, might have been pastorally redeployed by the gymnasiarchs to teach the boys to honour appropriately the Julio-Claudian ruler-benefactors – and the Roman gods more generally – in the first-century (e.g. Stobaeus, *Eclogae* III 1.173: Sosiades no. 3 ["Worship the gods"]; Sosiades no. 59 ["Honour benefactions"]; Sosiades no. 65 ["Honour the good ones"]; IKyzikos II 2 Col. 2 no. 20 ["Worship divinity"]). On Paul's subtle response to the imperial rulers – simultaneously honoring (Rom 13:7b) and demoting them (13:1b, 2a, 4a, 4b, 6b; cf. 1 Cor 8:4–6) – see J.R. Harrison, *Paul and the Imperial Authorities at Thessalonica and Rome*, WUNT I 273 (Tübingen: Mohr Siebeck, 2011), 271–323.

[73] Danker, *Benefactor*, § 17. For further examples of the crowning of gymnasiarchs and ephebes, see IPriene 114 (84 BC); Hands, *Charities*, §D56; Austin, *The Hellenistic World*, § 136. For the erection of an honorific statue, see IEph Ia 6 (II cent. BC).

[74] IEph Ia 6 (II cent. BC). On emulation, see Judge, "The Teacher as Moral Exemplar." An inscription from Kyme (R.A. Kearsley, "A Civic Benefactor of the First Century in Asia Minor," *New Docs* 7 [1994]: 233–41, § 10) notes how Kleanax's provision of *paideia* for his son Sarapion encouraged the boy to become a civic benefactor like his father: "(Kleanax) took thought for the boy's education in letters, and provided for the people a man worthy of his family, Sarapion (by name), and a protector and helper, one who has in many ways has already displayed zeal toward the city through his own manly deeds."

We have seen how the honours of gymnasiarchs were prominently listed for the emulation of posterity. Paul, too, upholds a principle of christocentric emulation that is transferred to the apostles and co-workers in the gospel (Rom 15:7–9; 1 Cor 11:1; 2 Cor 8:1–5, 9 [cf. 6:10]; Gal 6:17; Eph 5:1–2; Phil 2:4–5; 3:17; 1 Thess 1:6–7; 2:14; 2 Thess 3:7).[75] He gives honour to those service is worthy of special honour (e.g. Rom 16:1–23; 1 Cor 16:10; 2 Cor 8:16–24; Phil 3:19–30; Col 4:7–17). Paul's use of honour terminology is too widespread to claim that he subverts first-century honorific culture, notwithstanding the fact that he democratises the allocation of honour (Rom 12:10b) and extends it to the base of the social pyramid (1 Cor 12:24).

But what was Paul's attitude to the coronal honoring of illustrious men?[76] Paul and the early believers reject these coronal honours or formulate them differently in a bold re-definition of civic honour. First, Paul postponed the allocation of crowns until the eschaton (1 Cor 9:25; Phil 4:1; 1 Thess 2:19; cf. 2 Tim 2:5; 4:8; Jam 1:12; 1 Peter 5:4; Rev 2:10; 3:11), though both Paul and 1 Peter recognise the possibility of Christian benefactors receiving honours (including crowns) from the ruling authorities (Rom 13:3b; cf. 13:7b; 1 Pet 2:14–16).[77] Second, there was little interest in the wide variety of Hellenistic crown-types or the other civic honours. In this respect, Paul dismissed the Isthmian coronal honours as "fading" (φθαρτός: 1 Cor 9:25). Third, Paul and the early believers viewed the crowning ritual as a corporate experience. While the *demos* of a Hellenistic city-state did occasionally crown another city-state (IAssos 8; Demosthenes, *De Cor* 92–93), usually the ritual was reserved for members of the civic elite or local dignitaries such as the gymnasiarch. Only the decrees of the local associations – which aped the honorific conventions of the Hellenistic city-states – extended their titles, awards and privileges down the social ladder. As noted, Paul and the early believers democritised the coronal honour and postponed its conferral to the eschaton.

Moreover, in crowning the *ekklesia* at the eschaton, Paul claims that God had inverted social hierarchy and status (1 Cor 1:26–29; cf. Matt 19:28–30; Luke 14:7–11). The apostle's portrait of Christ – the unrequited Benefactor requited by God – underscores this reversal. Christ, the infinitely rich Benefactor reduced to destitute slave status (Phil 2:7–8; 2 Cor 8:9), had suffered profound dishonour (1 Cor 1:23; 2 Cor 13:4a; Gal 3:13b). But exalted by God's intervention,

---

[75] For general discussion, see Judge, "The Teacher as Moral Exemplar." On Paul's exhortatory use of positive and negative models, see Ben Witherington III, *Friendship and Finances in Philippi: The Letter of Paul to the Philippians* (Valley Forge: Trinity Press International, 1994), 19–20.

[76] For discussion, see J.R. Harrison, "A Share in All the Sacrifices," *New Docs* 9 (2002): 1–3, § 1; *idem*, "'The Fading Crown': Divine Honour and the Early Christians," *JTS* 54.2 (2003): 493–529.

[77] B.W. Winter, *Seek the Welfare of the City: Christians as Benefactors and Citizens* (Grand Rapids: Eerdmans, 1994), 25–40.

He became the focal point of divine honour (Phil 2:9–11; Rom 1:4; cf. Eph 1:20–21). In the heavenly court, however, God remains the object of all adoration and honour: so, at the eschaton, Christ is made subject to his Father so that God may be all in all (1 Cor 15:28). Thus, in democratising the crowning ritual and redirecting honour towards Christ and supremely to God, Paul was engaging in a critique of the Graeco-Roman honour system, at least in its coronal expression.

5.2.5. The Exclusivist Ethos of Gymnasiarchal Law

Finally, an intriguing insight into the exclusivist ethos of the gymnasium and its personnel is found in the Macedonia gymnasiarchal law at Verroia:

> Concerning those who are not to enter the gymnasium. No slave is to disrobe in the gymnasium, not any freedman, not their sons, nor cripples (ἀπάλαιστρος), nor homosexuals (ἡται[ρ]ευκώς: literally, "one who has prostituted himself"), nor those engaged in commerce (τῶν ἀγοραίαι τέχνῃ κεχρημένων: literally, "using a marketplace skill"), nor drunkards, nor madmen. If the *gymnasiarchos* knowingly allows any of the aforementioned to be oiled, or continues to allow them after having received a report of them, he is to be penalised 1,000 drachmas.[78]

What is Paul's attitude to the maintenance of group boundaries? His stance is more complex than the exclusivism of the ancient gymnasia. While Paul sets clear group boundaries for the members of his house churches (e.g. 1 Cor 5:1–13; 6:9–11; 10:14–22; Gal 1:8–10; 2 Cor 6:14–7:1), he is socially and ethically more radical than the conservative legislators of the gymnasia. He resists exclusivism of all kinds – whether it was the elevation of rhetoric and pneumatic gifts over the "ordinary" *charismata*,[79] judgmental attitudes over food and calendar laws,[80] ethnic and gender bias,[81] or socially divisive actions.[82] Paul calls upon the believing wife or husband to live in peace with the unbelieving spouse (1 Cor 7:12–16); he seeks to restore an offending church leader to his community

---

[78] Miller, *Arete*, § 126. Austin (*The Hellenistic World*, § 137) translates "cripples" (ἀπάλαιστρος [LSJ: "not trained in the *palaestra*", "awkward"]) more literally as "if he has not been to the wrestling-school." In the view of T.K. Hubbard, ed., *Homosexuality in Greece and Rome* [Berkeley: University of California Press, 2003], 85 n. 102), ἀπάλαιστρος is "of uncertain meaning, but probably refers to those who are qualified to enter the gymnasium in other respects, but do not attend due to a lack of physical fitness". Hubbard transliterates ἀπάλαιστρος, not attempting an English translation. Perhaps ἀπάλαιστρος was a "catch-all" term intended to disqualify a range of physically deficient people from entering the wrestling school and gymnasium. It excluded those who did not have the requisite wrestling training and/or fitness. It also disqualified from wrestling those who were now physically disabled – presumably due to a competition injury or an accident.

[79] 1 Cor 1:12–13; 3:4–9, 16–22; 4:6, 14–20; 2 Cor 10:10; 11:6.

[80] Rom 14:3–4, 10, 13, 19; 1 Cor 8:1–13; 10:23–11:1; Gal 2:11–14.

[81] Rom 11:18; Gal 3:28; 6:15; Eph 2:11–22; Col 3:11.

[82] 1 Cor 11:17–22.

of faith (2 Cor 2:5–11; 7:12). What removes exclusivism from the church is the loving acceptance of the other person in light of the cross (Rom 14:15; 15:7; 1 Cor 8:11–12) and the unity of the Spirit arising from justification by faith (Rom 3:27–31; 1 Cor 3:16–17; Gal 3:28; 6:15; Col 3:11).

What is intriguing is the way that Paul relativises the social stigma attached to many of the despised groups listed in the gymnasiarchical law at Verroia. The master-slave hierarchy is inverted because of the new relationship of brotherhood established in Christ (1 Cor 7:22; Gal 3:28; Phlm 15–16). Drunkenness is condemned (Rom 13:13; 1 Cor 5:11; 6:10; Gal 5:21; Eph 5:18), but only as one vice among others. The gymnasiarchal law forbids the presence of homosexuals, probably because the gymnasium, if unsupervised, provided opportunities for pederasty.[83] But, in Paul's view, while homosexual sin is forbidden (Rom 1:24–28; 1 Cor 6:9–11), former homosexuals could experience the transforming newness of the resurrection life in the body of Christ in the same way as other believers (1 Cor 6:12).[84] While Paul never mentions explicitly the physically dis-

---

[83] See Miller, *Arete* [2004], 189–93; Vanhove, "Le gymnase," 72–74; cf. K.J. Dover, *Greek Homosexuality* (London: Duckworth, 1978). Note the law cited by Aeschines (*In Tim.* 12): "The superintendents (οἱ γυμνασιάρχαι) of the gymnasium shall under no conditions allow anyone who has reached the age of manhood to enter the contests of Hermes together with the boys. A gymnasiarch who does permit this and fails to keep such a person out of the gymnasium, shall be liable to the penalties prescribed for the seduction of free-born youth."

[84] Paul's terminology for same-sex relations differs from the gymnasiarchal law of Verroia in Macedonia (n. 78 *supra*). Whereas the Verroian law refers to the exclusion of male prostitutes (ἡται[ρ]ευκως) from the gymnasium, Paul excludes unrepentant μαλακοί and ἀρσενοκοῖται from God's eschatological Kingdom (1 Cor 6:9). Like several other Jewish writers (e.g. Josephus [*Ap.* 2.273: παρὰ φύσιν; Philo [*Spec. Laws* 3.39; *Abr.* 133–136: παρὰ φύσιν]; *T. Naph.* 3.3–4: ἐνήλλαξε τάξιν φύσεως), Paul speaks against the "unnaturalness" of same-sex relations (Rom 1:26: μετήλλαξαν τὴν φυσικὴν χρῆσιν εἰς τὴν παρὰ φύσιν; 1:27: ἀφέντες τὴν φυσικὴν χρῆσιν τῆς θηλείας), in contrast to the "naturalness" of married relations in Jewish thought (e.g. Gen 1:27–28; 2:24; Josephus, *Ap.* 2.199: κατὰ φύσιν). For Graeco-Roman sources on male prostitution and the relation of sexuality to 'nature', see Hubbard, *Homosexuality in Greece and Rome*, *s.v.* Index "Prostitution", "Nature". Several scholars have recently challenged this "Jewish" reading of Paul regarding sexual relations. In their view, the traditional approach above does not address the issue of same sex relations with historical and exegetical integrity because it is fraught with modern misconceptions about the construction of ancient sexuality. First, Martin ("*Arsenokoitês* and *Malakos*: Meanings and Consequences," in *Biblical Ethics and Homosexuality*, ed. R.L. Brawley [Louisville: Westminster/John Knox, 1996], 117–36) proposes that ancient constructions of sexuality are vastly different to modern sexist ideology. He argues that μαλακοί refers to those who are "effeminate", whereas in the vice lists ἀρσενοκοῖται denotes only economically exploitive sex. However, "effeminacy" was a feature of some Graeco-Roman constructions of homosexuality (Hubbard, *Homosexuality in Greece and Rome*, §§ 7.18, 8.20, 9.12 [cf. 3.10, 3.23]) and, from a Jewish viewpoint, it included the penetration of passive partners (Philo, *Spec. Leg.* 3.37–42; *Abr.* 135–136; cf. *Sib.Or.* 3.185–188, 595–600, 760–64). Contrary to Martin (*Arsenokoitês* and *Malakos*, 119), Paul, as a first-century Jew, probably derived the compound ἀρσενοκοιτῆς from the separate use of the words ἄρσην and κοιτῆς condemning homosexuality in Leviticus 18:22 and 20:13. The Levitical holiness code is the most obvious referent for Paul's use of the compound here, especially given that in Romans Paul also reapplies the LXX Levitical language for various types of sexual

abled (if ἀπάλαιστροι is correctly translated as "cripples"), they are subsumed under the rubric of Christ's power being displayed in weakness (1 Cor 1:18–29; 4:10–13; 2 Cor 4:7–12; 6:8–10; 11:16–12.10; 13:4).[85] As far as the despised trades, Paul did not baulk at socially stepping down to work with his hands as a slavish artisan (2 Cor 11:7; 1 Thess 2:9; cf. 4:11–1; 2 Thess 3:7–8).[86]

We turn to a discussion of the maxims from the Delphic canon found in the ancient gymnasia. What would Paul have made of their ethical agenda in the pastoral and social formation of the *epheboi*?

impurity between people of the opposite sex (ἄρσην: LXX Lev 15:24; κοιτῆς: LXX 20:21) to sexual impurity between people of the same sex (ἀκαθαρσία: Rom 1:24). Second, D. L. Balch ("Romans 1:24–27, Science, and Homosexuality," *CurTM* 25.6 [1998]: 433–40) claims that Paul only condemns *compulsive* same-sex relations, in a manner similar to the psychological portraits of sexual addiction in the medical treatises (i. e. pseudo-Aristotle, *Problemata*; Soranus, *Gynecology*). However, this distinction overlooks Paul's link of same-sex relations with his condemnation of idolatry and its inversion of inviolable creation boundaries (Rom 1:19–23, 25; cf. vv. 24, 26), a connection also made in the Jewish literature (e. g. Wis 14:12, 26–27; *T.Naph.* 3.2–4; *Ps-Phoc.* 3, 8; *Jub.* 20:6–8; 22:22; *T.Jac.* 7.20; Josephus, *Ap.* 2:273–275). Third, D.B. Martin ("Heterosexism and the Interpretation of Romans 1:18–32," *BibInt* 3 [1995]: 332–55) agues that in Romans 1 homosexual intercourse is not a symptom of a "Fall" from a pristine creation (Gen 1–3) but is more a symptom of Gentile idolatry and polytheism. S.K. Stowers (*A Rereading of Romans: Justice, Jews, and Cultures* [New Haven and London: Yale University Press, 1994]: 122–25) also proposes that Paul's rhetoric in Romans 1:18–32 originates in the widespread "decline of civilization" accounts in which unnatural behaviour and the loss of reason is a common motif. For Paul, however, same-sex relations blur the inviolable distinction between "male" and "female" that God established at the creation (Rom 1:26–27 [v. 26: αἱ θήλειαι αὐτῶν; v. 27: οἱ ἄρσενες; cf. LXX Gen 1:27: ἄρσεν καὶ θῆλυ), in the same way that idolatry and polytheism blurs God's own separation from his creation (Gen 1–2; Rom 1:21–23, 25; cf. vv. 24, 26). As P. F. Esler notes regarding Romans 1:21–27, (*Conflict and Identity in Romans: The Social Setting of Paul's Letter* [Minneapolis: Fortress, 2003], 149), "Paul is not concerned with the invention of idolatry for its own sake, although he does explain how it came about (1:21–23), nor does he put forward some diachronic narrative of decline." Instead, Paul portrays the manifestation of God's wrath (Rom 1:18) towards all human sinfulness against the backdrop of creation which not only reflects the invisible qualities of its Creator (1:20) but which also possesses inviolable boundaries that must not be violated by human beings (1:21–23, 26b, 27a).

[85] L. L. Welborn (*Paul, the Fool of Christ: A Study of 1 Corinthians 1–4 in the Comic-Philosophic Tradition* [London and New York: T&T Clark, 2005], 142–47) argues that "aesthetic disdain, uniting the weak and deformed with the crucified," belonged to the gallows humour of the cross. In the comic mimes, the socially inferior and the physically defective (often slaves and the poor) are regularly threatened with crucifixion. But, in Paul's thought, weakness and deformity becomes a locus for the demonstration of God's cruciform power and wisdom (1 Cor 1:18–19, 25; 2 Cor 13:4; cf. 2 Cor 8:9a; Phil 2:7).

[86] R. F. Hock, *The Social Context of Paul's Ministry* (Philadelphia: Fortress, 1980), *passim*; E. A. Judge, "The Social Identity of the First Christians: A Question of Method in Religious History," in *Social Distinctives of the Christians in the First Century: Pivotal Essays by E. A. Judge*, ed. D. M. Scholer (Peabody: Hendrickson, 2008), 117–35.

5.3. Paul and the Ethical Ideals of the Gymnasium

We have drawn attention to the fact that the study of ethics was an important part of the curriculum of the late Hellenistic gymnasia. Sosiades' collection of the maxims of the famous seven sages – cited *in extenso* by Stobaeus (Σωσιάδου τῶν ἑπτα; σοφῶν ὑοθῆκαι, from Stobaeus, *Eclogae* III 1.173) – was the foundational ethical curriculum taught to the *epheboi* in the Greek East. Sosiades is unknown to us, but his collection of the maxims of the seven sages is found in the fifth-century AD anthology of Stobaeus. These maxims, better known to us as the Delphic canon, had been inscribed at Delphi for all to see (Plato, *Prt.* 343A–B; *Chrm.* 165A; *Hipparch.* 229A; Plutarch, *Mor.* 385D–E).

Many of the Delphic maxims have been found inscribed – with minor variations – at the gymnasium (?) at Miletopolis in the Hellespont (IKyzikos II 2 col. 1 [IV–III cent. BC]). Another version of the Delphic canon has been found at the gymnasium of the ephebes at Thera (IG XII[3] 1020: IV cent. BC), though the Therean version is more fragmentary. Thus the ethics of the Delphic canon had spread throughout the eastern Mediterranean gymnasia. The widespread dissemination of the Delphic maxims and the meticulous care taken in their transmission can be gauged from their presence at Egypt (P. Ath. Univ. inv. 2782 [I/II cent. AD]) and at Aï-Khanum on the Oxus (Afghanistan).[87]

We will now compare the ethical curriculum of the gymnasia of Miletopolis and Thera with the ethical exhortations of Paul to his house churches. How would Paul have viewed the pastoral formation sponsored by the ancient gymnasium?

---

[87] On Egypt, see A. N. Oikonomides, "The Lost Delphic Inscription with the Commandments of the Seven and *P. Univ. Athen* 2782," *ZPE* 37 (1980): 179–83. In the case of Aï-Khanum, the Delphic maxims were inscribed on a third-century BC stele erected by Clearchus (of Soli?) in the sanctuary of Cineas, the founder of the city. In the epigram on the front base of the stele, Clearchus says that the maxims on the stele came from a copy that he had *personally* transcribed while at Delphi. See L. Robert, "De Delphes a l'Oxus: inscriptions grecques nouvelles de la Bactriane," *Comptes Rendues de l'Académie des Inscriptions et Belles Lettres*, (1968): 416–57; l'Institut Fernand Courby, *Nouveau choix d'inscriptions grecques* (Paris: Société d'édition Les Belles Lettres, 1971), § 37. Found among the excavations at Aï-Khanum by French archaeologists (1964–1978) was a limestone statue, found in a niche of the site of the the gymnasium, probably of the gymnasiarch Strato (first half of II cent. BC). See http//www.gg-art.com/news/photoshow/1285611.html, accessed 06.03.2017. For finds of Delphic canon sayings in other locations, see M. Huys, "P. Oxy. 61.4099: A Combination of Mythographic Lists with Sentences of the Seven Wise Men," *ZPE* 113 (1996): 205–12; R. Pintaudi and Pieter J. Sijpesteijn, "Ostraka di contenuto scolastico provenienti da Narmuthis," *ZPE* 76 (1989): 85–92, Nos. 5, 6; A. Papathomas, "14. Ein literarisches Fragment mit Sprüchen der Sieben Weisen," in "*... vor dem Papyrus sind alle Gleich!': papyrologische Beiträge zu Ehren von Bärbel Kramer (P. Kramer)*," ed. R. Eberhard et al. (Berlin and New York: De Gruyter, 2009), 163–69. For full discussion of the Delphic canon, see Chapter 6 in this volume. See also J. R. Harrison, "The Seven Sages, the Delphic Canon and Ethical Education in Antiquity," in Hauge and Pitts, *Ancient Education and Early Christianity*, 71–86.

5.3.1. Methodological Problems in Comparing the Delphic Canon with Paul

Before we compare the maxims of the Delphic canon with the writings of Paul, several methodological problems must be aired.

First, what significance do we attach to the presence of well-known semantic domains in the Delphic canon but which are absent from Paul's letters? Has the domain failed to capture Paul's interest or is the apostle avoiding it for some reason?[88] Does Paul resort to another semantic domain in order to express the same idea? If so, why? Does the domain retain nuances about which Paul is uneasy? It is difficult to answer definitively these questions. But an understanding of how Paul's semantic domains intersected with the ethical vocabulary of his day illuminates his approach to leadership formation.

Second, where there is an overlap of a semantic domain between Paul and the Delphic canon, the exegetical context of Paul's writings must be respected. Only then can we be sure that Paul is endorsing an ethical commonplace. The distinctiveness of Paul's gospel must not be blurred at the expense of semantic overlaps.

Third, in discussing the presence or absence of a semantic domain, the stance of Paul and the Delphic canon on various social issues should be examined within a spectrum of documentary and literary evidence. Then we will avoid the twin dangers of overstating the historical evidence or indulging in historical abstraction.

Fourth, the Delphic canon places the sages' maxims in the agonistic context of the ancient gymnasium. In the inscriptions of Miletopolis and Thera, the singular form of the imperative is always used. The focus of the sages is on the self-knowledge of the individual ("Know yourself": IG XII 3.1020 4). The overwhelming concern of Delphic ethics is self-interest ("Look after yourself": IKyzikos II 2 Col. 2 No. 4; "Look after your own things": IKyzikos II 2 Col. 1 No. 20; "Use your advantage": IKyzikos II 2 Col. 1 No. 25), self-control ("Nothing to excess": IG XII 3.1020 No. 3), and self-protection ("Avoid commitment: you'll pay for it": IG XII 3.1020 No. 1).[89] Social attitudes are canvassed only in so far as they impinge on the individual's maintenance of harmonious relationships with others. The social agenda of the sages is intended to enable individuals to establish self-sufficiency and to preserve concord when faced with social collisions.

Paul's ethical exhortations, by contrast, are embedded in rhetorically complex and highly argumentative epistles intended to be read out aloud to local

---

[88] For example, the maxim "flee hatred" (IKyzikos II 2 Col. 2 No. 28) is not used at all in Paul. Paul's advises believers to flee immorality (1 Cor 6:18) and idolatry (1 Cor 10:14).

[89] E. A. Judge, "Ancient Beginnings of the Modern World,", in *idem*, *Jerusalem and Athens: Cultural Transformation in Late Antiquity*, WUNT I 265 (Tübingen: Mohr Siebeck, 2010), 282–314, esp. 288–96, 305–09.

communities of faith (Col 4:16; 1 Thess 5:27). The frequent use of the plural imperative underscores Paul's intention that his house churches experience communal transformation in Christ, whether they were confronting external cultural pressures (Rom 12:1–2) or dealing with self-centered behaviour inside the house churches (Rom 13:9–10; 15:7–9; 1 Cor 10:33–11:1; Phil 2:3–5; Gal 5:14; 6:2). We can speak more definitively about the social context of Paul's ethical teaching than we can about the sages' teaching.

Fifth, our task of penetrating the social world of the Delphic maxims is made doubly difficult by the fact that "for all their apparent simplicity, or because of it, their meaning lay wide open to interpretation."[90] A clear translation of some of the maxims is problematical. We cannot discern the organisational principle behind Sodiades' canon, assuming that it had one.[91] Also the stele of Miletoplis includes elements not found in the canon of Sosiades (IKyzikos II 2 Col. 1 Nos.3, 4, 5; IKyzikos II 2 Col. 2 Nos.18, 19, 20), even though the stele probably carried the entire 147 maxims of Sosiades' collection.[92] Moreover, as E. A. Judge notes,[93] IKyzikos II 2 marginally varies Sosiades' order. The stele at Thera (IG XII 3.1020) is too fragmentary to draw any firm conclusion regarding its handling of the Delphic traditions. Whatever we make of these differences, the difficulty of comparing the Delphic canon to the Paul's ethical exhortations should be obvious. In many respects, the ethical commands of Jesus, found in different Synoptic contexts, provide a more congenial corpus for comparison with the Delphic canon than the epistles of Paul.

Notwithstanding, a comparison of the Delphic gymnasium curriculum with Paul's ethical teaching of his houses churches, while tentative in its conclusions, enables us to situate Paul's ethical ideals of leadership in the context of the late Hellenistic gymnasium.

5.3.2. Differences between Paul and the Delphic canon

Many of the Delphic maxims are sharply polarised to Paul's theological viewpoint. Two Delphic maxims (IKyzikos II 2 Col. 1 Nos.6 ["Allow for chance"], 7 ["Honour providence"]) assert that life should be lived out reverently before the hypostasised deities, Tyche and Pronoia, who control human affairs. Paul, however, proposes that believers cannot be separated from the love of the crucified, risen and reigning Christ (Rom 8:31–39; cf. Eph 1:19–21; 2.6), no matter what

---

[90] Judge, "Ancient Beginnings of the Modern World," 290.

[91] Over against Delphic canon, Paul's careful placement of select ethical traditions contributes rhetorically, contextually, and theologically to his overall argument. Note Paul's use of the Jesus tradition in Romans 12–15 in M. Thompson, *Clothed with Christ: The Example and Teaching of Jesus in Romans 12:1–15:13* (Sheffield: Sheffield Academic, 1991), *passim*.

[92] Judge, "Ancient Beginnings of the Modern World," 291.

[93] Judge, "Ancient Beginnings of the Modern World," 291.

their circumstances might be (contra: IKyzikos II 2 Col. 2 No. 17 ["Fear what controls you"]).

There are other collisions between the Delphic canon and Paul's theology. Oath-taking for Paul is a mark of his apostolic truthfulness before God (2 Cor 1:17–20, 23; 11:30–33), whereas a maxim from Miletopolis asserts that oath-taking is to be avoided (IKyzikos II 2 Col. 1 No. 8 ["Use no oath"]; cf. Matt 5:33–37). Conversely, the Delphic insistence that secrets be kept hidden (IKyzikos II 2 Col. 2 No. 16 ["Keep secrets hidden"]) does not square with Paul's sense of openness before God and others (Rom 2:16; 16:25; 1 Cor 14:25; Eph 5:12–13), or with the apocalyptic unveiling of all things in Christ (1 Cor 3:7–10; 10:11; Eph 3:3, 6). A maxim urging the cultivation of nobility (IKyzikos II 2 Col. 1 No. 17 ["Cultivate nobility/the family"]) sits uneasily with Paul's portrait of the social inversion accomplished through the cross (1 Cor 1:26–29). The (Stoic?) admonition to "toil gloriously" (IKyzikos II 2 Col. 2 No. 7; cf. IKyzikos II 2 Col. 1 No. 11 ["Pursue glory"]) and to persevere to the end (IKyzikos II 2 Col. 2 No. 1 ["Go though with it, unflinchingly"]) does not approximate the experience of weakness and power and of death and life in the ministry of the apostles (2 Cor 4:7–12; 6:4–10; 11:21–12:10; 13:4). The same could be said about the injunction "Don't boast in strength" (IKyzikos II 2 Col. 2 No. 23). It does not capture the social humiliation of Paul boasting in his weaknesses (2 Cor 11:30; 12:9b–10).

Further examples are easily multiplied. Being "sociable" and "approachable" (IKyzikos II 2 Col. 1 No. 19; IKyzikos II 2 Col. 2 No. 5) or practising consensus (IKyzikos II 2 Col. 2 No. 14 ["Pursue/practise consensus"]) is far removed from the Spirit-endowed κοινωνία ("fellowship") uniting converts. Although being "well spoken" was important in ephebic culture (IKyzikos II 2 Col. 1 No. 23; IKyzikos II 2 Col. 2 No. 26), Paul dismisses the importance of rhetorical eloquence (1 Cor 1:20; 2:3–5; 4:20; 2 Cor 10:10–11; 11:6; 1 Thess 2:5). Neither does the Delphic idea of acting promptly (IKyzikos II 2 Col. 2 No. 12), accepting one's opportunity (IKyzikos II 2 Col. 2 No. 21) or deliberating in time (IKyzikos II 2 Col. 2 No. 11) capture the eschatological "now" of Paul's gospel (Rom 5:6; 13:11; 1 Cor 7:29; 10:11b; 2 Cor 6:2; Gal 4:4; Eph 5:16; Col 4:5). Even the Delphic acceptance of "old age" (IKyzikos II 2 Col. 2 No. 24) obscures Paul's eschatological orientation. According to Paul, God is daily renewing the believer's inner nature in preparation for the "eternal weight of glory beyond all comparison" at the resurrection age (Rom 13:11; 2 Cor 3:17–18; cf. 5:8; Phil 1:21).

Finally, in place of Delphic knowledge of self (IG XII 3.1020 No. 4 ["Know/recognize yourself"]), Paul emphasises how the knowledge of God, founded upon the crucified and risen Christ, is mediated through His Spirit and evidenced in our love for the weak (Rom 8:26–27; Phil 3:10; 1 Cor 8:2; Eph 1:18). The Delphic injunction to "get wealth justly" (IKyzikos II 2 Col. 2 No. 30) also runs counter to Paul's theology of the incarnation. The apostle exhorts his converts to concentrate more on the divestment of wealth than its acquisition (2 Cor 8:1–5, 9). Indeed, Christ's poverty (2 Cor 8:9) serves as a paradigm for apostolic ministry generally (2 Cor 6:10; cf. 11:27; Phil 4:12).[94]

In sum, there is a significant divide between the understanding of leadership evinced by the ancient gymnasia and Paul's early house churches. The result of character formation envisaged in each case was fundamentally different.

5.3.3. Commonplaces between Paul and the Delphic canon

There are several Pauline commonplaces that have affinities with the ethics of the Delphic canon. Nonetheless, we must be sensitive to the distinctive emphases of the gospel that drive Paul's ethical exhortation. They firm in Paul's ethics of leadership, both in their social and ecclesiastical dimensions. A series of examples will establish the point.

First, the maxim "Reply at the right time" (IKyzikos II 2 Col. 2 No. 6) echoes Paul's sentiments regarding well-timed gracious speech (Col 4:5–6). However, the redemptive role which proper conduct and speech plays in persuading unbelievers lifts Paul's exhortation to a different level. Paul's aim was to transfer the unbeliever to Christ's inclusive community through the gracious example of transformed believers (Col 4.7–17).

Second, Paul speaks of fixing one's sight on what is unseen (2 Cor 4:18), whereas a Delphic maxim directs "Control your eye" (IKyzikos II 2 Col. 2 No. 9; cf. Matt 5:27–30). There is only a surface similarity here. Paul more emphasises the divine enlightenment of the eyes of the believer's heart (Eph 1:18; Gal 3:1) and the responsibility to do right in the sight of the Lord before everyone (Rom 12:17; 2 Cor 8:21). This interaction of divine transformation and the believer's responsibility unveils the apostle's understanding of moral accountability in leadership.

Third, Paul's emphasis on repentance is echoed in the Delphic canon ([ἁ]μαρτὼν μετανόει: IKyzikos II 2 Col. 2 No. 8 ["If you err, turn back"]), though the Delphic version does not carry Paul's God-centered focus (e.g. Rom 2:4; 2 Cor 7:9, 10; 12:21; 2 Tim 2:25). The same difference in focus, though more christologically centered in this case, marks off Delphic perseverance in faith (IKyzikos II 2 Col. 2 No. 29 ["Don't (give up?) trusting"]) from Paul's understanding of perseverance in faith (1 Cor 1:4–9; Phil 1:6 [cf. 2:12–13]).

Fourth, the Delphic insistence upon breaking up enmities or a quarrel (IKyzikos II 2 Col. 2 No. 22; cf. IKyzikos II 2 Col. 1 No. 16 ["Hold off your enemies") finds profound theological expression in Paul when he explains how God has extinguished the hostility of Jew and Gentile though the cross (Eph 2:14). Moreover, Paul draws upon the Jesus tradition to underscore love of

[94] See Harrison, *Paul's Language of Grace*, 250–56.

the enemy and the principle of non-retaliation (Rom 12:14–15, 19–21; cf. Matt 5:38–48; cf. IKyzikos II 2 Col. 2 No. 13 ["Mete out justice"]). In the Delphic canon there is no sense of a divinely transformed community that will break down social divisions through the reconciliation of antagonists.

These contrasts are boldly drawn, given our methodological cautions aired above. Undoubtedly, there were elements of Delphic ethics that Paul could wholeheartedly endorse or modify. For example, the Delphic maxim to "hold to training" (IKyzikos II 2 Col. 1 No. 10) is affirmed, though somewhat differently understood by Paul. He limits *paideia* to the parental oversight of children (Eph 6.4; cf. IKyzikos II 2 Col. 1 No. 25 ["Train your sons"]) and, if the Pastorals are Pauline, to the supervisory role of the Scriptures (2 Tim 3:16). Moreover, Paul deems virtue as a praiseworthy (Phil 4:8) in a manner reminiscent of the Delphic canon (IKyzikos II 2 Col. 1 No. 12 ["Praise virtue"]). Avoidance of evil (IKyzikos II 2 Col. 1 No. 18 ["Keep way from evil"]: cf. Rom 12:9; cf. 12:21; cf. 1 Thess 5:21), hatred of arrogance (IKyzikos II 2 Col. 1 No. 22 ["Hate arrogance"]; cf. Rom 12:10b, 16b), and faithfulness to agreements (IKyzikos II 2 Col. 2 No. 31 ["(Stick by) agreements"]; cf. 2 Cor 1:17–23) are also consonant with Paul's ethical concerns.

But while there are ethical commonplaces in Paul and the Delphic canon, Paul formulates their outworking corporately rather than individually. He focuses on the reconciliation wielded by God through the cross in the believing community; it creates sensitivity and receptivity towards the outsider; it creates a sense of accountability for group behaviour; and it eliminates deep-seated social, racial and gender barriers.

5.3.4. Case Study on the Reciprocity System: Paul and the Delphic Canon

Of considerable interest is the way that Paul omits semantic domains central to the Dephic canon and to the smooth operation of Graeco-Roman society. One such domain involves the ethos of "friendship", signified by the presence of φιλ-compounds. Attention to the duties of friendship (φιλία) is a constant refrain throughout the Delphic canon (IKyzikos II 2 Col. 1. Nos.1 ["Help your friends"], 9 ["Love friendship"], 15 ["Goodwill for friends"], 21 ["Favour a friend"]; IKyzikos II 2 Col. 2. Nos.2 ["Look kindly on all"], 10 ["Guard friendship"]), undoubtedly because it forms a central part of the Graeco-Roman reciprocity system.

Paul rarely uses φιλ-compounds of human love and avoids them entirely in regards to divine love.[95] Paul's overwhelming preference for ἀγάπη ("love"), ἀγαπητός ("beloved") and ἀγαπᾶν ("to love") is probably explained by the fact

95 E. A. Judge, "Moral Terms in the Eulogistic Tradition," *New Docs* 2 (1982): 105–106, at 106, § 83.

that the apostle wishes to differentiate God's love and its outworking from the operations of the Graeco-Roman reciprocity system (Rom 4:4–5; 11:5–6, 35; 13:6–10; 1 Cor 4:7). In this regard, C. Spicq observes – though he overstates the evidence – that "friendship is properly used only of a relationship between equals."[96] While this is true in most cases, Aristotle observes that there was the possibility of friendship between those who were not equals (parents and children, husbands and wives, rulers and subjects).[97] But the friendship was proportionate to their status and not necessarily permanent. Therefore, as a description of divine and human love, ἀγάπη was better suited to relationships involving parties of different status (inferiors/superiors). It allowed Paul to speak of enduring human relationships founded on divine love, which, in contrast to the status-riddled operation of φιλία, did not calculate in advance the reciprocal benefits to each party.

Two examples will throw extra light on our argument. The Delphic canon at Miletopolis underscores the difference in world-view between the sages and Paul in the exhortation "love friendship" (IKyzikos II 2 Col. 1. No. 9: [φ]ιλίαν ἀγάπα). By contrast, Paul – or the pseudonymous author of Colossians and Ephesians – uses the imperative ἀγαπᾶτε two times (Eph 5:25a; Col 3:19a). In each case the husband is to love his wife self-sacrificially with no expectation of return (Eph 5:25b; Col 3:19b). Similarly, even the harmless "Good-will for friends" (IKyzikos II 2 Col. 1. No. 15 [φίλους εὐνόει]) stands in contrast to Paul. If Ephesians is deemed an authentic Pauline epistle, the apostle advises slaves to render their service "with a good will as to the Lord (μετ ᾽ εὐνοίας δουλεύοντες) and not to men" (Eph 6:7). Human reciprocity should not be the motivation behind the slave's service to his earthly master, but rather his relationship to the heavenly exalted Lord. Even if Ephesians is not Pauline, the pseudonymous interpreter of the apostle understood his thought well.

By contrast, the maxim "Respect/pity supplicants" (IKyzikos II 2 Col. 1. No. 24: ἱκέτας ἐλέει) might be construed as an acknowledgement on the part of the Delphic ethical tradition that respect should be extended to those who, unlike φίλοι ("friends"), are not social equals. However, I would argue that the Delphic imperative (ἐλέει ["pity"]) does not uphold the positive social worth of the recipients of mercy. This is well illustrated by the famous inscription of the Roman ruler, Nero. Speaking of his (short-lived) decision to liberate Greece from Roman provincial rule (AD 67), Nero explains the reasons for his unprecedented act of generosity:

> Would that Greece were still at its peak as I grant you this gift, in order that more people might enjoy this favour of mine (μου τῆς χάριτος) ... At present it is not out of pity (οὐ

[96] C. Spicq, ἀγάπη, in *idem*, *Theological Lexicon of the New Testament, Volume 1* (Peabody: Hendrickson, 1999), 10–11.

[97] P. Atkinson, *Friendship and the Body of Christ* (Croydon: SPCK, 2004), 19.

δι ̓ ἔλεον) for you but out of good-will (ἀλλὰ δι ̓ εὔνοιαν) that I bestow this benefaction, and I give it in exchange (ἀμείβομαι) to your gods, whose forethought on land and sea I have always experienced, because they granted me the opportunity of conferring such benefits. Other leaders have liberated cities, [only Nero] a province.[98]

According to Nero, pity is only accorded to undeserving social inferiors, but this is decidedly not the case as far as the Greeks. Rather Nero displays good will towards the Greeks because their gods have cared for him, making Greece worthy of the return of imperial favour. The return of good-will (εὔνοια) for favour received (μου τῆς χάριτος) is the decisive characteristic of grace in antiquity, over against the different understanding of mercy (human and divine) in Second Temple Judaism and in early Christianity.[99] For Paul, divine mercy is extended to human beings (Rom 9:15–16, 18, 23; 11:30–12; 12:1; 15:9; 1 Cor 7:25; 2 Cor 4:1; Eph 2:4; Phil 2:27) and from person to person (Rom 12:8; Gal 6:16) precisely because God is merciful.

Finally, another domain illustrating the ethos of reciprocity is the language of grace, although it is minimally used in the Dephic canon at Miletopolis. Several maxims have come down to us in Sosiades' collection (Stobaeus, *Eclogae* III.1.173) that employ the language of grace to underscore the importance of munificence: φίλωι χαρίζου ("Favour a friend": *ibid.* III.1.175 [37]); ἔχων χαρίζου ("Do a favour when you can": *ibid.* III.1.175 [45]); χάριν ἐκτέλει ("Return a favour": *ibid.* III.1.175 [75]); χαρίζου ἀβλαβως ("Favour without harming": *ibid.* III.1.175 [136]). Only two instances are found on the gymnasium (?) stele at Miletopolis (IKyzikos II 2 Col. 1. No. 14: "Return a favour" [χάριν ἀπόδος]; IKyzikos II 2 Col. 1. No. 21: "Favour a friend" [φίλωι χαρίζου]) and there is no grace language preserved at Thera. While there is clear evidence that Paul does endorse reciprocity in certain contexts,[100] his understanding of divine grace is unilateral (or "unconditioned", to borrow Barclay's term) in its origin, founded on God's loving initiative, and engaging reciprocally a response of gratitude and participatory obedience from His dependents. Paul redefines the dynamics of the Graeco-Roman reciprocity system in terms of love rather than indebtedness (Rom 13:8–10).

---

[98] SIG³ 814.

[99] On mercy, see B.F. Harris ("The Idea of Mercy and Its Graeco-Roman Context") and E.A. Judge ("The Quest for Mercy in Late Antiquity") in P.T. O'Brien and D.G. Peterson, eds., *God Who is Rich in Mercy: Essays Presented to D.B. Knox* (Homebush West: Lancer, 1986), 89–105 and 107–21 respectively. The latter essay was reprinted in Judge, *Jerusalem and Athens*, 185–197. See also D. Konstan, *Pity Transformed* (London: Duckworth, 2001). For further ancient sources, see Harrison, *Paul's Language of Grace*, 286 n. 275.

[100] See Harrison, *Paul's Language of Grace*, 324–32. See now the magnum opus of J.M.G. Barclay, *Paul and the Gift* (Grand Rapids: Eerdmans, 2015). See also the excellent theses of Barclay's doctoral students: K.B. Wells, *Grace and Agency in Paul and Second Temple Judaism: Interpreting the Transformation of the Heart*, NovTSup 157 (Leiden and Boston: Brill, 2015); O. McFarland, *God and Grace in Philo and Paul*, NovTSup 164 (Leiden and Boston: Brill, 2015).

5.3.5. Case Study of the Ephesian Household Codes: Paul and the Delphic Canon

Finally, we come to a central tenet of the ancient household codes, distilled with disarming simplicity in IKyzikos II 2 Col. 2 No. 3: "Rule your wife" (γυναικὸς ἄρχ[ε]). Unfortunately, the brevity of the Delphic canon's formulation of the role of the *paterfamilias* works militates against any detailed appreciation of its household ethics.[101] I will briefly examine Paul's household codes against the backdrop of the Graeco-Roman literature, funerary epigrams, and honorific inscriptions touching on the role of each spouse in marriage.[102]

First, the Graeco-Roman literature embraces a spread of positions regarding female submission within the household, ranging from Aristotle's hierarchical rule of the *paterfamilias* within the household,[103] to a communion of common advantage,[104] to female submission as a strategy of tolerating her husband's faults,[105]

[101] On ancient household codes, see M. Dibelius, *An die Kolosser Epheser an Philemon* (Tübingen: Mohr Siebeck, 1953), 43–50, 93–96; J. E. Crouch, *The Origin and Intention of the Colossian Haustafel* (Göttingen: Vandenhoeck and Ruprecht, 1972); D. L. Balch, *Let Wives Be Submissive: The Domestic Code in I Peter* (Chico: Scholars, 1981); *idem*, "Household Codes," in *Greco-Roman Literature and the New Testament*, ed. D. E. Aune (Atlanta: Scholars, 1988), 25–50; D. C. Verner, *The Household of God: The Social World of the Pastoral Epistles* (Chico: Scholars, 1981); E. A. Judge, "A Woman's Behaviour," *New Docs* 6 (1992): 18–23, § 2; E. Best, "The Haustafel in Ephesians (Eph 5:22–6.9)," in *idem*, *Essays on Ephesians* (Edinburgh: T&T Clark, 1997), 189–203; A. R. Bevere, *Sharing in the Inheritance: Identity and the Moral Life in Colossians* (Sheffield: Sheffield Academic, 2003) 225–54; H. W. Hoehner, *Ephesians: An Exegetical Commentary* (Grand Rapids: Eerdmans, 2003) 720–29; R. W. Gehring, *House Church and Mission: The Importance of Household Structures in Early Christianity* (Peabody: Hendrickson, 2004 [Gmn. orig. 2000]) 229–60; K. Zamfir, *Men and Women in the Household of God: A Contextual Approach to Roles and Ministries in the Pastoral Epistles*, NTOA/SUNT 103 (Göttingen and Bristol: Vandenhoeck & Ruprecht, 2013); S. E. Porter, "Paul, Virtues, Vices, and Household Codes," in *Paul and the Graeco-Roman World: A Handbook Volume 2*, 2nd ed. (London and New York: T&T Clark, 2016), 369–90.

[102] If Ephesians, over against Colossians, is not an authentic Pauline epistle, then Paul's household code in Colossians is less distinctive in its first-century Graeco-Roman context because of Colossians' strong ethos of subordination as opposed to the more christologically focused mutual subordination of Ephesians.

[103] Aristotle, *Pol.* 1260a 9–14; *id.*, *NE* VIII 1160b–1161a; Arius Didymus, *Epitome of Aristotle* 145.5–18; 149.5–8; Philo, *Spec. Leg.* 3.169–171; *idem*, *Hyp.* 7.3.5; Josephus, *Ap.* 2.199; Gen. Mid. 3.12. While Plutarch approves partnership in the household (*Mor.* 140D), he does not endorse "autonomous" women either. See L. Foxhall, "Foreign Powers: Plutarch and Discourses of Domination in Roman Greece," in *Plutarch's* Advice to the Bride and Groom *and* A Consolation to His Wife*: English Translation, Commentary, Interpretative Essays, and Bibliography*, ed. S. B. Pomeroy (New York and Oxford: Oxford University Press, 1999), 138–50, esp. 145–47. Diogenes, *Ep.* 47 (A. J. Malherbe, *The Cynic Epistles* [Atlanta: Scholars, 1977]) speaks out against marriage *per se*.

[104] Callicratidas, *On the Felicity of Families* (K. S. Guthrie, *The Pythagorean Sourcebook and Library* [Grand Rapids: Phanes, 1987], 235–37); Xenephon, *Oec.* 7.17–19.

[105] Perictyone, *On the Harmony of a Woman* (Guthrie, *The Pythagorean Sourcebook*, 239–41); Theano, *Letter to Nicostrate* (I. M. Plant, ed., *Women Writers of Ancient Greece and Rome: An Anthology* [London: Equinox, 2004], § 15).

and, finally, to non-hierarchical relationships within the household.[106] In respect of the Delphic canon, the social stance of the gymnasium at Miletopolis on household relationships (IKyzikos II 2 Col. 2 No. 3) was probably that of Aristotle. By contrast, Paul's statements of theological principle (Gal 3:28; 1 Cor 11:11–12) and mutuality (1 Cor 7:1–5) leans more towards the "feminism" of Hierocles and Musonius Rufus than the hierarchical thought of Aristotle. A few examples will suffice. Paul's addition of the phrase, "as is fitting in the Lord," in Colossians 3:18 spells out the boundaries of wife's submission to her husband as much it provides its theological rationale.[107] In contrast to the Delphic canon (γυναικὸς ἄρχ[ε]), Paul commands husbands to love their wives (ἀγαπᾶτε τὰς γυναῖκας: Col 3:19a; Eph 5:25a, 33b).[108] Paul's telling addition to the love command in each case (Col 3:19b ["do not be harsh with them"]; Eph 5:25b ["just as Christ loved the church and gave himself up for her"]) redefines the role of the *paterfamilias* and undermines the Neopythagorean expectation that the wife should submissively tolerate the husband's faults (e.g. Perictyone, *On the Harmony of a Woman*; Theano, *Letter to Nicostrate*).

Second, the funerary epigrams and honorific inscriptions, "primarily discuss women as housewives, with little interest in their characters."[109] The woman is defined in relation to her husband and forbears as far as her virtues, including her role of submission. Because of the focus of our study on gymnasiarchs, we cite a first-century AD inscription honoring a female gymnasiarch who acted as a benefactor on behalf of Arneae:

> The people of Arneae and vicinity, to Lalla daughter of Timarchus son of Diotimus, their fellow citizen, wife of Diotimus son of Vassus; priestess of the Emperor's cult and gymnasiarch out of her resources, honoured five times, chaste, cultivated, devoted to her husband and a model of all virtue, surpassing in every respect. She has glorified her ancestor's virtues with the example of her own character. [Erected] in recognition of her virtue and good will.[110]

[106] Musonius Rufus, *Oration* XIII.A; Hierocles, *On Duties* ("On Marriage", 4.22.21–24: A.J. Malherbe, *Moral Exhortation: A Greco-Roman Sourcebook* [Philadelphia: Westminster, 1986], 100–04); Pliny, *Ep.* 4.19.17ff. See W. Klassen, "Musonius Rufus, Jesus and Paul: Three First-Century Feminists," in *From Jesus to Paul: Studies in Honour of Francis Wright Beare*, ed. P. Richardson and J.C. Hurd (Waterloo: Wilfrid Laurier University Press, 1984), 185–206.

[107] D.M. Hay (*Colossians* [Nashville: Abingdon, 2000], 143) notes: "'In the Lord' suggests not only motive but also limitation: the wife's ultimate 'lord' is not her husband." On the radical nature of Paul's thought in Colossians, see Gehring, *House Church and Mission*, 236–38. On submission traditions in the Pastorals, see B.W. Winter, *Roman Wives, Roman Widows: The Appearance of New Women and the Pauline Community* (Grand Rapids: Eerdmans, 2003).

[108] Gehring (*House Church and Mission*, 234 n. 24) notes that the "love" command is not unique, being present in select Graeco-Roman literature.

[109] R. Hawley, "Practising What You Preach: Plutarch's Sources and Treatment," in *Plutarch's* Advice to the Bride and Groom *and* A Consolation to His Wife*: English Translation, Commentary, Interpretative Essays, and Bibliography*, ed. S.B. Pomeroy (New York and Oxford: Oxford University Press, 1999), 116–17.

[110] Lefkowitz and Fant, *Women's Life in Greece and Rome*, § 429. For similar inscriptions and funerary epigrams, see Lefkowitz and Fant, *ibid.*, §§ 44, 191, 198–200, 428, 432; Hands,

For Paul, however, the role of the husband and wife is defined in relation to the risen Christ. Thus Paul gives the household codes a cruciform focus (Col 3:18; Eph 5:23b, 25–27, 29b). Moreover, the role of the husband and wife is of *equal* interest to Paul in comparison to the one-sided approach of the contemporary household codes.[111] The self-sacrificing role of the husband – over against patriarchal privilege – is especially highlighted in Ephesians.

Third, the ancient literary and documentary sources comment on how the gods establish a harmonious household as the wife submits to the divine order and to the *paterfamilias*. Maximus of Tyre speaks of divine reason regulating sexual love in marriage:

This is the sacred institution of the gods who preside over nuptials, over kindred, and the procreation of children ... the human race ... is gifted by (the) Divinity with reason, as that which is equivalent to every other possession. To this (the) Divinity also subjected amatory appetite, as a horse to the bridle, as a bow to the archer, as a ship to the helm, as an instrument to the artificer.[112]

Plutarch says that a married woman should recognize and only worship her husband's household gods, steering away from strange cults and foreign superstitions.[113] Perictione's *On the Harmony of Women* underscores the importance of correct worship on the wife's part,[114] as does the *laudatio Turiae* ("reverence [for the gods] without superstition").[115]

Significantly for the Ephesian context, an inscription of the consul Severus speaks of the goddess Harmonia, daughter of Aphrodite and Ares (Hesiod, *Theogony* 937), blessing his marriage with happiness:

... a model of every kind of virtue, a man who saved the city, eminent among the Greeks, princeps of the Italians, the dear father of the famous Quadratus, for whom Harmonia built a royal chamber for a happy married life ...[116]

Hierocles provides a late Stoic perspective on the divine ordering of the household:

... the beauty of a household consists in the yoking together of a husband and wife who are united to each other by fate, are consecrated to the gods who preside over weddings,

Charities, §§D.13, D.39; Austin, *The Hellenistic World*, § 204; G.H.R. Horsley, "A More Than Perfect Wife," *New Docs* 3 (1983): 33–36, § 8; *idem*, "A Women's Virtues," *New Docs* 3 (1983): 40–43, § 11; CIJ II 772; IEph III 683A; R. Lattimore, *Themes in Greek and Latin Epitaphs* (Urbana: University of Illinois Press, 1962), 275–80, 291–300. On chaste living in the Pythagorean tradition according to Melissa, see Plant, *Women Writers*, § 19.

[111] Hoehner, *Ephesians*, 724; Bevere, *Sharing in the Inheritance*, 232, 234.

[112] Maximus of Tyre, *Dissertation* 10.

[113] Plutarch, *Mor.* 140D.

[114] Plant, *Women Writers*.

[115] Horsley, "A More Than Perfect Wife," 33–36. See also Xenephon, *Oec.*, 7.8: "Did your wife sacrifice along with you and offer the same prayers?"

[116] IEph V 1539.

births, and houses, agree with each other and have all things in common, including their bodies, or their souls, and who exercise appropriate rule over the household and servants, take care in the rearing of their children, and pay an attention to the necessities of life which is neither intense nor slack, but moderate and fitting.[117]

Finally, Xenephon addresses the wife regarding the divine intent of marriage in this manner:

Wife, the gods seems to have shown much discernment in yoking together female and male, as we call them, so that the couple might constitute a partnership that is most beneficial to both of them. First of all, so that the various species of living creatures may not become extinct, this pair sleeps together for the purpose of procreation. Then this pairing provides offspring to support the partners in their own age, at least in the case of human beings.[118]

New Testament scholars need to be reminded of the religious dimension of marriage in antiquity, if the aforementioned evidence is representative.[119] The husband's hierarchical rule over his wife extended to cultic affairs, touching their sexual life and procreation of children as much as the division of labour within the household.[120] If Paul (or the pseudonymous author) recycled materials from Colossians for his letter to the Ephesians,[121] he expands upon the household codes, infusing the idea of the mutual submission of husband and wife (Eph 5:21, 22, 24, 25, 33) with a theology of the Spirit (5:18b),[122] the cross (5:24b, 25–27, 29b; cf. Mk 10:35–45), the Lordship of Christ over the church (5:23–24, 25–27, 30, 32; cf. 18b–20), and the creation narrative (5:31 [Gen 2:24]). Submission for each partner is motivated by reverence for Christ (Eph 5:21b). The wife submits to

---

117 Hierocles, *On Duties.* On Marriage (4.502; Malherbe, *Moral Exhortation*, 100–04). Musonius Rufus (*Oration* XIV *ll.* 9–17) posits that the deity created both sexes with "a strong desire for association and union with the other." Coupled with Musonius' Stoic monotheism, however, is the traditional polytheistic superintendence of marriage by the "great gods" (Hera, Eros and Aphrodite: *ibid.*, *ll.* 20–32).

118 Xenephon, *Oec.*, 7.18–19. Note the divine design of women for indoor work and men for outdoor work (*ibid.*, 7.22). Verner (*The Household of God*, 66), referring to an inscription (*OGIS* 308 [II cent. BC]: cf. Polybius 22.20), points to the piety and concord of Queen Apollonius Eusebes in her family life.

119 See the excellent discussion of Balch, *Let Wives Be Submissive*, 88–90.

120 Note L. Goesler's comment ("*Advice to the Bride and Groom*: Plutarch Gives a Detailed Account of His Views on Marriage," in *Plutarch's* Advice to the Bride and Groom *and* A Consolation to His Wife*: English Translation, Commentary, Interpretative Essays, and Bibliography*, ed. S.B. Pomeroy [New York and Oxford: Oxford University Press, 1999], 97–115, at 103): "Harmony between the married couple reaches its highest form in agreement about religious matters."

121 For discussion, see J.D.G. Dunn, *The Epistles to the Colossians and to Philemon* (Grand Rapids: Eerdmans, 1996), 36–37. On the five critical options regarding the relationship of Colossians to Ephesians, see Best, "The Haustafel in Ephesians (Eph 5:22–6:9)," 190.

122 On the dependence of the participle ὑποτασσόμενοι (Eph 5:21) upon the verb πληροῦσθε (5:18b), see Hoehner, *Ephesians*, 720; Gehring, *House Church and Mission*, 244.

the husband as unto Christ (5:22) and the husband loves and serves the wife as Christ unto her (5:25).[123]

Did Paul feel that his teaching in Colossians had not gone far enough, given his strong emphasis on unity and mutuality elsewhere (Rom 10:12; Gal 3:28; 1 Cor 7:1–5; 11:11–12; 12:13; Col 3:11)? His teaching in Ephesians represents a theological revision of the Colossian household codes, which, though relevant to their social setting, had not unfolded sufficiently the redemptive significance of Christ's death for household relations. Paul would have been aware that the Neopythagorean theology of harmony, hierarchical in the ancient literature,[124] and embraced in some honorific inscriptions,[125] expressed the divine ideal for marriage in antiquity. Even the late Stoicism of Hierocles, though more consensual in its model of household relations, consecrates marriage to the gods. Paul's theological response in Ephesians 5:18–33 provided the household with a redemptive, christological, and ecclesiastical framework that would transform the hierarchical relationship between the *paterfamilias* and his wife. Not only was Paul enhancing the church's unity (Eph 2:11–3:13; 4:1–6) in the household code (Eph 5:21–6.9) with a view to a Roman world intolerant of foreign cults,[126] he was also challenging the curriculum of the eastern Mediterranean gymnasia and demoting the Graeco-Roman gods from their privileged position as guardians of the household and its social relations.

5.4. Conclusion

This chapter has argued that Paul would still have been exposed to gymnasiarchal culture even if, as was the likelihood, he did not have the ephebic education of other first-century Jews. The inscriptions of the gymnasiarchs alerted the apostle to the pastoral and social values they held dear. Paul may have heard their honorific decrees heralded in prominent public places, or have listened to the popular philosophers preaching in the open air the maxims of the Delphic canon, the ethical curriculum of the gymnasia spanning Greece and Afghanistan. At the very least, some of Paul's Gentile converts probably asked him questions about the integration of their new faith with their ephebic past.

[123] On submission in Colossians an Ephesians, see Gehring, *House Church and Mission*, 234–35, 238, 244.

[124] Goesler ("*Advice to the Bride and Groom*," 101) observes: "Everything proceeds in harmonious unison and by mutual agreement between the married couple – but the husband is always the leader and the one who makes the decisions." For a fine inscriptional example of harmony between the husband (Euphrosynus) and wife (Epigone), see Hands, *Charities*, §D.13.

[125] See n. 118 *supra*.

[126] Hoehner, *Ephesians*, 727. See Balch, "Household Codes," 28; *idem*, *Let Wives Be Submissive*, *passim*.

Regarding the values of the gymnasiarchal inscriptions, Paul's thought converges with the gymnasiarchs on many important issues of benefaction culture. But while Paul acknowledges the centrality of ancestral tradition, he exposes the futility of its boasting. His pastoral approach to those under his care is (not unexpectedly) less masculine in its tenor than the gymnasiarchs, preferring to explain his pastoral technique with maternal and paternal images. Benefaction, for Paul, paradoxically revolved around an impoverished and dishonoured benefactor as opposed to the icons of civic virtue lauded by the gymnasium. Significant echoes of Pauline ethics are found in the gymnasiarchal inscriptions, but these ethical commonplaces are sharply differentiated by the dynamic of the Spirit in the believer's life. Paul agrees with the *gymnasiarchoi* as to the importance of returning honour to human beings and to God, but he dismisses the coronal awards of athletes as "fading" and postpones the believer's crowning to the eschaton. The exclusivist ethos of the gymnasiarchal law at Verroia also stands in contrast to the inclusiveness of Paul's house churches.

There were also areas of overlap and divergence between Paul and the maxims of the Delphic canon. Whereas the Delphic canon teaches self-sufficiency through individual self-control, Paul inculcates in his communities the sufficiency of Christ through inter-dependant members of His body ministering to each other. Paul's understanding of grace differed from the Delphic canon in that it upended reciprocity rituals, divesting them of their hierarchical status, and pinpricking the expectation of commensurate return. Paul also challenges the "ruling" role traditionally attributed to the *paterfamilias* in the Delphic canon, presenting a cruciform alternative that would bring about harmony in the household in a radically different way to late Stoic and Neopythagorean thought.

A new pastoral dynamic, founded on the crucified and risen Christ, had emerged for the *epheboi* to consider as an alternate route of honour and self-control. The honouring of the weak in the body of Christ supplanted the agonistic world of civic honour and the selflessness of the Servant-Benefactor was to inform all social relationships, whether in the polis or in the household. Another pathway of ethical transformation had begun, moving from Jerusalem to Rome, and beyond.

Chapter 6

Paul, the Delphic Canon and the Ephebic Ethical Curriculum

The intersection of the Delphic canon with the New Testament documents has not captured the attention of New Testament researchers.[1] E.A. Judge, at the 1992 International SBL meeting (Melbourne, Australia), presented an unpublished paper on the Delphic canon and its relation to the Synoptic ethical imperatives. In his view, the Synoptic hortatory tradition was the closest New Testament approximation of genre to the Delphic canon. Judge provided a complete translation of Sosiades' collection of the sayings of the seven sages, along with a presentation of the extant documentary evidence, the latter replicating the majority of the canon's sayings.[2] J.R. Harrison, in a discussion of the pastoral formation implemented in the ancient gymnasium,[3] touched on the ethical curricu-

---

[1] I am deeply grateful to Professor Giovanni B. Bazzana, Harvard Divinity School, for his incisive response to a preliminary version of this chapter at the 69th General Meeting of SNTS at Sgezed, Hungary, 2014. I profited immensely from his helpful suggestions and from the conversation with other colleagues present at the *Papyrology, Epigraphy and the New Testament* Session. I have noted Professor Bazanna's contributions in the footnotes below. This chapter also incorporates elements of a much shorter article that appeared as J.R. Harrison, "The Seven Sages, The Delphic Canon and Ethical Education in Antiquity," in *Ancient Education and Early Christianity*, ed. M.R. Hauge and A.W. Pitts (London and New York: Bloomsbury T&T Clark, 2016), 71–86.

[2] E.A. Judge's translation of Sosiades, including the documentnary texts, was published as part of the documentary materials distributed at his final lecture at Macquarie University, titled "Ancient Beginnings of the Modern World," in the *Ancient History in a Modern University* Conference, on 13 July 1993. Readers may now access this lecture, with its English translation of Sosiades, in E.A. Judge, *Jerusalem and Athens: Cultural Transformation in Antiquity*, WUNT I 265, ed. A. Nobbs (Tübingen: Mohr Siebeck, 2010), 281–314, the translation being located at 305–09, with brief commentary on 288–96. I will refer to individual maxims from Sosiades' collection only by number, noting the documentary evidence only if the maxim is not present in Sosiades, or is a variant upon Sosiades' rendering. In addition to Sosiades' unattributed collection of the 147 sayings of the seven sages (O. Hense, *Ioannis Stobaei Anthologii Libri Duo Posteriores Vol. 1* [Berlin: Weidmann, 1894], § 173, 125–28), there is also Demetrius of Phaleron's attributed collection of the same sayings (*ibid.*, § 172, 111–25). The latter are grouped under the name of each sage, accompanied by his patronymic and birthplace, along with the verb ἔφη introducing the sayings belonging to each sage. However, the collection of Sosiades – who was a contemporary of Demetrius of Phaleron (350–280 BC) – is the definitive presentation, having been confirmed as a collection of maxims, as we will see, by the eastern Mediterranean documentary evidence.

[3] J.R. Harrison, "Paul and the Gymnasiarchs: Two Approaches to Pastoral Formation in Antiquity," in *Paul: Jew, Greek, and Roman. Pauline* Studies, PAST 5, ed. S.E. Porter (Leiden: Brill, 2008), 141–78. This now appears, revised, as Chapter 5.

lum of the Delphic canon and the inscriptional exempla of the gymnasiarchs, focusing on three case studies to demonstrate the similarities and differences of its ethical construct in comparison to the moral agenda promoted in the Pauline literature. D.E. Aune has also discussed Plutarch's depiction of the symposium of the seven sages (*Mor.* 146B–164D), discussing the New Testament's transmission of Jesus' ethical logia and its presentation of symposia,[4] positing an interesting "parallel" between the seven ages and the seven deacons of the early church (Acts 6:3).[5] Most recently, D. Zeller has studied the Greek gnomic wisdom sayings genre and compared it with Paul's ethical exhortation in Romans 12, noting briefly the sayings of the seven sages (in the versions of both Sosiades and Demetrius of Phaleron) as an example of the genre.[6] Apart from these four brief forays in the area, no one else (excluding my 2016 publication, noted above) has devoted an extended discussion of the intersection of the two ethical traditions.

Equally surprising, however, is the relatively scant attention paid to the Delphic canon in English scholarship, whereas European scholars have covered the ethical traditions of the seven sages in several important monographs. There the traditions relating to the men are comprehensively covered,[7] with a detailed study of the impact of several of their sayings in the ancient and modern litera-

---

[4] D.E. Aune, "Septem Sapientium Convivium," in *Plutarch's Ethical Writings and Early Christian Literature*, ed. D. Betz (Leiden: Brill, 1978), 51–105.

[5] Aune, "Septem Sapientium Convivium," 56 n. 19.

[6] D. Zeller, "Pauline Paraenesis in Romans 12 and Greek Gnomic Wisdom," in *Greco-Roman Culture and the New Testament: Studies Commemorating the Centennial of the Pontifical Biblical Institute*, ed. D.E. Aune and F.E. Brenk (Leiden and Boston: Brill, 2012), 73–86, at 76–77.

[7] O. Barkowski, "Sieben Weise," *RE* II A/2 (1923): 2242–64; W. Wiersma, "The Seven Sages and the Prize of Wisdom," *Mnemosyne* 1.2 (1933–34): 150–54; B. Snell, *Leben und Meinungen der sieben Weisen*: *Griechische und lateinische Quellen erläutert und übertragen* (Munich: Heimeran Verlag, 1938; 4th ed., 1971); A. Mosshammer, "The Epoch of the Seven Sages," *California Studies in Classical Antiquity* 9 (1976): 165–80; D. Fehling, *Die sieben Weisen und die frühgriechische Chronologie: eine traditionsgeschichtliche Studie* (Bern: P. Lang, 1985); A.N. Oikonomides, "Records of 'The Commandments of the Seven Wise Men' in the 3rd c. BC: The Revered Greek 'Reading-book' of the Hellenistic World," *Classical Bulletin* 63 (1987): 67–76; R.P. Martin, "The Seven Sages as Performers of Wisdom," in *Cultural Poetics in Archaic Greece: Cult, Performance, Politics*, ed., C. Dougherty and L. Kurke (Oxford: Oxford University Press, 1998), 108–28; J. Bollansée, "Fact and Fiction, Falsehood and Truth. D. Fehling and Ancient Legendry about the Seven Sages," *Museum Helveticum* 56 (1999): 65–75; A. Busine, *Les Sept Sages de la Grèce antique. Transmission et utilisation d'un patrimonie légendaire d'Hérodote à Plutarque* (Paris: De Boccard, 2002); I. Ramelli, ed. and tr., *I Setti sapienti: vite e opinioni nell' edizione di Bruno Snell* (Milan: Bompiani, 2005), 7–32; J. Engels, *Die sieben Weisen: Leben, Lehren und Legenden* (Munich: Verlag C.H. Beck, 2010); L. Kurke, *Aesopic Conversations: Popular Tradition, Cultural Dialogue, and the Invention of Greek Prose* (Princeton and Oxford: Princeton University Press, 2011), 102–15. More generally, see A.W. Nightingale, "Sages, Sophists, and Philosophers: Greek Wisdom Literature," in *Literature in the Greek and Roman Worlds: A New Perspective*, ed. O. Taplin (Oxford: Oxford University Press, 2000), 156–91; J. Althoff and D. Zeller, eds., *Die Worte der Sieben Weisen*, Texte zur Forschung Bd. 89 (Darmstadt: WBG, 2006).

ture. Moreover, a consensus had emerged, founded on the work of R. P. Martin,[8] which located the sages as significant actors upon the social and political stage rather than in the development of abstract ideas and the evolution of philosophical movements.[9] However, I. Ramelli has challenged this construct, arguing that the Greeks themselves debated whether the sages belonged to the history of philosophy or not.[10] Thus, in the case of the seven sages, wisdom and philosophy were not quite as widely separated as Martin posits.[11] More recently, J. Engels has steered a middle course, situating the seven sages within a high "wisdom" tradition. They purvey practical philosophy in a poetic and aphoristic genre and espouse both ethics and political philosophy, upon which the later philosophical movements built their moral edifice.[12] Last, L. Kurke has explored the development of Sophia, as it shifted from practical wisdom to philosophy, highlighting its links with Apollo at Dephi and the transmission of the ethical tradition of the seven sages at the site.[13] Given the fluidity of the category of "sophist" and "philosopher" in the fifth century BC, [14] it is likely that the aphorisms of the seven sages operated at a more sophisticated ideological level

---

[8] Martin ("The Seven Sages as Performers of Wisdom") concludes that the seven sages were practitioners of practical wisdom: they reveal sagacity through their poetic composition, political adeptness, competitive public performance and religious activities as a sacrificial *collegium*.

[9] Note Aristotle's depiction of the seven sages in "political" garb in his coverage of the five progressive stages of wisdom: "Again, they concerned themselves with political affairs and invented law and all things that hold cities together. And this conception they called *sophia*; for such men were the Seven sages, men who had invented certain forms of political excellence" (Aristotle, *On Philosophy*, Fragment 8 [W.D. Ross, *Aristotelis Fragmenta Selecta* (Oxford: Clarendon Press, 1955], though the attribution to Aristotle is not necessarily secure [cf. Kurke, *Aesopic Conversations*, 96 n. 2]). In similar vein, see Plutarch, *Vit. Sol.*, 3.4; Diogenes Laertius, 1.40.

[10] Ramelli, *I Setti sapienti*, 9–15. The debate over whether the "barbarians" or the Greeks invented philosophy (Diogenes Laertius 1.1–11), Ramelli argues, reflects earlier Greek debates about whether the "sages" (*sophoi*, *sophistai*) were to be considered philosophers (*philosophoi*) or not. Therefore Diogenes (c. late II–early III cent. AD) wanted to demonstrate the priority of the Greek claim because Christianity was equipping itself with philosophical structures and was being presented as a "philosophy" (Ramelli, *I Setti sapienti*, 9). On Diogenes Laertius' discussion of the seven sages, see Engels, *Die sieben Weisen*, 33–40. On the difficulty of analysing the sources cited by Diogenes and evaluating their reliability, see Busine, *Les Sept* Sages, 55–56.

[11] See the comments of Diogenes Laertius 1.12.

[12] Engels, *Die sieben Weisen*, 92–93. Engels (*ibid.*, 92) states: "Nevertheless, the Wise men did not strive after the establishment of an abstract philosophical teaching system, and, hence, they did not even write any systematic instructive writings. Ethics and political philosophy completely dominate in their aphorisms, (with the result that) the later central disciplines of Greek philosophy, physics, metaphysics, dialectics or logic are completely absent or are completely pushed in the background."

[13] Kurke, *Aesopic Conversations*, 102–15.

[14] See G.E.R. Lloyd, *The Revolutions of Wisdom: Studies in the Claims and Practice of Ancient Greek Science* (Berkeley: University of California Press, 1987), 93; Nightingale "Sages, Sophists, and Philosophers"; H. Tell, *Plato's Counterfeit Sophists* (Cambridge, MA and London: Center for Hellenic Studies, 2011), 19.

in the civic life of the polis and the private life of the household than has been previously appreciated,[15] with the likelihood that they formed an integrated curriculum that could be passed down for the instruction of future generations in wise living.

Other than the study of A. N. Oikonomides,[16] little analysis of Sosiades' collection of the sayings has occurred, apart from the narrowly focused discussions of the extant documents, epigraphic and papyrological, of the Delphic canon found in fragmentary form throughout the eastern Mediterranean basin.[17] There has been no sustained discussion as to whether there is a pedagogic intentionality behind the Delphic canon or, indeed, what its primary pedagogic context actually was. Why was the canon inscribed so widely across the eastern Mediterranean basin? And what is the significance of the location of some of the finds? What spawned this widespread geographic interest in its ethical teachings? Further, the existence of common terminology and the use of "doublets" and (occasionally) "triplets" throughout the collection have been overlooked. How are paradoxes and contradictions in ethical advice handled in the collection of maxims?[18] Why are they there? Ultimately, what is the ethical curriculum of the Delphic canon and its rationale in a private and public context?

---

[15] However, the seven sages are also satirised in a tavern at Ostia (c. AD 100). Several of the sages (Solon, Thales, Chilon, Bias) are depicted seated in wall paintings with Latin texts above them, dispensing pompous opinions on the refined art of defecation to twenty four Romans, who are presented in the lower register seated in a latrine-like line. The latter offer practical advice in Latin on correct bowel movements. Clearly, the disjunction between the abstract concerns of "philosophers" and the practicalities of real life is being highlighted. For translations of the Latin texts and pictures of the wall paintings, see www.ostia-antica.org/regio 3/10/10-2.htm (accessed 25.04.2014). For discussion, see J. R. Clarke, "High and Low: Mocking Philosophers in the Tavern of the Seven Sages," in *The Art of Citizens, Soldiers and Freedmen in the Roman World*, ed. E. D'Ambra and G. P. R. Métraux (Oxford: Archaeopress, 2006), 47–57; Engel, *Die sieben Weisen*, 113–14. We will not discuss the other Roman traditions regarding the seven sages (e.g. Cicero, *De or.* 3.137; *Resp.* 1.80; *Amic.* 7; *Fin.* 2.3.7; *Parad.* 1.8). For discussion, see Engel, *Die sieben Weisen*, 26–29.

[16] Oikonomides, "Records of 'The Commandments of the Seven Wise Men'." Althoff and Zeller (*Die Worte der Sieben Weisen*, 61–71) provide a brief introduction and a German translation.

[17] For the inscription at Thera (Aegean), see *IG* XI 3 (1898), 1020. For the inscription at Miletopolis (near Cyzicus, Hellespont, Asia Minor), see F. W. Hasluck, "Inscriptions from the Cyzicus District," *JHS* 27 (1907): 61–67; *SIG*³ 1268; *Die Inschriften von Kyzikos und Umgebung. Teil II. Miletopolis: Inschriften und* Denkmäler, Inschriften griechisher Städte aus Kleinsaien 26, ed. E. Schwertheim (Bonn: Habelt, 1983), § 2. For the inscription at Aï Khanum on the Oxus in Afghanistan, see L. Robert, "De Delphes à l'Oxus: inscriptions grecques nouvelles de la Bactriane," *Comptes Rendus de l'Académie des Inscriptions et Belles Lettres* 112.3 (1968): 416–57; Institut Fernand-Courby, *Nouveau choix d'inscriptions grecques: textes, traductions, commentaires* (Paris: Les Belles Lettres, 1971), 183–85 § 37; G. H. R. Horsley, "Speak No Evil," *New Docs* 4 (1987): 42–46, at 44–45, § 13. For the papyrus at Egypt, see A. N. Oikonomides, "The Lost Delphic Inscription with the Commandments of the Seven and *P. Univ. Athen* 2782," *ZPE* 37 (1980): 179–83.

[18] For a study of other types of maxims in the Graeco-Roman world and their relevance to

This chapter will explore the harmonious understanding of one's self and the gods inculcated in the Delphic curriculum of the ancient gymnasium, as well as the wide array of social relations that impacted upon the household and the polis, with a view to the resolution of potential conflicts residing therein in ways that promoted social cohesion. The paradox at the core of the Delphic collection can be summarised thus: how did one shelter oneself from the unexpected vicissitudes of Fortune and still cultivate the finely tuned balance of indifference and responsibility that was requisite for social order, household harmony and personal happiness? This is the heart of the ethical dilemma underlying the Delphic canon. The article brings the Delphic canon into dialogue with the Aristotelian tradition of the "ethical mean", as well as select case studies of select honorific inscriptions from Delphi and Ephesus relating to the moral education of the *epheboi* and *neoi*. Hopefully, this selection of literary and documentary evidence will situate the Delphic canon in its wider pedagogic, exemplary, philosophic, honorific and civic context. A final section will discuss the intersection of the Delphic Canon with 1 Corinthians, with a view to exploring the possibility that the socially powerful within the Corinthian house churches were influenced in their values by the *paideia* ("education") of the ancient gymnasium.

6.1. Delphi and the Philosophic Tradition of the Seven Sages

6.1.1. The Literary Tradition from Herodotus to Plutarch

The beginning of the literary tradition about the relationship of the seven sages with Delphi is announced implicitly rather than explicitly.[19] The tradition of Herodotus about the visit of the seven sages to the court of Croesus at Sardis

Paul, see R. A. Ramsaran, *Liberating Words: Paul's Use of Rhetorical Maxims in 1 Corinthians 8–10* (Valley Forge: Trinity Press international, 1996); *idem*, "Paul and Maxims," in *Paul and the Graeco-Roman World: A Handbook Volume 2*, J.P. Sampley, 2nd ed. (London and New York: T&T Clark, 2016), 116–46.

[19] Busine (*Les Sept Sages*, 35) states: "In the text of Herodotus, the strict correspondence between the words of the sage Solon and Delphic ideology is only implicit." The seven sages, who as a group flourished from the late VII to early VI cent. BC (Mosshammer, "The Epoch of the Seven Sages"), are identified by Plato as Thales of Miletus, Pittacus of Mytilene, Bias of Priene, Solon of Athens, Cleobulus of Lindus, Myson of Chen, and Chilon of Sparta (*Prot.* 343a; cf. *Hipp. Maj.* 281c: Pitticus, Bias, Thales only). However, while the "seven" are precisely identifiable in Plato's tradition, a complex debate existed in antiquity regarding their number and identity. Hermippus, drawing upon non-Athenian traditions from the Ptolemaic library from Alexandria (Engel, *Die sieben Weisen*, 22), asserts that there were seventeen *sophoi*, a much wider group that Plato's circle of seven (D.L. 1.42). Dicaerchus and Hippobutus claim, respectively, that there were ten or twelve *sophoi* (D.L. 1.41–42). See Engel (*Die sieben Weisen*, 9–78, esp. 39ff) who discusses the twenty-one *sophoi* who appear at one point or another in the ancient lists. Further, the ancient authorities disagree as to which figures actually belonged to the Seven, as the discussion of Diogenes Laertius demonstrates (D.L.

(*Hist.* 1:29) finds its culmination in the famous story about Solon's encounters with the king (1:30–32).[20] While Delphi or its oracles are not mentioned in the vignette, Solon, in response to Croesus' question about the locus of true happiness (*Hist.* 1:30), asserts the superiority of several Greek ideals over Croesus' inflated estimation of himself (1:30–31),[21] as well as warning him about the jealousy of the divinity and its aptness to stir things up (1:32). The irony is potent for those familiar with the Delphic maxims: Croesus has lived his life to entire excess ("Nothing in excess") and did not know his own finitude and vulnerability to fortune ("Know yourself"). In spite of Croesus' beneficence to the Delphic oracle (*Hist.* 1.50–51, 92),[22] the king lives in total violation of its wisdom traditions.[23] However, the situation is vastly different in the case of Solon. In Busine's view, Solon, in contrast to the other sages mentioned by Herodotus (Bias, Pittacus, Thales), is depicted by the historian not only as a careful legislator but also as a sophist: consequently, Solon engages in philosophy and has a reputation for wisdom (cf. Plato, *Tim.* 20d).[24]

1.41). Kurke (*Aesopic Conversations*, 104 n. 25, 131–132, 135) points to traditions that link Aesop with the seven sages – although Aesop is excluded in all the lists – and notes his prominent position in front of the seven sages in a statue group (Agathias, *Palatine Anthology* 16.332), as well as his presence with them at the court of Croesus (D.L. 9.26–28). Kurke (*Aesopic Conversations*, 125–58) argues that Aesop, by employing the "indirect" fable, issued a "low" challenge to the "higher" wisdom of the sages (e.g. Solon), thereby eliminating the possibility of politically offending Croesus. Last, Bollansée ("Fact and Fiction"; cf. Busine, *Les Sept* Sages, 29–30; Engel, *Die sieben Weisen*, 9–15) has decisively rebutted Fehling's proposal (*Die sieben Weisen*, 13) that the seven sages were Plato's invention, thereby reinstating the possibility of a genuine oral origin for the early stories about the seven sages (cf. Martin, "The Seven Sages," 126 n. 22). For a discussion of the sayings of the seven sages from the archaic to classical eras of Greece, see M. Asper, "‚Literatursoziologisches' zu den Sprüchen der Sieben Weisen," in Althoff and Zeller, *Die Worte der Sieben Weisen*, 85–103.

[20] However, note the conflicting traditions: "Archetimus of Syracuse describes their meeting at the court of Cypselus, on which occasion he himself happened to be present; for which Epherus substitutes a meeting without Thales at the court of Croesus" (Diogenes Laertius 1.40). The latter tradition, which reports the absence of Thales at Sardis, is contradicted by the letter of Periander of Corinth (Diogenes Laertius 1.99) to the seven sages, which affirms that *all* were present at the court of Croesus: "I learn that last year you met in Sardis at the Lydian court."

[21] For full discussion, see C. Pelling, "Educating Croesus: Talking and Learning in Herodotus' Lydian *Logos*," *Classical Antiquity* 25.1 (2006): 141–47, esp. 146–49; Busine, *Les Sept Sages*, 14.

[22] H.W. Parke, "Croesus and Delphi," *GRBS* 25.3 (1984): 209–32. Additionally, see H.I. Flower, "Herodotus and the Delphic Traditions about Croesus," in *Georgica: Greek Studies in Honour of George Cawkwell*, ed. M.A. Flower and M. Toher (London 1991), 57–77.

[23] C.C. Chiasson ("Herodotus' Prologue and the Greek Poetic Tradition," *Histos* 6 [2012]: 114–43, at 136) writes: "... the Herodotean Croesus is portrayed as a non-Greek, Asiatic 'other' with a perspective on material wealth that (for all his generosity to Delphic Apollo) proves disastrously shortsighted. For as long as Croesus possesses his Eastern riches and monarchy, he is unable to appreciate the Hellenic wisdom expounded by Solon ..." See also *id.*, "The Herodotean Solon," *GRBS* 27 (1986): 249–62.

[24] Busine, *Les Sept Sages*, 26.

The first explicit reference to the connection between Delphi and the sages occurs in Plato. Plato says that the seven sages, purported to be proponents of Spartan wisdom and culture, produced "pithy, memorable sayings" (*Prot.* 343b). In an important statement regarding their authoritative status, Plato notes that

> they jointly dedicated as the first fruits of their wisdom to Apollo in his temple in Delphi, inscribing there the maxims now on everyone's lips: "Know yourself" and "Nothing in excess."[25]

In *Charmides* 164d–165a (cf. Plutarch, *Mor.* 385D, 392A), Plato reaffirms the Delphic ethical tradition. Plato states, through the mouthpiece of Critias, that the inscriptions "Know yourself" and "Be temperate" were placed in the temple with the intention that both sayings would coalesce in an indissoluble moral unity in the lives of those entering the precinct. Properly understood, the two sayings represent the god's "greeting" to his initiates in the sanctuary of Delphi rather than a piece of casual "advice". "Self-knowledge" only comes through the virtue of *sophrosune* ("temperance"). Plato also adds that other sayings such as "Nothing too much" and "Pledges lead to perdition" were only added later inside Apollo's precinct.[26]

An intriguing admission, however, is also made regarding Delphi's reputation for oracular ambiguity. In regards to the "greeting" offered by the maxims to those who enter Apollo's sanctuary, it is said that the god "speaks very darkly, as a seer would do" (*Charm.* 164e). In other words, precisely because the meaning of the maxims or their interconnection was not always immediately clear, as was the case with the puzzling conjunction of "temperance" and "self-knowledge", it is likely that subsequent maxims were dedicated in the temple to clarify, nuance, and expand the growing collection. Therefore, we have to reckon with the cryptic, paradoxical and contradictory elements of Sosiades' rendering of the Delphic canon and in its documentary versions, because this "riddling" character lies at the core of Delphi's pedagogical and ethical tradition.[27]

---

[25] Plato, *Prot.* 343b.

[26] On the date and conflicting traditions regarding the place where the two famous maxims and the capital letter E were inscribed on the temple at Delphi (pre-546 BC?), as well as their re-inscribing in Roman times, see E. G. Wilkens, *The Delphic Maxims in Literature* (Chicago: University of Chicago Press, 1929): 1–8.

[27] The "indirect and riddling style" of the Delphi oracle (Kurke, *Aesopic Conversations*, 111) is beautifully captured in the comment of Heraclitus: "the lord whose oracle is at Delphi neither speaks, nor hides, but signifies" (H. Diels and W. Kranz, *Die Fragmente der* Vorsokratiker, 10th ed. [Berlin: Weidmann, 1960; orig. 1934], §B93). On the "riddling" traditions of Delphi, see Plato, *Apol.* 21b3–4. See also Plutarch (*Mor.* 385C; cf. 386E–F ["ambiguous oracles"]): "... it seems only natural that the greater part of what concerns the god should be concealed in riddles, and should call for some account of the wherefore and an explanation of its cause."

The Delphic priest Plutarch (c. 45–125 AD) is an ideal source for exploring the connections of the seven sages with Delphi.[28] In his treatise *The E at Delphi*, Plutarch says that the original *five* "sophists" – Chilon, Thales, Solon, Bias and Pittacus – were intimidated by the Cleobulus, the despot of the Lindians, and by the tyrant Periander of Corinth. The latter two rulers had circulated throughout Greece their own "wisdom" sayings, similar to the five original sages, by virtue of their power and patronage. The original five

> did not like this at all, but were loath to expose the imposture or to arouse open hatred over a question of repute, or to carry through a contest against such powerful men; they met here by themselves and, after conferring together, dedicated that one of the letters which is fifth in alphabetical order and which stands for the number five, thus testifying for themselves before the god that they were five, and renouncing and rejecting the seventh and the sixth as having no connection with themselves.[29]

Plutarch concedes that the third inscription of the capital Epsilon in the *pronaos* (vestibule) of the Delphic sanctuary, which was added to the other two famous inscriptions of "Know yourself" and "Nothing in excess", was only one of three Epsilons inscribed over the period the sanctuary. There was the wooden "E" of the seven sages, dating from the time of the seven sages (early VI cent. BC), but destroyed by fire in 548 BC; there was the brazen "E" of the Athenians, probably belonging to the Alcmeonid temple replacing the one burnt down; last, there was also the golden "E" erected by Livia, Augustus' wife, and present at Plutarch's time (*Mor.* 385F–386A).[30] Furthermore, the actual meaning of the "E" is uncertain, with Plutarch's treatise voicing six possibilities: it is either symbolic of the original five sages (*Mor.* 385F), the Apolline Sun (386A–B), enquiries to the god prefaced by "if" (386B-D), human logic (386D–387D), mystical powers associated with the number "five" (387F–391D), or, last, represents a form of welcome by the god (391E–392A).

Clearly, the significance of the Epsilon was unknown to Plutarch, though its potency as a fetish continued through the ages. What then do we make of Plutarch's original suggestion, noted above (*Mor.* 385F)? Probably Plutarch wanted to link the Delphic Epsilon traditions of his own age with the venerable wisdom traditions of the seven sages, though a grain of truth might conceivably underlie his proposal. But the enigmatic nature of the Epsilon symbol in the Delphic sanctuary provided him with the perfect opportunity to forge precisely

[28] On Plutarch's Delphic connections, see Plutarch, *Mor.* 785e, 792f and CIG 1713. For discussion, see R. Lamberton, *Plutarch* (Chelsea, MI: Sheridan books, 2001), 52–54; A. Casanova, "Plutarch as Apollo's Priest at Delphi," in *Plutarch in the Religious and Philosophical Discourse of Late Antiquity*, ed. L.R. Lanzillotta and I.M.O. Gallarte (Leiden: Brill, 2012), 159–70.

[29] Plutarch, *Mor.* 385E–F.

[30] See W.N. Bates, "The E of the Temple at Delphi," *AJA* 29 (1925): 239–46; K. Berman and L.A. Losada, "The Mysterious E at Delphi: A Solution," *ZPE* 17 (1975): 115–17; A.T. Hodge, "The Mystery of Apollo's E at Delphi," *AJA* 85.1 (1981): 83–84.

such a connection. Since debate about the significance of the Epsilon was unresolved in his own age, one more speculation about its origins would not matter. Undoubtedly, the long debate as to which sage was the wisest, exemplified in the story of the "passing of the tripod" at Delphi, is another example of the same tendency (Plutarch, *Sol.* 4.1–4; Diogenes Laertius, 1.28–32; Diodorus 9.3.1–3; 9.13.2).[31]

There were, however, alternative traditions to a Delphic meeting of the seven sages. Plutarch's treatise, *The Dinner of the Seven Wise Men*, presents an imaginative reconstruction of the visit of the seven sages to the court of Periander at Corinth.[32] Aesop and Neiloxenos are added to the dinner conversation, enhancing the informal association of Aesop with the sages (n. 19 *supra*), along with the females Melissa and Eumetis, who maintain a discreet silence (*Mor.* 154B) during the period of their attendance (150D–155E), and who leave before the conclusion of the symposium (155E). The work becomes a forum for Plutarch's rendering of the seven sage's teaching in Platonic garb,[33] as well as a discussion of *oikonomia*, concentrating the management of tyrannous states (*Mor.* 147A–D, 151E–152C, 154C–F) and everyday households (154F–160B).

While there is no direct reference to the seven sages being present at the sanctuary of Delphi in this treatise, it is significant that Plutarch refers to the legend about the harpist Arion, recounted by Herodotus (1.23–24). Plutarch presents the harpist Arion, who was subsequently saved from drowning by dolphins (*Mor.* 161d–f), singing initially to Pythian Apollo in supplication for his own safety and that of his fellow sailors (*Mor.* 161e–d). By this stratagem Plutarch connects the legend with the foundation story of Delphi, in which the dolphin god Apollo ("Delphinios") leads Cretan sailors to establish his sanctuary in the mountain (*Homeric Hymn to Pythian Apollo* 388–544). Plutarch's link with Delphic origins in this instance finds confirmation in the dolphin motifs exhibited on the early coinage of the city and on a Delphic tripod, unearthed at Ostia and now exhibited in the Museum of Paris.[34] In this treatise, as Busine ob-

[31] See Wiersma, "The Seven Sages."

[32] Diogenes Laertius (1.40–41) reports several alternative traditions to the Delphic meeting: meetings at the court of Cypselus and Periander (Corinth), the court of Croesus (Sardis), and the Pan-Ionian festival at Mycale (cf. Plutarch, *Sol.* 4.1). For discussion, see Aune, "Septem Sapientium Convivium"; J. Mossman, "Plutarch's Dinner of the Seven Wise Men and Its Place in Symposium Literature," in *Plutarch and His Intellectual World: Essays on Plutarch*, ed. J. Mossman (London: Duckworth, 1997), 119–40; Engel, *Die sieben Weisen*, 30–33; Busine, *Les Sept Sages*, 93–102.

[33] See Busine, *Les Sept Sages*, 98–99. Among the Platonic motifs are superiority of the soul to the body and, relatedly, their dichotomy (Plutarch, *Mor.* 163e; 159e–160a), as well as dreams as the medium of revelation (146d, 158f–159a) and the philanthropic nature of the sage (148d). Busine (*Les Sept Sages*, 101) postulates that Plutarch is presenting the seven sages as "Platonisers" who reflect the concerns of the erudite Greeks of the early Roman Empire.

[34] For Delphic coins with dolphins, see B.V. Head, *A Catalogue of the Greek Coins of the British Museum: Central Greece. Locris, Phocis, Boetia and Euboea* (London: Longmans and

serves,[35] Plutarch both rescues from neglect and updates several Delphic themes. By Plutarch's time, dolphin symbolism no longer appeared on the imperial coins of Delphi, having been mostly replaced by an emphasis on the god Apollo, among other motifs, presumably because of Augustus' close association with the deity.[36] Plutarch, therefore, returns to and contemporises traditional Delphic motifs.

What indicates that Sosiades' distillation of the oral wisdom tradition emanating from the seven sages was reliable and reflected the centrality of Delphi in its formation and dissemination?

6.1.2. Sosiades' Collection

6.1.2.1. Its Pedagogic Intentionality

At the outset, the question arises why we are concentrating on the canon of Sosiades, which lists 147 sayings of the seven sages, as opposed to the canon of Demetrius of Phaleron, which groups the sayings around the originator of each saying, with the addition of ἔφη (n. 2 *supra*). Apart from the confirmation of Sosiades' collection of sayings in the documentary evidence, discussed below, there are disagreements within the Delphic tradition as to which sage articulated various of the sayings (Diogenes Laertius 1.41).[37] Thus Sosiades' unattributed collection of sayings is less problematic than it initially appears in comparison to the attributed collection of Demetrius of Phaleron.[38] What we have to discern is whether there is a pedagogic intentionality about Sosiades' collection that would render it more likely to be memorised over the period of its transmission.

This chapter will argue that because some of the inscriptions replicating Sosiades' collection were found in ancient gymnasia, the wisdom sayings of the

---

Co., 1884), 24–27. At the museum of Paris there is a sculptured marble of the Delphic tripod with a lyre and dolphins, among several other motifs (P. Dodwell, *A Classical and Topographical Tour through Greece during the Years 1801, 1805, and 1806. Volume 1* [London: Rodwell and Martin, 1819], 193).

[35] Busine, *Les Sept Sages*, 101.

[36] J.F. Miller, *Apollo, Augustus and the Poets* (Cambridge: Cambridge University Press, 2009). For the imperial coins of Delphi, see Head, *A Catalogue of the Greek Coins*, xxxiv–xxxiv, 28–31.

[37] Aune ("Septem Sapientium Convivium," 55) writes: "Most attributions of such sayings or apophthegmata to particular ancient authorities are tendentious, based on rather what an ideal wise man should have said rather than on what he in fact actually said." In this regard, Diogenes Laertius 1.41 states: "Their utterances are variously reported, and are attributed now to one now to the other."

[38] Oikonomides ("The Lost Delphic Inscription," 180 n.7) states regarding the collection of Demetrius of Phaleron: "In a way it represents the efforts of Post-Aristotelean philosophers to attribute what could be attributed to each one of 'The Seven', separating thus their personal contributions to philosophy from the survivals of oral wisdom attributed to 'The Seven' as an undistinguishable group."

seven sages represented the ephebic ethical curriculum across the eastern Mediterranean basin. While no overarching organisational principle within Sosiades' collection has been found, the repetition of terminology and motifs throughout the collection point to the intentionality of the curriculum taught. The acknowledgement of the gods and providence provides the framework of the cosmic order, whereas in the terrestrial sphere the hierarchy of household relations establishes the wider social concord. Engagement with the complex social relations of the polis is underscored, given that the ephebes would become civic leaders of the future. Moreover, true virtue in this context will be achieved by aiming at the median point between behavioural extremes, a motif that would find its flowering under Aristotle. But, paradoxically, in this intricate web of social engagement, the maintenance of personal indifference by the cultivation of self is paramount. In this tension between personal indifference and social engagement, the health of the established order would be maintained. At its core, therefore, Sosiades' collection is a deeply conservative ethical construct, inculcating mores that would reinforce the social status quo and the entrenched privilege of the civic elites.

What terminological motifs recur in the Delphic canon and what mnemonic formulae are used to facilitate its formative ethical agenda?

6.1.2.2. Indications of Structure: Recurring Terminology, "Doublets" and "Triplets"

One structural element that shapes the teaching of Sosiades' collection is the presence of common terminology, indicating key motifs for the readers to consider. Several examples will suffice. Attention to the duties of friendship (φιλία, φιλοφρονέομαι) is a constant refrain throughout the Delphic canon (Sosiades 15 ["Help your friends"], 20 ["Love friendship"], 28 ["Goodwill for friends"], 37 ["Favour a friend"], 93 ["Look kindly on all"], 105 ["Guard friendship"]; cf. Aristotle, *Eth. nic.* 8.1.1–8.14.4), undoubtedly because it forms a central part of the Graeco-Roman reciprocity system. In regards to the latter, several maxims have come down to us in Sosiades' collection that employ the language of "grace" (χάρις, χαρίζομαι) to underscore the importance of munificence: 37 ("Favour a friend"), 45 ("Do a favour when you can"), 75 ("Return a favour"), 136 ("Favour without harming"). There is little doubt that the Delphic canon keeps the intricacies of social obligation in sharp focus here, including its pitfalls if the rituals of reciprocity and status go astray. Consequently, the centrality of honorific culture is heavily underscored (τίμα), whether it is honouring the hearth (13), providence (18), benefactions (59), and the good ones (65), or the praise of virtue (ἐπαίνει ἀρετήν: 26) and the concern for and pursuit of reputation (δόξαν μὴ λεῖπε: 118; δόξαν δίωκε: 22). The dominant social values are totally conventional in this scenario.

Another repeated strain is the tension between sensitivity to the outworking of "providence"/"fortune"/"good fortune" (πρόνοια: 18; τύχη: 68, 77, 142; εὐτυχίαν: 76) and sensitivity to the opportunities and exigencies of time (καιρός: 10, 39, 98, 103, 111). Thus one's ability to be indifferent to vicissitudes of life and yet to engage its demands astutely is upheld by this tension in the Delphic canon. Without caution before fortune and the critical moments of time, "arrogance" is the inevitable outcome (ὕβρις: 41, 83; ὑβρίζειν: 130). But where the disciplined individual embraces this tension, the pursuit and practice of justice becomes the norm (27, 84 [δίκαια], 64 [δίκαιως], 145 [δίκαιος]; cf. Aristotle, *Eth. nic.* 5.1.1–5.5.3), as well as one's submission to the just elites ("Yield to the just" [ἡττῶ ὑπὸ δικαίου]: 5). In sum, the recurring terminological emphasis on various motifs throughout Sosiades' collection enables the reader to discern what are the wider ethical contours in which all moral decision-making should be made.

Two other rhetorical devices help to give shape to the ethical intention of Sosiades' collection of maxims: the use of "doublets" and "triplets". Whether these are mnemonic clues to the transmission of the oral tradition either originating with the seven sages or their tradents, or whether they represent the redaction of the oral tradition over the period of the inscribing of collection, is impossible to determine. First, in the case of the triad, an A/B/A structure emerges, with the central maxim (B) being a specific ethical response to the overarching schema (A/A). Thus, in the strongly hierarchical world-view of the Delphic canon, submission to the god/gods and submission to the laws of the polis are equally mandatory. Similarly, in an honorific culture, where the praise of the socially powerful and their virtue is *de rigueur*, criticism *per se* is ruled out as a socially acceptable attitude. The "triplets" below help us to see the hierarchical focus of the Delphic canon more clearly:

Sosiades	*Magnifying the divine*	*Specific Ethical Response*
1	Follow God (A)	
2		Obey the law (B)
3	Worship the gods (A)	

Sosiades	*Magnifying honorific culture*	*Specific Ethical Response*
24	Compliment a gentleman (A)	
25		Criticise no-one (B)
26	Praise virtue (A)	

Second, in the case of the "doublets", the two maxims focus on a motif, with the second maxim qualifying, expanding or providing a thematic contrast to the first maxim. The intriguing interrelation of the two maxims forces the reader to consider the overall social and personal consequences of the moral ethic promoted.[39] Although we cannot discern an overarching organisational principle

[39] Being teachable: Sosiades 6 ("Learn your lesson") and 7 ("Listen and learn"). Responsible self-interest: Sosiades 33 ("Look after your own things") and 34 ("Lay off those of others").

behind Sosiades' collection, assuming for the moment that it might have had one, the presence of common terminology throughout and the mnemonic clues of "doublets" and "triplets" assures us that there was a pedagogic coherence about the Delphic canon rather than it being an entirely random assortment of the teaching of the seven sages.

6.1.3. The Eastern Mediterranean Documentary Evidence

6.1.3.1. The Finds, Their Location and Significance

We turn now to the documentary evidence confirming Sosiades' collection of the sayings of the seven sages.[40] Many of the Delphic maxims from Sosiades' collection have been found inscribed – with minor variations – at (most likely) the gymnasium at Miletopolis in the Hellespont (IKyzikos II 2 Cols. 1 and 2 [IV–III cent. BC]).[41] Another version of the Delphic canon has been found at the gymnasium of the ephebes at Thera (IG XII[3] 1020: IV cent. BC), though

---

The right use of time: Sosiades 39 ("Save time") and 40 ("Look to the future"). Benefaction rituals: Sosiades 58 ("Give what you mean to") and 59 ("Honour benefactions"). Prayer and providence: Sosiades 76 ("Pray for good fortune") and 77 ("Accept the outcome"). Gracious speech: Sosiades 81 ("Detest reproach") and 82 ("Hold your tongue"). Household relations: Sosiades 94 ("Don't curse your sons") and 95 ("Rule your wife"). Intergenerational relations: Sosiades 126 ("Respect the elder") and 127 ("Teach the younger").

[40] In addition to the Judge English translation (n. 2 *supra*), the inscriptional and papyrus remains of the Delphic canon, discussed below, are helpfully set out, with a full translation of Sosiades' 147 maxims, in A. N. Oikonomides, "Records of the 'Commandments of the Seven Wise Men' in the 3rd c. BC: The Revered 'Greek-Reading Book' of the Hellenistic World," *CB* 63 (1987): 67–76, esp. 71–72, 75–76. For another English translation of Sosiades' collection, accompanied by the Greek text, see B. Radice and G. Mardersteig, *Delphika grammata: The Sayings of the Seven Sages of Greece* (Verona: Officina Bodoni, 1976), not sighted by me. See, too, the German translation of J. Althoff and D. Zeller, "Antike Textzeugnisse und Überlieferungsgeschichte," in Althoff and Zeller, *Die Worte der Sieben Weisen*, 5–81. The translations of Judge and Oikonomides do not incorporate P. Oxy. 61.4099 or P. Kramer 14 (nn. 45, 47 *infra*), but for the text P. Oxy. 61.4099, see the German translation of Althoff and Zeller, "Antike Textzeugnisse," 73–76.

[41] IKyzikos II 2 Col. 1 reproduces 25 maxims from Sosaides' collection out of the 25 maxims presented, whereas IKyzikos II 2 Col. 2 lists another 31 of Sosiades' maxims out of the 31 maxims presented. Hasluck ("Inscriptions from the Cyzicus District, 1906," 62–63) dates the stele, on the basis of its orthography and lettering, to c. 300 BC. G. Mendel ("Catalogue des monuments grecs, romains et byzantins du Musée Impérial Ottoman de Brousse," *BCH* 33 [1909]: 402–04, § 401) notes that the stele was fixed on a base by four crampons, the holes for the attachment of which are still visible in the lower part. He speculates that it was likely to have been placed in the gymnasium of Miletopolis, pointing to version of Sosiades' collection found at the gymnasium of Thera (IG XII[3] 1020: IV cent. BC). He refers to the Pergameme copy of Hermes of Alcamene (citing AM XXIX, p. 180, in *idem*, "Catalogue des monuments," 404), which was found in the lower level terrace of the gymnasium. Its column shaft carried below the dedication the famous Delphic maxim: γνῶθι σαυτόν. The parallels are compelling, I believe, establishing the likelihood of the Miletopolis gymnasium was the original site of the stele, even though Hasluck gave no indication where the stone was subsequently located.

the Therean version is more fragmentary.[42] Thus the ethics of the Delphic canon had spread throughout the eastern Mediterranean gymnasia. The widespread dissemination of the Delphic maxims and the meticulous care taken in their transmission can be gauged from their presence at Egypt (P. Ath. Univ. inv. 2782 [III cent. BC]).[43] The original editor of the papyrus suggested that it represented a "school-exercise".[44] Once again we are steered towards a pedagogic intention for the collection of Sosiades. This has been confirmed by the find of a teacher's handbook displaying select Delphic maxims as a model for student handwriting in an Oxyrhynchus papyrus (P. Oxy. 61.4099: I cent. AD).[45] Two second to third-century AD ostraka have Delphic maxims inscribed on them, probably exercises in student alphabet training.[46] Finally, a fragmentary second-century AD Viennese papyrus (P. Kramer 14) has been published with several sayings from Sosiades' collection again present.[47] Undoubtedly, more papyrus and epigraphic fragments of Sosiades' rendering of the Delphic canon will appear in the future. But enough has been said to demonstrate that a clear pedagogic intention underlies the collection of Sosiades, with its ethical curriculum being taught from the preparatory school to the gymnasium, spanning the period from the fourth century BC right through to the third century AD.

In the case of the Aï-Khanum stele on the Oxus (Afghanistan), Clearchus (of Soli?) had erected the stone in the tomb-shrine of the sanctuary of the city's founder, Cineas, from a copy that he had personally inscribed while at Delphi.[48]

---

[42] IG XII(3) 1020 has only 3 maxims from Sosiades' collection out of the 4 maxims presented. The editor, Hillier von Gaertingen, believes the inscription to have come from the "epheborum gymnasium." However, Oikonomides ("Records of the 'Commandments of the Seven Wise Men'," 72) challenges von Gaertingen's restorations in *ll.* 1–2, suggesting alternate sayings from Sosiades' collection to be the originals.

[43] See A.N. Oikonomides, "The Lost Delphic Inscription with the Commandments of the Seven and P. Univ. Athen. 2782," *ZPE* 37 (1980): 179–83. *P. Ath. Univ. inv.* 2782 replicates 8 maxims from Sosaides' collection out of the 10 maxims presented. Oikonomides, however, revised the dating of the papyrus from the first to the second century AD in his 1980 article ("Records of the 'Commandments of the Seven Wise Men'") to the third century BC in his 1987 article ("The Lost Delphic Inscription").

[44] Oikonomides, "The Lost Delphic Inscription," 181

[45] M. Huys, "P. Oxy. 61.4099: A Combination of Mythographic Lists with Sentences of the Seven Wise Men," *ZPE* 113 (1996): 205–12. P. Oxy. 61.4099 has 14 maxims from Sosiades' collection out of the 15 maxims presented.

[46] R. Pintaudi and Pieter J. Sijpesteijn, "Ostraka di contenuto scolastico provenienti da Narmuthis," *ZPE* 76 (1989): 85–92, nos. 5, 6. I am indebted to Professor G.B. Bazanna, Harvard Divinity School, for this and the previous reference.

[47] A. Papathomas, "14. Ein literarisches Fragment mit Sprüchen der Sieben Weisen," in *'... vor dem Papyrus sind alle Gleich!': papyrologische Beiträge zu Ehren von Bärbel Kramer (P. Kramer)*, ed. R. Eberhard et al. (Berlin and New York: Walter de Gruyter, 2009), 163–69. I am again grateful to Professor G.B. Bazanna for this reference. P. Kramer 14 has only 2 maxims from Sosiades' collection out of the 5 maxims presented.

[48] See Robert, "De Delphes à l'Oxus"; cf. On Aï-Khanum, see Paul Bernard, *Ai Khanoum on the Oxus: A Hellenistic City in Central Asia*, (London: Oxford University Press, 1967); D.W. MacDowell and M. Taddei, "The Greek City of Aï-Khanum," in F.R. Allchin and

Although not placed in a gymnasium in this instance, the antiquity and hallowed status of the text is again underscored by its prestigious placement in the city. Consequently, its foundational importance for the continuing civic life of the polis is ensured. Only the base of the original stele remains, as well as another small fragment of the stele, with the last five of Sosiades' maxims squeezed on the right side of the base, because, as Robert argued,[49] they were not able to be fitted on the stele above. Robert identifies the peripatetic philosopher Clearchus as the famous pupil of Aristotle, mentioned in Josephus, *Ap.* 1.22.[50] This suggestion would also raise the possibility, as we will argue, that the Aristotelian ethical "mean" is a useful construct for understanding the Delphic canon's pedagogic intent.

Recently, however, J. Lerner has heavily attacked this identification, dismissing Robert's construct as entirely speculative. Moreover, he argues on the basis of paleographic criteria that the (allegedly) earlier inscriptions of Cineas' sanctuary belong to a later period (210–170 BC), as opposed to Robert's earlier dating of them (300–275 BC).[51] If Lerner's critique of Robert's identification is correct, and the otherwise unknown Clearchus is merely a citizen of Aï-Khanum who went to Delphi to copy the maxims in c. 210–170 BC, we have to ask the purpose of his unofficial visit and return. In agreement with Lerner, R. Mairs argues that our inscription is a later addition to a pre-existing founder shrine. Clearchus' inscribing of the Delphic canon in the sanctuary, therefore, represents an attempt to increase the city's status by supplementing the existing foundation of Cineas with the international reputation of the sanctuary of Delphi for oracles and ethical wisdom. As Mairs observes regarding Clearchus,

> ... his personal copying of the maxims could have been regarded as a kind of consultation by proxy, an attempt to give the founder – and his foundation – a connection with Delphi which they did not have in any literal sense.[52]

N. Hammond, eds., *The Archaeology of Afghanistan from Earliest Times to the Timurid Period* (London: Academic Press, 1978), 218–32. F. L. Holt, "Discovering the Lost History of Ancient Afghanistan: Hellenistic Bactria in the Light of Recent Archaeological and Historical Research," *AncW* 9 (1984): 3–11. On Crinus, see Robert, "De Delphes à l'Oxus," 432–43; Oikonomides, "The Lost Delphic Inscription," 180 n. 6.

[49] Robert, "De Delphes à l'Oxus," 429–30.

[50] Robert, "De Delphes à l'Oxus," 442–54.

[51] J. Lerner ("Correcting the Early History of Ay Kanom," *Archäologische Mitteilungen aus Iran und Turan* 35/36 [2003/2004]: 372–410, esp. 393–94, reported in SEG 54 [1567]) argues for a later date for the Aï-Khanum maxims than Robert, who famously proposed 300–275 BC. Instead Lerner posits that Clearchus was a citizen of Aï-Khanum who, having gone to Dephi and copied down the maxims, returned to his city and "had them set up at the temenos upon his return in the waning years of the 3rd cent. or in the first quarter of the 2nd cent. BC."

[52] R. Mairs, "The Founder's Shrine and the Foundation of Ai Khanoum," in *Foundation Myths in Ancient Societies: Dialogues and Discourses*, ed. N. Mac Sweeney (Philadelphia: University of Pennsylvania Press, 2015), 103–28, at 116.

Also the likelihood was that Aï-Khanum had to be protected from the constant threat of the nearby Scythian culture, in the same way that Delphi had to be protected from the Gauls.[53] The Hellenisation of Aï-Khanum had continued apace, with its citizens worshipping the patron deities of Greek *paideia*, Hemes and Heracles, as a dedication in the gymnasium demonstrates (SEG 38 [1550]).[54] Thus Clearchus' insertion of the Delphic canon in the tomb-shrine of Cineas ensured the continuing triumph of Greek moral values, education and social conventions at the frontier of the barbarian hordes. The remains of the Aï-Khanum inscription are as follows:

Text of Sosiades	Aï-Khanum base, right	
143 παῖς ὢν κόσμιος ἴσθι	1. παῖς ὢν κόσμιος γίνου	As a child be well behaved,
144 ἡβων ἐκρατής	2. ἡβων ἐκρατής	in youth restrained,
145 μέσος δίκαιος	3. μέσος δίκαιος	in middle life just,
146 πρεσβύτης εὔλογος	4. πρεσβύτης εὔλογος	in old age reasonable/prudent
147 τελευτῶν ἄλυπος	5. τελευτῶν ἄλυπος	at the end not worrying.

Aï-Khanum base, front, epigram
Ἀνδρῶν τοι ταῦτα παλαιοτέρων ἀνάκει[τα]ι
ῥήματα ἀριγνώτων Πυθοῖ ἐν ἠγαθέαι
ἔνφεν ταῦτ[α] Κλέαρχος ἐπιφραδέως ἀναγράψας
εἵσατο τηλαυγῆ Κινέου ἐν τεμένει

These wise words of men of long ago are dedicated
as sayings of the famous in most holy Pytho,
where Clearchus carefully wrote them out,
putting them up to shine afar in the sanctuary of Cineas.[55]

Small fragment of the inscription found 1 metre away from the Aï-Khanum base
[...]
ε[ὐλόγει πάντας]
φιλόσοφ[ος γίνου]
[...]

[...]
S[peak well of everyone]
[Be] a lover of wisd[om] (or [Take up] philosop[hy])
[...]

[53] F. L. Holt, *Thundering Zeus: The Making of Hellenistic Bactria* (Berkeley and Los Angeles: University of California Press, 1999), 45–46.

[54] Holt, *Thundering Zeus*, 43–44.

[55] For a photo of the base of the column bearing Clearchus' epigram, see P. Thonemann, *The Hellenistic Age* (Oxford: Oxford University Press, 2016), 4 Figure 1.

The final fragment above, heavily restored, confirms that the entire stele was inscribed with Sosiades' collection, with maxims 47 and 48 remaining on the stone, if Robert's identification is correct. It is also intriguing, if Lerner and Mairs have successfully trumped Robert's dating arguments, how the authority of Delphic wisdom is being invoked at the edges of the Greek world, with a view to enhancing local foundation myths and buttressing Hellenistic *paideia* over against the incursions of barbarian culture. Elsewhere in the Eastern Mediterranean basin, as we have seen, Sosiades' collection is at the centre of the ethical and social ephebic curriculum of the gymnasium, even penetrating the humble writing-exercises of school children. A final question remains: how reliably does the documentary evidence replicate Sosiades' collection?

6.1.3.2. Local Variations in Tradition

While there is substantial agreement of the documentary evidence with Sosiades' collection, the documentary order is not always the same, sometimes omitting sayings within Sosiades' sequence, and on other occasions adding entirely new sayings to Sosiades' collection.[56] We will deal first with the evidence of the papyri. In the case of the 8 maxims of P.Athen.Univ.inv.2782, the sole addition is "Obey a good man" (no. 2), with only one maxim of the remaining seven replicating Sosiades' exact sequence of maxims. As far as the 15 maxims in P. Oxy. 61.4099, the maxim "Conciliate all" (Z. no. 24) is the only addition to Sosiades.[57] Though two of the maxims have slight variations in the Greek, the order of Sosiades is followed across his collection, with only three sayings departing from the sequence of Sosiades (52: "Pray for what is possible"; 59: "Honour benefaction"; 55: "Give back what you take"). Regarding P. Bremer 14, only two of the five maxims come from Sosiades' collection (103: "take time to think"; 109: "Fear what controls you"). The additions are "esteem what is just" (P. Bremer 14 Kol. II no. 9), "despise no-one" (Kol. II no. 10), and "abide by agreements" (Kol. II no. 12).

We turn now to the evidence of the inscriptions. In the case of the Aï-Khanum stele, noted above, maxims 47 and 48 of Sosiades are found faintly on the fragment of the stele independent of the base, whereas the final five maxims of Sosiades (143–147) are found in correct sequence on the base. As far as the 25 maxims of IKyzikos II 2 Col. 1, there are only three additions (nos. 3 ["Flee injustice"], 4 ["Attest as is holy"], 5 ["Subdue pleasure"]), with only 5 maxims (nos. 6, 14, 21, 22, 23) not reflecting Sosiades' precise sequence, and also with omissions to Sosiades' sequence. *I Kyzikos* II 2 Col. 2 comprises 31 maxims,

[56] For new sayings added to Sosiades' collection, see P.Athen.Univ. inv. 2782 no. 2; IKyzikos II 2 Col. 1 nos. 3, 4, 5; IG XII 3.1020 no. 2; IKyzikos II 2 Col. 2 nos. 15, 19, 20, 27, 29, 31; P. Oxy. 61.4099 (n. 45 below).

[57] Althoff and Zeller, "Antike Textzeugnisse," 75 no. 24.

covering the sequence of Sosiades 92–117, with four omissions of Sosiades' maxims (nos. 94, 100, 106, 110), five additions to Sosiades' collection (nos. 15 ["Despise no-one"], 18 ["Trust to time"], 19 ["Don't speak to please"], 20 ["Worship divinity"], 29 ["Don't [give up?] trusting"]), and two relocations in Sosiades' order (nos. 13 and 25 moved to Sosiades 84 and 110 respectively). Last, regarding the four maxims of IG XII 3.1020 (Thera), the maxims are scattered singly across Sosiades' collection (8, 38, 69), with one highly restored and uncertain addition (no. 2: σ[πουδαῖα μελέτα(?)]). The evidence is too fragmentary to come to any conclusion about the degree to which the Therean inscription reflects the structure of Sosiades' collection.

What is so impressive about the documentary evidence is its replication of the wording and sequence of Sosiades' collection in the vast majority of cases, as well as its strong state of textual preservation. Further, the additions to Sosiades' collection are (relatively speaking) minor, comprising 15 new sayings augmenting the 79 authentic sayings from Sosiades' collection that are found in the documentary evidence. In other words, variations from the text of Sosiades are largely inconsequential in the documentary evidence, comprising additions, relocations and omissions. The collection of Sosiades, made at the same time as the version of Demetrius of Phaleron (350–280 BC),[58] is not an arbitrary invention of its collector, but reflects the oral traditions of the seven wise men that were given widespread documentary expression from the fourth century BC onwards. The fluidity of the oral tradition about the sayings of the seven sages is reflected *locally* in the additions to the copies at Kyzikos and Thera, but clearly the Delphic inscriptional tradition set strong parameters for Sosiades and the steles erected in other cities from the fourth century BC onwards.

6.2. The Pedagogical Context of the Delphic Canon: The Honorific Inscriptions, Paideia *and Virtue*

Before I examine the Delphic canon in depth, it is important to situate its moral ethos within the wider pedagogical context, so that we can better understand its intent regarding moral formation and the clientele whom its redactors had in mind in erecting the copies in the first place. Given that two of our inscriptions of the Delphic canon were found in the gymnasia of the eastern Mediterranean and that the papyrus was likely to be a school exercise, the honorific inscriptions relating to *paideia* reflect this context better as opposed to the writings of the peripatetic philosophers or the established philosophical schools.[59] As not-

[58] L. Zhmud, *Pythagoras and the Early Pythagoreans* (Oxford: Oxford University Press, 2012), 153 n. 76.

[59] On the ethical sophistication of late Hellenistic decrees, see B. D. Gray, "Philosophy of Education and the Late Hellenistic Polis," in *Epigraphical Approaches to the Post-Classical*

ed, the ethics of the seven sages, from whom the Delphic canon derived, were formulated in the political tussles of public life and the public inscriptions articulate a similar civic ethos. I will concentrate on the elitist values articulated in an inscription from Dephi, where the canon was originally inscribed, and one from Ephesus, chosen for the richness of its vocabulary.[60] Each honorand is either involved in the supervision and teaching of the *epheboi* and *neoi* in the gymnasium,[61] or is sponsoring *paideia* within his city. We will see that some of the ubiquitous formulae of the honorific inscriptions are taken up and expanded in the Delphic canon, showing us how the religious, civic and exemplary focus of the honorific inscriptions were consonant with the ethics of the seven sages.[62]

First, an honorific inscription from Phokis, Delphi (AD 1–17) honours its recipient, Artemidoros, from the city of Mazakene and also an Athenian citizen, with this decree (FD III 4:59 *ll.* 1–19):

1. ἀγαθῇ τύχῃ.
Διόδωρος Φιλονίκου εἶπεν· ἐπειδὴ Ἀρτεμίδωρος Εὐβούλου Μαζακηνό[ς],
ὁ καὶ Ἀθηναῖος, εὐσεβῶς μὲν διάκειται ποτὶ τὸ ἱαρὸν τοῦ Ἀπόλλωνος τοῦ Πυθίο[υ]
εὐνοϊκῶς δὲ καὶ ποτὶ τὰν πόλιν τῶν Δελφῶν, ἀεί τινος ἀγαθοῦ παραίτιος γ[ι]-
5. νόμενος τῇ τε πόλει καὶ τῶι θεῷ, καὶ ἐπὶ τῶν ἡγουμένων καὶ καθ' ἰδίαν, σπουδῆ[ς]
καὶ φιλοτιμίας οὐδὲν ἐνλείπων τοῖς ἐντυνχάνουσιν, φιλοτι<μού>μεν[ος]
δὲ διὰ παντὸς ὡς ὑπὲρ ἰδίας πατρίδος καὶ πολιτῶν, καί, τοῖς ἀρίστοι[ς]
καὶ πρώτοις τῶν πολιτῶν συνβαλλόμενος {ει} εἰς προκοπὴν παιδ<ε>ίας
καὶ λόγων, ἀγαθοὺς ἄνδρας καὶ τῇ πόλει τῶν Δε<λ>φῶν κατασκευάζε[ι]·
10. ἐ<πὶ> τούτο[ι]ς οὖν ἅπασι, σπανίοις καὶ ἀγ[α]θοῖς οὖσιν ἔργοις, οἷς ὁ ἀνὴ[ρ]
ἀδιαλ<ε>ίπτως ἐνδ<ε>ίκ<ν>υται, δεδόχθαι τ[ῇ] πόλ<ε>ι τῶν Δελφῶν ἐπαινέσ[αι]
τε τὸν ἄνδρα, καὶ δεδόσθαι αὐτῷ παρὰ τῆς πόλεως προξενίαν, πολειτείαν, ἀτέλε[ι]-
αν, προμαντείαν, γῆς καὶ οἰκίας [ἔνκτησ]ιν, προεδρίαν ἐν πᾶσι τοῖς ἀγῶσιν ο[ἷς]
[ἡ] πόλις τίθησι, καὶ αὐτῷ καὶ ἐκ[γόνοις ἰσο]πολειτείαν, προδικίαν, καὶ τἆλλα τ[εί]-
15. [μια] πάντα ὅσα καὶ τοῖς ἀγ[αθοῖς ἀνδράσι κ]αὶ εὐεργέταις καὶ προξένοις τῆς
[πόλεως ὑπ]άρχει, ἀναγρ[άψαι δὲ τάσδε τὰς] τειμ[ὰς ἐν τῷ ἐπ]ιφανεστάτῳ [τό]-
[πῳ τοῦ ἱεροῦ τοῦ Ἀπόλλωνος, καὶ ἀποστεῖλαι τὸ ἀντίγραφον τοῦ ψηφίσματος τοῦ]-
[δε πρὸς τ]ὴν πόλιν τῶν Μ[αζακη]νῶν δι' ἐπι[σ]τολῆ[ς ὑ]πὸ [σφρ]αγῖ[δι τῇ δημοσί]ᾳ,
[ἐγγ]ράψαντας τοὺς ἄρχοντα[ς τ]ῆς πόλεως τάσδε τὰς τιμάς.

Polis, ed. P. Martzavou and N. Papazarkadas (Oxford: Oxford University Press, 2013), 233–54, esp. 234–36.

60 For comparisons of the vocabulary of the inscriptions with Plutarch and Dio Chrysostom, see (respectively) C. Panagopoulos, "Vocabulaire et mentalité dans les Moralia de Plutarque," *DHA* 3 (1977): 197–235; M.-H. Quet, "Rhétorique, culture et politique: Le fonctionnement du discours idéologique chez Dion de Pruse et dans les Moralia de Plutarque," *DHA* 4 (1978): 51–119.

61 For a full investigation of gymnasiarchal ethics, see Harrison, "Paul and the Gymnasiarchs," reproduced as Chapter 5.

62 On the basis of several inscriptions (ISestos 1, IIasos 98, IPriene 112), Gray ("Philosophy of Education and the Late Hellenistic Polis," 238) argues that education in the Hellenistic gymnasia not only focused on psychological processes but also on polis structures, institutions and civic values.

1. To Good Fortune.
   Diodorus son of Philonikus said: "Since Artemidorus son of Euboulus from Mazakene,
   also from Athens, is piously disposed to the holy place of Pythia[n] Apollo
   and also kindly (disposed) to the city of Delphi, always being partially the cause of something
5. good both for the city and the god, both in the presence of the rulers and privately, in zeal
   and in love of honour forsaking nothing for the petitioners, but contributing
   liberally continually for his own country and citizens, and, (along) with the best
   and first of the citizens contributing to the advancement of education
   and oratory, he also equips good men for the city of Delphi;
10. therefore on the basis of all these things, which are rare and good works, which the man
   unceasingly takes upon (himself), it was decided by the city of Delphi both to praise
   and give him from the city public friendship, citizenship, exemption from
   the public burdens, possession of land and house, front seat in all the games which
   the city holds, equality of civic rights to him and (his) descendants, the office of advocate, and all
15. the other valued (honours) and (seeing) how many are at hand for good men and benefactors and public
   guests of the city, to inscribe these honours in the most conspicuous place
   of the temple of Apollo, and to send a copy of this decree
   to the city of Mazakene, by means of a letter under public seal,
   the rulers of the city having inscribed these honours."[63]

Several aspects of the Delphic decree resonate with the canon, both at a religious and social level. First, the formulaic dedication to fortune introducing the decree ("To Good Fortune": FD III 4:59 *l.* 1) finds a more nuanced expression in the teaching of the Delphic canon. Its readers are encouraged to allow for chance (Sosiades 68 [IKyzikos II 2 Col. 1 no. 6]: τύχην νόμιζε), honour providence (Sosiades 18 [IKyzikos II 2 Col. 1 no. 7]: πρόνοιαν τίμα), accept the outcome (Sosiades 77: τύχην στέργε), not to trust in fortune (Sosiades 142: τυχῆι μὴ πίστευε), sympathise with misfortune (Sosiades 135: ἀτυχοῦντι συνάχθου) and pray for good fortune (Sosiades 76: εὐτυχίαν εὔχου). Moreover, the emphasis on Pythian Apollo and its temple in the inscription (FD III 4:59 *ll.* 3, 5, 17) would find its counterpart in the Delphic canon's "admire oracles" (Sosiades 123: χρησμοὺς

[63] Note the similar inscription at Delphi (FD IV: 59 *ll.* 4–8) to Leukinios Likinios the grammarian, who

... taught the boys letters truly and
earnestly, and in all times displays the same choice, (and) having been the head
of preparatory teaching and of the young men (τῶ[ν ν]έων), makes himself worthy of nobleness towards all and of piety (εὐσεβείας) towards the god and of good will towards
the city; ...

θαύμαζε) and the submission to and worship of the god advocated throughout (Sosiades 1, 3 [P.Athen.Univ. inv. 2782 nos. 1, 4]; IKyzikos II 2 Col. 2 no. 20). In the cases above, we gain insight into why the redactors of the Delphic canon were keen to move their students into a full-orbed ethical response to fortune and the gods so that their life would embrace the divine more holistically.

However, the social attitudes enunciated in the Delphic decree and the Delphic canon have a common elitist base. Artemidorus is said to have contributed "with the best (ἀρίστοι[ς]) and first (πρώτοις) of the citizens to the advancement of education (παιδ<ε>ίας) and oratory (λόγων)," equipping "good men (ἀγαφοὺς ἄνδρας) for the city of Delphi" (FD III 4:59 *ll.* 7–8; cf. *ll.* 15–16; Aristotle, *Eth. nic.* 5.2.11). It is particularly emphasised that he does this not as a citizen of Delphi, but acting towards its people as if he were a citizen of the city. In the case of the Delphic canon, the *ephebes* are also encouraged to cultivate the powerful elites by various strategies. They are to obey and honour the good man (P.Athen.Univ. inv. 2782 no. 2: τοῦ ἀγαθοῦ πείθου; Sosiades 65: ἀγαθοὺς τίμα),[64] compliment a gentleman (Sosiades 24: καλὸν εὖ λέγε; alternatively, "praise what is fine"), mix with the wise (Sosiades 53: σοφοῖς χρῶ), cultivate nobility (Sosiades 30: εὐγένειαν ἄσκει), and get sons of the well-born (Sosiades 138: ἐξ εὐγενῶν γέννα). The "elite consciousness" apparent in the Delphic canon points to the social constituency of the students being educated for leadership within the cities of the eastern Mediterranean basin. Expressed in another way, the *ephebes* were to stick to their social lot (Sosiades 71).

In terms of the curriculum taught and its ethical lifestyle, there are terminological overlaps between the Delphic decree and the Delpic canon. "Zeal" terminology is used in both documents, though the Delphic canon's maxim is heavily restored (FD III 4:59 *l.* 6: σπουδῆ[ς [cf. IEph Ia 6 *l.* 33: τὴν σπουδήν, below]; IG XII 3.1020, no. 2: σ[πουδαῖα μελέτα (?)]). Similarly, παιδεία is also employed, though from the differing perspectives of the benefactor providing "for the advancement of education" (FD III 4:59 *l.* 8: παιδ<ε>ίας) and of the student receiving its benefits (Sosiades 21: παιδείας ἀντέχου; IKyzikos II 2 Col. 1 no. 10: παιδείας ἔχω; cf. Aristotle, *Eth. nic.* 5.2.10). The benefactor's advancement of oratory (FD III 4:59 *l.* 9: λόγων) is also reflected on the Delphic canon's attention to wise speech in a variety of strategic contexts (Sosiades 47 [Aï-Khanum stele 2], 70, 91). In the case of the Delphic decree, φιλοτιμία and its cognates is a circumlocution for the benefactor's financial generosity. Although the imperative τίμα is used in the Delphic canon in a wide range of contexts (e.g. Sosiades 13, 18 [IKyzikos II 2 Col. 1 no. 7], 59, 65), we have seen that χάρις and its cognates is the semantic domain employed for the extension of beneficence and its reciprocal obligations in the Delphic canon. Even where the same terminology

---

[64] See F. W. Danker, *Benefactor: Epigraphic Study of a Graeco-Roman and New Testament Semantic Field* (St Louis: Clayton Publishing House, 1982), 318–20.

is not used, similar ethical sentiments are reflected in different terminology: "kindly" (FD III 4:59 *l.* 4: εὐνοϊκῶς) and "look kindly on all" (Sosiades 93 [IKyzikos II 2 Col. 1 no. 2]: φιλοφρόνει πᾶσιν). Last, intriguingly, the ubiquitous inscriptional word employed for the benefactor's generosity to the gods, their premises and cult personnel – εὐσέβεια and its cognates (cf. FD III 4:59 *l.* 3: εὐσεβῶς; FD IV: 59 *l.* 7: εὐσεβείας) – is missing from the Delphic canon, though piety towards the gods is conveyed by the imperatives τίμα (Sosiades 13, 18), σέβου (Sosiades 3 [P.Athen.Univ. inv. 2782 no. 4]), and προσκύνει (IKyzikos II 2 Col. 2. no. 20).

Second, an Ephesian inscription (IEph Ia 6: II cent. AD) is fascinating because its emphasis is as much on the ethical lifestyle that the gymnasiarch Diodorus transmitted to his young charges as on his own virtues. Thus the decree, fragmentary at places, is a valuable test-case for the impact of values of the Delphic canon in the lives of the young men in the gymnasium (IEph Ia 6 *ll.* 1–37):

1. ἔδοξεν τῆι βουλῆι καὶ τῶι δήμω̣ι̣· Μ̣ίθρης Ἀστέου εἶπεν· προ-
[γραψαμέ]νω̣ν̣ ε̣ἰς̣ τ̣ὴ̣ν̣ βουλὴν τῶν ἀποδεδειγμένων ὑπὸ
[τῶν νέων] Ὀνη[σα]γόρου τοῦ Ἀρτεμιδώρου, Ἑρμ[οκρ]άτου τοῦ
[– κ]αὶ ὑπὲρ Ἀστυάνακτος τοῦ Χαρμολάου Ἀπο-
5. [–]ο[.] ὑπὲρ τι̣μ̣ῶν Διοδώρωι Μέντορος ὅτ[ι]
[αἱρε]θεὶς [γ]υμνασίαρχ[ο]ς τῶν νέων εἰς τὸν ἐνια̣[υτὸν]
[τ]ὸ̣ν̣ ἐ̣πὶ Ἡρακ[λ]είτου [πρ]υ̣τάνεως καλ̣[–]
ἐν [τοῖς] κατὰ τὴν ἀρχὴν [. c.5 .]ραφη[–]
φ[. . c.8 …] ἑ̣α̣υτὸν π̣α̣ρ̣έ̣χων π̣ρ̣οσαξι[–]
10. [–] καὶ τῆς [. c.6 . .] βουλ̣ῆς περι[–]
[–]οετο̣[.] ἐ̣λ̣α̣ίου θ<ἐ>σεως ἐπεμελήθη [–]
[–]ίου οὐκ ἠμέλ̣ησεν δὲ οὐδὲ τῆς τῶν ν[έων]
[–] κ̣α̣ὶ ε̣ὐκοσμίας α̣ἰδῶ παρασκευάζω̣ν̣
[–]ου καταστολῆς καὶ σωφροσύνης τὴν ἀνα-
15. [στ]ρ̣[ο]φὴν ποιούμενος διὰ παντὸς ἐν τῶι τόπ̣ωι, προ-
[ενό]η̣σεν δὲ καὶ τῆς τῶν νέων εὐανδρίας προτρεπόμενο[ς]
[αὐ]τοὺς πρός τε τὰ γυμνάσια καὶ φιλοπονίαν σωματι-
κήν τ̣ε̣ κ̣αὶ ψυχικὴν περὶ πλείστου ποιούμενος ἕνεκεν τοῦ
καὶ λόγωι καὶ ἔργωι συνεπαυξηθῆναι τὸ τῶν νέων ἀξίωμα
20. πρεπόντως τῆι τε περὶ τὸν τόπον διὰ προγόνων ὑπαρχούση[ι]
σεμνότητι καὶ δόξη{ς} τῶν τε λοιπῶν τῶν κατὰ τὸ γυμνάσιον <ἐ>π[ε]-
μελήθη μισοπονήρως τε καὶ φιλαγάθως, ἐν οὐθενὶ ἐνλείπων τῶ[ν]
πρὸς τιμὴν καὶ δόξαν ἀνηκόντων χάριν τοῦ μνήμης ἀξίαν κα[ὶ ἐ]-
π̣αίνου καταστῆσαι τὴν οὖσαν περὶ αὐτὸν αἵρεσιν πρὸς τὰ κάλλ[ισ]-
25. τα· ἀνθ' ὧν οἱ ἔφηβοι καὶ οἱ νέοι τὰς καταξίας προαιρούμενοι κατατ[ί]-
θεσθαι χάριτας ἔκριναν ἐπισήμου τιμῆς, ἀξιώσαντες στῆσαι α[ὐ]-
τ̣οῦ ἀνδριάντα ἐν τῶι γυμνασίωι, προτρεπόμενοι πάντας
ζηλωτὰς γίνεσθαι τῶν καλλίστων πράξεων, ἀποδείξ[αν]-
τες ἄνδρας τοὺς προγραψ<ο>μένους ὑπὲρ τῶν τιμῶν, [οἳ]
30. καὶ ἐπελθόντες ἐπὶ τὸν δῆμον ἐνεφάνισαν περὶ τού-
των· καὶ ὁ δῆμος ἐπεγνωκὼς τὴν τἀνδρὸς φιλοδοξία[ν]

τε καὶ δικαιοσύνην καὶ τὴν γεγενημένην ἐξ αὐτοῦ π[ε]-
ρὶ τὸ γυμνάσιον ἐν πᾶσι τοῖς κατὰ τὴν ἀρχὴν σπουδήν τ̣[ε]
[κ]α̣ὶ ἐπιμέλειαν συνκατέθετο τοῖς παρακαλουμένοις·
35. ὅπως οὖν σταθῇ Διοδώρου ἀνδριὰς ἐν τῶι γυμνασίωι πρ[ὸ]
τῆς στοᾶς τῆς κειμένης πρὸς ἀνατολὴν καὶ [ἐ]π̣ιγρα̣[φῇ]
[ἐ]πὶ τῆς βάσεως [–]

1. Decided by the council and people; Mithres, son of Asteas, moved (it).
on a proposal to the council by those delegated from
[the young men]: Onesagoras, son of Artemiodorus, Hermocrates, son of
[...], and, in lieu of Astyanax, son of Charmolaos, Apo-
5. [..., son of ...], concerning honours for Diodorus, son of Mentor, since
having been elected gymnasiarch of the young men for the year
under Heraclitus as president, (very) well [he conducted himself (?)]
in the matters under his charge [...], [...]
[...] making himself available ... [...]
10. [...] and of the [...] council concerning
[...] ... he took care of the supply of oil [...]
[of ...] he was not neglectful, nor in the case of the y[oung men]
[of their ...] and good bearing, treating them with respect,
[and ...] with understatement and moderation
15. in all respects arranging his life-style in this place,
and he gave attention also to the quality of the young men, both guiding
them in training and, as for love of effort both in body
and in soul, making much of it for the sake of
the reputation of the young men being fostered both in word and deed
20. as befitted both the place's inherited
dignity and fame, and for the remaining gymnasium affairs he took
care, hating the bad and loving the good, in nothing neglectful of what
relates to honour and fame for the sake of the memorable and
praiseworthy establishment of his existing preference for the best.
25. Wherefore the ephebes and young men, desiring very deservedly to register
thanks, decided upon this signal honour, deeming it fit to set up
his statue in the gymnasium, guiding everyone
to become emulators of excellent deeds, delegating
men to bring forward a proposal for the honours, who
30. also approached the people and dilated upon them.
And the people, being familiar both with the man's love of fame
and with his justness, and with his demonstrated
enthusiasm for the gymnasium in everything to do with his charge
and his care (for it), agreed with what was urged.
35. Then so that the statue of Diodorus may stand in the gymnasium before
the stoa that lies to the east, and that there may be inscribed
upon its base [–]

At the outset, it must be recognized that several elements of the ethics of this Ephesian inscription stand outside the semantic domain of the Delphic canon: εὐκοσμία, καταστολή, σωφροσύνη, φιλοπονία and ἐπιμέλεια. Yet there are still several areas of significant overlap: the motif of "justness" (δικαιοσύνη) in the Ephesian inscription (IEph Ia 6 *l.* 32) is heavily elaborated in the Delphic canon (Sosiades 5 [P.Athen.Univ. inv. 2782 no. 8], 27 [IKyzikos II 2 Col. 1 no. 13], 64, 84, 145; IKyzikos II 2 Col. 1 no. 3; IKyzikos II 2 Col. 2 no. 30). The concern for "reputation" (φιλοδοξία) enunciated in the Ephesian inscription (IEph Ia 6 *l.* 31) is also found in the Delphic canon (Sosiades 22 [IKyzikos II 2 Col. 1 no. 11: δόξαν δίωκε], 118 [δόξαν μὴ λεῖπε]). The motif of Diodorus' respect (αἰδῶ) towards the students (IEph Ia 6 *l.* 13) is more extensive in the Delphic canon, ranging from respect for parents (Sosiades 4: γονεῖς αἰδοῦ [P.Athen.Univ. inv. 2782 no. 5]), respect for the elder (Sosiades 126: πρεσβύτερον αἰδοῦ) and, significantly, for oneself (Sosiades 129: σεαυτὸν αἰδοῦ). Finally, Diodorus' direction of the *neoi* in word and deed (IEph Ia 6 *l.* 19: λόγωι καὶ ἔργωι) captures not only the Delphic canon's emphasis on nuanced rhetoric, noted above, but also its moral "work" ethic ("Work at what's worth having": [Sosiades 79])

The striking phrase "hating the bad and loving the good (μισοπονέρως τε καὶ φιλαγάθως)," used of Diodorus (IEph Ia 6 *l.* 22; cf. Rom 12:9; 12:21; 1 Thess 5:21), is also caught up in the Delphic canon in various ways, though with largely different terminology. The reader is to keep away from evil (Sosiades 31: κακίας ἀπέχου [IKyzikos II 2 Col. 1 no. 18]) and to hate evil (Sosiades 119: κακίαν μίσει). But the Ephesian "loving the good" is understood in a patronal manner in the Delphic canon, with the reader being encouraged to honour the "good ones" (Sosiades 65: ἀγαθοὺς τίμα). Not surprisingly, honorific culture is present in both the Ephesian inscription and the Delphic canon. Diodorus' devotion to what is praiseworthy (IEph Ia 6 *l.* 24: ἐπαίνου) is summed up in the Delphic canon as the praise of ἀρετή (Sosiades 26: ἐπαίνει ἀρετήν; IKyzikos II 2 Col. 1 no. 12), a word ubiquitously attributed to benefactors in the honorific inscriptions.[65]

As we have seen, different language can be used with similar intent or synonymous meaning. Diodorus' moderation (σωφροσύνη: IEph Ia 6 *l.* 14) nicely encapsulates the famous Delphic maxim "nothing to excess" (Sosiades 38: μηδὲν ἄγαν [IG XII 30.1020 no. 3]). However, terminology can be used quite differently. For instance, the the *epheboi* and *neoi* are guided to become "emulators (ζηλωτὰς γίνεσθαι) of excellent deeds" (IEph Ia 6 *l.* 28), whereas in the Delphic canon the reader is to pursue wisdom (Sosiades 23: σοφίαν ζήλου).

In conclusion, in considering the intersection between the honorific inscriptions and the Delphic canon, there are significant overlaps of ethical terminology. But, as would be expected, the moral precepts of the seven sages often provide a more expanded and nuanced version of the single moral quality found in

[65] On ἀρετή, see J. Gerlach, ΑΝΗΡ ΑΓΑΘΟΣ (München: J. Lehmaier, 1932), esp. 7–14 on the inscriptional evidence; Danker, *Benefactor*, 318; M.J. Payne, ARETAS ENEKEN: *Honors to Romans and Italians in Greece from 26 to 27 BC* (PhD diss., Michigan State University, 1984), *passim*.

the honorific inscriptions, or expresses the same concept in different words. Significantly, there is a common elitist social viewpoint throughout the honorific inscriptions and the Delphic canon. However, precisely because of the civic focus of the honorific inscriptions, the ethos of self-sufficiency and household ethics present in the Delphic canon are bypassed. In other words, a truncated moral viewpoint emerges if we focus exclusively on the Delphic canon's ethics in their civic expression and how that is reflected in the honorific inscriptions. The other ideological dimensions of the Delphic canon morality remain to be explored in our next section.

Notwithstanding, it is clear that, as far as the public careers for which the *epheboi* and *neoi* were trained in the gymnasium, the ethical code of the seven sages would remain *de rigueur* for the young men from elite families aspiring to leadership within the polis. This is why the later redactors of the Delphic canon continued to inscribe the precepts of the seven sages on steles in the prominent places in the eastern Mediterranean gymnasia for centuries after the death of the sages, and why grammarians and philosophers still chose to set them as preparatory school exercises, aiming thereby at the ethical transformation of each new generation that they taught. Where intersection with the thought of Aristotle's *Nichomachean Ethics* occurs, this is indicated.

6.3. Case Studies in the Ethical Curriculum of the Delphic Canon

6.3.1. Acknowledging the Gods and Providence

We have already touched on the role of providence in the Delphic canon.[66] A prayerful sensitivity to and acceptance of the interventions of providence is advocated in the Delphic canon, with sympathy being extended to those whom fortune strikes down (cf. Aristotle, *Eth. nic.* 1.9.1–3; 1.10.12–13; 4.3.19–21).[67] Consequently, *hubris* is an inappropriate character trait for those familiar with the vagaries of fortune (41: "Hate arrogance" [ὕβριν μίσει; IKyzikos II 2 Col. 1 no. 22]; 83: "Repel arrogance" [ὕβριν ἀμύνου]; 130: "Don't begin raging" [μὴ ἄρχε ὑβρίζειν]).[68] Shame is therefore to be respected (74) and risks to be taken reasonably (120).

[66] See P. Fisk, *Divine Providence in Philo of Alexandria*, TSAJ 77 (Tübingen: Mohr Siebeck, 1999); P. D'Hoine and G. Van Riel, eds., *Fate, Providence and Moral Responsibility in Ancient, Medieval and Early Modern Thought* (Leuven: Leuven University, 2014).

[67] The references to the text of Sosiades below will only be numerical, with supporting documentary references shown in brackets as required. For a full discussion of the motifs of the Delphic canon against the backdrop of Greek ethics, see D. Zeller, "Die Worte der Sieben Weisen–ein Zeugnis volkstümlicher griechischer Ethik," in Althoff and Zeller, *Die Worte der Sieben Weisen*, 107–58.

[68] See N.R.E. Fisher, *Hybris: A Study in the Values of Honour and Shame in Ancient Greece* (Warminster: Aris & Phillips, 1992).

In the case of the god/gods, as we have seen, oracular phenomena are endorsed at a general level, thereby legitimizing the oracles of Zeus at Dodona, Apollo at Delphi, and the various other oracular sites of antiquity. Presumably more popular eastern Mediterranean expressions of the oracular mentality would have also been included under this prophetic rubric (e.g. Acts 16:16a: ἔχουσαν πνεῦμα πύθωνα; 16:16b: αὐτῆς μαντευομένη) and, in early imperial times, the oracles given in honour of the Julian house.[69] Moreover, as we have established, the Delphic canon highlights the necessity of honouring the god/gods, providence and the hearth by a series of imperatives: τίμα, σέβου and προσκύνει (cf. Aristotle, *Eth. nic.* 1.12.3–4).

However, prayer is deeply conservative in the Delphic canon, being constrained in its expectation (Sosiades 52: "Pray for what is possible" [εὔχου δυνατά]), in sharp contrast to the open-ended expectation of Paul (Eph 3:20: ποιῆσαι ὑπερεκπερισσοῦ ὧν αἰτούμεθα ἢ νοοῦμεν).[70] The god/gods, therefore, are the foundation of the hierarchical world-view of the Delphic canon, even if the correlations between the divine realm and the human society are articulated in different ways to the literature of Second Temple Judaism and early Christianity.

6.3.2. Ruling the Household

The hierarchy of the divine realm is reflected within the household relations of the Delphic canon. Parents should be honoured (4 [P.Athen.Univ. inv. 2782 no. 5]; cf. Aristotle, *Eth. nic.* 8.14.4), but wives are to be ruled by their husbands (95: γυναικὸς ἄρχε [IKyzikos II 2 Col. 2 no. 3]; Aristotle, *Eth. nic.* 8.10.5–6; 8.11.4).[71] Sons are to be trained by (presumably) their fathers (44: [IKyzikos II 2 Col. 1 no. 25]), but neither should sons be cursed (94: υἱοῖς μὴ καταρῶ; cf. Eph 6:4; Col 3:21). More positively, the Delphic canon commands the *neoi* to "love those you rear" (124: οὓς τρέφεις ἀγάπα; Aristotle, *Eth. nic.* 8.12.2–3). The twin con-

[69] See S.R. Llewelyn, "Faithful Words," *New Docs* 9 (2002): 9–14, at *ll.* 1–7, § 5:
I, Gaurus, having obtained the prophets'
faithful words and inscribed
the victory of Caesar and the contests
of the gods, through whom by prayers
I grasped all things from start to
finish, and repaying ungrudgingly
the gifts I exult.

[70] On prayer in Graeco-Roman antiquity, see H.S. Versnel, "Religious Mentality in Ancient Prayer," in *idem*, *Faith, Hope and Worship: Aspects of Religious Mentality in the Ancient World* (Leiden: Brill, 1981), 1–64; P.W. van der Horst, "Silent Prayer in Antiquity," *Numen* 41.1 (1994): 1–25; P.W. van der Horst and G. Sterling, *Prayer in Antiquity: Greco-Roman, Jewish and Christian Prayers* (Notre Dame: University of Notre Dame Press, 2000); S. Pulleyn, *Prayer in Greek Religion* (Oxford: Clarendon Press, 1997); P.W. van der Horst and J.H. Newman, *Early Jewish Prayers in Greek* (Berlin: De Gruyter, 2008).

[71] For discussion of the maxim Sosiades 95, see Harrison, "Paul and the Gymnasiarchs," reproduced as Chapter 5.

cerns of social status and family wealth emerge in the advice given to the *ephe-boi* and *neoi* regarding marriage. Above all, they should intend to marry (9: γαμεῖν μέλλε). Further, they were to produce sons of the "well-born" (138: ἐξ εὐγενῶν γέννα). Elite families faced the very real challenge of transmitting inter-generational wealth, status and power, which was constantly put under threat by the high infant and childhood mortality of antiquity. Thus it was strategic to establish elite marriage alliances, producing a son to leave the estate to and a daughter though whose elite marriage the family could acquire a substantial dowry.[72]

Last, weddings are to be kept in check (67: γάμους κράτει [alternatively: "master wedding-feasts" or "control your liaisons"]), though the precise social background of the maxim is uncertain. Here we are confronted by the problem of the changing conventions regarding marriage, family status and dowries spanning the classical era to the early Roman period: how do we determine the original life-situation of the saying under the seven sages and the changed life-situation of its redactors?[73] Which meaning, if recoverable, has priority? The one constant in this scenario is the elitist perspective evinced (cf. Aristotle, *Eth. nic.* 4.1.12–13; 4.2.13–19). Is the maxim advising the son to be careful regarding the unwise multiplication of marriage, either via remarriage upon the death or the divorce of his spouse, with the consequent possibility of dowry disputes,[74] or, alternatively, the divisive issues aroused by differences of social status? Or is the point of concern the control of the wedding-feast itself, with its subtle cultural issues now lost to us?[75] We simply do not know. Either way, the

[72] A. Zuiderhoek, "Oligarchs and Benefactors: Elite Demography and Euergetism in the Greek East of the Roman Empire," in *Political Culture in the Greek City after the Classical Age*, ed. O.M. van Nijf and R. Alston (Leuven: Peeters, 2011), 185–96, esp. 186–87.

[73] The evidence of Theognis (VI cent. BC) perhaps helps us to see the original context of Sosiades' maxim (67). Some elite families, faced with the threat of non-elite social climbers (*Work and Days* 53–58), faced impoverishment because of this new challenge to their traditional public role (173–178, 667–670). Such families sought to salvage their influence by marriages with the wealthy non-elites (183–196, 1109–1114). Is this the type of marriage that, according to the Delphic canon (Sosiades 67), has to be kept in check because it dilutes the aristocracy? See K.A. Raaflaub, "Poets, Lawgivers, and the Beginnings of Political Reflection in Archaic Greece," in *The Cambridge History of Greek and Roman Political Thought*, ed. C.J. Rowe and M. Schofield (Cambridge; Cambridge University Press, 2000), 23–29, esp. 38–39. In a Roman context, the Augustan marriage laws, so A. Wallace-Hadrill argues ("Family and Inheritance in the Augustan Marriage Laws," *PCPS* 27 [1981]: 58–80), were designed to stabalise the transmission of property and social status. See also S. Dixon, "The Marriage Alliance in the Roman Elite," *Journal of Family History* 10 (1985): 353–78.

[74] For dowry disputes in the papyri and Roman law codes, see M.R. Lefkowitz and M.B. Fant, *Women's Life in Greece and Rome: A Source Book in* Translation, 3rd ed. (London: Duckworth, 2005), §§ 104–06, 137, 149–50. On social status and marriage in the Roman law codes, see *ibid.*, §§ 128–129.

[75] On Roman marriages and their rituals, see K.K. Hersch, *The Roman Wedding: Ritual and Meaning in Antiquity* (Cambridge: Cambridge University Press, 2010).

ritual of marriage can be problematical when elite families are involved, requiring careful supervision by fathers and sons.

6.3.3. Maintaining Indifference by the Cultivation of Self

How, then, were the *epheboi* and *neoi* to maintain an unruffled indifference to the blows of fortune, while pursuing a lifestyle of commitment to the welfare of polis commensurate with the provincial elites to whom they belonged? The Delphic answer is found conceptually in a triad of self, summed up in three σεαυτόν maxims. These congregate around the motifs of self-knowledge, self-control, and self-interest.[76] By means of a careful consideration of the σεαυτόν maxims, the character of the *ephebos* and *neos* is imbued with integrity (54: "Test character" [ἦθος δοκίμαζε]; "Be ashamed of falsehood": IKyzikos II 2 Col. 2 no. 27), prudence (17) and wisdom (23, 53). The cultivation of Delphic indifference is seen in the absence of worry (90, 133, 137) and envy (60) or, alternatively, the praise (or deprecation?) of hope (62), and not suspecting anyone (56).

First, the famous Delphic maxim, "Know/Recognise yourself" (8: σαυτὸν ἴσθι [IG XII 3.1020, no. 4]), is given ethical expression through the language of "knowledge": "Know that you are a stranger" (12), "Act on knowledge" (50), and "Speak when you know" (88). In each case, an accurate self-knowledge does not lead to self-absorption but rather to an astute self-awareness that expresses itself in informed actions and speech.

Second, the famous Delphic maxims, "Control yourself" (14: ἄρχε σεαυτοῦ) and "Nothing to excess" (38: μηδὲν ἄγαν [IG XII 3.1020, no. 3]), find a series of ethical applications within the wider canon. Thus, in terms of self-control, the wise man keeps his temper (16), subdues pleasure (IKyzikos II 2 Col. 1 no. 5), envies no-one (60), controls his expenses (72), is satisfied with what he has (73), controls his eye (102), keeps secrets (108 [IKyzikos II 2 Col. 2 no. 16]), and, last, fears what controls him (109 [IKyzikos II 2 Col. 2 no. 17]). Intriguing, too, is the way the Delphic canon articulates the progressive loss of self-control if self-discipline is not brought to bear in each instance: anger (16 [IKyzikos II 2 Col. 1 no. 2], enmity (29 [IKyzikos II 2 Col. 1 no. 16]), violence (89) and murder (51), Finally, the link between the two famous Delphic maxims (14, 38), noted above, is crucial. Self-control provides the restraint required for the avoidance of moral excess, whether that is a myopic quest for virtue that leads to disaster – such as the unrestrained quest for glory – or a reckless plunge into moral dissolution.

Third, another important σεαυτόν maxim from the Delphic canon is "Look after yourself" (96: σεαυτὸν εὖ ποίει [IKyzikos II 2 Col. 2 no. 4]). The "self-interest" underlying the Delphic canon is the final strut to the triad of self, men-

[76] Aristotle, *Eth. nic.* 9.8.7 (cf. 9.8.11): "Therefore the good man ought to be a lover of self (φίλαυτον)."

tioned above. As such, a considered focus on the self allows the *epheboi* and *neoi* to develop the internal resilience required in order to avoid the extremes of vices and virtues that would divert them from the ethical mean. Thus they are to look for advantage (110 [IKyzikos II 2 Col. 2 no. 25]), avoid any commitment or pledge because they will pay for it (69 [IG XII 3.1020 no. 1]), look after their own things (33 [IKyzikos II 2 Col. 1 no. 20]), accept their opportunity (111 [IKyzikos II 2 Col. 2 no. 21]) and take care (61).

6.3.4. Engaging in Social Relations in the Polis

The Delphic canon, despite its relentless singular imperatives and concentration upon the virtues of the self, is nevertheless interested in how ethics are lived out in social relations, especially within the context of the ancient polis. At the outset, we will bypass the clear indications of social elitism and the maintenance of the social convention of friendship in the Delphic because they have already been highlighted.[77] But what other motifs appear in the Delphic maxims that would equip the *ephebos* and *neos* for his civic context?

First, honorific culture, with its relentless quest for glory, features prominently in the ethical maxims. We have already seen that the imperative τίμα is an important leitmotiv in the Delphic canon (cf. Aristotle, *Eth. nic.* 1.4.4–5; 4.3.17–18; 4.4.1–6), whether it is honouring the hearth (13), providence (18 [IKyzikos II 2 Col. 1 no. 7]), benefactions (59), or the "good ones" (65). The forefathers of the city are also to be crowned (131), the standard honorific award in the eulogistic inscriptions.[78] Also the quest for glory features throughout the Delphic canon (22: 'Pursue glory'; 99: "Toil gloriously" [IKyzikos II 2 Col. 1 no. 7]). The glory accrued is either be military (132: "Die for your country") or personal (118: "Don't let your reputation go"). Precisely because glory is passed from generation to generation, the dead should not be mocked (134).

Second, an interesting emphasis within the canon is on the relationship between the generations. A doublet captures the teaching well: 'Respect the elder (126); "Teach the younger" (127). However, given that the inscriptional copies of the Delphic canon were erected in the gymnasia, the pedagogic culture of the gymnasium that is to be instilled in the young men is of intrinsic interest to the Delphic canon. Hence, in highly traditional terms, they are to hold to training (21: παιδείας ἀντέχου [IKyzikos II 2 Col. 1 no. 10]) and take up philosophy (48).

[77] See D. Konstan, *Friendship in the Classical World* (Cambridge: Cambridge University Press, 1997).

[78] See J. R. Harrison, "'The Fading Crown': Divine Honour and the Early Christians," *JTS* 54.2 (2003): 493–529; W. Slater, "The Victor's Return, and the Categories of Games," in *Epigraphical Approaches to the Postclassical Polis: Fourth Century BC to Second Century AD*, ed. P. Martzavou and N. Papazarkadas (Oxford: Oxford University Press, 2013), 39–63.

Third, avoiding civic and personal strife is another important moral emphasis to be instilled in the *epheboi* and *neoi*. The Delphic canon features the well-known motif of *homonoia* ("Practise/Pursue consensus": 107 [ὁμόνοιαν δίωκε]; IKyzikos II 2 Col. 2 no. 14, [ὁμόνοι[αν] ἄσκει]; cf. Aristotle, *Eth. nic.* 9.6.1–4), a word employed by the popular philosophers in discussing intercity rivalries (Dio Chrysostom, *Or.* 37–41).[79] Another word unveiling the destructive rivalries present within the civic context is *eris* ("Hate strife": 80 [ἔριν μίσει]). Hesiod attributes a positive and a negative role to *eris* in his *Works and Days* (*ll.* 14–23), either referring to a competitive striving which is beneficial for the welfare of the community, or, conversely, to a negative striving that results in war and contention. Clearly the original sage responsible for the maxim opted for the negative connotation of the word.

Fourth, the traditional benefaction system, with its rituals of reciprocity (Aristotle, *Eth. nic.* 4.3.24–25; 8.13.7–9; 8.14.4),[80] is endorsed in the Delphic canon through the language of grace (χάρις and cognates): 37 ("Favour a friend"), 45 ("Do a favour when you can"), 75 ("Return a favour" [I Kyzikos II 2 Col. 1 no. 14]), and 136 ("Favour without harming").[81] The last maxim is revealing because of its acknowledgement of how easily benefaction rituals can go astray if they are not handled with care.[82] The maxim "Give what you mean to" (58) carries considerable social force when one remembers Dio Chrysostom's public shame (*Or.* 40.3–4) over not providing promptly enough the public works that he had promised to his native city Prusa (139: "Make no-one a promise").[83] Conversely, the language of "honour" (τιμάω) is linked to reciprocity rituals in the return of honour for benefactions (58: "Honour benefactions"; cf. 55: "Give back what you take/receive" [λαβὼν ἀπόδος]). Therefore *pistis*, on behalf of the benefactor and the recipient, is paramount if the reciprocity system is to work smoothly (IKyzikos II 2 Col. 2 no. 29: "Don't [give up?] trusting" [πιστεύων μὴ α[–]).[84]

---

[79] See H.C. Baldry, *The Unity of Mankind in Greek Thought* (Cambridge: Cambridge University Press, 1965); A.R.R. Sheppard, "Homonoia in the Greek Cities of the Roman Empire," *Anc.Soc.* 15–17 (1984–1986): 229–52; D.B. Martin, *The Corinthian Body* (Chelsea: Yale University Press, 1995), 38–68. On the Concordia-Homonoia cult, see G. Thériault, *Le culte d'Homonoia dans les cités grecques* (Lyon-Québec: Collection Maison de l'Orient 26, série épigraphique 3, 1996). On the *homonoia* coinage of Asia Minor, see J.P. Lotz, "The 'Homonoia' Coins of Asia Minor and Ephesians 1:21," *TynBul* 50.2 (1999): 173–88.

[80] See J.R. Harrison, *Paul's Language of Grace in Its Graeco-Roman Context*, WUNT II 172 (Tübingen: Mohr Siebeck, 2003).

[81] Aristotle (*Eth. nic.* 5.5.7) refers to the shrine of the Graces being placed in a public place as a perpetual reminder to return a kindness.

[82] Dio Chrysostom, *Or.* 68–72, 78.

[83] Dio Chrysostom, *Or.* 40.312–13.

[84] See B. Cueto, *Paul's Understanding of* pistis *in Its Graeco-Roman Context* (PhD diss., Dallas Theological Seminary, 2012); T. Morgan, *Roman Faith and Christian Faith:* Pistis *and* Fides *in the Early Roman Empire and Early Churches* (Oxford and New York: Oxford University Press, 2015).

Furthermore, in the benefaction system, there is to be "respect" or "pity" for supplicants (42: ἱκέτας αἰδοῦ [IKyzikos II 2 Col. 1 no. 24: ἱκέτας ἐλέει]). We should not confuse here the Christian concept of "mercy" with Graeco-Roman "mercy" and "pity": "mercy" (*clementia*), as Seneca informs us, was to be extended to suppliants, not "pity" (*misericordia*). The wise man, guided by *clementia*, has a serenity that is not clouded – in the viewpoint of the Stoics – by the plight of others, or by strong emotions such as sorrow (Seneca, *Clem.* 2.4–5; 2.7.1, 3).[85] Thus Sosiades' version, articulating "respect" for suppliants, is be preferred to the Kyzikos' inscriptional rendering of "pity", given the several occurrences of "respect" in the Delphic canon (4 [P.Athen.Univ. inv. 2782 no. 5], 126, 129).

Fifth, the Delphic canon sponsors a lifestyle of social engagement through the *ephebos* and *neos* learning to pause and listen to those he encounters (7: "Listen and learn"; 35: "Always listen"; 78: "Look and listen"), as well as being sociable (32 [IKyzikos II 2 Col. 1 no. 19]), approachable (97), fitting in with everyone (43), and considerate (106).

Sixth, in view of the prominence of public oaths in civic rituals in antiquity,[86] the maxim "Use no oath" (19 [IKyzikos II 2 Col. 1 no. 8]) is perhaps surprising. The maxim may well be limited to the sphere of personal relations, being in harmony with "Make no-one a promise" (39). More likely, however, the saying is a terse reminder about the drastic consequences of the divine curses invoked upon those who violate their oaths, as the loyalty oaths to the early imperial rulers illustrate.[87] In such a context, it is better to make no oath at all if one is reluctant to make full commitment to its agreed terms.

6.3.5. Virtue as the Median Point between Behavioural Extremes

How are these diverse motifs integrated within the lifestyle of those committed to the ethical paradigms of the Delphic canon? In my opinion, the seven sages anticipate in their thought, to some degree, the "ethical mean" of Aristotle's *Nichomachean Ethics* (2.2.1–2.9.9). Most probably, the redactors of the Delphic canon would possibly have been familiar with Aristotle's moral theory in this regard, and in what follows I will point to areas of Aristotelian intersection throughout.[88] Consequently, we have to negotiate the ethical paradoxes within

[85] For discussion, see Harrison, *Paul and the Imperial Authorities*, 297–99. Additionally, see D. Konstan, *Pity Transformed* (London: Duckworth, 2001).

[86] C.G. Williamson, "'As God is my witness': Civic Oaths in Ritual Space as a Means Towards Rational Cooperation in the Hellenistic Polis," in *Cults, Creeds and Identities in the Greek City after the Classical Age*, ed. R. Alston et al. (Leuven: Peeters, 2013), 119–74.

[87] See Harrison, *Paul's Language of Grace*, 238–41; J.R. Harrison, "Who is the 'Lord of Grace'? Jesus' Parables in Imperial Context," in *Border: Terms, Ideologies and Performances*, WUNT I 336, ed. A. Weissenrieder (Tübingen: Mohr Siebeck, 2016), 383–417.

[88] Gray ("Philosophy of Education," 248–53) argues that late Hellenistic benefactors of gymnasia and *paideia* reflected the impact of Aristotle's thought in their emphasis upon pre-

the Delphic maxims. A few examples will suffice. In terms of finances, one maxim (72) advises "Control expenses", while another (85) stipulates "Use your money". Regarding the issue of personal trust, one maxim warns the reader to fear a trap (46) whereas the advice of another is to suspect no one (56). In a couplet that highlights a contradictory contrast, one maxim stipulates "Don't regret your action" (100), whereas the subsequent maxim commands "If you err, turn back" (101: ἁμαρτάνων μετανόει [IKyzikos II 2 Col. 2 no. 8]). Finally, in another couplet, the considered maxim "Deliberate in time" (103: [IKyzikos II 2 Col. 2 no. 11]; cf. 10: "Pick your time") finds a much more pressing alternative in "Act promptly" (104: IKyzikos II 2 Col. 2 no. 12).

How do we handle such "contradictory" advice, given that there is no recoverable context for understanding each maxim? Is it simply a case of "situation" ethics where each maxim is appropriate for its life-context, to be applied to the particular circumstances that providence allots? Or did the later redactors, well aware of the contradictions, leave them in the Delphic canon unaltered, knowing that the context for the seven sages' sayings was not retrievable? Either option is possible, but I suspect that the redactors subscribed to the Aristotelian idea of an "ethical mean" which, in view of the self-discipline promoted by the σεαυτόν sayings (§ 6.3.3, *supra*), meant that the "contradictory" maxims provided "boundary markers" by which the *epheboi* and *neoi* were to live responsibly (cf. Aristotle, *Eth. nic.* 3.11.8; 4.3.26–28). Thus, diverted from the excesses of virtue and vice by these "contradictory" maxims, the *epheboi* and *neoi* charted their course confidently in morally difficult times.

This suggestion, I propose, is confirmed by other data within the collection of maxims. Within the Delphic canon there are warnings against behavioural extremes negating self-control,[89] whereas there are also exhortations of obedience to behavioural norms enhancing self-control.[90] Clearly, in Aristotle's ethics, a disciplined life steers between the extremes of behavior,[91] lest a vice be-

serving and promoting civic solidarity. As Gray (*ibid.*, 253) concludes, "... it is a result of shared culture and possible diffusion of philosophical ideas." I am proposing that Aristotelian influences also shaped the pedagogical intentions of the early Hellenistic redactors of the Delphic canon as they related its ethics to civic and personal life. The later Hellenistic readers of the canon, too, would probably have understood its diverse teaching in light of the Aristotelian ethical "mean".

[89] E.g., arrogance: 41 (IKyzikos II 2 Col. 1 no. 22); 83; 130. Worry: 137. Envy: 60. Despising others (IKyzikos II 2 Col. 2 no. 15). Temper: 94; IKyzikos II 2 Col. 1 no. 2. Enmity, hatred, and murder: 29 (I Kyzikos II 2 Col. 1 no. 16); 51; 112 (IKyzikos II 2 Col. 2 no. 22); 116 (IKyzikos II 2 Col. 2 no. 28); 125. Slander: 63. Strife: 80.

[90] E.g., "Attest as is holy" and "Judge as is holy": IKyzikos II 2 Col. 1 no. 4; 49. Justice: 16 (IKyzikos II 2 Col. 1 no. 2); 27 (IKyzikos II 2 Col. 1 no. 13); 64; 66; 84 (IKyzikos II 2 Col. 2 no. 13). Repentance: 101 (IKyzikos II 2 Col. 2 no. 8). Prudence: 17. Wisdom: 23; 53. Testing character: 54. Praising hope and virtue: 62; 26 (IKyzikos II 2 Col. 1 no. 12). Modesty: 74. Being considerate and sociable: 106; 32 (IKyzikos II 2 Col. 1 no. 19).

[91] Aristotle, *Eth. nic.* 2.2.7; 2.6.12–14, 20; 2.7.4; 2.9.1; 3.7.13; 4.1.1; 4.1.24; 4.4.4–5; 4.5.1; 4.5.15; 4.8.5; 5.1.1–2; 5.3.1; 5.3.12; 5.4.7.

comes an accustomed habit, or a virtue deteriorates into excessive behaviour. A disciplined life, lived out under providence and exhibiting piety towards the god(s), fosters lasting harmony within the household and the polis. By heeding this ethical curriculum, the *epheboi* and *neoi* would develop into the elite leaders of the polis, ensuring thereby the perpetuation of the divinely ordained hierarchy of the "best".

Last, we might ask what the Delphic canon expected of the *ephebos* and *neos* beyond their life in the gymnasium? Perhaps it could be summed up in two propositions: maintain the training of the gymnasium (21 [IKyzikos II 2 Col. 1 no. 10], 44 [IKyzikos II 2 Col. 1 no. 25], 48 [Aï-Khanum stele 2], 121) and, in light of that precious deposit, learn to age graciously as a mortal (11 [IKyzikos II 2 Col. 2 no. 18, 141, 143–147]; cf. Aristotle, *Eth. nic.* 6.11.7; 9.2.8–9).

We now turn to our discussion of the possibility that *some* among the small but influential elite of the Corinthian house churches (1 Cor 1:26: οὐ πολλοὶ σοφοὶ κατὰ σάρκα, οὐ πολλοὶ δυνατοί, οὐ πολλοὶ εὐγενεῖς) were influenced by the moral and social values of the curriculum of the ancient gymnasium. How did Paul counter their elitist ideology in 1 Corinthians?

6.4. Paul's Pedagogy of Ethical Transformation and the "Wisdom" of the Corinthian Elite

6.4.1. R. S. Dutch and the Impact of Ephebic Culture on the Educated Corinthian Elite

R. S. Dutch has argued that the education model of the ancient gymnasium influenced the educated elite in the Corinthian house churches.[92] Previous scholarship, Dutch observes, has understood the status conflict in the Corinthian house churches from the perspective of several educational models (i. e. the suf-

[92] R. S. Dutch, *The Educated Elite in 1 Corinthians: Education and Community Conflict in Graeco-Roman Context*, JSNTS 271 (London and New York: T&T Clark, 2005). See also now A. G. White, *Where is the Wise Man? Graeco-Roman Education as a Background to the Divisions in 1 Corinthians 1–4*, LNTS 536 (London: Bloomsbury T&T Clark, 2015). On the ancient gymnasium, see J. Delorme, *Le Gymnase: Étude sur les monuments consacrés à l'éducation en Grèce* (Paris: Éditions E. de Boccard, 1960); O. Tzachou-Alexandri, "The Gymnasium: An Institution for Athletic and Education," in *idem*, ed., *Mind and Body: Athletic Contests in Antiquity* (Athens: Ministry of Culture, The National Hellenic Committee I.C.O.M., 1989); D. Vanhove "Le gymnase," in *idem*, *Le sport dans le Grèce antique: Du jeu à la compétition* (Bruxelles: Universiteit Gent, 1992), 57–75; N. M. Kennel, *The Gymnasium of Virtue: Education and Culture in Ancient Sparta* (Chapel Hill: University of North Carolina Press, 1995); D. Kah and P. Scholz, eds., *Das hellenistische Gymnasion* (Berlin: Akademie Verlag, 2004). On the Corinthian elite, see the nuanced summary and evaluation of recent research in L. L. Welborn, *An End to Enmity: Paul and the "Wrongdoer" of Second Corinthians* (Berlin and Boston: De Gruyter, 2011), 230–82.

fering sage, rhetorical education, Epicurean psychagogy, etc.),[93] but he correctly notes that the pedagogic context of the ancient gymnasium context has been ignored in modern discussion. Dutch explores the culture of the gymnasium at Corinth, airing the likelihood that some of the educated elite in the house churches, including Jews, had an ephebic education,[94] either at Corinth or elsewhere (e.g. Egypt), given the mobility of elites in the empire. However, Dutch does not ask to what degree Paul might have been exposed personally to the curriculum and values of the ancient gymnasium, or, indeed, what contact he could have had with *epheboi*, *neoi* and travelling athletes.[95]

The Corinthian believing elite, Dutch proposes, gloried in their ephebic education, transferring the cultural values of *paideia* to their new faith.[96] He sums up the implications in this manner:

> Ephebic education, with its time-honoured status, as an elite system was in conflict with the ethos of the Pauline ἐκκλησία. Conflict in gymnasium and games, and education as a status-determinant, ran counter to the weakness that the apostle Paul portrays to the elite.[97]

To establish his thesis, Dutch examines Paul's engagement with athletic imagery (1 Cor 9:24–27) in its Isthmian games context. Paul's contrast of "milk" and "meat" – applied to the immaturity of Corinthians' spirituality (3:1–4) – belonged to the wider arsenal of pedagogic metaphors, with Philo and Epictetus, in particular, employing the same contrast to highlight the difference between the "milk" of the preliminary Greek gymnasium education and the solid food of philosophy. Dutch links other Pauline images to ephebic pedagogic contexts (1 Cor 1:20; 3:5–9; 4:6) and argues convincingly for the gymnasium context of Paul's reference to the removal of circumcision (1 Cor 7:17–24).[98]

However, Dutch is less successful in establishing a clear connection between the gymnasium and Paul's "fatherhood" imagery (1 Cor 4:15) due to its widespread use in various contexts.[99] Moreover, methodologically speaking, much of Paul's imagery (e.g. 1:20; 3:5–9; 4:6; 9:24–27) was visually ubiquitous in the eastern Mediterranean basin and multivalent in its reference, so it did not neces-

---

93 Dutch, *The Educated Elite*, 58–91.

94 Dutch, *The Educated Elite*, 95–167.

95 See Harrison, "Paul and the Gymnasiarchs," reproduced in Chapter 5.

96 Dutch, *The Educated Elite*, 302.

97 Dutch, *The Educated Elite*, 302.

98 Dutch, *The Educated Elite*, 215–99.

99 See J.R. Harrison, "The Politics of Family Beneficence: Paul's "Parenthood" in First-Century Context (2 Cor 12:14–16)," in *Theologizing in the Corinthian Conflict: Studies in Exegesis and Theology of 2 Corinthians*, ed. R. Beiringer et al. (Leuven: Peeters, 2013), 399–426. "Family" metaphors occur in benefaction decrees as well. It is said of the benefactor in CIG II 2059 that he, giving himself unsparingly to his country, was as a "brother" to the citizens of his own age, to elders as a "son", and to children as a "father". W.P. Clark (*Benefactions and Endowments in Greek Antiquity* [unpub. PhD diss. thesis, University of Chicago, 1928], 261) notes that this decree is highly unusual because it is rare to see "any sign of deep feeling or a sense of 'social solidarity'" on the part of donors in honorific decrees.

sarily require a *specific* gymnasium context.[100] More fundamentally, Dutch largely works at the level of metaphor in Paul's writings, positing a common discourse between Paul's imagery and the ephebic values of the Corinthian educated elite, though the imagery is polemically slanted against the immature Corinthians. Two issues emerge from this overview of Dutch's innovative work.

First, as I have observed elsewhere,[101] Dutch does not enter sufficiently into the important task of cultural *synkrisis* ("comparison"), where the differences, as much as the similarities, between Paul's gospel and the surrounding Graeco-Roman culture are just as revealing as the "parallels" posited by the *Religionsgeschichtliche Schule.* This is not meant to diminish Dutch's valuable contribution to Corinthian studies, but simply to observe that he does not firm in the finer contours of the gymnasium's ethical curriculum against which Paul argues. Second, if my arguments about the elementary school and gymnasium context of the Delphic canon are correct,[102] then we are able to reconstruct many of the cultural assumptions of the educated Corinthian elite from the moral values advocated in the Delphic canon. This is why a comparison of the canon with 1 Corinthians is a valuable addition to previous research on the educational background to the status conflict in the Corinthian house churches. Here we have the opportunity to test beyond the boundaries of "metaphor" the likelihood that Paul is interacting critically with the values of the ephebic curriculum in 1 Corinthians.

6.4.2. Paul, the Ephebic Curriculum, and the Educated Elite in 1 Corinthians

6.4.2.1. Paul and the Gods

In the Delphic canon the curriculum of the ancient gymnasium included piety towards the god/gods. Some of the educated Corinthian believers may well have felt that the gods, while now harmless players in the cosmos (1 Cor 8:4b), none-

---

[100] See J.R. Harrison, "Paul and the Athletic Ideal in Antiquity: A Case Study in Wrestling with Word and Image," in *Paul's World*, PAST 4, ed. S.E. Porter (Leiden: Brill, 2007), 81–109.

[101] Harrison, "Paul and the Gymnasiarchs," 143.

[102] We are not suggesting, however, that the gymnasium was the *only* venue for the continued promotion of the Delphic canon in antiquity. Many aspects of the canon were widely conveyed in the ancient literature (Wilkens, *The Delphic Maxims in Literature*). Nor are we implying that the Corinthians would *only* have had familiarity with the Delphic maxims through the gymnasium-educated elites of the city, whose moral values may have influenced the small inner circle of the socially pretentious within the Corinthian congregation (1 Cor 1:26: "not many wise by human standards"). Undoubtedly maxims of the Delphic canon influenced many of the topoi of popular philosophy from the seventh century BC well into the third century AD. Even the moral exhortation of professional rhetoricians such as Isocrates (436–338 BC) reflected the maxims of the Delphic canon. As Professor Bazzana observed in his written (and verbal) response to my original paper at SNTS in 2014, two Delphic maxims, θεοὺς σέβου (Sosiades 3) and γονεῖς αἰδοῦ (Sosiades 4), "reappear in a slightly mutated form in paragraph 16 of the *Ad Demonicum* (Τοὺς μὲν θεοὺς φοβοῦ, τοὺς δὲ γονεῖς τίμα, τοὺς δὲ φίλους αἰσχύνου, τοῖς δὲ νόμοις πείθου)."

theless belonged to the everyday rituals of civil society, which, as prominent citizens, they still had to engage in culturally in order to maintain their connections and status. Paul's references to the "gods" in 1 Corinthians occurs in his strong condemnation of idolatry (1 Cor 5:11; 6:9), especially in regards to the hubristic behavior and judgemental attitudes of the Corinthian "strong" towards the "weak" regarding food offered to idols and participation in idol's feasts at temples (8:1, 4–5, 7, 10:7, 14, 19–21; 12:2). Precisely because the "strong" were attached to the civic benefits and upward mobility provided by the Federal imperial cult and games held at Corinth,[103] their civic participation in the cultic celebrations of the Julio-Claudian calendar was *de rigeur.*[104]

Paul's strategy in terms of his wide-ranging denunciation of idolatry is thoroughly Jewish (1 Cor 8:4b ["an idol is nothing at all": Deut 6:4–9; 11:13–21; Num 15:34–41], 5a ["so-called gods"], 6a ["one god": Deut 6:4; Ps 136:2–3]; 10:7 [LXX Ex 32:6]; 12:2b ["mute idols": Hab 2:18–18; Isa 46:7; Jer 10:5; Pss 115:5; 136:16]), reflecting the Isaianic denunciation of idolatry (Isa 44:9–20; 46:5–7), among other texts from Second Temple Judaism.[105] Not only does Paul's christologically modified monotheism (1 Cor 8:6) undermine the Graeco-Roman pantheon of deities (8:5b: "gods ... in heaven"), but also it challenges the status-riddled claims of the imperial cult and its clients (8:5b: "gods ... on earth").

In regards to 1 Corinthians 12:2, a lead curse tablet found in the Koutsongila cemetery at Roman Cenchreae (SEG 57.332: mid I cent. AD, or late III cent. AD) is an intriguing find. It is a prayer against a thief who had stolen an item of clothing, with the result that the author of the curse summons the chthonic deities for assistance. The supernatural power of Lord (κυρίος) Abrasax is invoked: "... take revenge and completely mow down the son of Caecil(i)us, O Lord Chan Sêreira Abrasax!" Two texts on a rectangular lead tablet, found in the debris of the southeast quarter of the Sanctuary of Demeter and Kore at Corinth (IV cent. AD), also address the gods of the underworld, either Katachthonois Hermes or Hades, with "lordship" (κυρίος) language: "Lord gods of the underworld –"; "Lord, expose them and – cut their hearts, Lord, by means of the gods of the underworld. THE [- - -]."[106] Possibly we see here something of the con-

[103] See B.W. Winter, *After Paul Left Corinth: The Influence of Secular Ethics and Social Change* (Eerdmans: Grand Rapids, 2001), 269–86.

[104] See, for example, the festival calendar of an Italian temple of Augustus (CIL X 8375: AD 4–14). Tr. F.C. Grant, ed., *Ancient Roman Religion* (New York: The Library of Religion, 1957), 184–85.

[105] E.g. 1 Cor 10:7: cf. Philo, *Mos.* 2.161–162, 270; *Ebr.* 95; *Spec.* 1.79; *LAB* 12; *t. Sotah* 3:10. 1 Cor 12:2b: *Genesis Rabbah* 84:10; *m. Sanh.* 7b. See R.E. Ciampa and B.S. Rosner, *The First Letter to the Corinthians* (Grand Rapids: Eerdmans, 2010) for discussion of the individual texts and references. Additionally, see J.D. Fantin, *The Lord of the Entire World: Lord Jesus, a Challenge to Lord Caesar?* (Sheffield: Sheffield Phoenix Press, 2011), 225–31.

[106] R.S. Stroud, *Corinth Volume XVIII.6. The Sanctuary of Dememter and Kore: The Inscriptions* (Princeton: American School of Classical Studies at Athens, 2013), § 127.

ceptual backdrop to Paul's warning to the Corinthians, including those living in the port city of Cenchreae and at Corinth itself, about being led astray by demonic idols, as they had been in their pre-conversion days (1 Cor 12:2; cf. 10:7, 14–22).

Believers who are led by the Spirit of God, Paul avers, can never say "Let Jesus be cursed!": rather they will always confess "Jesus is Lord" (1 Cor 12:3). Paul was well aware of the various counterfeits of spiritual power available in the ancient world and wanted the Corinthian believers to be absolutely clear about the consequences of their confessional and experiential commitment to the risen Christ. In conclusion, because of their sympathies for the imperial cult and, in other cases, a notional commitment to the "harmless" idolatry of the gymnasium *paideia*, the "strong" at Corinth risked sinning against Christ by judging the "weak" (1 Cor 8:11–12; cf. 2 Cor 13:4) and by sabotaging their own faith through a high-handed disobedience (6:9–11; 10:14–22).

6.4.2.2. Paul and Hierarchy in the Ancient Household and in the Household of God

Paul's comments on the ancient household are indirect in 1 Corinthians. They are either made in response to the Corinthian "ascetics" (7:1, 7a, 8b), who were horrified by the prevailing sexual immorality and, by reaction, were proposing to shun marriage (1 Cor 5:1–3; 6:12–20; 10:5);[107] or alternatively, they were addressed to combat Corinthian divisions over the appropriate attire for the sexes in the worship service (11:2–16). First, over against the hierarchical rule of the husband over the wife in the Delphic canon, Paul's emphasis on the appropriateness of marriage in an immoral and passing age (1 Cor 7:9, 28, 36, 38a) and, consequently, the importance of mutuality in sexual relations, articulates a different vision of human relationships for the ascetics (7:2–7), as does his upending of the hierarchy of master-slave status in Christ for Corinthian believers generally (7:22–23; 12:13).

Second, in contrast to the Delphic canon's directive to produce children from the "well-born", Paul endorses the charism of singleness in service of Christ (1 Cor 7:7 [χάρισμα ἐκ θεοῦ], 8, 27b, 32–35, 38b). Paul's stance could possibly be seen as directed at Augustus' legislation promoting marriage and procreation in the case of men and women (Dion. Hal., 9.22.2; Cassius Dio, *Hist.* 56; Suet., *Aug.* 34).[108] However, whereas Augustus' legislation was aimed at the elites of the state,[109] Paul's intention was to spare the Corinthians from the severity of

[107] See H. Chadwick, "'All Things to All Men' (1 Cor 9:22)," *NTS* 1 (1954–1955): 261–75.

[108] Most recently, see D. A. Reed, *Paul on Marriage and Singleness: Reading 1 Corinthians with the Augustan Marriage Laws* (ThD, University of St. Michael's College, 2013).

[109] See Wallace-Hadrill, "Family and Inheritance."

the famine conditions, viewed eschatologically (1 Cor 7:29–31), precipitating the "present crisis" at Corinth (7:26).[110]

Third, Paul's hierarchicalism, based on creation and Christology, addresses the Corinthian divisions regarding propriety in prayer and prophecy in public worship (1 Cor 11:4–5). The apostle appeals to three parallel relationships of "headship" and "subordination" in order to persuade the Corinthians, living in a Roman colony, to be sensitive to Rome's cultural norms in public worship:[111] that is, Christ and man (1 Cor 11:3a), husband and wife (11:3c, 7–8 [Gen 1:26–27; cf. *Genesis Rabbah* 8:9]),[112] and God and Christ (11:3c). The crescendo culminating the final pairing of God and Christ demonstrates that the "subordinate" partner does not necessarily possess inferior status in the relationship.[113] Christ, while subjected to the Father at the eschaton (1 Cor 15:28), is nevertheless the risen "Lord of glory" (2:8) and the Mediator of creation and salvation (8:6b). Thus Paul corrects the possible implication of an oppressive hierarchical understanding of male and female relationships by underscoring their mutual interdependence in creation and their common identity in God and Christ (1 Cor 11:11–12 [Gen 2:18; cf. 1:27]; v. 11b: ἐν κυρίῳ; v. 12b: τὰ δὲ πάντα ἐκ τοῦ θεοῦ).

I suspect that, given the hierarchical nature of Graeco-Roman society and its gendered order in sanctuary spaces,[114] Paul is trying to negotiate room for a more humane outcome relationally, socially and culturally in the ancient household and in the household of God, so that the Christian community can exhibit more clearly its unity in the Spirit (1 Cor 12:13). In this respect, the Delphic canon's concern for *homonoia* may be seen to have resonances with the apostle's agenda of healing the divided Corinthian church (1 Cor 1:10–13; 3:16–17; 12:4–6, 12–13, 25). But, while there is a nuanced hierarchy in Paul's thought regarding gender relations in the Body of Christ, it is certainly not to be equated with the absolute "rule" over the wife mandated in the Delphic canon. Furthermore, the focus of the pericope (1 Cor 11:3–17) is "ritual discourse firmly situated within the section dealing with ritual gatherings" and not "marital ethics".[115]

Fourth, the same could also be said about the sharply hierarchical text of 1 Corinthians 14:34–35, which is contextually limited to the public evaluation of prophecy in the Body of Christ (14:26–33, esp. v. 29b), as opposed to prophe-

---

[110] See B.W. Winter, "Secular and Christian Responses to Christian Famines," *TynBul* 40 (1989): 86–106; J.R. Harrison, "Times of Necessity," *New Docs* 9 (2002): 7–8, § 4; Reed, *Paul on Marriage and Singleness*, 73–79.

[111] See C.L. Thompson, "Hairstyles, Head-Coverings, and St. Paul: Portraits from Roman Corinth," *Biblical Archaeologist* 51.2 (1988): 99–15; D.W. Gill, "The Importance of Roman Portraiture for Head Coverings in 1 Corinthians 11:2–16," *TynBul* 41.2 (1990): 245–60.

[112] Ciampa and Rosner, *The First Letter to the Corinthians*, 524.

[113] Contra, see J. Økland, *Women in Their Place: Paul and the Discourse of Gender and Sanctuary Space* (London and New York: T&T Clark, 2004), 176–77.

[114] Økland, *Women in Their Place*, 78–130, 224–51.

[115] Økland, *Women in Their Place*, 177.

cy per se (11:5). As with the Delphic canon, oracular speech is highly valued in the Christian assembly (1 Cor 14:3, 4b–5, 6b, 22–26, 29–33), even if in Paul's view it is differently understood to the Delphic model, being orchestrated by the Spirit rather than by the enquirer's question at the sanctuary (Plutarch, *Mor.* 408C).[116] Similarly, in the gifting of the Body of Christ, there is a clearly developed hierarchy among the members (1 Cor 12:28: "first ... second ... third ... then"). However, this hierarchical approach is offset against other equally important interpersonal dynamics. Paul has already established the mutuality of the gifting for the common good (1 Cor 12:7–11), their interdependence as members of the Body of Christ (12:14–21), and the empathy of their common spiritual experience (12:26)

6.4.2.3. Paul and the Cult of the Self

We have noted the centrality of the σεαυτόν maxims in the Delphic canon. In Paul's view, this myopic focus on self, characteristic of the behaviour of the "strong" at Corinth, was anathema for the believer. The Delphic maxim σαυτὸν ἴσθι ("Know yourself") is countered by Paul's noetic emphasis on the Spirit as the revealer of the depths of divine wisdom in the cross of Christ (1 Cor 1:30; 2:9–15, 16b). The *gnosis* of the Corinthian "strong", although orthodox in its belief (1 Cor 8:4b), lacked humility and overlooked how God's covenantal knowledge of his people should be expressed in a cruciform love for fellow believers (8:1–3). In sum, Paul's costly denial of personal rights and pastoral identification with differing ethnic and socio-cultural groups (1 Cor 9:1–22) was ironically based on the athletic self-discipline of the gymnasium (9:23–27; cf. Sosiades 14: "Control yourself" [ἄρχε σεαυτοῦ]), but stripped of its self-centered and self-serving outcomes (Sosiades 51: "Look after yourself" [σεαυτὸν εὖ ποίει]; cf. 1 Cor 10:33; 13:1–13).

6.4.2.4. Paul, Elitism and the Inversion of Honour in Social Relations

The apostle pinpricks the elitism of the Delphic canon and its educated protégés when he reminds the Corinthian believers in 1 Corinthians 1:26 that the σοφοί ("wise"), δυνατοί ("powerful"), and εὐγενεῖς ("well-born") only comprised a small (but highly influential) part of the Corinthian house churches. This is the social constituency from which the *epheboi* and *neoi* of the ancient gymnasium were also drawn, as well as civic benefactors such as Artemidorus and Diodorus, discussed above. Instead, precisely because of the divine foolishness and weakness of the cross (1 Cor 1:18–25; 2 Cor 13:4), God had chosen instead the "fool-

[116] B. Witherington, *Conflict and Community in Corinth: A Socio-Rhetorical Commentary on 1 and 2 Corinthians* (Grand Rapids: Eerdmans, 1995), 287.

ish" (τὰ μωρὰ τοῦ κόσμου), the "weak" (τὰ ἀσθενῆ τοῦ κόσμου), the "low-born" (τὰ ἀγενῆ τοῦ κόσμου), and "the things that are not" (τὰ μὴ ὄντα) to be his elect (1 Cor 1:27–28). By contrast, in the estimation of the Graeco-Roman elites, the lower class Corinthian believers are "despised" objects (1 Cor 1:28b: τὰ ἐξουθενημένα).

The rationale for Paul's radical social upending was God's intention to shame (καταισχύνῃ) the "wise" and "strong" and to nullify (καταργήσῃ) the "things that are" (1 Cor 1:27–28). While Paul's terminology of social "honour" in 1 Corinthians 1:26 cleverly alludes to Jeremiah's call to the wise, mighty and wealthy not to boast in their status and possessions (Jer 9:22–23),[117] the terminology of "dishonour" nevertheless denotes accurately the low social status of the majority of the Corinthians believers (1 Cor 1:27–28). The language of "foolishness" and "weakness" (1:27; cf. 4:10) evokes the marginalised world of the moronic and physically deformed fools of the ancient mime troops, with the result that the Corinthian lower classes are depicted by Paul as objects of derision (1:28: ἐξουθενημένα) and are objectified in a denigrating manner.[118]

This shocking disembowelment of elitist social attitudes on the part of the apostle is pushed to breaking point in the savage pericope of 1 Corinthians 4:8–13. In 1 Corinthians 4:8, Paul depicts the self-satisfied Corinthians as Stoic philosopher-kings satiated with the wisdom and eloquence of their preferred teacher Apollos (1 Cor 1:12; 3:4, 6, 21–23; 4:6),[119] considered by the fickle Corinthians to be superior to their rhetorically inferior apostle (cf. 1:12, 17–31; 2:1–7; 3:4–9, 21–23; 4:6–7, 18–20).[120] The Delphic canon's repeated emphasis on "wise" speech (Sosiades 47 [Aï-Khanum stele 2], 70, 91) is consonant with the widespread adulation showered upon orators in antiquity. In the case of Roman Corinth, orators were regularly honoured in the public inscriptions: Publius Aelius Sospinus, an agonothete, for his "upright character and general excellence,"[121] the "good orator" Maecius Faustinus for "his upright character",[122] and Poseidoni-

[117] Ciampa and Rosner, *The First Letter to the Corinthians*, 104–05.

[118] See L.L. Welborn, *Paul, the Fool of Christ: A Study of 1 Corinthians 1–4 in the Comic-Philosophic Tradition* (London and New York: T&T Clark, 2005), 147–48.

[119] On Graeco-Roman rhetoric and the Corinthian Epistles, see D. Litfin, *St. Paul's Theology of Proclamation: 1 Corinthians 1–4 and Greco-Roman Rhetoric*, SNTSMS 79 (Cambridge: Cambridge University Press, 1994); B.W. Winter, *Philo and Paul among the Sophists*, SNTSMS 96 (Cambridge: Cambridge University Press, 1996); B.K. Peterson, *Eloquence and the Proclamation of the Gospel in Corinth* SBLDS 163 (Atlanta: Scholars Press, 1998); P.J. Hartin, *Apollos: Paul's Partner or Rival?* (Collegeville: Liturgical Press, 2009); C. Mihaila, *The Paul-Apollos Relationship and Paul's Stance toward Graeco-Roman Rhetoric*, LNTS 401 (London: T&T Clark, 2009).

[120] W.A. Meeks, *The Origins of Christian Morality: The First Two Centuries* (New Haven/London: Yale University Press, 1993), 63. See Cicero, *Mur.* 29.61 (cf. 1 Cor 4:8; 2 Cor 6:10).

[121] J.H. Kent, *Corinth Vol. VIII Part III The Inscriptions 1926–1950* (Princeton: The American School of Classical Studies at Athens, 1966), § 226 (third quarter of II cent. AD), abbreviated as IKorinthKent.

[122] IKorinthKent § 264 (mid II cent. AD). Similarly, *ibid.*, § 268: "[The city] by vote of the

us for his primacy as an orator (πρῶτός τε ῥήτο[ρ]).[123] While these moral accolades are entirely conventional, the Corinthian inscriptions underscore the city's obsession with rhetoric because of the precedence and moral reputation it conveyed for its practitioners, as well as the deflected glory it accrued for the sponsors of particular orators. Consequently, some of the Corinthian believers were seduced in their evaluation of their teachers by precisely this rhetorical "celebrity circuit".

Responding to their conceit, Paul renders his apostolate in imagery derived from the gladiatorial arena, depicting the apostles as criminals facing capital punishment in the last event on the day's program (ἐσχάτους: v. 9a), and condemned to fight to the death in a spectacle for all (ἀγγέλοις καὶ ἀνθρόποις).[124] Equally viable, however, is L.L. Welborn's suggestion that imagery of the theatre (θέατρον: v. 9b) underlies Paul's language in vv. 9–11. The apostles are the fools of the mime shows staged (ἀπέδεξεν: v. 9a) by God, involving naked and hungry morons who were beaten up for the audience's amusement, and who were belittled with the vulgar insults traded by the fools in the mime troops (κάθαρμα, περίφημα: cf. 1 Cor 4:13).[125]

The relation of honorific culture to the ancient theatre is also worth considering here. The wealthy elites and other dignitaries were given reserved front row seats of honour in the theatre,[126] the archaeological remains of which are still present in the theatres of Priene, Aphrodisias and Hierapolis.[127] The dishon-

city council (erected this monument to) Marcus Valerius Taurinus, son of Marcus, [a – – – philosopher (and) a good orator] because of [his fine character]"; *ibid.*, § 268: "Peducaeus Cestianus the Apollonian orator."

[123] IKorinthKent § 307 (end of II cent. AD). For other "orator" inscriptions asserting the precedence of the honorand, see IG VII 106 *ll.* 10–11 (Megaris): καί πρῶτον Πανέλληνα, ῥήτορα; *MAMA* 6 List 149, 162 *ll.* 5–6 (Phrygia): [ῥήτ]ορα καὶ πρῶτον [ἐν] τῇ πόλει.

[124] Ciampa and Rosner, *The First Letter to the Corinthians*, 181–82. See now J.R. Unwin, *Subversive Spectacles: The Struggles and Deaths of Paul and Seneca* (PhD thesis, Macquarie University, 2017).

[125] Welborn, *Paul, the Fool of Christ*, 246–47.

[126] The benefactor Poseidippos is honoured with "the front seats at the theatre and the first place in a procession and (the privilege of) eating in the public festivals" (SEG 11 948: Provenance: Cardamylae).

[127] For Priene, see E. Akurgl, *Ancient Civilizations and Ruins of* Turkey, 10th ed. (Istanbul: Net Turistik Yatinlar, 2007), 198, Plate 67 (top). For Aphrodisias, see K.T. Erim, *Aphrodisias: City of Venus Aphrodite* (London: Muller, Blond and White, 1986), 83 (lower picture). See P. Scherrer, ed. (*Ephesus: The New* Guide, rev. ed. [Turkey: Ege Yyinlari, 2000], 160) on inscriptions reserving seats at the theatre of Ephesus for socially important civic groups. Among the few Ephesian fragmentary remains, note: "To individuals from Keramus, a place that was granted by Ulpius Aristocratus, the high priest of Asia of the temples in Ephesus;" "(Place of) the most illustrious (?) council;" "(Place of) … the council of elders;" "(Place of) the *strategos,* leader of the council(?)." For these Ephesian theatre seating inscriptions and their epigraphic references, see T. Jones, *Seating and Spectacle in the Graeco-Roman World* (PhD diss. McMaster University, 2008), 337. For inscriptions reserving seats of honour at the theatre of Aphrodisias, see *ibid.*, 319–26; at the theatre of Hierapolis, *ibid.*, 344–45.

oured apostles, by contrast, shuffle last of all into the theatre, appointed to die or perform there for the entertainment of the highly honoured, including the celestial audience (1 Cor 4:9b). Irrespective of how we interpret the imagery, Paul's explosive contrasts of v. 10 are savage in their irony, contrasting the perceived honour of Corinthian believers and their teachers with the dishonour of the apostles:

The suffering apostles	*The Corinthian believers*
fools (μωροί) because of Christ	wise (φρόνιμοι) in Christ
weak (ἀσθενεῖς)	strong (ἰσχυροί)
dishonourable (ἄτιμοι)	honourable (ἔνδοξοι)

In Paul's portrait of the apostolic life, there is no hint that dishonour is somehow wrong (1 Cor 4:11–12a: cf. "until the present hour", v. 11a; cf. 2 Cor 6:8a: διὰ δόξης καὶ ἀτιμίας [cf. Aristotle, *Eth. nic.* 2.7.7; 4.3.17–20]). Rather in v. 10 Paul contrasts the self-sacrifice and shame of apostolic ministry in service of Christ (1 Cor 4:12b–13) over against the status-riddled rivalries of the Corinthians (4:7–8; cf. 3:1–3, 18, 21; 4:3, 6–7). The responses of the apostles ("bless", "endure", "implore": vv. 12b–13a) to rejection ("reviled", "persecuted", "slandered": vv. 12b–13a) reflect Christ's humble response to dishonour and provocation in his ministry (Matt 5:44; Lk 6:27; 23:34; 1 Pet 2:22–23). Christ's exemplum (2 Cor 10:1: διὰ τῆς πραΰτητος καὶ ἐπιεικείας τοῦ Χριστοῦ; cf. Matt 11:29b) had become for Paul the litmus test for assessing how the perpetrators and circumstances of dishonour should be responded to in each instance.

Not only is the general elitism of the Delphic canon challenged in such a construct, but also, more specifically, its policy of honouring only the good and powerful is exposed as socially bankrupt in Christian ministry. For Paul, then, the least honourable and weakest member is to be the most honourable and indispensable in the Body of Christ (1 Cor 12:22–25). Consequently, the poor were not to be humiliated at the Lord's Supper by the self-serving and preferential behaviour of the wealthy Corinthian elites (1 Cor 11:17–22; cf. Aristotle, *Eth. nic.* 4.2.13). Last, more could be said on issues of the reciprocation of honour and the progress of the Jerusalem collection (1 Cor 16:1–4). But, suffice it to say, at the time of the composition of 1 Corinthians, the issue of (potentially catastrophic) dishonour, arising from the Corinthian failure to finalise collection, had not yet emerged (cf. 2 Cor 9:1–5).[128] Notwithstanding, it is worth remembering that the Delphic canon was alert to how quickly benefaction rituals could unravel to the detriment of the giver and receiver (Sosiades 136 ["Favour without harming"]). Thus the issue of honour, notwithstanding Paul's inversion of its rituals, would remain a point of contention between the apostle and his Corinthian converts.

---

[128] See Harrison, *Paul's Language of Grace*, 294–324.

6.5. Conclusion

This chapter, which is the first major study of the intentionality of the Delphic canon, has argued that the maxims of the famous seven sages were adopted throughout the Eastern Mediterranean gymnasia and the preparatory schools for the ethical guidance of their young charges in the Hellenistic age and early Roman Empire. Our extant documentary remains confirm the order of the late antiquity collection of Sosiades, previously dismissed as unreliable regarding its dominical traditions. The later redactors of the collection, including the obscure Clearchus, would, I have argued, have understood the contradictory traditions within the Delphic canon from the framework of Aristotle's (occasionally unnamed) ethical mean.[129] We have posited that the ethics of the public inscriptions honouring civic benefactors had points of convergence with the elitist world-view of the Delphic canon and with the philosophy of Aristotle. Thus the abiding and geographically widespread influence of the Delphic canon in shaping the thought of popular philosophy and ancient civic ethics has not been sufficiently taken into account by classical and New Testament scholars.

In terms of the pedagogic intentionality of the Delphic canon, I have proposed that the canon espouses the harmonious understanding of one's self and the gods, as well as concord (*homonoia*) in the wide array of social relations that impacted upon the household and the polis, with a view to the resolution of any potential conflicts residing therein. The *epheboi* and *neoi* were taught to shelter themselves from the unexpected vicissitudes of Fortune, while still cultivating the finely tuned balance of indifference and responsibility requisite for social order and personal happiness. The word-view advocated, however, is entirely elitist.

In agreement with R.S. Dutch, I have explored the proposal that the Corinthian elite in 1 Corinthians was enamored by the elitist values of the *paideia* inculcated in the gymnasia of the eastern Mediterranean basin. This is not to suggest that this perspective entirely explains the complex melee of problems that the apostle faced at Corinth. But the addition of the "background" evidence of the Delphic canon allows us important apertures of insight into the (largely invisible to us) conversations occurring behind Paul's text and how the apostle framed his response in reaction to them. Paul's attack on the traditional gods and the upward mobility offered by the imperial cult at Corinth exposed the

[129] The Delphic canon does not nominate specific virtues for the "mean" and specific vices for the "deficit" and "excess", in the same way that Aristotle does. Rather the contradictory maxims in the Delphic canon function as "boundary markers" for charting a safe route to the unspecified ethical mean. However, Aristotle does speak on one occasion of the "unnamed" ethical mean: "Such is the middle character, although it has no name" (*Eth. nic.* 4.6.9). It is likely that the redactors of the Delphic canon thought about its impact in this more general way.

insensitive and self-serving behavior of the Corinthian elite towards the "weak" within the house churches. The hierarchical structure of ancient society made it more likely that self-centeredness would remain the ethical norm. Thus the apostle works towards a more nuanced understanding of hierarchy where more humane outcomes in social relations could emerge. Paul pinpricks the inflated cult of "Self" at Corinth, advocating instead a cruciform denial of personal rights and an incarnational identification with the "weak" and "foolish", as opposed to the "strong' and "wise" (cf. 2 Cor 8:9; 13:4). Last, Paul's breathtaking inversion of "honour" rituals in the Corinthian correspondence mark out the apostle as an innovative social thinker whose impact would ultimately change the boasting culture of antiquity and prepare the way for the triumph of humility and modesty as "virtues", in contrast to the stance of Aristotle (*Eth. nic.* 2.7.14; 4.9.1–8), in the evolution of Western thought.

Chapter 7

The Imitation of the Great Man in Antiquity: Paul's Inversion of a Cultural Icon

7.1. Introduction to the Scholarly Debate on the Motif of Imitation in Paul's Letters

There is no scholarly discussion of *mimesis* (μίμησις: "imitation") that covers the sweep of the ancient literary and documentary evidence. In approaching the topic, modern scholars have gravitated towards the development of aesthetics as an intellectual discipline, analysing the seminal contribution that Plato and Aristotle made to Western literary and artistic theory. In particular, the momentous collision between Plato and Aristotle over the nature of *mimesis* has generated an avalanche of scholarship.[1] In the *Republic*, Plato portrays Socrates as

[1] The literature on the debate between Plato and Aristotle is voluminous. See J. Tate, "Imitation in Plato's *Republic*," *CQ* 22 (1928): 16–23; *idem*, "Plato and Imitation," *CQ* 26 (1932): 161–68; W.J. Verdenius, Mimesis: *Plato's Doctrine of Artistic Imitation* (Leiden: Brill, 1949); H. Koller, *Die* Mimesis *in der Antike* (Bern: Francke, 1954); G. Else, "'Imitation' in the Fifth Century," *CPh* 53 (1958): 73–90; O.B. Hardison, "Epigone: An Aristotelian Imitation," in *Aristotle's Poetics*, ed. L. Golden and O.B. Hardison (Englewood Cliffs: Prentice Hall, 1968), 281–96; L. Golden, "Plato's Concept of *Mimesis*," *British Journal of Aesthetics* 15 (1975–1976): 118–31; *idem*, *Aristotle on Tragic and Comic Mimesis* (Atlanta: Scholars Press, 1992); K.F. Morrison, *The Mimetic Tradition of Reform in the West* (Princeton: Princeton University Press, 1982), 5–31; E. Belfiore, "A Theory of Imitation in Plato's Republic," *TAPA* 114 (1984): 121–46; A. Nehamas, "Plato on Imitation and Poetry in *Republic* 10," in *Plato on Beauty, Wisdom, and the Arts*, ed. J.M. Moravcsik and P. Temko (Totowa: Rowman and Allenheld, 1982), 47–78; P. Woodruff, "Plato on *Mimesis*," in *Encyclopaedia of Aesthetics Volume 3*, ed. M. Kelly (New York: Oxford University Press, 1998), 521–23; S. Halliwell, *The Aesthetics of Mimesis: Ancient Texts, Modern Problems* (Princeton: Princeton University Press, 2002); B. Earle, "Plato, Aristotle, and the Imitation of Reason," *Philosophy and Literature* 27.2 (2003): 382–401; S. Tsitsiridis, "*Mimesis* and Understanding: An Interpretation of Aristotle's *Politics* 4.1448B4–19a," in *Mimesis: The New Critical Idiom*, ed. M. Potolsky (New York and London: Routledge, 2006), 15–46; M. Potolsky, *Mimesis* (Abingden: Routledge, 2006); *idem*, "Poetry Is More Philosophical than History: Aristotle on *Mimesis* and Form," *The Review of Metaphysics* 64.2 (2010): 303–36; *idem*, "Plato on *Mimesis and* Mirrors," *Philosophy and Literature* 36.1 (2012): 187–95; J. Risser, "On the Threefold Sense of *Mimesis* in Plato's Republic, *Epoché* 17.2 (2013): 249–56; W.B. Stevenson, "From Catharsis to Wonder: Tragic *Mimesis* In Aristotle's *Poetics* and the Catholic Imagination," *Logos* 20.1 (2017): 64–75. Ironically, literary scholars have brought the classical debate on aesthetics into dialogue with the Christian gospels, a discussion that New Testament scholars have not pursued. Note the comment of O.D. Baban (*On the Road Encounters in Luke-Acts: Hellenistic* Mimesis *and Luke's Theology of the Way* [Milton Keynes: Paternoster, 2006], 73): "Contemporary NT scholarship has explored sur-

arguing that poetry imitates reality.[2] Subsequently, Socrates asserts that the artist – whether poet, painter or tragedian – only captures a reflection of the world at a third remove from its true essence.[3] In the view of Plato, therefore, only those artists who imitate noble actions should be allowed into the ideal state.[4] Although Aristotle agrees with Plato that the ideal work of art should express what it seeks to imitate,[5] his view is diametrically opposed to Plato's because of its cathartic rationale: that is, when people view evil actions in a dramatic performance of tragedy, they can be emancipated from the desire to act badly by being moved to pity.[6] This philosophical debate is central to the devel-

---

prisingly little how deeply *mimesis* was ingrained in Hellenistic story-telling, and, hence, in NT writings." E. Auerbach (*Mimesis: The Representation of Reality in Western Literature* [New York: Anchor Books, 1957, Gmn. orig. 1946]) argues that modern Western realism, emanating from the early nineteenth century French realist writers (Stendahl, Balzac), broke aesthetically from the classical rule of distinct levels of style. In seeking precedents for this, Auerbach posits that the *first* break with the classical tradition came about because of the Christian gospel: "It was the story of Christ, with its ruthless mixture of everyday reality and the highest and most sublime tragedy, which had conquered the classical rule of styles" (*ibid.*, 490). However, the same comment could apply equally to Paul's graphic portrait of the incarnate and crucified Christ as "weak", "poor" and "foolish" (1 Cor 1:18–30; 2 Cor 8:9; 13:4). On the social and artistic dimensions of the Pauline metaphors of foolishness and poverty, see J. R. Harrison, *Paul's Language of Grace in Its Graeco-Roman Context*, WUNT II 172 (Tübingen: Mohr Siebeck, 2003) 250–68; L. L. Welborn, *Paul, the Fool of Christ: A Study of 1 Corinthians 1–4 in the Comic-Philosophic Tradition* (London and New York: Continuum, 2005), *passim*.

[2] Plato, *Resp.* 3.392d–398b.

[3] Plato, *Resp.* 10.597e: "Then this will also be true of a tragedian, if indeed he is an imitator and is by nature third (τὸν τοῦ τρίτου ἄρα γεννήματος ἀπὸ τῆς φύσεως μιμητὴν καλεῖς) from the king and the truth, as are all other imitators." In Plato's view, *mimesis* is removed from reality because two other creators already exist: namely, ὁ φυτουργός (the real maker of the world in its divine essence: *Resp.* 10.597d) and ὁ δημιουργός (the craftsman who creates images of the divine essence: *Resp.* 10.596c–d). Thus *mimesis* struggles to replicate the original divine essence of the world because of its excessive distance from the original: it merely provides an appearance, a phantasm, an inferior copy of a copy (*Resp.* 10.598b; *Soph.* 236b). Plato, however, does speak positively of the accuracy of *mimesis* in representing reality (Plato, *Leg.* 668a–b; *Tim.* 47b–c). In this regard, Baban (*On the Road Encounters in Luke-Acts*, 91–92) correctly notes that Plato's view of *mimesis* is "ambiguous, dualistic" (*ibid.*, 92), sometimes accepting imitation within specific constrictions, but normally excluding it in other contexts.

[4] Plato, *Resp.* 3.395a–3.396d. However, Plato brought a series of charges against poet-tragedians such as Homer and wanted to ban the poetic arts. For discussion, see Baban, *On the Road Encounters in Luke-Acts*, 92–93. In Plato's view, there is no worthwhile knowledge purveyed by poetry (*Apol.* 22b–c; *Ion* 534a) because it relies on inspiration (*Ion* 34b–e; *Phaedr.* 245a) and propagates falsehoods (*Resp.* 1.337–3.391). Poetry is idiosyncratic and irrational (*Resp.* 10.605c), articulating private opinion as opposed to universal truth (*Prot.* 347c–e). In sum, *mimesis* is "an inferior child born of inferior parents" (*Resp.* 10.603b). It would be preferable for the ideal state to exclude all imitation (*Resp.* 10.595a) and to eliminate poetry entirely from Greek culture (10.607a).

[5] Aristotle, *Poet.* 6.1450a; 9.1451b; 23.1459a; 24.1460b; 25.1461b; 26.1461b–1462b. Cf. *idem*, *Phys.* 2.2.194a: "art imitates nature." Moreover, art brings to completion nature's deficiencies (*idem*, *Phys.* 2.2.199a; *Pol.* 7.17.1337a). For an excellent discussion, see Morrison, *The Mimetic Tradition*, 10–26.

[6] Aristotle, *Poet.* 1449b 24–28: "Tragedy is the *mimesis* of a serious and complete action of

opment of the Western intellectual tradition in the arts and in ethics. However, the failure of many modern scholars to move outside of the confines of the ancient debate on the role of *mimesis* in aesthetics has meant that the public context of imitation in civic life remains largely unexplored. The centrality of honour culture in the Greek East and the Latin West ensured that the imitation of the "great man" was a vital dimension of civic ethics in antiquity: but, inexplicably, this has been little discussed by classicists and New Testament scholars alike.[7]

This consuming interest in aesthetics on the part of classicists and literary theorists is not unexpected: it simply reflects the sharply focused discussion of the ancient philosophers on *mimesis* in antiquity. K.F. Morrison observes that the Greek philosophers had nominated three areas in which *mimesis* occurred: namely, (a) the realm of nature; (b) the realm of art; and (c) the realm of moral reproduction, facilitated by the mediation of nature and art. Morrison concludes that Paul, as a mimetic thinker, concentrates on the third realm at the expense of the other two realms, whereas Philo embraces all three realms in his thought.[8] Morrison's comment helps us to situate Paul as ethical thinker who drew selectively on the mimetic traditions in the Graeco-Roman world and Second Temple Judaism. In the case of New Testament scholars, however, few have been willing to explore the Graeco-Roman context of "imitation," with a view to relating its evidence to the mimetic concerns of Paul's letters. The oversight is surprising, given the overlap of the language of imitation (μιμητής: "imitator"; μιμεῖσθαι: "to imitate") in the Graeco-Roman and early Christian traditions.[9]

---

some magnitude; in language embellished in various ways in its different parts; in dramatic, not narrative form; achieving though pity and fear, the catharsis of such passions." See K.F. Morrison, *The Mimetic Tradition*, 21–22; N. Pappas, "Aristotle," in *The Routledge Companion to Aesthetics*, ed. B. Gaut and D. McIver Lopes (London and New York: Routledge, 2001), 15–26. Plutarch, too, refers to the educative value of negative examples as much as positive mimetic examples (*Demetr.* 1.4–6). See also *Socratics* 28.10 (A.J. Malherbe, *The Cynic Epistles* [Atlanta: Scholars Press, 1977], 291).

[7] Note the comment of J.E. Lendon regarding the link between honour and imitation (*Empire of Honour: The Art of Government of the Roman World* [Oxford: Oxford University Press, 1997], 46): "A natural consequence of the ascription of honour by the aristocratic community, of aristocrats regulating their conduct by close attention to the opinion of those around them, was the ostentatious imitation of celebrated men."

[8] Morrison, *The Mimetic Tradition*, 42, 47. In the case of Philo, the evidence regarding μιμέομαι and its cognates is categorised as follows: (a) the realm of nature: *LA* 1.48; 2.4; *Opif.* 25, 133, 139; *Migr.* 40; *Heres.* 165; *Aet.* 15; (b) the realm of art: *Mut.* 208; (c) the realm of moral reproduction: *Sac.* 65; *Mos.* 1.303, 158; 2.11; 4.173, 188; *Virt.* 66, 161, 168; *QG* 1.64a; *LA* 1.45; *Sac.* 30, 86; *Det.* 45, 83; *Post.* 135, 185; *Migr.* 133, 149, 164; *Heres.* 112; *Abr.* 38; *Decal.* 111, 114; *Spec.* 2.2, 135; *Prob.* 94; *Aet.* 2; *Legat.* 86–87. In the case of Josephus, the evidence regarding μιμέομαι and its cognates is categorised as follows: (a) the realm of nature, in contrast to Philo, is bypassed; (b) the realm of art: *AJ* 1.19; (c) various individuals: *AJ* 1.12, 68; 4.154; 5.98, 129; 6.143, 341, 347; 7.126; 8.193, 196, 251, 300, 315, 316; 9.44, 99, 243, 282; 12.203; 13.5; 15.271; 17.109, 110, 244; *Ap* 2.130, 270, 283.

[9] For the Pauline "imitation" terminology, see μιμητὴς γίνεσθαι ("to become an imitator"):

So far, there have only been three major works written in English devoted exclusively to the motif of "imitation" in the letters of Paul.[10] First, W.H. de Boer's important monograph, published in 1962, still remains an important exegetical discussion of the topic. However, although de Boer thoroughly investigates the Jewish context of imitation, he only briefly explores the Graeco-Roman writers, concentrating mainly on the cosmological thought of Hippocrates and the aesthetics of Plato.[11] Consequently, de Boer ignores the civic context of Graeco-Roman *mimesis*, a methodological flaw in his study. According to de Boer, the mimetic context of the teacher-pupil relationship in the Greek world was determinative for Paul.[12]

However, de Boer's "educational" model for Pauline *mimesis* does not do justice to the urban context of Paul's ministry. Although Paul sometimes casts himself in the role of the "gentle" philosopher with his converts (1 Thess 2:1–12),[13] he carried out his missionary outreach in the eastern Mediterranean *poleis* in ways that do not easily align with the teaching practice of contemporary philosophers. He does not fit the model of the teacher who lectured permanently at an established philosophical school (*pace*, Acts 19:9–10), or who travelled city-to-city begging like the Cynics (1 Thess 2:5–9; 2 Thess 3:7–8; 1 Cor 9:1–18; 2 Cor 12:14–15), or who, like the fee-charging sophists, was sponsored salon-to-salon by the wealthy elite (*pace*, Rom 16:1–2, 23; Acts 16:14).[14] New Testament

1 Thess 1:6; 2:14; 1 Cor 4:16; 11:1; Eph 5:1; μιμεῖσθαι ("to imitate"): 2 Thess 3:7, 9; συμμιμηταὶ γίνεσθαι ("to become imitators together"): Phil 3:17.

[10] W.P. de Boer (*The Imitation of Paul: an Exegetical Study* [Kampen: J.H. Kok, 1962], xii) notes: "The literature specifically dealing with the subject of the imitation of Paul is very limited." The judgement of de Boer still remains largely true almost five decades later. We will bypass H.D. Betz's suggestion that Paul's understanding of imitation is derived from the mystery cults (*Nachfolge und Nachahmung Jesu Christi im Neuen Testament* [Tübingen: Mohr Siebeck, 1967], 48–83). For a sound critique of the methodological flaws underlying Betz's case, see V.A. Copan, *Saint Paul as Spiritual Director: An Analysis of the Concept of the Imitation of Paul with the Implications and Applications to the Practice of Spiritual Direction* (Nottingham: Paternoster, 2007), 43. B. Fiore (*The Function of Personal Example in the Socratic and Pastoral Epistles* [Rome: Biblical Institute Press, 1986], *passim*) has extensively explored the teacher-pupil relationship from the perspective of the Socratic tradition in the Pastoral Epistles of the "Pauline School". However, since we are exploring the civic context of imitation, we will not discuss the mimetic context of the teacher-pupil relationship, except where the inscriptional evidence eulogises a tutor (§ 7.2.4.1).

[11] See de Boer, *The Imitation of Paul*, 1–50. The earlier work of E.J. Tinsley (*The Imitation of God in Christ: An Essay on the Biblical Basis of Christian Spirituality* [London: SCM Press, 1960], 27–64) demonstrates the same unbalanced emphasis as W.H. de Boer's monograph in regards to the Graeco-Roman evidence. For a more comprehensive coverage, see W. Michaelis, "μιμεῖσθαι," *TDNT* 4 (1967): 659–74.

[12] De Boer, *The Imitation of Paul*, 25.

[13] A.J. Malherbe, *Paul and the Popular Philosophers* (Fortress: Minneapolis, 1989), 35–66.

[14] See E.A. Judge, "First Impressions of St Paul," and "The Early Christians as a Scholastic Community," in *idem*, *The First Christians in the Roman World: Augustan and Roman Essays*, WUNT I 229, ed. J.R. Harrison (Tübingen: Mohr Siebeck, 2008), respectively, 410–15, 526–52. For a "Cynic" model of Paul, see F.C. Downing, *Cynics, Paul and the Pauline*

scholars like de Boer would have been better served in investigating how the mimetic models of civic leadership in the late Hellenistic age – articulated in the eulogistic inscriptions of local city benefactors and visually reinforced by their statues in the public spaces – interacted with the pattern of leadership in Paul's house churches.[15] This is the mimetic context of the house churches in which Paul ministered city-by-city in the eastern Mediterranean basin.

Further, E. A. Judge has argued from a careful study of the Latin names found in the inscriptions of the eastern Mediterranean *poleis* that Paul's co-workers and the chief patrons within his network of communities were drawn from the socially advantaged who were used to travel on business – i. e. Roman citizens and those with Latin status – in the Roman world.[16] Thus the late republican and early imperial understanding of *imitatio* represents another important paradigm of leadership, overlooked by classical and New Testament scholars, which should be considered in our study. How did Paul's understanding of mimetic leadership engage with the paradigm of leadership found in the statue program of the *forum Augusti*? Augustus had intended that his conception of his place in history – revealed in the *Res Gestae* and in his elaborate statue program in the forum – should be emulated by a new generation of Roman leaders.[17] The visual and documentary evidence, therefore, has been sidelined in

Churches (London and New York: Routledge, 1998). Downing (*ibid.*, 194–202) also proposes that there are Cynic resonances to Paul's call to his converts to imitate himself (1 Cor 11:1). However, R.F. Hock's criticism (*The Social Context of Paul's Ministry: Tentmaking and Apostleship* [Fortress: Philadelphia, 1980], 37, 65) of Judge's portrait of Paul as a "sophist" – which was heavily dependent on the Acts' evidence – does have a certain force. While Paul moved among the houses of the patronal elite at various stages in his missionary career, attracting thereby high-placed patrons (e. g. Rom 16:1–2, 23; Acts 16:14) and influential Latin co-workers (E. A. Judge, "The Roman Base of Paul's Mission," in *idem*, *The First Christians*, 553–67), normally he provided his own funding by working in a socially humiliating trade (Acts 16:14–15; 18:3; 1 Cor 4:11–12; 9:12, 15; 2 Cor 11:7; 1 Thess 2:9; 2 Thess 3:7–8). For an alternate interpretation of σκηνοποιός ("tentmaker") as "maker of stage properties," see Welborn, *Paul, the Fool of Christ*, 111–12.

[15] F.W. Danker's *Benefactor: Epigraphic Study of a Graeco-Roman and New Testament Semantic Field* (St Louis: Clayton Publishing House, 1982) is an outstanding example of the "civic" analysis of leadership in antiquity that I am advocating. For additional works alert to the civic context of Pauline ethics, see W. Meeks, *The First Urban Christians: The Social World of the Apostle Paul* (New Haven: Yale University Press, 1983); *idem*, *The Origins of Christian Morality: The First Two Centuries* (New Haven: Yale University Press, 1993); L. L. Welborn, *Politics and Rhetoric in the Corinthian Epistles* (Macon: Mercer University Press, 1997); B. Blumenfeld, *The Political Paul: Justice, Democracy and Kingship in a Hellenistic Framework* (Sheffield: Sheffield Academic Press, 2001); J. R. Harrison, "Paul and the Gymnasiarchs: Two Approaches to Pastoral Formation in Antiquity," in *Paul: Jew, Greek, and* Roman, PAST 5, ed. S. E. Porter (Brill: Leiden, 2008), 141–78, reproduced as Chapter 5 in this volume.

[16] Judge, "The Roman Base of Paul's Mission."

[17] Lendon (*Empire of Honour*, 129–30) is sensitive to the imitation of the imperial ruler in antiquity. J. K. Hardin (*Galatians and the Imperial Cult: A Critical Analysis of the First-Century Social Context of Paul's Letter* [Tübingen: Mohr Siebeck, 2008], 67, 71–78, 124) points out that that a Latin copy of the *Res Gestae* existed at Pisidian Antioch which Paul visited

discussions of "imitation" in antiquity and its relation to Paul's thought never effectively explored.[18] As a result, the continuity and discontinuity of Paul's leadership ethos with the mimetic traditions of his Graeco-Roman contemporaries has been underestimated in each case.

Second, E.A. Castelli's stimulating monograph on imitation is, in my opinion, too ideologically driven. She comes to the ancient texts and the epistles of Paul with *a priori* suppositions about the nature of power, overlooking how the subtleties of the honour system shaped power relations in antiquity.[19] In viewing Pauline imitation from a Foucaultian perspective,[20] Castelli inevitably distorts the apostle's social and ethical stance.[21] In the view of Castelli, Paul's hierarchical understanding of imitation enforces ideological sameness upon his house churches and denies social exclusivity (i.e. difference). But, in not engaging with the inscriptional evidence relating to imitation in the late Hellenistic and early imperial period, Castelli does not sufficiently reckon with the urban context of Paul's ministry and the mimetic paradigms of leadership that were found throughout the eastern Mediterranean *poleis*.[22] Like de Boer, she argues that the Graeco-Roman educational context provides the lens for understanding Paul's view of imitation.[23]

Paul, I will argue, was urging his urban believers to imitate the crucified Christ over against the much fêted "great men" of the first-century world, each with his own network of hierarchically based patronage. The apostle's establishment of alternate benefactor communities in Mediterranean cities meant that the mimetic ethos of ancient benefaction culture was firmly in his sights as he sought to redefine in Christ the experience and expression of divine and human beneficence for his converts. In this chapter, I will argue that Paul sponsors a model of imitation which up-ends Graeco-Roman conventions of patronal

---

(Acts 14:14–50). Whether Paul as a Roman citizen had any facility in Latin is unknown, though his intention to evangelise in the Latin West probably points to a rudimentary ability in the language on his part (Rom 15:24). See the careful analysis of S.E. Porter, "Did Paul Speak Latin?" in *Paul: Jew, Greek and Roman*, PAST 5, ed. S.E. Porter (Leiden: Brill: 2008), 289–308.

[18] For a methodological discussion of Paul's interaction with the visual evidence of antiquity, see J.R. Harrison, "Paul and the Athletic Ideal in Antiquity: A Case Study in Wrestling with Word and Image," in *Paul's World*, PAST 4, ed. S.E. Porter (Leiden: Brill, 2007), 81–109, reproduced as Chapter 4 in this volume.

[19] See Lendon, *Empire of Honour, passim.*

[20] E.A. Castelli, *Imitating Paul: A Discourse of Power* (Louisville: Westminster John Knox Press, 1991), 35–58.

[21] See the extensive critique of Castelli's work in Copan, *Saint Paul as Spiritual Director*, 181–218.

[22] Castelli, *Imitating Paul*, 59–87. Castelli's discussion of the Graeco-Roman literary evidence is more extensive than W.H. De Boer's selection, touching on various models of imitation (aesthetic, cosmological, theological, royal, pedagogical and ethical) in antiquity. However, Castelli does not explore the documentary and visual evidence relating to imitation.

[23] Castelli, *Imitating Paul*, 84–85.

power, without thereby diminishing the social importance of traditional benefaction ethics and its rewards.[24]

Third, the recent book of V.A. Copan is an excellent exegetical and pastoral analysis of the role of imitation in Paul's spiritual formation of his converts.[25] Particularly valuable is Copan's discussion of contemporary spiritual therapy,[26] as well as his decisive rebuttal of the imposition of Foucault's sociological models upon the Pauline texts.[27] Also he covers the Graeco-Roman context of imitation in a less blinkered manner than the discussions of de Boer and Castelli.[28] He posits a series of mimetic models (i.e. parent-child, leader-people, teacher-student, human-divine) – Graeco-Roman and Jewish – as impacting upon Paul.[29] But, once again, the civic context (i.e. Copan's "leader-people" model) is insufficiently examined, overlooking the documentary and visual evidence of the eastern and western Mediterranean *poleis*. Nor does Copan satisfactorily integrate the Graeco-Roman background materials with his exegesis in a way that differentiates Paul's understanding of imitation from the competing models found in antiquity.[30]

Two articles have helpfully focused on important aspects of the mimetic tradition in Graeco-Roman antiquity: namely, E.A. Judge's discussion of imitation within the honorific culture of the Ephesian inscriptions,[31] and H. Crouzel's examination of the widespread motif of the imitation of the gods.[32] Judge, in particular, takes seriously the urban context of the Ephesian believers to whom Paul was writing. More recently, in a satisfying study, R.A. Burridge has discussed theologically Paul's understanding of the "imitation" of Jesus,[33] with

[24] This paragraph draws from J.R. Harrison, *Paul's Language of Grace*, 315 n.99. For a more positive evaluation of Castelli's monograph, see D.M. Reis, "Following in Paul's Footsteps: *Mimesis* and Power in Ignatius of Antioch," in *Trajectories through the New Testament and the Apostolic Fathers*, ed. A.F. Gregory and C. Tuckett (Oxford: Oxford University Press, 2005), 287–306, esp. 288–93.

[25] Copan, *Saint Paul as Spiritual Director.*

[26] Copan, *Saint Paul as Spiritual Director*, 25–37, 229–65.

[27] Copan, *Saint Paul as Spiritual Director*, 181–218.

[28] Copan, *Saint Paul as Spiritual Director*, 40–71.

[29] Copan, *Saint Paul as Spiritual Director*, 44, 48–51, 54–61.

[30] The only example of integration is found in Copan, *Saint Paul as Spiritual Director*, 101–02.

[31] E.A. Judge, "The Teacher as Moral Exemplar in Paul and in the Inscriptions of Ephesus," in *idem*, *Social Distinctives of the Christians in the First-Century: Pivotal Essays by E.A. Judge*, ed. D.M. Scholer (Peabody: Hendrickson, 2008), 175–88.

[32] H. Crouzel, "L'imitation et la suite de dieu et du Christ dans les premiers siècles chrétiens ainsi que leurs sources gréco-romaines et hébraïques," *JAC* 21 (1978): 7–41.

[33] R.A. Burridge, *Imitating Jesus: An Inclusive Approach to New Testament Ethics* (Grand Rapids: Eerdmans, 2007), 81–154. For additional theological discussions of "imitation" in Paul's thought, see D.M. Stanley, "'Become Imitators of Me': The Pauline Conception of Apostolic Tradition," *Bib* 40 (1959): 859–77; J. Jervell, *Imago Dei. Gen. 1, 26 f, in Spätjudentum, in der Gnosis und in den paulinischen Briefen* (Göttingen: Vandenhoeck & Ruprecht, 1960), 171–336; A. Schulz, *Nachfolgen und Nachahmen: Studien über das Verhältnis der neu-*

a strong emphasis on its social implications for Paul's house churches and twenty-first century society.[34] However, we still do not gain any appreciation of how Paul's understanding of "imitation" interacted with the mimetic traditions of his Graeco-Roman contemporaries.

---

testamentlichen Jüngerschaft zur urchristlichen Vorbildethik (München: Köschel-Verlag, 1962), *passim*; Betz, *Nachfolge und Nachahmung Jesu Christi*, 48–83; E. Güttgemanns, *Der leidende Apostel und sein Herr* (Göttingen: Vandenhoeck & Ruprecht, 1966), *passim*; P. Gutierrez, *La paternité spirituelle selon Saint Paul* (Paris: J. Gabalda, 1968), 178–88; J.H. Schütz, *Paul and the Anatomy of Apostolic Authority*, SNTSMS 26 (Cambridge: Cambridge University Press, 1975), 226–32; B. Sanders, "Imitating Paul: 1 Cor 4:16," *HTR* 74.4 (1981): 353–63; L. Hurtado, "Jesus as Lordly Example in Philippians 2:5–11," in *From Jesus to Paul: Studies in Honour of Francis Wright Beare*, ed. P. Richardson and J.C. Hurd (Waterloo: Wilfrid Laurier University Press, 1984), 113–26; D.M. Stanley, "Imitation in Paul's Letters: Its Significance for His Relationship to Jesus and to His Own Christian Foundations," in Richardson and Hurd, *From Jesus to Paul*, 127–41; R.G. Hammerton-Kelly, "A Girardian Interpretation of Paul: Rivalry, *Mimesis*, and Victimage in the Corinthian Correspondence," *Semeia* 33 (1985): 65–81; W.S. Kurtz, "Kenotic Imitation of Paul and of Christ in Philippians 2 and 3," in *Discipleship in the New Testament*, ed. F.F. Segovia (Philadelphia: Fortress, 1985), 103–26; G. Lyons, *Pauline Autobiography: Towards a New Understanding* (Atlanta: Scholrs Press, 1985), 226–32; B. Fiore, *The Function of Personal Example*, 164–90; *idem*, "Paul, Exemplification, and Imitation," in *Paul in the Greco-Roman World: A Handbook Volume 1*, ed. J.P. Sampley, 2nd ed. (London and New York: T&T Clark, 2016), 169–95; N. Onwu, "*Mimetes* Hypothesis: A Key to the Understanding of Pauline Paraenesis," *AJBS* 1.2 (1986), 95–112; A. Reinhartz, "On the Meaning of the Pauline Exhortation: '*mimetai mou ginesthe* – Become Imitators of Me'," *SR* 16 (1987): 393–403; E.R. Best, *Paul and His Converts* (Edinburgh: T&T Clark, 1988), 59–72; M.A. Getty, "The Imitation of Paul in the Letters to the Thessalonians," in *The Thessalonian Correspondence*, ed. R.F. Collins and N. Baumert (Leuven: Leuven University Press, 1990): 277–83; K.F. Morrison, *The Mimetic Tradition*, 41–48; S.E. Fowl, *The Story of Christ in the Ethics of Paul* (Sheffield: JSOT, 1990); *idem*, "Imitation of Paul/of Christ," in *Dictionary of Paul and His Letters*, ed. G.F. Hawthorne et al. (Downers Grove and Leicester: IVP, 1993), 428–31; L.L. Belleville, "'Imitate Me, Just As I Imitate Christ': Discipleship in the Corinthian Correspondence," in *Patterns of Discipleship in the New Testament*, ed. R.L. Longenecker (Grand Rapids: Eerdmans, 1996), 120–42; A.D. Clarke, "'Be Imitators of Me': Paul's Model of Leadership," *TynBul* 49.2 (1998): 329–60; B.J. Dodd, "The Story of Christ and the Imitation of Paul in Philippians 2–3," in *Where Christology Began: Essays on Philippians 2*, ed. R.P. Martin and B.J. Dodd (Louisville: Westminster John Knox Press, 1998), 154–60; R.L. Plummer, "Imitation of Paul and the Church's Missionary Role in 1 Corinthians," *JETS* 44.2 (2001): 219–35; S. Kim, "*Imitatio Christi* (1 Corinthians 11:1): How Paul Imitates Jesus Christ in Dealing with Idol Food (1 Corinthians 8–10)," *BBR* 13.2 (2003): 193–26; K. Ehrensperger, *Paul and the Dynamics of Power: Communication and Interaction in the Early Christ-Movement* (London and New York: T&T Clark, 2009), 137–54. The dissertation of D.M. Williams (*The Imitation of Christ in Paul with Special Reference to Paul as Teacher* [PhD diss. Columbia University, 1967]) was unavailable to me. Somewhat unexpectedly, books on Pauline theology and New Testament ethics devote little space to the motif of "imitation" in Paul: e.g. L. Cerfaux, *Christ in the Theology of Paul* (New York: Herder and Herder, 1959), Index *s.v.* "Imitation"; *idem*, *The Christian in the Theology of Paul* (New York: Herder and Herder, 1967), Index *s.v.* "Imitation of Christ"; W. Furnish, *Theology and Ethics in Paul* (Nashville: Abingdon, 1968), 222–24; W. Schrage, *The Ethics of the New Testament* (Edinburgh: T&T Clark 1988 [Gmn. orig. 1982]), 208–09; J.D.G. Dunn, *The Theology of Paul the Apostle* (Grand Rapids: Eerdmans, 1998), Index of Subjects *s.v. Imitatio Christi*.

[34] Burridge, *Imitating Jesus*, 116–18.

Other New Testament scholars have plumbed the *exempla* tradition,[35] drawing on Graeco-Roman historiographical and biographical models, as a backdrop to understanding the rhetorical strategies of comparison and imitation employed in the New Testament writings. This discussion has been mostly carried out in relation to Luke-Acts, the Thessalonian epistles and Hebrews.[36] B. Witherington III, however, has drawn attention to Paul's sophisticated rhetorical use of positive and negative examples that the Philippian believers were either to imitate or avoid if there was to be *concordia* in the house churches.[37] M.M. Mitchell has also highlighted the summons to imitation found in the *exempla* of deliberative rhetoric, arguing that Paul adopted this rhetorical tactic in several places in 1 Corinthians.[38] Finally, S.E. Fowl has shown how Paul employs the story of Jesus as a paradigm to inculcate ethical transformation in his house churches, whereas B.R. Gaventa has demonstrated how Paul's autobiography in Galatians 1–2 is intended to have paradigmatic force in Paul's theological argument.[39] The rhetorical conventions of the *exempla* tradition, too, have to be kept in mind when we analyse Paul's response to the inscriptional eulogies of the great man and the commemoration of his virtue for the imitation of posterity.

---

[35] For discussion of the use of *exempla* as a rhetorical genre, see K. Alewell, *Über das rhetorische παραδειγμα. Theorie, Beispielsammlung, Verwendung in der römischen Literatur der Kaiserzeit* (Leipzig: Hoffman, 1913); H.W. Litchfield, "National *Exempla Virtutis* in Roman Literature," *HSCP* 25 (1914): 1–71; A. Lumpe, "*Exemplum*," *RAC* 6 (1966): 1229–57; S. Perlman, "The Historical Example, Its Use and Importance as Political Propaganda in the Attic Orators," in *Scripta Hierosolymitana VII: Studies in History*, ed. A. Fuks and I. Halpern (Jerusalem: Magnes, 1961), 150–66; E. Eyben, "The Concrete Ideal in the Life of the Young Roman," *L'Antiquité Classique* 41 (1972): 200–17; J.R. Fears, "The Cult of Virtues and Roman Imperial Ideology," *ANRW* 2.17.2 (1981): 827–48; G. Maslakov, "Valerius Maximus and Roman Historiography: A Study of the *Exempla* Tradition," *ANRW* 2.32.1 (1984): 437–96; C. Skidmore, *Practical Ethics for Roman Gentlemen: The Work of Valerius Maximus* (Exeter: University of Exeter Press, 1996), 3–27.

[36] In relation to Acts, see W.S. Kurz, "Narrative Models for Imitation in Luke-Acts," in *Greeks, Romans, and Christians: Essays in Honor of Abraham J. Malherbe*, ed. D.L. Balch et al. (Minneapolis: Fortress, 1990), 171–81; G.J. Steyne, "Luke's Use of MIMHSIS? Re-opening the Debate," in *The Scriptures in the Gospels*, ed. C.M. Tuckett (Leuven: Leuven University Press, 1997), 551–57; A.C. Clark, *Parallel Lives: The Relation of Paul to the Apostles in the Lucan Perspective* (Carlisle: Paternoster, 2001); Baban, *On the Road Encounters in Luke-Acts*, 73–140. In relation to Hebrews, see M.R. Cosby, *The Rhetorical Composition and Function of Hebrews 11 in Light of Example Lists in Antiquity* (Macon: Mercer University Press, 1988); P.M. Eisenbaum, *The Jewish Heroes of Christian History: Hebrews 11 in Literary Context* (Atlanta: Scholars Press, 1997). On imitation in the Thessalonian epistles, see Malherbe, *Paul and the Popular Philosophers*, Index of Subjects *s.v.* "Imitation."

[37] B. Witherington III, *Friendship and Finances in Philippi: The Letter of Paul to the Philippians* (Valley Forge: Trinity Press International, 1994), 19–20.

[38] M.M. Mitchell, *Paul and the Rhetoric of Reconciliation: An Exegetical Investigation of the Language and Composition of 1 Corinthians* (Louisville: Westminster John Knox Press, 1992), 39–60.

[39] Fowl, *The Story of Christ*, *passim*; B.R. Gaventa, "Galatians 1 and 2: Autobiography as Paradigm," *NovT* 28.4 (1986): 309–26.

We turn now to an investigation of the mimetic concerns of civic leadership in the late Hellenistic age and the early imperial period (§ 7.2.1–§ 7.2.5). In § 7.3 we will consider how Paul's gospel overturns the iconic status of the "great man" and replaces it with a new understanding of the function and status of leadership in the community of Christ. Here we will range more widely than the passages employing "imitation" terminology. We will then be better placed to discuss how Paul's language of "imitation", within its exegetical context, engaged the civic paradigms of virtue (§ 7.4).

In concentrating on the evidence relating to the civic context of imitation, we are not suggesting that this is the only Graeco-Roman model of imitation that elicited a theological and social response from Paul in his letters. As noted, V. A. Copan correctly isolates a diversity of models in the Jewish and Graeco-Roman evidence. But we are proposing that New Testament scholars (with the exception of F. W. Danker and E. A. Judge) have overlooked the important "civic" band of literary, documentary and visual evidence, a methodological oversight of some importance, given that Paul's converts were urban believers. Moreover, it provides us with another valuable lens to view the intersection of Paul's gospel with the first-century society of the eastern Mediterranean basin. The study, therefore, represents another step in researching the background of the Pauline house churches "city by city, institution by institution," social convention by social convention.[40]

7.2. The Imitation of the "Great Man" in Antiquity: A Survey of the Literary, Documentary and Visual Evidence

7.2.1. Introduction

At the outset, we need to identify the evidence to be investigated relating to the "great man" in antiquity, with a special focus on the civic context in the Latin West and the Greek East. First, Roman nobles competed with each other in order to surpass the fame of their family forebears, with a view to enhancing their own house's prestige. Models of ancestral or personal virtue were held forth for the imitation of future generations. In imperial times, this culminated in the ruler becoming the embodiment of all virtue with the triumph of the Julio-Claudian house over its rivals.

Second, models of virtue were celebrated not only in literary memorials (e. g. *Res Gestae*) but were also represented architecturally in the statue program of

---

[40] See E. A. Judge, "The Social Identity of the First Christians: A Question of Method in Religious History," in *idem*, *Social Distinctives of the Christians in the First Century: Pivotal Essays by E. A. Judge*, ed. D. M. Scholer (Peabody: Hendrickson, 2008), 117–35, at 135.

the Augustan forum, with its two lines of Roman leaders culminating in Augustus as *Pater Patriae*.[41]

Third, the Greek honorific inscriptions of the eastern Mediterranean basin allude to ancestral glory in eulogising public benefactors or, alternatively, establish the benefactor as the yardstick of virtue for imitation by new benefactors. Latin inscriptions honouring soldiers in the early empire reveal the same phenomenon.

Fourth, the literary comparison of famous Greeks and Romans in the writings of Plutarch, Valerius Maximus and the anonymous *De Viris Illustribus* serve the conservative function of either maintaining the ancient ethical tradition or reinforcing socially acceptable paradigms of leadership of the past for future generations.

7.2.2. The Imitation of Ancestral Glory in the Roman Republic and in the Early Imperial Age

The Roman nobility – comprising a narrow group of aristocratic families whose descendents had held the consulship – boasted in prominent examples of ancestral glory for each new generation to imitate and surpass.[42] This is well illustrated by the epitaphs of the republican Scipionic family. The Scipionic epitaphs set out the pedigrees (filiation, magistracies, military victories and official posts, priesthoods, Board memberships etc.) of each of the deceased members of the family.[43] The ethos evinced by the epitaphs points to the vitality of the Roman nobleman's replication of ancestral glory.

Two epitaphs in particular demonstrate clearly this culture of ancestral imitation. Gnaeus Cornelius Scipio Hispanus (*praetor peregrinus*, 139 BC) lists his magistracies and then adds this highly revealing *elogium*:

> By my good conduct I heaped virtues on the virtues of my clan: I begat a family and sought to equal the exploits of my father. I upheld the praise (*laudem*) of my ancestors, so that they were glad that I was created of their line. My honours have ennobled (*nobilitavit honor*) my stock.[44]

This epitaph sums up succinctly the world-view of the Roman *nobiles* ("nobles"). The ancestral virtues of the noble house had to be replenished by each new gen-

---

[41] For full discussion, see J. R. Harrison, *Paul and the Imperial Authorities at Thessalonica and Rome* (Tübingen: Mohr Siebeck, 2011), 190–95.

[42] On the Roman nobility, see M. Geltzer, *The Roman Nobility* (Oxford: Blackwell, 1969: Gmn. orig. 1912).

[43] For discussion, see R.E. Smith, *The Aristocratic Epoch in Latin Literature* (Sydney: Australasian Medical Publishing 1947), 8–10.

[44] E.H. Warmington, *Remains of Old Latin: Archaic Inscriptions* (Cambridge, Mass.: Harvard University, 1953), 'Epitaphs', § 10. For all the Scipionic epitaphs, see *ibid.*, "Epitaphs," §§ 1–10.

eration. The praise accorded the ancestors placed enormous expectations on each new generation of nobles. Each noble had to equal (and, hopefully, surpass) by virtuous conduct the achievements of the ancestors,[45] with the exploits of the immediate father being the starting point. If this replication of ancestral merit was successfully carried out by each new generation, the *nobilitas* of the family was rendered even more noble and virtuous. Remarkably, the dead ancestors are depicted as still vitally interested in the replenishment of the family honour attached to their line.[46]

What happens, however, if the noble's life was prematurely cut short by his death before he could add to his ancestral glory? The answer is given with moving simplicity in the epitaph of a young Scipio who had only achieved "the honoured cap of Jupiter's priest" before he died:

> Death caused all your virtues, honour, good report and valiance, your glory (*gloria*) and your talents to be short-lived. If you had been allowed long life in which to enjoy them, an easy thing it would been for you to surpass by great deeds the glory of your ancestors (*gloriam maiorum*). Wherefore, O Publius Cornelius Scipio, begotten son of Publius, joyfully does earth take you to her bosom.[47]

Here we see how the Scipios handled their less successful members, when their advancement in the *cursus honorum* was either cut short by death, as was the case with Publius Cornelius Scipio above,[48] or by a lack of significant magistracies, as was the case with the two family members named Lucius Cornelius Scipio below. The *elogium* of Lucius Cornelius Scipio, the twenty-year-old who died c. 160 BC without achieving any magistracies at all, adds somewhat self-consciously: "Whose life but not his honour fell short of honours, he that lies here was never outdone in virtue."[49] This *elogium* is particularly interesting because it demonstrates that whereas *virtus* had been understood to be an active demonstration of leadership in the public arena, in this case *virtus* is conceived as an inner quality that animated the honour of Lucius, notwithstanding his lack of any public profile.

---

[45] Note that Cicero (*Fam.* 12.7.2) also speaks of the *nobilis* surpassing his own accomplishments: "do your utmost to surpass yourself in enhancing your own glory."

[46] Note the comment of D.C. Earl ("Political Terminology in Plautus," *Historia* 9.1 [1960]: 235–43, at 242) regarding the role of *virtus* in Plautus and the Scipionic elogia: "(*Virtus*) consists in the gaining of pre-eminent *gloria* by the winning of office and the participation in public life. It concerns not only the individual but the whole family, not only its living members but the dead members and the unborn posterity as well."

[47] Warmington, *Remains of Old Latin*, "Epitaphs," § 5. Smith (*The Aristocratic Epoch*, 10) observes: "We see the constancy of the ideal, consisting still in public honours and public office, to the extent that even where the dead man took no part in public life, the only comment is on what he would have done had he lived longer."

[48] See also Warmington, *Remains of Old Latin*, "Epitaphs," § 8: "Cornelius Scipio Asiagenus Nevershorn, son of Lucius, grandson of Lucius, sixteen years of age."

[49] Warmington, *Remains of Old Latin*, "Epitaphs," § 6.

Similarly, the *elogium* of another Lucius Cornelius Scipio, the thirty-three-year old quaestor (167 BC) and tribune of the soldiers, finds refuge in ancestral honour: "His father vanquished King Antiochus."[50] Thus these less known Scipios are made to avoid scrutiny of posterity by basking in the *gloria* of more famous relatives or by vaunting what could have been if circumstances had been otherwise.[51]

In the late republic, Cicero strengthens the motif of the replication of ancestral glory by linking it strongly to the language of "imitation." He sums up the early republican quest for ancestral glory by reference to the celebrated military *exempla* of the leading Roman noble houses:

... it is almost an instinct in the human race that members of a family which has won credit in some particular line ardently pursue distinction, seeing that the virtues of their fathers are perpetuated by the speech and recollection of the world; so did Scipio emulate the military renown of Paulus; so also did his son emulate Maximus; so also Publius Decius was imitated (*imitatus est*) by his son in the sacrificing of his life and in the very manner of his death.[52]

Elsewhere Cicero argues that the preservation of the liberty of the republic could only be preserved when the heroes of the republic are imitated:

Accordingly let us imitate (*imitemur*) men like our Bruti, Camilli, Ahalae, Decii, Curii, Fabricii, Maximi, Scipiones, Lentulii, Aemilii, and countless others, who firmly established the *res publica*, whom, indeed, I reckon among the company and number of the immortal gods.[53]

---

[50] Warmington, *Remains of Old Latin*, "Epitaphs," §7.

[51] Even the more famous Scipios were not immune from criticism. Smith (*The Aristocratic Epoch*, 21–22) refers to the fragment of the dramatist Naevius (d. 210 BC) which exposes the youthful sexual indiscretions of the great Scipio (Gellius, 7.8.5):

Even him whose hand did oft
Accomplish mighty exploits gloriously
Whose deeds wane not, but live on to this day,
The one outstanding man in all the world,
Him, with a single mantle, his own father
Dragged from a lady-love's arms.

[52] Cicero, *Rab. Post.* 1.2. See also *idem*, *Cael.* 30.72; *Div. Caec.* 8.25. Cf. Tacitus, *Hist.* 2.68: "Keep and preserve, Conscript Fathers, a man of such ready counsels, that every age may be furnished with its teacher, and that our young men may imitate Regulus, just as our old men imitate (*imitentur*) Marcellus and Crispus."

[53] Cicero, *Sest.* 68.143. After citing several illustrious defenders of the *res publica*, Cicero says: "Imitate these examples (*haec imitamini*), I beg you in the name of the immortal gods, you who aspire to honour, praise and glory! These examples are glorious, they are superhuman, they are immortal; they are proclaimed in common talk, are committed to the records of history, are handed down to posterity" (*ibid.*, 47.101). See also Cicero, *Arch.* 14. Note, too, Quintilian, *Inst.* 12.2.29–30: "It is still more important that we should know and ponder continually all the noblest sayings and deeds that have been handed down to us from ancient times ...Who will teach courage, justice, loyalty, self-control, simplicity and contempt of grief better than men like Fabricus, Curius, Regulus, Decious, Mucius and countless others? For if the Greeks can bear away the palm for moral purposes, Rome can produce more striking examples of moral performance, which is a far greater thing." For an excellent discussion on the

In his speeches, Cicero sometimes singles out particular family members as worthy of imitation. This was a rhetorical ploy on Cicero's part designed to undermine those who accused unfairly faithful allies of the republic. For example, Castor had accused his grandfather, Deiotarus, the Galatian king and a loyal client of Rome, of dancing drunk and naked at a banquet. Cicero responds bluntly in this manner:

This king is an exemplar of all the virtues, as I think you, Caesar, know well enough; but in nothing is he more remarkable and more admirable than in his sobriety ... It would have been more becoming in you, Castor, to model yourself (*imitari*) on the character and principles of your grandfather than to malign a good and noble man through the lips of a runaway. But even had you possessed a grandfather who was a dancer, instead of a man to whom one might look for an ideal of honour and propriety, even so such slanders would be ill applied to a man of his years.[54]

Moreover, as a *novus homo* ("new man"), Cicero was highly sensitive to the influential family clients and the ancestral *exempla* that ensured the political dominance of the leading consular families in Rome for so long and which had ensured their replenishment generation by generation. Cicero, as the first in his family to achieve the consulship, did not have such ancestral advantages. Thus, while Cicero urges the Roman nobles to seek the traditional paths of ancestral glory by imitating worthy *exempla*, he still reserves a significant place for the *novi homines* ("new men") who were the first to achieve consular distinction without the advantage of any illustrious family models to imitate:

You, young Romans, who are nobles by birth, I rouse you to imitate the example of your ancestors (*ad maiorum vestrorum imitationem excitabo*); and you who can win nobility by your talents and virtue, I will exhort to follow that career in which many new men (*novi homines*) have covered themselves with honour and glory.[55]

Finally, Cicero, as a *novus homo*, has no compunction in appealing to himself as an example worthy of imitation. In a piece of special pleading, Cicero argues that he had selflessly resigned his consulship so that he could extinguish the conflagration of the Catilinarian conspiracy in 63 BC, thereby preserving the liberty of the *res publica*:

Imitate me (*Imitare me*), whom you have always praised, who resigned a province organised and equipped by the Senate, so that, dismissing every other thought, I might quench the conflagration that was devouring my country.[56]

---

specific virtuous individuals that Romans admired and imitated, see E. Ryben, "The Concrete Ideal in the Life of the Young Roman," *L'Antiquité classique* 41 (1972): 200–17. Additionally, see Skidmore, *Practical Ethics*, 13–21. On the precise virtues to be imitated and the individuals embodying them, see the excellent coverages of Alewell, *Über das rhetorische* παραδειγμα, 54–86; Litchfield, "National *Exempla Virtutis*," 9, 28–35.

[54] Cicero, *Deiot.* 10.26, 28.

[55] Cicero, *Sest.* 64.136.

[56] Cicero, *Phil.* 11.10.

What happened to this republican ideal of the imitation of ancestral virtue in the early imperial period, given that the influence of the noble families waned before the onslaught of the triumphant Julio-Claudian rulers?[57] The answer of Tacitus (*Ann.* 3.55) is that his age still furnished worthy models to imitate: "Nor was everything better in the past, but our own age too has produced many specimens of excellence and culture for posterity to imitate (*imitanda posteris*)." Although not stated in this instance, Tacitus would have had his father-in-law, Cn. Iulius Agricola (AD 49–93), the governor of Britain, in firmly view here as an outstanding example of virtue during the tyranny of Domitian.

More importantly, as J.E. Lendon observes,[58] the ruler was now the man most worthy of imitation in the empire. Tacitus informs us that a reform had occurred in the Roman aristocracy (*Ann.* 3.55; cf. *Hist.* 2.68) when Vespasian became the moral exemplar among the social elite.[59] Dio Chrysostom, too, contrasts the unrestrained infatuation of Nero with music with the more restrained approach of Trajan to popular culture: "How much better it would be to imitate (μιμεῖσθαι) the present ruler in his devotion to culture and reason" (*Or.* 32.60). Thus a significant shift had occurred in the conventions of ancestral imitation. Just as ancestral glory was increasingly concentrated in the Julio-Claudian rulers because their house had eclipsed all the aristocratic competitors by virtue of their patronage and military superiority,[60] so too the ruler had now become the embodiment of exemplary virtue.[61] Consequently, Seneca advises the young Nero that the state will reflect his image if he dispenses mercy to his dependents – worthy citizens and allies – in the imperial body (*Clem.* 2.2.1):

> That kindness of your heart will be recounted, will be diffused little by little throughout the whole body of the empire (*per omne imperii corpus*), and all things will be moulded into your likeness (*in similitudinem tuam formabuntur*). It is from the head (*a capite*) that comes the health of the body; it is through it that all the parts are lively and alert or languid and drooping according as their animating spirit has life or withers. There will be

[57] See especially Juvenal, *Sat.* 8.1–38 on the decline of the Roman nobility. For commentary, see J. Henderson, *Figuring Out Roman Nobility* (Exeter: University of Exeter Press, 1997).

[58] Lendon, *Empire of Honour,* 129–30.

[59] Tacitus, *Ann.* 3.55: "But the main promoter of the stricter code was Vespasian, himself of the old school in his person and table. Thenceforward, deference to the Princeps and the love of emulating him (*aemulandi amor*) proved more powerful than legal sanctions and deterrents."

[60] See Harrison, *Paul and the Imperial Authorities*, 201–69.

[61] On the teaching of the Pythagorean political theorists and the popular philosophers regarding the king imitating the gods and his subjects imitating the king, see Harrison, *Paul and the Imperial Authorities*, 279–87. P. Oakes (*Philippians: From People to Letter*, SNTSMS 110 [Cambridge: Cambridge University Press, 2001], 173) draws attention to Velleius Paterculus' appeal to Tiberius as a paradigm of virtue (2.126.4): "... the best of emperors teaches his citizens to do right by doing it, and though he is the greatest among us in authority, he is still greater in the example he sets."

citizens, there will be allies worthy of this goodness (*hac bonitate*), and uprightness (*recti mores*) will return to the whole world; your hands will everywhere be spared.[62]

In conclusion, as the imperial age unfolded from the house of the Julio-Claudians to the Flavian household, the role of the ruler as the embodiment of virtue expanded into role of a benefactor who dispensed grace through the Virtues. The Roman ruler, as the world-benefactor and the providentially appointed agent of the Roman gods, was ideally placed to render benefits to his dependents through the cult of the Virtues and to project his official image at a popular level throughout the empire by the means of specific hypostasised Virtues.[63]

7.2.3. The Forum Augustum *and Julian Conceptions of Rule*

The contribution of *forum Augustum* to our understanding of the motif of "imitation" of the great man in the early imperial period has not fired the interest of New Testament scholars.[64] Prior to the Augustan era, the ostentatious tomb monuments of the late republican *nobiles* ("nobles") expressed their self-aggrandisement as they sought to outdo each other in a quest for ancestral glory. What

[62] Unashamedly flattering the young Nero, Seneca (*Clem.* 1.1) diminishes the importance of the reigns of Augustus and Tiberius, positing that Nero was the only model worthy of imitation in the Julio-Claudian line. In saying this, Seneca ignores the iconic legacy of imitation that Augustus left to posterity (*Res Gestae* 8.5):

Thanks are rendered to you; no human being has ever been so dear to another as you are to the people of Rome – its great and lasting blessing. But it is a mighty burden that you have taken upon yourself; no one today speaks of the deified Augustus or the early years of Tiberius Caesar, or seeks for any model he would have you copy than yourself (*quod te imitari velit, exemplar extra te quaerit*); the standard for your principate is the foretaste you have given. This would indeed have been difficult if that goodness of yours were not innate but only assumed for a moment.

[63] J.R. Fears, "The Cult of Virtues and Roman Imperial Ideology," *ANRW* 2.17.2 (1981): 827–948. See also H. Axtell, *The Deification of Abstract Ideas in Roman Literature and Inscriptions* (Chicago: University of Chicago Press, 1907); A. Wallace-Hadrill, "The Emperor and His Virtues," *Historia* 30 (1981): 298–323.

[64] On the Roman forum, see P. Romanelli, *The Roman Forum*, 2nd ed. (Rome: Instituto Poligrafico Dello Stato, 1955); M. Grant, *The Roman Forum* (London: Weidenfeld & Nicolson, 1970); F. Coarelli, *Il Foro Romano* (Rome: Quasar, 1992); D. Favro, *The Urban Image of Augustan Rome* (Cambridge: Cambridge University, 1996). For ancient texts on the *forum Augustum*, see D.R. Dudley, *Urbs Romana: A Source Book of Classical Texts on the City and Its Monuments* (London: Phaidon, 1967), 123–29. On the *forum Augustum*, see H.T. Rowell, "The Forum and the Funeral Images of Augustus," *Memoirs of the American Academy in Rome* 17 (1940): 131–43; E.A. Judge, "On Judging the Merits of Augustus," in *idem*, *The First Christians*, 224–313, esp. 235–39; *idem*, "The Eulogistic Inscriptions of the Augustan Forum," in *idem*, *The First Christians*, 165–81; J.C. Anderson, *The Historical Topography of the Impeira Fora* (Bruxelles: Latomus, 1984), 65–100; P. Zanker, *The Power of Images in the Age of Augustus* (Ann Arbor: University of Michigan, 1990), 201–05; G. Sauron, QVIS DEVM? *L'expression plastique des ideologies politques et religieuses à Rome* (Rome: École Française de Rome, 1994), 525–36. What follows draws upon Harrison, *Paul and the Imperial Authorities*, 170–77.

had been essentially private monuments became public monuments on a grand scale with the erection of the Theatre of Pompey and the Forum of Caesar in the mid-first century BC.[65] By then the glorification of the "great man" in Roman history had reached unprecedented architectural heights. But, with the triumph of Octavian at Actium and the inability of the republican *nobiles* ("nobles") to compete against the new world benefactor, the grandiose monuments of the *familia Caesaris* were enlarged and integrated into the public life and mythology of Rome.[66]

The forum developed out of Augustus' desire to avenge his adoptive father's assassination at the Battle of Philippi in 42 BC. On the eve of the battle, Octavian vowed that he would construct a temple to Mars Ultor, should he be victorious (Suetonius, *Aug.* 29.2; Ovid, *Fasti* 5.569–578; cf. *Res Gestae* 21.1). Forty years later Augustus fulfilled his long-delayed vow when the temple was opened (2 BC), though in different form than he envisaged because the temple was now included as part of his forum project. In addition to commemorating the deeds of Julius Caesar by means of the temple, the forum was intended to relieve congestion in the existing *forum Romanum* by expanding its facilities for public business. Additionally, the victory tokens (e.g. crowns, sceptres) of returned *triumphators* were to be placed in the sanctuary of Mars Ultor, and governors on their way to military provinces took their leave there (Suetonius, *Aug.* 29.2).

More important is the design of the forum and the ideological purposes served by the portrait statue programme. The temple of Mars Ultor faced the South West, with the result that Mars Ultor faced the statue of Julius Caesar, Augustus' adoptive father, which was located prominently in the *forum Iulium*. The *forum Augustum* was set at right angles to the *forum Iulium*, with two semicircular bays (*exedrae*) jutting out on the South East and North West sides of the forum. Arrayed around the two *exedrae* and porticoes of the forum were statues of famous republican leaders (*principes*) and of the ancestors of the Julian nobility. Each line of republican and Julian luminaries radiated from a different founding-hero of Rome, the republican statues expanding outwards from South East *exedra*, the Julian statues from the North West *exedra*.[67] As Ovid (*Fasti* 5.563–566; cf. Dio Cassius 56.34.2; Pliny [the Elder], *NH* 22.7.13; Aul. Gell. *Noc. Att.*, 10.11.10) explains for the observer,

[65] See Zanker, *Power of Images*, 11–31.

[66] See P.J.E. Davies, *Death and the Emperor: Roman Imperial Funerary Monuments from Augustus to Marcus Aurelius* (Cambridge: Cambridge University, 2000), *passim*. The sitting rooms of Nero's Golden House, a Roman *domus* and garden of "cosmic" proportions (M. Bradley, "Fool's Gold: Colour, Culture, Innovation, and Madness in Nero's Golden House," *Apollo: The International Magazine of the Arts* [July 2002]: 35–44), exceeded all the land owned by illustrious Republican generals (Pliny the Elder, *NH* 36.111).

[67] Judge ("The Eulogistic Inscriptions," 175–76) lists the republican *principes*.

On the one side (one) sees Aeneas laden with his precious burden, and so many members of Julian nobility. On the other (one) sees Ilia's son Romulus bearing on his shoulder the arms of the (conquered) general, and the splendid records of action (inscribed) beneath (the statues of the) men arranged in order.[68]

Each statue was adorned with a distinctive emblem relevant to his career, and below each statue were boldly lettered laudatory inscriptions (*elogia fori Augusti*) that catalogued each man's career achievements. While there is a heavy concentration upon magistracies and military triumphs in the catalogues – many which prefigured Augustus' illustrious career in the *Res Gestae* – there are features in the careers of the republican luminaries that proleptically and symbolically point forward to the civic and moral grounds for Augustus' unprecedented *auctoritas* (*Res Gestae* 34.1, 3). As E.A. Judge observes,[69] each inscription focused on an episode that involved the republican leader in "political crisis management," that is, handling a desperate situation that imperilled Rome. Each inscriptional vignette of "crisis management" pointed forward to the decisive way that Augustus had extinguished the civil wars tearing apart the Roman republic (*Res Gestae* 34.1) and had returned his official powers (*potestas*) without recalcitrance to their owners, namely, the senate, the magistrates, and the people (34.1, 3). By exalting his *auctoritas* – his personal dignity and influence in the widest sense[70] – over his rank, Augustus defined exemplary virtue for future generations. Roman history had found its culmination in Augustus and he provided the yardstick of *virtus* ("virtue") for all future rulers of Rome.

In the *Res Gestae* inscribed on bronze tablets in front of his nearby mausoleum (Suetonius, *Aug.* 101.4), Augustus states that the revival of exemplary ancestral practices (*multa exempla mairorum*) in his legislative program formed part of a much wider transmission of "exemplary practises to posterity for their imitation" during his principate (*Res Gestae* 8:5: *ipse multarum rerum exempla imitanda posteris tradidi*). Undoubtedly, the *forum Augustum* formed a pivotal part of this Augustan culture of imitation.

Suetonius (*Aug.* 31.5) provides us insight into Augustus' motives in dedicating statues in triumphal form in the two porticoes of the forum. Augustus had declared in an edict

I have contrived this to lead the citizens to require me, while I live, and the rulers of later times as well, to attain the standard (*ad exemplar*) set by those worthies of old.

---

[68] Zanker (*Power of Images*, 201) notes: "In the Forum of Augustus, in the central niches of the two large *exedrae*, Aeneas and Romulus stood as counterparts of Mars and Venus ... Venus' grandson was depicted fleeing from Troy in flames, the son of Mars as *triumphator*. The juxtaposition was not intended to measure the two heroes against one another, but to celebrate their deeds as the embodiments of two complimentary virtues."

[69] Judge, "The Eulogistic Inscriptions," 169.

[70] *Res Gestae* 30.1: "I was the leading citizen (*princeps*)"; 34.3: "I excelled all in influence (*auctoritate*)."

The forum became one of the hallowed viewing places for Augustus' civic and military honours:

During my thirteenth consulship the senate and equestrian order and people of Rome unanimously saluted me father of my country and voted that this should be inscribed in the vestibule of my house, in the Julian senate house and in the Augustan forum beneath the chariot which had been set up in my honour by ruling of the senate.[71]

What, then, do we learn from the fragments of the *elogia fori Augusti* about the fulfilment of the Roman ideals of leadership in Augustus?[72] Three examples will suffice, illustrating important facets of Augustus' propaganda concerning his rule.

First, given the overflow of Augustus' beneficence (e.g. *Res Gestae* 15–24: cf. §7.5.2 *infra*), we observe how comprehensively Augustus replicated and surpassed the beneficence of the republican *principes*. Of Manius Valerius, for example, the statue inscription says that "on his own initiative the Senate freed the people from heavy debt" (ILS 50; cf. *Res Gestae* 15). In the statue inscriptions of Appius Claudius Caecus (ILS 54) and Gaius Marius (ILS 59), we see how both men combined their military role with that of civic benefactor.[73] In the case of Caecus' beneficence, the inscription states that "In his censorship he laid the Appian Way and built an aqueduct into the city; he built the temple of Belonna." Regarding Marius' beneficence, we learn from the inscription that "From the Cimbric and Teutonic spoils he built as victor a temple to Honour and Virtue."[74] In reading these *elogia*, literate Roman residents would be aware that Augustus, like the *principes*, juggled the roles of general and benefactor during his principate, but on a vastly greater scale in terms of their scope and longevity.

Second, in the statue inscriptions the piety of the republican *principes* – a feature of Augustus' rule to which he draws attention (*Res Gestae* 7.3; 9–12; 19; 24; 29.2) and one which his critics derided – is demonstrated by their commitment to the traditional cults in times of crisis. Thus it is said of L. Albinus that

---

[71] *Res Gestae* 35.1.

[72] Anderson (*Historical Topography*, 82) observes regarding the number of *triumphatores* originally represented: "The extant inscriptions from the Forum also fail us, as we have no way of determining from the fragments how many *triumphatores* were represented, or which ones were in the hemicycles and which in the porticos."

[73] Note, however, the military parallel between Augustus and Gaius Marius. Augustus (*Res Gestae* 1.1): "I successfully championed the liberty of the republic when it was oppressed by the tyranny of a faction." Gaius Marius (ILS 59): "while consul for the sixth time, he freed the republic when it was troubled by the revolt of tribunes of the plebs and praetors, who had seized the Capitol under arms."

[74] Anderson (*Historical Topography*, 83) observes regarding the *elogia fori Augusti* that "Temples built by four of these men were restored by Augustus in confirmation of Suetonius' statement that Augustus restored the works of great generals preserving the original inscriptions (*Aug.* 31.1)."

"when the Gauls were besieging the Capitol, he led the vestal virgins down to Caere, and there made it his concern that the solemn rites and ceremonies were not interrupted" (ILS 51). Similarly, L. Papirius Cursor "returned to Rome to renew his auspices" (ILS 53). In the *Res Gestae*, however, Augustus underlines his superiority to the *principes* of the *forum Augustum* through his telling references to the vestal virgins and the auspices. In Augustus' case, the vestal virgins made an annual sacrifice in honour of his return to Rome from Syria (*Res Gestae* 11), and the army of the Dacians was defeated and routed under his auspices (*Res Gestae* 30.2). The republican *principes* of the statue inscriptions only anticipate in rudimentary form Augustus' piety and the central position he assumed in the state cult.

Third, a final elogium honours Quintus Fabius Maximus. Fabius Maximus had rescued the legion of Mucinius from military disaster and earned thereby from the grateful soldiers the title "Father of the Legion":

> Quintus Fabius Maximus, son of Quintus, twice a dictator, five times consul, censor, twice interrex, curule aedile, twice quaestor, twice tribune of the soldiers, pontifex, augur. In his first consulship he subdued the Ligures and triumphed over them. In his third and fourth he tamed Hannibal by dogging his heels though rampant after numerous victories. As dictator he came to the aid of the magister equitum, Minucius, whose *imperium* the people had ranked equal with the dictator's, and of his routed army, and on that occasion was named 'father' by the army of Minucius. When consul for the fifth time he captured Tarentum, and triumphed. He was considered the most cautious general of his age and the most skilled in military matters. He was chosen *princeps senatus* at two Lustra.[75]

What was so impressive about Fabius Maximus' selfless and magnanimous act was that the Senate had previously snubbed him by giving his military subordinate, Mucinius, the same official power as himself.[76] Fabius Maximus' honour, however, was excelled by the unprecedented honour, "Father of his Country", which the Roman people pressed upon Augustus for saving them from a century of civil war (*Res Gestae* 35; cf. Suetonius, *Aug.* 58; Horace, *Carm.* 2.1.2.45ff). Once again, within the "typological" conventions of leadership articulated in the *forum Augustum*, we see how Augustus surpassed the best of his republican forebears and became the iconic model of political crisis management for future generations.

---

[75] ILS 56. Cicero had the title of "parent of his fatherland" bestowed unofficially upon him for suppressing the Catilinarian conspiracy and the title was later officially granted to Julius Caesar (Dio 44.4.4; Suetonius, *Jul.* 85). In the case of Cicero and Caesar, however, the title did not come to have the all-defining status that it assumed in Augustus' career; nor did the Roman people and Senate press the title upon Fabius Maximus, Cicero and Caesar with the same relentless insistence that they did with Augustus.

[76] For full discussion of Fabius Maximus' selfless act in the Roman annalistic tradition, see Harrison, *Paul and the Imperial Authorities*, 174–76.

7.2.4. The Honorific Inscriptions and the Imitation of the "Great Man"

7.2.4.1. The Greek Public Inscriptions

The Greek public inscriptions resort to the language of "imitation" and "emulation" in eulogising benefactors and teachers in the eastern Mediterranean world and in encouraging uncommitted members of wealthy elite in the city to assume the mantle of benefactor. Four Greek inscriptions reveal the culture of imitation that was promoted by the erection of inscriptions in the public spaces of the city.

First, a first-century AD inscription from Mantinea, Antigonea (Greek mainland), praises the wife of Euphrosynus, Epigone, for her replication of her husband's piety towards the gods:

For they were linked together in a union of body and mind in their lives and they shared a common and undivided concern in always seeking to go beyond the other in devoting themselves to the performance of good deeds; thus, they rebuilt the temples which had been in utter ruins and they added dining-rooms to those existing and they provided the [religious] societies with treasuries, extending their piety not only to the gods but to the places themselves. Epigone, indeed, a woman of saintly dignity and devoted to her husband, imitated his example (μειμησαμένη τὸν γαμήσαντα) herself by taking up the priesthood ordained for every priestess, worshipping the gods reverently at sacrificial expense, in providing all men alike with a festive banquet.[77]

Second, an inscription of Antiochus I of Kommagene, recounting the regulations for cultic observance at his burial shrine, concludes with a personal vignette of the piety that his descendents should display towards the gods. What is intriguing is the *do ut des* mentality ("I give in order that I may receive") underlying the inscription. The propitiation of the gods towards the homeland of Kommagene, as well as the maintenance of their favour towards its royal house, is entirely dependent on the mimetic ethos of the descendants of Antiochus I:

Through these, as well as many other ways, I have set forth for the benefit of my children and my descendants a clear impression of the piety one ought to show towards the gods and one's ancestors, and I expect them to imitate this fine example (καλὸν ὑπόδειγμα μιμήσασθαι) and ever increase the honours that are part of their family heritage, and that they will likewise, when they reach the peak of their own lives, add to my honours and magnify the glory of their ancestral house. And if they all do this, it is my prayer that all the gods of Persia and Macedonia and the homeland of Kommagene should remain propitiate and grant them every favour.[78]

Third, an Athenian decree (261/260 BC) honouring the Zeno, the father of Stoicism, sets out the rationale for Zeno's honours in mimetic terms. The focus

[77] IG V 2(268). Tr. A.R. Hands, *Charities and Social Aid in Greece and Rome* (London and Southampton: Thames and Hudson, 1968), §D.14.
[78] OGIS 383 (mid. I. cent. BC). Tr. Danker, *Benefactor*, § 41.

is upon the way that young men saw in Zeno's personal example the Stoic self-control (σωφροσύνη) about which he taught:

Since Zeno, son of Mnaseas, from Kition, having been involved with philosophy for many years in the city, both in other ways continued to be a good man (ἀνὴρ ἀγαθός), and by urging those young men who entered into association with him toward excellence (ἀρετήν) and self-control (σωφροσύνην), he stimulated them toward the very best things (τὰ βέλτιστα), having offered to all as an example his own life (παράδειγμα τὸν ἴδιον βίον) which was in agreement with the theories he professed ...[79]

Fourth, in a letter of Attalus II praising Arist[---], the tutor of Attalos III, the same mimetic concerns are highlighted. The character of the tutor provided an impetus for the moral transformation of young men that he taught:

And he was much the more highly regarded by us not only by reason of his being in rhetorical skill [and t]radition superior to many, but because also in character he seemed worthy of every [praise] and very suited to keeping company with a young man. For it is manifest to everyone that those who are naturally gentlemen amongst the young are zealous (ζηλοῦσι) for the training [of their] masters.[80]

There are other mimetic features of the eastern Mediterranean inscriptions that need discussion. In the "manifesto" clause of the honorific inscriptions, for example, there is regular mention of how the public honouring of benefactors stimulates other benefactors to imitate the beneficence of the honorand.[81] A decree of Sestos (c. 133–120 BC), in honour of the gymnasiarch Menas, concludes with this rousing call to the imitation of exceptional civic benefactors for the good of the city:

Therefore, in order that all people might know that Sestos is hospitable to men of exceptional character and ability, especially those who from their earliest youth have shown themselves devoted to the common good and have given priority to the winning of a glorious reputation, and that the People might not appear remiss in their gratitude, and that also all others, as they see the people bestowing honours on exceptional men, might emulate the noblest qualities (ζηλωταὶ μὲν τῶν καλλίστων γίνωται) and be moved on to virtue, to the end that the common good might be advanced as all aim ever to win a reputation for doing something beneficial for our home city ...[82]

---

[79] The decree is cited in Diogenes Laertius, 7.10–12. Tr. S.M. Burstein, ed., *The Hellenistic Age from the Battle of Ipsos to the Death of Kleopatra VII* (Cambridge: Cambridge University Press, 1985), § 59.

[80] IEph II 202 (150–140 BC: Provenance: Ephesus). Tr. Burstein, *The Hellenistic Age*, § 90. For a discussion of the decree, see R. Saunders, "Attalus, Paul and PAIDEIA: The Contribution of *I. Eph. 202* to Pauline Studies," in *Ancient History in a Modern University. Volume II: Early Christianity, Late Antiquity, and Beyond*, ed. T.W. Hillard et al. (Grand Rapids: Eerdmans, 1998), 175–83. On the imitation of Cynic teachers, see *Crates* 20.13; *Diogenes* 14. 4. See Malherbe, *The Cynic Epistles*, 70, 108 respectively.

[81] On the "manifesto" clause of the honorific inscriptions, see Harrison, *Paul's Language of Grace*, 40–43.

[82] OGIS 339. Tr. Danker, *Benefactor*, § 17. Note, too, Michel 1553 (Danker, *Benefactor*, § 21: c. 250 BC): "[so that] the members might be prompted to emulate (([ἐ]φάμιλλον) one an-

In another Ephesian inscription, the statue of Diodorus the gymnasiarch is set up in the gymnasium with the intention of "guiding everyone to become emulators of excellent deeds (ζηλῶτας γίνεσθαι τῶν καλλίστων πράξεων)."[83] Some inscriptions also mention a son following his father's example in his policies towards city-states.[84] Other inscriptions refer to benefactors either exceeding the generosity of their ancestors[85] or emulating their moral qualities.[86] Thus the imitation of ancestral virtue in the Greek East was just as much an important incentive motivating ethical behaviour as it was in the Latin West.

7.2.4.2. The Latin Public Inscriptions

Turning to the Latin inscriptions of the early imperial period, the ethos of imitation is also present, even though, as noted (§ 7.2.2), the Julio-Claudian rulers had become the supreme model of virtue. In a revealing epitaph from the Flavian period, cited by J. E. Lendon,[87] a soldier portrays himself as the unprecedented paradigm of military prowess, effectively leaving no room for others to excel his achievements.

---

other in generous service to the membership (knowing) that they will be honoured accordingly and that the Association of the Sarapiastae will find a further way to reward them as they continue their benefactions in the future."

[83] IEph Ia 6 (II BC: Provenance: Ephesus).

[84] E.g. C.B. Welles, *Royal Correspondence in the Hellenistic Period: A Study in Greek Epigraphy* (rpt. Chicago; Ares Publishers, 1974: orig. London, 1934), § 32: "in the future I shall try following my father's example to aid you in furthering them in whatever matters you summon me or I myself think of"; *ibid.*, § 14: "I have in former times shown all zeal in behalf of your city both through a gift of land and through care in all other matters as was proper because I saw that our father was kindly disposed toward the city and was the author of many benefits for you and had relieved you of harsh and oppressive taxes and tolls which certain of the kings had imposed." The literary evidence confirms this emphasis. Amidst a list of duties (Pseudo-Isocrates, *Demon.* 9–15) occurs this paraenesis: "I have produced a sample of the nature of Hipponicus, after whom you should pattern your life as after an example, regarding his conduct as your law, and striving to imitate and emulate your father's virtue." Cited A.J. Malhebe, *Moral Exhortation, a Greco-Roman Sourcebook* (Philadelphia: Westminster Press, 1986), 126. See also Pliny, *Ep.* 8.13: "he whom nature designed you should most resemble, is, of all others, the person whom you should most imitate!"

[85] Hands, *Charities*, §D.46: "in this going beyond the generous gifts of his forefathers"; *ibid.*, §D.69: "maintaining the good relations with the people inherited from his ancestors." Danker, *Benefactor*, § 24: "not only surpassed the generosity of his ancestors in his public services to the city and in his generosity toward the Synod both individually and collectively, but also matched the enthusiasm of many superintendents of the contests who have been especially generous toward us."

[86] Danker, *Benefactor*, § 19: "and (further assuring him) that (Opramoas) already from his earliest youth even until now has been emulating his ancestors' majestic qualities and generosity."

[87] Lendon, *Empire of Honour*, 245. The text (ILS 2558) can be found in E.M. Smallwood, ed., *Documents Illustrating the Principates of Nerva, Trajan, and Hadrian* (Cambridge: Cambridge University Press, 1966), § 336. Precise provenance unknown, but given as "near the Danube".

While this type of exalted boasting was standard fare for the Julio-Claudian world-benefactors, it is unconventional for a soldier in the imperial era to make such bold claims unabashed. The inflated boasting of Cornelius Gallus about his military exploits in Egypt in 29 BC drew Augustus' wrath and the renunciation of his friendship, resulting in Gallus' suicide in 26 BC.[88] The chilling consequences of overreaching oneself before the ruler was a lesson learned by Caesar's military retinue from that time onwards: even minor military officials were careful to acknowledge in their inscriptions the importance of the patronage of the ruler.[89]

Although deference toward the ruler is shown in our inscription ("With Hadrian watching"), the solder magnifies his role at the expense of his rivals. Indeed, the mention of Hadrian only serves to enhance his prestige indirectly. Even bolder is the soldier's claim that his only exemplar is himself:

Once I was most renowned on the Pannonian shore;
amidst a thousand Batavians the strongest;
With Hadrian watching I swam the huge waters
of Danube's deep in arms.
While a bolt from my bow hung in the air –
while it fell – I hit and shattered with another arrow.
Neither Roman or Barbarian, no soldier with his spear,
no Parthian with his bow, could defeat me.
Here I lie. My deeds I have entrusted to the memory of this stone.
Whether another after me will emulate my deeds (*mea facta sequ[a]tur*) has yet to be seen.
I am the first who did such things: my own exemplar (*exemplo mihi*).

The inscription, therefore, is graphic testimony to the tenacity of the rhetorical conventions regarding the imitation of the "great man" in antiquity, notwithstanding the fact that the ruler in the early imperial period had become the paradigm of all virtue.

7.2.5. The Literary Exempla and the Imitation of the Great Man

We have already noted M.M. Mitchell's discussion of how rhetoricians like Isocrates resorted to proof by example and the call to imitation when using deliberative rhetoric, especially in cases where the orator wanted to establish concord in the city-state.[90] We might also profitably refer in this regard to Dio Chrysostom (*Or.* 31.118) who, when discussing the conventions of praising and criticising famous city-states like Athens, offers this guideline:

[88] See E.A. Judge, "*Veni. Vidi. Vici*, and the Inscription of Cornelius Gallus," in *idem*, *The First Christians*, 72–75.

[89] For discussion, see Harrison, *Paul and the Imperial Authorities*, 225–32; now further expanded in J.R. Harrison, "The Erasure of Honour: Paul and the Politics of Dishonour," *TynBul* 66.2 (2016): 161–84.

[90] Mitchell, *Rhetoric of Reconciliation*, 60–64.

For as it is the custom of all men to recount the admirable institutions and practices which are found among other peoples for the purpose of encouraging eager emulation (ζήλου) of them, we should not in the same way mention any bad practice that is current elsewhere for the sake of encouraging imitation of it (ὥστε μιμεῖσθαι), but, on the contrary, only in order that one's people may be on their guard against it and may not fall unawares into that sort of thing.

But, as important as the mimetic concerns of civic rhetoric might be for our purposes, there is little point in covering territory well worn by Mitchell. Another fruitful field of enquiry is the Greek and Latin corpus of collectors of *exempla*. New Testament scholars have not as yet examined these writings in discussions of imitation in the letters of Paul. These works ranged from biographical vignettes of famous figures (*De Viris Illustribus*; Valerius Maximus) to Plutarch's full-fledged program of biographical comparison.[91] What light do these works throw on the mimetic ethos of antiquity?

7.2.5.1. *The* ΣΥΓΚΡΙΣΙΣ *of Plutarch*

Plutarch's biographies, which compare leading Romans with their Greek counterparts, are infused with moralistic purpose. The intent of Plutarch was to provide moral *exempla* for the leading men of his day so that a new generation of leaders might be raised up in the civic and military arena. Plutarch observes in the *Life of Pericles* 1.4, 2.4:

We find these examples in the actions of good men, which implant an eager rivalry and a keen desire to imitate them (εἰς μίμησιν) in the minds of those who sought them out, whereas our admiration for other forms of action does not immediately prompt us to do the same ourselves ... These, then, are the reasons which have impelled me to persevere in my biographical writings, and which I have therefore devoted this tenth book to the lives of Pericles and of Fabius Maximus, who staged such a land war with Hannibal. The two men possessed many virtues in common ...

In order to help his readers visualise more clearly his paradigm of mimetic leadership, Plutarch prefaced his parallel lives with a comparison (συγκρίσις) of each Roman and Greek leader that he was discussing.[92] Eighteen of these compari-

[91] Cornelius Nepos' *On the Great Generals of Foreign Nations* is left out of consideration, notwithstanding the fact that the work belongs to the ancient corpus of *exempla* and has close affinity, as Alewell notes (*Über das rhetorische* παραδειγμα, 48), with Valerius Maximus in its rhetorical genre. However, in contrast to Valerius Maximus and Plutarch, Nepos does not engage in *explicit* moralistic reflection, especially in regards to the "imitation" motif, within his work. For coverage of the authors and *exempla* comprising the Roman corpus of rhetorical literature, see Alewell, *ibid.*, 100–18.

[92] For occurrences of μιμεῖσθαι and cognates in Plutarch's *Lives*, see *Publ.* 10.2; *Cat. Maj.* 9.4; 19.7; *Pomp.* 60.4; *Cat. Min.* 65.10; 73.6; *Ti. C. Gracch.* 7.1; *Demetr.* 11.2; *Ant.* 17.4; *Arat.* 1.5; 38.9; *Alex.* 4.3; *Sol.* 31.4; *Dem.* 14.2; *Cic.* 42.3; *Demetr.* 1.6; 22.1; 52.6; *Dio.* 21.6. It is beyond the scope of this chapter to explore Plutarch's extensive use of the language of "imitation" in the *Moralia*.

sons have come down to us intact. At first sight, Plutarch's comparisons do not seem to throw light on the mimetic concerns of Paul's occasion-bound letters. On the three occasions where Plutarch resorts to the language of "imitation" in the comparisons,[93] he does not employ it with the imperatival force of Paul's letters. Plutarch prefers to concentrate on the character traits that contributed to each man's power and authority,[94] thereby making his moral points in ways appropriate to the biographical genre, but in a manner remote from Paul's formation of communities in Christ.

Notwithstanding, Plutarch's programme of biographical comparison exhibits several general points of convergence with Paul, even if he comes to vastly different conclusions regarding the ethos of leadership. For example, Plutarch provides a clear blueprint of what the true leader should be like;[95] he reflects on the interplay between Fortune and character in the development of a leader;[96] he critiques the morality of the subjects of his biographies;[97] he reflects on the leader's attitude to and use of wealth;[98] he highlights the importance of leaders establishing civic concord by persuasion;[99] and, last, he employs the familiar ethical motifs of his culture (e.g. the endangered benefactor) in order to convey the integrity of a leader.[100]

A more meaningful dialogue between Plutarch's programme of biographical comparison and the ethical concerns of Paul's epistles becomes possible when we remember that Paul employs christological narrative patterns (2 Cor 8:9;

---

[93] Plutarch, *Comp. Ag. Cleom. Ti. Gracch.* 5.3: "Lycurgus, whom he professed to imitate (μιμεῖσθαι)) ..." *Idem*, *Comp. Ages. Pomp.* 4.4: "there were many plains, ten thousand cities, and a whole earth which (Pompey's) great resources by sea afforded him had he wished to imitate (μιμεῖσθαι) Maximus, or Marius, or Lucullus, or Agesilaüs." *Idem*, *Comp. Sol. Publ.* 1.1: "There is, then, something peculiar in this comparison (ταύτην τὴν σύγκρισιν), and something that has not been true of any other thus far, namely, that the second imitated (γεγονέναι μιμητήν) the first, and the first bore witness for the second."

[94] Plutarch, *Comp. Dem. Cic.* 3.2: "But what is thought and said most of all to reveal and test the character of a man, namely power and authority (ἐξουσία καὶ ἀρχή), which rouses every passion and uncovers every baseness, this Demosthenes did not have."

[95] E.g. Plutarch, *Comp. Thes. Rom.* 2.1–2; *Comp. Lyc. Num.* 1.2; *Comp. Alc. Cor.* 1.4; *Comp. Ages. Pomp.* 3.3–4; *Comp. Nic. Crass.* 2.3–5; *Comp. Arist. Cat.* 3.1.

[96] Plutarch, *Comp. Thes. Rom.* 3.1; *Comp. Arist. Cat.* 2.4; *Comp. Cim. Luc.* 3.6; *Comp. Nic. Crass.* 5.1.

[97] See Plutarch's philosophical critique of styles of leadership in *Comp. Cim. Luc.* 1.1–4. Note, too, Plutarch's negative attitude to the pursuit of δόξα, an attitude consonant with the Greek ethical tradition, in *Comp. Dem. Cic.* 2.1–2.

[98] Plutarch, *Comp. Lys. Sull.* 3.1–2; *Comp. Alc. Cor.* 3.1–2.

[99] Plutarch, *Comp. Lyc. Num.* 4.8: "he changed the whole state by force of persuasion alone (πάντα πειθοῖ μεταβαλεῖν) and ... by his wisdom and justice (he) won the hearts of all the citizens and brought them into harmony (συναρμόσαντα)"; *idem*, *Comp. Nic. Crass.* 2.3–5: "[Nicias'] love of peace, indeed, had something godlike (θεῖος) about it."

[100] Plutarch, *Comp. Dion. Brut.* 1.3: "yet of his own accord he hazarded a peril (ἑκὼν κίνδυνον) so great in order to save Sicily (σῶσαι Σικελίαν)." On the "endangered benefactor" motif, see Danker, *Benefactor*, 417–27.

Phil 2:5–11) in order to transform communal life within his house churches. An interesting intersection occurs in Plutarch's discussion of the acceptance or rejection of absolute power by rulers and the quality of rule that emerged from their decision. Solon and Publicola are contrasted in this manner:

Moreover, though Solon rightly and justly plumes himself on rejecting absolute power even when the circumstances offered it to him and his fellow citizens were willing that he should take it, it redounds no less to the honour of Publicola that, when he had received a tyrannical power, he made it more democratic and did not use even the prerogatives which were his by right of possession.[101]

It is against this type of paradigmatic narrative that Paul's gentile audiences would have been able assess, if only by contrast, the nature and scope of Jesus' radical divestment of status and power in Philippians 2:5–11 and its social implications for humility and selflessness in their corporate relations. It also helps us to understand sympathetically Paul's refusal to play the role of a tyrant over his Corinthian converts (2 Cor 11:20–21), as opposed to the interloping super-apostles.[102]

Finally, we find another intriguing intersection between Paul and Plutarch when the biographer compares the stance of Aristides and Cato towards wealth. Whereas Cato increased his wealth,

Aristides, on the other hand, was so poor (τῇ πενίᾳ) as to bring his righteousness (τὴν δικαιοσύνην) into dispute, as ruining a household, reducing a man to beggary (πτωχοποιόν), and profiting everybody rather than its possessor ... He is not helpful to others, while heedless of himself and his family. Indeed, the poverty of Aristides would seem to have been a blemish on his political career, if, as most writers state, he had not foresight enough to leave his poor daughters a marriage portion, or even the cost of his own burial ... Whereas, though Aristides was foremost of the Greeks, the abject poverty (ἄπορος πενία) of his descendants forced some to ply a fortune-teller's trade, and others, for very want, to solicit the public bounty, while it robbed them all of every ambition to excel, or even to be worthy of their great ancestor.[103]

Here we see registered with graphic horror the reaction of the ancients to the idea that a benefactor like Aristides might, inconceivably, so impoverish himself that he would no longer be a "day-labour" (πένης) but a "beggar" (πτωχός).[104] Such a decision was ultimately inimical to his family and himself, no matter its benefits to others, because it deprived his family of the ability to maintain or surpass their ancestral honour. The immensity of the cultural shame involved in

---

[101] Plutarch, *Comp. Sol. Publ.* 2.3.

[102] See S.B. Andrews, "Enslaving, Devouring, Exploiting, Self-Exalting, and Striking: 2 Cor 11:19–20 and the Tyranny of Paul's Opponents," in *Society of Biblical Literature 1997 Seminar Papers*, ed. anon. (Atlanta: Society of Biblical Literature, 1997), 460–90.

[103] Plutarch, *Comp. Arist. Cat.* 3.3, 5–6.

[104] On rhetorical paradigms of poverty, see Alewell, *Über das rhetorische* παραδειγμα, 56–60.

Aristides' self-impoverishment provokes Plutarch to reappraise the dishonour of poverty and thus construe Aristides' "reprehensible" actions as being in reality "noble":

> Poverty (πενία) is never dishonourable (αἰσχρόν) in itself, but only when it is a mark of sloth, intemperance, extravagance, or thoughtlessness. When, on the other hand, it is the handmaid of a sober, industrious, righteous, and brave man, who devotes all his powers to the service of the people, it is the sign of a lofty spirit that harbours no mean thoughts.[105]

This comparison of Cato and Aristides provides us keen insight into profound shock with which the self-destitution of Christ in 2 Corinthian 8:9 (δι' ὑμας ἐπτώχευσεν) would have been heard. It also allows us to appreciate the sheer delight for contemporary auditors to learn – in an unexpected reversal of cultural expectations – that Christ's dependents were left enriched (ἵνα ὑμεις πλουτήσητε) rather than impoverished through his divestment of wealth (τῇ ἐκείνου πτωχείᾳ). It also underscores the social force that a paradigmatic narrative could acquire for an audience when wielded by skilled writers such as Plutarch and the apostle Paul.

7.2.5.2. De Viris Illustribus

Another important collector of *exempla* is the writer of the anonymous *De Viris Illustribus* ("Deeds of famous Men"). This anonymous collection of seventy-seven biographical sketches stretches from King Proca, Romulus' great-grandfather, to the Roman general Pompey, defender of the *res publica* in the face of Caesar's onslaught. There is little doubt that this list of republican luminaries, prefaced by the Roman kings (*De Viris Illustribus* 1–9), is intended to depict a cavalcade of virtue (10–77) culminating in Pompey the Great. The *exempla* are designed for the replication of posterity, presumably from the age of the Caesars onwards. On the rare occasion where the language of "imitation" and "example" is used, it refers to the maintenance of the cult and ancestral piety (*De Viris Illustribus* 4 [*imitatur*], 7 [*exemplo*], 27 [*exemplum patris imitatus*]).

The imitation, therefore, is more conceived collectively than individually as far as the *exempla* enumerated. It is the cumulative force of republican virtue that is the writer's focus here as opposed to the virtue of isolated republican individuals. In this regard, the absence of moralistic commentary interrupting each sparse narrative allows readers to draw their own conclusions in an impres-

[105] Plutarch, *Comp. Arist. Cat.* 4.1. Note how Plutarch (*ibid.*, 4.5–6) concludes (somewhat defensively) regarding Aristides: "Great is the simple life, and great its independence, but only because it frees a man from the anxious desire of superfluous things. Hence it was that Aristides, as we are told, remarked at the trial of Callias, that only those who were poor in spite of themselves (τοῖς ἀκουσίως πενομένοις) should be ashamed of their poverty (αἰσχύνεσθαι πενίαν); those who, like himself, chose poverty, should glory in it."

sionistic way as to why the republican leaders were so great. Significantly, the figure of Caesar is bypassed, apart from the symbolism of the telling episode where Caesar – strategically recounted in the final sentence of the work – is reduced to tears when Pompey's head was presented to him in an Egyptian covering (*De Viris Illustribus* 77). In sum, the transformation envisaged for each new generation in *De Viris Illustribus* consisted in conformity to an idealised past and the reinvigoration of Rome's future leadership through a renewed commitment to its republican legacy.

7.2.5.3. Facta et Dicta Memorabilia

Finally, we turn to Valerius Maximus' *Facta et Dicta Memorabilia* ("Memorable Doings and Sayings"), composed during the reign of Tiberius (AD 14–37). Divided into short chapters, the work provides *exempla* – Roman and foreign – for the consideration of posterity.[106] The *exempla* congregate in the fields of virtue and vice, religious practice and ancestral custom.[107] The work evinces a strong senatorial perspective towards the republican past, but, over against the *De Viris Illustribus*, Valerius Maximus endorses enthusiastically the new imperial order (Valerius Maximus 3.2.19).[108] The aim of the work is set out clearly at the outset (1. praef.):

> I have determined to select from famous authors and arrange the deeds and sayings worthy of memorial (*memoratu digna*) of the Roman City and external nations, too widely scattered in other sources to be briefly discovered, to the end that those wishing to take examples may be spared the labour of lengthy search.

Valerius Maximus also makes it plain that he is totally committed to Roman mimetic culture:

> At dinners the elders used to recite poems to the flute on the noble deeds of their forebears to make the young more eager to imitate them (*quo ad ea initanda iuventutum*

[106] For helpful discussion of the genre of the work, see Alewell, *Über das rhetorische* παραδειγμα, 36–53; Maslakov, "Valerius Maximus," *passim*; Skidmore, *Practical Ethics*, 31–50.

[107] On the moral purpose of the work, see Skidmore, *Practical Ethics*, 53–82.

[108] For Julius Caesar, see Valerius Maximus 3.2.19: "bright glory of the stars, as formerly of arms and the gown, the divine Julius, surest image of true valour." For Augustus, see Valerius Maximus 2.8.7: "with (the oak wreath) the doorposts of the August dwelling triumph in eternal glory." For Tiberius, see Valerius Maximus 1. praef.: "Caesar, surest foundation of the fatherland, in whose charge the unanimous will of the gods and men has placed the governance of land and sea, by whose celestial providence the virtues of which I shall tell are most kindly fostered and the vices most sternly punished." There is no need to dismiss Valerius Maximus' adulation of Tiberius as "conventional" for his age and, therefore, insincere. As J. Hellegouarc'h ("Etat présent des travaux sur l''Histoire Romaine' de Velléius Paterculus," *ANRW* 2.32.1 [1984]: 401–36, at 427) observes, "Velléius a servi sous Tibère et on peut parfaitement admettre qu'il ait eu de l'admiration pour lui; il est le représenant d'une classe sociale, composée d'officiers et de fonctionnaires, qui est naturellement attachée et soumise à l'empereur."

alacriorem redderent). What more splendid and more useful too than this contest? Youth gave appropriate honour to grey hairs, age that had travelled the course of manhood attended those entering on active life with fostering encouragement. What Athens, what school of philosophy, what alen-born studies should I prefer to this domestic discipline?

In this regard, while the motif of "glory" appears regularly throughout the work (esp. 8.14), our author makes it plain that "glory" emanates pre-eminently from Roman *exempla*. Speaking of examples of military discipline, Valerius comments regarding the great difficulty in representing accurately examples of glory in a glorious culture:

Give any one of these (examples) to communities no matter how a famous and they will seem amply furnished with the glory of military discipline. But our city ... has filled the entire globe with every kind of marvellous examples ... Therefore I too, Postumius Tubertus and Manlius Torquatus, strictest guardians of warlike concerns, feel hesitation as I include you in memorial narrative, because I perceive that overwhelmed by the weight of the glory you have deserved I shall reveal the insufficiency of my abilities rather than present your virtue in its proper light.[109]

Notwithstanding, Valerius Maximus parades a range of *exempla*, Roman and foreign, in which the language of "imitation" is specifically used. The models are variegated but decisive in their impact. Crassus imitated Romulus in his dedication of the *spoila opima* to Jupiter (3.2.4: *imitari*). Anaxarchus emulated the fortitude of Nearchus (3.3 ext. 3: *aemulus*). M. Curius was the "consummate pattern of Roman frugality (*exactissima norma Romanae frugalitatis*)" and, simultaneously, "a clearly established model of bravery (*fortitudinis perfectissimum specimen*)" (4.3.5a). Porcia M. Cato's daughter, upon hearing that her husband Brutus had been killed at Philippi, imitated (*imitata*) her father's "manly end with a woman's spirit" by placing burning coals in her mouth (4.6.5). M. Cotta emulated the filial piety (*hanc pietatem aemulatus*) of the young Manilius towards his father L. Manilius Torquatus by defending his own father at trial (5.4.4). Finally, Valerius Maximus (5.8.3; cf. Polybius, 6.53.1–6.54.4) reveals why the Roman nobles decked their houses with funeral masks and their pedigrees below them in the first part of the house:

For he saw that within the hall where he sat was placed the mask of Torquatus the Imperious, conspicuous in its severity, and as a very wise man he bethought himself that the effigies of a man's ancestors with their labels are placed in the first part of the house in order that their descendants should not only read of their virtues but imitate them (*imitarentur*).[110]

To conclude, the crucial difference between the *De Viris Illustribus* and *Facta et Dicta Memorabilia* lies in the forward-looking outlook of Valerius Maximus: the glory of the republican houses had culminated in the glory of the trium-

---

[109] Valerius Maximus 2.7.6.

[110] See also Pliny the Elder, *Nat.* 35.3.7; Sallust, *Bell. Jug.* 4.

phant Julio-Claudian house, whereas, in the former work, Caesar's tears over Pompey's decapitation (*De Viris Illustribus* 77) underscores with pathos the decline in exemplary virtue during the reign of the Julio-Claudians.

7.3. Paul's Inversion of Contemporary Models of Exemplary Virtue

In this section we will demonstrate how Paul's gospel interacts with the iconic status of the "great man" in Graeco-Roman antiquity, the paradigm of which was discussed in §§ 7.2.2–7.2.5. In response, we will proceed in the same order.

First, in response to the "boasting" culture of the Scipionic *elogia* and the imitation of the ancestral "glory" articulated in Cicero's speeches (§ 7.2.2),[111] Paul underscores that boasting is excluded by the law of "faith" over against the law of "works" (Rom 3:28; 4:2–3). The gospel of Christ crucified, with its radical reversal of human standards, reduces to nothing the accolades of status – past and present – so that no one could boast before God (1 Cor 1:26–27). There is one "Lord of glory" even if the rulers of this age did not recognise him (2 Cor 2:8). For Paul, the believer's "boasting" arises from the wonder of our new status in Christ (1 Cor 1:30–31); it celebrates God's missionary work through his appointed vessels as opposed to the self-commendation of the "super-apostles" (2 Cor 10:18); it rejoices in the progress of converts towards the day of Christ (Phil 2:16). Experientially, Paul boasts in his weakness (2 Cor 11:30; 12:6) because Christ's sufferings (Col 1:24) rob him of his self-sufficiency and open him up to the discovery of divine power amidst weakness (2 Cor 12:9–10). In sum, Paul gutted the Roman boasting system of its anthropocentric basis as he considered the social and theological implications of 'dying and rising' in Christ against the backdrop of the agonistic culture of the first-century.

While the glory of ancestral culture presented advantages for the Jew (Rom 9:1–5; cf. Phil 5:5–6; Gal 1:14), the only legitimate ancestral inheritance that would secure "glory" for Jew and Gentile before God was the justifying faith of Abraham and Isaac, our "fathers" (Rom 4:1–25; 9:10; Gal 3:6–14) Moreover, although transformation in glory has begun already through the Lord who is Spirit (2 Cor 3:18; cf. Gal 3:14; 5:16–26), Paul postpones the full attainment of glory until the arrival of the eschaton (Rom 8:18–21; 2 Cor 4:17–18; Phil 3:20–21).

We have seen that Cicero called upon the narrow clique of the Senatorial *optimates* to imitate him in defence of the *res publica* (§ 7.2.2). By contrast, Paul is more constricted in the locus of his imitation but wider in the scope of his appeal: "Imitate me as I imitate Christ" (1 Cor 11:1: μιμηταί μου γίνεσθε καθὼς κἀγὼ Χριστοῦ). Christ, who had become "all things to all people" in his cruci-

[111] On ancestral glory in Cicero, see Harrison, *Paul and the Imperial Authorities*, 212–19.

fixion, provides the paradigm for Paul's pastoral ministry. Rather than enshrining the rights of one particular group (e.g. Cicero's *optimates*), Paul accommodates to different ethnic and cultural groups by selflessly surrendering his rights (1 Cor 9:19–23), with a view to establishing communities in Christ that would unite diverse groups rather than divide them into warring factions.

Whereas the Julio-Claudian and Flavian propaganda asserted that the ruler had became the embodiment of all virtue, Paul demotes the ruler to the subordinate status of God's 'servant' (Rom 13:4, 6) who, like the rest of humanity, awaits the arrival of eschatological judgement (13:11–13). Moreover, Christ's "virtue" has been democratised throughout the body of Christ (Rom 5:18b, 19b; 8:29). The extension of mercy, the prerogative of Nero in the imperial body, was now the preserve of believers of believers in the body of Christ (Rom 12:1, 8b).

Second, the iconic Augustus – the fulfilment of republican history and the yardstick of virtue for Roman leaders past and future (§ 7.2.3) – had been outshone by the Benefactor of the ages. Romans 5:12–21 explodes with the language of "grace" and "overflow" – formulaic in the imperial propaganda – as Paul describes the superiority of the reign of grace in Christ.[112] Whereas Augustus had descended from the line of Romulus and the line of Aeneas, Paul reconfigures humanity in Romans 5:6–10 into two new lines of virtue that culminate in disappointment: one might conceivably die for the "benefactor" (ὑπὲρ γὰρ τοῦ ἀγαθοῦ) from the Greek world or the "righteous" man (ὑπὲρ δικαίου) from the Jewish world, but no one would die for dishonourable humanity. Seemingly, in terms of "crisis management" of humanity, there was no hope of any soteriological solution to humanity's desperate plight. The reason was clear. In the Graeco-Roman honour system, grace calculated the likelihood of its reciprocation in advance: Nero's mercy, for example, would only be extended to *worthy* citizens and allies in the imperial body (§ 7.2.2).

But, at the "right" time (Rom 5:6: ἔτι κατὰ καιρόν) – both in terms of God's timing and the desperate situation of his dependents – a dishonoured benefactor chose to die in an act of grace for his impious enemies (5:6b [ὑπὲρ ἀσεβῶν], 8b [ἔτι ἁμαρτωλῶν], 10a [ἐχθροὶ ὄντες]). By means of this undiscriminating and foolish act of beneficence on behalf of ungrateful dependents (Rom 1:21; 1 Cor 1:18–25), Christ managed the universal crisis that Augustus and the other heroes of the *forum Augustum* could not solve: the Adamic reign of sin and death (Rom 5:12–21). Christ, the τέλος of salvation history (Rom 10:4: "goal", "end"), fulfilled the law by absorbing its curse in his own person on the cross (Gal 3:10–14; Col 2:13–14), so that the blessing of Abraham might come by faith to humanity through the promised Spirit (Gal 3:14b).[113] As a result, instead of

[112] For discussion, see J. R. Harrison, "Paul, Eschatology and the Augustan Age of Grace," *TynBul* 50.1 (1999): 79–91.

[113] For discussion, see Harrison, *Paul and the Imperial Authorities*, 190–97.

the accolade *Pater Patriae* being the preserve of Augustus, believers had the extraordinary privilege of addressing God as *abba*, "Father", through the indwelling Spirit (Rom 8:15; Gal 4:6; cf. Mark 14:36). Paul's counter-imperial family, which crossed the social and ethnic divide of antiquity, had supplanted the Julio-Claudian networks of privilege and obligation with a new set of social relations that would ultimately transform the ancient world.

Third, the honorific inscriptions of the eastern Mediterranean basin, infused with mimetic concerns (§ 7.2.4), are open to the same criticisms that Paul launched against the Roman ideal of glory, outlined above. With their carefully tabulated lists of benefactions, priesthoods, gymnasiarchal service, and so on, the eulogistic inscriptions fall prey to Paul's savage parody of Graeco-Roman honorific culture in 2 Corinthians 11:16–30. Paul "foolishly" boasts in the inflated rhetorical style of the honorific inscriptions, but robs their content of validity by boasting in a shameful catalogue of weakness.[114] Even the prized boast of being an endangered benefactor (2 Cor 11:26: κινδύνοις) is subverted by his grandiloquent oath that he, like Demosthenes, was the cowardly benefactor who abandoned the city in the hour of crisis (2 Cor 11:30–32).[115] In the end, Paul portrays himself as a comic figure playing a series of stereotyped roles in the passing mime shows of antiquity – an abject figure of ridicule like his crucified Lord.[116] Only such brutal self-derision on Paul's part could shock the self-satisfied Corinthians to reappraise their client-patron relationship with their boastful "super-apostles."

Fourth, whereas the carefully constructed paradigms of virtue found in the collectors of *exempla* (Plutarch's ΣΥΓΚΡΙΣΙΣ, *De Viris Illustribus*, Valerius Maximus: §§ 7.2.5.1–7.2.5.3) venerated the idealised past, the emphasis of Paul is upon the transforming newness of the reign of grace in the present (Rom 7:6; Gal 6:15; 2 Cor 5:17), with a view to the inconceivably glorious arrival of the new creation in the future (Rom 8:18–25; 1 Cor 15:42–49; 2 Cor 4:16–18).

Of particular interest is the paradigm of the "impoverished benefactor" in antiquity,[117] as Plutarch's heated debate about the social legitimacy of Aristides' divestment of wealth illustrates. Ancient cities ensured that benefactors were not reduced to the humiliation of being either a πένης ("day-labourer", "poor man") or a πτωχός ("beggar", "pauper"): the honour of being deemed ἀλειτούργητος ("free from public services") for a specified period enabled the benefactor to have enough breathing space to recoup his depleted reserves. However, a benefactor who let his reserves slide to the level of becoming a πτωχός was morally,

[114] For discussion, see J. R. Harrison, "In Quest of the Third Heaven: Paul and His Apocalyptic Imitators," *VC* 58.1 (2004): 24–55, esp. 46–55.

[115] See Harrison, *Paul's Language of Grace*, 335–40.

[116] L. L. Welborn, "The Runaway Paul," *HTR* 92.2 (1999): 115–63.

[117] For discussion, see Harrison, *Paul's Language of Grace*, 250–56.

as the Anonymous Iamblichi note, κακός ("bad").[118] Useless as a benefactor, therefore, Christ had been disqualified as a paradigm of virtue. Such was the momentum of the social dishonour that Christ had experienced in becoming God's impoverished benefactor for the salvation of the ungrateful (2 Cor 8:9) and in being an exemplar of unstinting grace for his suffering apostles (6:10). Only God's glorious vindication of his dishonoured benefactor reversed this crippling social stigma (Phil 2:9–11) and enriched his dependents beyond their wildest dreams (2 Cor 8:9b).

There is little doubt, therefore, that Paul is debunking the adulation of the "great man" in antiquity, no matter the social and cultural context or the eulogistic genre employed to celebrate his status. Paul does not thereby dismiss the conventions of honorific culture towards the powerful (Rom 13:7b), but sets them in the new context of mutual honouring as an expression of love (12:10; 13:8–10), with special emphasis on the priority of the weak as far as the extension of honour within the body of Christ (1 Cor 12:23–24). In sum, Paul's figure of the crucified and impoverished benefactor triumphed over the powerful luminaries of antiquity by virtue of his impartial offer of overflowing beneficence to the unworthy, through his "crisis management" of the cosmic forces holding humanity hostage to sin and death, and by means of his flawless "virtue" being freely transferred to his dependents.

However, a final issue demands clarification. How does Paul's language of "imitation" contribute to the demise of the "great man"? The issue must be addressed because E. Castelli has powerfully argued Paul has employed his parental imagery in order to impose hierarchically μίμησις of himself upon his converts as a strategy of conformity.[119] In other words, if Castelli is correct, Paul merely dismantles one hierarchy – the imitation of the great man in antiquity – in order to impose another hierarchy upon his house churches. This, in my opinion, distorts the social intention of Paul's parental metaphors and his language of imitation.

7.4. Paul's Language of "Imitation" and Civic Paradigms of Virtue

In this section I will argue that Paul undermined the status of the "great man" in antiquity by linking a cruciform model of discipleship to the corporate *mimesis* that the apostle sponsored within his house churches. In particular, Paul's experience of Christ's resurrection power in the humiliation of weakness radically reshaped his understanding of social relations in ways that were antithetical to the values of the Graeco-Roman elite. Consequently, Paul's mimetic

---

[118] Harrison, *Paul's Language of Grace*, 264–68.
[119] See Castelli, *Imitating Paul*, 98–111, 115–16.

ethos became a subversive force for social transformation within the eastern Mediterranean *poleis* as the first believers articulated a new understanding of leadership that challenged the hierarchical, agonistic and honour-driven models of antiquity.

In the case of the church at Thessalonica, the believers imitated the suffering apostles and the Lord by persevering in their persecutions and receiving God's word with Spirit-inspired joy (1 Thess 1:6: ὑμεῖς μιμηταὶ ἡμῶν ἐγενήθητε καὶ τοῦ κυρίου). Paul's use of the passive ἐγενήθητε in verse 6, as many scholars have observed, points to God's agency in producing a Christ-centred imitation in the lives of the believers. The Thessalonians had also imitated the churches of God in Judea by not wilting under the heavy persecution of their countrymen (1 Thess 2:14: ὑμεῖς γὰρ μιμηταὶ, ἐγενήθητε, ἀδελφοί, τῶν ἐκκλησιῶν τοῦ θεοῦ τῶν οὐσῶν ἐν τῇ Ἰουδαίᾳ). Finally, Paul encouraged his converts to imitate him as an artisan who worked with his own hands (cf. 1 Cor 4:12) instead of being dependent on wealthy Roman patrons (2 Thess 3:7: δεῖ μιμεῖσθαι ἡμᾶς; 3:9: ἵνα ἑαυτοὺς τύπον δῶμεν ὑμῖν εἰς τὸ μιμεῖσθαι ἡμᾶς; cf. 1 Thess 2:9), including, if B.W. Winter is correct, Thessalonian politarchs such as Aristarchus (Acts 19:29; 20:4).[120]

Paul's mimetic ethos addresses two significant areas of urban life at Thessalonica for the first Christians. First, Paul transforms the social humiliation of persecution for the Thessalonians at the hands of their countrymen by interpreting the believer's suffering as a replication of the sufferings of the earthly Jesus.[121] Second, the paradigm of mimetic behaviour was extended to the work life of believers. Paul warned the Thessalonians against becoming increasingly dependent on the patronage of the wealthy, even though there were serious corn shortages in the empire in AD 51 due to famine (Tacitus, *Ann.* 12.43).[122] In this regard, Paul insisted that certain believers at Thessalonica were to abandon their parasitic dependence upon Roman networks of patronage for (presumably) the corn dole, as well as their dependence upon the support of wealthy Christian patrons in the city.[123] Rather, in imitation of their apostle's personal financial policy, these believers were not to insist upon their perceived "rights" (2 Thess 3:9a) or burden the "great men" of Thessalonica with further demands for financial support (3:8b). Consequently, Paul's mimetic ethos began to chal-

---

[120] B.W. Winter, *Seek the Welfare of the City: Christians as Benefactors and Citizens of the City* (Carlisle: Paternoster Press, 1994), 46.

[121] Note the observation of Stanley ("'Become Imitators of Me'", 866): "... Paul conceived his apostolic vocation as a prolongation of Jesus' role as the Suffering Servant of Yahweh." Further, see *idem*, "The Theme of the Servant of Yahweh in Primitive Christian Soteriology, and Its Transposition by St Paul," *Bib.* 16 (1954): 385–425; L.J. Windsor, *Paul and the Vocation of Israel: How Paul's Jewish Identity Informs His Apostolic Ministry, with Special Reference to Romans* (Berlin and Boston: De Gruyter, 2014), 96–111.

[122] Winter, *Seek the Welfare of the City*, 53–55.

[123] On the Roman benefaction culture of Thessalonica, see especially H.L. Hendrix, *Thessalonians Honor Romans* (PhD diss., Harvard University, 1984).

lenge the traditional structures of the benefaction system and the social dominance of the benefactor in antiquity. In a radical reversal of social custom, the Thessalonian believers themselves were to assume the role of benefactor vacated by the "great man", performing acts of beneficence for the needy through their house-church networks and from their own resources (2 Thess 3:12–13: μη ἐγκακήσητε καλοποιοῦντες; cf. Gal 6:9: τὸ καλὸν ποιοῦντες μὴ ἐγκακῶμεν), notwithstanding the personal cost (cf. 2 Cor 8:1–5).[124]

In the case of the Corinthian house churches, factionalism had erupted among the believers as to whether Paul or Apollos was the more rhetorically accomplished teacher (1 Cor 1:10–16; 3:1–9, 16–17, 21–23; 4:6–7, 15), a contest that Paul, along with Apollos (4:6a), disavowed (1:20; 2:1–5; 4:20).[125] In reply, Paul encouraged his converts to imitate their "weak" and "dishonourable" apostle (1 Cor 4:16: μιμηταί μου γίνεσθε), whose socially humiliating ministry is depicted in verses 9–13.[126] Thus another significant status-indicator of the "great man" in antiquity – rhetorical eloquence – is here debunked by Paul's graphic portrayal of his self-lowering on behalf of others. Although it has been claimed that in this instance Paul is imposing conformity on his converts by means of his appeal to "fatherhood" (1 Cor 4:16–17), it is very clear that Paul as a parent wanted to approach his children in a spirit of loving gentleness (4:21: ἐν ἀγάπῃ πνεύματί τε πραΰτητος; cf. 2 Cor 10:1: πραΰτητος; Matt 11:29: ὅτι πραΰς εἰμι) rather than adopting the harsh tone of a disciplinarian (ἐν ῥάβδῳ).[127]

---

[124] Note the observation of B. W. Winter (*After Paul Left Corinth: The Influence of Secular Ethics and Social Change* [Grand Rapids: Eerdmans, 2001], 185): "... Paul revolutionised the benefaction tradition by demanding that Christian clients no longer remain 'in the old ranking system' as the full-time paid retainers of patrons but rather become benefactors ... For Christians it was not the transformation of the role of clients but its demise."

[125] For a very helpful coverage of the topic, see D. Litfin, *St Paul's Theology of Proclamation: 1 Corinthians 1–4 and Greco-Roman Rhetoric*, SNTSMS 79 (Cambridge: Cambridge University Press, 1994); B. W. Winter, *Philo and Paul among the Sophists*, SNTSMS 96 (Cambridge: Cambridge University Press, 1996); B. K. Peterson, *Eloquence and the Proclamation of the Gospel in Corinth,* SBLDS 163 (Atlanta: Scholars Press, 1998); C. Mihaila, *The Paul-Apollos Relationship and Paul's Stance toward Graeco-Roman Rhetoric*, SBLDS 402 (London: T&T Clark, 2009); P. J. Hartin, *Apollos: Paul's Partner or Rival?* (Collegeville: Liturgical Press, 2009).

[126] For an outstanding discussion of Paul's social metaphors in 1 Cor 4:9–13, see Welborn, *Paul, the Fool of Christ*, 52–86.

[127] For Castelli's arguments, see above. S. S. Bartchy ("Who Should Be Called Father? Paul of Tarsus between the Jesus Tradition and *Patria Potestas*," *BTB* 33.4 [2003]: 135–47, at 146, original emphasis) makes this comment about Paul's purported patriarchal attitudes: "Paul's apparent goal was not the creation of an egalitarian community in the political sense, but a *well-functioning family* in the kinship sense. In this family, each surrogate member used his or her strengths, whatever they were, to enrich the quality of life for the family rather than for themselves as individuals. Thus I contend that Paul was anti-patriarchal while *not* being egalitarian. His vision is that of a society of siblings, of surrogate brothers and siblings, not related by blood, but now bound together by something even deeper: the personally chosen, intentionally embraced, and shared commitment to the will of God the Compassionate."

In 1 Corinthians 11:1, Paul encourages his converts to imitate himself and Christ (μιμηταί μου γίνεσθε καθὼς κἀγὼ Χριστοῦ) by forgoing their right to eat meat offered to idols. The intention behind Paul's summons was that the factionalised Corinthians might thereby experience the unity that comes through mutual acceptance and the service of the weak in the body of Christ (1 Cor 9:19–23; 10:31–33). Here the rights of the "strong" – those who possessed the wealth and social mobility to enjoy "consecrated meat" at various cultic occasions – are bypassed in favour of the "weak" of the lower classes who could not afford to buy meat and who were scandalised by the "idolatrous" involvement of the "strong" in the cultic associations (1 Cor 8:9–11; 10:14–22, 23–24, 28–30).[128] Once again, we are witnessing how Paul's mimetic ethos restructures social relations in antiquity.

Moreover, in confining the paradigm of imitation to Christ alone (1 Cor 11:1b: καθὼς κἀγὼ Χριστου), Paul undermines the centrality of imperial *mimesis* in the first century (§§ 7.2.2–7.2.3). Paul counters the social agenda of the Julio-Claudian propaganda by saying that divine "justice" and "mercy" is mediated exclusively through the crucified Christ (Rom 3:25–26; 9:15–18; 11:31–32; 12:1; 1 Cor 7:25b; 2 Cor 1:3a; 4:1) as opposed to the Roman ruler, notwithstanding the ruler's legitimate role in maintaining social cohesion (Rom 13:4).[129] Christ rules with impartial justice over the nations as the Messianic Son and the risen Lord of the house of David (1 Cor 8:5–6; Rom 1:2–5; 2:5–16; 15:12; 16:25–27; cf. 2 Sam 7:11–16; Pss 2:1–12; 89:19–37; 110:1–7) and offers unsolicited mercy to the nations (Rom 9:23–26; 10:16–20).[130] By contrast, Augustus and Nero, sons of the apotheosised Caesar and Claudius respectively (1 Cor 8:5),[131] belong to this

---

[128] For a sociological analysis of 1 Corinthians 8:1–11:1, see G. Theissen, "The Strong and the Weak in Corinth: A Sociological Analysis of A Theological Quarrel," in *idem*, *The Social setting of Pauline Christianity: Essays on Corinth* (Philadelphia: Fortress Press, 1982), 121–43. On the cultic associations, see J.R. Harrison, "Paul and the Cultic Associations," *RTR* 58.1 (1999): 31–47, revised and expanded as Chapter 9 in this volume.

[129] For the demonstration of divine "justice" and "mercy" in Paul, see δικαιοῦν ("to declare and treat as righteous"): Rom 3:24, 26, 28, 30; 4:5; 5:1, 9; 8:30, 33. δίκαιος ("just"): Rom 1:17; 3:26. δικαίωμα ("acquittal"): Rom 5:16. δικαίωσις ("putting into a right relationship", "acquittal"): Rom 4:25; 5:18. οἰκτιρμός ("compassion", "mercy", "pity"): Rom 12:1; 2 Cor 1:3. ἔλεος: "mercy", "compassion": Rom 9:23; 11:31; Eph 2:4. ἐλεεῖν ("to be merciful", "to show kindness"): Rom 9:15, 16, 18; 11:31, 32; 1 Cor 7:25. On Paul's presentation of *clementia* ("mercy") and *iustitia* ("justice") in their imperial context, see N. Elliott, *The Arrogance of the Nations: Reading Romans in the Shadow of Empire* (Minneapolis: Fortress Press, 2008), 59–119. On the question of God's impartiality in relation to his judgement, see J.M. Bassler, *Divine Impartiality: Paul and a Theological Axiom* (Chico: Scholars Press, 1982).

[130] On the imperial context of 1 Cor 8:5–6, see B.W. Winter, *After Paul Left Corinth*, 269–86. More generally, see *idem*, *Divine Honours for the Caesars: The First Christians' Responses* (Grand Rapids: Eerdmans, 2015).

[131] For documentary evidence on Nero as the son of the divine Claudius, see D.C. Braund, *Augustus to Nero: A Sourcebook on Roman History 31 BC–AD 68* (London/Sydney: Croom and Helm, 1985), §§ 235, 240, 244. For documentary evidence on Augustus as the son of the

passing age (7:31). The dynasty of the Caesars, with its iconic line of "virtuous" rulers, did not understand the vast social and political reordering that had occurred in the shame of the cross (1 Cor 2:6b, 8; cf. 1:22–23). Consequently, the house of the Caesars, along with the rest of humanity, awaits God's eschatological judgement (Rom 2:5–16; 13:11–12; 16:20). This would have been a rebuff to those "strong" believers among the social elite at Corinth (1 Cor 1:26b) who attended the Isthmian games, resited from Corinth back to the Isthmia in the early fifties,[132] and who had participated there in the idolatrous temple feasts and public festivals held in honour of the imperial ruler and the members of his family (1 Cor 8:10; 10:14–22).[133] In considering the needs of the "weak" in the body of Christ (1 Cor 8:8–13; 9:22; 10:31–11:1), the "strong", with their commitment to the powerful imperial networks at Corinth, would have to imitate the crucified Christ instead of being moulded into the likeness of Nero as the head of the "body of the empire" (§ 7.2.1: Seneca, *Clem.* 2.2.1).

Finally, in Philippians 3:17 Paul encourages his converts to imitate himself (συμμιμηταί μου γίνεσθε), as well as others who had lived according to the example that he and Timothy had set at Philippi (τύπον ἡμᾶς: cf. Phil 1:1; 2:19–24). As far the local Philippians who imitated the apostolic paradigm, undoubtedly Paul had in mind the selfless Epaphroditus (Phil 2:25–30; 4:18). But what precisely was the point of 'imitation' that Paul wanted the Philippians to replicate? In context, Paul must be referring to his refusal to boast in his ancestral status and nomistic fidelity as a Jew, as well as in his missionary achievements as a believer (Phil 3:4b–8; cf. Gal 1:14).[134] Paul's abandonment of achievement and inheritance is explained by the fact that he had gained by faith in Christ the gift of righteousness of God (Phil 3:9). However, somewhat unexpectedly, Paul's knowledge of Christ's resurrection power was experienced in the fellowship of

---

divine Julius, see Braund, *ibid.*, *passim*; L.R. Taylor, *The Divinity of the Roman Emperor* (Middletown: American Philological Association, 1931), 270–83.

[132] For discussion of the date of the resiting of the games, see Harrison, "Paul and the Athletic Ideal," reproduced as Chapter 4 in this volume.

[133] See Winter, *After Paul Left Corinth*, 271–76, 278–86. Note, too, how imperial family members were also considered "godlike" in the honorific inscriptions: Julia ("New Aphrodite": IGR IV 114); Livia ("New Hera": IGR IV 249); Gaius (*Neos Theos*: IGR IV 1094); Drusilla ("New Aphrodite": SIG[3] 798). The gem and numismatic evidence also points to the apotheosis of imperial family members, see L.J. Kreitzer, *Striking New Images: Roman Imperial Coinage and the New Testament World* (Sheffield: Sheffield Academic Press, 1996), 69–98. For the apotheosis of Caesar, watched by Augustus and his heirs, see the Belvedere altar (Rome, 12–2 BC). For the relief, see M. Beard, et al., ed., *Religions of Rome Volume 1: A History* (Cambridge: Cambridge University Press, 1998), 187 fig. 4.3.d.

[134] R.T. France (*Philippians* [Leicester; IVP, 1959], 145, original emphasis) notes in regards to the change of tense from the perfect to the present in verses 7 (ἥγημαι: "I have considered") to 8 (ἡγοῦμαι: "I consider"): "In the scales of his choice all the privileges he could claim as a Jew (verses 5–7) and as a Christian (verse 8) were offset by inestimable gain. This is stated in terms of *knowledge* (cf. verse 10) which is described in such a way as to leave the reader in no doubt about its uniqueness."

his sufferings and in daily conformity to his death, with a view to the eschatological resurrection (Phil 3:10–11). Precisely because Paul overturned any "confidence in the flesh" (Phil 3:3b, 4a, 4b) at the foot of the cross (3:10), the boasting culture of Graeco-Roman antiquity – with its catalogues of achievement and virtue – was sidelined in the Western intellectual tradition. Progressively humility would emerge as the crowning virtue of the "great" man.

What, then, was the dynamic that differentiated Paul's understanding of *mimesis* from that of his Graeco-Roman contemporaries? First, Paul confronted his auditors with the choice of conformity to this world (Rom 12:2) or to the image of Christ (8:29).[135] The status of Christ as "the image of the invisible God and the first-born of every creature" (Col 1:15) reduced the boastful luminaries of the Graeco-Roman world to insignificance. The choice between models, therefore, could not have been clearer. Second, the transformation of believers into Christ's glorious likeness had already begun in the present age through the Spirit (2 Cor 3:17–18; Col 3:10–11) and was given sharp behavioural focus in daily life by the example of the Father and Son (Eph 4:32–5:2; cf. 5:1: γίνεσθε οὖς μιμηταὶ τοῦ θεοῦ). Third, the death and resurrection of Christ had ensured the conformity of believers to the model of the risen Christ in the age to come (Rom 6:5; 8:19–21; 1 Cor 15:49; Phil 3:21). Fourth, as noted, it was ultimately the *cruciform* nature of Jesus' call to mimetic discipleship (Mark 8:34–38; cf. 1 Cor 1:18–25; 2 Cor 4:7–12; 13:4) and his example of humility and service (Mark 10:35–45; Luke 22:24–27; John 13:1–17; cf. Phil 2:5–8; Rom 15:7; 2 Cor 10:1; Col 3:13) that triumphed over the Graeco-Roman preoccupation with inherited status, individual achievement, and self-advertisement. Paul, a meticulous imitator of Christ, understood well the cost and glory of this alternate social order that was powerfully manifesting itself in his house churches.[136]

---

[135] Morrison, *The Mimetic Tradition*, 42.

[136] Note the comment of Judge ("The Teacher as Moral Exemplar," 187): "The idea of imitation offered a means of expressing the replication of Christ's experience, especially in social relations, that could be passed on in turn to those who believed in him."

Chapter 8

Paul and Ancient Civic Ethics: Redefining the Canon of Honour in the Graeco-Roman World

8.1. Prolegomena to Civic Virtue in the Greek East

8.1.1. The Quest for Honour from the Late Hellenistic to the Early Imperial Age

8.1.1.1. Paul's Language of "Honour" and "Shame"

From the late Hellenistic to the Julio-Claudian age the quest for civic honour underwent a constriction that reoriented its focus in the Greek East and Latin West. However, civic ethics remained undiminished in this renegotiation of honorific protocols between the provincial and imperial elites. The canon of honour in the eulogistic inscriptions provided a paradigm for those who sought honour in the public arena by serving the city. The virtues belonging to this canon were allocated as accolades to the honoree in order to provoke further benefits from the honorand and to provide an incentive for other benefactors to benefit the city.[1] Thus the "honour" system maintained social cohesion throughout the Roman empire and provided avenues of upward social mobility for its aspirants in the Mediterranean world.[2] Conversely, it assigned dishonour to those who violated its ethos of reciprocity by the "sin" of ingratitude, or who were insufficiently cautious regarding the protocols of honour under Julio-Claudian rule.[3]

Because Paul's Gentile converts were acculturated to the ethical values of the honour system, Paul's gospel had to engage its boasting, reciprocity ethos, and ethics.[4] This reordering of the hierarchy eof civic esteem occurred through the

[1] J.R. Harrison, *Paul's Language of Grace in Its Graeco-Roman* Context, WUNT II 172 (Tübingen: Mohr Siebeck, 2003), 40–43.

[2] J.E. Lendon, *Empire of Honour: The Art of Government in the Roman World* (rpt. Oxford: Oxford University Press, 2002).

[3] On the fate of Cornelius Gallus, see J.R. Harrison, *Paul and the Imperial Authorities at Thessalonica and Rome: A Study in the Conflict of Ideology*, WUNT I 273 (Tübingen, Mohr Siebeck, 2011), 228–30. For a more extended coverage, see *idem*, "The Erasure of Honour: Paul and the Politics of Dishonour," *TynBul* 66.2 (2016): 161–84.

[4] J.R. Harrison, "Paul's House Churches and the Cultic Associations," *RTR* 58.1 (1999): 31–44, esp. 45–47, reproduced and expanded as Chapter 9 in this volume; *idem*, "The Brothers as the "Glory of Christ" (2 Cor 8:23): Paul's *Doxa* Terminology in Its Ancient Benefaction Context," *NovT* 52 (2010): 156–88, esp. 181–87. On the dependence of Thessalonian believers on the city benefactors (2 Thess 3:6–13), see B.W. Winter, "'If a man does not wish to work ...'.

apostle's critique of the honour system and its ethics (Rom 12:3b, 10b; 13:7b–10; 1 Cor 12:24b–25) and, more positively, by his teaching on God's empowerment of marginalised believers (1 Cor 4:9–13; 2 Cor 4:7–12; 6:3–10; 11:16–12:10; 13:4) and the eschatological reversal of their dishonour (Rom 8:33–34; Phil 3:17–21). When Paul claims that he is not "ashamed of the gospel" (Rom 1:16: Οὐ γὰρ ἐπαισχύνομαι τὸ εὐαγγέλιον), he locates his gospel not only within the rhetoric of "honour" and "shame" discourse,[5] but also he highlights Christ's journey from the "foolishness" and "weakness" of the cross to his divine vindication as the risen and returning Lord (Rom 5:6–8; 6:4b; 1 Cor 1:18–31; 2 Cor 8:9; 13:4; Gal 3:13; Phil 2:5–11).[6] His ungrateful dependents are transferred by an act of grace from the divine wrath, aroused by their dishonouring of the Creator (Rom 1:18–32), to their participation in the glory of Christ's righteousness (Rom 5:18–19; 8:17–21, 29–30; 2 Cor 3:18; 4:17–18; 5:21; Phil 3:9–11).[7] Paul unveils a wide array of "honour" and "shame" terminology to explain the theological, ecclesiastical, and social consequences of this transfer.[8] This semantic domain, apart from δοξά and its cognates,[9] has been little studied against the backdrop of honorific rituals in the inscriptions and monuments of the eastern

A Cultural and Historical Setting for 2 Thessalonians," *TynBul* 40.2 (1989): 305–15. On the Roman benefactors at Thessalonica, see H. Hendrix, *Thessalonicans Honor Romans* (Th.D. diss., Harvard University, 1984); *idem*, "Beyond 'Imperial Cult' and 'Cults of Magistrates'," in *Society of Biblical Literature 1986 Seminar Papers*, ed. H.R. Kent (Chico: Scholars Press, 1986), 301–08; *idem*, "Benefactor/Patron Networks in the Urban Environment: Evidence from Thessalonica," *Semeia* 56 (1992): 39–58.

[5] D.A. deSilva, *The Hope of Glory: Honor Discourse and New Testament Interpretation* (Collegeville: Liturgical, 1999); *idem*, *Honor, Patronage and Purity: Unlocking New Testament Culture* (Downers Grove: IVP, 2002); R. Jewett, "Paul, Shame and Honor," in *Paul in the Greco-Roman World*, ed. J.P. Sampley (Harrisburg: Trinity Press International, 2003), 551–74; H. Neyrey, *New Testament Understanding of the Divine* (Minneapolis: Fortress, 2004), 144–90; J. Hellerman, *Reconstructing Honor in Roman Philippi: Carmen Christi as Cursus Pudorum*, SNTSMS 132 (Cambridge, Cambridge University Press, 2005); T. Finney, *Honour and Conflict in the Ancient World: 1 Corinthians in Its Greco-Roman Social Setting*, LNTS 460 (London: T&T Clark, 2011); R. McRae, "Eating with Honor: The Corinthian Lord's Supper in Light of Voluntary Association Meal Practices," *JBL* 130.1 (2011): 165–181; D.A. deSilva, "Paul, Honor, and Shame," in *Paul in the Greco-Roman World: A Handbook Volume 2*, ed. J.P. Sampley, 2nd ed. (London and New York: T&T Clark, 2016), 26–47. More generally, see D.L. Cairns, *Aidōs: The Psychology and Ethics of Honor and Shame in Ancient Greek Literature* (Oxford: Oxford University Press, 1993); D.A. deSilva, "Investigating Honor Discourse: Guidelines from Classical Rhetoricians," *SBL 1997 Seminar Papers* (Atlanta: Scholars Press, 1977), 491–525; J.R. Harrison, "The 'Fading Crown': Divine Honour and the Early Christians," *JTS* 54.2 (2003): 493–529; M.T. Finney, *Honour and Conflict in the Ancient World: 1 Corinthians in Its Greco-Roman Social Setting* LNTS 460 (London and New York: Bloomsbury/T&T Clark, 2012).

[6] M.D. Hooker, *Not Ashamed of the Gospel: New Testament Interpretations of the Death of Christ* (Grand Rapids: Eerdmans, 1994), 20–46.

[7] R. Jewett, *Romans*, Hermeneia (Minneapolis: Fortress, 2007), 46–53, 136–37.

[8] J.P. Louw and E.A. Nida, eds., *Greek-English Lexicon*, 2 Vols. (New York: United Bible Societies, 1988), Vol. 2 *s.v.* English Index: "honor/able", "shame/ful(ly)/less(ness)".

[9] J.R. Harrison, "Paul and the Roman Ideal of Glory in the Epistle to the Romans," in *The*

Mediterranean cities. However, New Testament studies have discussed honour from a modern sociological perspective,[10] applying honour discourse to Pauline exegesis.

What changes occurred to the Hellenistic "honour" system with the arrival of the Julio-Claudian rulers? What remained the same in terms of its ethical framework? What role did the local associations play in the allocation of honour, whether they were eulogising the Roman ruler, their benefactors and members?

8.1.1.2. The Concentration of Virtue and Honour in the Julio-Claudian Rulers

The quest of the Roman noble to equal and surpass the glory of his ancestors had led to such a heated competition for precedence among the leading families of the late republic that traditional conventions were overthrown and the state was plunged into a century of bloody civil war. The carnage was finally stopped when Augustus triumphed at the battle of Actium (31 BC), with the result that nobody could compete with the military power of the new ruler, exceed his grace as benefactor of the world, or outstrip his influence mediated through his *clientelae* across the empire. The quest for glory became constricted for the old noble houses, with the result that the language of "glory" became the preserve of Augustus and the members of the Julio-Claudian house.[11] The aristocratic elites of the cities in Greek East, including Ephesus, were dependent upon the grace of Augustus for the sponsorship of civic projects and for advancement within the *cursus honorum* ("course of honours").[12] Consequently, the Mediterranean elites in the provinces competed for the ruler's patronage, highlighted their achievements in the *cursus honorum* under his sponsorship, and reciprocated his munificence with honorific rituals.[13]

Epistle to the Romans, BETL 226, ed. U. Schnelle (Leuven and Walpole: Peeters, 2009), 323–63; *idem*, "The Brothers"; *idem*, "Paul and the Imperial Authorities," 201–69.

[10] On honour in classical and social-scientific studies, see Jewett, "Paul, Shame and Honor," 566–69.

[11] Harrison, *Paul and the Imperial Authorities*, 201–69, esp. 225–32.

[12] J.R. Harrison, "The 'Grace' of Augustus Paves a Street at Ephesus," *New Docs* 10 (2012): 59–63, § 11.

[13] In the I. cent. AD Corinthian inscriptions (J.H. Kent, *Corinth Volume VIII Part III: The Inscriptions, 1926–1950* [Princeton: American School of Classical Studies at Athens, 1966]; = IKorinthKent), the civic officials of Corinth replicate the conventions of Roman republican boasting, though imperially reconfigured. The magistracies are listed according to the progression of the *cursus honorum* (IKorinthKent §§ 149–164), with numerical tabulation of repeated magistracies (§§ 150, 158) and vignettes highlighting singular achievements. However, the *duoviri* (city councilors) spotlight their imperial priesthoods (§ 155: "pontifex"; § 157: "imperial priest of Neptune"; § 157: "priest of Britannic Victory") and their role in honouring apotheosised members of the imperial house (§ 153: "he introduced [poetry contests in honour of] the divine Julia Augusta"). They also boast in their achievements as *agonothetes* in organising the imperial games (§ 151: "[the first] to preside over the Isthmian games under the

At one level, the quest for honour among the civic elites of the Greek East exhibited continuity with the ruler cult of the past under the Julio-Claudians. However, the opportunities for the surviving noble houses at Rome in the Latin West to display publicly their ancestral honour in military triumphs was restricted by Augustus to the lesser triumph of the *ovatio* in 19 BC, the triumph proper now being confined to the victories of the ruler and his family. The public ceremony of the funeral, once a means of aristocratic self-advertisement, became a ritual reserved for the imperial family.[14] Other elements of discontinuity became apparent in the veneration of the ruler's presence through the cult of the virtues,[15] and in the obligation of recipients of the ruler's patronage to acknowledge him for their promotion in the *cursus honorum*.[16] Thus the ancestral honour of civic and royal luminaries in the Greek East was now viewed in the light of the vastly superior glory of Julio-Claudian house that had conquered the world and become its benefactor.[17] Even where the beneficence of the aristocratic provincial families does not explicitly acknowledge the ruler's patronage in the *cursus honorum*, its association with the imperial order is indicated in subtle ways (e.g. involvement in sponsoring local imperial games). With each transition of power during the Julio-Claudian period, the elites of the Greek East sought to make contact with the new ruler and his officials to preserve their patronage and honour under the new regime.[18] Moreover, the opportunities for social mo-

---

sponsorship of Colonia Laus Julia Corinthiensis"; § 154: "the first man to schedule the Caesarian games ahead of the Isthmian games").

[14] G.S. Sumi, *Ceremony and Power: Performing Politics in Rome Between Republic and Empire* (Ann Arbor: University of Michigan Press, 2005), 247–61. On imperial triumphs between 19 BC–AD 71, see M. Beard, *The Roman Triumph* (Cambridge, MA: The Belknap Press of Harvard University, 2007), 61–71.

[15] On the cult of the "virtues" see H. Mattingly, "The Emperor and His Clients," in *Essays on Roman Culture: The Todd Memorial Lectures*, ed. A.J. Dunston (Sarasota: Hakkert, 1976), 182–84; J.R. Fears, "The Cult of Virtues and Roman Imperial Ideology," *ANRW* II 17.2 (1981): 827–948. On the *virtus* of the Roman ruler, see Harrison, *Paul and the Imperial Authorities*, 138–41. On the virtues and the imperial coinage, see H. Mattingly, "The Roman 'Virtues'," *HTR* 30.2 (1937): 103–17; A. Wallace-Hadrill, "The Emperor and His Virtues," *Historia* 30.3 (1981): 298–323; C.F. Noreña, *Imperial Ideas in the Roman West: Representation, Circulation, Power* (Cambridge: Cambridge University Press, 2011): 371–02.

[16] The senatorial, equestrian and military protégés of Augustus acknowledge their indebtedness to the ruler for their posts in the inscriptions (Harrison, *Paul and the Imperial Authorities*, 229–30 n. 92), as do the powerful Ephesian elites by adding the epithets φιλοσέβαστος and φιλόκαισαρ to their names (S. van Tilborg, *Reading John in Ephesus* [Leiden: Brill, 1996], 197–98); P.A. Harland, *Associations, Synagogues, and Congregations: Claiming a Place in Ancient Mediterranean Society* [Minneapolis: Fortress, 2003], 125). R. Miles ("Communicating Culture, Identity and Power," in *Experiencing Rome: Culture, Identity and Power in the Roman Empire*, ed. J. Huskinson [London, Routledge, 2000], 35) observes regarding the extravagant Philopappos Monument at Athens (AD 114–116): "although the inscription portrays Philopappos as a powerful man, at the same time it displays the superior power of the Roman emperor himself."

[17] On SIG^3 798, see Harrison, *Paul and the Imperial Authorities,* 142–43.

[18] See J.R. Harrison, "Diplomacy over Tiberius' Accession," *New Docs* 10 (2012): 64–75, § 12.

bility and the acquisition of honour had been expanded by the ruler's civil and military administration, posts which new aspirants contested. Paradoxically, even free citizens were willing to become slaves in the imperial bureaucracy (*familia Caesaris*) in order to achieve the honour of its posts in the *cursus honorum*.[19]

However, the pace of competition among the Greek civic elites for honour became more heated in the imperial period. A. Zuiderhoek has argued that the upsurge of beneficence in the Eastern provinces in the first and second centuries AD "led to an increasing oligarchisation of social and political life in the cities, and a surge in elite incomes."[20] Disparities arose in the citizen body because of elite wealth and political power, with the result that social tension was never far from the surface. This potential for social rifts was subdued by elite gift giving. Society was redefined as "a sequence of hierarchically ordered status groups" instead of being, as was the Classical ideal, a "group of political equals" (*isonomia*).[21] Zuiderhoek claims that the consequence for civic ethics was that the canon of moral honorifics continued as normal,[22] but, gradually, a discontinuity began to emerge:

> What particularly stands out in the Greek honorific epigraphy especially of the Empire is the baroque exuberance of the language of praise. Such was the power of the citizen-oligarch of the Empire's eastern cities, and hence their need for legitimation, that merely showing one's virtue was no longer deemed sufficient. Benefactors had to show that they were *very, very good*, *in both words and deeds*, that is, in terms of the benefactions made, liturgies fulfilled and offices held on the one hand, and in terms of the honorific rewards received in exchange for such achievement on the other.[23]

Zuiderhoek's claim is confirmed in the Greek East by the 29 columns of decrees and letters honoring the Lycian benefactor, Opramoas of Rhodiapolis (c. AD 144).[24] There is also the long inscription detailing the endowment of the Ephesian benefactor, Caius Vibius Salutaris (IEph. Ia 27), as well as the extravagant monuments honouring Zoilos of Aphrodite and Philopappos of Athens (n. 16 *supra*). In the Latin West, too, the exuberant self-advertisement of the elites was

[19] G.H.R. Horsley, "Joining the Household of Caesar," *New Docs* 3 (1983): 7–9, § 1.

[20] A. Zuiderhoek, "Feeding the Citizens: Municipal Grain funds and Civic Benefactors in the Roman East," in *Feeding the Ancient Greek City*, G-RHSGCCA 1, ed. R. Alston and O.M. van Nyt (Leuven et al.: Peeters, 2008), 159–80, at 173.

[21] Zuiderhoek, "Feeding the Citizens," 174.

[22] Zuiderhoek, "Feeding the Citizens," 174.

[23] Zuiderhoek, "Feeding the Citizens," 175 (my emphasis).

[24] IGR III 739. F.W. Danker, *Benefactor: Epigraphic Study of Graeco-Roman and New Testament Semantic Field* (St. Louis: Clayton Publishing House, 1982), § 19; A. D'Hautcourt, "Public Finances and Private Generosity: The Example of Opramoas in Roman Lycia," *Journal of Economics, Business and Law* 5 (2003): 39–63, esp. 42–43; A. Zuiderhoek, *The Politics of Munificence in the Roman Empire: Citizens, Elites and Benefactors in Asia Minor* (Cambridge: Cambridge University Press, 2009), 122–25.

evidenced in late republican Rome by their construction of large ostentatious monuments.[25]

However, a fundamental question remains: to what extent did the quest for the acquisition of honour reach the base of the social pyramid in the I cent. AD?

8.1.1.3. Alternative Paths of Honour: Upward Mobility and the Local Associations

With the displacement of the Hellenistic ruler cult by the Julio-Claudian house and the shift of political fortunes that this heralded, the significance of the city-state (*polis*) as "the *controlling* factor in people's lives" declined to some degree.[26] As Danker notes, "more intimate types of association became popular."[27] Consequently, the small clubs and cultic associations flourished in the Greek East during the first century and beyond.[28] Care has to be exercised here, lest we imply, as Danker does, that there was either a disjunction between the local associations and moribund life of the polis, or that the membership of the local associations had little to do with the civic honour system of the local polis. Both implications have been challenged by recent research.[29] However, Danker is correct in saying that the local associations imitated the "bureaucratic" diction and syntax of the late Hellenistic city-state decrees, not only assigning honour to the socially elite benefactors of their clubs, but also allocating honour to their non-elite members. Members of the associations were of diverse social status, including among their constituency the urban poor, slaves, and freedmen,[30] and all the members appropriated, by virtue of their membership, the honorific titles and rituals of the association decrees.[31] As Danker explains,

[25] Harrison, *Paul and the Imperial Authorities*, 170–71.

[26] Danker, *Benefactor*, 26 (my emphasis).

[27] Danker, *Benefactor.*

[28] See E. A. Judge, *The First Christians in the Roman World: Augustan and New Testament Essays*, WUNT I 229, ed. J. R. Harrison (Tübingen: Mohr Siebeck, 2008), 596–668; R. S. Ascough et al., ed., *Associations in the Greco-Roman World: A Source Book* (Waco: Baylor University Press, 2012), 277–360; J. S. Kloppenborg and R. S. Ascough, eds., *Graeco-Roman Associations. Texts, Translations and Commentary. Attica, Central Greece, Macedonia, Thrace: Volume 1* (Berlin: De Gruyter, 2013); P. A. Harland, *Greco-Roman Associations: Texts, Translations and Commentary. II. North Coast of the Black Sea, Asia Minor*, BZNW 204 (Berlin and Boston: De Gruyter, 2014).

[29] Harland, *Associations, Synagogues, and Congregations*, 89–112. See K. Verboven ("The Associative Order: Status and Ethos Among Roman Businessmen in Late Republic and Early Empire," *Athenaeum* 95 [2007]: 861–93, at 870) on how associations enhanced civic life in cooperation with the civic authorities.

[30] S. G. Wilson, "Voluntary Associations: An Overview," in *Voluntary Associations in the Graeco-Roman World*, ed. J. S. Kloppenborg and S. G. Wilson (London and New York: Routledge, 2003), 1–15, esp. 10–11.

[31] Note the hierarchy of offices in the Bacchic Society (SIG^3 1109 *ll.* 1–10, 117–127: Provenance: Athens [164/165 AD]). But hierarchy is restricted in the feasts: "All members are, how-

... these clubs and associations affected the diction and syntax of the council chambers of city-states or of the chanceries of the Ptolemies or of the Seleucids. This diction and syntax brought to verbal expression deeply imbedded cultural values. For a brief moment, as is the case in a variety of deistic societies popular since the French Revolution, their members could play the role of esteemed civil service officials, of members of councils, and planning committees.[32]

In sum, a democratisation of honour occurred among groups outside of the patronage networks of the eastern provincial elites, though, as we have seen, obligation to the Roman ruler was not overlooked in the process,[33] and the upwardly mobile and elite members of the associations still pursued the traditional paths of honour within the polis (cf. n. 31 *supra*). Moreover, an upward mobility occurred within the hierarchy of the association, as its members sought the positions offered.[34] Furthermore, the decrees of the cultic associations, if Ephesus is representative, articulated a fusion of indigenous civic and imperial honours, so that the ruler's patronage would be maintained.[35] The civic authorities and the associations worked together harmoniously, in terms of their honour and cultic systems, provided that the associations did not create civic disturbances (Acts 19:38–40; IEph II 215; Pliny, *Ep.* 10.33–34, 93–94).[36] As Verboven concludes, "the hierarchic structure of the associations and the emphasis placed on honour and the display of honour within the associations reflected the situation in Roman society at large and helped to perpetuate the system"[37]. Finally, the

ever, eligible for the roles of the deities" (*ibid.*, *ll.* 126–127). A democratisation of honour occurs in the Society's recognition of the special honours and achievements of any member: "Any member who receives a legacy, or special honour (τειμήν), or change in status, shall make a drink-offering worthy of his new status" (*ibid.*, *ll.* 127–128). These achievements included receipt of citizen status, athletic prizes and civic honours (*ibid.*, *ll.* 128–137). Elite association members could attain public honours within the polis, while experiencing through their Society "alternate" paths of honour (Verboven, "The Associative Order," 882–86). For a sketch of and commentary on the inscribed column of the Bacchus Society and its iconography, see Harland, *Associations, Synagogues, and Congregations*, 82–83.

[32] F. W. Danker, "On Stones and Benefactors," *CurTM* 8.6 (1981): 351–56, at 352; Verboven, "The Associative Order," 869–71.

[33] For eastern association decrees honouring I. cent. Roman rulers, see Ascough, Harland, and Kloppenborg, *Associations*, §§ 108, 114, 124, 160, 190, 208.

[34] Verboven, "The Associative Order," 871 n. 57.

[35] P. A. Harland, "Honours and Worship: Emperors, Imperial Cults and Associations at Ephesus (First to Third Centuries CE)," *SR* 25 (1996): 319–34; *idem*, *Associations, Synagogues, and Congregations*, 115–36; van Tilborg, *Reading John in Ephesus*, 142–43.

[36] I. Arnaoutoglou, "Roman Law and *Collegia* in Asia Minor," *RIDA* 43 (2002): 27–44; Harland, *Associations, Synagogues, and Congregations*, 161–73, esp. 168–73.

[37] Verboven, "The Associative Order," 886. In the Silvanus association of Philippi (P. Pilhofer, *Philippi. Band II: Katalog der Inschriften von Philippi. 2. Auflage*, WUNT I 119 [Tübingen: Mohr Siebeck, 2009], § 164/L001) members gave minute benefactions to the association for statues and Temple repairs in comparison to the donations of wealthy benefactors for civic projects. For example, the wealthy Philippian benefactor, Lucius Decimus Bassus (*ibid.*, § 213/L347 [II cent. AD]), gave 30,000 sesterces to build the western fountain in the forum. Hellerman (*Reconstructing Honor*, 104) concludes: "We are obviously dealing with

grandiloquent language of moral praise, noted above, is also evident in the honorific decrees of the associations.[38]

To what extent does this honorific culture – conveyed in the decrees of the eastern Mediterranean elites and the local associations – inculcate ethics in the readers of the honorific inscriptions? What has modern scholarship said about this issue?

8.1.2. Civic Ethics and the Quest for Honour: A Survey of Modern Scholarship

8.1.2.1. Key Studies in Civic Ethics

The relation between civic ethics and the quest for honour in the public inscriptions has periodically ignited the interest of scholars. However, the focus of New Testament scholarship has been mostly upon the impact of popular philosophy upon Pauline ethics,[39] the Delphic canon and the *paideia* of the ancient gymnasium,[40] the ancient ethos of imitation,[41] the Stoic sage and his suffering.[42] Classical scholars have investigated the *arete* and *virtus* of the great man[43], the

---

two distinct levels of social status, with correspondingly different amounts of money available for benefaction. Nevertheless, the social values and behaviour of the two status groups mirror one another in a remarkable way."

[38] Ascough, Harland, and Kloppenborg, *Associations*, §§ 184, 212, 223, 224, 306.

[39] On the scholarly literature, see Harland, *Paul's Language of Grace*, pp. 168–69. Additionally, see J. T. Fitzgerald, *Friendship, Flattery, and Frankness of Speech: Studies on Friendship in the New Testament* (Leiden: Brill, 1996); *idem*, *Greco-Roman Perspectives on Friendship* (Atlanta: Scholars Press, 1997); T. Engberg-Pederson, *Paul and the Stoics* (Louisville: Westminster John Knox Press, 2000); *idem*, *Cosmology and the Self in the Apostle Paul: The Material Spirit* (Oxford: Oxford University Press, 2010); D. M. Scholer, ed., *Social Distinctives of the Christians in the First Century: Pivotal Essays by E. A. Judge* (Peabody: Hendrickson, 2008), 1–56 ("The Social Pattern of the Christian Groups in the First Century"), 73–97 ("St Paul and Classical Society"), 73–115; *idem*, "St Paul and Socrates", *The First Christians in the Roman* World, 670–83; *idem*, "'*Antike und Christentum*': Some Recent Work from Cologne", *Jerusalem and* Athens, WUNT I 265, ed. A. Nobbs (Tübingen: Mohr Siebeck, 2010): 69–79.

[40] R. S. Dutch, *The Educated Elite in 1 Corinthians: Education and Community Conflict in Graeco-Roman Context*, JSNTS 271 (London and New York: T&T Clark/Continuum, 2005); J. R. Harrison, "Paul and the Gymnasiarchs: Two Approaches to Pastoral Formation in Antiquity," in *Paul: Jew, Greek, and Roman*, PAST 5, ed. S. E. Porter (Leiden: Brill, 2008), 141–78, reproduced as Chapter 5 in this volume.

[41] B. Fiore, *The Function of Personal Example in the Socratic and Pastoral Epistles* (Rome: Biblical Institute Press, 1986); J. R. Harrison, "The Imitation of the Great Man in Antiquity: Paul's Inversion of a Cultural Icon," in *Christian Origins and Classical Culture: Social and Literary Contexts for the New Testament*, ed. S. E. Porter and A. W. Pitts (Leiden: Brill, 2013), 213–54, reproduced as Chapter 7 in this volume.

[42] J. T. Fitzgerald, *Cracks in an Earthen Vessel: An Examination of the Catalogues of Hardship in the Corinthian Correspondence*, SBLDS 99 (Atlanta: Scholars Press, 1988).

[43] J. Gerlach, ΑΝΗΡ ΑΓΑΘΟΣ (Munich: J. Lehmaier, 1932), esp. 7–14 on the inscriptional evidence. See also M. McDonnell, *Roman Manliness: Virtus and the Roman Republic* (Cambridge: Cambridge University Press, 2006).

"motive" formulae of the Greek inscriptions,[44] and the intersection of ethics in the literary and inscriptional evidence of the Greek East.[45]

However, C. Panagopoulos and M.-H. Quet, have opened up important perspectives on civic ethics. Panagopoulos argues that "the system of public *elogia* … functions well as the principal ideological regulator of Greek society under the Empire."[46] The inscriptional civic ideals ensured the domination of the local notables over the lower classes,[47] though this was secured by the property and inheritances of the municipal aristocracy, as well as by their posts as senior civil servants in the imperial bureaucracy. This domination extended to the small independent producers, who were excluded from the civic magistracies,[48] though their mercantile metaphors impacted contemporary authors (e.g. Dio Chrysostom, *Or.* 31).[49] By contrast, Quet focuses on the "ideological function" of Dio Chrysostom's rhetoric.[50] She argues that Plutarch and Dio Chrysostom employed their rhetoric to redefine, among the philosophical traditions, a "true Greek culture." This "would be compatible with the new social and political structures and allow the Greeks from cities to believe and feel free in the Roman Empire."[51]

However, the most significant work on civic ethics, overlooked by New Testament scholars, is E. Forbis' exhaustive study of the municipal virtues in the imperial period in the Latin West.[52] She assembles 482 honorary Latin texts – listed region by region in an Appendix[53] – commemorating the virtues and benefactions of men and women of all social classes. The inscriptions are drawn from municipal Italy, with the exception of Rome, and date from the late Republic to the third century AD. Forbis identifies the virtues pertaining to benefaction,[54] as well as the virtues animating patronage. She isolates the virtues pertinent to administration and politics,[55] differentiating them from the person-

---

44 E. Nachmanson, "Zu den Motivformeln der griechischen Ehreninschriften," *Eranos* 11 (1911): 180–96; M.J. Payne, ARETAS ENEKEN: *Honors to Romans and Italians in Greece from 26 to 27 BC* (PhD diss., Michigan State University, 1984).

45 C. Panagopoulos, "Vocabulaire et mentalité dans les Moralia de Plutarque," *DHA* 3 (1977): 197–235, at 235; M.-H. Quet, "Rhétorique, culture et politique: Le fonctionnement du discours idéologique chez Dion de Pruse et dans les Moralia de Plutarque," *DHA* 4 (1978): 51–119.

46 Panagopoulos, "Vocabulaire et mentalité," 233.

47 Panagopoulos, "Vocabulaire et mentalité."

48 Panagopoulos, "Vocabulaire et mentalité," 197

49 Panagopoulos, "Vocabulaire et mentalité."

50 Quet, "Rhétorique, culture et politique," 77.

51 Quet, "Rhétorique, culture et politique," 52.

52 E. Forbis, *Municipal Virtues in the Roman Empire: The Evidence of Italian Honorary Inscriptions* (Stuttgart and Leipzig: B.G. Teubner, 1996). Note Zuiderhoek ("Feeding the Citizens: The Politics of Munificence") on the hierarchicalism and competitiveness of civic ethics under the Empire.

53 Forbis, *Municipal Virtues*, 105–232.

54 Forbis, *Municipal Virtues*, 29–43.

55 Forbis, *Municipal Virtues*, 61–82

al and moral virtues.[56] Consequently, "communal application of personal moral virtue was the ideal."[57] The language of moral virtue represents a description of the honorand's responsibilities in daily community life as opposed to being "a form of ornamental flattery."[58]

Forbis observes that "the notion of *honor* often represents the public's settling of accounts after receiving a *beneficium*". As she elaborates,

> The opportunity afforded by praise language in honorary inscriptions was not used to embellish the beneficiaries' grateful posture, but pressed in unadorned and often abbreviated *honoris causa* formulas so as not to detract from praise of the honorand's virtues and achievements. As integral parts of public monuments experienced by many passers-by, honorary texts capitalized on circumstance by focusing attention on the honorand as an *exemplum* of virtue to be admired, and more importantly, to be emulated.[59]

Thus the summons to exceptional virtues (e.g. *rarissimus, singuaris, incomparabilis*) in public inscriptions did not set an ethical standard too high to attain in municipal life. Rather it stimulated the opposite reaction. As Forbis explains, "the distinguished individual who set seemingly incomparable standards provoked a perfect opportunity to capture the attention of competitive onlookers."[60]

Finally, Forbis contends that the promulgation of municipal ethics in Italy embraced and recognized the marginalised sectors of society (a conclusion diverging from Panagopoulos):

> Women and freedmen especially, realizing that personal integrity or chastity alone were inconsequential at their level of civic involvement, saw their best opportunity for public recognition in various forms of financial largesse.[61]

As far as civic ethics and honour in the Greek East, F.W. Danker explored the semantic field of benefaction that emerges from the Mediterranean epigraphic evidence. In profiling benefactors, Danker discusses the variegated terminology that defines the benefactor ethically and socially.[62] Another chapter is devoted to the sacrifice made by benefactor in exposing themselves to "danger" on behalf of their clients, a common motif of the honorific inscriptions.[63] Curiously, however, Danker's coverage of the terminology of "honour" itself is very brief,

---

[56] Forbis, *Municipal Virtues*, 83–90.

[57] Forbis, *Municipal Virtues*, 96. Forbis (*ibid.*) observes: "The language of praise in honorary texts was the voice of communities, elite and populace alike, articulating their desires for a prosperous and happy existence. To this end, the voice did concede the importance of moral virtue."

[58] Forbis, *Municipal Virtues*, 97.

[59] Forbis, *Municipal Virtues*, 12. Rather than being "ornamental flattery," the inscriptional language of praise "was directed primarily at those most involved in a community's daily life to describe their local responsibilities" (*ibid.*, 97).

[60] Forbis, *Municipal Virtues*, 90.

[61] Forbis, *Municipal Virtues*, 98.

[62] Danker, *Benefactor*, 317–92.

[63] Danker, *Benefactor*, 416–35.

being confined solely to *philotimia*.[64] E.A. Judge and R. Saunders have added local colour to Danker's picture by discussing the ethical terminology of the Ephesian inscriptions.[65]

Finally, Hellerman has investigated the hierarchical *cursus honorum* ("course of honour") in the Philippian inscriptions, arguing that Christ's descent from glory in Philippians 2:5–8 represents a counter-cultural *cursus pudorum* ("course of shame").[66] While Hellerman's thesis is finely argued, he has overlooked the rare occasions where "dishonor" becomes an issue in the honorific inscriptions. What light does this throw on Paul's theological reflection on cultural dishonour? What would some of Paul's "dishonoured" auditors have made of his reconfiguration of honour?[67] Conversely, what elements of honorific culture does Paul endorse and for what reasons?

8.1.2.2. Issues for Investigation

Several important issues emerge from our discussion above, overlooked in classical and New Testament scholarship. We will conduct an investigation of the interrelationship between honour and civic ethics in the inscriptional evidence of the Greek East, focusing on inscriptions, where relevant, from the eastern cities of Paul's house churches (Philippi, Thessalonica, Corinth, Ephesus). In order to understand further the civic context of honour and its canon of virtue in the house churches of Paul, we will also explore the honoring of luminaries in the eulogistic inscriptions and bring that corpus of evidence into dialogue with the moral accolades accorded to individuals on the honorific monuments and statues erected in ancient cities. By contrast, we will also highlight the occasions where the disruptive force of dishonour undermines the reciprocation of favour with civic honour, the positive social transaction routinely expected in antiquity. From there, having explored the literary (i.e. Dio Chrysostom), inscriptional and visual evidence relating to "honour" and "dishonor", we will evaluate Paul's language of "honour" and "shame" and its ethical implications for civil society.

---

[64] Danker, *Benefactor*, 328–29.

[65] E.A. Judge, "The Teacher as Moral Exemplar in Paul and in the Inscriptions of Ephesus," in *idem*, *Social Distinctives*, 175–188; R. Saunders, "Attalus, Paul *and PAIDEIA: The Contribution of I. Eph. 202 to Pauline Studies*," in *Ancient History in a Modern University. Volume II: Early Christianity, Late Antiquity, and Beyond*, ed. T.W. Hillard (Grand Rapids: Eerdmans, 1998), 175–83.

[66] Hellerman, *Reconstructing Honor*, 88–109, 129–56.

[67] Hellerman, *Reconstructing Honor*, 148–56, 161–66.

8.2. Ancient Civic Ethics: Issues of "Honour" and "Dishonour"

8.2.1. The Eastern Mediterranean Inscriptions: A Profile of Civic Honour

8.2.1.1. "Zeal" for Honour and the Inculcation of Civic Ethics

It is important to understand the interplay between the allocation of civic honour and the ethical and social incentives it generates, not only for the benefactor but also for the city councils that dispense the honours and for those who would acquire civic recognition. In an honorific decree from Thessalonica (Sept. 95 BC), the Thessalonican gymnasiarch Paramonos is eulogised: he "has e[ngag]ed very eagerly in the oversight of the office with [grace and] dignity, zealously (ἐκτενῆ) offering himself among those who provide for public expenses and increasing the customary honours ... for the gods and Roman benefactors."[68] On account of Paramonos' propriety and attendance to all expenses, the Thesssalonicans honoured their benefactor with a crown, statue and inscribed stele in the gymnasium. The rationale for these honours is not only the reciprocation of gratitude but also the hope that other – including the elite young men of the gymnasium conferring the honours – would be transformed into zealous civic benefactors like the gymnasiarch:

> ... it is good that those who aspire to public re[cog]nition (φιλοδόξ̣ω̣) obtain the appropriate honours so that others also when they consider the honours bestowed by The Youths might strive (ζηλωταὶ γίνωνται) for similar honours.[69]

A moral impetus in munificence, therefore, is unleashed by the city publicly honoring its benefactors, both in terms of the People's own reputation as grateful recipients of grace and of the character formation of the city's benefactors. A decree in honour of Menas of Sestos (c. 130–120 BC) unfolds the city's ethical and financial motivations with this clause:

> Therefore, in order that all might know that Sestos is hospitable to (lit. "manifestly honours") men of exceptional character and ability, especially those who from their earliest youth have shown themselves devoted to a glorious reputation (φιλοτίμους γινομένους), that the People might not be remiss in their gratitude (ἐν χάριτος ἀπόδοσει), and that also all others, as they see the People bestowing honours on exceptional men, might emulate the noblest qualities (ζηλωταί μὲν τῶν καλλίστων γίνωνται) and be moved to *arete* (πρὸς ἀρετήν: lit. "towards virtue"), to the end that the common good might be advanced as all

---

[68] C. Edson, ed., *Inscriptiones Graecae Epiri, Macedoniae, Thraciae, Scythiae. Pars II: Inscriptiones Macedoniae. Fasciculus I: Inscriptiones Thessalonicae et Viciniae* (Berlin: De Gruyter, 1972; = IG X 2.1), §4 *ll.* 7–11. Tr. Hendrix, "Benefactor/Patron Networks," 43–45.

[69] IG X 2.1, §4 *ll.* 16–19. The Ephesian Council and People, after considering the benefactions of the gymnasiarch Diodorus (IEph Ia 6 *ll.* 26–27: II cent. BC), decided "to set up his statue in the gymnasium, guiding everyone to become emulators (ζηλωτὰς γίνεσθαι) of excellent deeds." Cf. Ascough, Harland, and Kloppenborg, *Associations*, §20; Harrison, "Paul and the Gymnasiarchs."

aim ever to win a reputation (πρὸς τό φιλοδοξεῖν) for doing something beneficial for our home city.[70]

8.2.1.2. "Surpassing" Honour

Not only were civic luminaries expected to acquire honour, but also they were required to surpass their competitors and outshine the honour of previous generations. A variety of motifs express this ethical impetus. An Ephesian stele for the benefactor Titus Flavius Damianus is "erected by those in the agora for the honour of a man in all things incomparable (ἀσυνκρίτου)."[71] The Organisation of Peoples and Tribes in Asia honours Herostratos because he "has excelled (διενένκαντα) in trust and excellence and justice and piety," having exercised the greatest zeal on its behalf.[72] A Spartan doctor is also described as "going beyond all limits in the nobility of his spirit towards us,"[73] and Opramoas has "displayed unparalleled philanthropies in his home towns."[74] Another inscription speaks of the "exceptional and unparalleled generosity and munificence" of its benefactor.[75] In each case, what is highlighted is the ability of the benefactors to transcend not only the expectations of the city in their beneficence and personal self-sacrifice, but also to surpass, according to the polished rhetoric of the decree, the highest standards of civic ethics in the cities of the eastern Mediterranean basin.

We have seen, too, in the case of Roman Corinth, that the Latin honorific inscriptions follow republican convention in using the language of primacy (*primus*) in highlighting the unprecedented nature of the honorand's achievement (n. 13 *supra*).[76] But, in the case of the inscription of Gaius Julius Spartiaticus (AD 55), this singular boast is brought into dialogue with the honorand's virtue and munificence: "the first of the Achaeans (*primo Achaeon*) to hold this office on account of his excellence (*virtutem*) and unsparing and most lavish generosity (*animosam fusissimamque munificientiam*) both to the divine family and to our colony."[77] The boasting conventions of the republican nobles are

---

[70] OGIS 339 *ll.* 86–93. Tr. Danker, *Benefactor*, § 17.

[71] IEph III 672 *ll.* 21–24. Cf. Ascough, Harland, and Kloppenborg, *Associations*, § 124: "because of his love of glory and incomparable goodwill toward the homeland."

[72] OGIS 438 *ll.* 7–9 (Provenance: Poimanenan, I. cent. BC). Tr. R. K. Sherk, *Rome and the Greek East to the Death of Augustus* (Cambridge: Cambridge University Press, 1984), § 58.

[73] IG V 1145 (Provenance: Gytheion, 86 BC). Tr. A. R. Hands, *Charities and Social Aid in Greece and Rome* (London and Southampton: Thames and Hudson, 1968), §D. 69.

[74] IGR III 739 col. V *l.* 104. Tr. Danker, *Benefactor*, § 19.

[75] Hands, *Charities and Social Aid*, §D. 46 (Provenance: Guelma [Libya], AD 250). See Danker, *Benefactor*, § 19 (IGR III 739 Col. V *ll.* 103–04 [133–120 BC]): "Opramoas himself has in the past displayed unparalleled philanthropies in his home towns."

[76] Additionally, SIG^3 495 (Provenance: Olbia, 230 BC). Tr. Hands, *Charities and Social Aid*, §D. 4: "he was the first to promise ..." (used twice).

[77] A. B. West, *Corinth VIII 2: Latin Inscriptions, 1986–1926* (Cambridge, MA: Harvard University Press, 1931; = IKorinthWest), § 68 *ll.* 9–12.

recognisable in the stylistic conventions used, but the focus now is upon the highest order of achievement in the imperial *cursus honorum*.

In the case of the inscriptions of the Roman veteran colony of Philippi, the *cursus honorum* is often military in its emphasis, along with its decorative honours.[78] While moral virtues are routinely not mentioned, the force of the ascending honours reverberates in praise of the soldier's *virtus* ("manliness"). This is seen in this honorific inscription from the reign of Domitian, with the soldiers who are erecting the inscription being keen to establish that they were *honorably* discharged:

For Lucius Tatinius Gnosus, son of Lucius, from the tribe Voltina, soldier of the fourth praetorian cohort, *singularis* and *beneficiarius tribuni*, adjutant, *beneficiarius praefecti praetorio*, *evocatus* of Augustus, who was given, as decorative honours, neckchains, bracelets, breastplates, and a golden wreath by the imperator Domitianius Caesar Augustus Germanicus, centurion of the fourth cohort of the watch, centurion *statorum*, centurion of the eleventh urban cohort, the veterans who had served under him in the cohort of the watch, who were dismissed with an honorable discharge (*honesta missione missi sunt*) (set up this inscription).[79]

8.2.1.3. The "Rivalry" Motif

The "rivalry" motif is evident in the inscription of Caius Vibius Salutaris (AD 104) who was crowned for his substantial bequest of statues to the imperial ruler and Ephesian Artemis. However, as we will see, there is an interesting reticence to go too far in the encouragement of rivalry. The decree demands that the return of coronal honour to benefactors in the present should correspond to the blessings that Artemis distributed to benefactors who had honoured the goddess in any age. This interrelation between the maintenance of divine honour and the return of coronal honour to benefactors was carefully articulated. The honours of the present age should be commensurate with those accorded to benefactors of past and also correspond to the "enjoyment" of honour experienced by Ephesian benefactors in the present. It was hoped that this careful tabulation of honour, past and present, would act as an incentive to a new generation of benefactors seeking the same honours in the future:

Since the men who are munificent in the case of the city, and on every occasion show the affection of genuine citizens, should have honours (χρὴ τυχεῖν τειμῶν) corresponding to the enjoyment to those who have done well to the city in the past, and is laid up for those who are wishing to rival (ἁμι[λλᾶσθαι]) them about similar things, and corresponding at the same time to the enjoyment of those who have been zealous to honour ([τοὺς]

[78] The imperial priesthoods and patronage are also a point of boasting at Philippi (Pilhofer, *Philippi*, 001/L027; 002/L028; 004/L030; 031/L121; 226/L334).

[79] Pilhofer, *Philippi*, 202/L313.

ἐσπουδα[κ]ότας τειμᾶν) the greatest goddess Artemis, from whom the most beautiful things come to all, it is fitting for them to be honoured by the city ...[80]

What is interesting about this inscription is that it is expected that there will be other prominent men at Ephesus who would want to rival (ἁμιλλᾶσθαι) the great men of the past in beneficence. But, significantly, there is no mention of "rivaling" the *other* leading men of the city *in the present*, as there is in honorific inscriptions elsewhere.[81] The paradigm for rivalry is focused entirely *on the past*. The omission is telling, although rivalry between the aristocratic families of Ephesus undeniably existed. Did the framers of the decree fear that they might provoke a heated competition among the elites that could undermine the *homonia* ("sameness of mind", "unity") of the city?[82] Alternatively, were they concerned that they might provoke the *invidia* ("envy") of other prominent citizens who had received lesser honours or, worse, no honours at all?[83] Or is it just another case of *not* challenging the honour of the Roman ruler and his house?[84] Whatever the truth, we witnessing in Ephesus, I believe, the invisible politics of honour in this summons of benefactors to rivalry.

8.2.1.4. The "Emulation" Motif

Since I have discussed this motif elsewhere,[85] I will confine myself to an Ephesian inscription not discussed in the previous publication. The proconsul of Asia, Paullus Fabius Persicus, encouraged the leading magistrates of the provinces to be upright and faithful in the conduct of the magistracy entrusted to them. They were to think constantly about what is useful for their entire province and

---

[80] IEph Ia, 27 *ll.* 8–14. See G.M. Rogers, *The Sacred Identity of Ephesos: Foundation Myths of a Roman City* (London: Routledge, 1991).

[81] See *Michel* 235 and SEG XXI 419, each using ἁμιλλᾶσφαι, in Harrison, *Paul's Language of Grace*, 317.

[82] Hands, *Charities and Social Aid*, §D. 54 (Provenance: Pergamum, II cent. BC): "praying to all the gods for the safety of the people and for their unity of heart (ὁμονοίαν)." J. Pouilloux, *Choix d'inscriptions Grecques* (Paris: Les Belles Lettres, 2003), § 21 (Provenance: Samos, 280 BC): "wanting that the citizens at variance once conciliated to live in friendship (ἐν ὁμονοίαι)." Cf. Ascough, Harland, and Kloppenborg, *Associations*, § 18: "the entire immigrant group lives in concord."

[83] See J.P. Lotz, "The *Homonoia* Coins of Asia Minor and Ephesians 1:21," *TynBul* 50.2 (1999): 173–78; Zuiderhoek, *The Politics of Munificence*, 67, 75, 95, 109; T.P. Lau, *The Politics of Peace: Ephesians, Dio Chrysostom and the Confucian Tradition*, NovTSup 133 (Leiden, Brill, 2010).

[84] The quaestor Publius Cornelius Scipio, possessing a famous republican noble name, rivals the benefactors of the past with his civic benefits, but he is careful not to overlook honour to Gaius Caesar: "zealous to make them rival those given in the past, and on the other hand to preserve equally the revered status (of Gaius)" (SEG XXIII 206 *ll.* 15–16; Provenance: Messene, AD 2). Tr. R.K. Sherk, *The Roman Empire: Augustus to Hadrian* (Cambridge: Cambridge University Press, 1988), § 18.

[85] Harrison, "The Imitation of the Great Man," 213–54, esp. 233–38.

the city in which they reside. Speaking about the example of the Roman ruler Claudius, the proconsul outlines the reason for his exhortation to the magistrates:

... I acknowledge that in regard to this my opinion is rather happily endorsed by the example (τῶι ὑποδείγματι) if the finest and in truth most just leader [i.e. Claudius], who has rendered the whole human race into his care by the finest and indeed the sweetest acts of philanthropy; and he has bestowed this gracious favour, the restoration to each person of (their) property.[86]

Notwithstanding the proconsul's flattery of the Roman ruler, we have to acknowledge that the proconsul of Asia wielded the selfless example of Claudius with rhetorical and political effect to underscore the necessity for probity on the part of the provincial magistrates.

8.2.1.5. The "Danger" Motif

Since F.W. Danker has discussed the "endangered" benefactor motif, we will only briefly touch on its significance for civic ethics.[87] The emphasis of this motif is either on the great dangers from which the honorand did not shirk in serving the people of his city,[88] or, alternatively, the great dangers from which he saved his people.[89] Even the association honorific decrees highlight this motif.[90] Here we encounter what might be loosely called the "service" ethic of antiquity. A late republican decree from Aphrodisias captures well the tenor of the "endangered" benefactor motif:

...] saviour and benefactor, having saved his country from many and great dangers (κινδύνων), having fought bravely in all the wars which beset his country, having guarded the forts entrusted to him by the city and preserved faith to the common interest (?) in the most difficult circumstances (πίστεις ἐν τοῖς ἀναγκαιοτάτος καιροῖς), having filled all the magistracies with integrity (καθαρῶς) and justice (δικα(ί)ως) and to the advantage of the city ...[91]

[86] I.Eph Ia. 18a *ll.* 11–17.

[87] Danker, *Benefactor*, 417–27.

[88] SIG³ 613A (Provenance: Delphi, 184–183 BC): "does not seek to avoid any hardship or danger which his enemies prepare for him." Tr. M.M. Austin, ed., *The Hellenistic World from Alexander to the Roman Conquest: A Selection of Ancient Sources in Translation*, 2nd ed. (Cambridge: Cambridge University Press, 2006), § 88.

[89] SIG³ 528 (Provenance: Cnossus, 221–219 BC): "Hermias being a good man showed then all his zeal on our behalf and saved them [from] great dangers." Tr. Austin, *The Hellenistic World*, § 144.

[90] See Ascough, Harland, and Kloppenborg, *Associations*, § 74.

[91] J. Reynolds, *Aphrodisias and Rome* (London: Society for the Promotion of Roman Studies, 1982), § 30 *ll.* 5–13. Additionally, *ibid.*, §§ 28, 31; Pouilloux, *Choix d'inscriptions Grecques*, §§ 4, 34.

8.2.1.6. *The "Word-Deed" Conjunction*

The combination of noble actions with finesse in words point to the holistic character transformation expected not only of benefactors but also in the people that they mentor.[92] Both the dative of the noun phrase (λόγῳ καὶ ἔργῳ) and the corresponding verbs in the participial phrase (λέγων καὶ πράσσων) are regularly used. The inscription of the Ephesian gymnasiarch Diodorus (II cent. BC) is remarkable not only for its articulation of ethical guidance provided for the young men of the gymnasium, but also for its heavy emphasis upon the moral probity of the gymnasiarch and his meticulous concern for the public reputation of the gymnasium:

> ... and he gave attention also to the quality of the young men, both guiding them in training and, as for love of effort both in body and in soul (σωματικήν τε καὶ ψυχικήν), making much of it for the sake of the reputation (τὸ τῶν νέων ἀξίωμα) of the young men being fostered both in word and deed (τοῦ καὶ λόγωι καὶ ἔργωι) as befitted both the place's existing inherited dignity and fame (περὶ τὸν τόπον διὰ προγόνων ὑπαρχούση[ι] καὶ δόξη[ς]), and for the remaining gymnasium affairs he took care, hating the bad and loving the good (μισοπονήρως τε καὶ φιλαγάθως), in nothing neglectful of what relates to honour and fame (πρὸς τιμὴν καὶ δόξαν) for the sake of the memorable and praiseworthy establishment of his existing preference for the best.[93]

8.2.1.7. *The Enhancement of Ancestral Fame and the "Eternity" of Honour for Posterity*

The responsibility of the benefactor to enhance ancestral honour and to secure honour in perpetuity before the watching eyes of posterity is underscored in the eulogistic inscriptions. The virtue of the benefactor and his family demonstrates its abiding quality by withstanding the forgetfulness of each new generation.[94] Thus an inscription from Ephesus unfolds the remarkable rollcall of ancestral glory belonging to the aristocratic Ephesian family of the Vedii. Vedia, a priestess of Artemis, had made the customary distributions to the guilds and completed the mysteries worthily of her family.[95] But the inscription also lists all the civic magistracies that her relatives had achieved: asiarch, high priest, priestess and *kosmetira*, *prytenis*, secretary and agonothete.[96] Indications of Roman rank (*eques*) and female social importance (*matrona stolata*: "woman wearing a

---

[92] See Danker, *Benefactor*, 339–40. Additionally, see Sherk, *The Roman Empire*, § 7. II. The East (E): "conducting his civic life to the best advantage of his city, in deed and word." Also, Austin, *The Hellenistic World*, § 98: "constantly says and does what is best for the people in all the magistracies."

[93] IEph Ia. 6 *ll.* 16–24.

[94] See n. 148 *infra*.

[95] IEph VII 1.3072 *ll.* 28–32. Cf. IEph III 730: "the benefactors descended from ancestors and a family (of benefactors)."

[96] IEph VII 1.3072 *ll.* 1–27.

stole") are emphasised, as well as imperial connections (*philosebastos*: "emperor-loving").[97] While Vedia's contribution to this rich repository of civic virtue has been modest, her inherited glory was incalculable.

Two examples of the replication and surpassing of ancestral honour will suffice. Atalanta, a widow, is described as a woman "adorned with both nobility and with a sense of what is right, and who reveals to the full the quality of a woman emulating by her exertions the accomplishments of her forefathers in their ambitious services toward the city."[98] The benefactor Conon, a life-long priest of the Augusti, is introduced in an imperial inscription as "a virtuous man and an ornament of our city." The inscription elaborates that "he excelled all ancestral honour (πᾶσαν φιλοτειμίαν προγονικὴν ὑπερβαλών) by his own zeal for the city."[99] Thus the virtuous example of the ancestral past impresses itself upon the intentions and actions of its descendants.

Finally, the outcome of exceptional civic ethics is never in doubt: immortal fame. An Ephesian inscription speaks of "the gymnasiarchs of the eternal gymnasiarchy (τῆς αἰωνίου γυμνασιαρχίας) in the account (?) of Artemis."[100] Sestos of Menos, it is said, intended to acquire "for himself and his family imperishable glory (δόξαν ἀ(ε)ίμνηστον)."[101] The Thessalonican bequest of a priestess of Dionysos states: "I bequest for my eternal memory two plethora of vineyards with the ditches."[102] Another benefactor is equally forthright: "My idea is to achieve immortality in making such a just and kindly disposal [of my property] and, in entrusting it to the city, I shall surely not fail in my aim."[103] Other phrases, celebrating the benefactor's "eternal memory", "everlasting praise" and "imperishable memorial", point in the same direction.[104]

We turn now to celebration of civic ethics in monuments and statuary: do we find the same heightening of civic virtue in the visual evidence as we have seen in the inscriptions?

---

[97] IEph VII 1.3072 *ll.* 8–9, 12, 18.

[98] Hands, *Charities and Social Aid*, §D. 39 (Provenance: Termissus, Pisidia [Asia Minor], late II cent. AD).

[99] J.R. Harrison, "Excels Ancestral Honours," *New Docs* 9 (2003): 20–21, § 9 *ll.* 10–13.

[100] IEph V 1500 *ll.* 13–14.

[101] OGIS 339 *ll.* 9–10. Tr. Danker, *Benefactor*, § 17.

[102] IG X. 2.1. 260 (III cent. AD). Tr. Ascough, Harland, and Kloppenborg, *Associations*, § 58.

[103] IG V 1.1208 (Provenance: Gytheion, AD 161–169). Tr. Hands, *Charities and Social Aid*, §D. 71.

[104] Respectively, Sherk, *Rome and the Greek East*, § 58; Hands, *Charities and Social Aid*, §§D. 54, 69.

8.2.2. *The Visual Evidence of the Honorific Monuments and Statuary of the Greek East*

8.2.2.1. *The Mausolem of Zoilos of Aphrodisias*

The career of Zoilos of Aphrodisias is so well known from the epigraphic record that the details need not detain us. He is a freedman of Augustus who went on to become a civic luminary at Aphrodisias, with the eulogistic inscriptions celebrating his benefactions, honours, and priesthoods.[105] In terms of iconographic sophistication, the Mausoluem of Zoilos was the Greek East equivalent of the Mausoleum of the Julii in the Latin West.[106] R.R. Smith has definitively discussed the monument, so I rely upon his conclusions.[107] The square marble mausoleum was built on a low, stepped platform, with a 1.85 m high paneled frieze set between angle piers. Nothing survives of the superstructure and only Side A of the decorated frieze is complete, although damaged.[108]

Side A shows a scene of personified Andreia ("Courage", i.e. Virtus) presenting Zoilos a shield on the left side of the panel,[109] whereas Timê ("Honour", i.e. Honos) crowns Zoilos on the right side.[110] Smith argues that the scene, highlighting the Roman context of Zoilos' career,[111] "celebrates Zoilos' courage in war, his status as a Roman citizen, and the honour (and wealth) he has won thereby."[112] Another scene shows Zoilos clad in a chlamys and travelling hat,[113] perhaps signifying his role as an ambassador. He is greeted by the Demos and is crowned by the Polis.[114] This scene, Smith argues, places Zoilos in a "Greek civic setting,"[115] mediating on behalf of Aphrodisias and its people in inter-city relations. Such ambassadors were honoured in the eulogistic inscriptions, with the emphasis being on their service at considerable personal risk.[116]

---

105 R.R.R. Smith, *Aphrodisias I: The Monument of C. Julius Zoilos* (Mainz: Philipp von Zabern, 1993), 4–10.

106 H. Rolland, *Le mausolée de Glanum* (Paris: Éditions du Centre Nationale de la Recherche Scientifique, 1969).

107 Smith, *Aphrodisias*.

108 Smith, *Aphrodisias*, 16 fig. 2, 25 fig. 5; plates 2, 33.

109 Smith, *Aphrodisias*, 25 fig. 5; plates 3–5. ἀνδρεία does not appear frequently in the honorific inscriptions: SIG³ 700 *l.* 35: "managing these worthily of (his) country and descendants, worthily of his own glory (τῆς ἰδίας δόξης) and courage (ἀνδρείας)." Additionally, SIG³ 1073 *l.* 5; OGIS 339 *l.* 71; 445 *l.* 5.

110 Smith, *Aphrodisias*, 25 fig. 5; plates 3, 6–7.

111 Smith, *Aphrodisias*, 61.

112 Smith, *Aphrodisias*, 60.

113 Smith, *Aphrodisias*, 25 fig. 5; plates 1, 12–14.

114 Smith, *Aphrodisias*, 25 fig. 5; plates 15–17.

115 Smith, *Aphrodisias*, 61.

116 Danker, *Benefactor*, § 12; Sherk, *Rome and the Greek East*, §§ 5, 65; S.M. Burstein, *The Hellenistic Age from the Battle of Ipsos to the Death of Kleopatra VII* (Cambridge: Cambridge University Press, 1985), § 55. The "endangered" benefactor motif is highlighted in the ambassadorial role: Hegesias "[thought] nothing of the dangers involved in the foreign travel, but

On Side B, Roma is shown seated, with her back to Andreia and her left arm draped over a shield.[117] Another damaged panel has only the inscribed fragment, Pistis ("Loyalty", "Faith"), remaining.[118] Whether this represents "Zoilos' Loyalty to Rome or the Good Faith between Rome and Zoilos" is hard to determine.[119] At the beginning of Side C, Aion ("Eternity") looks to the recent past: he leans intently with hand on chin and studies the illustrations of the achievements of Zoilos on the frieze.[120] It is uncertain whether the iconography is saying that Zoilos' deeds would stand the test of time, a view perhaps confirmed by the unplaced panel of Mneme ("Memory"), or, alternatively, whether this represents Zoilos' tribute to the Augustan *saeculum*.[121] However, the point is plain: either the indestructibility of Zoilos' civic virtue is highlighted or Zoilos' *pistis* to Augustus is affirmed.

Furthermore, the civic virtue of Zoilos is reaffirmed by the presence of Minos,[122] the precise placement of which in the sequence of panels is uncertain. Notwithstanding, the ancient eschatology is clear enough. The vindication of Zoilos' civic virtue before the underworld judges is assured because Minos was one of its senior judges.[123] Other figures of the frieze could be discussed, such as the unplaced male figure in the himation and the soldier (Side D), representing, respectively, the Greek civic life of Zoilos and his military prowess.[124] Suffice it to say, the monument of Zoilos celebrates the eternal virtue of Zoilos, as a Roman freedman of Augustus and as a Greek civic benefactor of Aphrodisias.[125] What we are witnessing in this Aphrodisian frieze is the heightening of civic virtue – a tendency observed in the honorific inscriptions and the mausoleum of the Julii in the Latin West – among the competitive elites of the early Empire.[126]

[considered] his own affairs [of less importance] than the city's interest" (SIG^3 591 *ll.* 13–15 [196–195 BC: Provenance: Lampsakos]: Sherk, *Rome and the Greek East*, § 5). Cf. Danker, *Benefactor* § 12: "in general ... risking body and soul in every perilous circumstance."

[117] Smith, *Aphrodisias*, 43 figs. 6–7; plates 18–19.

[118] Smith, *Aphrodisias,* 58 fig. 15, plate 28c. See Smith (*ibid.*, 58) for inscriptional examples of *pistis*. Cf. T. Morgan, *Roman Faith and Christian Faith:* Pistis *and* Fides *in the Early Roman Empire and Early Churches* (Oxford and New York: Oxford University Press, 2015); B. Cueto, *Paul's Understanding of* pistis *in Its Graeco-Roman Context*, (PhD diss., Dallas Theological Seminary, 2012).

[119] Smith, *Aphrodisias*, 61.

[120] Smith, *Aphrodisias*, 46 figs. 8–9; plates 21–22, 32.

[121] Harrison, *Paul and the Imperial Authorities*, 105–06.

[122] Smith, *Aphrodisias*, 50 fig. 12; plates 24–25.

[123] Smith, *Aphrodisias*, 61.

[124] Smith, *Aphrodisias*, 55–56; plates 26, 27.

[125] Smith, *Aphrodisias*, 66–67.

[126] Regarding the Hellenistic monument of Memmius at Ephesus, P. Scherrer, ed. (*Ephesus: The New Guide,* rev. ed. [Turkey, Ege Yyinlari, 2000], 96) comments: "Its re-erection as an architectural pastiche is more a modern interpretation than an illustration of an ancient edifice."

8.2.2.2. Civic Statuary: Honour at Ephesus and Isthmia

Apart from honorific monuments like those of Zoilos or Philopappos in the Greek East (n. 16 *supra*), the honorific statue, with an elogium on its base, promoted the civic ethics and the cultural identity of benefactors.[127] The arrangement of statues in tiers of niches decorating buildings was a means of public display favoured by benefactors and city councils.[128] Although few of these statues have survived both in situ and intact, the Library of Celsus at Ephesus is a conspicuous exception, even though the statues remaining are not the originals.[129] The honorific inscriptions extant on the remains of statue bases help us to reconstruct the lost statuary of ancient cities,[130] as do the inscriptional references to the gifts of statues.[131]

Four statues, each recessed in niches, flanked the three entrance doorways of the Library of Celsus. The dedicatee of the Library was a prominent Ephesian whose rise in the imperial administration was meteoric: a senator initially under Vespasian, a suffect consul under Domitian (AD 92), and a proconsul of Asia under Trajan (AD 105/106).[132] The four statues of Celsus personified his virtues as proconsul of Asia (*sophia* [Σοφία Κέλσου: "The wisdom of Celsus"]; *arete* ['Αρετὴ Κέλσου: "The virtue of Celsus"]; *ennoia* ["Εννοια Φιλίππου: "The intelligence of Philip", "idea"]; *episteme* ['Επιστήμη Κέλσου: "The knowledge of Celsus"]),[133] with two equestrian statues flanking the stairs, and possibly a statue in his crypt.[134] The will of Aquila, his son, specified that his statues should

[127] See R.R.R. Smith, "Cultural Choice and Political Identity in Honorific Statues in the Greek East," *JRS* 88 (1998): 56–93.

[128] V.M. Strocka (*The Celsus Library in Ephesus*, in anon., *Ancient Libraries in Anatolia: Libraries of Hattusha, Pergamon, Ephesus, Nysa* [Ankara: Middle East Technical University Library, 2003], 33–43, at 41–42) states regarding serials of honorary statues in the Empire: they "show the honoured person in different clothing and posture, hence in different roles that he played and that embodied different offices or 'virtues'."

[129] On the change of statues after the Ephesian earthquake of 262 AD and the (later) re-ascribing of Celsus' virtue of *ennoia* to the unknown Philip, see Scherrer, *Ephesus*, pp. 130–32. Sherrer observes that the four virtues, all originally ascribed to Celsus, are those "typically expected of all high-ranking Roman civil servants" (*ibid.*, 130). The reason for this particular change is obscure. Did Philip's generous funding of the new statues for the library occasion this re-ascription of honour to himself? Or, alternatively, is this a case of the opportunistic appropriation of Celsus' honour by a powerful Ephesian official of the mid III cent. AD, who decided to switch one of the replacement statues with his own eulogistic inscription (cf. Dio Chrysostom, *Or.* 31, *infra*)?

[130] For the inscriptions of the honorees on the plinths of statues in Kuretes Street at Ephesus, see Rogers, *The Sacred Identity of Ephesos*, 121 nn. 105–108.

[131] Note the procession of imperial statues provided for in the bequest of the Ephesian benefactor, Caius Vibius Salutaris (IEph Ia 27 *ll.* 28–31: AD 104). See Rogers, *The Sacred Identity of Ephesos*.

[132] On Celsus, see Strocka, *The Celsus Library in Ephesus*, 33–43.

[133] Respectively, IEph VII 5108, VII 5109, VII 5110, VII 5111.

[134] B. Burrell, "False Fronts: Separating the Imperial Cult from the Aedicular Façade in Roman Asia Minor," *AJA* 110 (2006): 437–69, at 455.

be hung with wreaths three times a year and that all other statues be decorated on his birthday feast.[135] The virtues of Celsus, therefore, were not only immortalized in stone but also celebrated by public coronal rituals and feasting each year, so that his memory would remain at the forefront of civic life and exemplary practice.

Last, inscribed on a statue base of white marble was the honorific epigram accorded to Nikias, an agonothetes, by his fellow officials. It was found in front of a semi-circular foundation at the northern edge of the Palaimonion area at Isthmia. The marble base and the bronze statue of Nikias had been later moved there from its original location in the forechamber of the Temple of Poseidon (*ll.* 4, 8), some thirteen km east of ancient Corinth. Although the inscription is undated, it is probably roughly contemporary with the early Roman period when the Palaimonion shrine was built (i.e. mid I. cent–mid II. cent). The inscription is set out below:

1 First (τὸν πρῶτον) among orators, pre-eminent (ἄριστον) as agonothetes,
Having acquired glory (κῦδος) in every public office–
For these achievements your colleagues in the office of agonothetes,
Erected a statue of you, Nikias, in the forechamber of Poseidon.
5 BY VOTE OF THE COUNCIL
He verily pours forth words like streams
At the mouths of ever flowing Rivers.
He stands, a portrait of bronze, before the Temple,
in the midst of pure hands, by purifying streams (of water);
10 And as a reward for his merit (Ἀντ' ἀρετῆς) he received [a gold crown(?)] by which they honoured (ἔτεισαν) him.
Readily, unfalteringly the athlothetai knew (your worth),
O Nikias, a great delight to the city; and to the young –
15 Citizens and strangers alike – how great a blessing nature (ἔφυς) has made you.[136]

Broneer argues that the two honours were conveyed on separate occasions. The first (a bronze statue) was awarded for Nikias' role as agonothetes (*ll.* 1–4), whereas the second (a gold crown?) – the lettering of which has been deliberately erased from the stone – was awarded for his oratorical ability (*ll.* 6–7, 10–11). Broneer speculates what circumstances may have provoked this official censure,[137] but, importantly, the erasure shows how quickly honour rituals were supplanted by dishonour when the honoree fell out of favour.

The conventional language of "preeminence" (πρῶτος, ἄριστος) and "glory" (κῦδος) is attached to the first honour (*l.* 1). Significantly, ceremonial hand washing occurred in a basin at the entrance of the Temple (*l.* 9), located just before the

[135] IEph VII 5113. Tr. S Strocka, *The Celsus Library*, 40.
[136] O. Broneer, "Excavations at Isthmia: Fourth Campaign, 1957–1958," *Hesperia* 28.4 (1959): 298–343, esp. 324–26 (§ 5). The line numbers used here correspond to Broneer's English translation, as opposed to the slightly different line numbers of the Greek.
[137] Broneer, "Excavations at Isthmia," 325–26.

pronaos (an open vestibule) where Nikias' statue had originally been erected (*ll.* 4, 8). Nikias' reputation before posterity was thereby invested with an aura of cultic purity by virtue of its association with the sacred space and activities of the Temple.[138]

In the case of the second (coronal?) honour (*ll.* 10–11), Nikias' oratorical power and personal worth ("a great delight to the city") is portrayed in such "exaggerated terms" that his civic virtue (ἀρετή) demands the reciprocation of honour.[139] His natural virtue (ἔφυς) is apparent to all generations: the citizens and non-citizens of the city, the mature *athlothetai* and the aspiring young (*ll.* 13–15). Again we are witnessing the inflated moral language that dominated "honour" discourse in the early Empire.[140]

We have seen, too, somewhat unexpectedly, the erasure of honour on the public statues and their dedications. We now turn to an investigation of dishonour in the inscriptions and papyri, as well as the orations of Dio Chrysostom.

8.2.2.3. The Eruption of Dishonour in a World of Honour

8.2.2.3.1. Handling Dishonour: The Evidence of the Inscriptions and Papyri

Since the honorific inscriptions were unreservedly positive, intended, as they were, to register the return of the recipient's gratitude to the benefactor and thereby elicit further beneficence from the honoree and other wealthy elites, it is difficult to discern a dark underside to the ancient benefaction system. Apart from the evidence of the epistolary theorists and the occasional papyrus, there is little evidence pointing to the breakdown of honour protocols.[141] Undoubtedly collisions arising from the honour system occurred more frequently than is registered in our primary sources. However, there are occasional tensions of the honour system aired in the inscriptions, indicating that its protocols had been violated (or were about to be), with the result that the rumblings of dishonour might damage social relations in the civic arena.

First, a Samian grain law legislates sanctions against those who commit financial misconduct in the administration of the elite-sponsored grain fund. As the decree stipulates, "... if he does not pay the interest to the man elected to be in charge of the grain supply, let him owe an equal amount as penalty ... and, besides the penalty, let him be registered as *atimos* ("dishonourable"), and let him

[138] Cf. Ascough, Harland, and Kloppenborg, *Associations*, § 212: "it was resolved by us to honour the man with a statue which will be set up in the most noticeable place in the metropolis, and a separate one for the competitors will be set up in the theatre as a most beautiful model of virtue for the spectators."

[139] Broneer, "Excavations at Isthmia," 325.

[140] See the inflated metaphorical language used of Kallimachos (OGIS 39 *ll.* 14–23 [Provenance: Thebes, AD March 39). Tr. Burstein, *The Hellenistic Age*, § 111.

[141] Harrison, *Paul's Language of Grace*, 70–72, 78, 82–83.

be *atimos* (ἔστω ἀτίμος) until he pays."[142] Here we see the nexus of honour with probity in financial affairs, whether that related to civic legislature or to the beneficence of the elites. Any violation of this ethical code led to the public imposition of dishonour upon the offender.

Second, in a third century BC papyrus,[143] the writer Aristeides seeks exemption from the liturgical service of securing the city's grain supply. As Aristeides explains, "I have had the misfortune to be proposed by the citizens as grain-buyer although I am not yet of the right age nor due for that burden, but [have been proposed by] certain persons out of jealousy."[144] If Aristeides is correct in his assessment of the motives of his adversaries, it seems that these unidentified people are resentful that he, a member of a prominent family, had been nominated by the citizens to ensure the continuance of the grain supply. Were his opponents jealous of the fact that he had been chosen by the citizens to act as an elite benefactor ahead of his legal age, and, concomitantly, ahead of themselves and their families as potential benefactors? Were they hoping that this upcoming and youthful member of the civic elite would buckle under the responsibilities of meeting the pressing demands of this liturgy, a potential outcome to which the papyrus itself bears witness? Here we see the pressure imposed by the demands of civic honour when a prominent citizen, of relative inexperience, is offered a difficult liturgy for the first time, a challenge also experienced by Dio Chrysostom, as we will see below. It also underscores the tensions and rivalries that emerge when wealthy elites competed for prestigious civic honours. The potential for dishonour, resulting in public shame, lurked below the surface in these transactions.

Third, an Athenian decree had been erected on stelae in honour of Euphron of Sicyon for his death in defending the democracy in 323/322 BC.[145] In 322 BC the subsequent oligarchic government spitefully destroyed the stelae.[146] This,

[142] SIG³ 976 (Provenance: Samos). Tr. R.S. Bagnall and P. Derow, eds., *The Hellenistic Period: Historical Sources in Translation*, new ed. (Oxford: Blackwell, 2004), § 75. The technical phrase ἔστω ἄτιμος ("let him be dishonoured") appeared 26 times, excluding restorations, in a web search of the inscriptions of all regions in the Packard Humanities Institute Epigraphy programme (sourced May 2013), whereas for ἀτιμία there were only 5 matches.

[143] P. Mich. I. 23 (257 BC). Tr. Bagnall and Derow, *The Hellenistic Period*, § 88.

[144] Note the fragmentary Latin inscription which speaks of the envy aroused by the elaborate honour – provocatively a gilded statue rather than the simpler marble statue – which had been accorded the benefactor: "(Those who were) anxious to please, in their innocence believing that something great was being proposed and hoping to bring me a gift, were bringing (me) ruin ... They made (me) a gilded (statue) with money produced from all sides. Great envy grew from the honour; the citizens, as if they were masters, attempted to drive (their) patron into exile" (CIL V 509 *ll.* 3–4, 7–9: Provenance: south of the Tridentine Alps, Italy; Julio-Claudian era). See F. Martin, "The Importance of Honorific Statues: A Case-Study," *BICS* 41 (1996): 53–70.

[145] SIG³ 310.

[146] SIG³ 317 (318/317 BC). Tr. Austin, *The Hellenistic World*, § 32.

however, was not the end of the matter. The demos restored the decree on new stelae in 318 BC when democratic government returned to Athens for one year. The decree articulates the virtue of Euphron's meritorious and beneficent death on behalf of the democracy, the dishonouring of his civic virtue by the malicious oligarchs, and the restoration and vindication of his honour by his grateful fellow democrats. As the decree eulogises Euphron,

> ... he preferred death at the hand of his enemies, [fighting] for the democracy, rather than to see his [own native city] or the rest of Greece enslaved; and [when] the people of Athens honoured him with [citizenship] and the other honours which are fitting for [benefactors], both himself and his descendants, because of his [merits and] because of the benefactions of his ancestors, the government of the oligarchy deprived [him] of his privileges [and] destroyed the stelae; but now since the people has [come back] and has [recovered] its laws and the democracy, with good fortune, be it resolved by all the people, that all the [privileges] granted by the [people] of Athens to Euphron in his honour should be confirmed, both for himself and his descendants, and that [the] secretary of the council should inscribe the [stelae] which were destroyed and in which the privileges were [recorded], and the decree, and dedicate one copy on the acropolis and the other near (the altar) of Zeus the Saviour, just as the people decreed [previously], and should also inscribe the present decree on both the stelae.[147]

At the end of the decree, the people of Athens states the motivation for its actions in 318 BC: "... so that all may know [that the people] of Athens, when a good deed is done to it, believes that it must honour not only the benefactors but their children as well and remember the benefactions it has received."[148] Thus the Athenian decree reminds us that a story about an executed and dishonoured benefactor, who was later vindicated to his place of honour because of his self-sacrifice on behalf of his dependents (cf. Phil 2:5–11), may not have been quite as surprising to ancient auditors as initially thought. Hellerman is correct in proposing that the *carmen Christi* in Philippians reflects a *cursus pudorum* ("a succession of ignominies") as opposed to a *cursus honorum* ("a course of honours [offices]"). The "social verticality of the colony of Roman Philippi" and its competitive grab for honour is underscored in the Philippian inscriptions.[149] Nonetheless, the motif of the loss and restoration of honour portrayed in Philippians 2:5–11 was not totally unprecedented, as this inscription reminds us.

Last, the vaunting of one's military victory over national enemies and, concomitantly, their public dishonouring, is seen in the placement of L. Aemilius Paullus' statue on a pillar formerly erected for King Perseus. The inscription on the base of the pillar states with pointed humiliation for the Macedonians their

---

[147] SIG³ 317 *ll.* 23–38.

[148] SIG³ 317 *ll.* 47–50. Note the funerary inscription that challenges its readers to remember honour, "knowing well that the heirs forget" (*IG.* XIII 8[561]: Pouilloux, *Choix d'inscriptions Grecques*, § 51.

[149] Hellerman, *Reconstructing Honor*, 129.

military subjugation: "Lucius Aemilius, son of Lucius, general, took (this pillar) from King Perseus and the Macedonians."[150]

8.2.2.3.2. Dishonour in the Orations of Dio Chrysostom (AD 40–110)

Dio's orations are an important source for revealing the tensions underlying the competitive world of the eastern Mediterranean civic elites, with its emphasis on ancestral achievement, inherited wealth and citizenship status, each of which Dio had acquired through his father and grandfather (41.6; 44.3–5; 46.2–5). We should not be beguiled, however, by Dio's (largely) favourable assessment of the imperial world when he became an adviser to Trajan.[151] As a beneficiary of the ruler's favour and honour, Dio could hardly have indicated otherwise. More likely, as V. Nutton observes, he "knew the reality behind the façade."[152] Dio's comments on the civic concord (*homonoia*) required between cities and citizens are designed to preserve what remained of the independence of Greek cities in the eastern provinces (*Or.* 38–41), while ensuring that the Romans did not intervene because of internal or external divisions among cities (*Or* 44.10; 46.14; 48.1–2).[153] Notwithstanding, Dio highlights the underside of imperial honour in Nero's plundering of the honorific monuments for his own personal consumption (*Or.* 3.148). Consequently, we will look at four cases of the dishonouring of benefactors in Dio's orations.

First, in the Rhodian oration (*Or.* 31), Dio addresses the issue of the recycling of old statues with new inscriptions at Rhodes for the honouring of the city's new crop of benefactor.[154] Dio argues that the actions of the Rhodians violated the reciprocation of honour at the heart of the benefaction system. Not only did it rob benefactors of gratitude and honour (31.8–9, 12, 36–37, 65), but also it blighted their illustrious careers with the *damnatio memoriae* reserved for tyrants and the treasonous (31.27–31). The Rhodians, Dio asserts, would show themselves superior to the rest of the world, including Rome its hegemon, by honouring their benefactors (31.161–162).[155]

---

[150] ILS 8884 (Provenance: Delphi, 168/168 BC). Tr. Sherk, *Rome and the Greek East*, §24.

[151] See C.P. Jones, *The Roman World of Dio Chrysostom* (Cambridge, MA: Harvard University Press, 1978).

[152] V. Nutton, "The Beneficial Ideology," in *Imperialism in the Ancient World*, ed. P.D.A. Garnsey and C.R. Whittaker (Cambridge: Cambridge University Press, 1978), 209–22, at 211.

[153] Nutton, "The Beneficial Ideology," 211–12; G. Salmeri, *Dio, Rome, and the Civic Life of Asia Minor*, in *Dio Chrysostom: Politics, Letters, and Philosophy*, ed. S. Swain (Oxford: Oxford University Press, 2000), 64.

[154] Harrison, "The Brothers," 170–74.

[155] Marcus Aurelius refused to let the ancient statues of emperors, kept in the council hall of Ephesus, to be diverted from their original honorific purpose by being renamed and transformed into images of himself and his family (IEph 1a 25 *ll.* 11–23 [AD 162/163]).

Second, in an oration delivered before his exile and conversion to his Cynic-Stoic mission, Dio discusses the danger posed by the unprovoked attack, arising from a bread riot, that had been launched by a mob against his family property and the residence of his neighbour (*Or.* 46.11, 12). The attack had stalled at the narrow lane close to Dio's estate (46.12–13), but the next morning the orator stated his case against the unruly mob at the town meeting called by the magistrates. Dio registers his incredulity that his family, as benefactors of the city (46.2–5), had been singled out with such rancour, including his neighbour ("what's-his-name"). He asserts that he had contributed substantially to civic liturgies and did not deserve this dishonour (46.6):

> ... I have performed for you the greatest liturgies, in fact no one in the city has more of them to his credit than I have. Yet you yourselves know that many are wealthier than I am. What is it, that makes you angry with me, and why of all the citizens have you singled out for dishonour (ἄτιμον) me and what's-his-name, and why do you threaten us with stoning and burning?

Dio denies the slur that he had manipulated the grain prices (46.7, 9–10) or had built a pretentious villa with colonnades and workshops near the city's hot springs (46.8) with a view to enhancing his prestige. The latter charge had originated, Dio claims, from the jealousy of the powerful citizens (46.9: "this is the injury some say the city is suffering at my hands!"). Nor is Dio backward in reminding his auditors that his grandfather earned his second fortune from imperial favour and had acquired for the city the protection and good-will of the Roman ruler, presumably Claudius (46.3–4). Here we see how the how the *invidia* of civic elites in the Greek East cut across social boundaries, causing not only danger to powerful individuals, but also temporarily blighting their families with dishonour.

Third, upon his return from exile (AD 96), Dio had decided to embellish his home city Prusa. His ambitious scheme consisted of civic refurbishment and expansion (45.12–14). It had been given approval in a letter from the Roman ruler (40.5; 47.13–14) and required Dio's cultivation of the proconsuls (47.21). Criticism of Dio erupted when this project demolished older structures and removed certain landmarks (Or 40: 8–9; 47:17, 19–20). But the building of a colonnade provoked the acrimony of his fellow citizens (47.15, 17, 19, 20, 21), stirring up opposition to the payment of subscriptions to the building fund (47.19). Dio had contributed to this project from his own funds at considerable expense (47.20, 21, 23). Notwithstanding, Dio's opponents besmirched his public honour, labelling him a "vagabond" and tiresome "chatterbox" (47.8, 16 ["nightingale"])[156] and accusing him of acting as an impious "tyrant" by "tearing down the city and all its shrines" (47.23–24; cf. 47.17).

---

[156] Presumably this denigrates Dio's conversion to the Cynic lifestyle ("vagabond") and his oratorical ability ("chatterbox").

In face of this attack on his honour, Dio refuses the well-meaning advice of his sole supporter at Prusa. Because Dio was familiar with the Roman ruler, his supporter suggested that Dio could enhance his status further by associating with the Roman glitterati: he should therefore abandon Prusa and visit other more grateful cities as an *amicus* ("friend") of the Romans (47.22). What is intriguing here is that Dio, a convert to the Cynic lifestyle, disavows the "royal" trappings of imperial status and honour, whether it is erecting at Prusa a golden ancestral house like the Nero's in the capital (47.14, 25) or wearing the royal purple (47.25). Rather, he asserts, his conversion is genuine, having adopted the Cynic long hair and coarse cloak (47.25: "miserable rag"; cf. 35.2). Instead, he rhetorically assumes the mantle not of the 'tyrant' but of the philosopher "king". For Dio, "being roundly abused, though doing kindly deeds, is also a mark of royalty" (47.25).

Fourth, in an earlier oration where the embellishment of Prusa was barely underway, Dio had to contend with the accusation that he had not lived up to the elaborate promise that he had made to his fellow-citizens. To be tardy in fulfilling one's promises places the benefactor in a position of indebtedness to his community.[157] Therefore the debt must be repaid with interest (40.3):

> For there is nothing more weighty, no debt bearing higher interest, than a favour (χάριτος) promised. Moreover, this is the shameful and bitter kind of loan (τὸ ἀναίσχυντον δάνειον καὶ πίκρον), when, as one might say, because of tardy payment the favour (ἡ χάρις) turns into an obligation, an obligation the settlement of which those who keep silent demand altogether more sternly than those who cry aloud.

Apart from what this reveals about the indebtedness imposed by the promise of grace on the part of benefactors, the language of "shame" and "bitterness" reveals the intensity of the dishonour faced by Dio because of his tardiness as a benefactor in meeting his promise to his community.

We turn to a study of the semantic domain of "honour" and "shame" in Paul's letters, with a view to isolating his evaluation of civic ethics in the cities where his house churches ministered.

[157] Harrison, *Paul's Language of Grace*, 312–13. Contra, M. A. Jennings, "Patronage and Rebuke in Paul's Persuasion in 2 Cor 8–9," *JGRChJ* 6 (2009): 107–27, at 119 n. 31.

8.3. The Apostle Paul and the Canon of Honour in the Greek East

8.3.1. Paul's Language of "Honour" and Its Engagement with the Graeco-Roman Honour System

8.3.1.1. τιμή and Its Cognates

The usage of τιμή and cognates in Paul's writings appears conventional in the majority of cases, though care needs to be taken because Paul brings socially challenging dimensions to his teaching on honour. In accord with the honorific inscriptions,[158] Paul endorses the quest for "glory" (δόξα), honour' (τιμή) and "immortality" (ἀφθαρσία), along with its moral focus of "doing good" (Rom 2:7). But he reminds the honour-driven Romans that it is God alone, not the civic elites or posterity, who impartially judges all works (2:5b–6, 10–11). God recompenses those who persevere in their moral endeavour with the eschatological reward of eternal life (2:7; 3:29–30). Although humans fall short of God's glory (3:19–20), believers are declared righteous in Christ by divine grace and thereby experience in the present the ethical transformation of the pneumatic power of the risen Christ (7:6b; 8:3–7, 11–13; 14:17). Paul underscores the right of the divine potter to allocate human vessels to "honorable" and "dishonorable" use (Rom 9:21: εἰς τιμήν, εἰς ἀτιμίαν). However, Paul does not display any reticence in rendering honour to faithful believers in the eulogistic manner of the inscriptions. His summons to hold "in esteem" the self-sacrificing Epaphroditus belongs to traditional honorific parlance (Phil 2:29: ἐντίμους) and it is reinforced by the inscriptional language of "liturgy" and "zeal" (2:25: λειτουργόν; 2:28: σπουδαιοτέρους) and by Paul's allusion to the "endangered" benefactor motif (2:30).

In a radical move, however, Paul challenges his auditors' social assumptions in discussing how honour rituals should operate in the Body of Christ. Rather than evincing a hierarchic understanding of honour that results in a heated competition to achieve precedence – either through the imperial *cursus honorum* or by means of the alternate pathways of recognition in the associations – Paul inverts the conventional operation of the honour system. Believers are to prefer one another in honour (12:10b: τῇ τιμῇ ἀλλήλους προηγούμενοι), associate with the lowly (τοῖς ταπεινοῖς σθναπαγόμενοι) as opposed to cultivating the wealthy and powerful (12:16b; cf. v. 3),[159] and act beneficently towards their

[158] The references to honour in Ephesians 6:2 (τίμα) reflect the LXX (Exod 20:12) or in the case of 1 Thessalonians 4:4 occur in a sexual context (ἐν τιμῇ).

[159] On the negative connotation of ταπεινός and cognates, see C. Spicq, *Theological Lexicon of the New Testament Volume* 3 (Peabody: Hendrickson, 1994), 369–71. Paul steps down socially (E. A. Judge, "The Social Identity of the First Christians: A Question of Method in Religious History," in *idem*, *Social Distinctives*, 117–35, at 132) by working *gratis* as an artisan while at Corinth (2 Cor 11:7: ἐμαυτὸν ταπεινῶν; cf. Lucian, *Somn*, 13; cf. R. F. Hock, *The Social Context of Paul's Ministry: Tentmaking and Apostleship* (Philadelphia: Fortress, 1980) and fears being humbled before God by the impenitence of the Corinthians (12:21: μου ταπεινώσῃ;

enemies (Rom 12:19–21; cf. Lk 6:35–36). The modus operandi of the ancient reciprocity system had been transformed by a new set of social relations.

This social perspective is reinforced in 1 Corinthians 12:23–24. Confronting Corinthian attitudes of "self-sufficiency" (*autarkeia*) within the Body of Christ (12:14–17, 19, 21), Paul emphasises that God's allocation of the members within the body is his prerogative (12:18), irrespective of whether the members are deemed "dishonorable" (ἃ αδοκοῦμεν ἀτιμότερα) or "more honourable" (τιμὴν περισσοτέραν). This diversity of God's allocation of members finds its harmonious outworking in the Spirit-given unity of the Body of Christ (12:13; cf. vv. 4, 7, 8, 9, 11). Thus Paul's understanding of unity, while reflecting some of the concerns of ancient benefactors for *homonia* in civic contexts (12:25a: ἵνα μὴ ᾖ σχίσμα ἐν τῷ σώματι; n. 82 *supra*), is a different social construct because of its pneumatic and ecclesial emphasis. Furthermore, Paul asserts that God has inverted the rituals of social honour in the Body of Christ (12:24b). The inferior member (τῷ ὑστερουμένῳ) is given the greater honour (περισσοτέραν δοὺς τιμήν); the "shameful" (τὰ ἀσχήμονα) have the "greater prominence" (εὐσχημοσύνην περισσοτέραν); the "dishonourable" (ἀτιμότερα) are the "more honourable" (τιμὴν περισσοτέραν); and, last, the "weaker" (ἀσθενέστερα) are "indispensable" (ἀναγκαῖά) (12:22–23). This remarkable conglomeration of "honour" and "dishonour"/"shame" terminology demonstrates that Paul is not only speaking literally about the clothing of the body and the value of the weaker and immodest bodily parts, but he is also applying the imagery metaphorically to social relations within the Body of Christ, with believers being encouraged to act in a unified manner amidst their diverse giftedness.[160] The only way for that to happen without competition and division is for the least honoured in the Body of Christ to become the most honoured in social interactions. The hierarchic and status-riddled operation of the civic honour system is thereby reconfigured.

In Romans 13:7b, Paul endorses the rendering of honour (τῷ τὴν τιμὴν τὴν τιμήν) to the imperial authorities – including, presumably, their provincial representatives, and other unspecified dignitaries – who govern the world. This perspective is reinforced by the language of the ruler's divine appointment (13:1b, 2b), the believer's submission to his authority (12:1a, 2–3a, 4b–5a, 6a), and the promise of the ruler's praise (ἔπαινον), should a wealthy believer performs civic benefactions on behalf of the community (τὸ ἀγαθὸν ποίει).[161] However, in Paul's construct, the Roman ruler is stripped of the eulogistic honours that were the hallmark of the imperial propaganda: namely, that the ruler was the image of

cf. Phil 4:12: οἶδα καὶ ταπεινοῦσθαι). On the relationship of Christ's self-humbling (Phil 2:8: ἐταπείνωσεν) to honour, see *infra*.

[160] On Seneca's "weakness" imagery (*Clem.* 1.4.1–1.5.1–2) regarding Nero as the "body of state", see Harrison, *Paul and the Imperial Authorities*, 294–95.

[161] B.W. Winter, "The Public Honoring of Christian Benefactors: Romans 13:3–4 and 1 Peter 2:14–15," *JSNT* 34 (1988): 87–103.

God, the vice-regent of God who was foreknown and commissioned by him, the embodiment of "animate law", the priestly intermediary between his people and the gods, the summation of divine virtue and wisdom, the head of the body politic, the soul of the *res publica*, and, finally, the world benefactor and the dispenser of mercy.[162] In reality, the Roman ruler was, in agreement with Old Testament perspectives,[163] merely the servant of God (13:4a, 4b, 6b). Moreover, in a chillingly prophetic warning (8:35; 13:5), given the imminence of Nero's persecution of Roman believers less than a decade later, Paul alerts the Roman believers that the ruler does not bear the sword in vain. In sum, the exalted language belonging to imperial honorific culture is counterbalanced by the apostle's use of the Old Testament rhetoric, which demoted the status of all earthly rulers to "servants" of YHWH. Last, the apostle's strong eschatological emphasis, which looked forward to the passing of the present world order (13:11–13), set in proper perspective the boastfulness underlying so much of honorific culture (1:30: ἀλαζόνας; 2:29b: ὁ ἔπαινος οὐκ ἐξ ἀνθρώπων ἀλλ' ἐκ τοῦ θεοῦ; 3:27: Ποῦ οὖν ἡ καύχησις;).[164]

8.3.1.2. δόξα and Its Cognates

Since I have already written about δόξα in its republican, imperial and Mediterranean honorific context, I will not revisit well-worn paths.[165] Instead I want to propose that the reason why Paul so frequently refers to δόξα and its cognates is not just because of its rich heritage in Second Temple Judaism, though that is certainly the primary consideration. In many respects, δόξα is the key honorific term, along with χάρις, that Paul chose to convey to early believers both the wonder of their new status in Christ in a world of honour and, concomitantly, the unsurpassable splendour of their divine Benefactor. Since δόξα was widely used in the inscriptions, the intersection of honorific perspectives from the eastern Mediterranean basin with the praise traditions of Second Temple Judaism allowed Paul to bring the culmination of glory in Christ into a rich cross-cultural dialogue in his letters.

Although Paul endorses the legitimacy of the human quest for glory (Rom 2:7, 10), the conviction of the apostle is that the glory of God has been and continues to be dishonoured by human idolatry and ingratitude (1:21, 23). There is no self-justifying subterfuge by which human beings can deflect the moral claims of divine glory (Rom 3:7) or claim that the participation in the covenantal glory of Israel is sufficient alone (Rom 9:4). In reality all humanity has fallen short in the quest for the glory of God (3:23). In this dire situation, God brought Israel's covenantal promises to their fulfilment in Christ, resulting in the magnifying of

[162] See Harrison, *Paul and the Imperial Authorities*, 277–99.
[163] Harrison, *Paul and the Imperial Authorities*, 300–08.
[164] Harrison, *Paul and the Imperial Authorities*, 308–23.
[165] See n. 9 *supra*.

the divine glory (Rom 9:23; 2 Cor 1:22; Phil 2:11). The glory of God, therefore, resides in Christ and his gospel (2 Cor 3:18; 4:4, 6). Consequently, the ancestral glory attached to the Mosaic covenant is a spent force in comparison to the new covenant of the Spirit (2 Cor 3:7, 8, 9, 10, 11, 13).

Furthermore, the resurrection age is suffused with divine glory (Rom 6:4), with the result that suffering humanity and the groaning creation is buoyed by the eschatological hope of glory (Rom 5:2; 8,17, 18; 2 Cor 4:17; Eph 1:18; Phil 1:10–11; 3:21; 1 Thess 2:12; 2 Thess 1:9). Rather than life being consumed by the quest for immortality through the surpassing of ancestral honour, as the eastern Mediterranean elites and associations believed,[166] for Paul the eternal glory of God is the unchanging foundation of the universe and its inhabitants (Rom 11:36; 16:27; Gal 1:5; Eph 3:21; 4:20). Thus Paul's motivation as an apostle is not glory from men (1 Thess 2:6) but rather the praise of God's glory (Eph 1:6, 12, 14; 2 Thess 1:12).

Having set out this vision of the denouement of glory in history, Paul unveils the social implications of glory in the body of Christ. Beneficence within the Body of Christ produces thanksgiving to the glory of God (2 Cor 4:15), with the result that the organizers of the Jerusalem collection are accorded the honorifics of glory (2 Cor 8:19, 23).[167] Mutual acceptance between Jew and Gentile redounds to the glory and mercy of God (Rom 15:7, 9), assuring Paul that his sufferings as the apostle of the Gentiles are the glory of his converts (Eph 3:13). Thus, in the present age, believers can remain confident in the glorious riches of Christ and his Spirit (Eph 3:16; Phil 4:19), experiencing transformation into Christ's likeness from glory to glory (2 Cor 3:18). In light of the glorious consummation of all things, believers need not be concerned about the loss of worldly honour in service of Christ (2 Cor 6:8), or, like their contemporaries, fear the erasure of their honour by those consumed with *invidia*.

8.3.1.3. ἔπαινος, δόκιμος *and Their Cognates*

A significant dimension to Paul's honorific use of ἔπαινος is his concentration upon the praise of God (Rom 15:11: ἐπαινεσάτωσαν [LXX Ps 117:1[116:1]]; Phil 1:11: ἔπαινον φεοῦ) and the praise received by believers from God at the eschaton (1 Cor 4:5: ὁ ἔπαινος ἀπὸ τοῦ φεοῦ).[168] In the remarkable sentence of Ephesians 1:3–14, reminiscent of inscriptional eulogies by virtue of its length and benefaction terminology,[169] Paul speaks of the praise of God's glorious

[166] See SIG³ Vol. 4 *s.v.* IV. δόξα.

[167] Harrison, "The Brothers."

[168] ἔπαινος is widespread in the honorific inscriptions (e.g. SEG 32:1243; 33:696; 34:1233; IG I³ 61; II² 883, 10998, 13040, 11309/12; XII. 1, 2, 9, 56, 100; TAM II 905).

[169] H.L. Hendrix, "On the Form and Ethos of Ephesians," *USQR* 42.4 (1988): 3–15; Harrison, *Paul's Language of Grace*, 242–47.

grace (Eph 1:6: ἔπαινον δόξης τῆς χάριτος αὐτοῦ) and the praise of his glory (1:12, 14: εἰς ἔπαινον δόξης). This honouring of God and his beneficence is enhanced by the sentence's eulogistic spiral, seamlessly connected by the "in Christ" motif and the stylized repetitions of the divine soteriological benefits from which the blessings flow.[170] In contrast to Paul's language of divine praise, the inscriptional word typically used for relations of benefactors towards the gods is *eusebeia* ("piety") and it refers routinely to the cultic benefactions paid for by civic luminaries.[171]

Intriguingly, in other cases, Paul does not polarise the approval of God over against the approval of men, whether in a civic or ecclesiastical context. Paul employs δόκιμος as an honorific in speaking of Apelles as "tested and approved in Christ" (Rom 16:10: τὸν δόκιμον). In another case, speaking about the importance of showing the qualities of righteousness, joy, and peace in the Spirit in the service of Christ (Rom 14:18b–19a; cf. Rom 7:6; 8:4; Gal 5:22), Paul states that one is to be pleasing to God and approved by men (14:19b: δόκιμος τοῖς ἀνφρώποις). Here we see in miniature how Paul brings the ethics of the Spirit into dialogue with the ethics of honorific culture and, concomitantly, how he affirms the importance of a praiseworthy reputation for believers in that context.

Paul, however, does employ ἔπαινος in the conventional manner of the inscriptions for the praise originating from human beings (Rom 2:29: οὐκ ἐξ ἀνθρόπων), including the praise of the Roman authorities for a civic benefactor (13:3b; e.g. IGR III 739 Cols. X–XII, XVII; c.f. IMilet 156).[172] However, Paul's primary focus, in contrast to honorific culture, is the praise that comes from God (2:29b: ἀλλ' ἐκ τοῦ θεοῦ). Consequently, he employs the eulogistic convention of praise to honour his co-workers for their work in the gospel (2 Cor 8:18: ὁ ἔπαινος ἐν εὐαγγελίῳ) or to praise the Corinthians for remembering their apostle and maintaining apostolic tradition (1 Cor 11:2: Ἐπαινῶ). Conversely, the language of praise can be wielded to shame his churches for their humiliation of the poor at the Lord's Supper when the apostle, in a world where honour is the dominant cultural value, withholds his praise from his fractious converts (1 Cor 11:17 [οὐκ ἐπαινῶ], 22 [ἐπαινέσω ὑμας;]).

---

[170] C. Masson (*L'Épître de Paul aux Éphésiens* [Neuchâtel, Delachaux & Niestle, 1953], 149) comments: "one is struck by the fullness of the language, its liturgical majesty, its perceptible rhythm from beginning to end." On the "in Christ" motif (Eph 1:3a, 10a, 12b; "in him": 1:4a, 9b, 10b; "in whom": 1:7a, 11a, 13a, 13b), see C.R. Campbell, *Paul and Union with Christ: An Exegetical and Theological Study* (Grand Rapids: Zondervan, 2012). Repetitions: "praise" (ἔπαινος: 1:6, 12, 14); "blessing" (εὐλεγητος, εὐλεγέω, εὐλογία: 1:3); "glory" (δόξα: 1:6a, 12a, 14b); "grace" (χάρις, χάριζομαι: 1:6a, 6b, 7b); "will" (θέλμα: 1:5b, 9b, 11b); "good pleasure" (εὐδοκία: 1:5b, 9b); "predestination" (προορίζω: 1:5a, 11a); "redemption" (ἀπολύτρωσις: 1:7a, 14a); "Spirit/spiritual" (πνευματικός, πμεῦμα: 1:3b, 13b).

[171] See SIG³ Vol. 4 *s.v.* IV. εὐσέβεια. For Ephesian examples, see IEph II 213; IV 1200, 1288.

[172] Danker, *Benefactor*, § 19; Ascough, Harland, and Kloppenborg, § 178.

Finally, in Philippians 4:8, Paul suggests a series of eight qualities worthy of consideration for the believer. While the scope of these qualities is deliberatively kept open (the eightfold repetition of the introductory ὅσα ["whatever"]), three of the qualities, grouped together at the end of the list, belong to the Mediterranean world of honorific culture: εὔφημα ("well-spoken of"),[173] ἀρετή ("virtue"), and ἔπαινος ("praise"). Clearly, for Paul, one's civic reputation was to be guarded, held in honour, and contemplated by believers in engaging civic life.

In the case of δόκιμος, the word appears in honorific contexts in the inscriptions.[174] But Paul's usage of the word refocuses the attention of his converts on divine approval as opposed to human approval. Paul was faced at Corinth with a challenge to his apostolic gospel and status from the intruding "super apostles" (2 Cor 11:1–6, 13–15, 21b–23a), who, some Corinthians believed, were rhetorically, ethically and pneumatically superior to Paul (10:1, 10; 11:6–15, 21–23; 12,1, 11–18). In replying to these interlopers, Paul spoofs honorific conventions by boasting in his apostolic weakness and failures (2 Cor 11:16–12:10). With biting irony the apostle employs the boasting conventions of the honorific inscriptions (11:16–18, 21, 30; 12:1, 5–6, 9)[175] – including the motifs of the "endangered" benefactor, "surpassing" virtue, and "ancestral fame" (*supra*: 11:23: περισσοτέρως, ὑπερβαλλόντως; 11:26: κινδύνοις; 11:22–23a) – but he parodies their eulogistic intent by means of (what in his opponents' view would have been) an ineffective *apologia* because of its shameful content (12:19: ἀπολογούμεθα). An important aspect of Paul's defence is his conviction that the one who commends him/herself is not "approved" (δόκιμος), but the one whom God commends is "approved". In the case of the Corinthian church, Paul argues, the approval of God is paramount in assessing the reputation of the apostle and his converts (2 Cor 13:5–7: δοκιμάζετε, ἀδόκιμοι, δόκιμοι). In sum, Paul's strategy challenges from a divine perspective the catalogues of virtue and achievement celebrated in the honorific inscriptions and monuments, as well as the Corinthian commendation of the interloping "apostles" (2 Cor 12:11; cf. 3:1).

8.3.1.4. ὑπερυφόω

In Philippians 2:9a Paul states that God exalted Christ (ὑπερύψωσεν: lit. "raised to the highest position"), having depicted his self-emptying (ἑαυτὸν ἐκένωσεν) and self-humbling (ἐτσαπείνωσεν ἑαυτόν) in vv. 7–8, culminating in the shame, weakness and foolishness of the cross (v. 8b; cf. 1 Cor 1:18–31; 2 Cor 13:4;

[173] Although much rarer than ἀρετή and ἔπαινος in the inscriptions, εὔφηος appears in the honorific contexts (e.g. SEG 37:479; 50:572) and in the Delphic ethical canon (SIG³ 1268 *l.* 23: "be well-spoken" [ε]ὔφημος γίνου).

[174] SIG³ 867 *l.* 20: "a most esteemed (δοκιμωτάτου) man and worthy of all honour and praise."

[175] J.R. Harrison, "In Quest of the Third Heaven: Paul and His Apocalyptic Imitators," *VC* 58.1 (2004): 24–55, esp. pp. 46–55; Harrison, *Paul's Language of Grace*, 335–40.

Gal 2:13), known to us through the literary and iconographic evidence.[176] ὑπερυφόω does not appear in the honorific inscriptions, but the accompanying language of honour, even if derived from the Old Testament (vv. 10–11a; cf. Is 45:18–23, esp. v. 23), would have registered with auditors familiar with eulogistic culture. The phrase "name above every name" (2:9b) would have ironically evoked the honorific epithets vaunted by the republican nobles,[177] the Roman ruler Nero,[178] the competitive Mediterranean cities and their elites (e.g. the Ephesian Vedii *supra*),[179] and the ancient associations, with their grandiloquent titles for members.[180] The descent of Christ from equality with God (2:5) to servile and cruciform dishonour (2:7–8) challenged counter-culturally the ascent to honour through the *cursus honorum* at Roman Philippi and at other Roman colonies such as Corinth (n. 16 *supra*).[181] Paradoxically, even in Christ's triumph as the vindicated Lord of all, there is self-effacement: his acceptance of universal honour at his heavenly coronation (2:10–11a) is deflected to the glory of God the Father (2:11b). A new narrative of honour had started to emerge in the ancient world, but it was not without precedent in the case of the dishonoured benefactor, Euphron of Sicyon, in Athens (*supra*). Paul's narrative stood in contrast to those figures of exceptional merit, the "endangered" benefactor, who sacrificed themselves for their city, but whose honour remained intact in the process of commitment to their dependents. In the instance of Christ's *cursus pudorum*, the dishonour incurred had been so demeaning and unprecedented (Rom 5:6–8), given the status of the one dishonoured (2:6), that God had to intervene to restore its loss and enhance its glory.

8.3.2. Paul's Language of "Shame" and the Graeco-Roman Honour System

We have noted the scarcity of "dishonour" terminology in the inscriptions apart from one technical term (n. 142 *supra*). In Paul's letters not only is "dishonour"

---

[176] M. Hengel, *Crucifixion in the Ancient World and the Folly of the Message of the* Cross (Philadelphia: Fortress, 1977); L. L. Welborn, *Paul, the Fool of Christ: A Study of 1 Corinthians 1–4 in the Comic-Philosophic Tradition* (Edinburgh: T&T Clark, 2005), 131–47; G. Samuelson, *Crucifixion in Antiquity: An Enquiry into the Background and Significance of the New Testament Terminology*, WUNT II 310, 2nd ed. (Tübingen, Mohr Siebeck, 2013); L.W. Hurtado, "The Staurogram: Earliest Depiction of Jesus Crucifixion," *BAR* 39.2 (2013): 49–52, 63; B. Witherington III, "Images of Crucifixion: Fresh Evidence," *BAR* 39.2 (2013): 28, 66; J.G. Cook, *Crucifixion in the Mediterranean World*, WUNT I 327 (Tübingen: Mohr Siebeck, 2014).

[177] Harrison, *Paul and the Imperial Authorities*, 332.

[178] Sherk, *The Roman Empire*, § 71.

[179] Spicq (*Theological Lexicon Volume* 1, 363–64 n. 9) cites the imperial decree (MAMA VI 6[2]) recounting a dispute over the names or ranks of various cities. Apparently, some cities had been granted new glory (καινῇ δόξῃ) and became increasingly self-important because of the receipt of their titles.

[180] Danker, *Benefactor*, § 22.

[181] Hellerman, *Reconstructing Honour*, 128–56.

terminology frequent but also its spread of terminology is impressive. Clearly something unusual is occurring here that has to be accounted for. We will focus on those texts directly relevant to the experience of dishonour in a civic context. ταπεινός and its cognates have been briefly touched on and will be omitted from discussion (n. 159 *supra*).

8.3.2.1. ἀτιμία, ἐντρέπω, αἰσχύνομαι *and* καταισχύνω

In 1 Corinthians 4:8, Paul depicts the self-satisfied Corinthians as Stoic philosopher-kings satiated with the wisdom and eloquence of their preferred teachers, considered by the fickle Corinthians to be superior to their rhetorically inferior apostle (cf. 1:12, 17–31; 2:1–7; 3:4–9, 21–23; 4:6–7, 18–20).[182] Responding to their conceit, Paul renders his apostolate in imagery arguably derived from the gladiatorial arena, depicting the apostles as criminals facing capital punishment in the last event on the day's program (ἐσχάτους: v. 9a), and condemned to fight to the death in a spectacle for all (ἀγγέλοις καὶ ἀνθρόποις).[183] Equally viable is L.L. Welborn's suggestion that imagery of the theatre (θέατρον: v. 9b) underlies Paul's language in vv. 9–11. The apostles are the fools of the mime shows staged (ἀπέδεξεν: v. 9a) by God, involving naked and hungry morons who were beaten up for the audience's amusement, and who were belittled with the vulgar insults traded by the fools in the mime troops (κάθαρμα, περίφημα: cf. 4:13).[184]

The relation of honorific culture to the ancient theatre is also worth considering here. The wealthy elites and other dignitaries were given reserved front row seats of honour in the theatre,[185] the archaeological remains of which are still present in the theatres of Priene, Aphrodisias and Hierapolis.[186] The dishonoured apostles, by contrast, shuffle last of all into the theatre, appointed to die or perform there for the entertainment of the highly honoured, including the celestial audience (4:9b). However we interpret the imagery, Paul's explosive contrasts of v. 10 are savage in their irony, contrasting the perceived honour of Corinthian believers and their teachers with the dishonour of the apostles:

---

[182] W.A. Meeks, *The Origins of Christian Morality: The First Two Centuries* (New Haven and London: Yale University Press, 1993), 63. See Cicero, *Mur.* 29.61 (cf. 1 Cor 4:8; 2 Cor 6:10).

[183] R.E. Ciampa and B.S. Rosner, *The First Letter to* the Corinthians, Pillar (Grand Rapids: Eerdmans, 2010), 181–82.

[184] Welborn, *Paul, the Fool of Christ*, 246–47.

[185] The benefactor Poseidippos is honoured with "the front seats at the theatre and the first place in a procession and (the privilege of) eating in the public festivals" (SEG XI 948: Provenance: Cardamylae).

[186] For Priene, see E. Akurgl, *Ancient Civilizations and Ruins of* Turkey, 10th ed. (Istanbul: Net Turistik Yatinlar, 2007), 198, plates 67 (top). For Aphrodisias, see K.T. Erin, *Aphrodisias: City of Venus Aphrodite* (London: Muller, Blond and White, 1986), 83 (lower picture). See Scherrer (*Ephesus*, 160) on inscriptions reserving seats at the theatre of Ephesus for socially important civic groups. Cf. Ascough, Harland, and Kloppenborg, *Associations*, §§ 183, 199.

The suffering apostles	*The Corinthian believers*
"fools (μωροί) because of Christ"	"wise (φρόνιμοι) in Christ"
"weak" (ἀσθενεῖς)	"strong" (ἰσχυροί)
"dishonourable" (ἄτιμοι)	"honourable" (ἔνδοξοι)

In Paul's portrait of the apostolic life, there is no hint that dishonour is somehow wrong (4:11–12a: cf. "until the present hour", v. 11a). Rather in v. 10 Paul contrasts the self-sacrifice and shame of apostolic ministry in service of Christ (4:12b–13) over against the status-riddled rivalries of the Corinthians (4:7–8; cf. 3:1–3, 18, 21; 4:3, 6–7). The responses of the apostles ("bless", "endure", "implore": vv. 12b–13a) to rejection ("reviled", "persecuted", "slandered": vv. 12b–13a) reflect Christ's humble response to dishonour and provocation in his ministry (Matt 5:44; Lk 6:27; 23:34; 1 Pet 2:22–23). His exemplum (2 Cor 10:1: διὰ τῆς πραΰτητος καὶ ἐπιεικείας τοῦ Χριστοῦ; cf. Matt 11:29b) had become for Paul the litmus test for assessing how the perpetrators and circumstances of dishonour should be responded to in each instance.

Paul has already established that God has chosen the foolish and weak – the "nothings" of this world (1:29) – to shame (ἵνα καταισχύνῃ) the wise and strong (1:27), a fact confirmed by the social constituency of the Corinthian church (1:26: οὐ πολλοί). Consequently, Paul challenges those Corinthians humiliating the poor by their insensitive behaviour at the Lord's Supper (11:22: καταισχύνετε). Paul, however, is genuine in saying that he does not intend to shame his converts (1 Cor 4:14: Οὐκ ἐντρέπων), though, with the Thessalonicans, he employs the language of shame to warn the disobedient (2 Thess 3:14–15: ἵνα ἐντραπῇ [v. 14]).[187]

Another case of the same phenomenon is found in 2 Corinthians 6:8. Responding to Corinthian annoyance over his inconsistent visitation (2 Cor 1:15–23), to his collision with a local leader (2:5–11; 7:12), and to the Corinthian support for the letter-bearing intruders (3:1b), Paul unveils another catalogue of cruciform discipleship (2 Cor 6:4–10). Verses 8–9a pivots four categorisations of "honour" and "shame" to describe the apostolic experience of ministry:

The accolades of honorific culture	*The dishonour of apostolic ministry*
"honour" (δόξης)	"dishonor" (ἀτιμίας)
"good repute" (εὐφημίας)	"ill repute" (δυσφημίας)
"true" (ἀληθεῖς)	"imposters" (πλάνοι)
"being well-known" (ἐπιγινωσκόμενοι)	"being unknown" (ἀγνοούμενοι)

Apart from ἀληθεῖς, the accolades are found in the honorific inscriptions.[188] For Paul the experience of honour and dishonour are two different experiences of

[187] The Corinthian tardiness in finalising the Jerusalem collection shames the apostle (2 Cor 9:4: καταισχυνθῶμεν ἡμεῖς), though note their positive response to Titus' visit (7:4: οὐ κατησχύνθην). However, Paul is not ashamed to boast in his apostolic authority when he is building up his converts (2 Cor 10:8: οὐκ αἰσχυνθήσομαι).

[188] εὐφημίας: IG XII 5(653); IMylasa 71; IMagnesia 32 (ἕ[νεκ]εν εὐφημί[α]ς καὶ δόξης). ἐπιγινώσκοντες: IG VII 4130, 4131; IGLSyr III 2 [1183]; IG XII 5 653 *ll.* 41–44: "Therefore in

legitimate and praiseworthy service of Christ. In this instance, Paul explains more fully why this is the case. The "imitation" motif appears again, with the parallel made between the apostles as "impoverished" benefactors and the dishonour of Christ as the "impoverished" benefactor *par excellence* (2 Cor 6:10; 8:9).[189] But, additionally, the resurrection power of Christ is highlighted in the lives of the apostles, ensuring that dishonour is not the final evaluation of their work. As Paul explains, we are regarded as "dying and behold we live, as being punished and not being put to death" (2 Cor 6:9b). Just as God intervened to vindicate the honour of his dishonoured benefactor (Phil 2:9–11), so it was with his apostles. As Paul said of his eschatological hope to the Philippians, neither life in Christ nor death in Christ held shame for him anymore (Phil 1:20: ἐν οὐδενι αἰσχυνθήσομαι; Rom 5:5: ἡ δὲ ἐλπὶς οὐ καταισχύνει; 9:33b; 10:11: οὐ καταισχυνθήσεται).

8.3.2.2. δειγματίζω ἐν παρρησίᾳ

H. Schlier observes of the rare word δειγματίζω in Colossians 2:15, not used in the honorific inscriptions, that it carries the sense "to make a public exhibition".[190] It belongs to the Roman parlance of the display of vanquished foes in a triumphal procession.[191] The shaming of opponents in the imagery enhances the honour of Christ, the cosmic *triumphator*, who parades his enemies before him. Two pieces of evidence, one literary, the other numismatic, will illustrate the depth of the "shame" culture invoked.

First, the triumph of the Roman general, Paullus Aemilius Lepidus, over the Macedonian king, Perseus, at the battle of Pydna (168 BC) was celebrated in a demeaning manner for the conquered in the triumphal procession back at Rome. Plutarch (*Life of Aemilius Paullus*, 33.3–34.4) describes the triumphal procession, focusing initially on the plight of Perseus' three children, and, after exposing the total humiliation of Perseus, despises his cowardice with a departing sneer:

Behind the children and their train of attendants walked Perseus himself, clad in a dark robe and wearing the high boots of his country, but the magnitude of his evils made him resemble one who is utterly dumbfounded and bewildered. He, too, was followed by a company of friends and intimates, whose faces were heavy with grief, and whose tearful gaze continually fixed upon Perseus gave the spectators to understand that it was his misfortune that they bewailed, and their own fate least of all concerned them. And yet

---

order that the People, being thankful, may also manifestly honour both the good and worthy according to its power, and that many others may devote themselves (to beneficence) knowing well (ἐπιγινώσκοντες) the nobleness and goodness of the city."

[189] Harrison, *Paul's Language of Grace*, 250–56; Ascough, Harland, and Kloppenborg, *Associations*, § 289.

[190] H. Schlier, "δειγματίζω," *TDNT* 2 (1964): 31–32.

[191] Schlier, "δειγματίζω," 31.

Perseus had sent to Aemilius begging not to be led in the procession and asking to be left out of the triumph. But, Aemilius, in mockery, as it would seem, of the king's cowardice and love of life, had said: "But this at least was in his power before, and is so now, if he should wish it", *signifying death in preference to disgrace*; for this, however, the coward had not the heart, but was made weak by no one knows what hopes, and became a part of his own spoils.

Second, on a denarius commemorating the victory, Lepidus places his hand on the victory trophy, with Perseus standing nearby shame-facedly with his two sons.[192] Thus Paul, through his strategic choice of triumphal imagery, has depicted God's public shaming of cosmic opponents on behalf of enslaved humanity through the shame of the cross (Col 2:13–15: ἐν αὐτῷ [v. 15b]).[193] One of the great Roman civic rituals, reserved for the Roman ruler and his house, had been subverted for Christ and his dependents.

8.4. Conclusion

Accolades of civic honour motivated eastern Mediterranean elites to act ethically on behalf of their cities, either as benefactors of the community, or by seeking the praise of the Roman ruler through posts in the imperial *cursus honorum*. The constriction of honour and the virtues to the ruler meant that indebtedness to him had to be acknowledged, and that an inappropriately prominent public profile was to be avoided. Notwithstanding, grandiloquent moral language and the monumental iconography became more pronounced and competitive in the imperial age. Paul's denunciation of boasting and the moral failure of humanity should be viewed as much against this backdrop as the traditional Jewish polemics against Gentile immorality and idolatry.

This emphasis on civic virtue was democratised through non-elite aspirants gaining recognition via the imperial *cursus honorum* and by means of the alternate pathways of honour opened up through the local associations. Wealthy businessmen could continue to achieve simultaneously civic honour in the public arena and private honour as association benefactors; the socially marginalized could compete for honorific posts in the associations even though they were the "nothings" of the world. Either way, the associations, reflecting I cent. AD Graeco-Roman society, were hierarchically organised, with members competing in an upwardly mobile quest for honour.

The inscriptional language of honour portrays what was ethically expected of civic luminaries. The monumental iconography (e.g. Zoilos of Aphrodisias) and honorific statuary (e.g. Celsus of Ephesus, Nikias of Isthmia) spotlighted the

[192] E. A. Sydenham, *The Coinage of the Roman Republic* (London: Spink, 1952), § 926.

[193] Cicero, *Verr.* 2.171: "the cross of agony"; *Rab. Post.* 4.13: "'Veil his head, hang him to the tree of shame"'; *idem*, 5.16: "the dread of the cross."

civic virtues of their recipients in the public spaces. Nevertheless, the blight of social dishonour created tensions within this system of civic esteem, originating from the *invidia* of political rivals or unfulfilled promises in the case of Dio Chrysostom, or from the slurs of civic opponents in the cases of Euphron of Sicyon, Nikias of Isthmia, and Aristeides. Therefore Paul's extensive use of the language of "shame" in this context is just as remarkable as his rich semantic domain of honorific terminology.

Paul's ethical thought addresses the believer's experience of "honour" and "dishonor" in civic, ecclesiastical, and family contexts (Eph 6:2; cf. 1 Tim 5:3–4), without diminishing the centrality of honour for civil society or underplaying the shame of dishonor in the cost of discipleship. The apostle endorses honorific culture, but subjects its culture of relentless boasting to eschatological judgement. Instead, the apostle denies honour for himself but allocates it to others. The reason for Paul's decision is plain. The hierarchical and status-riddled expression of honour in Graeco-Roman society had been overturned by God's gracious election of the foolish, weak, low and despised to his covenant people (1 Cor 1:26–29 [v. 28a: ἐξουθενημέμα]).

The least honoured, therefore, are to be the most honoured in the Body of Christ and believers are to outdo each other in giving honour to others. Paul highlights the extraordinary status of all believers, explaining that they participate in the glory of their risen and reigning Benefactor in the present and at the eschaton. All praise, therefore, is focused on God, with Christ being the supreme example of this in his ministry to others. However, Paul, depending on his pastoral situation, can commend others with honorifics, withhold praise, or use "shame" language to stimulate ethical change among believers.

Thus the divine vindication of Christ as the "dishonoured" and "impoverished" Benefactor is the touchstone for Paul's reconfiguration of honorific society in the Body of Christ and its relations with the outside world. The Roman ruler is demoted to "servant: status, irrespective of the exalted rhetoric popularly employed in his praise, but, significantly, his honour was to be upheld and his laws obeyed. Consequently, the wealthy believer was encouraged to achieve the ruler's praise through munificence. More generally, Paul brings the believer's experience of the Spirit and the renewal of the mind into ethical dialogue with Graeco-Roman honorific culture. The believer's experience of "honour" and "dishonor" is the inevitable outcome of the self-denying ministry modeled upon the crucified, risen, and reigning Christ. This christocentric narrative of cruciform "shame" and vindicated "honour" would enable believers to continue to serve others selflessly and humbly within the house churches and the city at large, ignoring the stigma of social dishonour and not being seduced by the trappings of honorific status.

Chapter 9

Paul's House Churches and the Cultic Associations

9.1. *Modern Scholarship on the Local Associations*

In the Hellenistic era many decrees were erected in honour of benefactors by small clubs and cultic associations (θίασος, *collegium*). These associations offered fellowship and feasting under the patronage of various deities or heroes, both in temples and in private homes.[1] They also provided mutual assistance in difficult times, as well as funerary services. Critics of early Christianity, such as Pliny (*Ep.* 96.6–8) and Celsus (Origen, *Against Celsus* 1.1; 8.17), identified house churches with the cultic associations of their times.[2] It is no surprise, then, to see that Tertullian (*Apologeticus* 38.1) strongly differentiated the Christian "associations" and their personnel – distinguished, in his view, by ἀγάπη – from their Graeco-Roman counterparts.

Initially, New Testament scholars were slow to explore this promising terrain. In three pioneering articles published between 1876 and 1881, the German scholar, Georg Heinrici, argued that the early church modelled itself on the structure of Greek associations.[3] In 1881 an English scholar, Edwin Hatch, ex-

[1] For an example of a household *collegium*, see *CIL* VI (948)10261–63: *collegium quod est in domo Sergiae Paullinae* ("The Association in the home of Sergia Paullina"). For other examples, see H.O. Maier, *The Social Setting of the Ministry as Reflected in the Writings of Hermas, Clement and Ignatius* (Waterloo: Wilfrid Laurier, 1991), 22.

[2] Pliny, *Ep.* 9.8: "(the Christians) had in fact given up this practice since my edict, based on your instructions, which banned all political *societies* (*hetaerias*)." Origen, *Against Celsus* 1.1: "Celsus' first main point in his desire to attack Christianity is that the Christians secretly make associations with one another contrary to the laws, because 'societies which are public are allowed by the laws, but *secret societies* are illegal'." *Idem*, *Against Celsus* 8.17: "After this Celsus says that we 'avoid setting up altars and images and temples,' since, he thinks, it is 'a sure token of *an obscure and secret society*'." For discussion, see R.L. Wilken, "Collegia, Philosophical Schools, and Theology," in *The Catacombs and the Colosseum: The Roman Empire as the Setting of Primitive Christianity*, ed. S. Benko and J.J. O'Rourke (Valley Forge: Judson Press, 1971), 279–86; *idem*, *The Christians as the Romans Saw Them* (New Haven and London: Yale University Press, 1984), 31–47.

[3] On Heinrici's contribution, see A. Malherbe, *Social Aspects of Early Christianity*. 2nd ed. (Philadelphia: Fortress, 1983), 87–91. For the two articles were Heinrici suggested that the house churches were modelled on associations, see G. Heinrici, "Die Christengemeinden Korinths und die religiösen Genossenschaften der Griechen," *ZWT* 19 (1876): 465–526; *idem*, "Zur Geschichte der Anfänge paulinischer Gemeinden," *ZWT* 20 (1877): 89–130.

panded upon Heinrici's initial foray.[4] The views of Heinrici and Hatch were largely dismissed and consiged to the history of scholarship. E.A. Judge revived the issue in 1960,[5] but the ground-breaking article within the discipline was that of S.C. Barton and G.H. R Horsley (1981).[6] The authors, in a detailed discussion of a Philadelphian cult group, drew several points of comparison and contrast between the early house churches and the associations.[7]

In his 1998 article, S.K. Stowers persuasively argues that Barton and Horsley had misinterpreted the nature of the Philadephian cult group they discussed.[8] In Stowers' view, the Philadelphian inscription belongs to a traditional Greek *oikos* cult, without any overtones of "other-worldy salvation" or mystery cult. Moreover, the presence of free men, free women and household slaves in the cult is in accord with the traditional Greek household and does not necessarily point to an egalitarian ethos. Finally, according to Stowers, the ethics of the inscription are typical of the behaviour demanded by many of the cults.[9]

[4] E. Hatch, *The Organisation of the Early Christian Churches* (Oxford and Cambridge: Rivingtons, 1881), 26–54. For discussion of Hatch's contribution to the discipline, see J.S. Kloppenborg, "Edwin Hatch, Churches, and *Collegia*," in *Origins and Method: Towards a New Understanding of Judaism and Christianity*, JSNTSup 86, ed. B.H. McLean (Sheffield: JSOT Press, 1993), 212–37.

[5] E.A. Judge, "The Social Pattern of Christian Groups in the First Century," in *Social Distinctives of the Christians in the First Century: Pivotal Essays by E.A. Judge*, ed. D.M. Scholer (Peabody: Hendrickson, 2009), 1–71, at 27–34.

[6] S.C. Barton, and G.H.R. Horsley, "A Hellenistic Cult Group and the New Testament Churches," *JAC* 24 (1981): 7–41.

[7] See the new discussion of the inscription by J.C. Hanges, *Paul, Founder of Churches: A Study in Light of the Evidence for the Role of "Founder-Figures" in the Hellenistic-Roman Period*, WUNT I 292 (Tübingen: Mohr Siebeck, 2012), 260–304.

[8] S.K. Stowers, "A Cult from Philadelphia: Oikos Relation or Cultic Association?," in *The Early Church in Its Context: Essays in Honour of Everett Ferguson*, ed. A.J. Malherbe et al. (Leiden: Brill, 1998), 287–301.

[9] For additional discussion of the associations in twentieth-century scholarship, R.S. Ascough, "The Completion of a Religious Duty: The Background of 2 Cor 8:1–15," *NTS* 42.4 (1996): 584–99; V. Branick, *The House Church in the Writings of Paul* (Wilmington: Michael Glazier, 1989): 46–49; A.E.R. Boak, "The Organisation of Gilds in Greco-Roman Egypt," *TAPhA* 68 (1937): 212–20; L. Wm. Countryman, "Patrons and Officers in Club and Church," *SBL 1977 Seminar Papers*, ed. P. Achtemeier (Missoula: Scholars Press, 1978), 135–41; *idem*, *The Rich Christian in the Church of the Early Empire: Contradictions and Accommodations* (New York and Toronto: Edward Mellen Press, 1980), 162–71; F.W. Danker, "Associations, Clubs, Thiasoi," in D.N. Freedman, ed., *Anchor Bible Dictionary* Vol. 1 (New York: Doubleday, 1992): 501–03; E.E. Ellis, *Pauline Theology: Ministry and Society* (Grand Rapids: Eerdmans, 1989), 123–47; C.A. Forbes, *Neoi: A Contribution to the Study of Greek Associations* (Middletown: American Philological Association, 1933); *idem*, "Ancient Athletic Guilds," *CPh* 50 (1955): 238–52; P. Foucart, *Des Associations religieuses chez les Grecs: thiases, éranes, orgéons* (Paris: Klincksieck, 1873); M. Ginsburg, "Roman Military Clubs and Their Social Functions," *TAPhA* 71 (1940): 149–56; G.H.R. Horsley, "A Fishing Cartel in First-Century Ephesos," *New Docs* 5 (1989): 95–114, §5; J. Kloppenborg and S. Wilson, eds., *Voluntary Associations in the Graeco-Roman World* (London: Routledge, 1996); B.H. McLean, "The Agrippinilla Inscription: Religious Associations and Early Church Formation," in *Origins and Method: Towards a New Understanding of Judaism and Christianity. Essays in Honour of*

However, since the arrival of R.S. Ascough's pioneering monograph comparing the Macedonian associations with the Thessalonian and Philippian house churches in 2003,[10] an ongoing revolution and revitalisation of the discipline has occurred that shows no indication of waning, and, if anything, is gaining momentum.[11] What characterises the recent New Testament scholarship on the associations – emanating in large part from J. Kloppenborg (University of Toronto) and his doctoral students (R.S. Asough, P.A. Harland, R. Last)[12] – is its methodological caution and meticulous historical and social analysis of the association inscriptions and papyri. Instead of positing direct dependence of the first Christians upon association paradigms and practices, in the vein of the nineteenth century *Religionsgeschichtliche Schule*, these scholars have translated and discussed the association inscriptions as a useful databank of comparanda for the analysis of the New Testament documents and the early Christian communities. The association documents throw indirect light on the organisation, constituency, and processes of the early Christian churches by virtue of their mutual similarities, but, significantly, distinctive aspects of the ethos of the early churches is acknowledged in this new wave of scholarship and thus the historic trap of "parallelomania" is avoided.

John C. Hurd, JSNTSup 86, ed. B.H. McLean (Sheffield: JSOT Press, 1993), 239–70; W.A. Meeks, *The First Urban Christians* (New Haven: Yale University Press, 1983), 77–80; A.D. Nock, "The Historical Importance of Cult Associations," *CR* 38 (1924): 105–09; C.H. Roberts, T.C. Skeat and A.D. Nock, "The Gild of Zeus Hypsistos," *HTR* 29 (1936): 39–87; M.N. Tod, "Clubs and Societies in the Greek World," in *idem*, *Ancient Inscriptions: Sidelights on Greek History* (Chicago: Ares, 1932), 71–96; J.-P. Waltzing, *Étude historique sur les corporations professionnelles chez les romains*, Vols I–IV (Louvain: Charles Peeters, 1895–1900); W.L. Willis, *Idol Meat in Corinth: The Pauline Argument in 1 Corinthians 8 and 10*, SBLDS 68 (Chico: Scholars Press, 1985), 49–52; L. Migeotte, *Les souscriptions publiques dans les cités grecques* (Geneva: Librairie Droz, 1992); O. van Nijf, *The Civic World of Professional Associations in the Roman East* (Amsterdam: J.C. Gieben, 1997); R.S. Ascough, *What are They Saying about the Formation of Pauline Churches?* (Mahwah: Paulist Press, 1998).

[10] R.S. Ascough, *Paul's Macedonian Associations: The Social Context of Philippians and 1 Thessalonians*, WUNT II 161 (Tübingen: Mohr Siebeck, 2003); *idem*, "Of Memory and Meals: Greco-Roman Associations and the Early Jesus-Group at Thessalonikê," in *From Roman to Early Christian Thessalonikê: Studies in Religion and Archaeology*, Harvard Theological Studies 74, ed. L. Nasrallah et al. (Harvard: Harvard Divinity School, 2010), 49–72; *idem*, "Redescribing the Thessalonians' 'Mission' in Light of Graeco-Roman Associations," *NTS* 60.1 (2014): 61–82; P.M. Nigdelis, "Voluntary Associations in Roman Thessalonikê: In Search of Identity and Support in a Cosmopolitan Society," in Nasrallah, *From Roman to Early Christian Thessalonikê*, 12–47.

[11] R.S. Ascough, "What Are They Now Saying About Christ Groups and Associations?" *Currents in Biblical Research* 13.2 (2015): 207–44; *idem*, "Paul and Associations," in *Paul in the Greco-Roman World: A Handbook Volume 1*, ed. J.P. Sampley, 2nd ed. (London and New York: T&T Clark, 2016), 68–89.

[12] Not excusively, however. Note, for example, P. Ismard, *La cité des réseaux. Athènes et ses associations VIe–Ier siècle av. J.-C.* (Paris: Publications de la Sorbonne, 2010); P. Fröhlich and P. Hamon, eds., *Groupes et associations dans les cités grecques (IIIe siècle av. J.-C.–IIe siècle ap. J.-C)* (Geneva: Librairie Droz, 2013).

Furthermore, in a contribution of immense value to New Testament scholars, a vast corpus of the association inscriptions has been translated into English,[13] with an extensive annotated bibliography included,[14] now graced by the addition of John Kloppenborg's online Oxford Bibliography "Associations in the Greco-Roman World."[15] Accompanying these rich resources is the publication of the projected four volume series *Greco-Roman Associations: Texts, Translations and Commentary*, published by De Gruyter, with two volumes having appeared so far.[16] In addition to the publication information regarding the texts chosen, the monument on which the inscription was found is described, the Greek or Latin text is provided with epigraphic notes, and a translation rendered with commentary and bibliography. Finally, in addition to this rich research output and resources, reference should also be made to the Copenhagen Associations Project, based at the University of Copenhagen, the aim of which is to investigate the private associations of the Classical, Hellenistic and Roman worlds (500 BC–c. AD 300).[17] Conferences, symposia, research projects, and publications constitute the activities undertaken by their staff.

What key articles and books have appeared on the association context of the early churches so far in this century? The following list is necessarily truncated and is thus representative of a wider range of scholarship. In a pioneering work R. A. Ascough persuasively argues that Paul and the Macedonian Christian communities shared "the same discursive field as the voluntary associations,"[18] providing convenient analogues for understanding the communal structures of Paul's churches at Thessalonica and Philippi, their financial practices and internal social cohesion, among many other features.[19] In the same year P. A. Harland's major study of the ancient associations, synagogues, and Christian congregations in Asia Minor appeared, establishing that there was considerably less tension between the Roman ruler and the local associations than is suggested in

[13] R. S. Ascough, et al., eds. *Associations in the Greco-Roman World: A Source Book* (Waco: Baylor University Press, 2012).

[14] An online and expanding version of the association inscriptions, titled *Associations in the Greco-Roman World: An Expanding Collection of Inscriptions, Papyri, and Other Sources in Translation*, now exists. See www.http://philipharland.com/greco-roman-associations/, accessed 20.03.2017.

[15] See www. http://oxfordbibliographies.com/view/document/obo.../obo-9780195393361-0064.x... accessed 19.03.2017.

[16] See J. S. Kloppenborg, P. A. Harland, and R. S. Ascough, *Greco-Roman Associations: Texts, Translations, and Commentary. I. Attica, Central Greek, Macedonia, Thrace*, BZNW 181 (Berlin: De Gruyter, 2011); P. A. Harland, *Greco-Roman Associations: Texts, Translations and Commentary. II. North Coast of the Black Sea, Asia Minor*, BZNW 204 (Berlin and Boston: De Gruyter, 2014).

[17] See www.http://copenhagenassociations.saxo.ku.dk, accessed 20.03.2017.

[18] Ascough, *Paul's Macedonian Associations*, 190.

[19] See also the ground-breaking research of J. M. Ogereau, *Paul's Koinonia with the Philippians: A Socio-Historical Investigation of a Pauline Economic Partnership*, WUNT II 377 (Tübingen: Mohr Siebeck, 2014).

modern scholarship, and highlighting the important role that occupational identity and networks played in the asociations and the early churches.[20] E.A. Judge revisited the issue in 2008 in his discussion of whether the churches competed with the cult-groups, arguing that five distinctives differentiated the churches from the cultic associations: namely, the preoccupation of the early Christians with ideas; the reorientation of their understanding of history towards the future; their focus on the reconstruction of community; their emphasis on the divine gifting of each person; and the inauguration of a new start as the basis for these distinctives.[21] From the 1990's onwards J.S. Kloppenborg has published a series of incisive articles on association classification, membership, conduct, organisation, dissafiliation and discourse.[22] J.M.G. Barclay has written a very helpful piece comparing the practices of the ancient associations regarding money matters and meetings with the practices of the early Christians, including in his discussion the ancient Jewish evidence.[23]

Finally, in seminal and carefully researched book, R. Last has made an intriguing case for even closer parity between the association inscriptions and the Corinthian house churches.[24] Because our focus is on the Corinthians espistles, greater space will be devoted to Last's argument than our preceeding coverage. Last argues that the typical Corinthian house church comprised 9–10 members, with the addition of a guest, positing in a powerful piece of scholarship that Gaius was not Paul's "host" (ξένος) but rather his "guest" (ξένος) at the Christ-meeting, in a reflection of association practices.[25] The members of the

---

[20] P.A. Harland, *Associations, Synagogues and Congregations: Claiming a Place in Ancient Mediterranean Society* (Minneapolis: Fortress, 2003).

[21] E.A. Judge, "Did the Churches Compete with Cult Groups?," in *idem*, The *First Christians in the Roman World: Augustan and New Testament Essays*, WUNT I 229, ed. J.R. Harrison (Tübingen: Mohr Siebeck, 2008), 597–618.

[22] See J.S. Kloppenborg, "Collegia and *Thiasoi*: Issues in Function, Taxonomy and Membership," in Kloppenborg and Wilson, *Voluntary Associations in the Graeco-Roman World*, 16–30; "Greco-Roman *Thiasoi*, the *Ekklêsia* at Corinth, and Conflict Management," in *Redescribing Paul and the Corinthians*, Early Christianity and Its Literature 5, ed. R. Cameron and M.P. Miller (Atlanta: SBL Press, 2011), 187–218; *idem*, "Disaffiliation in Associations and the ἀποσυναγωγός of John," *HTSTeologieseStudies/Theological Studies* 67 (2011): 1–16; *idem*, "Membership Practices in Pauline Christ Groups," *Early Christianity* 4 (2013): 183–215; *idem*, "The Moralising of Discourse in Graeco-Roman Associations," in "'*The One Who Sows Bountifully': Essays in Honor of Stanley K. Stowers*, ed. C.K. Hodge et al. (Providence: Brown Judaic Studies, 2013), 215–28.

[23] J.M.G. Barclay, "Money and Meetings: Group Formation among Diaspora Jews and Early Christians," in *idem*, *Pauline Churches and Diaspora Jews*, WUNT I 275 (Tübingen: Mohr Siebeck, 2011), 108–21.

[24] For details, see R. Last, *The Pauline Church and the Corinthian Ekklêsia: Greco-Roman Associations in Comparative Context*, SNTSMS 164 (Cambridge: Cambridge University Press, 2016).

[25] Last, *The Pauline Church and the Corinthian Ekklêsia*, 61–71, 131–33. See also J.S. Kloppenborg, "Gaius the Roman Guest," *NTS* 63.4. (2017): 534–49. While the meaning of "host" (ξένος) in Romans 16:23 may be justified by the prior reference to "hospitality"

house churches belonged to a "middling" socio-economic level rather than the abject poor,[26] having adequate resources for their "club" membership.[27] Fees were imposed upon the believing members, not only for the provision of meals but also for a common fund for projects such as the Jerusalem collection.[28] The early Christians reflected the same honorific culture in their meetings as the ancient associations, including crowning rituals;[29] formal-office holding was avialable to all members, as in the associations, though the tenure of the elected officials was temporary.[30] In sum, a great debt of gratitude is owed to these scholars because of the quality of their research into the local associations in the eastern Mediterranean.

The Corinthian epistles provide us the most detailed profile of the operation of Paul's house churches, but, in choosing them as starting point for comparison with the ancient associations, we are not suggesting that that the church at Corinth is representative of all the other early Christian communities in the eastern Mediterranean basin.[31] Needless to say, it would be methodologically sound to compare the Corinthian *ekklesia* with the cult associations of Corinth and Cenchreae. But the extant inscriptional evidence for associations in both cities is sparse, with the available inscriptions postdating the New Testament period. There is a second century AD monument erected by the Association (*collegium*) of the Lares to honour the imperial house at Corinth, a fragmentary reference to a thiasos, and an association tombstone at nearby Cenchreae.[32] Un-

---

(φιλοξενία: Rom 12:13), Last demonstrates from an impressive array of the association documentary evidence that the meaning of ξένος is "guest" (Last, *The Pauline Church and the Corinthian Ekklêsia*,, 67–68). If Last is correct, it is interesting to speculate why Paul was bringing Gaius as his "guest" to the Christian meeting. Was it an evangelistic strategy on Paul's part aimed at exposing Gaius to the gospel? If Gaius was an elite Corinthian official, a postion much challenged in recent scholarship, then Paul was perhaps according a high status individual a significant honour within the Corinthians Body of Christ by means of his personal invitation as an apostle (Rom 13:7), or introducing Gaius, if he were a recent covert, to the assembled believers for the first time. Certainty is unachievable.

[26] Last, *The Pauline Church and the Corinthian Ekklêsia*, 3–4, 83–89, 91–96, 112–18.

[27] Last, *The Pauline Church and the Corinthian Ekklêsia*, 83–89, 91–96, 112–26, 135–47.

[28] Last, *The Pauline Church and the Corinthian Ekklêsia*, 137–48, 166–76. See also Ascough, "Paul and Associations," 81–86. On translocal links, the association inscriptions, and the Jerusalem collection, see D.J. Downs, *The Offering of the Gentiles: Paul's Collection for Jerusalem in Its Chronological, Cultural, and Cultural Contexts*, WUNT II 248 (Tübingen: Mohr Siebeck, 2008), 112–15.

[29] Last, *The Pauline Church and the Corinthian Ekklêsia*, 1–3, 5–20, 83–86, 149–62, 179–81.

[30] Last, *The Pauline Church and the Corinthian Ekklêsia*, 1–20, 83–86, 183–212.

[31] Ascough, "Of Memory and Meals," 58.

[32] J.H. Kent, *Corinth VIII/3: The Inscriptions 1926–50* (Princeton: American School of Classical Studies at Athens, 1966), § 62. There is also a fragmentary inscription (44BC–AD 267) mentioning a *thiasos* ("society") in Corinth (Kent, *Corinth*, § 308 = Ascough, *Associations in the Greco-Roman World*, § 26). In nearby Cenchreae (Rom 16:1–2), there is a tombstone (Roman period) of a member of a "cowherd" association devoted to the worship of Dionysius (*IG* IV 207 = Ascough, *Associations in the Greco-Roman World*, § 25). Puzzling,

fortunately, the literary evidence fares no better: we have a reference to the *thiasos* of Kotys,[33] but nothing else. However, the reference to a "synagogue" association, in Acts 18:4–8 (vv. 4, 7: τῇ συναγωγῇ; v. 8: ὁ ἀρχισυνάγωγος) and in other possible documentary evidence (ἀρχ[ισυνάγωγ]ος),[34] should not be overlooked in discussing the Corinthian evidence for associations. In conclusion, the paucity of local epigraphic evidence for Corinthian associations forces us to look elsewhere for interesting intersections with the Corinthian epistles.

This chapter will examine the *charismatic* nature of Paul's Corinthian house churches against the backdrop of the documentary evidence of five cultic/*oikos* associations. These are

(a) the Rule of Iobacchoi (*SIG*³ 1109: c. 164/165 AD);[35]
(b) the Rule of the Andanian mysteries (*SIG*³ 736: 92/91 BC);
(c) the Philadelphian Association (*SIG*³ 985: late II–I cent. BC);
(d) the Gild of Zeus Hypsistos (*P. Lond.* 2710: 69–58 BC);
(e) Statutes of the College of Diana and Antinous at Lanuvium, Italy (Dessau, ILS § 7212: AD 136).[36]

however, is the claim of Last (*The Pauline Church and the Corinthian Ekklêsia*, 77 n. 120) that B. J. Meritt, *Corinth Vol. VIII Part 1: Greek Inscriptions 1896–1927* (Cambridge, Mass.: Harvard University Press, 1931), §§ 1–10 and Kent, *Corinth*, §§ 46, 306–07, 309–310 are all association inscriptions. The spread of tell-tale terminology for the associations (pace, e.g. Kent, *Corinth*, §§ 62 [COLLEGIO LARVM], 308 [τοῦ θιάσου]) is not present. Neither Meritt or Kent give any indication that these are association decrees, though Kent, *Corinth*, § 310 *may* be one such case, given Kent's very cautious but non-commital comment: "The wording suggests that the document may have contained official minutes of *some* religious gathering" (*ibid.*, 123, emphasis mine). Further, some of these decrees are so fragmentary and heavily restored that the conclusion of an association context is not warranted (Meritt, *Corinth*, § 1, 6, 7–9; Kent, *Corinth*, § 309). Perhaps Last has assumed that because some honorands are being eulogised for benefactions and achievements (e.g. Meritt, *Corinth*, §§ 2–3, 4, 10; Kent, *Corinth*, §§ 46, 306–07), the honorific context must be a local association, or, at the very least, such civic honorands were most likely members and benefactors of local associations. The latter assumption may well be true, but there is no evidence from these inscriptions that this is so. In sum, Last overestimates the number of Corinthian inscriptions that can be defintively shown to be association decrees. For a full-scale response to Last's case, see B. Eckhardt, "The Eighteen Associations of Corinth," *GRBS* 56 (2016): 646–62. I am grateful to Richard Last for drawing my attention to Eckhardt's article in private correspondence. Last's extensive response to Eckhardt is set out in an appendix of his forthcoming Mohr Siebeck book titled *The Other Christian Groups of Late Antiquity: Neighbourhood Networks, Occupational Guilds, and Trans-Local Writers' Organizations.*

[33] A. Adler, ed., *Suidae Lexicon* 1.2 (Stuttgart: B. G. Teubner, 1967), θιασώτης Κότυος, § 381.

[34] See G. H. R. Horsley, "An *archsynagogos* of Corinth?" *New Docs* 4 (1987): 213–20, § 113.

[35] See Ascough, *Associations in the Greco-Roman World*, 14, Figure 1, for a sketch of the inscribed column of the *Iobacchoi.*

[36] Tr. F. W. Danker, *Benefactor: Epigraphic Study of a Graeco-Roman and New Testament Semantic Field* (St. Louis: Clayton, 1982), § 22; M. W. Meyer, *The Ancient Mysteries: A Sourcebook* (San Francisco: HarperSanFranciso, 1987), 49–59; Barton, and Horsley, "A Hellenistic Cult Group"; Roberts, Skeat and Nock, "The Gild of Zeus Hypsistos"; N. Lewis and M. Reinhold, eds, *Roman Civilzation. Sourcebook II: The Empire,* 3rd ed. (New York: Columbia

Although these documentary choices retrace some of the well-worn paths of previous scholars,[37] the association inscriptions from the Peloponnese, southern, central and northern Greece, and the southern edges of continental Europe (the Lower Danube and Bosporan Kingdom), will also be discussed by way of addition. This will compensate for the paucity of Corinthian association inscriptions by bringing into dailogue a wide geographic spread of Greek documentary evidence to the north and south of Roman Corinth.[38]

The chapter is structured as follows. First, the connection between divine χάρις ("favour") and the *giftedness* of Christ's body is briefly discussed. The focus is on the *charismatic* nature of Paul's house churches and how that was expressed socially in a manner different, it will be argued, to the cultic associations. Second, the differences between Paul's house-churches and the Graeco-Roman cultic associations, based on our selection, are explored. Third, an investigation of their common features may help us better understand some of the problems that plagued the early Christian house churches. Fourth, in order to appreciate better to what extent social levelling occurs in the cultic associations and the early Christian communities, two further important association inscriptions higlighting the importance of *philia* in social relations ("friendship") will be examined, again supplementing the five well-known inscriptions discussed above. What distinctive understandings emerge between both groups regaring the social dynamics between members? Fifth, what light does this background material throw on the situation at Corinth?

9.2. The Corinthian House Churches as Charismatic Communities

In grappling with Paul's understanding of χάρισμα in its Graeco-Roman context, we are immediately confronted with the problem that the earliest assured occurrence of the word in Greek literature is from the second century AD (Alciphron, *Ep.* 3.17.4).[39] On the Jewish side, the evidence is equally unpromising.

University Press, 1990), 186–88. On Paul's exposure to the associations, see Branick, *The House Church*, 49.

[37] Ascough, *Associations in the Greco-Roman World*, 1–2.

[38] Note, however, the acute warning of Barclay ("Money and Meetings," 108): "The greater our knowledge of ancient 'associations', the harder it comes to identify their 'essential' characteristics, since the evidence, scattered over several centuries and over a wide geographical area, points to an incredible variety of names, forms, memberships and purposes."

[39] On χάρισμα in Paul, see G.P. Wetter, *Charis: Ein Beitrag zur Geschichte des ältesten Christentums* (Leipzig: J.C. Hinrichs, 1913), 168–87; J. Wobbe, *Der Charis-Gedanke bei Paulus: Ein Beitrag zur neutestamentlichen Theologie* (Münster: Aschendorffsche Verlagsbuchhandlung, 1932), 63–75; A.C. Piepkorn, "*Charisma* in the New Testament and the Apostolic Fathers," *CTM* 42.6 (1971): 369–89; U. Brockhaus, *Charisma und Amt: Die paulinische Charismenlehre auf dem Hintergrund der frühchristlichen Gemeindefunktionen* (Wuppertal: Theologischer Verlag, 1972), *passim*; H. Conzelmann, "χάρισμα," *TDNT* 9 (1974): 402–06;

The evidence of the Jewish apocrypha is textually suspect (cf. the variant readings of *Sir.* 7:33 [cod. B] and 38:30 [cod. S]). The Jewish pseudepigraphic work, the *Sibylline Oracles*, describes the soul as a "gracious gift of God" (*Sib. Or.* 2:54): but this appears in a passage which is clearly a Christian interpolation. The twofold occurrence of χάρισμα in Philo, referring to the "free grace of God" dispensed in creation (*Leg. All.* 3.78), probably represents the first time in antiquity that the word was used with theological reference.[40]

It is likely, then, that Paul borrowed χάρισμα from contemporary colloquial language – with the sense of "gift" or "present" – and was the first to use it as a technical term.[41] Nevertheless, several of Paul's uses of χάρισμα ("gift") retain a general non-technical sense. χάρισμα refers three times to the beneficent act of God in Christ which secures righteousness (Rom 5:15a, 16b) and eternal life for his dependants (6:23). Acts of divine beneficence toward individuals are also embraced by χάρισμα: Paul's delivery from deadly peril in Asia through the prayer of his fellow Christians (2 Cor 1:11); or, again, the gift of celibacy which

---

J. D. G. Dunn, *Jesus and the Spirit: A Study of the Religious and Charismatic Experience of Jesus and the First Christians as Reflected in the New Testament* (London: SCM, 1975): 205–07, 259–300; H. A. Lombard, "Charisma and Church Office," *Neot* 10 (1976): 31–52; F. S. Malan, "The Relationship Between Apostleship and Office in the Theology of Paul," *Neot* 10 (1976): 53–68; R. Banks, *Paul's Idea of Community: The Early House Churches in Their Historical Setting*, 2nd ed. (Peabody: Hendrickson, 1994: orig. edit. 1978), 88–108; R. Y. K. Fung, "Ministry, Community and Spiritual Gifts," *EvQ* 66.1 (1984): 3–20; N. Baumert, "Charisma und Amt bei Paulus," in *L'apôtre Paul: personnalité, style et conception du ministère*, BETL 73, ed. A. Vanhoye (Leuven: Leven University Press/Uitgeverig: Peeters, 1986), 203–28; D. S. Lim, *The Servant Nature of the Church in the Pauline Corpus* (Ph.D. diss., Fuller Theological Seminary, 1987), 138–58; D. Zeller, *Charis bei Philon und Paulus*, Stuttgarter Bibelstudien 142 (Stuttgart: Verl. Kath. Bibelwerk, 1990), 185–89; E. Nardoni, "The Concept of Charism in Paul," *CBQ* 55.1 (1993): 68–80; M. Turner, *The Holy Spirit and Spiritual Gifts Then and Now* (Carlisle: Paternoster, 1996), 261–85; *ibid.*, "Modern Linguistics and the New Testament," in *Hearing the New Testament: Strategies for Interpretation*, ed. J. B. Green (Grand Rapids: Eerdmans, 1995), 146–74, at 156–65; O. McFarland, *God and Grace in Philo and Paul*, NovT-Sup 164 (Leiden and Boston: Brill, 2016), 192–224. J. M. G. Barclay (*Paul and the Gift* [Eerdmans: Grand Rapids, 2015]) does not address χάρισμα, presumably because it will be a substantial focus of his subsequent volume on grace, currently being written.

[40] The position of Zeller, *Charis bei Philon und Paulus*, 36 n. 21. By contrast, Banks (*Paul's Idea of Community*, 91) unnecessarily plays down the theological content of Philo's reference. Contrary to Zeller, Brockhaus (*Charisma und Amt*, 128) claims that the earliest and clearest reference to χαρίσμα in the extant Greek literature is that of Paul. This is because there remains text-critical argument among scholars concerning the presence of χάρισμα in *Leg. All.* 3.78. See also Wobbe (*Der Charis-Gedanke bei Paulus*, 64) and Conzelmann ("χάρισμα," 403 n. 4). Either way, Paul embarks on the most extended and original use of χάρισμα in antiquity. Note the comment of McFarland (*God and Grace in Philo and Paul*, 68 n. 14): "Philo uses a variety of terms to describe the world as a gift: χάρις, χάρισμα, δῶρον, δωρεά, εὐεργεσία." χάρισμα, then, clearly does not acquire the same technical sense or theological versatility as it does in Paul. It is simply one among several options of grace and benefaction language that Philo employs in speaking of God's bountiful gift in creation.

[41] These are the positions respectively of Nardoni ("The Concept of Charism," 69) and Banks (*Paul's Idea of Community*, 91).

enables Christians (single and married) to exercise self control over their sexual desires (1 Cor 7:7).[42]

But χάρις and χάρισμα acquire a specific technical connotation when they designate the manifestation and operation of divine grace either within the nation of Israel (Rom 11:29: τὰ χαρίσματα [cf. 9:4]) or the body of Christ (χάρις: Eph 4:7; χάρισμα: Rom 1:11; 12:6; 1 Cor 1:7; 12:4, 9, 28, 30–31; cf. 1 Tim 4:14; 2 Tim 1:6).

Four important conclusions can be drawn from Paul's technical use of χάρισμα.

(1) Paul does not regard χάρις and χάρισμα as interchangeable. Rather, χάρισμα ("gift") is the direct result of God's χάρις ("favour").[43] Therefore the rich variety of gifting within Christ's church is a product of divine grace (Rom 12:6: χαρίσματα κατὰ τήν χάριν; 1 Cor 1:7 [cf. v. 4]).

(2) The eschatological fullness of the Spirit is grounds for the diversity of gifting.[44] The Spirit helps Christians to understand the gifts bestowed on them by God (2 Cor 2:12: τὰ ὑπὸ τοῦ θεοῦ χαρισθέντα) and animates the gifts themselves (Rom 1:11: χάρισμα πνευματικόν; 1 Cor 12:1: πεπὶ τῶν πνευματικῶν; 1 Cor 12:7: ἡ φανέρωσις τοῦ πνεύματος). At the sovereign discretion of the Spirit (1 Cor 12:11: καθὼς βούλεται), each member of Christ's body is apportioned a gift (or gifts). Nonetheless, despite the centrality of the Spirit in this process (1 Cor 12:4, 8 , 9, 11: τὸ αὐτὸ πνεῦμα), the Father and the Son (12:4–6) are equally the source of the unity and diversity within the body of Christ.[45]

(3) God equips his church with giftted people (χάρις: Eph 4:7, 11; cf. 1 Cor 12:28), along with their specific ministries (χαρίσματα: Rom 1:11; 1 Cor 1:7; 12:4, 9, 28, 30–31; cf. 1 Tim 4:14; 2 Tim 1:6).

(4) The χαρίσματα promote a variety of social relationships that ultimately invert the hierarchical structure of Graeco-Roman society.[46] There occurs a reciprocal exchange that mutually strengthens and encourages Christians (Rom 1:11–12). Unity in the Spirit among believers (1 Cor 12:12–13) enables them to work together in love (12:31–14:1) and for the "common good"

[42] On 1 Corinthians 7:7, see especially Dunn, *Jesus and the Spirit*, 206–07.

[43] Nardoni, "The Concept of Charism," 71.

[44] Zeller, *Charis bei Philon und Paulus*, 186. Note L. Cerfaux's observation ("La théologie de la grâce selon Saint Paul," *VSpir* 83 [1950]: 5–19, at 11): "Les charismes sont l'explosion extérieure d'un don l'intérieur ou de la présence de l'Esprit."

[45] Cerfaux ("Les charismes," 11) says that in 1 Cor 12:4–6 we are presented "un panorama *trinitaire*."

[46] Note the astute comment of E. A. Judge on Paul's body imagery ("Demythologizing the Church: What is the Meaning of 'The Body of Christ'?" in *idem*, *The First Christians in the Roman World: Augustan and New Testament Essays*, WUNT I 229, ed. J. R. Harrison [Tübingen: Mohr Siebeck, 2008], 568–85, at 581): "this leads to the conclusion that what Paul is regularly concerned with is the question of status and the social obligations consequent upon faith in Christ, and that his use of body language is designed to raise these to the highest place in the estimation of his readers."

> (12:7). This is variously understood as the edification of Christ's body (14:3–5, 17, 12, 26), its equipment for service through the grace-gifts (Eph 4:11–12), and its growth toward fullness in Christ (Eph 1:22–23; 4:12–13; Col 1:18–19; 2:19). Each Christian, as an interdependent and complementary member of Christ's body (Rom 12:4–8; 1 Cor 12:12–27), is uniquely gifted and therefore indispensable in its overall health.

In this regard, Paul's body metaphor summons Christians to abandon the Cynic-Stoic ideal of "self-sufficiency" (αὐτάρκεια: cf. 1 Cor 12:14–21, 25b–26). It asserts the unity of Christ's church (12:4–6, 12–13) in contrast to the fragile concord of the body politic (Republican and Caesarian); it undermines the pecking order of the *cursus honorum* ("course of offices") at Rome and in the colonies (12:22–25a); it overturns the entrenched social power of the καλοκἀγαθός in honouring the socially disenfranchised (12:22–25a).[47]

How, then, does Paul's understanding of the *charismatic* body of Christ differ from the ethos of the voluntary religious associations?

9.3. Differences between Paul's House Churches and the Cultic Associations

Each of our associations is cultic, with little emphasis on divine beneficence (apart from the Philadelphian association: SIG³ 985, *ll.* 60–64). But Paul's communities can hardly be described as cultic. All the traditional practices of cultic ritual were absent. The apostle underscores this by transferring Jewish cultic terminology to the believers themselves and to their ministries.[48] Also each as-

---

[47] On αὐτάρκεια ("self-sufficiency"), see A.N.M. Rich, "The Cynic Conception of *Autarkeia*," *Mnemosyne* 9 (1956): 23–29; G. Kittel, "αὐτάρκεια," *TDNT* 1 (1964): 466–67; A.J. Malherbe, "Paul's Self-Sufficiency (Philippians 4:11)," in *Friendship, Flattery and Frankness of Speech: Studies on Friendship in the New Testament World*, NovTSup 82, ed. J.T. Fitzgerald (Leiden: Brill, 1996), 125–39. On the republican and Caesarian body metaphors, see E.A. Judge, "Contemporary Political Models for the Inter-Relations of the New Testament Churches," in *idem*, *The First Christians in the Roman World*, 586–96; G. Theissen, *Social Reality and the Early Christians: Theology, Ethics, and the World of the New Testament* (Edinburgh: T&T Clark, 1992), 196–201. On the *cursus honorum* at Corinth and Paul's discussion of gifts, see A.D. Clarke, *Secular and Christian Leadership in Corinth: A Socio-Historical and Exegetical Study of 1 Corinthians 1–6*, AGJU 18 (Leiden: Brill, 1993), 13–18; B. Witherington III, *Conflict and Community in Corinth: A Socio-Rhetorical Commentary on 1 and 2 Corinthians* (Grand Rapids: Eerdmans, 1995), 259–61; J.R. Harrison, "Paul and the *agōnothetai* at Corinth: Engaging the Civic Values of Antiquity," in *The First Urban Churches. Volume 2: Roman Corinth*, ed. J.R. Harrison and L.L. Welborn (Atlanta: SBL Press, 2016), 271–326, at 291–305.

[48] See the fine discussion of J.D.G. Dunn, *The Theology of Paul the Apostle* (Grand Rapids: Eerdmans, 1998), 543–48. See also M. Newton, *The Concept of Purity at Qumran and in the Letters of Paul*, SNTSMS 53 (Cambridge: Cambridge University Press, 1985), 52–78.

sociation survives on the generosity of human benefactors, the payment of compulsory fees, and the imposition of various fines for the misdemeanours of their members. By contrast, Paul envisages local communities of believers, inaugurated by God's salvific patronage, which proclaim his beneficence and act as benefactors on his behalf.[49]

There is no notion of the *giftedness* of each member in the cultic associations, as there is in Paul's house churches. The closest approximation occurs in the *Rule of the Iobacchoi*. There "every member is expected to participate in word or deed or confer some special benefit and shall pay monthly the contribution for the wine" (SIG³ 1109 *ll.* 45–46).[50] The emphasis upon "word" and "deed" is interesting here, arguably reflecting the division of word and deed ministries in 1 Corinthians 12:7–11 and 12:27–30. But when we try to define precisely from the epigraphic context what are the serving and speaking actvities that the *Iobacchoi* undertake we are left with something fundamentally different. The members of the *Iobacchoi* association

(a) contribute the monthly dues for the wine (SIG³ 1109 *ll.* 45–50);
(b) verbally approve the rules of the association (SIG³ 1109 *ll.* 10–25);
(c) take part in the assigned roles pertaining to the dramatic presentation and sacred rites of the society's celebrations "with all propriety and in good taste" (SIG³ 1109 *ll.* 63–66, 111–126);
(d) deliver speeches, though only with the recognition of the priest and vice-priest (SIG³ 1109 *ll.* 108–111);
(e) uphold and promote the honour of one's Bacchic society over against other Bacchic societies (*SIG*³ 1109 *ll.* 26–27).

In sum, there is no sense here, in contrast to Paul, that the god has unexpectedly and mercifully called the *Iobacchoi* association members into an interconnected family of grace,[51] where each member has been divinely gifted to minis-

---

[49] Danker, *Benefactor*, 156.

[50] Ascough (*Associations in the Greco-Roman World*, §7) translates: "Each member shall speak and act and be zealous for the association, contributing to the fixed monthly dues for wine."

[51] However, the terminology of fictive parenthood ("mother," "father") and brotherhood is found in the association inscriptions. See P.A. Harland, "Familial Dimensions of Group Identity: 'Brothers' (ἀδελφοί) in Associations of the Greek East," *JBL* 124 (2005): 491–513; *idem*, "Familial Dimensions of Group Identity (II): 'Mothers' and 'Fathers' in Associations and Synagogues of the Greek World," *JSNTPHRP* 38 (2007): 57–79; *idem*, *Dynamics of Identity in the World of the Early Christians: Associations, Judeans, and Cultural Minorities* (New York: Continuum/T&T Clark, 2009), 63–96. For πατήρ, see Ascough, *Associations in the Greco-Roman World*, §§46, 88, 91, 319, 322, 329H, 329K. For ἀδελφός, see Ascough, *Associations in the Greco-Roman World*, §88, 92, 215. For mothers of sygagogues, see B.J. Brooten, *Women Leaders in the Ancient Synagogue: Inscriptional Evidence and Background Issues*, Brown Judaic Studies 46 (Atlanta: Scholars Press, 1982), 57 (*mater*), 59 (μήτηρ), 60 (*mater*), 61 (*pateressa*). Even the language of adoption (cf. Rom 8:14: πνεῦμα υἱοθεσίας) is used: "the adopted brothers (εἰσποιητοὶ ἀδελφοί) who revere Theos Hypistos inscribed their names alongside the

ter to those within the group and outside it, with a view to ushering new members into their family so that they might know and obey the risen and reigning Christ, while impartially caring for those in need irrespective of their gender, ethnicity, or social status (Rom 10:12; 1 Cor 12:13; Gal 3:28) until the eschatological renewal of all creation occurs. Paul's understanding of the role of the gifted believers in the Body of Christ is more wide-ranging in its scope, focus, spread of activities, and gifting. There is, admittedly, an interesting "eschatological" and ritualistic similarity to early Christianity in that the priest of the association of the *Iobacchoi* makes a drink-offering "for the return of Bakchos" in its meetings (SIG³ 1109 *l.* 114; cf. 1 Cor 11:25–26 [v. 26: ἄχρις οὗ ἔλθῇ]). However, the reference is cultic its sacrificial expression and location specific: it is the return of Bakchos to *Athens* that is envisaged,[52] not the establishment of the new heavens and a new earth which is precipated by Christ's parousia in the early Christian tradition. Similarities between cross-cultural traditions do not necessarily point to actual conceptual correspondence.

Further, there is little understanding of ethical conduct being grounded in and transformed by divine grace. To be sure, the Philadelphian association (SIG³ 985 *ll.* 15–51) and the *Rule of the Andanian mysteries* (SIG³ 736 Sect. 1) make various ethical vows to the deities. While there is a strong interest in sexual self-control in association inscriptions, this is hardly regarded as a χάρισμα from God (cf. 1 Cor 7:7). Instead the gods demand obedience, dispensing grace to those who obey and punishments to those who transgress (SIG³ 985 *ll.* 45–51). According to Paul, grace is the real dynamic behind Christian ethics: it touches believers as much in their language (χάρις: Eph 4:29; Col 4:6) as in the weightier matters of personal reconciliation (χαρίζεσθαι: 2 Cor 2:7, 10; 12:13; Eph 4:32; Col 3:13; Phlm 22).

Finally, the *Rule of the Iobacchoi* strove to enhance the social status of its members by recognising their attainment of new civic honours and by highlighting recent personal achievements (SIG³ 1109 *ll.* 127–136). While Paul endorsed the appropriateness of honouring fellow Christians (Rom 12:10b; 1 Cor 12:26b), there was no room for inflated self-importance (Rom 12:3) or for dishonouring the weak in the body of Christ (1 Cor 12:22–25). Furthermore, the *Rule of the Iobacchoi* vaunted its superiority over the other Bacchic societies

Elder Name (Ascough, *Associations in the Greco-Roman World*, § 92)." While the fictive familial terminology is certainly present in the association inscriptions, there is no sense, as there is in the Pauline epistles, that the god initiates the family relationship by an unconditioned act of grace towards former enemies (cf. Rom 5:6–8). Moreover, Paul argues that believers, because they are adopted children of God's family (Rom 8:15b, 16b; Gal 4:5), are now indwelt by the Spirit of Christ (8:15b–16a) and, as eschatological heirs to God's glory (8:17, 30b), are given unprecedented access to the Father through Christ (Αββα ὁ πατήρ: Mark 14:36; Rom 8:15b; Gal 4:6). The family terminology of the Pauline house churches surpasses the heart-felt bonhomie amongst brothers of the associations feasts in the scope of its theological application.

[52] Danker, *Benefactor*, 164.

(SIG³ 1109 *l.* 27). But, for Paul, the wild olive was not entitled to boast over the branches (Rom 11:17–18). Divine grace had become the great social leveller in the body of Christ.[53]

It is also worth noting that the cultic associations mimicked the honours and status rituals of patronal society by arrogating to themselves the official titles, special privileges and honorific crowns which were the preserve of civic luminaries.[54] We might ask to what extent Paul engages in a critique of the Graeco-Roman patronal system. E. A. Judge has correctly observed that Paul subverts the patronal system –based as it was on the obligation of a socially inferior client to a socially superior patron – by subjecting everyone to a common Master who outshines all.[55] The terminology of servitude and subordination that Paul universally applies to social relations within the body of Christ undermines the status conventions associated with the reciprocity system.[56] The honorific titles and privileges accorded the officials and patrons of the Sarapis association (Michel, Suppl. 1553), the sacred association of the Great Mother (Michel, Recueil 984), and the Bacchic society (SIG³ 1109) are absent from Paul's house

---

[53] S.J. Case (*The Social Origins of Christianity* [New York: Baker and Taylor, 1923], 134) writes: "No herald in the Christian assemblies announced, after the model of the Eleusinian mysteries, that admission to the cult was open only to those who could meet specified tests of a ritual or moral sort."

[54] Note the comment of F.W. Danker ("On Stones and Benefactors," *CurTM* 8.6 [1981], 351–56, at 352):

> In a world in which ordinary individuals had little contribution to make in the formation of their political destiny, the small groups offered some semblance of corporate dynamics. And like the United Kingdom, which endeavours through pomp and pageant to suggest a political reality that is no more, these clubs and associations affected the diction and syntax of city-states or of the chanceries of the Ptolemies or of the Seleucids. This diction and syntax brought to verbal expression deeply imbedded cultural values. For a brief moment ... their members could play the role of esteemed civil service officials, of members of councils and planning committees.

The benefactors of the local associations were also honoured. An association decree from Delos (*I. Délos* IV 1521: II cent. BC), in praise of a father and his son, apportions the following honours:

> it was resolved to praise both together and to honour each of them with a gold crown and with a bronze image and to set up (the image) in whatever (place) they prefer; and that they receive in addition the fitting privilege of entrance to the guild, having an honoured place for reclining (at the guild banquets), being free of all public service and that in the course of each drinking-bout both be honoured in the guild with a proclamation.

[55] E.A. Judge, "Paul as a Radical Critic of Society," in Scholer, *Social Distincives of the Christians*, 99–115. Elsewhere, Judge ("The Reaction against Classical Education in the New Testament," in *idem*, *The First Christians in the Roman World*, 709–16, at 716) writes of Paul: "... he deliberately tore down the structure of privilege with which his followers wished to surround him. In its place he set out a fundamentally new pattern of human realtions in which each is endowed by God with gifts to contribute to the upbuilding of others."

[56] Judge, "Paul as a Radical Critic," 107. This is not to deny, however, that elements of association friendship language (e.g. συνεργοί ["fellow-workers"], φίλοι ["friends"], ἀδελφοί ["brothers"]) appear in New Testament community language (Ascough, *Paul's Macedonian Associations*, 139–40. See also Ascough's pertinent remarks on Acts 2:44 (*ibid.*, 30 n. 73).

churches.[57] Significantly, regarding the reciprocation of honour, the weakest was to be accorded the greatest honour in the body of Christ (1 Cor 12:22–26).

The differences, then, between Paul's house churches and the cultic associations are apparent. But what about the similarities?

9.4. Similarities between Paul's House Churches and the Cultic Associations

Each of the associations gives clear instructions regarding the organisation of the group and its officials, as well as the social attitudes and behaviour expected of members. The central preoccupations of the associations, as revealed in our documents, reflect some of the issues that Paul struggled with in his house churches. I will summarise these under six points.

First, the regulations of the associations state that participants should be orderly in their behaviour and exhibit reverence during cultic activities. A desire for concord, the maintenance of socially appropriate roles, and avoidance of hubris are paramount.[58] The *Rule of the Andanian mysteries* demands that initiations into the mysteries be carried out "reverently and in a fully lawful manner."[59] The disorderly and impious are to be scourged and excluded from the mysteries.[60] The *Lanuvium College of Diana and Antinous* and the *Rule of Iobacchoi* will not tolerate either disruptive behaviour or abusive and insolent language.[61] So offenders are fined or excluded from meetings.[62] Moreover, in the *Rule of Iobacchoi*, the victims of such injustice should not air their charges publicly, but bring them privately to the priest or arch-Bakchos.[63] The charter of the Bacchic society also insisted that "No one shall deliver a speech without recognition by the priest or the vice-priest."[64]

[57] Danker, *Benefactor*, §§20, 21, 22. See L.M. White ("Social Authority in the House Church Setting and Ephesians 4:1–16," *ResQ* [29.4 1987], 209–28, at 221 n. 49) for additional examples.

[58] On the disorderly conduct and sexual immorality associated with ancient feasts, see respectively G. Paul, "Symposia and Deipna in Plutarch's *Lives* and in Other Historical Writings," in *Dining in a Classical Context*, ed. W.J. Slater (Ann Arbor: University of Michigan Press, 1991), 157–69, esp. 159ff; A. Booth, "The Age for Reclining and Its Attendant Perils," in Slater, *Dining in a Classical Context*, 105–20. Also see Willis, *Idol Meat in Corinth*, 56–61, esp. Athenaeus 420e (cited at 61).

[59] SIG³ 736 § 1.

[60] SIG³ 736 § 9.

[61] Dessau, ILS, § 7212 *Pag. II. ll.* 25–29. SIG³ 1109 *ll.* 74–91.

[62] Dessau, ILS, § 7212 *Pag. II. ll.* 25–29. SIG³ 1109 *ll.* 74–91.

[63] SIG³ 1109 *ll.*64–65, 91–93. New members of the *Lanuvium College of Diana and Antinous* are to read the Society's by-laws carefully "so as not to find cause for complaint later or bequeath a lawsuit to your heir" (Dessau, ILS, § 7212 *Pag. I. ll.* 17–19). Moreover, "no patron or patroness, master or mistress, or creditor have any right of claim against this Society unless he has been named heir in a will" (Dessau, *ILS*, § 7212 *Pag. I.* 37–38–*Pag. II. ll.* 1–2).

[64] SIG³ 1109 *ll.*108–110.

Paul, too, struggled to maintain group cohesion in his house churches. He was concerned about Corinthian divisions at the Lord's supper (1 Cor 11:17–34) and the divisive use of χαρίσματα at worship services (1 Cor 13:1–13, 14:1–39). He sharply criticised the Corinthian practice of taking fellow believers publicly to court (1 Cor 6:1–8). He encouraged the prophets in the assembly to speak one at time, in turn, so that the brethren listening might be edified by what was said (1 Cor 14:29–39).

Also revealing for our purposes is the charter of the *Gild of Zeus Hypsistos*. It stipulates that

> It shall not be permissible for any one of them to . . . . or to make factions (σχίματα) or to leave the brotherhood of the president for another, or for men to enter into one another's pedigrees at the banquet or to abuse one another or to chatter or to indict or accuse one another or to resign for the course of the year or again to bring the drinkings to nought ...[65]

If the editors are correct in regarding σχίματα as an error for σχίσματα ("factions"), we are reminded of Paul's strictures against the factionalism at Corinth (σχίσματα: 1 Cor 1:10; 11:18; 12:25).[66] The fear that association members might go to another brotherhood, hosted by a different president, throws light on the Corinthian rivalry over their "sophistic schools" and rhetors (1 Cor 1:12; 3:4, 21–22a; 4:6).[67] The concern over disruptive "chatter" at association banquets also finds a counterpart in Paul's house churches (1 Cor 14:33–36).

---

[65] P. Lond. 2710 *ll*.13–18.

[66] Roberts, Skeat and Nock ("The Gild of Zeus Hypsistos", 51) air the possibility that σχίματα is an error for σχήματα. The editors dismiss this option because σχῆμα ("position of dignity, status") is regularly used in the singular and is not found in the plural. For cultic background to the "I am of Paul/Apollos/Cephas/Christ" σχίσματα (1 Cor 1:12), see the reference of B.W. Winter ("Theological and Ethical Responses to Religious Pluralism – 1 Corinthians 1–10," *TynBul* 41.2 [1990], 209–26, at 224 n. 54) to the Corinthian cup of Aphrodite, which was inscribed τᾶς Ἀφροδίτας ἐμι ("I am of Aphrodite", "I belong to Aphrodite": Kent, *Corinth VIII/3: The Inscriptions 1926–50*, § 3). S.M. Pogoloff (*Logos and Sophia: The Rhetorical Situation of 1 Corinthians* [Atlanta: Scholars Press, 1990], 251 n. 50) draws attention to the fact that the *titles* of collegia took the genitive form (e.g. οἱ ἐκ τῆς τοῦ Διὸς Ὑψίστοῦ συνόδου: *P. Lond.* 2710 *l.* 4). This background material poses an intriguing question. Do the Corinthian σχίσματα reflect the divisive behaviour of the voluntary associations? This is possible when one considers the fact that the Corinthians had once been idol worshippers (1 Cor 12:2). Also the "strong" at Corinth were participating in idols' feasts at temples (1 Cor 8:10; 10:14ff). These feasts would either have been civic (e.g. imperial: 1 Cor 8:5 [λεγόμενοι θεοὶ ... ἐπὶ γῆς, ὥσπερ εἰσὶν θεοὶ πολλοὶ καὶ κύριοι πολλοί]; cf. Kent, *Corinth VIII/3: The Inscriptions 1926–50*, § 62) or association festivities, or other more private functions. Presumably the "strong" felt that there was little necessity for any change in their behaviour, whether they attended the association banquets or the "love feasts" of the early church (cf. 2 Peter 2:13; Jude 12). Further, they provided theological justification for their participation in both the association and house church feasts (1 Cor 8:1a, 4b).

[67] On the issue, see D. Litfin, *St. Paul's Theology of Proclamation: 1 Corinthians 1–4 and Greco-Roman Rhetoric*, SNTSMS 79 (Cambridge: Cambridge University Press, 1994); S.M. Pogoloff, *Logos and Sophia*; B.W. Winter, *Philo and Paul among the Sophists*, SNTSMS 96

Instead, Paul spotlights Corinthian unity in Christ (1 Cor 3:16–17; 12:13). For Paul, the partisan boasting of the Corinthians (1 Cor 3:21a; 4:7b) misunderstands the servant role of God's leaders who abandon the trappings of social status for the sake of the gospel (3:3–22; 4:1–7; 4:8–18).[68] Moreover, it ignores the fact that God's election has overturned the social pecking order (1 Cor 1:28–29) and that, by means of the cross, He has located all wisdom in Christ (1:21, 24b–25, 30–31). Further, it impoverishes the riches of God's grace given to the body of Christ (1 Cor 1:5; 3:21–22; 4:7): it denies the diversity of God's gifting which, instead of being a point of contention, promotes unity among the Corinthian house churches (3:5–17; 12:4–11). Finally, the apostle dismisses as "foolishness" all boasting in pedigrees (2 Cor 11:21–12:10; Phil 3:4–6; cf. 1 Cor 3:21; 4:6–7). The mark of true humility (1 Cor 1:29, 31; 3:21; 4:7; cf. 2 Cor 10:15–15; 11:16–32; 12:1–10) and love (13:4b) is the refusal to boast.

Second, women should not violate public decorum. The *Rule of the Andanian mysteries* states that "None of the women are to wear gold, or rouge, or white makeup, or hair band, or braided hair, or shoes made of anything but felt or leather from sacrificial victims."[69] This is similar to the mind-set of the author of the Pastorals (1 Tim 2:9–10). Paul's disquiet over the Corinthian women praying and prophesying with heads uncovered (1 Cor 11:1–16) reflects this wider cultural concern for appropriate sexual and cultic roles.[70]

In the associations, illicit sexual conduct can provoke the gods' wrath. In the Philadelphian association, a sexually immoral person is refused entry into the house because the gods who watch over the household will punish all transgres-

(Cambridge: Cambridge University Press, 1997). It is worth mentioning that the cultic associations and the various *symposia* had regular contact with rhetoricians. For example, Herodes Atticus, the distinguished Athenian sophist and philanthropist, is perhaps to be identified with the "Claudius Atticus", the priest-benefactor of the Athenian Bacchic Society (SIG³ 1109: Danker, *Benefactor*, § 22). Our literary texts emphasise the presence of eloquent orators at banquets. Lucian (*On Salaried Posts in Great Houses*, 27) presents a Greek philosopher who, when hired by a wealthy Roman, fears that the owner of a troupe of dancing girls – among others – will eclipse his oratory at the after-dinner entertainment. As the philosopher bemoans, "most of all when your favour is rivalled by a cinaedus or a dancing-master or an Alexandrian dwarf who recites Ionics. How could you be on a par, though, with those who render these services to passion and carry notes about in their clothing? ... You would be glad, I think, to become a composer of erotic ditties, or at all events to be able to sing them properly when somebody else had composed them: for you see where precedence and favour go!" It is possible (but not provable) that some of Paul's wealthy patrons may have hosted lectures given by wandering philosophers in their salons prior to their conversion. Was it precisely such patrons who drew invidious comparisons between Paul and other more rhetorically and philosophically gifted luminaries at Corinth (2 Cor 10:3–11)? On the entertainment offered to guests over dinner, see Jones, "Dinner Theater," 185–98. On eloquence at dinner, see Pogoloff, *Logos and Sophia*, 237–71.

[68] See Clarke, *Secular and Christian Leadership*, *passim*.

[69] SIG³ 736 § 4.

[70] See the comments of Danker (*Benefactor*, 164) regarding "the secondary position accorded ... to priestesses in relation to priests in Graeco-Roman cults."

sors.[71] So, likewise, Paul consigns the incestuous man at Corinth to the realm of Satan outside the church (1 Cor 5:1ff) and forbids participation in cultic prostitution (1 Cor 6:12–20; 10:7–8).[72]

Third, the management of the association funds must be carried out by men of integrity. This is emphasised in the *Lanuvium College of Diana and Antinous* and in the *Rule of the Andanian mysteries.*[73] The situation is delicately poised for Paul. Facing accusations that he had been deceitful in his administration of the Jerusalem collection (2 Cor 12:16–18), Paul attests to the probity of the delegates of the Gentile churches who were accompanying him with the collection (2 Cor 8:16–26).[74]

Fourth, our documents reveal that association officials could reasonably expect remuneration, honour and submission from association members. The *quinquennalis* of the *Lanuvium College of Diana and Antinous*, for example, receives a double share in the distributions during his tenure of office. Thereafter, he will receive a share and a half as a mark of honour for the honest discharge of his duties.[75] This is reminiscent of the Pastorals' exhortation that the teaching-preaching elder is worthy of the "double honour" (1 Tim 5:17). Paul avers his right as an apostle to financial support (1 Cor 9:1–18; Gal 6:6), notwithstanding his refusal of payment at Corinth.

Regarding submission, the *Gild of Zeus Hypsistos* states that "all are to obey (ὑπακούσειν) the president and servant in matters pertaining to the corpora-

[71] SIG³ 985 *ll.* 25–35.

[72] H. Conzelmann (*1 Corinthians* [Philadelphia 1975: Gmn. orig. 1969], 12, esp. n. 97) and J. Murphy-O'Connor (*St. Paul's Corinth: Texts and Archaeology. Third Revised and Expanded Edition* [Wilmington: Michael Glazier, 2002], 55–57) have sharply criticised the assumption that Roman Corinth returned to the (so-called) "sacred prostitution" of the pre-146 BC polis. Such stereotypes not only misrepresent, to some degree, the Corinthian evidence but also the morality of the Graeco-Roman world more generally. On the latter, see F. W. Danker, *A Century of Greco-Roman Philology Featuring the American Philological Association and the Society of Biblical Literature* (Atlanta: Scholars Press, 1988), 131–41, esp. 136 n. 18. Witherington III (*Conflict and Community in Corinth*, 13–14 n. 34) helpfully points to the presence of hetaerae and prostitutes at association and cultic feasts – in private homes and in temple precincts – as background to 1 Cor 6:12–26, 10:7–8. In this regard, note the messenger's invitation to the Bacchic festival – cited in Willis, *Idol Meat in Corinth*, 58 – from Aristophanes' *Acharians* (*ll.* 1085–1090):

> Come at once to supper, and bring your pitcher, and your supper-chest. The priest of Bacchus sends to fetch you thither. And do be quick; you keep the supper waiting. For all things else are ready and prepared: the couches, tables, sofa-cushions, rugs, wreaths, sweetmeats, myrrh, the harlotry are there.

[73] Dessau, ILS, § 7212 *Pag. I. ll.* 28–33. SIG³ 736 § 11.

[74] For Paul's use of inscriptional motifs of rivalry and imitation to encourage the completion of the Jerusalem collection, see J. R. Harrison, *Paul's Language of Grace in Its Graeco-Roman Context*, WUNT II 172 (Tübingen: Mohr Siebeck, 2003), 314–21; cf. Ascough, "The Completion of a Religious Duty."

[75] Dessau, ILS, § 7212 *Pag. II. ll.* 17–23.

tion."[76] Paul (or pseudonymous author) could be equally blunt: "If anyone does not obey (ὑπακούει) our instruction in this letter, take special note of him. Do not associate with him, in order that he may feel ashamed" (2 Thess 3:14).[77]

Fifth, association benefactors should be publicly honoured in a worthy fashion. The benefactor of the *Gild of Zeus Hypsistos* is said to be "worthy (ἄξιος) of the place and of the company."[78] Similarly Paul exhorts that Phoebe, as a προστάτις of the Corinthians at Cenchrea, be received "worthily (ἄξιως) of the saints," in recompense of her benefactions (Rom 16:1–2).

Sixth, at the other end of the social scale, slaves find a place of refuge in the cult of the *Andanian mysteries.*[79] Paul, by contrast, sets out to redefine household relationships at Corinth by inverting the hierarchy of social status: the slave is the Lord's freedman and the master Christ's slave (1 Cor 7:22; cf. Gal 3:28). However, the *Lanuvium College of Diana and Antinous* provides an interesting contrast to Paul's house churches. The Lanuvium by-laws required that slaves donate an amphora of good wine to the College upon emancipation.[80] Paul, in returning Onesimus back to Philemon's house church (Phlm 2), reverses the direction of social obligation. Philemon is to welcome Onesimus back as a "dear brother" (Phlm 16), as an extension of Paul's apostolic presence (Phlm 17), and as a co-worker in Christ (Phlm 11–13). There is a delicious twist of humour in the social reversal envisaged. As J. Koenig writes,

> Here the screw turns, but not without laughter. Philemon, the expert in hospitality, is bidden to receive his own slave as a guest, indeed as an emissary from the apostle who must be honoured as the latter's own presence.[81]

Having discussed our five major association inscriptions enunciated for study at the beginning of the chapter, in the next section we will now analyse the role of φιλία in the social relations of the cultic associations, along with honorific and social concord motifs emanating from inscriptions from the Greek peninsula and beyond. In this way, as we argued, the lack of substantive association inscriptions from Corinth will be partially overcome. In each case, it will be argued that the apostle Paul interacts with the challenges posed by the cultic associations, either by choosing alternative semantic domains to φιλία, or by engaging in detailed critique of the ethos of the local associations.

---

[76] P. Lond. 2710 *ll.* 10–11. The rod-bearers of the *Rule of the Andanian Mysteries* "are to be obedient to those who oversee the mysteries" (SIG³ 736 § 10).

[77] On Paul's authority and his expectation of obedience from his house churches, see C. E. Glad, *Paul and Philodemus: Adaptibility in Epicurean and Early Christian Psychagogy*, NovTSup 81 (Leiden: Brill, 1995), 205–08.

[78] P. Lond. 2710 *ll.* 6–7.

[79] SIG³ 736 § 16.

[80] Dessau, ILS, § 7212 *Pag. II. ll.* 8–9.

[81] J. Koenig, *New Testament Hospitality: Partnership with Strangers as Promise and Salvation* (Philadelphia: Fortress, 1985), 79.

9.5. The Issue of Honorific Rituals and Social Relationships: Comparing the Cultic Associations and the House Churches

9.5.1. Paul, Friendship and the Cultic Associations

Our first inscription, IG II² 1275 (Attica: III–II cent. BC), set out below, recounts the responsibilities of the association members towards each other. What is striking is the strong emphasis on "friendship" as the basis for mutual obligation in social relationships. The decree is fragmentary at the beginning (*ll.* 1–4), but from the second half of line 4 the ethos underlying association relationships emerges forcefully:

1 – δέ τις αι
– ναι κατασ-
– αι̣α τῶν θιασ-
[ωτῶν – – – – – – – – εἰὰν δέ τι]ς αὐτῶν ἀπογίγνητ-
5 [αι, φράσ]ει ἢ ὑὸ[ς ἢ μήτηρ? ἢ π]ατὴρ ἢ ὅς ἂν οἰκειότατ-
ος εἶ τοῦ θίασου, τοῦ δ' ἀπογιγνομένου̣ ἰέναι ἐπ' ἐ-
χφορὰν καὶ αὐτοὺς καὶ τοὺς φίλους ἅπαντας καὶ ἄ-
ν τις ἀδικῆται, β̣οηθεῖν καὶ αὐτοὺς καὶ τοὺς φί-
λ̣ους ἅπαντας, ὅπως ἂν πάντες εἰδῶσιν ὅτι καὶ
10 εἰς τοὺς θεοὺς εὐσ̣εβοῦμεν καὶ εἰς τοὺς φίλους· τα-
ῦ̣τα δὲ ποιοῦσιν αὐτοῖς πολλὰ κἀγαθὰ καὶ ἐγγόν-
οις καὶ προγόνοις. ἐπειδὰν δὲ κυρώσωσι τὸν νόμον οἱ θιασῶται, μηθὲν εἶναι τοῦ νόμου κυριώτερ-
ον· εἰὰν δέ τις παρὰ τὸν νόμον ἢ εἴπει ἢ πράξει, κα-
15 τηγορίαν αὐτοῦ εἶναι τῶι βουλομένωι τῶν θιασωτῶ-
ν, καὶ ἂν ἕλει αὐτὸν τιμάτωσαν αὐτὸν καθότι ἂν δο-
κεῖ τῶι κοινῶι.[82]

…
… of the *thiasōtai* of the association
5 … and if any of them should die … or a son or a … or a father or whoever is
his closest relative in the association, and they shall attend the cortège –
both the members and all the friends. And if a member should be
wronged, they and all the friends shall come to his assistance, so that
10 everyone might know that we show piety to the gods and to our friends.
To those who do these things, (may) many blessings come upon them,
their descendants and their ancestors. Whenever the *thiasōtai* have
ratified this law, let there be nothing to take precedence over it. And if
someone should either speak or act in contravention of the law, an
15 accusation against him may be lodged by any of the *thiasōtai* who so
wishes; and if he convicts him, let them assess the penalty, whatever
seems appropriate to the association.

---

[82] For the translation and commentary, see Kloppenborg, Harland, and Ascough, *Greco-Roman Associations*, Vol. I, § 8. I am grateful to Professor Kloppenborg for drawing my attention to this inscription and providing the English translation.

Two areas of social obligation emerge in this association inscription. The first area of obligation involves responsibilities at the funeral cortège of dead members: both the members and all the "friends" (*l.* 7: τοὺς φίλους ἅπαντας) of the association are to attend the procession. The significance of a (possible) distinction between "members" and "friends" is not clear from the text. It may be just a manner of self-designation within the associations, underscoring the fact that all the members are actually friends.[83] But what might IG II² 1275 mean if there is indeed a distinction being made between the two groups, one not obvious to us now? Perhaps the φίλοι have been guests of the association in the past and they still retain strong connections with members of the associations. They could be ex-members of the association who have departed on good-terms with the members, but who maintain civic or professional contact with members of the association: alternatively, they may be initiates or guests awaiting full membership. Certainty, in my opinion, is unobtainable, other than trying to discern from each inscription whether there is a distinction being made, and, if so, what might be its significance.[84]

The second area of obligation involves the rescue of members who have been wronged: what precisely is the issue or the occasion envisaged is again difficult to determine, irrespective of whether we are speaking about a misdemeanour that has occurred inside or outside the association. In all probability, the language is deliberately kept imprecise so that a variety of occasions and misdemeanours are covered. Once again, the members and friends are to render assistance to the wronged man. The motive of piety on the part of association (*l.* 10: εὐσ̣εβοῦμεν) towards the gods and the friends undergirds the extension of assistance. In sum, the public reputation of the association before its tutelary deities and its citizen-friends is paramount. Seemingly, irrespective of the social status of association members and their friends, a social levelling occurs through the mutual commitment of each member to each other and to the god.

---

[83] Harland, *Associations, Synagogues, and Congregations*, 33: "There are numerous occasions of association members referring to one another as 'friends' in inscriptions, often as a self-designation or title of the group itself."

[84] The terminology of friendship elsewhere in the association degrees usually points to self-designations. For example, the grave inscription of Apollonios, erected by an association of "friends" (φίλοι), does not reveal anything more than friendship is the ethos of the association and represents the self-designation of the group (Ascough, *Associations in the Greco-Roman World*, §219 [Seleucia]; cf. similarly, the "friendship association" [συμβίωσις φιλία] in *ibid.*, §242 [Tenos]). An association inscription of the mysteries from Rome links "initiates" (μύθσται) and "friends" (φίλοι) so closely together that both words are obviously self-designations of members of the group (*ibid.*, §327 [III–IV cent. AD]). The "companions" (ἑταῖροι) of the elder Ophelion and "close friends" (συνήθεις φίλοι) of Sakerdos, the high-priest and benefactor-head of the gymnasium, are most likely self-designations for the same members of the group, as the absence of the article before συνήθεις φίλοι probably indicates (*ibid.*, §99 [Prusa near Olympus: I cent. AD]).

Second, at Athens, to the east of the Parthenon, a late second-century AD statute of a club (ἔρανος) sets out the rules for admission to association membership:

[εἰς?] μνήμην φθιμένοις καὶ ἀλλήλους ἀν-
[έθηκ]αν
24 ἄρχων μὲν Ταύρισκος, ἀτὰρ μὴν Μου
νιχιὼν ἦν,
ὀκτ[ω]καιδεκάτῃ δ' ἔρανον σύναγον
φίλοι ἄνδρες
καὶ κοινῇ βουλῇ θεσμὸν φιλίης ὑπέ-
γραψαν.
30 νόμος ἐρανιστῶν.
[μη]δενὶ ἐξέστω ἰσι[έν]αι ἰς τὴν σεμνοτάτην
σύνοδον τῶν ἐρανιστῶν πρὶν ἂν δοκι-
μασθῇ εἴ ἐστι ἁ[γν]ὸς καὶ εὐσεβὴς καὶ ἀγ-
α[θ]ός· δοκιμα[ζέ]τω δὲ ὁ προστάτης [καὶ]
35 [ὁ] ἀρχιεραγιστὴς καὶ ὁ γ[ρ]αμματεὺς κα[ὶ]
[οἱ] ταμίαι καὶ σύνδικοι· ἔστωσαν δὲ ο[ὗ]-
[τ]οι κληρωτοὶ κατὰ ἔ[το]ς χωρὶς πρ [[ισπρ]] οστάτ[ου] {προστάτου}
ὁμολείτωρ δὲ ἔ [[ι]] στω {ἔστω} δ[ιὰ] βίου αὐτο[ῦ]
ὁ ἐπὶ ἡρώου καταλιφθείς· αὐξανέτω δ[ὲ]
40 ὁ ἔρανος ἐπιφιλοτειμίαις· εἰ δέ τις μά-
χας ἢ θορύβους κεινῶν φαίνοιτο,
ἐκβαλλέσθω τοῦ ἐράνου ζημιού-
μενος [[ε]] Ἀττ[ι]καῖς κε΄ ἢ πληγαῖς αἰκ [[αικ]] ιζό-
μενος {αἰκιζόμενος} ταῖς διπλαῖς πέ [[τ]] ρα {πέρα} κρίσεως.

(17 lines missing due to damage)
... set up this in the memory of the dead and the others ...
(5 lines too damaged to translate) ...
Tauriscus was archon, and it was
on the 18th of Munichion that men friends
formed a club and by common consent dictated the rule of friendship.
30 Members' Law
No one is to enter the solemn meeting of the members before being tested for honesty, piety and respectability. The test is to be made by the patron and | the club president and secretary and the treasurers and the adjudicators. They are to be set up by lot annually except for the patron. Joint-administrator for life shall
40 be the one left in charge of the tomb. Let the club thrive | on benefactions. But if anyone seems to be stirring up fighting or uproar he is to be thrown out of the club with a fine of 25 Attics or double the flogging that has been determined.[85]

Again the dynamic of social relations within the club, as was the case with the previous inscription, is φιλία ("friendship"). The membership of the club is

[85] Lines 18–19 in the Greek translation are translated into English by Ascough, *Associations in the Greco-Roman World*, § 8. The rest of the translation in English (*ll.* 24–44 in the Greek) comes from Judge, "Did the Churches Compete with Cult Groups?," 616–17.

male, bonded together as friends (φίλοι), and the law governing interactions among the members is designated "the rule of friendship" (θεσμὸν φιλίης). However, the club does not reflect the open commensality of the Jesus community towards the economically and socially marginalised, the outcast, the ritually impure, and sinners (Mark 2:14–17; 10:21, 31; Luke 15:1; 18:10–14; 19:2; Matt 5:3// Luke 6:20; Matt 11:5//Luke 7:22; Matt 11:19//Luke 7:34; Matt 23:12//Luke 14:11).[86] Rather the officials of the club test potential candidates before their admission for their probity and good character: only those who are ἁγνός, εὐσεβής, and ἀγαθός are eligible.[87] Moreover, the social dynamics of friendship enunciated in this inscription are not united by any philosophical or religious interests.[88] As E. A. Judge comments about the identity of the φίλοι,

> They are those employees and servants of the patron and tomb-heir who wish to maintain the link through to an honourable burial. They are financing this jointly, and in the meantime enjoying a good time at regular drinking or dining parties. Any sacrifices offered will have been safely performed before the fun began.[89]

What is the attitude of the apostle Paul towards the ethos of friendship in the association inscriptions? Paul is wary of employing φιλ-compounds (φιλαδελφία: Rom 12:10; 1Thess 4:9; φιλέω: 1 Cor 16:22; φίλημα: 1 Cor 16:20; 2 Cor 13:20), bypassing φιλία entirely.[90] By contrast, the Gospel of John uses φιλέω extensively (John 5:20; 11:3, 36; 12:25; 15:19; 16:27; 20:2; 21:15, 17 [2x]). Moreover, in a remarkable appropriation of the Graeco-Roman ideals of friendship,[91] John presents Christ as (a) elevating the servant status of the disciples to the esteemed status of friends, (b) revealing the Father's words to his intimate friends, (c)

---

[86] See J. D. G. Dunn, *Jesus Remembered. Christianity in the Making: Volume 1* (Grand Rapids: Eerdmans, 2003), 516–41; C. S. Keener, *The Historical Jesus of the Gospels* (Grand Rapids: Eerdmans, 2009), 210–12; T. Holmén, "Jesus and the Purity Pradigm," in *Handbook for the Study of the Historical Jesus. Volume 3: The Historical Jesus*, ed. T. Holmén and S. E. Porter (Leiden and Boston: Brill, 2011), 2709–44 B. Chilton, "Jesus and Sinners and Outcasts," in Holmén and Porter, *Handbook for the Study of the Historical Jesus. Volume* 3, 2801–33.

[87] The precise nunace of the translation of ἁ[γν]ός (*l.* 33) is unclear, either being "pure", if one understands the word in a cultic context (e. g. Ascough, *Associations in the Greco-Roman World*, § 8), or relating to financial probity (e. g. Judge, "Did the Churches Compete with Cult Groups?," 617), if one considers the word to be relating to the club's thriving benefactions and its collection of fines.

[88] Judge, "Did the Churches Compete with Cult Groups?," 602.

[89] Judge, "Did the Churches Compete with Cult Groups?," 602.

[90] Scholars have argued that Philippians 4:10–20 is a letter of "friendship", but this is an overstatment. See J. Reumann, *Philippians: A New Translation with Introduction and Commentary* (New Haven and London: Yale University Press, 2008), 678–85.

[91] On friendship in the Graeco-Roman and New Testament world, see J. T. Fitzgerald, *Friendship, Flattery, and Frankness of Speech: Studies on Friendship in the New Testament* (Leiden: Brill, 1996); *id.*, *Greco-Roman Perspectives on Friendship* (Atlanta: Scholars Press, 1997); D. Konstan, *Friendship in the Classical World* (Cambridge: Cambridge University Press, 1997).

dying for his dependent friends,[92] and (d) summoning his loyal friends to obedience (φιλοί: John 15:13, 14, 15; cf. 3:29; 11:1; 19:12) – the latter being the characteristic response of a grateful disciple.[93]

This contrast, therefore, between the Gospel of John and the local associations over against the apostle Paul in regards to the dynamics of friendship in community relations is potent. Why does Paul avoid φίλια and φιλ-compounds and what is his preferred discourse of community in the Corinthian epistles?[94] It is difficult to determine with certainty why a writer pays little attention to a semantic domain at the expense of others. It could simply be that a particular domain provides greater opportunities to create flashes of cultural and hermeneutical recognition in the minds of its original auditors than an alternative domain. But in the case of φίλια and its φιλ-compounds, the political context of the Roman colony of Corinth, with its powerful provincial elites, may explain why the apostle avoided friendship terminology as semantic domain for relationships between believers. The Latin equivalent of φίλια, *amicitia*, charted the shifting political alliances of the elites in republican and imperial Rome,[95] capturing not only the hierarchical relationships of patrons and clients (Cicero, *Amic.* 9.31; *idem*, *Fam.* 4.2.3) but also the more intimate friendships between social equals and unequals (*Fam.* 19.69–70; 20.71–73). However, as E.A. Judge notes, friendship in antiquity was "an integral part of the whole social apparatus,"[96] being inherently unequal in its social expression notwithstanding its occasions of intimacy, and therefore was always potentially a "perilous" relationship."[97] The furious competition for status, clients and magistracies that this system entailed (Cicero, *Amic.* 17.63–64), with its cycles of obligation and coun-

---

[92] C.S. Keener (*The Gospel of John: A Commentary. Volume Two* (Peabody: Hendrickson, 2003), 1014) posits regarding the pericipe of John 15:12–17: "Though an allusion to patronal friendship is possible in this passage, the Greco-Roman ideals of loyalty, intimacy and sharing are more likely in view." While I agree with the overall thrust of what Keener says, the patronal image of friendship may well underlie the death of Christ on behalf of his friends and dependents (John 15:13), notwithstanding the prior "friend of the bridegroom" reference (3:29). However, patronal φιλία in John 15:13 is redefined by the greater love of Christ precipitating it (15:13a: μείζονα ταύτης ἀγάπην οὐδεὶς ἔχει). On the relationship between love and friendship, see Cicero, *Amic.* 8.26–27; Seneca, *Ep.* 81, 112.

[93] On friendship in the Gospel of John, see J.M. Ford, *Redeemer – Friend and Mother: Salvation in Antiquity and in the Gospel of John* (Minneapolis: Fortress, 1997). See especially the discussion of Keener, *The Gospel of John*, 1004–15.

[94] Paul's avoidance of φίλια and φιλ-compounds cannot be explained by a purported disinterest in φίλια in the literature of Second Temple Judaism. The motif of friendship, as A.J. Köstenberger observes (*John* [Grand Rapids: Baker Academic, 2004], 458), was a "subject of extended reflection in Second Temple wisdom literature (esp. Sir. 6:5–17)."

[95] On *amicitia* as a political concept in republican Rome, see J. Hellegouar'h, *Le vocabulaire Latin des relations et des partis politiques sous la* République (Paris: Les Belles Lwttres, 1963), 41–62.

[96] Judge, "Paul as a Radical Critic," 105.

[97] Judge, "Paul as a Radical Critic," 105.

ter-obligation (8.26),[98] as well as the rituals of friendship and enmity as relationships evolved and dissolved (Cicero, *Amic.* 10.34–35; 21.76–77; 22:85), was anathema for the harmonious working of the Body of Christ at Corinth. In terms of Paul's preferred discourse for communal relations in the Corinthian epistles, the answer is statistically clear: ἀγάπη ("love") and its cognates dominate all.[99] Their occurrence vastly exceeds another possible communal candidate: κοινωνία ("fellowship", "communion": 1 Cor 1:9; 10:16 [2x]; 2 Cor 6:14; 8:14; 9:13; 13:13), κοινωνός ("partner": 1 Cor 10:18, 20; 2 Cor 1:7; 8:23).[100] The answer for the predominance of ἀγάπη and its cognates in Paul's writings is probably dominical: ἀγάπη is Jesus' summary of the Mosaic Law (Mark 12:28–34; Matt 22:36–40; cf. Rom 13:8–10; Gal 6:2). Paul's indebtedness to the Jesus tradition in this instance could not be clearer.

9.5.2. Paul, the World of Honour, and Social Concord in the Body of Christ

Our selection of association inscriptions from the Greek cities to the north and south of Corinth, touching the edges of Lower Danube basin and the Bosporan Kingdom, reveal the centrality of honour in the cultic associations. How does Paul engage their honorific conventions and redefine their rationale in distinguishing the Christian house churches from the ubiquitous local cultic associations? Several key motifs will be addressed.

First, the Roman ruler is regularly honoured in the association inscriptions,[101] testifying to the prominence of the imperial cult throughout the Greek peninsula at the local association level. We have also already seen that there was a II. century AD monument erected by the Association (*collegium*) of the Lares to honour the imperial house at Corinth (n. 32 *supra*). Corinth would have undoutedly had its first-century association equivalents. Paul, however, adopts in the epistle to the Romans a more ambiguous approach towards the ruler, encouraging his converts to render him honour as God's appointee and pay their taxes (Rom 13:1–7), yet simultaneously reducing him to "servant" status in the same way as the LXX does the rulers of the nations, thereby divesting him of his

---

[98] On the key phrase in Cicero, *Amic.* 8.26 ("so that by the giving and receiving of favours": *ut dandis recipiendisque meritis*), its relationship to εἰς λόγον δόσεως καὶ λήμψεως in Phil 4:15 ("in the matter of giving and receiving"), and the financial implications of "friendship" within Roman senatorial circles, see Ogereau, *Paul's Koinonia with the Philippians*, 274–77.

[99] ἀγάπη: 1 Cor 4:21; 8:1; 13:1, 2, 3, 4, 8, 13; 14:1; 16:14, 24; 2 Cor 2:2, 4; 5:14; 6:6; 8:7, 8, 24; 13:11, 13. ἀγαπάω: 1 Cor 2:9; 8:3; 2 Cor 9:7; 11:11; 12:15. ἀγαπητός: 1 Cor 4:14, 17; 10:14; 15:58; 2 Cor 7:1; 12:19.

[100] See G. Panikulam, *Koinônia in the New Testament: A Dynamic Expression of Christian Life* (Rome: Biblical Institute Press, 1979); Ogereau, *Paul's Koinonia with the Philippians.*

[101] Augustus: Ascough, *Associations in the Greco-Roman World*, § 32 (27 BC–14 AD). Pertinax: *ibid.*, § 64 (AD 196–198). "Household of the Augusti": *ibid.*, § 67 (II–III cent. AD). Marcus Aurelius: *ibid.*, § 71 (AD 222–235). "Salvation of the Augusti": *ibid.*, § 72 (AD 150–200).

stratospheric accolades in the imperial propaganda of the eastern Mediterranean.[102] In the case of the Corinthian epistles, Paul critiques the quasi-divine status accorded the Julio-Claudian household in the Greek East (1 Cor 8:5–6; v. 5: "so-called gods either in heaven and on earth").[103] The confessional name for the exalted Christ (1 Cor 8:6: "Lord" [κύριος]), the mediator of all creation (8:6b), has imperial reference, given the increasing attribution of *kyrios* language to Nero in inscriptions and papyri from the sixties onwards.[104] It is likely that this language was already informally abroad in the early fifties. Consequently, Paul warns about his Corinthian converts about the dangers associated with idolatry in the civic temples (1 Cor 10:14–22), including not only the religious excesses of the indigenous cults but also the seductive ubiquity of the imperial cult at Roman Corinth.

This critique is extended by Paul when he highlighs the ignorance of "the rulers of this age" regarding God's plan, which has been "decreed before the ages for our glory" (1 Cor 2:7). Indeed, if the rulers had been aware of God's intentions they would not have crucified the "Lord of glory" (2:8), Paul avers. For Paul, the glorious destination of the Corinthian believers finds its culmination in Christ, the risen and glorious Lord of all history. The concentration of "glory" in the powerful Julio-Claudian house, which had extinguished the traditional republican quest of the Roman nobles for ancestral glory,[105] has been shamed by the weakness and foolishness of the cross (1 Cor 1:23–25).

Furthermore, the triumph of the cross, confimed by Christ's resurrection and coming parousia (1 Cor 15:20–28; cf. Phil 2:9–11), opens up a continuous renewal for believers through the revelatory agency of the Spirit of the risen Christ (καθάπερ ἀπὸ κυρίου πνεύματος: 2 Cor 3:18b).[106] Not only do believers behold and reflect the Lord's glory (τὴν δόξαν κυρίου: 2 Cor 3:18a), but also they are transformed into his image in the present age (τὴν αὐτὴν εἰκόνα μεταμορφούμεθα: 2 Cor 3:18b; cf. Gen 1:26–27; 5:1; Rom 8:29–30; 2 Cor 4:4, 6; Eph 4:23; Col 3:10).[107] The phrase εἰς δόξαν ("to glory": 2 Cor 3:18b) presages the eschatological meta-

---

[102] J.R. Harrison, *Paul and the Imperial Authorities at Thessalonica and Rome: A Study in the Conflict of Ideology*, WUNT I 273 (Tübingen: Mohr Siebeck, 2011), 271–323.

[103] See B.W. Winter, *After Paul Left Corinth: The Influence of Secular Ethics and Social Change* (Grand Rapids: Eerdmans, 2001), 269–86.

[104] J.D. Fantin, *The Lord of the Entire World: Lord Jesus, a Challenge to Lord Caesar?* (Sheffield: Sheffield Phoenix Press, 2011), 196–202.

[105] Harrison, *Paul and the Imperial Authorities*, 205–32.

[106] On καθάπερ ἀπὸ κυρίου πνεύματος (2 Cor 3:18b) as a reference to the Spirit of Christ, see P.W. Barnett, *The Second Epistle to the Corinthians* (Grand Rapids: Eerdmans, 1997), 208–09 n.54.

[107] On the connection between "the glory of the Lord: (2 Cor 3:18a) and "the same image" (2 Cor 3:18b), note the observation of J.-F. Collange (*Énigmes de la deuxième épître de Paul aux Corinthiens* SNTSMS 18 [Cambridge: Cambridge University Press, 1972], 121): "le Christ est le miroir dans lequel le chrétien contemple l'image de dieu (Gen. 1:26s), qu'il est appelé à devenir lui-même."

morphosis of believers to Christ's body of glory (cf. 1 Cor 15:49; Phil 3:21; Col 3:4).[108] Thus Paul has no hesitation in designating the messengers of the churches accompanying the Jerusalem collection as "the glory of Christ" (δόξα Χριστοῦ).[109] Not only are believers being currently transformed and will be fully transformed at the eschatological age, but, unexpectedly, their ministries of the Spirit (1 Cor 12:4–31) reflect increasingly the glory of their eschatological destination (cf. 2 Cor 3:7–18) and glorify God in the present evil age (2 Cor 9:13a: δοξάντες τὸν θεόν). In sum, the Julio-Claudian *cursus honorum* opened up for the provincial elites and the upwardly mobile at Corinth by the Roman ruler and his governors is replaced by an infinitely more glorious service for *all* believers in the Body of Christ at the present and this honouring of Christ would find its culmination in eschatological glory.

Second, another feature of the world of honour in the association inscriptions are the awards of crowns, statues or images, shields, and plaques to benefactors and members of the associations for their services, noted above.[110] What is said in the association inscriptions about the crowns themselves is revealing. A few examples will suffice. Members contributing a gold stater for the construction of a temple will receive "a crown of honour for life," whereas those offering 30 silver drachmas will be granted "a crown of glory during the triennial festival for life."[111] Ariston, who saved the People "on every occasion and in every danger," is honoured with a crown "in perpetuity."[112] The initiates of Dionysos at Thessalonica are to wear a crown of roses during the Rose Festival,[113] whereas another association from decree the region of Attica stipulates that "Everyone is to wear a wreath in honour of the god."[114] In particular, R. Last, as we have seen, argues that the early Christians would have adopted coronal rituals at their meetings on the basis of the comparanda of the association inscriptions.

However, the distinctive early Christian rhetoric regarding coronal rituals is overlooked in this process. The New Testament writers consistently postpone the allocation of crowns until the eschaton (1 Cor 9:25; Phil 4:1; 1 Thess 2:19; 1 Tim 2:5; 4:8; Jas 1:12; 1 Peter 5:4; Rev 2:10; 3:11). Indeed, the famous coronal

---

[108] Barnett, *Corinthians*, 320.

[109] J.R. Harrison, "The Brothers as the 'Glory of Christ' (2 Cor 8:23): Paul's *Doxa* Terminology in Its Ancient Benefaction Context," *NovT* 52.2 (2010): 156–88.

[110] Award of shield and image of a civic leader and association member: Ascough, *Associations in the Greco-Roman World*, § 5 (Athens: 112/111 BC). Award of gold cowns to supervisors of the sanctuary, accompanied by two wreaths incised on the relief below the inscription: *ibid.*, § 12 (Piraeus, Athens: 329/328 BC). Award of olive wreath, with a commendation inside an engraved wreath: Ascough, *ibid.*, § 16 (Piraeus, Athens: 300/299 BC); cf. *ibid.*, § 14 (also with the erection of a statue). Erection of image, to be crowned at every sacrifice, and a plaque: *ibid.*, § 20 (Piraeus, Athens: 178/177 BC).

[111] Ascough, *Associations in the Greco-Roman World*, § 72 (Histria: AD 150–200).

[112] Ascough, *Associations in the Greco-Roman World*, § 74 (Kallatis: AD 12–14).

[113] Ascough, *Associations in the Greco-Roman World*, § 58 (Thessalonica: III cent. AD).

[114] Ascough, *Associations in the Greco-Roman World*, § 9 (Liopesi: early II cent. AD).

honour of the Isthmian games is dismissed in 1 Corinthians 9:25 as "perishable" (φθαρτός) as opposed to the "imperishable" eschatological crown (ἄφθαρτος).[115] Elsewhere I have argued that John's stinging denunciation of idolatry, his multiple-visioned presentation of the grandeur of the throne room of God and his Lamb (Rev 4–5, 7, 14), and his inversion of crowning rituals (Rev 4:10) critiqued the imperial theology of victory and its widespread iconographic rendering of coronal rituals.[116] Nor must we forget the early Christian indebtedness to Jewish terminology that undergirds the New Testament descriptions of the "crown of glory" (1 Peter 5:4) and the "crown of righteousness" (2 Tim 4:8).[117] Consequently there was little interest in the wide variety of Hellenistic crown-types on the part of early Christians. This highly qualified coronal rhetoric, with its strong eschatological focus, continued in Tertullian's *De corona militis.* What prompts this early Christian dismissal of contemporary crowning rituals? Perhaps the mock royal investiture of Christ with a crown of thorns and purple cloak (Mark 15:17: ἀκάνθινον στέφανον), prefacing the shame of the cross (cf. Cicero, *Rab. Post.* 4.13) and his forsaken death (Mark 15:34), underscored for the early Christians that they too, like Christ, had to wait for their exaltation in honour. It is unlikely, given this precedent, that the early Christians would have introduced the association coronal rituals into their love feasts, preferring instead to redefine their rationale in the manner enunciated above.

Of interest, too, is the application of the language of "eternity" to the honours conferred. We hear of "eternal honour and goodwill" being exercised towards Marcus for erecting a pillar from his own resources to the Bacceion of the Asians,[118] whereas in the same inscription the Roman ruler Septimius Severus (AD 193–211) is wished "health, victory and eternal duration." Finally, the Eueian priestess of Prinophoros sums up her claim for immortality in the memory of posterity with these words: "I bequeath for my eternal memory two *plethra* of vineyards with the ditches, in order that from the income sacrifices not less than five denarii may be burned for me."[119] The apostle Paul employs the language of eternity very sparingly in the Corinthian epistles, but strikingly focuses on afflictions preparing believers for the excessive weight of eternal glory to come (2 Cor 4:17: "ὑπερβολὴν αἰώνιον βάρος δόξης"). Believers have to concentrate on what is eternal (4:17: αἰώνια), as opposed to what is earthly, because their destiny is the bodily resurrection, described by the apostle as "a building from God, a house not made with human hands, eternal (5:1: αἰώνιον) in the

[115] For full discussion, see Chapter 4.

[116] See J.R. Harrison, "'The Fading Crown': Divine Honour and the Early Christians," *JTS* 54.2 (2003): 493–529, at 509–18. See also *idem*, "A Share in All the Sacrifices," *New Docs* 9 (2002): 1–3, § 1.

[117] For details, see Harrison, , "'The Fading Crown'," 508–09.

[118] Ascough, *Associations in the Greco-Roman World*, § 64 (Perinthos: AD 196–198).

[119] Ascough, *Associations in the Greco-Roman World*, § 58 (Thessalonica: III cent. AD).

heavens." In line with the Old Testament, Paul's focus on eternity is theocentric, rejecting all human claims to eternal glory (cf. Rom 3:23), whether that comes from civilisations like ancient Chaldea (Isa 47:7) or from members of the local associations in his own era. What drives Paul's theocentric focus is its concentration on the resurrection, paradoxically entered by suffering, another reflection of how the soteriological narrative of the crucified and risen Christ shapes the lives of believers. By contrast, the Old Testament language of eternity ranges more widely, with only one text speaking of all humans having to go to their eternal home, death (Eccl 12:5; cf. 3:11).[120]

Third, the rivalry for honour among association members is underscored in the association inscriptions. The association inscriptions highlight the commendations and crowning of benefactors "so that that there might be rivalry among the rest who aspire to honour, knowing that they will receive thanks befitting those who are benefactors of the association of sacrificing associates."[121] The establishment of an association of Sarapis, precipitated by an epiphany of the god in a dream incubation in a sanctuary, was effected when a divine letter, left under the pillow of Xenainetos, commanded the recipient to establish the cult with the help of his hated political rival.[122] Finally, the rivalry to excel the previous benefactors of an association is underscored when Ariston is eulogised thus: "although young, he displayed more ambition towards the citizens than those who were chosen earlier as benefactors."[123] There is little doubt that Paul uses the inscriptional motifs of rivalry (2 Cor 9:1–4) and imitation (2 Cor 8:1–4, 9) in order to pressure the recalcitrant Corinthians to finalise their preparations for and completion of their contribution to the Jerusalem connection. Here is a clear similarity in Paul's approach to the association decrees and the world of benefaction. However, the apostle does not do this at the expense of what has primacy for him: χάρις and ἀγάπη.[124]

Fourth, in addition to the rules governing disruptive behaviour in the association inscriptions, there is occasionally a strong emphasis on "concord" as a desirable value between different ethnic groups, indigenous and immigrant, in

---

[120] The language of eternity refers to God (Gen 21:33; [Dt 33:27: NRSV footnote only]; 1 Sam 15:29; Isa 26:4; Pss 90:1–2; 93:2; 102:27–28; 119:89; 139:16), his pleasures and blessings (Pss 16:11; 21:6), his kingdom (Dan 4:3, 34) and eternal creation (Hab 3:6). On God as eternal, see E. Jacob, *Theology of the Old Testament* [London: Hodder and Stoughton, 1958), 38, 52, 318–19; Th. C. Vriezen, *An Outline of Old Testament Theology* (Oxford: Basil Blackwell, 1958), 180–83.

[121] Ascough, *Associations in the Greco-Roman World*, § 20 (Piraeus, Athens: 178/177 BC). See *ibid.*, § 16 (Piraeus, Athens: 300/299 BC; cf. *ibid.*, § 17): "This is so that others will also be ambitious toward the society members, knowing that they will receive thanks from the society members commensurate with the benefactions."

[122] Ascough, *Associations in the Greco-Roman World*, § 52 (Thessalonica: I–II cent. AD).

[123] Ascough, *Associations in the Greco-Roman World*, § 74 (Kallatis: AD 12–15).

[124] See Harrison, *Paul's Language of Grace*, 314–21.

the common cultic worship of a deity in a particular city.[125] A Thracian group, who alone of all the immigrant groups had been permitted to build a sanctuary to the goddess Bendis in the Asty in Athens, were permitted to join the Athenians in their procession to the Bendis shrine in the Piraeus. The Athenian priest and priestess of Bendis at the Piraeus were to deliver a prayer during the sacrifices for the Thracian group in the Asty. The prayer, the association inscription informs us, was

> for the sacrificing associates who are in the Asty, so that when these things take place and the entire immigrant group lives in concord (ὁμονοοῦντος παντὸς τοῦ ἔθ[νους]), the sacrifices and other rites shall be made to the gods, in accordance with both the ancestral customs of the Thracians and the laws of the city. So that it will turn out well and in a manner reflecting piety for the entire immigrant group in matters concerning the gods.[126]

There are some interesting resonances here with the thought of the apostle Paul. The Jewish believers, Paul tells us, would yearn for their Gentile Corinthian brethren upon the delivery of the Jerusalem collection and pray for them because of the surpassing grace of God given to the Gentiles (2 Cor 9:14: τὴν ὑπερβάλλοθσιν ψάριν τοῦ θεῷ). Although the cultures are vastly different – processional and cultic at the shrine of Bendeis at the Piraeus as opposed to Paul's collection for the poor processing to Jerusalem – nevertheless the reconciliation of different ethnic groups (cf. 1 Cor 12:13b) and the establishment of concord (cf. 1 Cor 10:10–11; 3:5–9, 21–23; 10:17; 12:4–13; 14:33) through prayer, while differently understood in each case, is an intriguing correspondence.[127] Finally, as M. Mitchell has demonstrated long ago, Paul, in addressing the divisions within the Corinthian church, drew upon motifs from the well-known deliberative speeches on concord (ὁμόνοια), a prized political and association value, in treating the subject of disunity within the Corinthian church.[128]

What conclusions do we draw from this additional evidence from the association inscriptions drawn from the Greek peninsula? Once again, there were elements of common concern between the cultic associations and the early Christian *ekklêsiae* as they handled group tensions and the issues posed by different ethnicities, rendered honour to the Roman ruler and other association members, and sponsored rivalry in beneficence for the common good. Indeed, Paul drew upon rhetorical conventions from the honorific inscriptions and the de-

---

[125] As far as the social and gender composition of associations, it should be noted that the Spartans legislated that each group should have a diverse membership of women, slaves and freedmen so that the state's ideology was reaffimed across the entire social constituency. See Ascough, *Associations in the Greco-Roman World*, § 29.

[126] Ascough, *Associations in the Greco-Roman World*, § 18, *ll.* 23–27 (Piraeus, Athens: 240/239 BC).

[127] See Harrison, *Paul's Language of Grace*, 271–72.

[128] See M. M. Mitchell, *Paul and the Rhetoric of Reconciliation: An Exegetical Investigation of the Language and Composition of 1 Corinthians* (Louisville:Westminster/John Knox Press, 1992), 60–64.

liberative speeches on concord in addressing some of these issues, while avoiding prominent rhetorical conventions in other cases. Notwithstanding, Paul critiques many aspects of honorific and imperial culture, sometimes re-defining its dynamics and rationale in light of the traditions of the LXX and the apocalyptic gospel of Christ crucified and risen. In so doing, the apostle sometimes reaffirmed central institutions and customs of eastern Mediterranean society, on other occasions redefined them or postponed them eschatologically in light of the gospel revelation, and in other instances rejected them outright as Christ's new creation (2 Cor 5:17; cf. Gal 6:15) erupted with all its social novelty. It is this complexity of response which makes Paul's thought simultaneously so fascinating and challenging. But because of the scholarly work of Ascough, Harland, Kloppenborg, and Last over the last quarter of a century, we are much better placed, due to their meticulous attention to comparanda, to make informed decisions about the subtle nuances of Paul's thought on his house churches in their ancient association context.

9.6. Competing Paradigms of Group Identity at Corinth

What light, then, does this wealth of material throw on the situation at Corinth? I suggest that what we are witnessing are two competing paradigms of group identity. Certain Corinthian believers may have viewed the Christian assembly as a cultic association (or *collegium*) and ignored the attendant threat of divisiveness and idolatry.[129] This is not to suggest that these believers imported an explicit agenda from the cultic associations into the house churches.[130] Rather, due to their hubristic behaviour,[131] they simply assumed that the social practices and attitudes of the associations were transferable to a Christian context. There was sufficient theological warrant, in their view, to justify their stance.[132]

[129] This is the suggestion of Witherington III, *Conflict and Community in Corinth*, 245.

[130] I am not suggesting that the cultic associations explain everything in 1 Corinthians – in the vein of the "over-realised eschatology" (e.g. A.C. Thiselton, "Realized Eschatology at Corinth," *NTS* 24 [1977–1978], 510–26) and "gnostic" hypotheses (e.g. W. Schmithals, *Gnosticism in Corinth: An Investigation of the Letters to the Corinthians* [Nashville 1971]). Rather it forms part of the general background that makes up first century Corinth. Note that the "over-realised eschatology" hypothesis (1 Cor 4:8), popular with some commentators (e.g. G.D. Fee, *The First Epistle to the Corinthians*, NICNT [Grand Rapids: Eerdmans, 1987], 12–13), over-interprets a Cynic-Stoic commonplace. See J.T. Fitzgerald, *Cracks in an Earthen Vessel: An Examination of the Catalogues of Hardships in the Corinthian Correspondence* (Atlanta 1988), 135–37; W.A. Meeks, *The Origins of Christian Morality: The First Two Centuries* (New Haven and London: Yale University Press, 1993), 132.

[131] φυσιόω: 1 Cor 4:6, 18, 19; 5:2; 8:1; 13:4. καυχάομαι and cognates: 1 Cor 1:29, 31; 3:21; 4:7; 5:6; 9:15, 16; 13:3. On Corinthian hubristic behaviour, see P. Marshall, *Enmity in Corinth: Social Conventions in Paul's Relations with the Corinthians*, WUNT II 23 (Tübingen: Mohr Siebeck, 1987), 194–218; Clarke, *Secular and Christian Leadership*, 74–77, 95–99.

[132] See our comments in n. 66 *supra*.

Each of our associations was aware of the potential for social discord at their meetings and formulated strict stipulations to counterbalance this tendency. However, a wealthy and socially pretentious minority in the Corinthian churches hosted their Christian "*collegia*" and competed among themselves for status and pedigrees. They sought to be patrons of visiting "sophists" like Apollos or Paul (1 Cor 1:12; 3:4, 21–22, 4:6a, 6b);[133] they coveted marriage dowries by entering irregular sexual alliances (5:1–13);[134] they were adversaries in secular law courts (6:1–8).[135] Status-conscious males wore Roman cultic head-coverings in the Christian assembly (1 Cor 11:4, 7a);[136] they hosted a Lord's supper divided by wealth and status (11:18–34);[137] and, as priestly patrons, they sought to dispense benefits to those who had died unbaptised (1 Cor 15:29).[138] Finally the

[133] See our comments in n. 67 *supra*.

[134] J.K. Chow, *Patronage and Power: A Study of Social Networks in Corinth*, JSNTSup. 75 (Sheffield: JSOT Press, 1992), 130–41; Clarke, *Secular and Christian Leadership*, 73–78.

[135] Chow, *Patronage and Power*, 123–30; Clarke, *Secular and Christian Leadership*, 59–71; A.C. Mitchell, "Rich and Poor in the Courts of Corinth: Litigiousness and Status in 1 Corinthians 6:1–11," *NTS* 39.1 (1993): 562–86; B.W. Winter, *Seek the Welfare of the City: Christians as Benefactors and Citizens* (Grand Rapids: Eerdmans, 1994), 106–21.

[136] See especially D.W. Gill, "The Importance of Roman Portraiture for Head Coverings in 1 Corinthians 11:2–16," *TynBul* 41.2 (1990): 245–60. Also R.E. Oster, "Use, Misuse and Neglect of Archaeological Evidence in Some Modern Works on 1 Corinthians (1Cor 7,1–5; 8,10; 11,2–16; 12,14–26)," *ZNW* 83.1 (1992): 52–73; *idem*, "When Men Wore Veils to Worship: The Historical Context of 1 Corinthians 11:4," *NTS* 34 (1988): 481–505; C.L. Thompson, "Hairstyles, Head-Coverings, and St. Paul: Portraits from Roman Corinth," *BA* 51.2 (1988): 99–115; Witherington *Conflict and Community in Corinth*, 232–35. For an entirely theological approach to 1 Corinthians 11:7–9, see A.C. Thiselton, *The First Epistle to the Corinthians*, NIGTC (Grand Rapids/Carlisle: Eerdmans/Paternoster, 2000), 834–37; D.E. Garland, *1 Corinthians*, ECNT (Grand Rapids: Baker Academic, 2003), 522–24; R.E. Ciampa and B.S. Rosner, *The First Letter to the Corinthians* (Grand Rapids/Nottingham: Eerdmans/Apollos, 2010), 522–29. While such commentaries effectively unfold the Jewish background to gender relations in 1 Cor 11:2–16, and, concomitantly, what is appropriate culturally in a worship context, the status issues associated with *men's* headwear in a Roman context (1 Cor 11:7a), important in the competitive Julian colony of Corinth, are easily overlooked.

[137] J. Murphy-O'Connor, "House Churches and the Eucharist: Archaeological Light from Paul's Corinth," *The Bible Today* 22.1 (1984): 32–38; P. Lampe, "The Corinthian Eucharistic Dinner Party: Exegesis of a Cultural Context (1 Cor 11:17–34)," *Affirmation* 4.2 (1991): 1–15; B. Witherington III, *Conflict and Community in Corinth*, 241–52; L.L. Welborn, "Inequality in Roman Corinth: Evidence from Diverse Sources Evaluated by a Neo-Ricardian Model," in *The First Urban Churches 2: Roman Corinth*, ed. J.R. Harrison and L.L. Welborn (Atlanta: SBL Press, 2016), 47–84. However, see Last (*The Pauline Church and the Corinthian Ekklêsia*, 201–02), who explores 1 Corinthians 11:18–34 against the practices of the ancient associations. In the view of Last (*ibid.*, 212), the pericope "speaks in passing about some of the most routine experiences of associations: selection of leaders, displays of equality and inequality at banquets, and conflict between officers and regular members." In other words, the issue is not socio-economic inequality within the Body of Christ but revolves around the intricacies of association procedures. For a full and convincing statement of the socio-economic interpretation, see L.L. Welborn, "The Polis and the Poor," in *The First Urban Churches 1: Methodological Considerations*, ed. J.R. Harrison and L.L. Welborn (Atlanta: SBL Press, 2015), 189–243.

[138] Chow, *Patronage and Power*, 157–66.

strong despised the socially weak who, unlike themselves, did not participate in the idolatrous civic celebrations (1 Cor 8–10).[139]

Paul provided another paradigm of community: a *charismatic* community, founded on divine grace, which inverted all the trappings of social status (1 Cor 12:21–26). The cross of Christ had overturned the community of the wise and powerful and had exalted the community of the weak and foolish in its place (1 Cor 1:18ff, esp. 27–29).[140] It was a community where Jew and Greek, slave and free, could live in concord and mutual service (1 Cor 12:13).

The issue, however, was not resolved in Paul's favour. At the time of Paul's third visit to the Corinthians, his converts still clung to the model of cultic associations, the excesses of which were disavowed by many association decrees. We see this in 2 Corinthians 12:20–21. There Paul, appealing for unity and peace (2 Cor 13:11), laments:

> I am afraid that when I come I may not find you as I want you to be ... I fear that there may be quarrelling, jealousy, outbursts of anger, factions, slander, gossip, arrogance, and disorder ... I will be grieved over many who have sinned earlier and have not repented of impurity, sexual sin and debauchery in which they have indulged.

---

[139] Chow, *Patronage and Power*, 154–57; K. Ehrensperger, *Paul at the Crossroads of Cultures: Theologizing in the Space Between* (London and New York: Bloomsbury T&T Clark, 2015), 175–213.

[140] See D.G. Horrell, *The Social Ethos of the Corinthian Correspondence: Interests and Ideology from 1 Corinthians to 1 Clement* (Edinburgh: T&T Clark, 1996), 131–37; R. Penna, "The Wisdom of the Cross and Its Foolishness as Foundation of the Church," in *idem*, *Paul the Apostle: Wisdom and Folly of the Cross. Volume 2*. Tr. T.P. Wahl (Collegeville: Michael Glazier, 1996), 45–60; R. Pickett, *The Cross in Corinth: The Social Significance of the Death of Jesus*, JSNTSup 143 (Sheffield: Sheffiled Academic Press, 1997); L.L. Welborn, *Paul, the Fool of Christ: A Study of 1 Corinthians 1–4 in the Comic-Philosophic Tradition*, JSNTSup 293 (London and New York: T&T Clark, 2005); M.R. Malcolm, *Paul and the Rhetoric of Reversal in 1 Corinthians: The Impact of Paul's Gospel on His Macro-Rhetoric*, SNTSMS 155 (Cambridge: Cambridge University Press, 2013).

Chapter 10

Conclusion

10.1. Celebrity Culture, the "Great Man," and the Apostle Paul

At the outset of this study, ancient and modern celebrity culture was compared. In the case of the Graeco-Roman world, the "great man" embodied the ethical paradigms that ensured the smooth operation of civic life in its variegated expresions. The ancestral virtue of the elite houses was refreshed generation-by-generation as each new family luminary strove to equal and suprass the fame of their forebears. Ancient writers such as Plutarch, Valerius Maximus, and the anonymous author of *De Viris Illustribus* presented models of civic and military virtue for the imitation of posterity, whereas the eulogistic inscriptions, along with their accompanying statues, celebrated the achievements and moral character of the honorand for perpetuity. This competitive culture of public esteem ensured that the social and political status quo was replenished by each new generation of the elites. Convention, informed by exempla from the past and the present, undergirded the deep conservatism of ancient society.

In the modern period, Thomas Carlyle nominated political leaders as the inheritors of this heroic mantle in his famous 1840 book on the "great man". In the western intellectual tradition, Nietzsche's "*Übermensch*" ("Superman") and Søren Kierkegaard's "Knight of Faith", introduced respectively in *Thus Spake Zarathustra* (1885) and in *Fear and Trembling* (1843),[1] had clear affinities with Carlyle's "great man" tradition by virtue of the elevation of these mythic figures over what was common. Each figure possessed the will power and faith to triumph over the ordinary and thereby achieve social progress. Other thinkers took up Carlyle's ideological baton at the time and in the ensuing years. The German philosopher Georg Hegel (1770–1831), a contemporary of Carlyle, proposed that heroic men were those clear-sighted thinkers of practical action who became conduits for the *Geist*, or God-Spirit, in the world.[2] William H. Mal-

[1] On Nietzsche's "*Übermensch*", see M. Knoll, "The 'Übermensch' as a Social and Political Task: A Study in the Continuity of Nietzsche's Political Thought," in *Nietzsche as a Political Philosopher*, ed. M. Knoll and B. Stocker (Berlin and Boston: De Gruyter, 2014), 239–66. For discussion of Kierkegaard's "Knight of Faith", see M. Gabriel, *Subjectivity and Religious Truth in the Philosophy of Søren Kierkegaard* (Macon: Mercer University Press, 2010), 153–64.

[2] G. Hegel, *Lectures on the Philosophy of History* (1837). Note Section 2 Paragraph 33: "World-historical men – the Heroes of an epoch – must, therefore, be recognised as its clear-sighted ones; their deeds, their words are the best of that time. Great men have formed

lock (1849–1923), the English novelist and economic writer, vigorously defended Carlyle's thesis.[3] Nevertheless, he did not dismiss the contribution to social progress that was made by lesser gifted men.[4] Oswald Spengler (1880–1936) would later argue that the great man, who, in his view, arose out of historical necessity,[5] could transition a culture from a phase of decline to another new phase.[6] In Spengler's view, the "great man" incarnated a spirit quaility that exalted a nation.[7] However, as we have seen, in 1896 the sociologist Herbert Spencer consigned the corpse of the "great man" theory to a long overdue grave. Spencer argued that only a sociological analysis of the history and culture of the period would allow the great man's contribution to his nation to be properly

purposes to satisfy themselves, not others ... For that Spirit which had taken this fresh step in history is the inmost soul of all individuals; but in a state of unconsciousness which the great men in question aroused." For the text, see "Hegel's Lectures on the Philosophy of History," accessed 09.09.2017, at https://www.marxists.org/reference/archive/hegel/works/hi/hicont-en.htm. For discussion of the following authors, I am indebted to the pseudonymous web article of Dewi Sant, "The Great Man of History and the Fallacy of Equality," accessed 09.09.2017, at https://sydneytrads.com/2014/07/16/dewi-sant/.

[3] W.H. Mallock, *Aristocracy and Evolution: A Study of the Rights, the Origin, and the Social Functions of the Wealthier Classes* (London: Adam and Charles Black, 1898).

[4] Mallock, *Aristocracy and Evolution*, 116: "Whatever is done by great men of the heroic type, something similar, if not so striking, is done by a number of lesser great men also; that whilst the action of the heroic great men is intermittent, the action of the lesser great men is constant; and that the latter, as a body, although not individually, do incalculably more to promote progress than the former."

[5] In the face of cultural decline, O. Spengler argues that a return to the sentimental past is an impossibility because historical necessity forces us to act in accordance with what remains viable in terms of cultural reinvigoration (*The Decline of the West*, Volume 2 [Oxford: Oxford University Press, 1923], 507): "For us, however, whom a Destiny has placed in this Culture and at this moment of its development – the moment when money is celebrating its last victories, and the Caesarism that is to succeed approaches with quiet, firm step – our direction, willed and obligatory at once, is set for us within narrow limits, and on any other terms life is not worth the living. We have not the freedom to reach to this or to that, but the freedom to do the necessary or to do nothing. And a task that historic necessity has set will be accomplished with the individual or against him."

[6] O. Spengler, *The Decline of the West*, 2 Vols. (Oxford: Oxford University Press, 1918, 1923; one volume edition, 1932). For discussion of Spengler's work, see N. Frye, "*The Decline of the West* by Oswald Spengler," *Daedalus* 103.1 (1974):1–13; B. Almén, "Prophets of the Decline: The Worldviews of Heinrich Schenker and Oswald Spengler," *Indiana Theory Review* 17.1 (1996): 1–24; R. Duchesne, "Oswald Spengler and the Faustian Soul of the West," *The Occidental Quarterly* 14.4 (2014–2015): 3–22.

[7] For example, speaking about European music and painting, O. Spenger airs his "great man" theory partially to counter the perception that contemporary artistic culture was in irredeemable decline (*The Decline of the West*, Volume 1 [Oxford: Oxford University Press, 1918], 294): "There have always been, for one great artist, a hundred superfluities who practised art, but so long as a great tradition (and *therefore* great art) endured even these achieved something worthy. We can forgive this hundred for existing, for in the ensemble of the tradition they were the footing for the individual great man. But to-day we have only these superfluities, and ten thousand of them, working art 'for a living' (as if that were a justification!). One thing is quite certain, that to-day every single art-school could be shut down without art being affected in the slightest."

understood in its context. No longer did the great man determine singehandedly the course of history, past, present or future.

But, ironically, with the advent of the celebrity cult from the 1780s onwards, a different type of "great man" was resurrected in the popular consciousness, irrespective of whether Garibaldi, Byron or Whitman was the real originator of the "public image" of modern social celebrity. However, the social hierarchy initially associated with this new movement was undermined progessively by photojournalism that bridged the distance between the aristocratic elites and mass audiences. Moreover, the democritising advent of reality TV and the Internet presented the opportunity of overnight international fame to the masses without any prerequsite of personal talent, elite status, or the possesion of wealth to succeed. In particular, the Web 2.0 phenomena spawned a "do-it-yourself celebrity" that opened up Andy Warhol's 15 minutes of fame to allcomers.

The virtual development of a non-hierarchical and viral form of fame that extended to the base of the social pyramid in our generation differentiates the modern celebrity circuit from its ancient counterpart. Contact with and the cultivation of the Graeco-Roman elites was generally the prerequiste for celebrity status. In the imperial age, the upwardly mobile career paths sponsored by the Roman ruler usually paved the way to fame and success in antiquity. Nevertheless, the contours of fame are easy to discern in the wider social landscape of Mediterranean antiquity when one takes into account the inscriptional evidence. Public eulogies of benefactors and generals, the heroisation of the dead in epitaphs, the elaborate funeral processions of the Julio-Claudian house, the rewards of agonistic competition (atheletics, chariot-racing, gladiatorial contests, entertainers), elite civic processions in honour of the gods, the provincial tours of the Roman ruler and the Ecumenical Synod of Dionysiac Artists, as well as numerous other pathways of celebrity: all disseminated the fame of civic luminaries throughout the Mediterranean basin.

However, in introducing the rationale of the book, it was suggested that this culture of ancestral promotion and self aggrandisment among the civic elites and their clients in antiquity sat uneasily with Christ's teaching on humility, his establishment of an alternative "servant" community of the marginalised, and his searing denunciation of the self-advertisement and self-serving power of the elites. This was partially recognised by the ancient historian Robert Garland but its significance was not fully appreciated. Paul's gospel of the "foolishness" and "weakness" of the cross ensured that Christ's *cursus pudorum* (Phil 2:5–8; cf. Gal 3:13) was the avenue to true greatness as opposed to the boastful *cursus honorum* of the upwardly mobile. Furthermore, cruciform humour in antiquity traded on the conceit that the crucified competed for social precedence by means of their more elevated postion on the cross or found the culmination of their athletic careers in literally flying past the earth-bound competitors standing below their crosses. The gospel portraits of the soldiers' mockery of Christ in an inverted royal investure ritual also posed the confronting question as to where true greatness resided.

We are witnessing here a collision of cultures in Paul's preaching of the cross (1 Cor 1:18–31; 4:18–19; 7:7:31; Gal 1:4): "Where is the wise man? Where is the scholar? Where is the philosopher of this age? Has not God made foolish the wisdom of the world?" (1 Cor 1:20).[8] While it is true to speak of Paul's adaption, reconfiguration, and transvaluation of Graeco-Roman social leitmotifs – noting also his endorsement of matters of cultural indifference and whatever else was socially and ethically consonant with his gospel (ὅσα: Phil 4:8)[9] – a critique of the hierarchical and elitist values antithetical to the gospel was nonetheless taking place. To be sure, Paul endorses the God-appointed hierarchy within the church (1 Cor 12:28–29; 14:32–38; 16:15–16; 1 Thess 5:12–13),[10] invokes his own apostolic authority in the face of opposition and misunderstanding (1 Cor 4:14–21; 9:1–11; 2 Cor 3:1–3; 10:7–17; 12:11–13; Gal 1:1, 8–9; 2:6–10),[11] points to the exemplum of church practice in responding to contention (1 Cor 7:17b; 11:16), and, more generally, urges submission to the divinely appointed authorities in Graeco-Roman society (Rom 13:1–7; cf. 1 Tim 2:1–2).[12] But Paul understands ministry as involving the self-effacting service and building up of the diversley gifted and mutually interdepedent members of the Body of Christ (1 Cor 3:5–9; 4:21–23; 9:12b, 15–18; 12:4–26; 14:3b, 5b, 12b; 2 Cor 4:5; Eph 4:11–13).[13] In this process of the redefinition of elite hierarchy, Paul configures the social relations

[8] See E. A. Judge, *Paul and the Conflict of Cultures: The Legacy of His Thought Today*, ed. J. R. Harrison (Eugene: Cascade Books, 2019).

[9] See J. P. Sampley, "Living in an Evil Aeon: Paul's Ambiguous Relation to Culture," in *Paul in the Greco-Roman World. A Handbook: Volume 2*, ed. J. P. Sampley, 2nd ed. (London and New York: Bloomsbury T&T Clark, 2017), 391–432. Sampley correctly speaks of Paul's revisionist view of the cross, shame and honour (*ibid.*, 415–21), attributing Paul's ambiguous relation to culture to the apostle's simultaneous apocalyptic disengagement and apocalyptic engagement with the world (*ibid.*, 421–32). More generally, see J. P. Sampley, *Walking Between the Times: Paul's Moral Reasoning* (Minneapolis: Fortress, 1991).

[10] Sampley, "Living in an Evil Aeon," 411. For discussion, see H. von Campenhausen, *Ecclesiastical Authority and Spiritual Power in the Church in the First Three Centuries* (London: Adam & Charles Black, 1969); B. Holmberg, *Paul and Power: The Structure of Authority in the Primitive Church as Reflected in the Pauline Epistles* (Philadelphia: Fortress, 1978); G. Shaw, *The Cost of Authority: Manipulation and Freedom in the New Testament* (London: SCM, 1984); J. W. McCant, "A Parodic Defense of Authority (2 Corinthians 10–13)," in *idem*, *2 Corinthians* (Sheffield: Sheffield Academic, 1999), 101–72; K. Ehrensperger, *Paul and the Dynamics of Power: Communication and Interaction in the Early Christ-Movement*, LNTS 325 (London and New York: T&T Clark, 2007).

[11] See J. H. Schütz, *Paul and the Anatomy of Apostolic Authority*, SNTSMS 26 (Cambridge: Cambridge University Press, 1975). Additionally, see C. K. Barrett, *The Signs of an Apostle* (Philadelphia: Fortress, 1972).

[12] For discussion, see J. R. Harrison, *Paul and the Imperial Authorities at Thessalonica and Rome: A Study in the Conflict of Ideology*, WUNT I 273 (Tübingen: Mohr Siebeck, 2011), 271–323.

[13] On mutuality, see K. Ehrensperger, *That We May Be Mutually Encouraged: Feminism and the New Perspective in Pauline Studies* (New York and London: T&T Clark, 2004).

and ecclesial life of believers around the motif of "dying and rising" with Christ.[14] Further, Paul defines his own apostolic vocation in light of the priestly and eschatological vocation of Israel (Rom 15:15–17), seeing its rationale articulated in his personal identification with the Isaianic "suffering servant" (δοῦλος: Rom 1:1–5, at v. 1 [Isa 49:1–6]; 2 Cor 5:14–6:10 [Isa 40–66]).[15] Christ's resurrection power, therefore, was experienced in cruciform weakness in the face of a self-assertive, boastful, and self-sufficient world (Rom 8: 31–39; 1 Cor 4:8–13; 15:31; 2 Cor 4:7–12; 6:1–10; 11:16–12:10; Gal 2:19–20; 6:14, 17; Phil 2:4–8; 3:10; Col 1:24).[16]

As far as the governing elites (1 Cor 2:8a: "the rulers of this age" [οὐδὲ τῶν ἀρχόντων τοῦ αἰῶνος]),[17] in Paul's view the Graeco-Roman and Jewish rulers were coming to nothing (2:6b) because the current age was passing away (7:31b), given the advent of the "fulfilment of the ages" in the Body of Christ (10:11b [τὰ τέλη τῶν αἰώνων]). The secret wisdom of God (1 Cor 2:7a) had bypassed the elite

---

[14] See R.C. Tannehill, *Dying and Rising with Christ: A Study in Pauline Theology* (Berlin: Alfred Töpelmann, 1967); M.J. Gorman, *Cruciformity: Paul's Narrative Spirituality of the Cross* (Grand Rapids: Eerdmans, 2001); *idem*, *Inhabiting the Cruciform God: Kenosis, Justification, and Theosis in Paul's Narrative Soteriology* (Grand Rapids: Eerdmans, 2001).

[15] See L.J. Windsor, *Paul and the Vocation of Israel: How Paul's Jewish Identity Informs His Apostolic Ministry, with Special Reference to Romans*, BZNW 205 (Berlin and Boston: De Gruyter, 2014), 96–139; pace, the more reserved and nuanced position of M. Gignilliat (*Paul and Isaiah's Servants: Paul's Theological Reading of Isaiah 40–66 in 2 Corinthians 5:14–6:10*, LNTS 330 [London and New York: T&T Clark, 2007]) regarding Paul's personal identification with the Isaianic servant in 2 Corinthians. Luke, however, is in no doubt on the issue in his depiction of Paul's mission (Acts 13:47 [Isa 49:6]).

[16] See D.A. Black, *Paul, Apostle of Weakness:* Astheneia *and Its Cognates in the Pauline Literature* (New York: Peter Lang, 1984); K.A. Plank, *Paul and the Irony of Affliction* (Atlanta: Scholars Press, 1987); A.E. Harvey, *Renewal Through Suffering: A Study of 2 Corinthians* (Edinburgh: T&T Clark, 1996); T.B. Savage, *Power through Weakness: Paul's Understanding of the Christian Ministry in 2 Corinthians*, SNTSMS 86 (Cambridge: Cambridge University Press, 1996); Gorman, *Cruciformity*, 268–303.

[17] It is beyond the scope of this chapter to discuss the complex issue regarding the identity of the ἄρχοντες in 1 Corinthians 2:6 and 2:8. It has been suggested that it refers to (a) demonic forces (H. Conzelmann, *1 Corinthians: A Commentary on the First Epistle to the Corinthians*, Hermeneia [Philadelphia: Fortress, 1975], 60–63), (b) angelic powers (G.B. Caird, *Principalities and Powers: A Study in Pauline Theology* [Oxford: Clarendon Press, 1956], 1–11), (c) human authorities (W. Carr, *Angels and Principalities: The Background Meaning and Development of the Pauline Phrase HAI ARCHAI KAI HAI EXOUSIAI*, SNTSMS 42 [Cambridge: Cambridge University Press, 1981], 118–20; R.E. Ciampa and B.S. Rosner, *The First Letter to the Corinthians* [Grand Rapids: Eerdmans, 2010], 121–27), (d) a combination of demonic and human influences (D.E. Garland, *1 Corinthians* [Grand Rapids: Baker Academic, 2003], 91–96), and (e) socio-political powers that collectively transcend individual actors on the historical stage (A.C. Thiselton, *The First Epistle to the Corinthians: A Commentary on the Greek Text* [Grand Rapids: Eerdmans, 2000], 233–39, at 238–39). It seems to me that 1 Corinthian 2:8 must include (at the very least) the human actors in the crucifixion of Christ: therefore, even if other suprahuman forces are operative, Paul nevertheless critiques the complicity of the contemporary politcal elites in Christ's death, underscoring how God's eternal plan was *apocalytically* revealed despite their efforts to the contrary.

authorities because God's plan was divinely hidden to their understanding (2:7a, 8a). Not only were they blind to the fact that they were crucifying the eternally glorious Son (1 Cor 10:4; Phil 2:6a),[18] but, ironically, they were, unknown to themselves, providentially elevating Christ to his rightful position of soteriological supremacy and unrivalled honour as the Lord of glory (1 Cor 2:8b [τὸν κύριον τῆς δόξης]) in the present age, because it was precisely through the shame of the cross that Christ would enter into his glorious place of exaltation over all (1 Cor 2:8b; 15:25, 27b; Phil 2:9–11). Not only was the ephemeral fame of the elites extinguished by the apocayptic revelation of God's hidden wisdom in Christ's cross and resurrection,[19] but also it had always been God's plan before the ages to transfer his glory to the "nothings of this world," that is, believers in Christ (1 Cor 2:7b; cf. 1:28b; 2 Cor 3:18). In this dramatic up-ending of the social order of antiquity, the power of the elites ("the things that are") was nullified and the inflated boasting of ancient celebrities was shamed before God (1:27b,

[18] The issue of the pre-incarnate glory of Christ is strongly contested in Philippians 2:6. J.D.G. Dunn (*Christology in the Making: An Inquiry into the Origins of the Doctrine* [London: SCM, 1980], 114–21) argues that in Philippians 2:6 an Adamic christology underlies Paul's thought (2:6a: ὃς ἐν μορφῇ θεοῦ), rejecting the traditional interpretation of the pre-existent Christ of eternal glory voluntarily becoming man and submitting to death. He postulates instead that Christ rejected Adam's temptation to assert himself before God, choosing instead to assume the fate of fallen Adam in his incarnation. In sum, there is no reference to Christ's pre-existence in Philippians 2:6 or at 2 Corinthians 8:9 (Dunn, *ibid.*, 121–23). According to Dunn (*ibid.*, 115), the crucial phrase ἐν μορφῇ θεοῦ (Phil 2:6a) alludes to Adam being made in the image of God and sharing in the divine glory, whereas μορφὴν δούλου (2:7a) denotes Christ's assumption of the fallen state of Adam who has lost his divine glory. On the diversity of interpretation of ἐν μορφῇ θεοῦ in relation to τὸ εἶναι ἴσα θεῷ, see N.T. Wright, "Jesus Christ is Lord: Philippians 2:5–11," in *idem, The Climax of the Covenant: Christ and the Law in Pauline Theology* (Edinburgh: T&T Clark, 1991), 56–98, at 81. Certainly the writings of Second Temple Judaism spoke of the original glory of Adam (4Q504 [4QDibHam[a] VII *Frag.* 8 *l.* 7]) and its loss through the fall (3 *Bar* 4.16 [Greek]). Nor does one want to deny the likelihood of implicit contrasts in Philippians 2:6–8 between the obedience of Christ and the disobedience of Adam (cf. Rom 5:12–21). But S.E. Fowl (*The Story of Christ in the Ethics of Paul: An Analysis of the Function of the Hymnic Material in the Pauline Corpus*, JSNTSSup. 36 [Sheffield: JSOT Press, 1990], 54), noting that Paul uses δόξα for "the visible manifestation of God's glory" (Rom 1:23; 1 Cor 11:7; 2 Cor 3:18; 4:6), concludes: "It seems most adequate, then, to take the μορφή of God as a reference to the glory, radiance and splendour by which God's majesty is made visible. By locating Christ in this glory, it conveys the majesty and splendour of his pre-incarnate state." However, contra, see G.F. Hawthorne, "In the Form of God and Equal with God," in *Where Christology Began: Essays on Philippians 2*, ed. R.P. Martin and B.J. Dodd (Louisville: Westminster John Knox Press, 1998), 96–110, at 99–100. The issue, therefore, remains impenetrably complex, with no easy solution. On δόξα and the semantic domain of "glory" in Second Temple Judaism, see Harrison, *Paul and the Imperial Authorities*, 232–54. Last, Paul does not speak, in contrast to the literature of the Dead Sea Scrolls and Second Temple Judaism, "of Adam's pre-fall glory being transferred to the righteous at the eschaton" (*ibid.*, 258; contrast Rom 8:29). This perhaps warns us against overpressing the implied Christ-Adam contrast by rejecting any suggestion of Christ's glorious pre-existence in Philippians 2:6: there were clear limits to the contrast in Paul's mind.

[19] See A.R. Brown, *The Cross and Human Transformation: Paul's Apocalyptic Word in 1 Corinthians* (Minneapolis: Fortress, 1995), 108–19.

28b–29), especially given the relentless approach of eschatological judgement (1 Cor 15:24–25) and the socially transformative advent of the new creation (2 Cor 5:17; cf. Gal 6:14–15).

Friedrich Nietzsche understood perfectly the ethical consequences of this radical re-evaluation of Graeco-Roman morality by the Judaeo-Christian tradition: it meant the destruction of the highly esteemed values of the Roman aristocratic elites and their society.[20] As Nietzsche venemously wrote,

> It was the Jews who, rejecting the aristocratic value equation (good = noble = powerful = beautiful = happy = blessed) ventured, with awe-inspiring consistency, to bring about a reversal and held it in the teeth of the most unfathomable hatred (the hatred of the powerless), saying: "Only those who suffer are good, only the poor, the powerless, the lowly are good; the suffering, the deprived, the sick, the ugly, are the only pious people, the only ones saved, salvation is for them alone, whereas you rich, the noble and powerful, you are eternally wicked, cruel, lustful, insatiate, godless, you will also be eternally wretched, cursed and damned!" ... We know *who* became heir to this Jewish revaluation ...[21]

What impact, then, would Paul's gospel have had in critiquing the boastful and elitist culture of the Roman world, particularly in its late republican and Augustan expressions? What difference did it make to the ancient athletic ideal, its educational institutions, and its ethical curriculum? How did the gospel interact with the eulogistic traditions of the "great man" and the civic ethics that the urban elites promoted? What alternative pathways of honour were available to those situated less honourably below the apex of the social pyramid or to those who were humiliated and marginalised at its base? What values and upward mobility did the ancient associations, with their elite patrons and socially variegated membership, promote for their members in this regard? How did the early Christians position themselves in such a contested social space?

10.2. Summary of Argument

In Chapters 2–3 the elite values of the late Roman republic and Augustan principate, eloquently espoused in the orations of Cicero and in the *Res Gestae* of Augustus, were investigated. In the case of Cicero, the hierarchical, competitive, and status-riddled quest for ancestral honour among the aristocratic elites – including recently admitted *novi homines* like Cicero – led inevitably to the outbreaks of enmity and the eventual dissolution of republican society. Cicero's orations help us to see how conventional ethical traditions were now in a state of flux and transition in the late republic. As far as traditional morality, career-

[20] F. Nietzsche, *On the Genealogy of Morality*, ed. K. A. Pearson and tr. C. Diethe (Cambridge: Cambridge University Press, 2006), First Essay, § 16 (pp. 32–33).

[21] Nietzsche, *On the Genealogy of Morality*, First Essay, § 7, (p. 13)

ists like Caesar, Cicero, opined, pursued "false gory" as opposed "true glory" with disastrous results for the republic. The *imitatio* of worthy forebears from the old Roman noble houses would increasingly be confined to the Julio-Claudian house, with the exemplum of Augustus being the paradigm for future rulers and senatorial magistrates of Rome. Even traditional values such as *humanitas* aroused in Cicero strong feelings of Roman ethnic superiority over the nations, whereas *clementia* would become the preserve of the Julian ruler who allocated his mercy to the "worthy". Last, Paul's preaching of the cross was in reality the Ciceronian "tree of shame" as far as Romans were concerned.

What is intriguing is how Paul's gospel seamlessly embraces both the elements of continuity and discontinuity that emerged between Cicero's graphic portrait of the disintegration of the Roman republic in his orations and the subsequent ascendancy of the Julian-Claudian house in the early empire. In its social relationships Paul's "Body of Christ" functioned not only as an radical alternative to Cicero's service of the "body of the republic" but also to the hegemony of Seneca's Neronian "body of state". The glory and mercy of God are soteriologically concentrated in Christ, but believers, having already been glorified by virtue of their justification and being daily transformed from glory to glory by the Spirit, become agents of mercy and honour towards others as opposed to being obsessed by the elite acquisition of pubic esteem in the celebrity circuit. The believer's imitation of Christ's unconditional acceptance of his enemies through the "tree of shame" ensured that the traditional hierarchies of obligation were reversed: the believer was equally obligated to Greek and barbarian, rendering to all, no matter their ethnicity, the perpetual debt of cruciform love. Unbeknown to the Romans at this early imperial stage, a collision of cultures had begun that would ultimately impact the western intellectual tradition and its cultural values.

In the case of Augustus, we noted the discrepancy between the primacy of the Roman ruler, as articulated in the public propaganda, and the reluctance of the ruler evinced in the *Res Gesate*, seen in Augustus' strict refusal to overshadow the honours of others, or to accept the extraordinary powers offered him, or to act in ways inimical to ancestral custom. A more paradoxical construction of the ruler's power emerged, rhetorically echoing the reluctance of Virgil's Aeneas, the mythological founder of Rome, who, significantly, was celebrated in the statue programme of the Augustan forum. But the vignettes of Augustus' equivocation in the *Res Gestae* are modified by the ruler's assumption of the "shepherd" role, adumbrated in Hellenistic kingship ideology, in times of national crisis. Augustus' decisive role in such contexts is further confirmed by his presentation of himself as an "endangered benefactor" in describing the scope and personal cost of his munificence. Thus the paradox of the "reluctant leader" had clearly defined limits when Augustus shouldered the responsibility for the state in dire times. His actions stood in contrast to the total withdrawal of his successor, Tiberius, from the demands of state during AD 26–31, stretching in his case the "reluctance" paradigm to breaking point.

Paul's understanding of apostolic leadership in 2 Corinthians 4:7–18 is an equally paradoxical and challenging construct. The apocalyptic antinomies characterising the present age of suffering (*2 En.* 66.6–8 [J]) – the termination of which is understood from an Enochic perspective (2 *En.* 67.1–68.4) – were unexpectedly confronted by the superior power of the weak and crucified Christ. In counterpoint to the Enochic traditions, the apostle illustrates the divine vindication of his suffering by means of the scriptural precedents of the righteous sufferer of the Psalms (2 Cor 4:13–14: Ps 116:10 [LXX 115:10]) and the suffering servant of Isaiah (2 Cor 4:5b; 6:2 [LXX Isa 49:8]). Notwithstanding the depth of their sufferings, the apostles experience the dying of Christ as an "apocalyptic" power at work in their weakness (2 Cor 4:10a, 11a, 12a), unleashing the grace of the resurrection life of Christ in the Corinthian converts (4:12b, 15), and effecting the inward renewal of the apostles themselves (4:16c; 6:9b). This entire pericope is framed by Paul's discussion of the apocalyptic glory of the new covenant of the Spirit (2 Cor 3:7–11), experienced transformatively in the present by believers (4:16b; cf. 3:18), with a view to the glory to come (4:14, 17–18; 5:1–5).

We argued that there were similarities between the Augustan conception of leadership and Paul's understanding of apostolic ministry. But why did the Pauline paradigm of "servant" leaders, who die daily on behalf of their dependents (1 Cor 15:31; 2 Cor 4:14b; 6:9b; 11:28–29), triumph in the western intellectual tradition? Undoubtedly, the issue is more complex than the brief suggestions offered at the end of Chapter 3. But, at the risk of generalisation, the paradigm of Augustan leadership ossified into an lifeless antiquarianism because its focus was the exemplary and idealised republican past. The traditional quest for glory on the part of the old noble houses had began to crumble under the onslaught of the careerists, Julius Caesar, and his triumviral associates, as they ruthlessly sought (what in Cicero's view) was "false glory." This quest became increasingly constricted with the advent of the triumphant Julian house and its Claudian heirs, with the result that, in the case of the remaining noble families of republican consular descent who had survived the civil war,[22] their social preeminence could no longer be maintained in the long term.[23]

By contrast, the forward-looking dynamism of Paul's communities of grace challenged the self-serving and self-promoting paradigms of Roman leadership.

[22] For a savage satire of the Roman nobility by Juvenal (late I.–early II. cent AD), see *Sat.* 8.1–275. For a commentary on the satire, see J. Henderson, *Figuring Out Roman Nobility: Juvenal's Eighth* Satire (Exeter: University of Exeter Press, 1997).

[23] M. Gelzer (*The Roman Nobility*, tr. R. Seager [Oxford: Basil Blackwell, 1969], 158) writes: "As soon as the opportunity of restoring exhausted finances by military operations or apt exploitation of provincial government was withdrawn, the nobles' position of power in society was sooner or later to come to an end of its own accord."

Furthermore, the communal dynamics of Christ's cruciform grace still pose today a moral alternative to Ayn Rand's advocacy of a rational individualism in objectivist ethics,[24] which, in her view, are best expressed in the "virtue of selfishness."[25] Warren Zevon's perceptive song, "Splendid Isolation," pithily sums up the social results of Rand's ethics for a modern world deluded by celebrity culture:

Michael Jackson in Disneyland
Don't have to share it with nobody else
Lock the gates, Goofy, take my hand
And lead me through the World of Self.[26]

In Chapters 4–6 the world of ancient athletics, including the elite educational institution of the gymnasium, along with its ethical curriculum of the Delphic canon, was explored. This perpective, I argued, gives us keen insight into the pedagogic intent of the civic ethics that animated the urban elites throughout the eastern Mediterranean basin. The Delphic canon, after all, was found inscribed in the gymnasia spanning ancient Delphi to modern Afghanistan and contributed to shaping the lives of the *epheboi and neoi*.

Chapter 4 focused upon the visual material evidence in discussing the ancient athletic ideal, an emphasis overlooked by most New Testament scholars. 1 Corinthians 9:24–27 was examined in its wider eastern Mediterranean and local Corinthian athletic context, adding to the visual evidence relevant literary texts where pertinent. It was argued that Paul emptied the athletic ideal of its elitism and agonistic individualism. In a pastoral context, the apostle to the Gentiles reapplied its sports imagery to the corporate discipline required for the believer's new life of adaptablity, identification, and flexibility, geared now to the diverse needs of the members of the Body of Christ. In becoming "all things to all people" in an ecclesial context (1 Cor 9:22b), Paul modelled himself on the crucified Christ (1 Cor 9:19b; 2 Cor 4:5), who had become "all things to all people" in his atoning death. In democritising the athletic ideal throughout the Body of Christ and postponing its coronal awards to the eschaton, Paul pinpricked the ancient veneration of the "great man" in the ancient celebrity circuit,

[24] A. Rand, *The Virtue of Selfishness* (New York: Signet, 1961), 27: "The Objectivist ethics holds that human good does not require human sacrifices and cannot be achieved by the sacrifice of anyone to anyone. It holds that the rational interests of men do not clash – that there is no conflict of interests among men who do not desire the unearned, who do not make sacrifices nor accept them, who deal with one another as traders, giving value for value."

[25] Rand, *The Virtue of Selfishness*, 27: "The idea that man's self-interest can be served only by a non-sacrificial relationship with others has never occurred to those humanitarian apostles of unselfishness, who proclaim their desire to achieve the brotherhood of men. And it will not occur to them, or to anyone, so long as the concept 'rational' is omitted from the context of 'values,' 'desires,' 'self-interest' and ethics."

[26] The song is found in Warren Zevon's 1989 album, *Transverse City*, released by Virgin Records.

both in its civic and sporting contexts. The soteriological imperative of the mutual acceptance of Jew, Gentile, and the weak (1 Cor 9:19–22; 2 Cor 11:29; cf. Rom 15:1–3, 7–13), which was necessary for the outworking of Christ's resurrection life in the Corinthian house churches, had total priority.

In Chapter 5 a portrait of the ethics of the gymnasiarch, the leader and benefactor of the gymnasium, was extracted from the evidence of the public inscriptions honouring him. The ideals of ancient civic leaders, exemplified by the gymnasiarch, were revealed therein. First, the upholding and surpassing of ancestral honour was the key motivation for the gymnasiarch. Significantly, Paul sees the heated contemporary quest for ancestral honour as a misguided exercise, choosing instead to highlight in a Jewish context its culmination in the crucified and risen Christ (2 Cor 11:22–12:10; Gal 1:14–24; Phil 3:4–11). Second, the pastoral attitude of the gymnasiarch showed several interesting overlaps with Paul, including the convergence of "word" and "deed" in personal transformation and the centrality of unity and beneficence for corporate relations. Nevertheless, Paul has distinctive elements in his ethical exhortation, including the paradoxical exemplum of an impoverished benefactor as an incentive for generosity and apostolic ministry (2 Cor 8:9; cf. 6:10b; 8:1–4) and the work of the Spirit in establishing fellowship and loving unity among believers (Rom 14:16; 1 Cor 12:13; Phil 2:1–2). Third, the ethics of the gymnasiarch articulated in the eulogistic inscriptions are largely circumlocutions for his beneficence (e.g. "zeal", "good-will", "righteousness", etc.), though certain inscriptional phrases ("hating the bad and loving the good": IEph 1.6) are sometimes echoed in Paul (Rom 12:9; cf. 12:21; cf. 1 Thess 5:21). Paul has the theological and social versatility to adapt, reconfigure, revalue, or endorse ethical commonplaces, providing that they are either matters of indifference or congruent with the values of his Gospel. Fourth, the honours accorded to the gymnasiarch were discussed and Paul's radical reconfiguration of athletic honours has already been noted above. Fifth, the exclusivist ethos of the ancient gymnasium stood in contrast to Paul's opposition to exclusivism of all types within the Body of Christ.

In terms of the ethical curriculum of the gymnasium, differences and similarities existed between the exhortatory imperatives of the Dephic canon and those found in Paul's epistles. But the striking difference is that the Delphic canon uses the singular imperative whereas Paul uses the plural. The canon, therefore, is preparing the self-sufficient "great man" for future civic leadership, whereas Paul is exhorting established interdependent communities in Christ towards Christ's cruciform transformation that is wrought by the Spirit. The moral outcomes are significantly different despite the occasional overlaps in ethical attitudes. This was reinforced by two case studies that compared Paul's gospel with key social *modus operandi* in the Delphic Canon and antiquity more generally: namely, the ancient reciprocity system and the household codes.

In the case of the reciprocity sytem, Paul largely steered clear of the language of "friendship" (φιλία and cognates: cf. φιλαδελφία: Rom 12:10; 1 Thess 4:9; φιλέω: 1 Cor 16:22; φίλημα: Rom 16:20; 1 Cor 16:20; 2 Cor 13:12; 1 Thess 5:26) in what scholars consider the genuine epistles, with its occurrence being predominantly confined to the (pseudepigraphic?) Pastorals. The reason for Paul's hesitancy is possibly that the language of *amicitia* ("friendship") in Roman politics involved the status-riddled interchange of gifts and favours in a heated competition for clients. While the participants in the exchange avowed camaraderie, both in relationships involving equals and unequals, *amicitia* had denegerated by late republican times, if Cicero's *De Amicitia* is correct,[27] into "a commercial-style reckoning of advantages that harmed the gift-exchange so essential to friendship."[28] This culculated reckoning of advantage flew in the face of the divine ἀγάπη and χάρις revealed in Christ, which bonded parties of different social status in a mutually levelling faith under a common Lord. This transformative experience summoned the believer to demonstrate an indebtedness of love to all human beings, including the enemy (Rom 13:8–10; cf. 12:17–21). By contrast, the Ciceronian interplay between *amor* and *amicitia*, noted above (*supra*, n. 27), shows how the Roman nobles viewed the protocols of liberality and beneficence towards friends and clients: it is a class-bound understanding of "love," reserved entirely for the political alliances of the elites. Last, in the case of household relations, the maxim of the Delphic canon, "Rule your wife," leans more towards the hierarchical thought of Aristotle as opposed the "feminism" of Hierocles and Musonius Rufus, whereas Paul, in Ephesians 5:21–33, reflects the latter perspective, though with redemptive, christological, and ecclesiastical distinctives informing his social thought in this instance.

In Chapter 6 it was argued that the Delphic canon – the ephebic ethical curriculum of the eastern Mediteranean gymnasia – had a pedagogic intentionality in its design. The canon acknowledged the traditional gods and the role of Providence, with the divine order determining the hierarchy of household relations. The *neoi* and *epheboi* were to maintain indifference by cultivating the Self and engaging in harmonious social relations within the polis. Virtue was achieved

---

[27] Cicero roots *amicitia* in an understanding of love (*amor*) as opposed to a hope for gain (*Amic.* 9.30–31; cf. 9.29). The mutual love between Gaius Laelius Sapiens the orator (b. 188 BC), the imaginary intelocutor in Cicero's *De Amicitia*, and the recently deceased Scipio Africanus Minor (d. 129 BC), is depicted by Cicero thus: "Although many and great advantages did ensue from our friendship, still the beginnings of our love did not spring from the hope of gain. For as men of our class are generous and liberal (*benefici liberalesque*), not for the purpose of demanding repayment – for we do not put our favours out at interest, but are by nature given to acts of kindness (*liberalitem*) – so we believe that friendship (*amicitiam*) is desirable, not because we are influenced by hope of gain, but because the entire profit is in the love itself (*in ipso amore*)."

[28] N. Coffee, *Gift and Gain: How Money Transformed Ancient Rome* (Oxford: Oxford University Press, 2017), 104. For Ciceronian references, see 231 n. 15.

by steering an Aristotelian middle course between behavioural extremes. In agreement with R.S. Dutch,[29] it was proposed that the Corinthian believing elite had absorbed the educational values of the ancient gymnasium, though, I would add, their ethical formation had been primarily acquired through the pedagogical inculcation of the Delphic canon. Consequently, in 1 Corinthians Paul denounces idolatry, qualifies hierarchical understandings of male and female relations in marriage, denounces the cult of Self, and inverts elitist understandings of honour in social relations. Paul's innovative thought paved the way for the triumph of humility and modesty as "virtues" over the traditional classical paradigms, thereby loosening the stranglehold of the Aristotelian mean upon western thought.

In Chapter 7 the "great man" theory of ethical instruction in antiquity was explored by a close examination of the ancient evidence: namely, the pursuit of ancestral models of glory in the late republican and early imperial age, the imitation of republican luminaries in the statue programme of the Augustan Forum, the eulogising of the "great man" in the Greek and Latin honorific inscriptions, and various literary exempla canonising the "great man". In response, Paul inverted the contemporary models of exemplary virtue by

- discarding the old culture of Roman boasting for a new culture of humility based upon the work of Christ;
- depicting the *telos* of history as being located in Christ as opposed to the iconic Augustus;
- parodying Graeco-Roman honorific culture through a shameful catalogue of his apostolic weaknesses, modelled on the weakness of the crucified Christ (2 Cor 13:4), over against more worthy catalogues of personal achievement;
- replacing conventional exempla of beneficence with the unconventional exemplum of Christ the "impoverished benefactor" (2 Cor 8:9).

Paul's mimetic traditions in 1 Thessalonians transform the humiliation of the Thessalonian believers because their sufferings replicate the sufferings of Christ. Furthermore, the Thessalonian believers assume the role of benefactor – traditionally the preserve of the "great man" – by carrying out acts of beneficence for the needy through their house-church networks and from their own resources. In the case of the Corinthian and Philippian epistles, Christ is the object of imitation, but believers, in assuming this role, also became role-models for other believers (1 Cor 11:1; 2 Cor 8:9 [cf. vv. 1–4]; Phil 3:17). There is, at one level, a continuity here with Roman convention where, generation-by-generation, the *nobiles* modelled themselves on ancestral models of virtue, but it is with a view to (hopefully) surpassing the paradigm. In the case of the early

[29] R.S. Dutch, *The Educated Elite in 1 Corinthians: Education and Community Conflict in Graeco-Roman Context*, JSNTS 271 (London and New York: T&T Clark, 2005).

Christian *imitatio*, what is remarkable and, indeed, repulsive to Romans, is that the model of imitation for believers is cruciform. Not is there any sense that the exemplum of Christ can ever be surpassed: rather it represents an inexhaustible fountain of grace from which the believer draws by faith and to which he or she is obediently conformed.

In Chapter 8 the canon of "honour" in Graeco-Roman antiquity was explored, focusing initially upon the concentration of honour in the Julio-Claudian house during the early imperial period, as well as the alternative pathways of honour opened up for the more socially marginalised members of the local associations. An inscriptional profile of honour was collated, revolving around the motifs of "zeal", "surpassing" excellence, "rivalry", "emulation", the "endangered benefactor" motif, the "word-deed" conjunction, and the "eternal" enhancement of "ancestral fame". Upon further examination of the visual evidence of honorific monuments and statuary, the eruptions of dishonour that frequently occurred in social relations were also discussed, drawing upon relevant evidence from the inscriptions, the papyri, and Dio Chrysostom. After an exhaustive analysis of Paul's variegated language of "honour" and "shame" and its engagement with the honour system of the Greek East, it was argued that the divine vindication of Christ as the "dishonoured" and "impoverished" benefactor was the driving force behind Paul's reconfiguration of honorific society in the Body of Christ and its wider relations with the outside world.

In Chapter 9 a comparison between the early house churches and the local Graeco-Roman associations was conducted. After a coverage of nineteenth to twentieth-century scholarship on the ancient associations, the important twenty-first century scholarly contributions by (what might be called) the "Toronto School" on associations were highlighted: namely, the works of Richard Ascough, Philip Harland, John Kloppenborg, and Richard Last. A series of inscriptional case studies, supported by a wider selection of inscriptional evidence from the Greek East, formed the background for a comparison of the local associations with the Pauline house churches as *charismatic* communities. After highlighting the similarities and differences between the associations and Paul's house churches, the important role of φιλία ("friendship") in the life of the associations was explored. Whereas this dynamic was of intense interest to the author of the Gospel of John (φιλοί: 15:13, 14, 15; cf. 3:29; 11:1; 19:12), Paul, as we have seen, largely avoided "friendship" terminology. The world of honour and concord in the association inscriptions simultaneously touches upon and diverges from the concerns of the apostle Paul in his epistles. Paul reaffirms the important institutions and customs of eastern Mediterranean society, but, more often than not, he redefines their operations, eschatologically postpones their incentives in light of his Gospel, and occasionally rejects outright their rationale. Finally, it was argued that the divisive behaviour of the "strong" in the Corinthian house-churches perhaps reflected their pre-Christian involvement in the local associations at Corinth, with the result that they mistakenly assumed that the social dynamics of both groups were commensurate in ethos.

10.3. Future Research

The previously published and new essays selected for this volume are united by a concentration upon civic ethics and the celebrity culture of antiquity. The value of such an approach becomes obvious when we situate Paul's gospel of the crucified Christ within the literary, archaeological, and inscriptional evidence and consider how the apostle proceeds to work out the ethical and social implications for his converts. What further pathways of research remain for New Testament scholars to venture down? A few suggestions are given below.

First, a major study remains to be written that brings Paul's moral universe into theological and social dialogue with Plutarch's *Moralia*, Dio Chrysostom's discourses, and the eulogistic inscriptions of the eastern Mediterranean basin. Two pioneering articles have already explored how the ethics of Plutarch and Dio Chrysostom reflected the moral discourse of the public inscriptions in the ancient cities.[30] In bringing Paul's letters into debate with the corpora of the ethical literature and the eulogistic inscriptions, we are able to asssess how the gospel either affirmed or collided with first-century civic ethics, as case may be, or how Paul treated them as matters of indifference in some instances. In particular, a substantial inscriptional study of the municipal ethics operative in the cities of the Italian peninsula (Italia) and in the Roman Greek East would be an invaluable ideological backdrop against which the ethical teaching of Paul in its urban context might be profitably assessed.[31] Additionally, in coming to grips with the thought of the apostle, the terminology and values of Plutarch and Dio Chrysostom that are omitted by Paul may well prove to be as important as those with which he interacts. Why does the apostle avoid various semantic domains that were vitally important in his civic world? We noted above, for example, the tantalising question posed by Paul's scant reference to the language of "friendship" in (what are deemed) his authentic epistles. This programme of research would provide a clearer understanding of the ideological, ethical, and social pressures that the early churches encountered and struggled with in their day-to-day urban interactions.

[30] C. Panagopoulos, "Vocabulaire et mentalité dans les Moralia de Plutarque," *DHA* 3 (1977): 197–235; M.-H. Quet, "Rhétorique, culture et politique: Le fonctionnement du discours idéologique chez Dion de Pruse et dans les Moralia de Plutarque," *DHA* 4 (1978): 51–119.

[31] See E. Forbis, *Municipal Virtues in the Roman Empire: The Evidence of Italian Honorary Inscriptions* (Stuttgart and Leipzig: B.G. Teubner, 1996). The counterpart in the Greek East, from a benefaction perspective, is F.W. Danker, *Benefactor: Epigraphic Study of a Graeco-Roman and New Testament Semantic Field* (St. Louis: Clayton Publishing Inc., 1982).

Second, Paul's civic and administrative terminology and his allusions to urban rituals and institutions need to be studied more intensively.[32] Gratifyingly, there has been a steady stream of studies on the terminology of civic magistracy in the letters of Paul and how such terms, when appropriated by the apostle, inform his self-understanding and ministry paradigms.[33] Moreover, we have seen in Chapter 5, for example, how a study of the gymnasiarch, not mentioned at all by Paul in his epistles, affords important insights into Paul's pastoral approach, equally by what is common and by what is distinctive in his approach and terminology. Even Paul's vague allusions to important civic magistrates such as the *agōnothetēs*, possibly referred to in Philippians 3:14, can inform studies of the civic context of Paul's epistles.[34] There remains, however, much to do. A study of the role of Paul as a κήρυξ (1 Tim 2:7; 2 Tim 1:11; cf. κήρυγμα [5x]; κηρύσσω [18x]) demands a full-scale monograph on the figure of the κήρυξ in his Graeco-roman context, with a special exegetical concentration on Paul's appropriation of "herald" terminology. Other words such as πολίτευμα (Phil 3:20; cf. πολιτεύομαι: Phil 1:27) could be profitably investigated, among other terms. Similarly, in terms of civic conventions, the numerous Ephesian citizenship decrees could be usefully studied against Paul's language of citizenship in Ephesians 2:12 and 19.[35] As one's engagement with the urban Mediterranean inscriptions deepens, more examples will inevitably turn up.

---

[32] Note the comment of B. Nongbri ("The Concept of Religion and the Study of Paul," *JJMJS* 2 [2015]: 1–26, at 22): "It seems to me that various Greek and Roman civic and administrative social formations might also yield interesting models for thinking about Pauline groups. Paul did, after all, address his letters to *ekklēsiai*, which he characterized as being part of a *politeuma*. In addition to such vocabulary, one can also consider practices, such as letter writing and the sending of emissaries, which were ubiquitous in the running of Roman civil administration."

[33] On magistracies of various sorts, see A. Bash, *Ambassadors for Christ: An Exploration of the Ambassadorial Language in the New Testament*, WUNT II 92 (Tübingen: Mohr Siebeck, 1997); J.K. Goodrich, *Paul as an Administrator of God in 1 Corinthians*, SNTSMS 152 (Cambridge: Cambridge University Press, 2012); A.G. White, "Servants, Not Intellectual Clients: The Significance of Paul's Role as an *Oikonomos* in 1 Cor 4:1 and 9:17," *ABR* 62 (2014): 44–57. On the role of the ἐκκλησία on Paul, see Y.-H. Park, *Paul's Ekklesia as a Civic Assembly: Understanding the People of God in Their Politico-Social World*, WUNT II 393 (Tübingen: Mohr Siebeck, 2015). On the urban ritual of *acclamatio* and its relevance to Paul's Corinthian correspondence, see B.J. Bitner, *Paul's Political Strategy in 1 Corinthians 1–4: Constitution and Covenant*, SNTSMS 163 (Cambridge: Cambridge University Press, 2015), 275–85.

[34] See J.R. Harrison, "Paul and the *agōnothetai* at Corinth: Engaging the Civic Values of Antiquity," in *The First Urban Churches. Volume 2: Roman Corinth*, ed. J.R. Harrison and L.L. Welborn (Atlanta: SBL Press, 2016), 271–326.

[35] See J.R. Harrison, "The Citizenship Decrees of Hellenistic Ephesus and the *Politeuma* of Roman Philippi: Evaluating Paul's 'Alternative' Citizenship in Epigraphic and Papyrological Context," in *New Documents Illustrating the History of Early Christianity. Volume 11: Ephesus*, ed. J.R. Harrison and B.J. Bitner (Grand Rapids: Eerdmans, forthcoming).

But, above all, what is required for civic ethics studies in a New Testament context is a volume similar to Danker's *Benefactor.* There needs to be, set out in Greek text and English translation, a selection of inscriptions from the biblical cities touching on important civic magistracies, including those mentioned in the New Testament, and, especially, in several instances, those that possess a rich ethical vocabulary for a comparison with Paul's moral terminology and motifs.[36] As a further supplement, a range of other inscriptions mentioning important civic rituals, prominent city institutions, social and religious conventions, should also be included. Finally, the addition of a series of essays explaining the exegetical, social, and historical significance of these inscriptions for the New Testament documents would be invaluable. This would enable us to see how the world and values of the elites in the biblical cities intersected with the first Christians in the eastern Mediterranean basin.

Third, and last, we have studied the elite ethical curriculum of the eastern Mediterranean gymnasia, embodied in the Delphic canon, in Chapter 6. But we must not forget that the Delphic canon also formed part of preparatory school-exercises. In other words, the canon, or at least individual sayings from the Seven Sages, belonged to popular morality as well. While popular morality in the Roman world has been studied extensively by T. Morgan,[37] the ethical impact of popular morality upon Paul's urban converts has been little considered. How did Paul's gospel intersect with such ethical viewpoints? For example, a study of the gnomai (moralising quotations) of the mid first-century slave and mime writer, Publilius Syrus (fl. 85–43 BC), would be valuable for the light thrown upon the moral world-view of Paul's Gentile converts and its possible interlocution with his gospel. Other forms of popular morality and their intersection with Paul's ethical and social thought are worth pursuing as well (e.g. fables: Babrius, Phaedrus; proverbs: ps.-Diogenianus, Zenobius, ps.-Plutarch, etc.).

In sum, scholalry studies of the civic context of Paul's gospel are beginning to flourish and undoubtedly will continue to open up new vistas regarding the thought and ministry of the urban apostle, whom Luke styled "a citizen of no mean city" (Acts 21:39).

[36] Such a list of 50 examples exists for the Ephesian inscriptions. See E. A. Judge, "Ethical Terms in St Paul and the Ephesian Inscriptions," in *The First Christians in the Roman World: Augustan and New Testament Essays*, WUNT I 229, ed. J. R. Harrison (Tübingen: Mohr Siebeck, 2008), 368–77, at 376–77.

[37] T. Morgan, *Popular Morality in the Early Roman Empire* (Cambridge: Cambridge University Press, 2007).

Bibliography

Abrams, Daniel M., and Mark J. Panaggio. "A Model Balancing Cooperation and Competition Can Explain Our Right-Handed World and the Dominance of Left-Handed Athletes." *Journal of the Royal Society Interface* 9.75 (2012): 2718–2722.

Achtemeier, Paul J. *The Quest for Unity in the New Testament Church.* Philadelphia: Fortress, 1987.

Adams, Edward. *The Earliest Christian Meeting Places: Almost Exclusively Houses?* Library of New Testament Studies 450. London and New York: Bloomsbury T&T Clark, 2013.

Adler, Ada, ed. *Suidae Lexicon.* Stuttgart: B.G. Teubner, 1967.

Agamben, Giorgio. *The Time that Remains: A Commentary on the Letter to the Romans.* Translated by Patricia Dailey. Stanford: Stanford University Press 2005.

Adcock, Frank E. "The Interpretation of Res Gestae Divi Augusti, 34.1." *Classical Quarterly* 1 (1951): 130–135.

Alföldi, Andreas. *Die monarchische Repräsentation im römischen Kaiserreiche.* Darmstadt: Wissenschaftliche Buchgesellschaft, 1970.

Almén, Byron. "Prophets of the Decline: The Worldviews of Heinrich Schenker and Oswald Spengler." *Indiana Theory Review* 17.1 (1996): 1–24.

Aitken, Ellen B., and Jennifer K. Berenson McLean, eds., trans. *Flavius Philostratus:* On Heroes. Atlanta: Society of Biblical Literature, 2001.

Akurgal, Ekrem. *Ancient Civilizations and Ruins of Turkey.* 10th edition. Istanbul: Net Turistik Yatinlar, 2007.

Alewell, Karl. Über das rhetorische ΠΑΡΑΔΕΙΓΜΑ. *Theorie, Beispielsammlung, Verwendung in der römischen Literatur der Kaiserzeit.* Leipzig: Hoffman, 1913.

Alexander, Christine. *Greek Athletics.* New York: Metropolitan Museum of Art, 1925.

Alexander, Patrick H., John F. Kutsko, James D. Ernest, Shirley A. Decker-Lucke, and David L. Petersen, eds. *The SBL Handbook of Style for Ancient Near Eastern, Biblical, and Early Christian Studies.* 2nd edition. Atlanta: SBL Press, 2014.

Allo, Ernest-Bernard. *Saint Paul: Première Épitre aux Corinthiens.* Paris: J. Gabalda, 1934.

Althoff, Jochen, and Dieter Zeller. "Antike Textzeugnisse und Überlieferungsgeschichte." Pages 5–81 in *Die Worte der Sieben Weisen.* Texte zur Forschung Bd. 89. Edited by Jochen Althoff and Dieter Zeller. Darmstadt: WBG, 2006.

–. eds. *Die Worte der Sieben Weisen.* Texte zur Forschung. Bd. 89. Darmstadt: WBG, 2006.

Amandry, Michel. *Le Monnayage des Duovirs Corinthiens.* BCH Supplement XV. Athens and Paris: École française d'Athènes, 1988.

–. "Le monnayage de la Res Publica Coloniae Philippensium." Pages 23–30 in *Sonderdruck aus Edith Schönert-Geiss zum 65.* Geburtstaged, Hrsg. S. Nomismatikos. Berlin: Akademie Verlag, 1998.

Anderson, James C. *The Historical Topography of the Imperial Fora*. Bruxelles: Latomus, 1984.

Andrews, Scott B. "Enslaving, Devouring, Exploiting, Self-Exalting, and Striking: 2 Cor 11:19–20 and the Tyranny of Paul's Opponents." Pages 460–490 in *Society of Biblical Literature 1997 Seminar Papers*. Edited by Anonymous. Atlanta: Society of Biblical Literature, 1997.

Andronicos, Manolis, Manolis Chatzidakis, and Vassos Karageorghis. *The Greek Museums*. London: Barrie & Jenkins, 1975.

Arapoyianni, Xeni. "Statuette of a Runner." Page 76 in Terence Measham, Elisabeth Spathari, and Paul Donnelly, *1000 Years of the Olympic Games: Treasures of Ancient Greece*. Sydney: Powerhouse Publishing, 2000.

Armstrong, Andrea J. *Roman Phrygia: Cities and Their Coinage*. PhD thesis. University College London, 1998.

Arnaoutoglou, Ilias. "Roman Law and *Collegia* in Asia Minor." *Revue internationale des droits de l'antiquité* 43 (2002): 27–44.

Ascough, Richard S. "The Completion of a Religious Duty: The Background of 2 Cor 8:1–15." *New Testament Studies* 42.4 (1996): 584–599.

–. *What are They Saying about the Formation of Pauline Churches?* Mahwah: Paulist Press, 1998.

–. *Paul's Thessalonian Associations: The Social Context of Philippians and 1 Thessalonians*. Wissenschaftliche Untersuchungen zum Neuen Testament II 161. Tübingen: Mohr Siebeck, 2003.

–. ed. *Religious Rivalries and the Struggle for Success in Sardis and Smyrna*. Studies in Christianity and Judaism 14. Waterloo: Wilfrid Laurier University Press, 2005.

–. "Of Memories and Meals: Greco-Roman Associations and the Early Jesus-Group at Thessalonikê." Pages 49–72 in *From Roman to Early Christian Thessalonikê: Studies in Religion and Archaeology*. Harvard Theological Studies 64. Edited by Laura Nasrallah, Charalambos Bakirtzis, and Steven J. Friesen. Cambridge, MA: Harvard University Press, 2010.

–. "Redescribing the Thessalonians' 'Mission' in Light of Graeco-Roman Associations." *New Testament Studies* 60.1 (2014): 61–82.

–. "What Are They Now Saying About Christ Groups and Associations?" *Currents in Biblical Research* 13.2 (2015): 207–244.

–. "Paul and Associations." Pages 68–89 in *Paul in the Greco-Roman World: A Handbook. Volume 1*. Edited by J. Paul Sampley. 2nd edition. London and New York: T&T Clark, 2016.

Ascough, Richard S., Philip A. Harland, and John S. Kloppenborg, eds. *Associations in the Greco-Roman World: A Sourcebook*. Waco: Baylor Press/De Gruyter, 2012.

Asper, Markus. "'Literatursoziologisches' zu den Sprüchen der Sieben Weisen." Pages 85–103 in *Die Worte der Sieben Weisen*. Texte zur Forschung. Bd. 89. Edited by Jochen Althoff and Dieter Zeller. Darmstadt: WBG, 2006.

Atkinson, Peter. *Friendship and the Body of Christ*. Croydon: SPCK, 2004.

Aune, David E. "Septem Sapientium Convivium." Pages 51–105 in *Plutarch's Ethical Writings and Early Christian Literature*. Edited by Hans Dieter Betz. Leiden: Brill, 1978.

Auerbach, Erich. *Mimesis: The Representation of Reality in Western Literature*. New York: Anchor Books, 1957; German original 1946.

Austin, Michel M. *The Hellenistic World from Alexander to the Roman Conquest: A Selection of Ancient Sources in Translation.* 2nd edition. Cambridge: Cambridge University Press, 1981.
Axtell, Harold. *The Deification of Abstract Ideas in Roman Literature and Inscriptions.* Chicago: University of Chicago Press, 1907.
Baban, Octavian D. *On the Road Encounters in Luke-Acts: Hellenistic* Mimesis *and Luke's Theology of the Way.* Milton Keynes: Paternoster, 2006.
Badian, Ernst. *Foreign Clientelae (264–70 BC).* Oxford: Clarendon Press, 1958.
Badiou, Alain. *Saint Paul: The Foundation of Universalism.* Stanford: Stanford University Press, 2003.
Bagnall, Roger S., and Peter Derow, eds. *The Hellenistic Period: Historical Sources in Translation.* Oxford: Blackwell, 2004.
Balch, David L. *Let Wives Be Submissive: The Domestic Code in 1 Peter.* Chico: Scholars, 1981.
–. "Household Codes." Pages 25–50 in *Greco-Roman Literature and the New Testament.* Edited by David E. Aune. Atlanta: Scholars, 1988.
–. "Romans 1:24–27, Science, and Homosexuality." *Currents in Theology and Mission* 25.6 (1998): 433–440.
–. "Paul's Portrait of Christ Crucified (Gal 3:1) in Light of Paintings and Sculptures of Suffering and Death in Pompeiian and Roman Houses." Pages 84–108 in *Early Christian Families in Context: An Interdisciplinary Dialogue.* Edited by David L. Balch and Carolyn A. Osiek. Grand Rapids: Eerdmans, 2003.
–. "Rich Pompeiian Houses, Shops for Rent, and the Huge Apartment Building in Herculaneum as Typical Spaces for Pauline House Churches." *Journal for the Study of the New Testament* 27.1 (2004): 27–46.
Baldry, Harold C. *The Unity of Mankind in Greek Thought.* Cambridge: Cambridge University Press, 1965.
Baldwin, Barry. *The Philogelos or Laughter-Lover.* Amsterdam: J. C. Gieben, 1982.
Balla, Peter. "2 Corinthians." Page 768 in *Commentary on the New Testament Use of the Old Testament.* Edited by Gregory K. Beale and Don A. Carson. Grand Rapids: Baker/Apollos, 2007.
Banks, Robert. *Paul's Idea of Community: The Early House Churches in Their Historical Setting.* 2nd edition. Peabody: Hendrickson, 1994.
Barclay, John M. G. "Money and Meetings: Group Formation among Diaspora Jews and Early Christians." Pages 108–121 in *Pauline Churches and Diaspora Jews.* Wissenschaftliche Untersuchungen zum Neuen Testament I 27. Edited by John M. G. Barclay. Tübingen: Mohr Siebeck, 2011.
–. *Paul and the Gift.* Grand Rapids: Eerdmans, 2015.
Barclay, William. *Educational Ideals in the Ancient World.* Grand Rapids: Eerdmans, 1974; original 1959.
Barentsen, Jack. *Emerging Leadership in the Pauline Mission: A Social Identity Perspective on Local Leadership Development in Corinth and Ephesus.* Princeton Theological Monograph Series 168. Eugene: Pickwick, 2011.
–. "Stephanas as Model Leader: A Social Identity Perspective on Community and Leadership (Mis)Formation in Corinth." *Journal of Biblical Perspectives in Leadership* 3.2 (2011): 3–13.
Barkowski, Otto. "Sieben Weise." *Realencyclopädie der classischen Altertumswissenschaft* II A/2 (1923): 2242–2264.

Barrett, Anthony A. *Caligula: The Corruption of Power*. London: B.T. Batsford, 1989.
Barrett, Charles K. *The Signs of an Apostle*. Philadelphia: Fortress, 1972.
–. *The Second Epistle to the Corinthians*. London: A & C Black, 1973.
Barnes, Timothy D. "Who Were the Nobility of the Roman Empire?" *Phoenix* 28.4 (1974): 444–449.
Barnett, Paul. *The Second Epistle to the Corinthians*. Grand Rapids: Eerdmans, 1997.
Bartchy, S. Scott. "Who Should Be Called Father? Paul of Tarsus between the Jesus Tradition and *Patria Potestas*." *Biblical Theology Bulletin* 33.4 (2003): 135–147.
Barton, Carlin A. *The Sorrows of Ancient Romans: The Gladiator and the Monster*. Princeton: Princeton University Press, 1993.
Barton, Stephen C. "Paul and the Cross: A Sociological Approach." *Theology* 85 (1982): 13–19.
–. "Food Rules, Sex Rules and the Prohibition of Idolatry. What's the Connection?" Pages 141–162 in *Idolatry: False Worship in the Bible, Early Judaism and Christianity*. Edited by Stephen C. Barton. London and New York: T&T Clark, 2007.
Barton, Stephen C., and Greg H.R. Horsley. "A Hellenistic Cult Group and the New Testament Churches." *Jahrbuch für Antike und Christentum* 24 (1981): 7–41.
Bash, Anthony. *Ambassadors for Christ: An Exploration of the Ambassadorial Language in the New Testament*. Wissenschaftliche Untersuchungen zum Neuen Testament II 92. Tübingen: Mohr Siebeck, 1997.
Bassler, Jouette M. *Divine Impartiality: Paul and a Theological Axiom*. Chico: Scholars, 1982.
Bates, William N. "The E of the Temple at Delphi." *American Journal of Archaeology* 29 (1925): 239–246.
Bauman, Richard. *Human Rights in Ancient Rome*. London: Routledge, 2000.
Baumert, Norbert. "Charisma und Amt bei Paulus." Pages 203–228 in *L'apôtre Paul: personnalité, style et conception du ministère*. Bibliotheca Ephemeridum Theologicarum Lovaniensium 73. Edited by Albert Vanhoye. Leuven: Leven University Press/ Uitgeverig: Peeters, 1986.
Beale, Gregory K. *We Become What We Worship: A Biblical Theology of Idolatry*. Downers Grove: IVP, 2008.
–. *A New Testament Biblical Theology: The Understanding of the Old Testament in the New*. Grand Rapids: Baker, 2011.
Beard, Mary. *The Roman Triumph*. Cambridge, MA: The Belknap Press of Harvard University, 2007.
Beard, Mary, John North, and Simon Price, eds. *Religions of Rome. Volume 1: A History*. Cambridge: Cambridge University Press, 1998.
Beazley, John D. *Attic Red-Figure Vase-Painters*. 2nd edition. Oxford: Clarendon, 1963.
Beer, David, and Ruth Penfold-Mounce. "Researching Glossy Topics: The Case of the Academic Study of Celebrity." *Celebrity Studies* 1.3 (2010): 360–365.
Beker, J. Christiaan. *Paul the Apostle: The Triumph of God in Life and Thought*. Edinburgh: T&T Clark, 1980.
Belfiore, Elizabeth. "A Theory of Imitation in Plato's Republic." *Transactions of the American Philological Association* 114 (1984): 121–146.
Bell, Sinclair. "Roman Chariot Racing Charioteers, Factions, Spectators." Pages 492–504 in *A Companion to Sport and Spectacle in Greek and Roman Antiquity*. Edited by Paul Christesen and Donald G. Kyle. Malden: Wiley-Blackwell, 2014.

Belleville, Linda L. *Reflections of Glory: Paul's Polemical Use of the Moses-Doxa Tradition in 2 Corinthians 3:1–18*. Journal for the Study of the New Testament Supplement 52. Sheffield: Sheffield Academic, 1991.

–. "'Imitate Me, Just As I Imitate Christ': Discipleship in the Corinthian Correspondence." Pages 120–142 in *Patterns of Discipleship in the New Testament*. Edited by Richard L. Longenecker. Grand Rapids: Eerdmans, 1996.

Bentley, Eric. *The Cult of the Superman: A Study of the Idea of Heroism in Carlyle and Nietzsche with Notes on Other Hero-Worshippers of Modern Times*. London: R. Hale, 1947.

Berenson, Edward. *Heroes of Empire: Five Charismatic Men and the Conquest of Africa*. Berkeley: University of California Press, 2011.

Berenson, Edward, and Eva Giloi, eds. *Constructing Charisma: Celebrity, Fame, and Power in Nineteenth-Century Europe*. New York: Berghahn Books, 2010.

Berman, Kathleen, and Luis A. Losada. "The Mysterious E at Delphi: A Solution." *Zeitschrift für Papyrologie und Epigraphik* 17 (1975): 115–117.

Bernard, Paul. *Ai Khanoum on the Oxus: A Hellenistic City in Central Asia*. London: Oxford University Press, 1967.

Best, Ernest R. *Paul and His Converts*. Edinburgh: T&T Clark, 1988.

–. "The Haustafel in Ephesians (Eph 5:22–6.9)." Pages 189–203 in Ernest R. Best, *Essays on Ephesians*. Edinburgh: T&T Clark, 1997.

Betz, Hans D. *Nachfolge und Nachahmung Jesu Christi im Neuen Testament*. Tübingen: Mohr Siebeck, 1967.

Bevere, Allan R. *Sharing in the Inheritance: Identity and the Moral Life in Colossians*. Sheffield: Sheffield Academic, 2003.

Bitner, Bradley J. "Coinage and Colonial Identity: Corinthian Numismatics and the Corinthian Correspondence." Pages 151–187 in *The First Urban Churches 1: Methodological Foundations*. Edited by James R. Harrison and Larry L. Welborn. Atlanta: SBL Press, 2015.

–. *Paul's Political Strategy in 1 Corinthians 1–4: Constitution and Covenant*. Society for New Testament Studies Monograph Series 163. Cambridge: Cambridge University Press, 2015.

Black, David A. *Paul, Apostle of Weakness:* Astheneia *and Its Cognates in the Pauline Literature*. New York: Peter Lang, 1984.

Blake, David H. *Walt Whitman and the Culture of American Celebrity*. New Haven and London: Yale University Press, 2006.

Blanton, Thomas R. *A Spiritual Economy: Gift Exchange in the Letters of Paul*. London and New Haven: Yale University Press, 2017.

Bleicken, Jochen. *Augustus: Eine Biographie*. Hamburg: Rowohlt, 2010.

Bloomer, W. Martin, ed. *A Companion to Ancient Education*. Chichester: Wiley Blackwell, 2015.

Blumenfeld, Bruno. *The Political Paul: Justice, Democracy and Kingship in a Hellenistic Framework*. Sheffield: Sheffield Academic, 2001.

Boak, Arthur E.R. "The Organisation of Gilds in Greco-Roman Egypt." *Transactions of the American Philological Association* 68 (1937): 212–220.

Bockmuehl, Markus. *Revelation and Mystery in Ancient Judaism and Pauline Christianity*. Grand Rapids: Eerdmans, 1990.

Bollansée, Jan. "Fact and Fiction, Falsehood and Truth. D. Fehling and Ancient Legendry about the Seven Sages." *Museum Helveticum* 56 (1999): 65–75.

Bonner, Stanley F. *Education in Ancient Rome: From the Elder Cato to the Younger Pliny*. London: Methuen, 1977.
Boorstin, Daniel J. *The Image: A Guide to Pseudo-events in America*. New York: Atheneum, 1961.
Booth, Alan. "The Age for Reclining and Its Attendant Perils." Pages 105–120 in *Dining in a Classical Context*. Edited by William J. Slater. Ann Arbor: University of Michigan Press, 1991.
Borgen, Peder. "'Yes', 'No', 'How Far?': The Participation of Jews and Christians in Pagan Cults." Pages 30–59 in *Paul in His Hellenistic Context*. Edited by Troels Engberg-Pedersen. Edinburgh: T&T Clark, 1994.
Bosworth, Brian. "Augustus, the *Res Gestae* and Hellenistic Theories of Apotheosis." *Journal of Roman Studies* 89 (1999): 1–18.
Bowman, Alan K., Edward Champlin, and Andrew Lintott, eds. *The Cambridge Ancient History X: The Augustan Empire 43 BC–AD 69*. 2nd edition. Cambridge: Cambridge University Press, 1996.
Bradley, Mark. "Fool's Gold: Colour, Culture, Innovation, and Madness in Nero's Golden House." *Apollo: The International Magazine of the Arts* (July 2002): 35–44.
Bragues, George. "Profiting with Honour: Cicero's Vision of Leadership." *Journal of Business Ethics* 97 (2010): 21–33.
Brändl, Martin. *Der Agon bei Paulus: Herkunft und Profil paulinischer Agonmetaphorik*. Wissenschaftliche Untersuchungen zum Neuen Testament II 222. Tübingen: Mohr Siebeck, 2006.
Branick, Vincent. *The House Church in the Writings of Paul*. Wilmington: Michael Glazier, 1989.
Braudy, Leo. *The Frenzy of Renown: Fame and Its History*. New York: Vintage Books, 1997.
Brockhaus, Ulrich. *Charisma und Amt: Die paulinische Charismenlehre auf dem Hintergrund der frühchristlichen Gemeindefunktionen*. Wuppertal: Theologischer Verlag, 1972.
Broneer, Oscar. *Corinth: Terracotta Lamps*. Cambridge, MA: Harvard University Press, 1930.
–. "Excavations at Isthmia: Fourth Campaign, 1957–1958." *Hesperia* 28.4 (1959): 298–343.
–. "The Isthmian Victory Crown." *American Journal of Archaeology* 66.3 (1962): 259–263.
–. *Isthmia II: Topography and Architecture*. Princeton: American School of Classical Studies at Athens, 1973.
Brookins, Timothy A. *Corinthian Wisdom, Stoic Philosophy, and the Ancient Economy*. Society for New Testament Studies Monograph Series 159. Cambridge: Cambridge University Press, 2014.
Brooten, Bernadette J. *Women Leaders in the Ancient Synagogue: Inscriptional Evidence and Background Issues*. Brown Judaic Studies 46. Atlanta: Scholars, 1982.
Brown, Alexandra R. *The Cross and Human Transformation: Paul's Apocalyptic Word in 1 Corinthians*. Minneapolis: Fortress, 1995.
Bruce, Frederick F. *1 and 2 Corinthians*. London: Oliphants, 1971.
Brunet, Stephen A. *Greek Athletes in the Roman World: The Evidence from Ephesus*. PhD dissertation. University of Texas, 1998.
Brunt, Peter A., and John M. Moore. *Res Gestae Divi Augusti: The Achievements of the Divine Augustus*. Oxford and New York: Oxford University Press, 1967.
Brunt, Peter A. "Princeps and Equites." *Journal of Roman Studies* 73 (1983): 42–75.

–. "The Role of the Senate in the Augustan Regime." *Classical Quarterly* (1984): 434–444.

Bultmann, Rudolf. *The Second Letter to the Corinthians*. Minneapolis: Augsburg, 1976.

Burrell, Barbara. "False Fronts: Separating the Imperial Cult from the Aedicular Façade in Roman Asia Minor." *American Journal of Archaeology* 110 (2006): 437–469.

Burridge, Richard A. *Imitating Jesus: An Inclusive Approach to New Testament Ethics*. Grand Rapids: Eerdmans, 2007.

Burstein, Stanley M., ed. *The Hellenistic Age from the Battle of Ipsos to the Death of Kleopatra VII*. Cambridge: Cambridge University Press, 1985.

Burtchaell, James T. *From Synagogue to Church: Public Services and Offices in the Earliest Christian Communities*. Cambridge: Cambridge University Press, 1992.

Busine, Aude. *Les Sept Sages de la Grèce antique. Transmission et utilisation d'un patrimonie légendaire d'Hérodote à Plutarque*. Paris: De Boccard, 2002.

Cadwallader, Alan H. "Assessing the Potential of Archaeological Discoveries for the Interpretation of New Testament Texts: The Case of a Gladiator Fragment from Colossae and the Letter to the Colossians." Pages 41–66 in *The First Urban Churches I: Methodological Foundations*. Edited by James R. Harrison and Larry L. Welborn. Atlanta: SBL Press, 2015.

–. "Paul and the Games." Pages 363–390 in *Paul in the Greco-Roman World: A Handbook. Volume 1*. Edited by J. Paul Sampley. 2nd edition. London and New York: T&T Clark, 2016.

Caird, G. Bradford. *Principalities and Powers: A Study in Pauline Theology*. Oxford: Clarendon Press, 1956.

Cairns, Douglas L. *Aidōs: The Psychology and Ethics of Honor and Shame in Ancient Greek Literature*. Oxford: Oxford University Press, 1993.

Cameron, Alan. *Porphyrius the Charioteer*. London: Oxford University Press, 1973.

–. *Circus Factions: Blues and Greens at Rome and Byzantium*. Oxford: Clarendon Press, 1976.

Campbell, Constantine R. *Paul and Union with Christ: An Exegetical and Theological Study*. Grand Rapids: Zondervan, 2012.

Campbell, R. Alastair. *The Elders: Seniority within Earliest Christianity*. Edinburgh: T&T Clark, 1994.

Canavan, Rosemary. *Clothing the Body of Christ at Colossae: A Visual Construction of Identity*. Wissenschaftliche Untersuchungen zum Neuen Testament II 334. Tübingen: Mohr Siebeck, 2012.

–. "Visual Exegesis: Interpreting Text in Dialogue with Its Visual Context." *Colloquium* 47.1 (2015): 141–151.

Capdetrey, Laurent, and Yves Lafond, eds. *La cité et ses élites: pratiques et représentation des formes de domination et de contrôle social dans les cités grecques. Actes du colloque de Poitiers, 19–20 octobre 2006*. Pessac: Ausonius, 2010.

Capes, David B. *Old Testament Yahweh Texts in Paul's Christology*. Wissenschaftliche Untersuchungen zum Neuen Testament II 47. Tübingen: Mohr Siebeck, 1992.

Caputo, John D., and Linda M. Alcoff, eds. *St Paul among the Philosophers*. Bloomington: Indiana University Press, 2009.

Carlyle, Thomas. *On Heroes, Hero-Worship, and the Heroic in History: Six Lectures*. New York: Longmans, Green, and Co., 1906; original London: Chapman and Hall, 1841.

Carr, A. Wesley. *Angels and Principalities: The Background Meaning and Development of the Pauline Phrase HAI ARCHAI KAI HAI EXOUSIAI*. Society for New Testament Studies Monograph Series 42. Cambridge: Cambridge University Press, 1981.

Carter, Michael. *The Presentation of Gladiatorial Spectacles in the Greek East: Roman Culture and Greek Identity.* PhD dissertation. McMaster University, 1999.

Casanova, Angelo. "Plutarch as Apollo's Priest at Delphi." Pages 159–170 in *Plutarch in the Religious and Philosophical Discourse of Late Antiquity.* Edited by Lautaro R. Lanzillotta and Israel M.O. Gallarte. Leiden: Brill, 2012.

Case, Shirley J. *The Social Origins of Christianity.* New York: Baker and Taylor, 1923.

Castelli, Elizabeth A. *Imitating Paul: A Discourse of Power.* Louisville: Westminster John Knox, 1991.

Cébeillac-Gervasoni, Mireille, and Laurent Lamoine, eds. *Les* élites *et leurs facettes: les* élites locales *dans le monde hellénistique et romain.* Rome: École française de Rome; Clermont-Ferrand: Presses universitaires Blaise-Pascal, 2003.

Cébeillac-Gervasoni, Mireille, Laurent Lamoine, and Frédéric Trément, eds. *Autocélébration des élites locales dans le monde romain: contextes, images, textes, IIe s. av. J.C.- IIIe s. ap. J.-C.* Clermont-Ferrand: Centre de recherche sur les civilisations antiques, 2004.

Cerfaux, Lucien. "La théologie de la grâce selon Saint Paul." *La vie spirituelle* 83 (1950): 5–19.

–. *Christ in the Theology of Paul.* New York: Herder and Herder, 1959.

–. *The Christian in the Theology of Paul.* New York: Herder and Herder, 1967.

Chadwick, Henry. "'All Things to All Men' (1 Cor 9:22)." *New Testament Studies* 1 (1954–1955): 261–275.

Champlin, Edward. *Nero.* Cambridge, MA and London: Harvard University Press, 2003.

Chankowski, Andrzej S. *L'Éphébie hellénistique: Étude d'une institution civique dans les cités grecques des îles de la Mer Égée et de l'Asie Mineure, Culture et cité 4.* Paris: De Boccard, 2010.

Chapple, Allan L. *Local Leadership in the Pauline Churches: Theological and Social Factors in Its Development. A Study Based on 1 Thessalonians, 1 Corinthians and Philippians.* PhD Dissertation. Durham University, 1984.

Charlesworth, Martin P. "The Refusal of Divine Honours: An Augustan Formula." *Papers of the British School at Rome* 15 (1939): 1–10.

Cheung, Alex T. *Idol Food in Corinth: Jewish Background and Pauline Legacy.* Journal for the Study of the New Testament Supplement 176. Sheffield: Sheffield Academic Press, 1999.

Chiasson, Charles C. "The Herodotean Solon." *Greek, Roman, and Byzantine Studies* 27 (1986): 249–262.

–. "Herodotus' Prologue and the Greek Poetic Tradition." *Histos* 6 (2012): 114–143.

Chilton, Bruce. "Jesus and Sinners and Outcasts." Pages 2801–2833 in *Handbook for the Study of the Historical Jesus. Volume 3: The Historical Jesus.* Edited by Tom Holmén and Stanley E. Porter. Leiden and Boston: Brill, 2011.

Chiusi, Tiziana, J. "'Fama' and 'Infamia' in the Roman Legal System: The Cases of Afrania and Lucretia." Pages 143–165 in *Judge and Jurist: Essays in Memory of Lord Rodger of Earlsferry.* Edited by Andrew Burrows, David Johnston, and Reinhard Zimmermann. Oxford: Oxford University Press, 2013.

Chow, John K. *Patronage and Power: A Study of Social Networks in Corinth.* Sheffield: Sheffield Academic, 1992.

Ciampa, Roy E., and Brian S. Rosner. *The First Letter to the Corinthians.* Grand Rapids: Eerdmans, 2010.

Clark, Andrew C. *Parallel Lives: The Relation of Paul to the Apostles in the Lucan Perspective.* Carlisle: Paternoster, 2001.

Clark, Wesley P. *Benefactions and Endowments in Greek Antiquity*. PhD dissertation. University of Chicago, 1928.
Clarke, Andrew D. *Secular and Christian Leadership in Corinth: A Socio-Historical and Exegetical Study of 1 Corinthians 1–6*. Leiden: Brill, 1993.
–. "'Be Imitators of Me': Paul's Model of Leadership." *Tyndale Bulletin* 49.2 (1998): 329–360.
–. *Serve the Community of the Church: Christians as Leaders and Ministers*. Grand Rapids: Eerdmans, 2000.
Clarke, John R. "High and Low: Mocking Philosophers in the Tavern of the Seven Sages." Pages 47–57 in *The Art of Citizens, Soldiers and Freedmen in the Roman World*. Edited by Eve D'Ambra and Guy P.R. Métraux. Oxford: Archaeopress, 2006.
Clarke, Martin L. *Higher Education in the Ancient World*. Albuquerque: University of New Mexico Press, 1971.
Coad, David. *The Metrosexual: Gender, Sexuality, and Sport*. Albany: State University of New York Press, 2008.
Coarelli, Filippo. *Il Foro Romano*. Rome: Quasar, 1992.
Coffee, Neil. *Gift and Gain: How Money Transformed Ancient Rome*. Oxford: Oxford University Press, 2017.
Collange, Jean-François. *Enigmes de la deuxième épître de Paul aux Corinthiens*. Society for New Testament Studies Monograph Series 18. Cambridge: Cambridge University Press, 1972.
Collins, John J. *Seers, Sibyls, and Sages in Hellenistic-Roman Judaism*. Leiden: Brill, 1997.
–. "What is Apocalyptic Literature?" Pages 1–16 in *The Oxford Book of Apocalyptic Literature*. Edited by John J. Collins. Oxford: Oxford University Press, 2014.
Collins, John N. *Diakonia: Re-interpreting the Ancient Sources*. Oxford: Oxford University Press, 1990.
Collins, Raymond F. *First Corinthians*. Collegeville: Michael Glazier/Liturgical Press, 1999.
Concannon, Cavan W. "'Not for an Olive Wreath, but Our Lives': Gladiators, Athletes, and Early Christian Bodies." *Journal of Biblical Literature* 133.1 (2014): 193–214.
Connolly, Joy. *The State of Speech: Rhetorical and Political Thought in Ancient Rome*. Princeton: Princeton University Press, 2007.
Conzelmann, Hans. "χάρισμα." Pages 402–406 in *Theological Dictionary of the New Testament. Volume IX*. Edited by Gerhard Kittel and Gerhard Friedrich. Translated by Geoffrey W. Bromiley. Grand Rapids: Eerdmans, 1967.
–. *1 Corinthians: A Commentary on the First Epistle to the Corinthians*. Philadelphia 1975; German original 1969.
Cook, John G. *Crucifixion in the Mediterranean World*. Wissenschaftliche Untersuchungen zum Neuen Testament I 327. Tübingen: Mohr Siebeck, 2014.
Cooley, Alison E. *Res Gestae Divi Augusti: Text, Translation, and Commentary*. Cambridge: Cambridge University Press, 2009.
Copan, Victor A. *Saint Paul as Spiritual Director: An Analysis of the Concept of the Imitation of Paul with the Implications and Applications to the Practice of Spiritual Direction*. Nottingham: Paternoster, 2007.
Cordiano, Giuseppe. *La Ginnasiarchia Nelle «Poleis» Dell'Occidente Mediterraneo Antico*. Studi e testi di storia antica diretti da Mauro Moggi 7. Pisa: Ediozi ETS, 1997.
Cosby, Michael R. *The Rhetorical Composition and Function of Hebrews 11 in Light of Example Lists in Antiquity*. Macon: Mercer University Press, 1988.

Countryman, L. William. "Patrons and Officers in Club and Church." Pages 135–141 in *SBL 1977 Seminar Papers*. Edited by Paul Achtemeier. Missoula: Scholars, 1978.
–. *The Rich Christian in the Church of the Early Empire: Contradictions and Accommodations*. New York and Toronto: Edward Mellen Press, 1980.
Cousar, Charles B. *A Theology of the Cross: The Death of Jesus in the Pauline Epistles*. Minneapolis: Fortress, 1990.
Cousland, J. Robert C. "Athletics." Pages 140–142 in *Dictionary of New Testament Background*. Edited by Craig A. Evans and Stanley E. Porter. Downers Grove-Leicester: IVP, 2000.
Crenshaw, James L. *Education in Ancient Israel: Across the Deadening Silence*. New York: Doubleday, 1998.
Crielard, Jan P., Vladimir Stissi, and Gert Jan van Wijngaarden, eds.*The Complex Past of Pottery: Production, Circulation and Consumption of Mycenaean and Greek Pottery*. Amsterdam: J.B. Gieben, 1999.
Crook, John A. "Augustus: Power, Authority, Achievement." Pages 113–146 in *The Cambridge Ancient History. Second Edition. X: The Augustan Empire 43 BC–AD 69*. Edited by Alan K. Bowman, Edward Champlin, and Andrew Lintott. Cambridge: Cambridge University Press, 1996.
–. "Political History, 30 BC to AD 14." Pages 70–112 in *The Cambridge Ancient History. Second Edition. X: The Augustan Empire 43 BC–AD 69*. Edited by Alan K. Bowman, Edward Champlin, and Andrew Lintott. Cambridge: Cambridge University Press, 1996.
Crook, Zeba A. *Reconceptualising Conversion: Patronage, Loyalty, and Conversion in the Religions of the Ancient Mediterranean*. Berlin and New York: De Gruyter, 2004.
Crouch, James E. *The Origin and Intention of the Colossian Haustafel*. Göttingen: Vandenhoeck & Ruprecht, 1972.
Crouzel, Henri. "L'imitation et la suite de dieu et du Christ dans les premiers siècles chrétiens ainsi que leurs sources gréco-romaines et hébraïques." *Jahrbuch für Antike und Christentum* 21 (1978): 7–41.
Crowther, Nigel B. "Male Beauty Contests in Greece: The *Euandria* and *Euexia*." *l'antiquité classique* (1985): 285–291.
Croy, N. Clayton. *Endurance in Suffering: Hebrews 12:1–13 in Its Rhetorical, Religious and Philosophical Context*. Cambridge: Cambridge University Press, 1998.
Csapo, Eric, and William J. Slater. *The Context of Ancient Drama*. Ann Arbor: University of Michigan Press, 1994.
Cueto, Bernard. *Paul's Understanding of* pistis *in Its Graeco-Roman Context*. PhD dissertation. Dallas Theological Seminary, 2012.
Cullmann, Oscar. *Prayer in the New Testament, with Answer from the New Testament for Today's Questions*. Translated by John Bowden. London: SCM, 1995.
Cullyer, Helen. *Greatness of Soul from Aristotle to Cicero: The Genealogy of a Virtue*. PhD thesis. Yale University, 1999.
Curty, Olivier. *Gymnasiarchika: recueil et analyse des inscriptions de l'époque hellénistique en l'honneur des gymnasiarques*. De l'archéologie à l'histoire, 64. Paris: De Boccard, 2015.
Curty, Olivier, and Marcel Piérart. *L'huile et l'argent, gymnasiarchie et évergétisme dans la Grèce hellénistique – Actes du colloque tenu à Fribourg, du 13 au 15 octobre 2005, publiés en l'honneur du Professeur Marcel Piérart à l'occasion de son 60e anniversaire*. Fribourg: Séminaire d'histoire ancienne, 2009.

Damon Cynthia. *Res Gestae Divi Augusti*. Bryn Mawr: Bryn Mawr College, 1995.
Danker, Frederick W. "On Stones and Benefactors." *Currents in Theology and Mission* 8.6 (1981): 351–356.
–. *Benefactor: Epigraphic Study of a Graeco-Roman and New Testament Semantic Field*. St. Louis: Clayton Publishing, 1982.
–. *A Century of Greco-Roman Philology Featuring the American Philological Association and the Society of Biblical Literature*. Atlanta: Scholars, 1988.
–. *II Corinthians*. Minneapolis: Augsburg, 1989.
–. "Associations, Clubs, Thiasoi." Pages 501–503 in *Anchor Bible Dictionary. Volume 1*. Edited by David N. Freedman. New York: Doubleday, 1992.
Dasen, Véronique. "*Infirmitas* or Not? Short-statured Persons in Ancient Greece." Pages 29–50 in *Infirmity in Antiquity and the Middle Ages: Social and Cultural Approaches*. Edited by Christian Krötzl, Katariina Mustakallio, and Jenni Kuuliala. London and New York: Routledge, 2015.
Davies, Penelope J.E. *Death and the Emperor: Roman Imperial Funerary Monuments from Augustus to Marcus Aurelius*. Austin: University of Texas Press, 2004.
de Boer, Willis P. *The Imitation of Paul: An Exegetical Study*. Kampen: J.H. Kok, 1962.
De Witt, Norman W. *St. Paul and Epicurus*. Minneapolis: University of Minnesota Press, 1954.
Delatte, Louis. *Les traités de la royauté d'Ecphante, Diotogène et Sthénidas*. Liége: Bibliothèque de la Faculté de Philosophie et Lettres de l'Université de Liége, 1942.
Deller, Ruth A. "Star Image, Celebrity Reality Television and the Fame Cycle." *Celebrity Studies* 7.3 (2016): 373–389.
Delorme, Jean. *Le Gymnase: Étude sur les monuments consacrés à l'éducation en Grèce*. Paris: De Boccard, 1960.
deSilva, David A. "The Noble Contest: Honor, Shame, and the Rhetorical Strategy of 4 Maccabees." *Journal for the Study of the New Testament* 13 (1995): 31–57.
–. "Investigating Honor Discourse: Guidelines from Classical Rhetoricians." Pages 491–525 in *SBL 1997 Seminar Papers*. Atlanta: Scholars, 1997.
–. *The Hope of Glory: Honor Discourse and New Testament Interpretation*. Collegeville: Liturgical, 1999.
–. *Honor, Patronage and Purity: Unlocking New Testament Culture*. Downers Grove: IVP, 2002.
–. "Paul, Honor, and Shame." Pages 26–47 in *Paul in the Greco-Roman World: A Handbook. Volume 2*. Edited by J. Paul Sampley. 2nd edition. London and New York: T&T Clark, 2016.
D'Hautcourt, Alexis. "Public Finances and Private Generosity: The Example of Opramoas in Roman Lycia." *Journal of Economics, Business and Law* 5 (2003): 39–63.
D'Hoine, Pieter, and Gerd Van Riel, eds. *Fate, Providence and Moral Responsibility in Ancient, Medieval and Early Modern Thought*. Leuven: Leuven University, 2014.
Dibelius, Martin. *An die Kolosser Epheser an Philemon*. Tübingen: Mohr Siebeck, 1953.
Diels, Hermann, and Walther Kranz. *Die Fragmente der Vorsokratiker*. 10th edition. Berlin: Weidmann, 1960; original 1934.
Dixon, Suzanne. "The Marriage Alliance in the Roman Elite." *Journal of Family History* 10 (1985): 353–738.
Dodd, Brian J. "The Story of Christ and the Imitation of Paul in Philippians 2–3." Pages 154–160 in *Where Christology Began: Essays on Philippians 2*. Edited by Ralph P. Martin and Brian J. Dodd. Louisville: Westminster John Knox Press, 1998.

Dodge, Hazel. "Amphitheaters in the Roman World." Pages 543–560 in *A Companion to Sport and Spectacle in Greek and Roman Antiquity*. Edited by Paul Christesen and Donald G. Kyle. Malden: Wiley-Blackwell, 2014.

Dodson, Joseph R., and David E. Briones, eds. *Paul and Seneca in Dialogue*. Leiden: Brill, 2017.

Dodwell, Edward. *A Classical and Topographical Tour through Greece during the Years 1801, 1805, and 1806. Volume 1*. London: Rodwell and Martin, 1819.

Donnelly, Paul. "Red-Figure Kylix." Page 100 in Terence Measham, Elisabeth Spathari, and Paul Donnelly, *1000 Years of the Olympic Games: Treasures of Ancient Greece*. Sydney: Powerhouse Publishing, 2000.

Doohan, Helen. *Leadership in Paul*. Wilmington: Michael Glazier, 1984.

Dover, Kenneth J. *Greek Homosexuality*. London: Duckworth, 1978.

Dowling, Melissa B. *Clemency and Cruelty in the Roman World*. Ann Arbor: University of Michigan, 2006.

Downing, F. Gerald. *Cynics, Paul and the Pauline Churches*. London and New York: Routledge, 1998.

Downs, David J. *The Offering of the Gentiles: Paul's Collection for Jerusalem in Its Chronological, Cultural, and Cultic Contexts*. Wissenschaftliche Untersuchungen zum Neuen Testament II 248. Tübingen: Mohr Siebeck, 2008.

Du Toit, Andrie B. "Shaping a Christian Lifestyle in the Roman Capital." Pages 371–403 in Andrie B. Du Toit, *Focusing on Paul: Persuasion and Theological Design in Romans and Galatians*. Beihefte zur Zeitschrift für die neutestamentliche Wissenschaft 151. Edited by Cilliers Breytenbach and David S. Du Toit. Berlin and New York: De Gruyter, 2007.

Duchesne, Ricardo. "Oswald Spengler and the Faustian Soul of the West." *The Occidental Quarterly* 14.4 (2014–2015): 3–22.

Dudley, Donald R. *Urbs Romana: A Source Book of Classical Texts on the City and Its Monuments*. London: Phaidon, 1967.

–. *The World of Tacitus*. London: Secker and Warburg, 1968.

Dumbrell, William J. "Paul's Use of Exodus 34 in 2 Corinthians 34." Pages 179–194 in *God Who is Rich in Mercy*. Edited by Peter T. O'Brien and David G. Peterson. Homebush West: Lancer, 1986.

Dunn, James D. G. *Jesus and the Spirit: A Study of the Religious and Charismatic Experience of Jesus and the First Christians as Reflected in the New Testament*. London: SCM, 1975.

–. *Christology in the Making: An Inquiry into the Origins of the Doctrine*. London: SCM, 1980.

–. *The Epistles to the Colossians and to Philemon*. Grand Rapids: Eerdmans, 1996.

–. *The Theology of Paul the Apostle*. Grand Rapids: Eerdmans, 1998.

–. *Jesus Remembered. Christianity in the Making. Volume 1*. Grand Rapids: Eerdmans, 2003.

Dupont, Jacques. ΣΥΝ ΧΡΙΣΤΩΙ: *L'Union avec le Christ suivant Saint Paul*. Paris: Desclée de Brouwer, 1952.

Dutch, Robert S. *The Educated Elite in 1 Corinthians: Education and Community Conflict in Graeco-Roman Context*. JSNTS 271. London and New York: T&T Clark, 2005.

Earl, Donald C. "Political Terminology in Plautus." *Historia* 9.1 (1960): 235–243.

–. *The Political Thought of Sallust*. Cambridge: Cambridge University Press, 1961.

–. *The Age of Augustus*. New York: Crown, 1968.

Earle, Bo. "Plato, Aristotle, and the Imitation of Reason." *Philosophy and Literature* 27.2 (2003): 382–401.
Earle, David M. *All Man!: Hemingway, 1950s Men's Magazines, and the Masculine Persona*. Kent: Kent State University Press, 2009.
Eck, Werner. *Da Senatus Consultum de. Cn. Pisone Patre*. Munich: Beck, 1996
–. *The Age of Augustus*. 2nd edition. Oxford: Blackwell, 2007.
Eckhardt, Benedikt. "The Eighteen Associations of Corinth." *Greek, Roman, and Byzantine Studies* 56 (2016): 646–662.
Edsall, Benjamin. "When Cicero and St Paul Agree: Intra-Group among Luperci and the Corinthian Believers." *Journal of Theological Studies* 64.1 (2013): 25–36.
Edson, Charles, ed. *Inscriptiones Graecae Epiri, Macedoniae, Thraciae, Scythiae. Pars II: Inscriptiones Macedoniae. Fasciculus I: Inscriptiones Thessalonicae et Viciniae*. Berlin: De Gruyter, 1972.
Edwards, Catharine. *The Politics of Immorality in Rome*. Cambridge: Cambridge University Press, 1993.
Edwards, Katharine M. *Corinth: Coins, 1896–1927*. Cambridge, MA: Harvard University Press, 1933.
Ehrensperger, Kathy. *That We May Be Mutually Encouraged: Feminism and the New Perspective in Pauline Studies*. New York and London: T&T Clark, 2004.
–. *Paul and the Dynamics of Power: Communication and Interaction in the Early Christ-Movement*. London and New York: T&T Clark, 2009.
–. *Paul at the Crossroads of Cultures: Theologizing in the Space Between*. London and New York: Bloomsbury: T&T Clark, 2015.
Eisenbaum, Pamela M. *The Jewish Heroes of Christian History: Hebrews 11 in Literary Context*. Atlanta: Scholars, 1997.
Elliott, Neil. *The Arrogance of Nations: Reading Romans in the Shadow of Empire*. Minneapolis: Fortress, 2008.
Ellis, E. Earle. *Pauline Theology: Ministry and Society*. Grand Rapids: Eerdmans, 1989.
Else, Gerald. "'Imitation' in the Fifth Century." *Classical Philology* 53 (1958): 73–90.
Engberg-Pedersen, Troels. *Paul and the Stoics*. Edinburgh: T&T Clark, 2000.
–. *Cosmology and the Self in the Apostle Paul: The Material Spirit*. Oxford: Oxford University Press, 2010.
Engels, Johannes. *Die sieben Weisen: Leben, Lehren und Legenden*. Munich: C.H. Beck, 2010.
Epstein, David F. *Personal Enmity in Roman Politics, 218–43 BC*. London: Croom Helm, 1987.
Eriksonas, Linas. *National Heroes and National Identities: Scotland, Norway and Lithuania*. Multiple Europes 26. Brussels: Peter Lang, 2005.
Erim, Kenan T. *Aphrodisias: City of Venus Aphrodite*. London: Muller, Blond and White, 1986.
Esler, Philip F. *Conflict and Identity in Romans: The Social Setting of Paul's Letter*. Minneapolis: Fortress, 2003.
–. "Paul and the Agon: Understanding a Pauline Motif in Its Cultural and Visual Context." Pages 356–384 in *Picturing the New Testament: Studies in Ancient Visual Images*. Wissenschaftliche Untersuchungen zum Neuen Testament II 193. Edited by Annette Weissenrieder, Friederike Wendt, and Petra von Gemünden. Tübingen: Mohr Siebeck, 2005.

Evangelos, Albanidis. "Educational Athletic Institutions in Thrace during the Hellenistic and Roman Periods." *ASSH Bulletin* 27 (1997): 15–20.

Everitt, Anthony. *Augustus: The Life of Rome's First Emperor.* New York: Augustus, 2006.

Eyben, Emiel. "The Concrete Ideal in the Life of the Young Roman." *L'Antiquité Classique* 41 (1972): 200–217.

Fantin, Joseph D. *The Lord of the Entire World: Lord Jesus, a Challenge to Lord Caesar?* Sheffield: Sheffield Phoenix Press, 2011.

Favro, Diane. *The Urban Image of Augustan Rome.* Cambridge: Cambridge University, 1996.

Fears, J. Rufus. "The Cult of Virtues and Roman Imperial Ideology." *Aufstieg und Niedergang der römischen Welt* 2.17.2 (1981): 827–848.

Fee, Gordon D. "Εἰδωλόθυτα Once Again: An Interpretation of 1 Corinthians 8–10." *Biblica* 61 (1980): 172–197.

–. *The First Epistle to the Corinthians.* Grand Rapids: Eerdmans, 1987.

–. *Pauline Christology: An Exegetical-Theological Study.* Peabody: Hendrickson, 2007.

Fehling, Detlev. *Die sieben Weisen und die frühgriechische Chronologie. Eine traditionsgeschichtliche Studie.* Bern: P. Lang, 1985.

Feldman, Louis H. *Jew and Gentile in the Ancient World.* Princeton: Princeton University Press, 1993.

Ferlinghetti, Lawrence. *These Are My Rivers: New and Selected Poems 1955–1993.* New York: New Directions, 1993.

Fernoux, Henri-Louis. *Notables et élites des cités de Bithynie aux époques hellénistique et romaine (IIIe siècle av. J.-C. –IIIe siècle ap. J.-C.). Essai d'histoire sociale.* Collection de la Maison de l'Orient et de la Méditerranée 31. Série Épigraphique et Historique 5. Paris: Collection de la Maison de l'Orient et de la Méditerranée, 2004.

Ferrario, Sarah Brown. *Historical Agency and the "Great Man" in Classical Greece.* Cambridge and New York: Cambridge University Press, 2014.

Ferris, Kerry O., and Scott R. Harris. *Stargazing: Celebrity, Fame, and Social Interaction.* New York and London: Routledge, 2011.

Finney, Mark T. *Honour and Conflict in the Ancient World: 1 Corinthians in its Greco-Roman Social Setting.* London and New York: Bloomsbury/T&T Clark, 2012.

Fiore, Benjamin. *The Function of Personal Example in the Socratic and Pastoral Epistles.* Rome: Biblical Institute Press, 1986.

–. "Paul, Exemplification, and Imitation." Pages 169–195 in *Paul in the Greco-Roman World: A Handbook.* Edited by J. Paul Sampley. 2nd edition. London and New York: T&T Clark, 2016.

Fisher, Nicolas R.E. Hybris*: A Study in the Values of Honour and Shame in Ancient Greece.* Warminster: Aris & Phillips, 1992.

Fitzgerald, F. Scott. "Echoes of the Jazz Age." *Scribner's Magazine* 90.5 (1931): 459–465.

Fitzgerald, John T. *Cracks in an Earthen Vessel: An Examination of the Catalogue of Hardships in the Corinthian Correspondence.* SBLSS 99. Atlanta: Scholars, 1988.

–. *Friendship, Flattery, and Frankness of Speech: Studies on Friendship in the New Testament.* Leiden: Brill, 1996.

–. *Greco-Roman Perspectives on Friendship.* Atlanta: Scholars, 1997.

Fitzgerald, John T., and L. Michael White. *The Tabula of Cebes.* Chico: Scholars, 1983.

Flower, Harriet I. "Herodotus and the Delphic Traditions about Croesus." Pages 57–77 in *Georgica: Greek Studies in Honour of George Cawkwell.* Edited by Michael A.

Flower and Mark Toher. London: University of London Institute of Classical Studies, 1991.

–. "Elite Self-Representation in Rome." Pages 271–285 in *The Oxford Handbook of Social Relations in the Roman World*. Edited by Michael Peachin. Oxford and New York: Oxford University Press, 2011.

Forbes, Clarence A. *NEOI: A Contribution to the Study of Greek Associations*. Middletown: American Philological Association, 1933.

–. "Ancient Athletic Guilds." *Classical Philology* 50 (1955): 238–252.

Forbis, Elizabeth. *Municipal Virtues in the Roman Empire: The Evidence of Italian Honorary Inscriptions*. Stuttgart and Leipzig: B. G. Teubner, 1996.

Ford, J. Massyngberde. *Redeemer – Friend and Mother: Salvation in Antiquity and in the Gospel of John*. Minneapolis: Fortress.

Fotopoulos, John. *Food Offered to Idols in Roman Corinth: A Socio-Rhetorical Reconstruction of 1 Corinthians 8:1–11:1*. Wissenschaftliche Untersuchungen zum Neuen Testament II 151. Tübingen: Mohr Siebeck, 2003.

Foucart, Paul. *Des Associations religieuses chez les Grecs: thiases, éranes, orgéons*. Paris: Klincksieck, 1873.

Fountoulakis, Andreas. "The Artists of Aphrodite." *L'antiquité classique* 69.1 (2000): 133–147.

Fowl, Stephen E. *The Story of Christ in the Ethics of Paul: An Analysis of the Function of the Hymnic Material in the Pauline Corpus*. JSNTSup. 36. Sheffield: JSOT Press, 1990.

–. "Imitation of Paul/of Christ." Pages 428–431 in *Dictionary of Paul and His Letters*. Edited by Gerald F. Hawthorne, Daniel G. Reid, and Ralph P. Martin. Downers Grove and Leicester: IVP, 1993.

Foxhall, Lin. "Foreign Powers: Plutarch and Discourses of Domination in Roman Greece." Pages 138–150 in *Plutarch's* Advice to the Bride and Groom *and* A Consolation to His Wife*: English Translation, Commentary, Interpretative Essays, and Bibliography*. Edited by Sarah B. Pomeroy. New York and Oxford: Oxford University Press, 1999.

France, Richard T. *Philippians*. Leicester; IVP, 1959.

Fredricksen, Paula. "Paul at the Races. Some Sports Fans Consider Athletics a Religion: It Used to Be." *Bible Review* 18.3 (2002): 12, 42.

Freyne, Sean. "Early Christianity and the Greek Athletic Ideal." Pages 93–100 in *Sport*. Edited by Gregory Baum and John Coleman. Edinburgh: T&T Clark, 1989.

Frick, Peter. *Divine Providence in Philo of Alexandria*. Texts and Studies in Ancient Judaism 77. Tübingen: Mohr Siebeck, 1999.

Friesen, Steven J. "Paul and Economics: The Jerusalem Collection as an Alternative to Patronage." Pages 27–54 in *Paul Unbound: Other Perspectives on the Apostle*. Edited by Mark D. Given. Peabody: Hendrickson, 2010.

Fröhlich, Pierre, and Patrice Hamon, eds. *Groupes et associations dans les cités grecques (IIIe siècle av. J.-C.–IIe siècle ap. J.-C.* Geneva: Librairie Droz, 2013.

Frye, Northrop. "*The Decline of the West* by Oswald Spengler." *Daedalus* 103.1 (1974): 1–13.

Fung, Ronald Y. K. "Ministry, Community and Spiritual Gifts." *Evangelical Quarterly* 66.1 (1984): 3–20.

Furnish, Victor P. *Theology and Ethics in Paul*. Nashville: Abingdon, 1968.

–. *II Corinthians*. New York: Doubleday, 1984.

Futrell, Alison. *The Roman Games: A Sourcebook*. Malden and Oxford: Blackwell, 2006.

Gabriel, Merigala. *Subjectivity and Religious Truth in the Philosophy of Søren Kierkegaard*. Macon: Mercer University Press, 2010.
Gaffney, John, and Diana Holmes. *Stardom in Postwar France.* New York: Berghahn Books, 2007.
Gagé, Jean. *Res Gestae Divi Augustae ex Monumentis Ancyrano et Antiocheno Latinis Ancyrano et Apolloniensi Graecis*. Paris: Les Belles Lettres, 1935.
Gager, John G. *The Origins of Anti-Semitism: Attitudes Towa rd Judaism in Pagan and Christian Antiquity*. New York and Oxford: Oxford University Press, 1985.
Gaines, Robert N. "Cicero, Philodemus, and the Development of Late Hellenistic Rhetorical Theory." Pages 91–100 in *Philodemus and the New Testament*. Novum Testamentum Supplement 111. Edited by John T. Fitzgerald, Dirk Obbink, and Glenn S. Holland. Leiden: Brill, 2004.
Galinsky, Karl. *Augustan Culture: An Interpretive Introduction*. Princeton: Princeton University Press, 1996.
Galow, Timothy W. *Writing Celebrity: Stein, Fitzgerald, and the Modern(ist) Art of Self-Fashioning*. New York: Palgrave Macmillan, 2011.
Gamson, Joshua. "The Unwatched Life Is Not Worth Living: The Elevation of the Ordinary in Celebrity Culture." *PMLA* 126.4 (2011): 1061–1069.
Garde-Hansen, Joanne. "Measuring Mourning with Online Media: Michael Jackson and Real-time Memories." *Celebrity Studies* 1.2. (2010): 233–235.
Gardiner, E. Norman. *Athletics of the Ancient World*. Chicago: Ares Publishers, 1930.
Garland, David E. *2 Corinthians*. Nashville: Broadman & Holman, 1999.
–. *1 Corinthians*. Grand Rapids: Baker Academic, 2003.
Garland, Robert. *Celebrity in Antiquity: From Media Tarts to Tabloid Queens*. London: Duckworth, 2006.
Garofalo, Daniela. "Communities in Mourning: Making Capital Out of Loss in Carlyle's Past and Present and Heroes." *Texas Studies in Literature and Language* 45.3 (2003): 293–314.
Garrison, Roman. "Paul's Use of the Athlete Metaphor in 1 Corinthians 9." Pages 95–104 in *The Graeco-Roman Context of Early Christian Literature*. Edited by Roman Garrison. Sheffield: Sheffield University Press, 1997.
Gauthier, Philippe. "Bienfaiteurs du gymnase au Létôon de Xanthos." *Revue des études grecques* 109.1 (1996): 1–34.
–. "Notes sur le rôle du gymnase dans les cités hellénistiques." Pages 531–550 in Philippe Gauthier, Études d'histoire et d'institutions grecques: choix d'écrits (édité et indexé par Denis Rousset). École pratique des hautes études, scienc*es historiques et philologiques – III.* Hautes études du monde gréco-romain 47. Genève: Librairie Droz, 2011.
–. "Un gymnasiarche honoré à Colophon." Pages 661–673 in Philippe Gauthier, Études d'histoire et d'institutions grecques: choix d'écrits (édité et indexé par Denis Rousset). École pratique des hautes études, scienc*es historiques et philologiques – III.* Hautes études du monde gréco-romain 47. Genève: Librairie Droz, 2011.
Gauthier, Philippe, and Miltiades B. Hatzopoulos. *La loi gymnasiarchique de Beroia*. Athens: Centre de recherches de l'antiquité grecque et romaine, 1993.
Gaventa, Beverly R. "Galatians 1 and 2: Autobiography as Paradigm." *Novum Testamentum* 28.4 (1986): 309–326.
Gebhard, Elizabeth R. "The Isthmian Games and the Sanctuary of Poseidon in the Early Empire." Pages 78–94 in *The Corinthia in the Roman Period*. Edited by Timothy E. Gregory. Ann Arbor: Journal of Roman Archaeology, 1993.

Gehring, Roger W. *House Church and Mission: The Importance of Household Structures in Early Christianity.* Peabody: Hendrickson, 2004; German original 2000.
Gelzer, Matthias. *The Roman Nobility.* Translated by Robin Seager. 2nd edition. Oxford: Basil Blackwell, 1975; German original 1912.
Georgi, Dieter. *The Opponents of Paul in Second Corinthians.* Edinburgh: T&T Clark, 1987.
Gerlach, Julius. ΑΝΗΡ ΑΓΑΘΟΣ. Munich: J. Lehmaier, 1932.
Getty, Mary A. "The Imitation of Paul in the Letters to the Thessalonians." Pages 277–283 in *The Thessalonian Correspondence.* Edited by Raymond F. Collins and Norbert Baumert. Leuven: Leuven University Press, 1990.
Giblin, Charles H. *In Hope of God's Glory.* New York: Herder and Herder, 1970.
Gibson, Margaret. "Guest Editorial: Some Thoughts on Celebrity Deaths: Steve Irwin and the Issue of Public Mourning." *Mortality* 12.1 (2007): 1–3.
Gildenhard, Ingo. *Creative Eloquence: The Construction of Reality in Cicero's Speeches.* Oxford and New York: Oxford University Press, 2011.
Gill, David W.J. "The Importance of Roman Portraiture for Head-coverings in 1 Cor 11:2–16." *Tyndale Bulletin* 41 (1990): 245–260.
Gignilliat, Mark. *Paul and Isaiah's Servants: Paul's Theological Reading of Isaiah 40–66 in 2 Corinthians 5:14–6:10.* Library of 330. London and New York: T&T Clark, 2007.
Gingras, Marie T. "Annalistic Format, Tacitean Themes and the Obituaries of 'Annals' 3." *Classical Journal* 87.3 (1992): 241–256.
Ginsburg, Michael. "Roman Military Clubs and Their Social Functions," *Transactions of the American Philological Association* 71 (1940): 149–156.
Glad, Clarence E. *Paul and Philodemus: Adaptability in Epicurean and Early Christian Psychagogy.* Novum Testamentum Supplement 81. Leiden: Brill, 1995.
Goesler, Lisette. "*Advice to the Bride and Groom*: Plutarch Gives a Detailed Account of His Views on Marriage." Pages 97–115 in *Plutarch's* Advice to the Bride and Groom *and* A Consolation to His Wife*: English Translation, Commentary, Interpretative Essays, and Bibliography.* Edited by Sarah B. Pomeroy. New York and Oxford: Oxford University Press, 1999.
Golden, Leon. "Plato's Concept of *Mimesis.*" *British Journal of Aesthetics* 15 (1975–1976): 118–131.
–. *Aristotle on Tragic and Comic Mimesis.* Atlanta: Scholars, 1992.
Gooch, Peter D. *Dangerous Food: 1 Corinthians 8–10 in Its Context.* Studies in Christianity and Judaism 5. Ontario: Wilfrid Laurier University Press, 1993.
Goodenough, Erwin R. "The Political Philosophy of Hellenistic Kingship." *Yale Classical Studies* 1 (1928): 55–102.
Goodrich, John K. *Paul as Administrator of God in 1 Corinthians.* Society for New Testament Studies Monograph Series 152. Cambridge: Cambridge University Press, 2012.
Gorman, Michael J. *Cruciformity: Paul's Narrative Spirituality of the Cross.* Grand Rapids: Eerdmans, 2001.
–. *Inhabiting the Cruciform God: Kenosis, Justification, and Theosis in Paul's Narrative Theology* Grand Rapids: Eerdmans, 2009.
Gosbell, Louise A. "*The Poor, the Crippled, the Blind, and the Lame*": *Physical and Sensory Disability in the Gospels of the New Testament.* Wissenschaftliche Untersuchungen zum Neuen Testament II 469. Tübingen: Mohr Siebeck, 2018.
Grabbe, Lester L. *Judaism from Cyrus to Hadrian.* London: SCM, 1992.

Grant, Frederick C., ed. *Ancient Roman Religion*. New York: The Library of Religion, 1957.

Grant, Michael. *Roman History from Coins: Some Uses of the Imperial Coinage to the Historian*. Cambridge: Cambridge University Press, 1968.

–. *The Roman Forum*. London: Weidenfeld & Nicolson, 1970.

Gray, Benjamin D. "Philosophy of Education and the Late Hellenistic Polis." Pages 233–254 in *Epigraphical Approaches to the Post-Classical Polis*. Edited by Paraskevi Martzavou and Nikolaos Papazarkadas. Oxford: Oxford University Press, 2013.

Griffin, Miriam T. *Nero: The End of a Dynasty*. New Haven/London: Yale University Press, 1984.

Gruen, Erich S. "The Roman Oligarchy: Image and Perception." Pages 215–234 in *Imperium Sine Fine: T.S. Roberts and the Roman Republic*. Edited by Jerzy Linderski. Stuttgart: Franz Steiner Verlag, 1966.

Guthrie, Kenneth S. *The Pythagorean Sourcebook and Library*. Grand Rapids: Phanes, 1987.

Gutierrez, Pedro. *La paternité spirituelle selon Saint Paul*. Paris: J. Gabalda, 1968.

Güttgemanns, Erhardt. *Der leidende Apostel und sein Herr*. Göttingen: Vandenhoeck & Ruprecht, 1966.

Habinek, Thomas, and Allesandro Schiesaro, eds. *The Roman Cultural Revolution*. Cambridge: Cambridge University Press, 1997.

Hadas-Lebel, Mireille. *Jerusalem against Rome*. Leuven/Dudley: Peeters, 2006.

Hafemann, Scott J. *Paul, Moses, and the History of Israel: The Letter/Spirit Contrast and the Argument from Scripture in 2 Corinthians 3*. Peabody: Hendrickson, 1996.

–. *2 Corinthians*. Grand Rapids: Zondervan, 2000.

Hall, Edith, and Rosie Wyles, eds. *New Directions in Ancient Pantomime*. New York: Oxford University Press, 2008.

Halliwell, Stephen. *The Aesthetics of Mimesis: Ancient Texts, Modern Problems*. Princeton: Princeton University Press, 2002.

Hammerton-Kelly, Robert G. "A Girardian Interpretation of Paul: Rivalry, *Mimesis*, and Victimage in the Corinthian Correspondence." *Semeia* 33 (1985): 65–81.

Hammond, Mason. "The Sincerity of Augustus." *Harvard Studies in Classical Philology* 69 (1965): 139–152.

Han, Cheon-Seoul. *Raised for Our Justification: An Investigation on the Significance of the Resurrection of Christ within the Theological Structure of Paul's Message*. Kampen: Uitgeverij Kok, 1995.

Hanchey, Daniel P. *Cicero the Dialogician: The Construction of Community at the End of the Republic*. PhD dissertation. University of Texas, 2009.

Hands, Arthur R. *Charities and Social Aid in Greece and Rome*. London and Southampton: Thames and Hudson, 1968.

Hanges, James C. *Paul, Founder of Churches: A Study in Light of the Evidence for the Role of "Founder-Figures" in the Hellenistic-Roman Period*. Wissenschaftliche Untersuchungen zum Neuen Testament I 292. Tübingen: Mohr Siebeck, 2012.

Hanson, Anthony T. *The Pioneer Ministry*. Revised edition. London: SPCK, 1975.

Hardie, Philip. *Rumour and Renown: Representations of* Fama *in Western Literature*. Cambridge: Cambridge University Press, 2012.

Hardison, Osborne B. "Epigone: An Aristotelian Imitation." Pages 281–296 in *Aristotle's Poetics*. Edited by Leon Golden and Osborne B. Hardison. Englewood Cliffs: Prentice Hall, 1968.

Hargreaves, Jennifer. *Heroines of Sport: The Politics of Difference and Identity*. London: Routledge, 2000.
Harland, Philip A. "Honours and Worship: Emperors, Imperial Cults and Associations at Ephesus (First to Third Centuries CE)." *Studies in Religion/Sciences Religieuses* 25 (1996): 319–334.
–. *Associations, Synagogues and Congregations: Claiming a Place in Ancient Mediterranean Society*. Minneapolis: Fortress, 2003.
–. "Familial Dimensions of Group Identity: 'Brothers' (ἀδελφοί) in Associations of the Greek East." *Journal of Biblical Literature* 124 (2005): 491–513.
–. "Familial Dimensions of Group Identity (II): 'Mothers' and 'Fathers' in Associations and Synagogues of the Greek World." *Journal for the Study of Judaism in the Persian, Hellenistic and Roman Period* 38 (2007): 57–79.
–. *Dynamics of Identity in the World of the Early Christians: Associations, Judeans, and Cultural Minorities*. New York: Continuum/T&T Clark, 2009.
–. *Greco-Roman Associations: Texts, Translations and Commentary. II. North Coast of the Black Sea, Asia Minor*. Beihefte zur Zeitschrift für die neutestamentliche Wissenschaft 204. Berlin and Boston: De Gruyter, 2014.
Harries, Jill. *Cicero and the Jurists: From Citizen's Law to Lawful State*. London: Duckworth, 2006.
Harris, Bruce F. "The Idea of Mercy and Its Graeco-Roman Context." Pages 89–105 in *God Who is Rich in Mercy: Essays Presented to D. B. Knox*. Edited by Peter T. O'Brien and David G. Peterson. Homebush West: Lancer, 1986 .
Harris, Harold A. *Greek Athletics and the Jews*. Cardiff: University of Wales Press, 1976.
Harris, Murray J. *The Second Epistle to the Corinthians*. Grand Rapids: Eerdmans, 2005.
Harrison, James R. "Paul and the Cultic Associations." *Reformed Theological Review* 58.1 (1999): 31–47.
–. "Paul, Eschatology and the Augustan Age of Grace." *Tyndale Bulletin* 50.1 (1999): 79–91.
–. "Paul's House Churches and the Cultic Associations." *Reformed Theological Review* 58.1 (1999): 31–44.
–. "Excels Ancestral Honours." *New Docs* 9 (2002): 20–21.
–. "A Share in All the Sacrifices." *New Docs* 9 (2002): 1–3.
–. "Times of Necessity." *New Docs* 9 (2002): 7–8.
–. "'The Fading Crown': Divine Honour and the Early Christians." *Journal of Theological Studies* 54.2 (2003): 493–529.
–. *Paul's Language of Grace in Its Graeco-Roman Context*. Wissenschaftliche Untersuchungen zum Neuen Testament II 172. Tübingen: Mohr Siebeck, 2003.
–. "In Quest of the Third Heaven: Paul and His Apocalyptic Imitators." *Vigiliae Christianae* 58.1 (2004): 24–55.
–. "Paul and the Athletic Ideal in Antiquity: A Case Study in Wrestling with Word and Image." Pages 81–109 in *Paul's World*. Pauline Studies 4. Edited by Stanley E. Porter. Leiden: Brill, 2008.
–. "Paul and the Gymnasiarchs: Two Approaches to Pastoral Formation in Antiquity." Pages 141–178 in *Paul: Jew, Greek, and Roman*. Pauline Studies, Pauline Studies 5. Edited by Stanley E. Porter. Leiden: Brill, 2008.
–. "Paul and the Roman Ideal of Glory in the Epistle to the Romans." Pages 323–363 in *The Epistle to the Romans*. Bibliotheca Ephemeridum Theologicarum Lovaniensium 226. Edited by Udo Schnelle. Leuven and Walpole: Peeters, 2009.

–. "The Brothers as the 'Glory of Christ' (2 Cor 8:23): Paul's Doxa Terminology in Its Ancient Benefaction Context." *Novum Testamentum* 52.2 (2010): 156–188.
–. "'More Than Conquerors' (Rom 8:37): Paul's Gospel and the Augustan Triumphal Arches of the Greek East and Latin West." *Buried History* 47 (2011): 3–21.
–. *Paul and the Imperial Authorities at Thessalonica and Rome: A Study in the Conflict of Ideology*. Wissenschaftliche Untersuchungen zum Neuen Testament I 273. Tübingen: Mohr Siebeck, 2011.
–. "Diplomacy over Tiberius Succession." *New Docs* 10 (2012): 64–75.
–. "Family Honour of a Priestess of Artemis." *New Docs* 10 (2012): 30–36.
–. "The 'Grace' of Augustus Paves a Street at Ephesus." *New Docs* 10 (2012): 59–63.
–. "Paul and the Social Relations of Death at Rome (Rom 5:14, 17, 21)." Pages 161–184 in *Paul and His Social Relations*. Pauline Studies 7. Edited by Stanley E. Porter. Leiden: Brill, 2012.
–. "Augustan Rome and the Body of Christ: A Comparison of the Social Vision of the Res Gestae and Paul's Letter to the Romans." *Harvard Theological Review* 106.1 (2013): 1–36.
–. "The Imitation of the Great Man in Antiquity: Paul's Inversion of a Cultural Icon." Pages 213–254 in *Christian Origins and Classical Culture: Social and Literary Contexts for the New Testament*. Edited by Stanley E. Porter and Andrew W. Pitts. Leiden: Brill, 2013.
–. "Paul's 'Indebtedness' to the Barbarian (Rom 1:14) in Latin West Perspective." *Novum Testamentum* 55.4 (2013): 311–348.
–. "Paul among the Romans." Pages 143–176 in *All Things to All Cultures: Paul Among Jews, Greeks, and Romans*. Edited by Mark Harding and Alanna Nobbs. Grand Rapids: Eerdmans, 2013.
–. "The Politics of Family Beneficence: Paul's "Parenthood" in First-Century Context (2 Cor 12:14–16)." Pages 399–426 in *Theologizing in the Corinthian Conflict: Studies in Exegesis and Theology of 2 Corinthians*. Edited by Reimund Beiringer, Dominika Kurek-Chomycz, and M. Marilou S. Ibita. Leuven: Peeters, 2013.
–. "The First Urban Churches: Introduction." Pages 1–40 in *The First Urban Churches. Volume 2: Roman Corinth*. Edited by James R. Harrison and Larry L. Welborn. Atlanta: SBL Press, 2016.
–. "The Erasure of Honour: Paul and the Politics of Dishonour." *Tyndale Bulletin* 66.2 (2016): 85–123.
–. "Paul and the *agōnothetai* at Corinth: Engaging the Civic Values of Antiquity." Pages 271–326 in *The First Urban Churches. Volume 2: Roman Corinth*. Edited by James R. Harrison and Larry L. Welborn. Atlanta: SBL Press, 2016.
–. "The Seven Sages, the Delphic Canon and Ethical Education in Antiquity." Pages 71–86 in *Ancient Education and Early Christianity*. Edited by Matthew R. Hauge and Andrew W. Pitts. London and New York: Bloomsbury T&T Clark, 2016.
–. "Sponsors of *Paideia*: Ephesian Benefactors, Civic Virtue and the New Testament." *Early Christianity* 7 (2016): 346–367.
–. "Who is the 'Lord of Grace'? Jesus' Parables in Imperial Context." Pages 383–417 in *Border: Terms, Ideologies and Performances*. Wissenschaftliche Untersuchungen zum Neuen Testament I 336. Edited by Annette Weissenrieder. Tübingen: Mohr Siebeck, 2016.

–. "The Persecution of Christians from Nero to Hadrian." Pages 266–300 in *Into All the World: Emergent Christianity in its Jewish and Greco-Roman Context.* Edited by Mark Harding and Alanna Nobbs. Grand Rapids: Eerdmans, 2017.
–. "The Citizenship Decrees of Hellenistic Ephesus and the *Politeuma* of Roman Philippi: Evaluating Paul's 'Alternative' Citizenship in Epigraphic and Papyrological Context." In *New Documents Illustrating the History of Early Christianity. Volume 11: Ephesus.* Edited by James R. Harrison and Bradley J. Bitner. Grand Rapids: Eerdmans, forthcoming.
Hartin, Patrick J. *Apollos: Paul's Partner or Rival?* Collegeville: Liturgical Press, 2009.
Harvey, Anthony E. *Renewal Through Suffering: A Study of 2 Corinthians.* Edinburgh: T&T Clark, 1996.
Harwood, Gwen. *Collected Poems 1943–1995.* Edited by Alison Hoddinott and Gregory Kratzmann. St Lucia: University of Queensland Press, 2003.
Hasluck, Frederick W. "Inscriptions from the Cyzicus District." *Journal of Hellenic Studies* 27 (1907): 61–67.
Hatch, Edwin. *The Organisation of the Early Christian Churches.* Oxford and Cambridge: Rivingtons, 1881.
Hauge, Matthew R., and Andrew W. Pitts, eds. *Ancient Education and Early Christianity.* London and New York: Bloomsbury T&T Clark, 2016.
Hawhee, Debra. *Bodily Arts: Athletic and Rhetorical Training in Antiquity.* PhD dissertation. The Pennsylvania State University, 2000.
Hawley, Richard. "Practising What You Preach: Plutarch's Sources and Treatment." Pages 116–117 in *Plutarch's* Advice to the Bride and Groom *and* A Consolation to His Wife*: English Translation, Commentary, Interpretative Essays, and Bibliography.* Edited by Sarah B. Pomeroy. New York and Oxford: Oxford University Press, 1999.
Hawthorne, Gerald F. "In the Form of God and Equal with God." Pages 96–110 in *Where Christology Began: Essays on Philippians 2.* Edited by Ralph P. Martin and Brian J. Dodd. Louisville: Westminster John Knox Press, 1998.
Hay, David M. *Colossians.* Nashville: Abingdon, 2000.
Head, Barclay V. *A Catalogue of the Greek Coins of the British Museum: Central Greece. Locris, Phocis, Boetia and Euboea.* London: Longmans, 1884.
Heinrici, Georg. "Die Christengemeinden Korinths und die religiösen Genossenschaften der Griechen." *Zeitschrift für wissenschaftliche Theologie* 19 (1876): 465–526.
–. "Zur Geschichte der Anfänge paulinischer Gemeinden." *Zeitschrift für wissenschaftliche Theologie* 20 (1877): 89–130.
Hellegouarc'h, Joseph. *Le vocabulaire Latin des relations et des partis politiques sous la* République. Paris: Les Belles Lettres, 1963.
–. "Etat présent des travaux sur l''Histoire Romaine' de Velléius Paterculus." *Aufstieg und Niedergang der römischen Welt* 2.32.1 (1984): 401–436.
Hellerman, Joseph. *Reconstructing Honor in Roman Philippi: Carmen Christi as* Cursus Pudorum. Society for New Testament Studies Monograph Series 132. Cambridge: Cambridge University Press, 2005.
–. *Embracing Shared Ministry: Power and Status in the Early Church and Why It Matters Today.* Grand Rapids: Kregel, 2013.
Hellmueller, Lea C., and Nina Aeschbacher. "Media and Celebrity: Production and Consumption of 'Well-Knownness'." *Communication and Research Trends* 29.4 (2010): 3–35.
Henderson, John. *Figuring Out Roman Nobility.* Exeter: University of Exeter Press, 1997.

Henderson, Walter E. "The Athletic Imagery of Paul." *Theological Educator* 56 (1997): 30–37.

Hendrix, Holland L. *Thessalonians Honor Romans.* PhD dissertation. Harvard University, 1984.

–. "Beyond 'Imperial Cult' and 'Cults of Magistrates'." Pages 301–308 in *Society of Biblical Literature 1986 Seminar Papers.* Edited by Harold R. Kent. Chico: Scholars, 1986.

–. "On the Form and Ethos of Ephesians." *Union Seminary Quarterly Review* 42.4 (1988): 3–15.

–. "Benefactor/Patron Networks in the Urban Environment: Evidence from Thessalonica." *Semeia* 56 (1992): 39–58.

Hengel, Martin. *Crucifixion in the Ancient World and the Folly of the Message of the Cross.* Philadelphia: Fortess, 1977.

Herbert, Zbigniew. *The Passion of our Lord painted by an anonymous hand from the circle of Rhenish Masters.* Page 209 in David Curzon, *The Gospels in Our Image: An Anthology of Twentieth-Century Poetry Based on Biblical Texts.* New York et al.: Harcourt Brace and Co., 1995.

Hersch, Karen K. *The Roman Wedding: Ritual and Meaning in Antiquity.* Cambridge: Cambridge University Press, 2010.

Herwitz, Daniel A. *The Star as Icon: Celebrity in the Age of Mass Consumption.* New York: Columbia University Press, 2008.

Hillard, Tom. "Augustus and the Evolution of Roman Concepts of Leadership." *Ancient History: Resources for Teachers* 38.2 (2011): 107–152.

Hock, Ronald F. *The Social Context of Paul's Ministry: Tentmaking and Apostleship.* Fortress: Philadelphia, 1980.

Hodge, A. Trevor. "The Mystery of Apollo's E at Delphi." *American Journal of Archaeology* 85.1 (1981): 83–84.

Hoehner, Harold. W. *Ephesians: An Exegetical Commentary.* Grand Rapids: Eerdmans, 2003.

Holmberg, Bengt. *Paul and Power: The Structure of Authority in the Primitive Churches as Reflected in the Pauline Epistles.* Philadelphia: Fortress, 1980.

Holmén, Tom. "Jesus and the Purity Paradigm." Pages 2709–2744 in *Handbook for the Study of the Historical Jesus. Volume 3: The Historical Jesus.* Edited by Tom Holmén and Stanley E. Porter. Leiden and Boston: Brill, 2011.

Hock, Ronald F. *The Social Context of Paul's Ministry: Tentmaking and Apostleship.* Philadelphia: Fortress, 1980.

Holt, Frank L. "Discovering the Lost History of Ancient Afghanistan: Hellenistic Bactria in the Light of Recent Archaeological and Historical Research." *The Ancient World* 9 (1984): 3–11.

–. *Thundering Zeus: The Making of Hellenistic Bactria.* Berkeley and Los Angeles: University of California Press, 1999.

Hooker, Morna D. *Not Ashamed of the Gospel: New Testament Interpretations of the Death of Christ.* Grand Rapids: Eerdmans, 1994.

Hornblower, Simon, and Anthony J.S. Spawforth. *The Oxford Classical Dictionary.* 3rd edition. Oxford: Oxford University Press, 1996.

Horrell, David G. *The Social Ethos of the Corinthian Correspondence: Interests and Ideology from 1 Corinthians to 1 Clement.* Edinburgh: T&T Clark, 1996.

–. "Idol-Food, Idolatry and Ethics in Paul." Pages 120–140 in *Idolatry: False Worship in the Bible, Early Judaism and Christianity*. Edited by Stephen C. Barton. London and New York: T&T Clark, 2007.
Horsley, Greg H.R. "Joining the Household of Caesar." *New Docs* 3 (1983): 7–9.
–. "A More Than Perfect Wife." *New Docs* 3 (1983): 33–36
–. "A Woman's Virtues." *New Docs* 3 (1983): 40–43.
–. "An *archsynagogos* of Corinth?" *New Docs* 4 (1987): 213–220.
–. "Speak No Evil." *New Docs* 4 (1987): 42–46.
–. "A Fishing Cartel in First-Century Ephesos." *New Docs* 5 (1989): 95–114.
Horsley, Greg H.R., and John A.L. Lee. "A Preliminary Checklist of Abbreviations of Greek Epigraphic Volumes." *Epigraphica* 66 (1994): 129–170.
Howe, P. David, and Andrew Parker. "Celebrating Imperfection: Sport, Disability, and Celebrity Culture." *Celebrity Studies* 3.3 (2012): 270–282.
Hubbard, Thomas K., ed. *Homosexuality in Greece and Rome*. Berkeley: University of California Press, 2003.
Hughes, Philip E. *The Second Epistle to the Corinthians*. Grand Rapids: Eerdmans, 1962.
Humphrey, John H. *Roman Circuses: Arenas for Chariot Racing*. Berkeley: University of California Press, 1986.
Hurtado, Larry W. "Jesus as Lordly Example in Philippians 2:5–11." Pages 113–126 in *From Jesus to Paul: Studies in Honour of Francis Wright Beare*. Edited by Peter Richardson and John C. Hurd. Waterloo: Wilfrid Laurier University Press, 1984.
–. *God in New Testament Theology*. Nashville: Abingdon, 2010.
–. "The Staurogram: Earliest Depiction of Jesus' Crucifixion." *Biblical Archaeology Review* 39.2 (2013): 49–52, 63.
Husband, Terence J. *Cicero and the Moral Education of Youth*. PhD thesis. Georgetown University, 2013.
Huys, Marc. "P. Oxy. 61.4099: A Combination of Mythographic Lists with Sentences of the Seven Wise Men." *Zeitschrift für Papyrologie und Epigraphik* 113 (1996): 205–212.
Inglis, Fred. *A Short History of Celebrity*. Princeton: Princeton University Press, 2010.
Institut Fernand Courby. *Nouveau choix d'inscriptions grecques: textes, traductions, commentaires*. Paris: Société d'édition Les Belles Lettres, 1971.
Ismard, Paulin. *La cité des réseaux. Athènes et ses associations VIe–Ier siècle av. J.-C.* Paris: Publications de la Sorbonne, 2010.
Jacob, Edmond. *Theology of the Old Testament*. London: Hodder and Stoughton, 1958.
Jacobi, Martin. "Bob Dylan and Collaboration." Pages 69–79 in *The Cambridge Companion to Bob Dylan*. Edited by Kevin J.H. Dettmar. Cambridge and New York: Cambridge University Press, 2009.
Jaeger, Werner. *Paideia: The Ideals of Greek Culture*. 3 volumes. Oxford: Blackwell, 1946.
Jaffe, Aaron. *Modernism and the Culture of Celebrity*. Cambridge and New York: Cambridge University Press, 2004.
Jennings, Mark A. "Patronage and Rebuke in Paul's Persuasion in 2 Cor 8–9." *Journal of Greco-Roman Christianity and Judaism* 6 (2009): 107–127.
Jervell, Jacob. *Imago Dei. Gen. 1, 26 f, in Spätjudentum, in der Gnosis und in den paulinischen Briefen*. Göttingen: Vandenhoeck & Ruprecht, 1960.
Jewett, Robert. "Tenement Churches and Communal Meals in the Early Church: The Implications of a Form-Critical Analysis of 2 Thessalonians 3:10." *Biblical Research* 38 (1993): 23–43.

–. "Paul, Shame and Honor." Pages 551–574 in *Paul in the Greco-Roman World*. Edited by J. Paul Sampley. Harrisburg: Trinity Press International, 2003.

–. *Romans: A Commentary*. Hermeneia. Minneapolis: Fortress, 2007.

Johnson, Allan C., Paul R. Coleman-Norton, and Frank C. Bourne. *Ancient Roman Statutes*. Austin: University of Texas Press, 1961.

Jones, Arnold H. M. *Augustus*. New York: Norton, 1970.

Jones, Brian W., and Robert D. Milns. *The Use of Documentary Evidence in the Study of Roman Imperial History*. Netley: Sydney University Press, 1984.

Jones, Christine H. *Bob Dylan and the End of the (Modern) World*. PhD dissertation. University of Texas, Dallas, 2013.

Jones, Christopher P. *The Roman World of Dio Chrysostom*. Cambridge, MA: Harvard University Press, 1978.

–. "Dinner Theatre." Page 198 in *Dining in a Classical Context*. Edited by William J. Slater. Ann Arbor: University of Michigan Press, 1991.

Jones, Max. "What Should Historians Do with Heroes? Reflections on Nineteenth- and Twentieth-Century Britain." *History Compass* 5.2 (2007): 439–454.

Jones, Tamara. *Seating and Spectacle in the Graeco-Roman World*. PhD dissertation. McMaster University, 2008.

Joubert, Stephan J. "Managing the Household: Paul as *Paterfamilias* of the Christian Household Group in Corinth." Pages 213–223 in *Modelling Early Christianity: Social-Scientific Studies of the New Testament in Its Context*. Edited by Philip F. Esler. London: Routledge, 1995.

–. *Paul as Benefactor: Reciprocity, Strategy and Theological Reflection in Paul's Collection*. Tübingen: Mohr Siebeck, 2000.

Judge, Edwin A. "The Roman Nobility: Study Guide No. 2." Macquarie University Ancient History Department, 1973.

–. "Moral Terms in the Eulogistic Tradition." *New Docs* 2 (1982): 105–106.

–. "The Quest for Mercy in Late Antiquity." Pages 107–121 in *God Who is Rich in Mercy: Essays Presented to D. B. Knox*. Edited by Peter T. O'Brien and David G. Peterson. Homebush West: Lancer, 1986.

–. "A Woman's Behaviour." *New Docs* 6 (1992): 18–23.

–. "The Augustan Republic: Tiberius and Claudius on Roman History." Pages 127–139 in Edwin A. Judge, *The First Christians in the Roman World: Augustan and New Testament Essays*. Wissenschaftliche Untersuchungen zum Neuen Testament I 229. Edited by James R. Harrison. Tübingen: Mohr Siebeck, 2008.

–. "Augustus in the *Res Gestae*." Pages 182–223 in Edwin A. Judge, *The First Christians in the Roman World: Augustan and New Testament Essays*. Wissenschaftliche Untersuchungen zum Neuen Testament I 229. Edited by James R. Harrison. Tübingen: Mohr Siebeck, 2008.

–. "Contemporary Political Models for the Inter-Relations of the New Testament Churches." Pages 586–96 in Edwin A. Judge, *The First Christians in the Roman World: Augustan and New Testament Essays*. Wissenschaftliche Untersuchungen zum Neuen Testament I 229. Edited by James R. Harrison. Tübingen: Mohr Siebeck, 2008.

–. "*Contemptu famae contemni* virtutes: On the Morality of Self-advertisement among the Romans." Pages 59–65 in Edwin A. Judge, *The First Christians in the Roman World: Augustan and New Testament Essays*. Wissenschaftliche Untersuchungen zum Neuen Testament I 229. Edited by James R. Harrison. Tübingen: Mohr Siebeck, 2008.

–. "Demythologising the Church: What is the Meaning of the 'Body of Christ'?" Pages 586–596 in Edwin A. Judge, *The First Christians in the Roman World: Augustan and New Testament Essays.* Wissenschaftliche Untersuchungen zum Neuen Testament I 229. Edited by James R. Harrison. Tübingen: Mohr Siebeck, 2008.

–. "Did the Churches Compete with Cult Groups?" Pages 597–618 in Edwin A. Judge, *The First Christians in the Roman World: Augustan and New Testament Essays.* Wissenschaftliche Untersuchungen zum Neuen Testament I 229. Edited by James R. Harrison. Tübingen: Mohr Siebeck, 2008.

–. "The Early Christians as a Scholastic Community." Pages 526–552 in Edwin A. Judge, *The First Christians in the Roman World: Augustan and New Testament Essays.* Wissenschaftliche Untersuchungen zum Neuen Testament I 229. Edited by James R. Harrison. Tübingen: Mohr Siebeck, 2008.

–. "Ethical Terms in St Paul and the Ephesian Inscriptions." Pages 368–377 in Edwin A. Judge, *The First Christians in the Roman World: Augustan and New Testament Essays.* Wissenschaftliche Untersuchungen zum Neuen Testament I 229. Edited by James R. Harrison. Tübingen: Mohr Siebeck, 2008.

–. "The Eulogistic Inscriptions of the Augustan Forum: Augustus on Roman History." Pages 52–58 in Edwin A. Judge, *The First Christians in the Roman World: Augustan and New Testament Essays.* Wissenschaftliche Untersuchungen zum Neuen Testament I 229. Edited by James R. Harrison. Tübingen: Mohr Siebeck, 2008.

–. "First Impressions of St Paul." Pages 410–415 in Edwin A. Judge, *The First Christians in the Roman World: Augustan and New Testament Essays.* Wissenschaftliche Untersuchungen zum Neuen Testament I 229. Edited by James R. Harrison. Tübingen: Mohr Siebeck, 2008.

–. "On Judging the Merits of Augustus." Pages 224–313 in Edwin A. Judge, *The First Christians in the Roman World: Augustan and New Testament Essays.* Wissenschaftliche Untersuchungen zum Neuen Testament I 229. Edited by James R. Harrison. Tübingen: Mohr Siebeck, 2008.

–. "The Real Basis of Augustan Power." Pages 116–120 in Edwin A. Judge, *The First Christians in the Roman World: Augustan and New Testament Essays.* Wissenschaftliche Untersuchungen zum Neuen Testament I 229. Edited by James R. Harrison. Tübingen: Mohr Siebeck, 2008.

–. "The Reaction against Classical Education in the New Testament." Pages 709–716 in Edwin A. Judge, *The First Christians in the Roman World: Augustan and New Testament Essays.* Wissenschaftliche Untersuchungen zum Neuen Testament I 229. Edited by James R. Harrison. Tübingen: Mohr Siebeck, 2008.

–. "*Res Publica Restituta*: A Modern Illusion?" Pages 140–64 in Edwin A. Judge, *The First Christians in the Roman World: Augustan and New Testament Essays.* Wissenschaftliche Untersuchungen zum Neuen Testament I 229. Edited by James R. Harrison. Tübingen: Mohr Siebeck, 2008.

–. "The Roman Base of Paul's Mission." Pages 553–567 in Edwin A. Judge, *The First Christians in the Roman World: Augustan and New Testament Essays.* Wissenschaftliche Untersuchungen zum Neuen Testament I 229. Edited by James R. Harrison. Tübingen: Mohr Siebeck, 2008.

–. "The Second Thoughts of Syme on Augustus." Pages 314–345 in Edwin A. Judge, *The First Christians in the Roman World: Augustan and New Testament Essays.* Wissenschaftliche Untersuchungen zum Neuen Testament I 229. Edited by James R. Harrison. Tübingen: Mohr Siebeck, 2008.

–. "St Paul and Socrates." Pages 670–683 in Edwin A. Judge, *The First Christians in the Roman World: Augustan and New Testament Essays.* Wissenschaftliche Untersuchungen zum Neuen Testament I 229. Edited by James R. Harrison. Tübingen: Mohr Siebeck, 2008.

–. "*Veni. Vidi. Vici*, and the Inscription of Cornelius Gallus." Pages 72–75 in Edwin A. Judge, *The First Christians in the Roman World: Augustan and New Testament Essays.* Wissenschaftliche Untersuchungen zum Neuen Testament I 229. Edited by James R. Harrison. Tübingen: Mohr Siebeck, 2008.

–. "The Social Identity of the First Christians: A Question of Method in Religious History." Pages 117–135 in *Social Distinctives of the Christians in the First Century: Pivotal Essays by E. A. Judge.* Edited by David M. Scholer. Peabody: Hendrickson, 2008.

–. "Paul as a Radical Critic of Society." Pages 99–115 in *Social Distinctives of the Christians in the First Century: Pivotal Essays by E. A. Judge.* Edited by David M. Scholer. Peabody: Hendrickson, 2008.

–. "The Social Pattern of Christian Groups in the First Century." Pages 27–34 in *Social Distinctives of the Christians in the First Century: Pivotal Essays by E. A. Judge.* Edited by David M. Scholer. Peabody: Hendrickson, 2008.

–. "The Teacher as Moral Exemplar in Paul and in the Inscriptions of Ephesus." Pages 175–188 in *Social Distinctives of the Christians in the First Century: Pivotal Essays by E. A. Judge.* Edited by David M. Scholer. Peabody: Hendrickson, 2008.

–. "Ancient Beginnings of the Modern World." Pages 282–314 in Edwin A. Judge, *Jerusalem and Athens: Cultural Transformation in Late Antiquity.* Wissenschaftliche Untersuchungen zum Neuen Testament I 265. Edited by Alanna Nobbs. Tübingen: Mohr Siebeck, 2010.

–. "'*Antike und Christentum*': Some Recent Work from Cologne." Pages 69–79 in Edwin A. Judge, *Jerusalem and Athens: Cultural Transformation in Late Antiquity.* Wissenschaftliche Untersuchungen zum Neuen Testament I 265. Edited by Alanna Nobbs. Tübingen: Mohr Siebeck, 2010.

–. "The Ecumenical Synod of Dionysiac Artists." Pages 137–139 in Edwin A. Judge, *Jerusalem and Athens: Cultural Transformation in Late Antiquity.* Wissenschaftliche Untersuchungen zum Neuen Testament I 265. Edited by Alanna Nobbs. Tübingen: Mohr Siebeck, 2010.

–. "The Crux of RG 34.1 Resolved? Augustus on 28 BC." *New Docs* 10 (2012): 55–58.

–. "Higher Education in the Pauline Churches." Pages 21–31 in *Learning and Teaching Theology: Some Ways Ahead.* Edited by Les Ball and James R. Harrison. Eugene: Wipf and Stock, 2015.

–. *Paul and the Conflict of Cultures: The Legacy of His Thought Today.* Edited by James R. Harrison. Eugene: Cascade Books, 2019.

–. "The Changing Idea of the Great Man." In *Paul and the Conflict of Cultures: The Legacy of His Thought Today.* Edited by James R. Harrison. Eugene: Cascade Books, forthcoming.

Kah, Daniel, and Peter Scholz, eds. *Das hellenistische Gymnasion.* Berlin: Akademie Verlag, 2004.

Kahl, Brigitte. *Galatians Re-Imagined: Reading with the Eyes of the Vanquished.* Minneapolis: Fortress, 2010.

Kajava, Mika. "When Did the Isthmian Games Return to the Isthmus? Rereading Corinth 8.3.153." *Classical Philology* 97 (2002): 168–178.

Kearsley, Rosalinde A. "A Civic Benefactor of the First Century in Asia Minor." *New Docs* 7 (1994): 233–241.

Keck, Leander E. *Romans*. Nashville: Abingdon, 2005.

Keel, Othmar. *The Symbolism of the Biblical World: Near Eastern Iconography and the Book of Psalms*. London: SPCK, 1978, German original 1972.

Keeline, Thomas J. *A Rhetorical Figure: Cicero in the Early Empire*. PhD dissertation. Harvard University, 2014.

Keener, Craig S. *The Gospel of John: A Commentary. Volume Two*. Peabody: Hendrickson, 2003.

–. *The Historical Jesus of the Gospels*. Grand Rapids: Eerdmans, 2009.

–. *Acts: An Exegetical Commentary. Volume 3: 15:1–23:35*. Grand Rapids: Baker Academic, 2014.

Kennell, Nigel M. *The Gymnasium of Virtue: Education and Culture in Ancient Sparta*. Chapel Hill: University of North Carolina Press, 1995.

–. "The Greek Ephebate in the Roman Period." Pages 175–194 in *Sport in the Cultures of the Ancient World: New Perspectives*. Edited by Zinon Papakonstantinou. Milton Park: Routledge, 2010.

Kent, John H. *Corinth Volume VIII Part III: The Inscriptions 1926–1950*. Princeton: American School of Classical Studies at Athens, 1966.

Kerkeslager, Allen. "Maintaining Jewish Identity in the Greek Gymnasium: A Jewish 'Load' in CPJ 3.519." *Journal for the Study of Judaism* 28 (1997): 12–33.

Kim, Seyoon. *The Origin of Paul's Gospel*. Grand Rapids: Eerdmans, 1982.

–. "*Imitatio Christi* (1 Corinthians 11:1): How Paul Imitates Jesus Christ in Dealing with Idol Food (1 Corinthians 8–10)." *Bulletin for Biblical Research* 13.2 (2003): 193–226.

Kittel, Gerhard. "αὐτάρκεια." Pages 466–467 in *Theological Dictionary of the New Testament. Volume I*. Edited by Gerhard Kittel and Gerhard Friedrich. Translated by Geoffrey W. Bromiley. Grand Rapids: Eerdmans, 1964.

Klassen, William. "Musonius Rufus, Jesus and Paul: Three First-Century Feminists." Pages 185–206 in *From Jesus to Paul: Studies in Honour of Francis Wright Beare*. Edited by Peter Richardson and John C. Hurd. Waterloo: Wilfrid Laurier University Press, 1984.

Kloppenborg, John S. "Edwin Hatch, Churches, and *Collegia*." Pages 212–237 in *Origins and Method: Towards a New Understanding of Judaism and Christianity*. Journal for the Study of the New Testament Supplement 86. Edited by Bradley H. McLean. Sheffield: JSOT Press, 1993.

–. "Collegia and *Thiasoi*: Issues in Function, Taxonomy and Membership." Pages 16–30 in *Voluntary Associations in the Graeco-Roman World*. Edited by John S. Kloppenborg and Stephen G. Wilson. London: Routledge, 1996.

–. "Disaffiliation in Associations and the ἀποσυναγωγός of John." *HTS Teologiese Studies/Theological Studies* 67 (2011): 1–16.

–. "Greco-Roman *Thiasoi*, the *Ekklêsia* at Corinth, and Conflict Management." Pages 187–218 in *Redescribing Paul and the Corinthians*. Early Christianity and Its Literature 5. Edited by Ron Cameron and Merrill P. Miller. Atlanta: SBL Press, 2011.

–. "Membership Practices in Pauline Christ Groups," *Early Christianity* 4 (2013): 183–215.

–. "The Moralising of Discourse in Graeco-Roman Associations." Pages 215–228 in *'The One Who Sows Bountifully': Essays in Honor of Stanley K. Stowers*. Edited by Caroline J. Hodge, Saul M. Olyan, Daniel Ullucci, and Emma Wasserman. Providence: Brown Judaic Studies, 2013.

–. "Gaius the Roman Guest." *New Testament Studies* 63.4 (2017): 534–549.

Kloppenborg, John S., and Richard S. Ascough, eds. *Graeco-Roman Associations. Texts, Translations and Commentary. Attica, Central Greece, Macedonia, Thrace: Volume 1.* Berlin: De Gruyter, 2011.

Kloppenborg, John S., and Stephen G. Wilson, eds. *Voluntary Associations in the Graeco-Roman World.* London: Routledge, 1996.

Knibbe, Dieter. "*Via Sacra Ephesiaca*: New Aspects of the Cult of Artemis." Pages 141–155 in *Ephesos: Metropolis of Asia. An Interdisciplinary Approach to Its Archaeology, Religion, and Culture.* Edited by Helmut Koester. Valley Forge: Trinity International Press, 1995.

Knoll, Manuel. "The '*Übermensch*' as a Social and Political Task: A Study in the Continuity of Nietzsche's Political Thought." Pages 239–266 in *Nietzsche as a Political Philosopher.* Edited by Manuel Knoll and Barry Stocker. Berlin and Boston: De Gruyter, 2014.

Koester, Helmut, ed. *Cities of Paul: Images and Interpretations from the Harvard New Testament Archaeology Project.* Minneapolis: Fortress, 2005.

Koenig, John. *New Testament Hospitality: Partnership with Strangers as Promise and Salvation.* Philadelphia: Fortress, 1985.

Koller, Hermann. *Die* Mimesis *in der Antike.* Bern: Francke, 1954.

Kondratieff, Eric. "Column and Coinage of C. Duilius." *Scripta classica Israelica* 23 (2004): 1–39.

Konstan, David. *Friendship in the Classical World.* Cambridge: Cambridge University Press, 1997.

–. *Pity Transformed.* London: Duckworth, 2001.

–. *Before Forgiveness: The Origins of a Moral Idea.* Cambridge: Cambridge University Press, 2010.

Köstenberger, Andreas J. *John.* Grand Rapids: Baker Academic, 2004.

Kreitzer, Larry J. *Striking New Images: Roman Imperial Coinage and the New Testament World.* Journal for the Study of the New Testament Supplement 134. Sheffield: Sheffield Academic Press, 1996.

Krentz. Edgar. "Paul, Games, and the Military." Page 352 in *Paul in the Greco-Roman World: A Handbook.* Edited by J. Paul Sampley. Harrisburg: Trinity Press, 2003.

Kurke, Leslie. *Aesopic Conversations: Popular Tradition, Cultural Dialogue, and the Invention of Greek Prose.* Princeton and Oxford: Princeton University Press, 2011.

Kurz, William S. "Kenotic Imitation of Paul and of Christ in Philippians 2 and 3." Pages 103–126 in *Discipleship in the New Testament.* Edited by Fernando F. Segovia. Philadelphia: Fortress, 1985.

–. "Narrative Models for Imitation in Luke-Acts." Pages 171–181 in *Greeks, Romans, and Christians: Essays in Honor of Abraham J. Malherbe.* Edited by David L. Balch, Everett Ferguson, and Wayne A. Meeks. Minneapolis: Fortress, 1990.

Kyle, Donald G. *Spectacles of Death in Ancient Rome.* London and New York: Routledge, 1998.

Lada-Richards, Ismene. *Silent Eloquence: Lucian and Pantomime Dancing.* London and New York: Bloomsbury Academic, 2007.

Lamberton, Robert. *Plutarch.* Chelsea, MI: Sheridan Books, 2001.

Lambrecht, Jan. "The nekrõsis of Jesus: Ministry and Suffering in 2 Cor 4:7–15." Pages 120–143 in *L'Apôtre Paul.* Edited by Albert Vanhoye. Leuven: Uitgeverij Peeters, 1986.

–. “The Eschatological Outlook in 2 Corinthians 4:7–15.” Pages 122–139 in *To Tell the Mystery: Essays on New Testament Eschatology in Honor of Robert H. Gundry*. Journal for the Study of the New Testament Supplement 100. Edited by Thomas E. Schmidt and Moises Silva. Sheffield: JSOT Press, 1994.

–. *Second Corinthians*. Collegeville: Michael Glazier, 1999.

Lampe, Peter. “The Corinthian Eucharistic Dinner Party: Exegesis of a Cultural Context (1 Cor 11:17–34).” *Affirmation* 4.2 (1991): 1–15.

Last, Richard. *The Pauline Church and the Corinthian* Ekklēsia*: Greco-Roman Associations in Comparative Context*. Society for New Testament Studies Monograph Series 164. Cambridge: Cambridge University Press, 2016.

–. *The Other Christian Groups of Late Antiquity: Neighbourhood Networks, Occupational Guilds, and Trans-Local Writers’ Organizations*. Forthcoming.

Lattimore, Richard. *Themes in Greek and Latin Epitaphs*. Urbana: University of Illinois Press, 1962.

Lau, Te-Li P. *The Politics of Peace: Ephesians, Dio Chrysostom and the Confucian Tradition*, Novum Testamentum Supplement 133. Leiden, Brill, 2010.

Lee, Michelle V. *Paul, the Stoics, and the Body of Christ*. Society for New Testament Studies Monograph Series 137. Cambridge: Cambridge University Press, 2006.

Leeman, Anton D. *Gloria: Cicero’s waardering van de roem en haar achtergrond in de Hellenistische wijsbe geerte en de Romeinse samenleving*. Diss. Leiden. Rotterdam: N.V. Drukkerij M. Wijt & Zonen, 1949.

Lee-Stectum, Parshia. “Dangerous Reputations: Charioteers and Magic in Fourth-Century Rome.” *Greece & Rome* 53.2 (2006): 224–234.

Lefkowitz, Mary R., and Maureen B. Fant. *Women’s Life in Greece and Rome: A Source Book in Translation*. 3rd edition. London: Duckworth, 2005.

Legras, Bernard. “Violence ou douceur: Les normes éducatives dans les sociétés grecque et romaine.” *Histoire de l’éducation* 118 (2008): 11–34.

Leithart, Peter J. *Gratitude: An Intellectual History*. Waco: Baylor University Press, 2014.

Lendon, Jon E. *Empire of Honour: The Art of Government in the Roman World*. Oxford: Oxford University Press, 2002. Reprint.

Leneghan, John O. *A Commentary on Cicero’s Oration*. De haruspicum responso. The Hague and Paris: Mouton, 1969.

Leppin, Hartmut. “Between Marginality and Celebrity: Entertainers and Entertainments in Roman Society.” Pages 660–678 in *The Oxford Handbook of Social Relations in the Roman World*. Edited by Michael Peachin. Oxford and New York: Oxford University Press, 2011.

Lerner, Jeffrey. “Correcting the Early History of Ay Kanom.” *Archäologische Mitteilungen aus Iran und Turan* 35/36 (2003/2004): 372–410.

Levick, Barbara. *Tiberius the Politician*. London: Croom Helm, 1976.

Lewis, Naphtali, and Meyer Reinhold, eds. *Roman Civilzation. Sourcebook II: The Empire*. 3rd edition. New York: Columbia University Press, 1990.

Lieb, Kristin J. *Gender, Branding, and the Modern Music Industry: The Social Construction of Female Popular Music Stars*. New York: Routledge, 2013.

Lim, David S. *The Servant Nature of the Church in the Pauline Corpus*. PhD dissertation. Fuller Theological Seminary, 1987.

Linkof, Ryan. *The Public Eye: Celebrity and Photojournalism in the Making of the British Tabloids, 1904–1938*. PhD thesis. University of Southern California, 2011.

Litchfield, Henry W. "National *Exempla Virtutis* in Roman Literature." *Harvard Studies in Classical Philology* 25 (1914): 1–71.

Litfin, A. Duane. *St. Paul's Theology of Proclamation: 1 Corinthians 1–4 and Greco-Roman Rhetoric*. Society for New Testament Studies Monograph Series 79. Cambridge and New York: Cambridge University, 1993.

Littler, Jo. "The New Victorians? Celebrity Charity and the Demise of the Welfare State." *Celebrity Studies* 6.4 (2015): 471–485.

Lloyd, Geoffrey E. R. *The Revolutions of Wisdom: Studies in the Claims and Practice of Ancient Greek Science*. Berkeley: University of California Press, 1987.

Llewelyn, Stephen R. "Faithful Words." *New Docs* 9 (2002): 9–14.

Lombard, Herman A. "Charisma and Church Office." *Neot* 10 (1976): 31–52.

Lopez, Davina C. *Apostle to the Conquered: Reimagining Paul's Mission*. Minneapolis: Fortress Press, 2008.

Lotz, John P. "The 'Homonoia' Coins of Asia Minor and Ephesians 1:21." *Tyndale Bulletin* 50.2 (1999): 173–188.

Louw, Johannes P., and Eugene A. Nida, eds. *Greek-English Lexicon*. 2 volumes. New York: United Bible Societies, 1988.

Luce, T. James. "Livy, Augustus and the Forum Augustum." Pages 123–138 in *Between Republic and Empire: Interpretations of Augustus and His Principate*. Edited by Kurt A. Raaflaub and Mark Toher. Oxford/Berkeley: University of California Press, 1990.

Lumpe, Adolf. "*Exemplum*." *Reallexikon für Antike und Christentum* 6 (1966): 1229–1257.

Lyons, George. *Pauline Autobiography: Towards a New Understanding*. Atlanta: Scholars, 1985.

MacDowell, Douglas W., and Maurizio Taddei. "The Greek City of Aï-Khanum." Pages 218–232 in *The Archaeology of Afghanistan from Earliest Times to the Timurid Period*. Edited by Raymond Allchin and Norman Hammond. London: Academic Press, 1978.

MacGillivray, Erlend D. "Re-evaluating Patronage and Reciprocity in Antiquity and New Testament Studies." *Journal of Greco-Roman Christianity and Judaism* 6 (2009): 37–81.

MacMullen, Ramsay. "What Difference Did Christianity Make?" *Historia* 35 (1986): 322–343.

Maier, Harry O. *The Social Setting of the Ministry as Reflected in the Writings of Hermas, Clement and Ignatius*. Waterloo: Wilfrid Laurier, 1991.

–. *Picturing Paul in Empire: Imperial Image, Text and Persuasion in Colossians, Ephesians and the Pastoral Epistles*. London and New York: Bloomsbury, T&T Clark, 2013.

–. "Come and See: The Promise of Visual Exegesis." *Colloquium* 47.1 (2015).

Mairs, Rachel. "The Founder's Shrine and the Foundation of Ai Khanoum." Pages 103–128 in *Foundation Myths in Ancient Societies: Dialogues and Discourses*. Edited by Naoíse Mac Sweeney. Philadelphia: University of Pennsylvania Press, 2015.

Malan, François S. "The Relationship Between Apostleship and Office in the Theology of Paul." *Neot* 10 (1976): 53–68.

Malcolm, Matthew R. *Paul and the Rhetoric of Reversal in 1 Corinthians: The Impact of Paul's Gospel on His Macro-Rhetoric*. Society for New Testament Studies Monograph Series 155. Cambridge: Cambridge University Press, 2013.

Malherbe, Abraham J. *The Cynic Epistles*. Atlanta: Scholars, 1977.

–. *Social Aspects of Early Christianity*. Philadelphia: Fortress, 1983.

–. *Moral Exhortation: A Greco-Roman Sourcebook*. Philadelphia: Westminster, 1986.

–. *Paul and the Thessalonians: The Philosophic Tradition of Pastoral Care*. Philadelphia: Fortress, 1987.
–. *Paul and the Popular Philosophers*. Minneapolis: Fortress, 1989.
–. "Paul's Self-Sufficiency (Philippians 4:11)." Pages 125–139 in *Friendship, Flattery and Frankness of Speech: Studies on Friendship in the New Testament World*. Novum Testamentum Supplement 82. Edited by John T. Fitzgerald. Leiden: Brill, 1996.
–. *Light from the Gentiles: Hellenistic Philosophy and Early Christianity. Collected Essays, 1959–2012, by Abraham J. Malherbe*. Edited by Carl R. Halladay, John T. Fitzgerald, James W. Thompson, and Gregory E. Sterling. Leiden and Boston: Brill, 2013.
Mallock, William H. *Aristocracy and Evolution: A Study of the Rights, the Origin, and the Social Functions of the Wealthier Classes*. London: Adam and Charles Black, 1898.
Mann, Christian. *'Um keinen Kranz, um das Leben kämpfen wir!': Gladiatoren im Osten des Römischen Reiches und die Frage der Romanisierung*. Studien zur Alten Geschichte, 14. Berlin: Antike, 2011.
Marrou, Henri-Irénée. *A History of Education in Antiquity*. London and New York: Sheed and Ward, 1956.
Marshall, P. David. *The Celebrity Culture Reader*. New York: Routledge, 2006.
–. *Celebrity and Power: Fame in Contemporary Culture*. Minneapolis: University of Minnesota Press, 1997.
–. "The Promotion and Presentation of the Self: Celebrity as a Marker of Presentational Media." *Celebrity Studies* 1.1 (2010): 35–48.
Marshall, Peter. *Enmity in Corinth: Social Conventions in Paul's Relations with the Corinthians*. Wissenschaftliche Untersuchungen zum Neuen Testament II 23. Tübingen: Mohr Siebeck, 1987.
Martin, Dale B. *The Corinthian Body*. New Haven and London: Yale University Press, 1995.
–. "*Arsenokoitês* and *Malakos*: Meanings and Consequences." Pages 117–136 in *Biblical Ethics and Homosexuality*. Edited by Robert L. Brawley. Louisville: Westminster/John Knox, 1996.
Martin, Freya. "The Importance of Honorific Statues: A Case-Study." *Bulletin of the Institute of Classical Studies* 41 (1996): 53–70.
Martin, Ralph P. *Reconciliation: A Study of Paul's Theology*. London: Marshall, Morgan and Scott, 1981.
–. *2 Corinthians*. Waco: Word, 1986.
–. "The Seven Sages as Performers of Wisdom." Pages 108–128 in *Cultural Poetics in Archaic Greece: Cult, Performance, Politics*. Edited by Carol Dougherty and Leslie Kurke. Oxford: Oxford University Press, 1998.
Martyn, J. Louis. *Theological Issues in the Letters of Paul*. Edinburgh: T&T Clark, 1997.
Maslakov, George. "Valerius Maximus and Roman Historiography: A Study of the *Exempla* Tradition." *Aufstieg und Niedergang der römischen Welt* 2.32.1 (1984): 437–496.
Masson, Charles. *L'Épître de Paul aux Éphésiens*. Neuchâtel, Delachaux & Niestle, 1953.
Mattingly, Harold. "The Roman 'Virtues'." *Harvard Theological Review* 30.2 (1937): 103–117.
–. "The Emperor and His Clients." Pages 182–184 in *Essays on Roman Culture: The Todd Memorial Lectures*. Edited by Arthur J. Dunston. Sarasota: Hakkert, 1976.
McCant, Jerry W. "A Parodic Defense of Authority (2 Corinthians 10–13)." Pages 101–172 in Jerry W. McCant, *2 Corinthians*. Sheffield: Sheffield Academic, 1999.

McDayter, Ghislaine. *Byromania and the Birth of Celebrity Culture*. Studies in the Long Nineteenth Century Literature. Albany: State University of New York Press, 2009.

McDonald, Brent, and Daniel Eagles. "Matthew Mitcham: The Narrative of a Gay Sporting Icon." *Celebrity Studies* 3.3 (2012): 297–318.

McDonnell, Myles. *Roman Manliness: Virtus and the Roman Republic*. Cambridge: Cambridge University Press, 2006.

McFarland, Orrey. *God and Grace in Philo and Paul*. Novum Testamentum Supplement 164. Leiden and Boston: Brill, 2015.

McLean, Bradley H. "The Agrippinilla Inscription: Religious Associations and Early Church Formation." Pages 239–270 in *Origins and Method: Towards a New Understanding of Judaism and Christianity. Essays in Honour of John C. Hurd*. Journal for the Study of the New Testament Supplement 86. Edited by Bradley H. McLean. Sheffield: JSOT Press, 1993.

McRae, Rachel. "Eating with Honor: The Corinthian Lord's Supper in Light of Voluntary Association Meal Practices." *Journal of Biblical Literature* 130.1 (2011): 165–181.

Measham, Terence, Elisabeth Spathari, and Paul Donnelly. *1000 Years of the Olympic Games: Treasures of Ancient Greece*. Sydney: Powerhouse Publishing, 2000.

Meeks, Wayne A. *The First Urban Christians: The Social World of the Apostle Paul*. New Haven: Yale University Press, 1983.

–. *The Origins of Christian Morality: The First Two Centuries*. New Haven and London: Yale University Press, 1993.

Meijer, Fik. *Chariot Racing in the Roman Empire: Spectacles in Rome and Constantinople*. Translated by Liz Waters. Baltimore: The Johns Hopkins University Press, 2010.

Mellor, Ronald. "The Goddess Roma." *Aufstieg und Niedergang der römischen Welt* 2.17.2 (1981): 998–999.

Mendel, Gustave. "Catalogue des monuments grecs, romains et byzantins du Musée Impérial Ottoman de Brousse." *Bulletin de correspondance hellénique* 33 (1909): 402–404.

Mendelson, Alan. *Secular Education in Philo of Alexandria*. Cincinnati: Hebrew Union College, 1982.

Merkelbach, Reinhold, Recep Meriç, Johannes Nollé, and Sencer Şahin. *Die Inschriften von Ephesos Teil VII, I*. Bonn: Rudolf Habelt Verlag, 1981.

Meritt, Benjamin D., ed. *Corinth Vol VIII. Part I: Greek Inscriptions 1896–1927*. Cambridge, Mass.: Harvard University Press, 1931.

Metzner, Rainer. "Paulus und der Wettkampf: Die Rolle des Sports in Leben und Verkündigung des Apostels (1 Kor 9.24–29; Phil 3.12–16)." *New Testament Studies* 46.4 (2000): 565–583.

Meyer, Marvin W. *The Ancient Mysteries: A Sourcebook*. San Francisco: HarperSanFranciso, 1987.

Michaelis, Wilhelm. "μιμεῖσθαι." Pages 659–674 in *Theological Dictionary of the New Testament. Volume IV*. Edited by Gerhard Kittel and Gerhard Friedrich. Translated by Geoffrey W. Bromiley. Grand Rapids: Eerdmans, 1967.

Migeotte, Leopold. *Les souscriptions publiques dans les cités grecques*. Geneva: Librairie Droz, 1992.

Mihaila, Corin. *The Paul-Apollos Relationship and Paul's Stance toward Graeco-Roman Rhetoric*. Library of New Testament Studies 402. London: T&T Clark, 2009.

Miles, Richard. "Communicating Culture, Identity and Power." Page 35 in *Experiencing Rome: Culture, Identity and Power in the Roman Empire*. Edited by Janet Huskinson. London, Routledge, 2000.

Millar, Fergus, ed. *La révolution romaine après Ronald Syme: bilans et perspectives*. Geneva: Fondation Hardt, 2000.

Miller, John F. *Apollo, Augustus and the Poets*. Cambridge: Cambridge University Press, 2009.

Miller, Stephen G. *Arete: Greek Sports from Ancient* Sources. 2nd edition. Berkeley and Los Angeles: University of California Press, 1991.

–. "The Organization and Functioning of the Olympic Games." Page 28 in *Sport and Festival in the Ancient Greek World*. Edited by David J. Philips and David Pritchard. Swansea: The Classical Press of Wales, 2003.

–. *Ancient Greek Athletics*. New Haven and London: Yale University Press, 2004.

Mitchell, Alan C. "Rich and Poor in the Courts of Corinth: Litigiousness and Status in 1 Corinthians 6:1–11." *New Testament Studies* 39.1 (1993): 562–586.

Mitchell, Margaret M. *Paul and the Rhetoric of Reconciliation: An Exegetical Investigation of the Language and Composition of 1 Corinthians*. Louisville: Westminster John Knox Press, 1992.

Mitchell, Stephen. "The Ionians of Paphlagonia." Page 95 in *Local Knowledge and Microidentities in the Imperial Greek World*. Greek Culture in the Roman World. Edited by Tim Whitmarsh. Cambridge and New York: Cambridge University Press, 2010.

Mohr, John W. "Cicero: Persons and Positions." Pages 123–132 in *Sociological Insights of Great Thinkers*. Edited by Christofer Edling and Jens Rydgren. Santa Barbara: Praeger, 2011.

Mole, Tom. *Byron's Romantic Celebrity: Industrial Culture and the Hermeneutic of Intimacy*. Houndmills and New York: Palgrave MacMillan, 2007.

Mommsen, Theodore. *Res Gestae Divi Augusti: Ex Monumentis Acyrano et Apolloniensi*. Berlin: Weidmann, 1883.

–. *History of Rome. Volume 5*. London: J.M. Dent, 1911.

Moo, Douglas. *The Epistle to the Romans*. Grand Rapids: Eerdmans, 1996.

Moretti, Luigi. *Inscrizioni agonistiche greche*. Roma: A. Signorelli, 1953.

Morgan, Teresa. *Popular Morality in the Early Roman Empire*. Cambridge: Cambridge University Press, 2007.

–. *Roman Faith and Christian Faith:* Pistis *and* Fides *in the Early Roman Empire and Early Churches*. Oxford: Oxford University Press, 2015.

Morris, Leon. *The Apostolic Preaching of the Cross*. 3rd edition. London: Tyndale Press, 1965.

–. *The Cross in the New Testament*. Exeter: Paternoster Press, 1967.

Morrison, Karl F. *The Mimetic Tradition of Reform in the West*. Princeton: Princeton University Press, 1982.

Murphy-O'Connor, Jerome. "House Churches and the Eucharist: Archaeological Light from Paul's Corinth." *The Bible Today* 22.1 (1984): 32–38.

–. "Corinth." Page 1138 in *The Anchor Bible Dictionary Volume I A–C*. Edited by David N. Freedman, Gary A. Herion, David F. Graf, and John D. Pleins. New York: Doubleday, 1992.

–. *St. Paul's Corinth: Texts and Archaeology. Third Revised and Expanded Edition*. Wilmington: Michael Glazier, 2002.

Nachmanson, Ernst. "Zu den Motivformeln der griechischen Ehreninschriften." *Eranos* 11 (1911): 180–196.

Nardoni, Enrique. "The Concept of Charism in Paul." *Catholic Biblical Quarterly* 55.1 (1993): 68–80.

Nehamas, Alexander. "Plato on Imitation and Poetry in *Republic* 10." Pages 47–78 in *Plato on Beauty, Wisdom, and the Arts*. Edited by Julius M. Moravcsik and Philip Temko. Totowa: Rowman and Allenheld, 1982.

Neraudau, Jean-Pierre. "La Fama dans la Rome Antique." *Médiévales* 12.24 (1993): 27–34.

Newman, Carey C. *Paul's Glory-Christology: Tradition and Rhetoric*. Novum Testamentum Supplement 69. Leiden: E.J. Brill, 1992.

Newton, Michael. *The Concept of Purity at Qumran and in the Letters of Paul*. Society for New Testament Studies Monograph Series 53. Cambridge: Cambridge University Press, 1985.

Neyrey, Jerome H. *New Testament Understanding of the Divine*. Minneapolis: Fortress, 2004.

Ng, Diana Y. *Manipulation of Memory: Public Buildings and Decorative Programs in Roman Cities of Asia Minor*. PhD dissertation. University of Michigan, 2007.

Nicorgski, Walter J. "Cicero and the Rebirth of Political Philosophy." *The Political Science Reviewer* 8 (1978): 63–101.

Nietzsche, Friedrich. *On the Genealogy of Morality*. Edited by Keith A. Pearson. Translated by Carol Diethe. Cambridge: Cambridge University Press, 2006.

Nigdelis, Pantelis M. "Voluntary Associations in Roman Thessalonikê: In Search of Identity and Support in a Cosmopolitan Society." Pages 12–47 in in *From Roman to Early Christian Thessalonikê: Studies in Religion and Archaeology*. Harvard Theological Studies 64. Edited by Laura Nasrallah, Charalambos Bakirtzis, and Steven J. Friesen. Cambridge, MA: Harvard University Press, 2010.

Nightingale, Andrea W. "Sages, Sophists, and Philosophers: Greek Wisdom Literature." Pages 156–191 in *Literature in the Greek and Roman Worlds: A New Perspective*. Edited by Oliver Taplin. Oxford: Oxford University Press, 2000.

Nock, Arthur D. "The Historical Importance of Cult Associations." *The Classical Review* 38 (1924): 105–109.

Nongbri, Brent. "The Concept of Religion and the Study of Paul." *Journal of the Jesus Movement in Its Jewish Setting* 2 (2015): 1–26.

Noreña, Carlos F. *Imperial Ideas in the Roman West: Representation, Circulation, Power*. Cambridge: Cambridge University Press, 2011.

Nutton, Vivian. "The Beneficial Ideology." Pages 209–222 in *Imperialism in the Ancient World*. Edited by Peter D.A. Garnsey and Charles R. Whittaker. Cambridge: Cambridge University Press, 1978.

Oakes, Peter E. "Epictetus (and the New Testament)." *Vox Evangelica* 23 (1993): 39–56.

–. *Philippians: From People to Letter*. Society for New Testament Studies Monograph Series 110. Cambridge: Cambridge University Press, 2001.

Oehler, Julius. "Gymnasiarch." *Realencyclopädie der classischen Altertumswissenschaft* 7 (1912): 2005–2008.

Ogereau, Julien M. *Paul's* Koinonia *with the Philippians: A Socio-Historical Investigation of a Pauline Economic Partnership*. Wissenschaftliche Untersuchungen zum Neuen Testament II 377. Tübingen: Mohr Siebeck, 2014.

O'Gorman, Ellen. *Irony and Misreading in the Annals of Tacitus*. Cambridge: Cambridge University Press, 2004.

Oikonomides, Alcibiade N. "The Lost Delphic Inscription with the Commandments of the Seven and *P. Univ. Athen* 2782." *Zeitschrift für Papyrologie und Epigraphik* 37 (1980): 179–183.

–. "Records of 'The Commandments of the Seven Wise Men' in the 3rd c. BC: The Revered Greek 'Reading-book' of the Hellenistic World." *Classical Bulletin* 63 (1987): 67–76.

Økland, Jorunn. *Women in Their Place: Paul and the Discourse of Gender and Sanctuary Space*. London and New York: T&T Clark, 2004.

Oliver, James H. *Greek Constitutions of Early Roman Emperors from Inscriptions and Papyri*. Philadelphia: American Philosophical Society, 1989.

Onwu, Nlenanya. "*Mimetes* Hypothesis: A Key to the Understanding of Pauline Paraenesis." *African Journal of Biblical Studies* 1.2 (1986): 95–112.

Oostendorp, Derk W. *Another Jesus: A Gospel of Jewish-Christian Superiority in II Corinthians*. Kampen: J.H. Kok, 1967.

Orth, Maureen. *The Importance of Being Famous: Behind the Scenes of the Celebrity-Industrial Complex*. New York: H. Holt, 2004.

Oster, Richard. "Numismatic Windows into the Social World of Early Christianity: A Methodological Enquiry." *Journal of Biblical Literature 101* (1982): 195–223.

–. "'Show me a denarius': Symbolism of Roman Coinage and Christian Beliefs." *Restoration Quarterly* 28.2 (1985–1986): 107–115.

–. "When Men Wore Veils to Worship: The Historical Context of 1 Corinthians 11:4." *New Testament Studies* 34 (1988): 481–505.

–. "Use, Misuse and Neglect of Archaeological Evidence in Some Modern Works on 1 Corinthians (1Cor 7,1–5; 8,10; 11,2–16; 12,14–26)." *Zeitschrift für die Neutestamentliche Wissenschaft* 83.1 (1992): 52–73.

Panagopoulos, Cécile. "Vocabulaire et mentalité dans les Moralia de Plutarque." *Dialogues d'histoire ancienne* 3 (1977): 197–235.

Panikulam, George. *Koinōnia in the New Testament: A Dynamic Expression of Christian Life*. Rome: Biblical Institute Press, 1979.

Pao, David W. *Thanksgiving: An Investigation of a Pauline Theme*. Downers Grove: IVP, 2002.

Papahatzis, Nicos. *Ancient Corinth: The Museums of Corinth, Isthmia and Sicyon*. Athens: Ekdotike Helados S.A., 1994.

Papathomas, Amphilochios. "Das agonistische Motiv 1 Kor 9.24ff. im Spiegel zeitgenössischer dokumentarischer Quellen." *New Testament Studies* 43.2 (1997): 223–241.

–. "14. Ein literarisches Fragment mit Sprüchen der Sieben Weisen." Pages 163–169 in '... *vor dem Papyrus sind alle Gleich!': Papyrologische Beiträge zu Ehren von Bärbel Kramer (P. Kramer)*. Edited by Raimar Eberhard, Holger Kockelmann, Stefan Pfeiffer, and Maren Schentuleit. Berlin and New York: De Gruyter, 2009.

Pappas, Nickolas. "Aristotle." Pages 15–26 in *The Routledge Companion to Aesthetics*. Edited by Berys Gaut and Dominic McIver Lopes. London and New York: Routledge, 2001.

Park, Young-Ho. *Paul's Ekklesia as a Civic Assembly: Understanding the People of God in Their Politico-Social World*. Wissenschaftliche Untersuchungen zum Neuen Testament II 393. Tübingen: Mohr Siebeck, 2015.

Parke, Herbert W. "Croesus and Delphi." *Greek, Roman, and Byzantine Studies* 25.3 (1984): 209–232.

Pate, Charles M. *Adam Christology as the Exegetical and Theological Substructure of 2 Corinthians 4:7–5:21.* Lanham: University Press of America, 1991.

Patrick, James. "Insights from Cicero on Paul's Reasoning in 1 Corinthians 12–14: Love Sandwich or Five Course Meal?" *Tyndale Bulletin* 55.1 (2004): 43–64.

Paul, George. "Symposia and Deipna in Plutarch's *Lives* and in Other Historical Writings." Pages 157–169 in *Dining in a Classical Context.* Edited by William J. Slater. Ann Arbor: University of Michigan Press, 1991.

Payne, Martha J. ARETAS ENEKEN: *Honors to Romans and Italians in Greece from 26 to 27 BC.* PhD dissertation. Michigan State University, 1984.

Pelling, Christopher. "Educating Croesus: Talking and Learning in Herodotus' Lydian *Logos.*" *Classical Antiquity* 25.1 (2006): 141–147.

Penna, Romano. "The Wisdom of the Cross and Its Foolishness as Foundation of the Church." In Romano Penna, *Paul the Apostle: Wisdom and Folly of the Cross. Volume 2.* Translated by Thomas P. Wahl. Collegeville: Michael Glazier, 1996.

Perlman, Shalom. "The Historical Example, Its Use and Importance as Political Propaganda in the Attic Orators." Pages 150–166 in *Scripta Hierosolymitana VII: Studies in History.* Edited by Alexander Fuks and Israel Halpern. Jerusalem: Magnes, 1961.

Peterlin, Davorin L. *Paul's Letter to the Philippians in the Light of Disunity in the Church.* Novum Testamentum Supplementp 79. Leiden et al.: Brill, 1995.

Peterson, Brian K. *Eloquence and the Proclamation of the Gospel in Corinth.* Society of Biblical Literature Dissertation Series 163. Atlanta: Scholars, 1998.

Pfitzner, Victor C. *Paul and the Agon Motif: Traditional Athletic Imagery in the Pauline Literature.* Leiden: Brill, 1967.

Pickett, Raymond. "The Death of Christ as Divine Patronage in Romans 5:1–11." *SBL Seminar Papers* 1993. 726–739.

–. *The Cross in Corinth: The Social Significance of the Death of Jesus.* Journal for the Study of the New Testament Supplement 143. Sheffield: Sheffield Academic Press, 1997.

Piepkorn, Arthur C. "Charisma in the New Testament and the Apostolic Fathers." *Concordia Theological Monthly* 42.6 (1971): 369–389.

Pietsch, Wolfgang. *Gladiatoren in Ephesos: Tod am Nachmittag. Eine Ausstellung im Ephesos Museum Seluk Seit 20. April 2002.* Wein: ÖAI, 2002.

Pilhofer, Peter. *Philippi. Band II: Katalog der Inschriften von Philippi. 2. Auflage.* Wissenschaftliche Untersuchungen zum Neuen Testament I 119. Tübingen: Mohr Siebeck, 2009.

Pintaudi, Rosario, and Pieter J. Sijpesteijn. "Ostraka di contenuto scolastico provenienti da Narmuthis." *Zeitschrift für Papyrologie und Epigraphik* 76 (1989): 85–92.

Plank, Karl A. *Paul and the Irony of Affliction.* Atlanta: Scholars, 1987.

Plant, Ian M., ed. *Women Writers of Ancient Greece and Rome: An Anthology.* London: Equinox, 2004.

Plass, Paul. *The Game of Death in Ancient Rome: Arena Sport and Political Suicide.* London: The University of Wisconsin Press, 1995.

Plummer, Robert L. "Imitation of Paul and the Church's Missionary Role in 1 Corinthians." *Journal of the Evangelical Theological Society* 44.2 (2001): 219–235.

Pogoloff, Stephen M. *Logos and Sophia: The Rhetorical Situation of 1 Corinthians.* Society of Biblical Literature Dissertation Series 134. Atlanta: Scholars, 1992.

Poliakov, Michael B. "Jacob, Jove, and Other Wrestlers: Reception of Greek Athletics by Jews and Christians in Antiquity." *Journal of Sport History* 11 (1984): 48–65.

–. *Combat Sports in the Ancient World: Competition, Violence, and Culture.* New Haven and London: Yale University Press, 1987.
Porter, Stanley E. "Did Paul Speak Latin?" Pages 289–308 in *Paul: Jew, Greek and Roman.* Pauline Studies 5. Edited by Stanley E. Porter. Leiden: Brill: 2008.
–. "Paul, Virtues, Vices, and Household Codes." Pages 369–390 in *Paul and the Graeco-Roman World: A Handbook. Volume 2.* 2nd edition. Edited by J. Paul Sampley. London and New York: T&T Clark, 2016.
Postman, Neil, and Camille Paglia. "Dinner Conversation: She Wants Her TV! He Wants His Book!" *Harpers Magazine* (March 1991): 44–55.
Potolsky, Matthew. *Mimesis.* Abingden: Routledge, 2006.
–. "Poetry Is More Philosophical than History: Aristotle on *Mimesis* and Form." *The Review of Metaphysics* 64.2 (2010): 303–336.
–. "Plato on *Mimesis and* Mirrors," *Philosophy and Literature* 36.1 (2012): 187–195.
Potter, David S. "Entertainers in the Roman Empire." Pages 256–325 in *Life, Death, and Entertainment in the Roman Empire.* Edited by David S. Potter and David J. Mattingly. Ann Arbor: The University of Michigan Press, 1999.
Pouilloux, Jean. *Choix d'inscriptions Grecques: textes, traductions et notes.* Paris: Société d'édition Les Belles Lettres, 1960.
Powell, Jonathan G.F., ed. *Cicero the Philosopher.* Oxford: Clarendon Press, 1995.
Prévert, Jacques. *Paroles: Selected Poems.* Translated by Lawrence Ferlinghetti. San Francisco: City Lights Books, 1958.
Price, John. *Everyday Heroism: Victorian Constructions of the Heroic Civilian.* London and New York: Bloomsbury Academic, 2014.
Price, Simon R.F. "Gods and Emperors: The Greek Language of the Roman Imperial Cult." *Journal of Hellenic Studies* 104 (1984): 79–95.
–. *Rituals and Power: The Roman Imperial Cult in Asia Minor.* Cambridge: Cambridge University Press, 1984.
Prigozy, Ruth. "Introduction: Scott, Zelda, and the Culture of Celebrity." Pages 1–27 in *The Cambridge Companion to Scott Fitzgerald.* Edited by Ruth Prigozy. Cambridge: Cambridge University Press 2002.
Provence, Thomas E. "'Who Is Sufficient for These Things?': An Exegesis of 2 Corinthians 2:15–3:18." *Novum Testamentum* 24.1 (1982): 54–81.
Pulleyn, Simon. *Prayer in Greek Religion.* Oxford: Clarendon Press, 1997.
Quet, Marie-Henriette. "Rhétorique, culture et politique: Le fonctionnement du discours idéologique chez Dion de Pruse et dans les Moralia de Plutarque." *Dialogues d'histoire ancienne* 4 (1978): 51–119.
Raaflaub, Kurt A. "Poets, Lawgivers, and the Beginnings of Political Reflection in Archaic Greece." Pages 23–29 in *The Cambridge History of Greek and Roman Political Thought.* Edited by Christopher J. Rowe and Malcolm Schofield. Cambridge: Cambridge University Press, 2000.
Radice, Betty, and Giovanni Mardersteig. *Delphika grammata: The Sayings of the Seven Sages of Greece.* Verona: Officina Bodoni, 1976.
Ramage, Edwin S. *The Nature and Purpose of Augustus' "Res Gestae".* Stuttgart: Franz Steiner Verlag, 1987.
Ramelli, Ilaria, ed. and trans. *I Setti sapienti: vite e opinioni nell'edizione di Bruno Snell.* Milan: Bompiani, 2005.
Ramsaran, Rollin A. *Liberating Words: Paul's Use of Rhetorical Maxims in 1 Corinthians 8–10.* Valley Forge: Trinity Press international, 1996.

–. "Paul and Maxims." Pages 116–146 in *Paul and the Graeco-Roman World: A Handbook. Volume 2.* Edited by J. Paul Sampley. 2nd edition. London and New York: T&T Clark, 2016.

Rand, Ayn. *The Virtue of Selfishness.* New York: Signet, 1961.

Ravid, Gilad, and Elizabeth Currid-Halkett. "The Social Structure of Celebrity: An Empirical Network Analysis of an Elite Population." *Celebrity Studies* 4.2 (2013): 182–201.

Reasoner, Mark. "The Theology of Romans 12:1–15:13." Pages 287–299 in *Pauline Theology Volume III: Romans.* Edited by David M. Hay and E. Elizabeth Johnson. Minneapolis: Fortress, 1995.

Reed, David A. *Paul on Marriage and Singleness: Reading 1 Corinthians with the Augustan Marriage Laws.* ThD, University of St. Michael's College, 2013.

Rehak, Paul. *Imperium and Cosmos: Augustus and the Northern Campius Martius.* Edited by John G. Younger. Wisconsin: University of Wisconsin Press, 2006.

Reinhartz, Adele. "On the Meaning of the Pauline Exhortation: '*mimetai mou ginesthe* – Become Imitators of Me'." Studies in Religion/Sciences Religieuses 16 (1987): 393–403.

Reis, David M. "Following in Paul's Footsteps: *Mimesis* and Power in Ignatius of Antioch." Pages 287–306 in *Trajectories through the New Testament and the Apostolic Fathers.* Edited by Andrew F. Gregory and Christopher Tuckett. Oxford: Oxford University Press, 2005.

Remer, Gary. "Political Oratory and Conversation: Cicero versus Deliberative Democracy." *Political Theory* (1999): 39–44.

Reumann, John. *Philippians: A New Translation with Introduction and Commentary.* New Haven and London: Yale University Press, 2008.

Renkin, Claire. "An Art Historian Reflects on Modes of Visual Exegesis." *Colloquium* 47.1 (2015): 158–161.

Reydams-Schils, Gretchen. *Roman Stoics: Self, Responsibility and Affection.* Chicago and London: University of Chicago Press, 2005.

Reynolds, Joyce. *Aphrodisias and Rome.* London: Society for the Promotion of Roman Studies, 1982.

Riall, Lucy. *Garibaldi: Invention of a Hero.* New Haven and London: Yale University Press, 2007.

–. "Garibaldi: The First Celebrity." *History Today* 57.8 (2007): 41–47.

Rice, Joshua. *Paul and Patronage: The Dynamics of Power in 1 Corinthians.* Eugene: Pickwick, 2013.

Rich, Audrey N.M. "The Cynic Conception of *Autarkeia*." *Mnemosyne* 9 (1956): 23–29.

Rich, John, and Jonathan H. C Williams. "Leges et iura P.R. restituit: A New Aureus of Octavian and the Settlement of 28–27 BC." *Numismatic Chronicle* 159 (1999): 169–213.

Richter, Gisela M.A. "Grotesques and the Mime." *American Journal of Archaeology* 17.2 (1913): 149–156.

Ridderbos, Herman. *Paul: An Outline of His Theology.* Grand Rapids: Eerdmans, 1975.

Ridley, Ronald. *The Emperor's Retrospect: Augustus' Res Gestae in Epigraphy, Historiography and Commentary.* Leuven and Dudley: Peeters, 2003.

Rilinger, Rolf. *Ordo und dignitas: Beiträge zur römischen Verfassungs- und Sozialgeschichte.* Stuttgart: Franz Steiner Verlag, 2007.

Risser, James. "On the Threefold Sense of *Mimesis* in Plato's Republic." *Epoché* 17.2 (2013): 249–256.

Ritti, Tullia, and Salim Yilmaz. *Gladiatori e venationes a Hierapolis di Frigia*. Rome: Accademia Naz. dei Lincei, 1998.

Robbins, Vernon K., Walter S. Melion, and Rory R. Jeal. *The Art of Visual Exegesis: Rhetoric, Texts, Images*. Emory Studies in Early Christianity 19. Atlanta: SBL Press, 2017.

Robert, Louis. "De Delphes a l'Oxus: inscriptions grecques nouvelles de la Bactriane." *Comptes Rendues de l'Académie des Inscriptions et Belles Lettres* (1968): 416–457.

–. *Les gladiateurs dans l'orient grec*. Amsterdam: Adolf M. Hakkert, 1971.

Roberts, Colin, H., Theodore C. Skeat, and Arthur D. Nock. "The Gild of Zeus Hypsistos." *Harvard Theological Review* 29 (1936): 39–87.

Robinson, Betsey A. "'Good Luck' from Corinth: A Mosaic of Allegory, Athletics, and Civic Identity." *American Journal of Archaeology* 116 (2012): 105–132.

Rogers, Guy M. *The Sacred Identity of Ephesos: Foundation Myths of a Roman City*. London and New York: Routledge, 1991.

–. *The Mysteries of Artemis of Ephesos: Cult, Polis, and Change in the Graeco-Roman World*. Synkrisis. New Haven and London: Yale University Press, 2012.

Rogers, Trent A. *God and the Idols: Representations of God in 1 Corinthians 8–10*. Wissenschaftliche Untersuchungen zum Neuen Testament II 427. Tübingen: Mohr Siebeck, 2016.

Rojek, Chris. *Celebrity*. London: Reaktion, 2001.

Rolland, Henri. *Le mausolée de Glanum*. Paris: Éditions du Centre Nationale de la Recherche Scientifique, 1969.

Romanelli, Pietro. *The Roman Forum*. 2nd edition. Rome: Instituto Poligrafico Dello Stato, 1955.

Ross, W. David. *Aristotelis Fragmenta Selecta*. Oxford: Clarendon Press, 1955.

Rostad, Aslak. *Human Transgression – Divine Retribution: A Study of Religious Transgressions and Punishments in Greek Cultic Regulations and Lydian-Phrygian Reconciliation Inscriptions*. PhD Thesis. University of Bergen, 2006.

Rousseau, Jean-Jacques. "Discourse on the Virtue a Hero Most Needs or On Heroic Virtue." In Jean-Jacques Rousseau, *The "Discourses" and Other Early Political Writings*. Edited by Victor Gourevitch. Cambridge Texts in the History of Political Thought. Cambridge: Cambridge University Press, 1997.

Rowell, Henry T. "The Forum and the Funeral Images of Augustus." *Memoirs of the American Academy in Rome* 17 (1940): 131–143.

Russell, David S. *The Method and Message of Jewish Apocalyptic 200 BC–AD 100*. London: SCM, 1964.

Saller, Richard P. "Promotion and Patronage in Equestrian Careers." *Journal of Roman Studies* 60 (1980): 38–49.

–. *Personal Patronage Under the Early Empire*. Cambridge: Cambridge University Press, 1982.

Salmeri, Giovanni. *Dio, Rome, and the Civic Life of Asia Minor*. Page 64 in *Dio Chrysostom: Politics, Letters, and Philosophy*. Edited by Simon Swain. Oxford: Oxford University Press, 2000.

Sampley, J. Paul. *Walking Between the Times: Paul's Moral Reasoning*. Minneapolis: Fortress, 1991.

–. "Living in an Evil Aeon: Paul's Ambiguous Relation to Culture." Pages 391–432 in *Paul in the Greco-Roman World. A Handbook: Volume 2*. Edited by J. Paul Sampley. 2nd edition. London and New York: Bloomsbury T&T Clark, 2017.

Samuelson, Gunnar. *Crucifixion in Antiquity: An Enquiry into the Background and Significance of the New Testament Terminology*. Wissenschaftliche Untersuchungen zum Neuen Testament II 310. 2nd edition. Tübingen: Mohr Siebeck, 2013.

Sanders, Boykin. "Imitating Paul: 1 Cor 4:16." *Harvard Theological Review* 74.4 (1981): 353–363.

Sansone, David. *Greek Athletics and the Genesis of Sport*. Berkeley and Los Angeles: University of California Press, 1988.

Saunders, Ross. "Attalus, Paul and PAIDEIA: The Contribution of I. Eph. 202 to Pauline Studies." Pages 175–183 in *Ancient History in a Modern University. Volume II: Early Christianity, Late Antiquity, and Beyond*. Edited by Tom W. Hillard, Rosalinde Kearsley, Charles E. V. Nixon, and Alanna M. Nobbs. Grand Rapids: Eerdmans, 1998.

Sauron, Gilles. QVIS DEVM? *L'expression plastique des ideologies politques et religieuses à Rome*. Rome: École Française de Rome, 1994.

Savage, Timothy B. *Power Through Weakness: A Historical and Exegetical Examination of Paul's Understanding of the Christian Ministry in 2 Corinthians*. Society for New Testament Studies Monograph Series 86. Cambridge: Cambridge University Press, 1996.

Schäfer, Peter. *Judeophobia: Attitudes towards the Jews in the Ancient World*. London and Cambridge, MA.: Harvard University Press, 1997.

Scheid, John. "Les prêtres officials sous les empereurs Julio-Claudiens." *Aufstieg und Niedergang der römischen Welt* 2.16.1 (1979): 610–654.

–. *Res Gestae Divi Augusti: hauts faits du divin Auguste*. Paris: Les Belles Lettres, 2007.

Scherrer, Peter, ed. *Ephesus: The New Guide*. Revised edition. Turkey: Ege Yyinlari, 2000.

Schickel, Richard. *Intimate Strangers: The Culture of Celebrity in America*. 2nd edition. Chicago: Ivan R. Dee, 2000; original 1985.

Schlier, Heirich. "δειγματίζω." Pages 31–32 in *Theological Dictionary of the New Testament. Volume II*. Edited by Gerhard Kittel and Gerhard Friedrich. Translated by Geoffrey W. Bromiley. Grand Rapids: Eerdmans, 1964.

Schmithals, Walter. *Gnosticism in Corinth: An Investigation of the Letters to the Corinthians*. Nashville 1971.

Schnelle, Udo. *Apostle Paul: His Life and Theology*. Grand Rapids: Baker Academic, 2005.

Scholer, David M., ed. *Social Distinctives of the Christians in the First Century: Pivotal Essays by E. A. Judge*. Peabody: Hendrickson, 2008.

Schrage, Wolfgang. *The Ethics of the New Testament*. Edinburgh: T&T Clark 1988; German original 1982.

Schreiner, Thomas R. *Paul, Apostle of God's Glory in Christ: A Pauline Theology*. Downers Grove: IVP, 2002.

Schulz, Anselm. *Nachfolgen und Nachahmen: Studien über das Verhältnis der neutestamentlichen Jüngerschaft zur urchristlichen Vorbildethik*. Munich: Köschel-Verlag, 1962.

Schütz, John H. *Paul and the Anatomy of Apostolic Authority*. Cambridge: Cambridge University Press, 1975.

Scroggs, Robin. *The Last Adam: A Study in Pauline Anthropology*. Philadelphia: Fortress, 1966.

Seager, Robin. *Tiberius*. 2nd edition. Oxford: Blackwell, 2005.

Seifrid, Mark A. *Justification by Faith: The Origin and Development of a Central Pauline Theme*. Leiden: Brill, 1992.

–. "Romans." Pages 680–681 in *Commentary on the New Testament Use of the Old Testament*. Edited by Gregory K. Beale and Don A. Carson. Grand Rapids: Baker/Apollos, 2007.

Sevenster, Jan N. *Paul and Seneca*. Novum Testamentum Supplement 4. Leiden: Brill, 1961.

Shaw, Graham. *The Cost of Authority: Manipulation and Freedom in the New Testament*. London: SCM, 1984.

Sheppard, Anthony R.R. "Homonoia in the Greek Cities of the Roman Empire." *Ancient Society* 15–17 (1984–1986): 229–252.

Sherk, Robert K. *Rome and the Geek East to The Death of Augustus*. Cambridge: Cambridge University Press, 1984.

–. *The Roman Empire: Augustus to Hadrian*. Translated Documents of Greece and Rome 6. Cambridge: Cambridge University Press, 1988.

Shi, Wenhua. *Paul's Message of the Cross as Body Language*. Wissenschaftliche Untersuchungen zum Neuen Testament II 254. Tübingen: Mohr Siebeck, 2008.

Shipe, Matthew. "The Twilight of the Superheroes: Philip Roth, Celebrity, and the End of Print Culture." Pages 101–118 in *Roth and Celebrity*. Edited by Aimee Pozorski. Lanham, MD: Lexington Books, 2013.

Short, Richard G. *Religion in Cicero*. PhD dissertation. Harvard University, 2012.

Shotter, David. *Augustus Caesar*. 2nd edition. London and New York: Routledge, 2005.

Shumway, David R. "Dylan as Cultural Icon." Pages 110–121 in *The Cambridge Companion to Bob Dylan*. Edited by Kevin J.H. Dettmar. Cambridge and New York: Cambridge University Press, 2009.

–. "Gatsby, the Jazz Age, and Luhrmann Land." *The Journal of the Gilded Age and Progressive Era* 14 (2015): 132–137.

Sijpesteijn, Pieter J. *Liste de gymnasiarques des métropoles de l'Égypte romaine*. Amsterdam: Adolf M. Hakkert, 1967.

Skidmore, Clive. *Practical Ethics for Roman Gentlemen: The Work of Valerius Maximus*. Exeter: University of Exeter Press, 1996.

Slater, William J. "The Pantomime Tiberius Iulius Apolaustus." *Greek, Roman, and Byzantine Studies* 36 (1995): 263–292.

–. "The Victor's Return, and the Categories of Games." Pages 39–63 in *Epigraphical Approaches to the Post-Classical Polis*. Edited by Paraskevi Martzavou and Nikolaos Papazarkadas. Oxford: Oxford University Press, 2013.

Smallwood, E. Mary., ed. *Documents Illustrating the Principates of Nerva, Trajan, and Hadrian*. Cambridge: Cambridge University Press, 1966.

Smethurst, Stanley E. "Politics and Morality in Cicero." *Phoenix* 9.3 (1955): 111–121.

Smith, Claire S. *Pauline Communities as "Scholastic Communities": A Study in the Vocabulary of "Teaching" in 1 Corinthians, 1 and 2 Timothy, and Titus*. Wissenschaftliche Untersuchungen zum Neuen Testament II 335. Tübingen: Mohr Siebeck, 2012.

Smith, Jacob. *The Thrill Makers: Celebrity, Masculinity, and Stunt Performance*. Berkeley: University of California Press, 2012.

Smith, Richard E. *The Aristocratic Epoch in Latin Literature*. Sydney: Australasian Medical Publishing, 1947.

Smith, Roland R.R. *Aphrodisias I: The Monument of C. Julius Zoilos*. Mainz: Philipp von Zabern, 1993.

–. "Cultural Choice and Political Identity in Honorific Statues in the Greek East." *Journal of Roman Studies* 88 (1998): 56–93.

Snell, Bruno. *Leben und Meinungen der sieben Weisen: Griechische und lateinische Quellen erläutert und übertragen.* 4th edition. Munich: Heimeran Verlag, 1971; original 1938.

Spannagel, Martin. *Exemplaria Principis: Untersuchungen zu Entstehung und Ausstattung des Augustusforums.* Heidelberg: Verlag Archäologie und Geschichte, 1999.

Spawforth, Anthony J.S. "Gymnasiarch." Page 659 in *The Oxford Classical Dictionary.* Edited by Simon Hornblower and Anthony J.S. Spawforth. 3rd edition. Oxford: Oxford University Press, 1996.

Spencer, Andrew C. *The Value of Imperial* Virtutes *in the* Tabula Siarensis *and the Senatus Consultum de Cn. Pisone Patre.* MA thesis. University of North Carolina, Chapel Hill, 2009.

Spencer, Herbert. *The Study of Sociology.* New York: D. Appleton, 1896.

Spicq, Ceslas. *Theological Lexicon of the New Testament.* 3 volumes. Peabody: Hendrickson, 1999.

Stanley, David M. "'Become Imitators of Me': The Pauline Conception of Apostolic Tradition." *Biblica* 40 (1959): 859–877.

–. "Imitation in Paul's Letters: Its Significance for His Relationship to Jesus and to His Own Christian Foundations." Pages 127–141 in *From Jesus to Paul: Studies in Honour of Francis Wright Beare.* Edited by Peter Richardson and John C. Hurd. Waterloo: Wilfrid Laurier University Press, 1984.

Stem, Rex. "Cicero as Orator and Philosopher: The Value of the *Pro Murena* for Ciceronian Political Thought." *The Review of Politics* 68 (2006): 206–231.

Stephens, Mark B., and Georgiane Deal. "The God Who Gives Generously: Honour, Praise, and Celebrity Culture," *Scottish Journal of Theology* 71.1 (2018): 52–66.

Sternheimer, Karen. *Celebrity Culture and the American Dream: Stardom and Mobility.* 2nd edition. New York: Routledge, 2015.

Stevenson, William B. "From Catharsis to Wonder: Tragic *Mimesis* In Aristotle's *Poetics* and the Catholic Imagination." *Logos* 20.1 (2017): 64–75.

Steyne, Gert J. "Luke's Use of MIMHSIS? Re-opening the Debate." Pages 551–557 in *The Scriptures in the Gospels.* Edited by Christopher M. Tuckett. Leuven: Leuven University Press, 1997.

Stockhausen, Carol K. *Moses' Veil and the Glory of the New Covenant.* Rome: Pontificio Istituto Biblico, 1989.

Stowers, Stanley K. *A Rereading of Romans: Justice, Jews, and Cultures.* New Haven and London: Yale University Press, 1994.

–. "A Cult from Philadelphia: Oikos Relation or Cultic Association?" Pages 287–301 in *The Early Church in Its Context: Essays in Honour of Everett Ferguson.* Edited by Abraham J. Malherbe, Frederick W. Norris, and James W. Thompson. Leiden: Brill, 1998.

Strocka, Volker M. *The Celsus Library in Ephesu.* Pages 33–43 in Anonymous, *Ancient Libraries in Anatolia: Libraries of Hattusha, Pergamon, Ephesus, Nysa.* Ankara: Middle East Technical University Library, 2003.

Stroud, Ronald S. *Corinth Volume XVIII.6. The Sanctuary of Dememter and Kore: The Inscriptions.* Princeton: American School of Classical Studies at Athens, 2013.

Strunk, Tom. *History after Liberty: Tacitus on Tyrants, Sycophants, and Republicans.* Ann Arbor: University of Michigan Press, 2017.

Strychacz, Thomas. "Masculinity." Pages 277–286 in *Ernest Hemingway in Context*. Edited by Debra A. Moddelmog and Suzanne Del Gizzo. Cambridge: Cambridge University Press, 2013.

Sumi, Geoffrey S. *Ceremony and Power: Performing Politics in Rome Between Republic and Empire*. Ann Arbor: University of Michigan Press, 2005.

Sumney, Jerry L. "The Place of 1 Corinthians 9:24–27 in Paul's Argument." *Journal of Biblical Literature* 119.2 (2000): 24–27.

Sutcliffe, Marcella P. "Negotiating the 'Garibaldi Moment' in Newcastle-upon-Tyne (1854–1861)." *Modern Italy* 15.2 (2010): 129–144.

Swaddling, Judith. *The Ancient Olympic Games*. 2nd edition. London: British Museum Press, 1999.

Sweet, Waldo E. *Sport and Recreation in Ancient Greece: A Sourcebook with Translations*. New York and Oxford: Oxford University Press, 1987.

Sydenham, Edward A. *The Coinage of the Roman Republic*. London: Spink, 1952.

Syme, Ronald. *The Roman Revolution*. Oxford: Oxford University Press, 1939.

–. "Obituaries in Tacitus." *AJP* 79 (1958): 18–31.

–. *Tacitus*. 2 volumes. Oxford: Oxford University Press, 1958.

Tadashi, Ino. *Paul's Use of Canonical and Non-canonical Wisdom Literature in Romans and the Corinthian Letters*. PhD thesis. Andrews University, 2003.

Tannehill, Robert C. *Dying and Rising with Christ: A Study in Pauline Theology*. Berlin: Alfred Töpelmann, 1967.

Tate, John. "Imitation in Plato's *Republic*." *Classical Quarterly* 22 (1928): 16–23.

–. "Plato and Imitation." *Classical Quarterly* 26 (1932): 161–168.

Taylor, Lily R. *The Divinity of the Roman Emperor*. Middletown: American Philological Association, 1931.

Tell, Hakan. *Plato's Counterfeit Sophists*. Cambridge, MA and London: Center for Hellenic Studies, 2011.

Theissen, Gerd. *The Social Setting of Pauline Christianity: Essays on Corinth*. Philadelphia: Fortress, 1982.

–. "The Strong and the Weak in Corinth: A Sociological Analysis of a Theological Quarrel." Pages 121–143 in *The Social Setting of Pauline Christianity: Essays on Corinth*. Edited by Gerd Theissen. Philadelphia: Fortress, 1982.

–. *Psychological Aspects of Pauline Theology*. Edinburgh: T&T Clark, 1987.

Theophilos, Michael P. "Ephesus and the Numismatic Background to 'νεωκόρος'." Pages 299–331 in *The First Urban Churches 3: Ephesus*. Edited by James R. Harrison and Larry L. Welborn. Atlanta: SBL Press, 2018.

Thériault, Gaétan. *Le culte d'Homonoia dans les cités grecques*. Lyon-Québec: Collection Maison de l'Orient 26, série épigraphique 3, 1996.

Thiselton, Anthony C. "Realized Eschatology at Corinth." *New Testament Studies* 24 (1977–1978): 510–526.

–. *The First Epistle to the Corinthians*. Carlisle: Eerdmans/Paternoster, 2000.

Thompson, Catherine L. "Hairstyles, Head-coverings, and St. Paul: Portraits from Roman Corinth." *The Biblical Archaeologist* 51 (1988): 99–115.

Thompson, Michael. *Clothed with Christ: The Example and Teaching of Jesus in Romans 12:1–15:13*. Journal for the Study of the New Testament Supplement 59. Sheffield: Sheffield Academic, 1991.

Thonemann, Peter. *The Hellenistic Age*. Oxford: Oxford University Press, 2016.

Thorsteinsson, Runar M. *Roman Christianity and Roman Stoicism: A Comparative Study of Ancient Morality*. Oxford: Oxford University Press, 2010.

Thrall, Margaret E. *The Second Epistle to the Corinthians. Volume I: I–VII*. Edinburgh: T&T Clark, 1994.

Tinsley, Ernest J. *The Imitation of God in Christ: An Essay on the Biblical Basis of Christian Spirituality*. London: SCM Press, 1960.

Tod, Marcus N. "Clubs and Societies in the Greek World." Pages 71–96 in Marcus N. Tod, *Ancient Inscriptions: Sidelights on Greek History*. Chicago: Ares, 1932.

Tomson, Peter J. *Paul and the Jewish Law: Halakha in the Letters of the Apostle to the Gentiles*. Minneapolis: Fortress, 1990

Toney, Carl N. *Paul's Inclusive Ethic: Resolving Community Conflicts and Promoting Mission in Romans 14–15*. Wissenschaftliche Untersuchungen zum Neuen Testament II 252. Tübingen: Mohr Siebeck, 2008.

Toussaint, Constant. *L'Hellénisme et l'apôtre Paul*. Paris: Émille Nourry, 1921.

Townsend, John T. "Ancient Education in the Time of the Early Roman Empire." Pages 139–163 in *The Catacombs and the Colosseum: The Roman Empire as the Setting of Early Christianity*. Edited by Stephen Benko and John J. O'Rourke. London: Oliphants, 1972.

Troncoso, Victor A. "The Hellenistic Gymnasium and the Pleasures of *Paideia*." *Symbolae Philologorum Posnaniensium Graecae et Latinae* 19 (2009): 71–84.

Tsitsiridis, Stavros. "*Mimesis* and Understanding: An Interpretation of Aristotle's *Politics* 4.1448B4–19a." Pages 15–46 in *Mimesis: The New Critical Idiom*. Edited by Matthew Potolsky. New York and London: Routledge, 2006.

Tsouvala, Georgia. "Women Members of a Gymnasium in the Roman East (ig iv 732)." Pages 111–23 in *Ancient Documents and Their Contexts: First North American Congress of Greek and Latin Epigraphy (2011)*. Brill Studies in Greek and Roman Epigraphy 5. Edited by John Bodel and Nora Dimitrova. Leiden: Brill, 2014.

Turner, Graeme, Frances Bonner, and P. David Marshall. *Fame Games: The Production of Celebrity in Australia*. Cambridge and New York: Cambridge University Press, 2000.

Turner, Max. "Modern Linguistics and the New Testament." Pages 146–174 in *Hearing the New Testament: Strategies for Interpretation*. Edited by Joel B. Green. Grand Rapids: Eerdmans, 1995.

–. *The Holy Spirit and Spiritual Gifts Then and Now*. Carlisle: Paternoster, 1996.

Twain, Mark. *Autobiography of Mark Twain. Volume 2*. Edited by Harriet E. Smith, Benjamin Griffin, Victor Fischer, Michael B. Frank, Sharon K. Goetz, Leslie D. Myrick, and Robert Hirst. Berkeley: University of California Press, 2013.

Tzachou-Alexandri, Olga. "The Gymnasium: An Institution for Athletic and Education." In *Mind and Body: Athletic Contests in Antiquity*. Edited by Olga Tzachou-Alexandri. Athens: Catalogue of the Exhibition, Ministry of Culture and the National Hellenic Committee [ICOM], 1989.

–. ed. *Mind and Body: Athletic Contests in Ancient Greece*. Athens: Catalogue of the Exhibition, Ministry of Culture and the National Hellenic Committee [ICOM], 1989.

Unwin, James R. *Subversive Spectacles: The Struggles and Deaths of Paul and Seneca*. PhD thesis, Macquarie University, 2017.

Valavanis, Panos. "La proclamation des vainqueurs aux Panathénées." *BCH* 114 (1990): 325–359.

–. *Games and Sanctuaries in Ancient Greece: Olympia, Delphi, Isthmia, Nemea, Athens.* Los Angeles: J. Paul Getty Museum, 2004.
van der Horst, Pieter W. "Silent Prayer in Antiquity." *Numen* 41.1 (1994): 1–25.
van der Horst, Pieter W., and G. Sterling. *Prayer in Antiquity: Greco-Roman, Jewish and Christian Prayers.* Notre Dame: University of Notre Dame Press, 2000.
van der Horst, Pieter W., and J.H. Newman. *Early Jewish Prayers in Greek.* Berlin: De Gruyter, 2008.
van Groningen, Bernard A. *Les gymnasiarques des métropoles de l'Égypte Romaine.* Groningue: Noordhoff, 1924.
van Krieken, Robert. *Celebrity Society.* New York and London: Routledge, 2012.
van Nijf, Onno. *The Civic World of Professional Associations in the Roman East.* Amsterdam: J.C. Gieben, 1997.
van Tilborg, Sjef. *Reading John in Ephesus.* Leiden: Brill, 1996.
Vanhove, Doris. "Le gymnase." Pages 57–75 in *Le sport dans le Grèce antique: Du jeu à la compétition.* Edited by Doris Vanhove. Bruxelles: Palais des Beaux-Arts/Universiteit Gent, 1992.
–. ed. *Le sport dans la Grèce antique: Du jeu à la compétition.* Bruxelles: Palais des Beaux-Arts/Universiteit Gent, 1992.
Verboven, Koenraad. "The Associative Order: Status and Ethos Among Roman Businessmen in Late Republic and Early Empire." *Athenaeum* 95 (2007): 861–893.
Verdenius, Willem J. Mimesis: *Plato's Doctrine of Artistic Imitation.* Leiden: Brill, 1949.
Verner, David C. *The Household of God: The Social World of the Pastoral Epistles.* Chico: Scholars, 1981.
Versnel, Henk S. "Religious Mentality in Ancient Prayer." Pages 1–64 in *Faith, Hope and Worship: Aspects of Religious Mentality in the Ancient World.* Edited by Henk S. Versnel. Leiden: Brill, 1981.
Volkmann, Hans. *Res Gestae Divi AVGVSTI: Das Monumentum Ancyranum.* Berlin: De Gruyter, 1969.
von Campenhausen, Hans. *Ecclesiastical Authority and Spiritual Power in the Church in the First Three Centuries.* London: Adam & Charles Black, 1969.
Vriezen, Theodorus C. *An Outline of Old Testament Theology.* Oxford: Basil Blackwell, 1958.
Walbank, Mary E. "Image and Cult: The Coinage of Roman Corinth." Pages 151–198 in *Corinth in Context: Comparative Studies on Religion and Society.* Edited by Steve J. Friesen, Daniel N. Schowalter, and James Walters. Leiden: Brill, 2011.
Wallace-Hadrill, Andrew. "The Emperor and His Virtues." *Historia* 30 (1981): 298–323.
–. "Family and Inheritance in the Augustan Marriage Laws." *Proceedings of the Cambridge Philological Society* 27 (1981): 58–80.
–. "Civilis Princeps: Between Citizen and King." *Journal of Roman Studies* 72 (1982): 32–48.
–. "The Golden Age and Sin in Augustan Ideology." *Past and Present* 95 (1982): 19–36.
Walters. James C. *Ethnic Issues in Paul's Letter to the Romans: Changing Self-Definitions in Earliest Roman Christianity.* Valley Forge: Trinity Press International, 1993.
Waltzing, Jean-Pierre. *Étude historique sur les corporations professionnelles chez les romains.* Volumes I–IV. Louvain: Charles Peeters, 1895–1900.
Warmington, Eric H. *Remains of Old Latin: Archaic Inscriptions.* Cambridge, MA: Harvard University, 1953.

Webb, Ruth. "The Nature and Representation of Competition in Pantomime and Mime." Pages 221–256 and 364–365 in *L'Organisation des spectacles dans le monde Romain*. Entretiens sur l'Antiquité classique 58. Edited by Kathleen Coleman and Jocelyne Nelis-Clément. Vandoeuvres and Genève: Fondation Hardt, 2011.

Weber Hans-Ruedi. *The Cross: Tradition and Interpretation*. Translated by Elke Jessett. London: SPCK, 1979; German original 1975.

Weir, Robert. "Commemorative Cash: the Coins of the Ancient and Modern Olympics." Pages 179–192 in *Onward to the Olympics: Historical Perspectives on the Olympic Games*. Edited by Gerald P. Schaus and Stephen R. Wenn. Waterloo: Wilfrid Laurier Press, 2007.

Welborn, Larry L. *Politics and Rhetoric in the Corinthian Epistles*. Macon: Mercer University Press, 1997.

–. "The Runaway Paul." *Harvard Theological Review* 92.2 (1999): 115–163.

–. *Paul, the Fool for Christ: A Study of 1 Corinthians 1–4 in the Comic-Philosophic Tradition*. London and New York: T&T Clark, 2005.

–. "'Extraction from the Mortal Site': Badiou on the Resurrection in Paul." *New Testament Studies* 55.3 (2009): 295–314.

–. *An End to Enmity: Paul and the "Wrongdoer" of Second Corinthians*. Berlin and Boston: De Gruyter, 2011.

–. *Paul's Summons to Messianic Life: Political Theology and the Coming Awakening*. New York: Columbia University Press, 2015.

–. "The Polis and the Poor." Pages 189–243 in *The First Urban Churches 1: Methodological Considerations*. Edited by James R. Harrison and Larry L. Welborn. Atlanta: SBL Press, 2015.

–. "Inequality in Roman Corinth: Evidence from Diverse Sources Evaluated by a Neo-Ricardian Model." Pages 47–84 in *The First Urban Churches 2: Roman Corinth*. Edited by James R. Harrison and Larry L. Welborn. Atlanta: SBL Press, 2016.

Welles, C. Bradford. *Royal Correspondence in the Hellenistic Period: A Study in Greek Epigraphy*. Chicago: Ares Publishers, 1974; original London, 1934.

Wells, Kyle B. *Grace and Agency in Paul and Second Temple Judaism: Interpreting the Transformation of the Heart*. Novum Testamentum Supplement 157. Leiden and Boston: Brill, 2015.

West, Allen B. *Corinth VIII 2: Latin Inscriptions, 1986–1926*. Cambridge, MA: Harvard University Press, 1931.

Wetter, Gillis P. *Charis: Ein Beitrag zur Geschichte des ältesten Christentums*. Leipzig: J.C. Hinrichs, 1913.

White, Adam G. "Servants, Not Intellectual Clients: The Significance of Paul's Role as an *Oikonomos* in 1 Cor 4:1 and 9:17." *Australian Biblical Review* 62 (2014): 44–57.

–. *Where is the Wise Man? Graeco-Roman Education as a Background to the Divisions in 1 Corinthians 1–4*. Library of New Testament Studies 536. Harrisburg: T&T Clark, 2015.

White, John L. *The Apostle of God: Paul and the Promise of Abraham*. Peabody: Hendrickson, 1999.

White, Joel R. "'Peace and Security' (1 Thessalonians 5:3): Is It Really a Roman Slogan?" *New Testament Studies* 59.3 (2013): 382–395.

White, L. Michael. "Social Authority in the House Church Setting and Ephesians 4:1–16." *ResQ* 29.4 (1987): 209–228.

Whittle, Sarah. *Covenant Renewal and the Consecration of the Gentiles in Romans.* Society for New Testament Studies Monograph Series 161 Cambridge: Cambridge University Press, 2015.

Wiedemann, Thomas E.J. *The Emperors and Gladiators.* London and New York: Routledge, 1992.

–. "Tiberius to Nero," Pages 198–255 in *The Cambridge Ancient History. Second Edition. X: The Augustan Empire 43 BC–AD 69.* Edited by Alan K. Bowman, Edward Champlin, and Andrew Lintott. Cambridge: Cambridge University Press, 1996.

Wiefel, Wolfgang. "The Jewish Community in Ancient Rome and the Origins of Roman Christianity." Pages 85–101 in *The Romans Debate: Revised and Expanded Edition.* Edited by Karl P. Donfried. 2nd edition. Peabody: Hendrickson, 1991.

Wiersma, William. "The Seven Sages and the Prize of Wisdom." *Mnemosyne* 1.2 (1933–34): 150–154.

Wiles, Gordon P. *Paul's Intercessory Prayers: The Significance of the Intercessory Prayer Passages in the Letters of Paul.* Society for New Testament Studies Monograph Series 24. Cambridge: Cambridge University Press, 1974.

Wilken, Robert L. "Collegia, Philosophical Schools, and Theology." Pages 279–286 in *The Catacombs and the Colosseum: The Roman Empire as the Setting of Primitive Christianity.* Edited by Stephen Benko and John J. O'Rourke. Valley Forge: Judson Press, 1971.

–. *The Christians as the Romans Saw Them.* New Haven and London: Yale University Press, 1984.

Wilkens, Eliza G. *The Delphic Maxims in Literature.* Chicago: University of Chicago Press, 1929.

Williams, David J. *Paul's Metaphors: Their Context and Character.* Peabody: Hendrickson, 1999.

Williams, Donald M. *The Imitation of Christ in Paul with Special Reference to Paul as Teacher.* PhD dissertation. Columbia University, 1967.

Williams, Margaret H. *The Jews among the Greeks and Romans: A Sourcebook.* London: Duckworth, 1998.

Williams, William C. *Pictures from Brueghel and Other Poems: Collected Poems 1950–1962.* New York: New Directions Books, 1962.

Williamson, Christina G. "'As God is my witness': Civic Oaths in Ritual Space as a Means Towards Rational Cooperation in the Hellenistic Polis." Pages 119–174 in *Cults, Creeds and Identities in the Greek City after the Classical Age.* Edited by Richard Alston, Onno M. van Nijf, and Christina G. Williamson. Leuven: Peeters, 2013.

–. *Paterson.* Revised edition. New York: New Directions, 1992.

Willis, Wendell L. *Idol Meat in Corinth: The Pauline Argument in 1 Corinthians 8 and 10.* SBL Dissertation Series 68. Chico: Scholars, 1985.

Wilson, Frances, ed. *Byromania: Portraits of the Artist in Nineteenth and Twentieth Century Culture.* Basingstoke: Palgrave Macmillan, 1999.

Wilson, Stephen G. "Voluntary Associations: An Overview." Pages 1–15 in *Voluntary Associations in the Graeco-Roman World.* Edited by John S. Kloppenborg and Stephen G. Wilson. London and New York: Routledge, 2003.

Wilson, Walter T. *Love Without Pretense: Romans 12:9–21 and Hellenistic-Jewish Wisdom Literature.* Wissenschaftliche Untersuchungen zum Neuen Testament II 46. Tübingen: Mohr Siebeck, 1991.

Windsor, Lionel J. *Paul and the Vocation of Israel: How Paul's Jewish Identity Informs His Apostolic Ministry, With Special Reference to Romans*. Beihefte zur Zeitschrift für die neutestamentliche Wissenschaft 205. Berlin and Boston: De Gruyter, 2014.

Winter, Bruce W. "The Public Honoring of Christian Benefactors: Romans 13:3–4 and 1 Peter 2:14–15." *Journal for the Study of the New Testament* 34 (1988): 87–103.

–. "'If a man does not wish to work ...'. A Cultural and Historical Setting for 2 Thessalonians." *Tyndale Bulletin* 40.2 (1989): 305–315.

–. "Secular and Christian Responses to Christian Famines." *Tyndale Bulletin* 40 (1989): 86–106.

–. "Theological and Ethical Responses to Religious Pluralism – 1 Corinthians 1–10." *Tyndale Bulletin* 41.2 (1990): 209–226.

–. *Seek the Welfare of the City: Christians as Benefactors and Citizens*. Carlisle/Grand Rapids: Paternoster/Eerdmans, 1994.

–. *Philo and Paul among the Sophists*. Society for New Testament Studies Monograph Series 96. Cambridge: Cambridge University Press, 1997.

–. *After Paul Left Corinth: The Influence of Secular Ethics and Social Change*. Eerdmans: Grand Rapids, 2001.

–. *Roman Wives, Roman Widows: The Appearance of New Women and the Pauline Community*. Grand Rapids: Eerdmans, 2003.

–. *Divine Honours for the Caesars: The First Christians' Responses*. Grand Rapids: Eerdmans, 2015.

Wiseman, Timothy P. "Cicero and the Body Politic." *Politica Antica* 1 (2012): 133–140.

Witherington III, Ben. "Not So Idle Thoughts about *Eidolothuton*." *Tyndale Bulletin* 44 (1993): 237–254.

–. *Friendship and Finances in Philippi: The Letter of Paul to the Philippians*. Valley Forge: Trinity Press International, 1994.

–. *Conflict and Community in Corinth: A Socio-Rhetorical commentary on 1 and 2 Corinthians*. Grand Rapids: Eerdmans, 1995.

–. "Images of Crucifixion: Fresh Evidence." *Biblical Archaeology Review* 39.2 (2013): 28, 66.

Wobbe, Joseph. *Der Charis-Gedanke bei Paulus: Ein Beitrag zur neutestamentlichen Theologie*. Münster: Aschendorffsche Verlagsbuchhandlung, 1932.

Wolter, Michael. *Paul: An Outline of His Theology*. Translated by Robert L. Brawley. Waco: Baylor University Press, 2015.

Wood, Neal. *Cicero's Social and Political Thought*. Berkeley and Los Angeles: University of California Press, 1988.

Woodruff, Paul. "Plato on *Mimesis*." Pages 521–523 in *Encyclopaedia of Aesthetics Volume 3*. Edited by Michael Kelly. New York: Oxford University Press, 1998.

Woolf, Raphael. *Cicero: The Philosophy of a Roman Sceptic*. London and New York: Routledge, 2015.

Wright, N. Thomas. "Jesus Christ is Lord: Philippians 2:5–11." Pages 56–98 in N. Thomas Wright, *The Climax of the Covenant: Christ and the Law in Pauline Theology*. Edinburgh: T&T Clark, 1991.

–. "Romans." Pages 423–770 in *New Interpreter's Bible. Volume X*. Edited by Leander E. Keck. Nashville: Abingdon, 2002.

Yavetz, Zvi. "*Existimatio*, *Fama*, and the Ides of March." *Harvard Studies in Classical Philology* 78 (1974): 35–65.

Young, Frances, and David F. Ford. *Meaning and Truth in 2 Corinthians*. Grand Rapids: Eerdmans, 1987.

Zamfir, Korinna. *Men and Women in the Household of God: A Contextual Approach to Roles and Ministries in the Pastoral Epistles*. Novum Testamentum Et Orbis Antiquus/ Studien zur Umwelt des Neuen Testaments 103. Göttingen and Bristol: Vandenhoeck & Ruprecht, 2013.

Zanker, Paul. *The Power of Images in the Age of Augustus*. Translated by Alan Shapiro. Ann Arbor: The University of Michigan Press, 1990.

Zeller, Dieter. *Charis bei Philon und Paulus*. Stuttgart: Verlag Katholisches Bibelwerk, 1990.

–. "Pauline Paraenesis in Romans 12 and Greek Gnomic Wisdom." Pages 73–86 in *Greco-Roman Culture and the New Testament: Studies Commemorating the Centennial of the Pontifical Biblical Institute*. Edited by David E. Aune and Frederick E. Brenk. Leiden and Boston: Brill, 2012.

Zhmud, Leonid. *Pythagoras and the Early Pythagoreans*. Oxford: Oxford University Press, 2012.

Zuiderhoek, Arjan. "Feeding the Citizens: Municipal Grain funds and Civic Benefactors in the Roman East." Pages 159–180 in *Feeding the Ancient Greek City*. Groningen-Royal Holloway Studies on the Greek City after the Classical Age 1. Edited by Richard Alston and Otto M. van Nijf. Leuven et al.: Peeters, 2008.

–. *The Politics of Munificence in the Roman Empire: Citizens, Elites and Benefactors in Asia Minor*. Cambridge: Cambridge University Press, 2009.

–. "Oligarchs and Benefactors: Elite Demography and Euergetism in the Greek East of the Roman Empire." Pages 185–196 in *Political Culture in the Greek City after the Classical Age*. Edited by Onno M. van Nijf and Richard Alston. Leuven: Peeters, 2011.

Index of References

Old Testament

Apocrypha

Pseudepigrapha

Rabbinic Literature

Qumran

New Testament

Ancient Literary Sources

Inscriptions

Papyri

Coins

Ostraca

Modern Author Index

Subject Index

Wissenschaftliche Untersuchungen zum Neuen Testament

WUNT I is an international series dealing with the entire field of early Christianity and its Jewish and Graeco-Roman environment. Its historical-philological profile and interdisciplinary outlook, which its long-term editor Martin Hengel was instrumental in establishing, is maintained by an international team of editors representing a wide range of the traditions and themes of New Testament scholarship. The sole criteria for acceptance to the series are the scholarly quality and lasting merit of the work being submitted. Apart from the specialist monographs of experienced researchers, some of which may be habilitations, *WUNT I* features collections of essays by renowned scholars, source material collections and editions as well as conference proceedings in the form of a handbook on themes central to the discipline.

WUNT II complements the first series by offering a publishing platform in paperback for outstanding writing by up-and-coming young researchers. Dissertations and monographs are presented alongside innovative conference volumes on fundamental themes of New Testament research. Like Series I, it is marked by a historical-philological character and an international orientation that transcends exegetical schools and subject boundaries. The academic quality of Series II is overseen by the same team of editors.

WUNT I:
ISSN: 0512-1604
Suggested citation: WUNT I
All available volumes can be found at *www.mohrsiebeck.com/wunt1*

WUNT II:
ISSN: 0340-9570
Suggested citation: WUNT II
All available volumes can be found at *www.mohrsiebeck.com/wunt2*

Mohr Siebeck
www.mohrsiebeck.com